Latino Education in the U.S.

Advisory Board

Antonia Darder, Professor
University of Illinois at Urbana–Champaign

Alfredo Benavides, Professor
University of Texas

Eugene García, Dean of the College of Education
Arizona State University

Juliana Lasta, doctoral candidate
Columbia University

Tracy Rodriguez, educational consultant and doctoral student
Columbia University

Latino Education in the U.S.

Edited by Lourdes Diaz Soto

ROWMAN & LITTLEFIELD EDUCATION
Lanham • New York • Toronto • Plymouth, UK

Published in the United States of America
by Rowman & Littlefield Education
A Division of Rowman & Littlefield Publishers, Inc.
A wholly owned subsidary of The Rowman & Littlefield Publishing Group, Inc.
4501 Forbes Boulevard, Suite 200, Lanham, Maryland 20706
www.rowmaneducation.com

Estover Road
Plymouth PL6 7PY
United Kingdom

British Library Cataloguing in Publication Information Available

The Praeger Publishers edition of this book was previously catalogued by the Library of Congress as follows:

The Praeger handbook of Latino education in the U.S. / edited by Lourdes Diaz Soto ;
foreword by Antonia Darder.
     p.   cm.
  Includes bibliographical references and index.
  1. Hispanic Americans—Education. I. Soto, Lourdes Diaz, 1945–
LC2669.P73 2007
371.829'68073—dc22   2006032638

ISBN- 13: 978-1-57886-710-3 (pbk. : alk. paper)
ISBN- 10: 1-57886-710-X (pbk. : alk. paper)

♾™ The paper used in this publication meets the minimum requirements of American National Standard for Information Sciences—Permanence of Paper for Printed Library Materials, ANSI/NISO Z39.48-1992.
Manufactured in the United States of America.

To our grandparents,
who toiled in the vineyards with humility
and hope in their hearts;

To our parents,
who worked in factories while seeking
social justice and equity;

To ourselves,
the radical lovers of hope and freedom;

And to our children,
who are the soul of an increasingly
Latinized nation.

Contents

Foreword

We have been roused from our slumbers, and may we never sink into repose until we have conveyed a clear and undisputed inheritance to posterity . . .

LULAC Constitution (1929)[1]

In perhaps no other domain of society is the growth of the Latino population in the United States more marked than in education.

Luis Moll and Richard Ruiz (2002)[2]

The more consciously people make their history, the more they clearly understand the difficulties that they have to confront in economic, social, and cultural domains.

Paulo Freire and Donaldo Macedo (1987)[3]

Latinos and Latinas in the U.S. waged many battles throughout the twentieth century to consciously make history. Although many of these community and legal efforts were left unnoted in the annals of the U.S. mainstream, many of their efforts were centered on achieving educational equality. As young Latinos and Latinas availed themselves of the hard-earned opportunities made possible by the civil rights movement of the 1960s and 1970s, a large number of committed Chicano, Puerto Rican, and other Latino college students chose to enter the field of education. Education, with its long-held promises of upward mobility, social privileges, and economic opportunities, represented for many Latinos a concrete place to expand community efforts for social emancipation, bringing these efforts into public educational institutions and the scholarly terrain of educational research.

Latino Education in the U.S. represents a timely and significant milestone in the history of educational literature on Latinos and schooling. It has been, undoubtedly, a daunting task. Nevertheless, the handbook serves as a long-awaited response to the late George Sanchez's (1934)[4] concern that there existed an "urgent need for greater public enlightenment" about the education of Latino children in the U.S. Seven decades after the publication of Sanchez's cautionary words in the Journal of Applied Psychology, many of the same educational problems he addressed throughout his lifetime persist in American public schools today. Many Latino children continue to face shameful barriers that obstruct their democratic participation and thwart their academic success.

Beyond the often-cited cultural conflicts, language differences, racialization, and class inequalities, major barriers within schools themselves are often just as responsible for the academic difficulties experienced by Latino students. These obstacles include classroom teachers who are ill prepared to engage the realities of low-income Latino communities, lack of sound pedagogical knowledge, curriculum that is disconnected from students' lives, social studies textbooks and educational materials that are inaccurate or irrelevant, assessment and testing practices that are inappropriate, schools with increasing impoverishment and segregation, and misguided views about Latino parents, just to name a few. There is no question that the serious impact of these barriers is well reflected in the contours of daily life, as well as in statistical portrayals of Latinos in the U.S., whether these be rates of educational completion, labor force participation, family income, or incarceration.

Given the economic constraints and relative youthfulness of the growing U.S. Latino population, our work as educators, activists, researchers, and theorists must engage openly the contradictions and conflicts that exist between the rhetoric of equality and the forces of inequality. This is a necessary step in our efforts to substantially transform the quality of education received by Latino and Latina students in the U.S. Moreover, this requires strong historical, political, and cultural knowledge of the theories and practices in the field, as well as the effective programs and resources specifically directed toward addressing the needs and ultimately improving the education of Latino students. Bringing this wealth of information together is precisely the difficult challenge that the editors and contributors of this groundbreaking handbook take on, with seriousness and fury.

Most important, the handbook's multifaceted approach to documenting Latino education—including major educational perspectives, policies and concerns, significant events, historical figures in the field, and major organizations—provides a comprehensive educational resource just at a time when we are contending, once again, with the rise of a new assimilationist wave in American society. Hence, this handbook represents more than simply a well-produced collection of historical facts, reports, and research about Latinos and education. *Latino Education in the U.S.* is a bold and conscious act of selfdetermination and a clear and undisputed inheritance to our posterity.

Antonia Darder
University of Illinois at Urbana–Champaign

NOTES

1. LULAC Constitution, ratified in 1929. See G. San Miguel Jr., "Roused from Our Slumbers," in A. Darder, R. D. Torres, & H. Gutie´rrez (Eds.), *Latinos and Education: A Critical Reader* (New York: Routledge, 1997), p. 66.

2. L. C. Moll & R. Ruiz, "The Schooling of Latino Children," in M. M. Saurez-Orozco & M. M. Paez (Eds.), *Latinos: Remaking America* (Berkeley: University of California Press, 2002), p. 362.

3. P. Freire & D. Macedo, *Literacy: Reading the Word and the World* (South Hadley, MA: Bergin & Garvey, 1987), p. 66.

4. G. I. Sanchez, "Bilingualism and Mental Measures: A Word of Caution," *Journal of Applied Psychology* 18 (1934), 765–772. Sanchez was one of the first Mexican American scholars to challenge the educational inequality faced by Spanish-speaking children of Mexican descent in the U.S.

Acknowledgments

I would like to express my sincere gratitude to each one of the contributors who so willingly shared his or her expertise and support. The children who shared their thoughts and photos merit a special note of thanks. This project was made possible only because of Marie Ellen Larcada's patience and encouragement throughout the pre-publication and publication process. The Advisory Board deserves credit for supporting and providing counsel for this work. Antonia Darder (author of the foreword) deserves special recognition for assisting in the recruitment of valuable contributions and for salient advice. *Gracias Antonia por tu apoyo*. I would also like to thank Shirley Steinberg, who helped to support the origination and contributors, as well as the "naming" of this handbook. Marta Soler from Universidad de Barcelona was gracious in recruiting colleagues for several pieces. In addition, I found the staff at the Library of Congress's photo-duplication office (especially Barbara Moore) extremely helpful, as were the staff at the University of Texas at San Antonio's Institute of Texan Cultures (in particular Patrick Lemelle). We are grateful to the colleagues who quickly endorsed our work, including Rodolfo D. Torres, Raymond Padilla, Sonia Nieto, and Pedro Noguera.

Introduction

A PEOPLE'S STRUGGLE

These headlines help to explain why Latino education in the U.S. has become "a people's struggle":

> "Census Bureau: Hispanics Lag in Education"
> > USAToday.com, June 19, 2001

> "An Education Crisis: Educating Latinos"
> > NPR special report, November 24–December 23, 2002,
> > > http://search.npr.org

> "Diverse Schools More Likely to Be Labeled as Failing, Study Says."
> > *New York Times*, December 24, 2003, p. 19

> "15 Years on the Bottom Rung"
> > *New York Times*, May 26, 2005, p. A9

It may be that in no other realm of the U.S. is the growth of the Latino/a population more evidenced than in education. The latest census data available to us note that there are 37.4 million Latinos/as, that one-third of us is less than 18 years old (younger population), and that the 13.3% of the population currently made up of Latinos is projected to grow to nearly *one-fourth* (24.4%) of the total U.S. population by the year 2050 (U.S. Census Bureau, 2002).

Many question the census data's accuracy. Others maintain that it presents evolving possibilities. I have relied on several sources of data for the purposes of this handbook (e.g., U.S. government census, Pew Hispanic Center, Rand Corporation, National Center for Educational Statistics, and numerous contemporary scholars), and all relay numerous challenges and opportunities. The challenges we are experiencing include the fact that as compared to the national average, our educational attainment is lower; our poverty rates are higher (22.6%), with 28% of our children under 18 years of age living in poverty; our school dropout rate is 27%; and our job participation is largely limited to service work, precision production, crafts, and repair and transportation occupations. Mexican Americans comprise our largest group (66.9%), followed by Puerto Ricans (8.6%), Central and South Americans (14.3%), Cubans (3.7%), and other Latino groups (6.5%).

The possibilities highlight the opportunities provided by a population significantly younger than the international average. While Latinos/as are a younger population, international comparisons show that the U.S. as a whole has more people aged 80 and over (U.S. Census Bureau, 2000). Thus Latino/a youth become an asset for our nation. School- and college-age youth (ages 5–24) comprise 37% of the Latino population, with projections of an 82% increase making education a "*matter of national significance*" (Pew Hispanic Center, 2002; emphasis added).

The intergenerational differences documented by Suro and Passel (2003) show that the younger generation Latino/a is a product of U.S. schools and represents cultural and political identities influenced by and yet differing from those of their immigrant parents. In addition,

their economic status will be determined largely by the course of an education system that is facing demands for change at almost every level. One prediction about second-generation Latinos, however, seems safe: Given their numbers, their future will *be a matter of national interest*. (p. 9; emphasis added.)

Contemporary Latinos/as comprise much of the hope for the American spirit. Latino/a youth—our children, our grandchildren, and our great-grandchildren—will comprise an increasingly large portion of the population. Those of us who are radical lovers of hope and freedom see the need to improve educational opportunities as an issue of social justice and equity. Others interested in desirable public investments can understand this need, given the Rand Report (1994) documenting how raising college participation levels can increase contributions to social security programs, tax revenues, and intergenerational strengthening of the nation's fabric.

NEED FOR THE VOLUME

In light of research evidence and demographic data there is a clear need to inform educators and the public of both the challenges and the opportunities for Latino/a learners in education. Although we cannot cover every aspect; this handbook highlights the current state of Latino education; discusses existing educational challenges and opportunities; and provides an essential reference for students, educators, scholars, and policymakers.

We invited scholars in the field to share their knowledge and wisdom about how to understand the complexities and diversity inherent in the educational needs of Latino/a learners. Although the task appears daunting, my colleagues and I will continue the dialogue to chart a space of educational equity. Our goal is to present a handbook that provides both an overview and a comprehensive understanding of the complex issues related to Latino/a education in the U.S. This volume is intended to serve as an essential reference for academic, school, and public libraries. In addition, it targets educators who are interested in making a difference in the lives of Latino/a learners and who work or plan to work as educators or community workers. We will continue the dialogue with existing findings and future possibilities.

SCHOOLS

The Pew Hispanic Center (2002) found that Latinos/as show tremendous faith in schools and school personnel. Immigrants in particular demonstrated optimism while also expressing a concern that the educational system does not always treat Latino/a students fairly: "Hispanic students lag because teachers are not able to cross the cultural divide . . . (while parents) are willing to assume some of the blame for not pushing their children hard enough" (p. 3). Parents indicated that they embrace educational reforms helping to improve schools while still maintaining their children in the public school system.

The National Center for Education Statistics (NCES, 2003–2008) documents a demographic shift from 1976 to 2026 when Latino/a and African American enrollment will grow from 23% to 70% of U.S. public schools. Latino students became the largest "minority" group in the year 2005, according to NCES. Latino/a students and African American students now comprise the majority of learners in urban schools while their presence is also being felt in rural schools (Moll & Ruiz, 2002). Garcia (2001) notes:

In the decades to come, it will be virtually impossible for a professional educator to serve in a school context, in which his or her students are not consequentially diverse—racially, culturally, and/or linguistically. (p. 26)

Educational institutions are clearly not meeting the challenge to provide an equitable education for Latino/a learners. A research project conducted by Meir and Stewart (1991) aptly describes the situation, "Un paso pa'lante y dos pa'tras" (One step forward and two steps back). Surveying 150 large school districts across the nation, these researchers found that Latino/a learners continue to be denied access to an equitable education.

Angela Valenzuela (1999) documents the "subtractive schooling" that U.S.-Mexican youth experience. Her discussion on a caring curriculum shows the need for schools to become more knowledgeable about the social and academic complexities affecting Mexican immigrant and Mexican American youth. Her call for an authentically caring pedagogy envisions an additive perspective.

An authentically caring pedagogy would not only cease subtracting students' cultural identities, it would also reverse its effects. It would build bridges wherever there are divisions and it would privilege biculturalism out of respect for the cultural integrity of their students. (p. 266)

HISPANIDAD/LATINO/A

David Theo Goldberg (1993) reminds us that the "category" of race has been linked to science, colonialism, reason, and morality in ways that have produced racialized discourses and racist practices. The category of race has permeated the formal, informal, and hidden curricula in our public and private spaces.

The challenge for the census takers is clear—who is "Hispanic"? How do you measure Hispanidad? The U.S. census data show that in 1990, 9% of the respondents identified themselves as Latino/a, whereas in the 2000 survey 12.5% did so, making this one of the fastest-growing demographic groups in the United States of America (http://censusscope.org). We come from similar extended family traditions and linguistic and cultural practices, yet vary by sociocultural and human complexities.

SEARCH FOR EDUCATIONAL EQUITY

The search for educational equity has been a long and arduous struggle by Latino/a children, families, and educators (Carger, 1996; Carrasquillo, 1991; Darder, Torres, & Gutiérrez, 1997; DiSipio & de la Garza, 1997; Garcia, 2001; Gaston Report, 1999; Nieto, 2000; Soto, 1997b; Tashakkori & Ochoa, 1999; Valdés, 1996; Valenzuela, 1991; Walsh, 1996; Zentella, 1997; and many others). Scholars and activists have documented educational civil rights activity in multiple communities across the nation. The complexity of the educational issues lies in part in the way schools view children. An inherent deficit is that children are categorized and labeled, yet rarely found to be gifted. Schools seldom see the linguistic and cultural gifts brought by Latino/Latina children and their families. What they do see reflects societal views and stereotypes.

The "American cultural idealism" is a travesty when "mainstream" communities in Arnhem (Bigler, 1999) and Steeltown (Soto, 1997b) wield their oppressive power to demoralize and victimize culturally and linguistically diverse peoples. In Steeltown an elder described how the community coped with racism: "*Tragamos, tragamos y tragamos*" (We swallowed, swallowed, and swallowed). They felt that if they remained quiet, the powerful ones would someday respect and care for their children. Their outrage exploded when they realized that the community voices were silenced and outmaneuvered. The award-winning 20-year-old bilingual education program was dismantled even after a prayerful, peaceful session before the local school board.

What license gives the privileged ones the right to disregard and mistreat whole groups of people? When will the bells of social justice ring to emancipate and liberate children growing up as *puentes tendidos* (extended bridges) or, as Maria Montessori so eloquently described, "as butterflies pinned to their desks"? I have asked myself these questions when viewing how a Westernized curriculum has dominated classrooms where diverse children cannot see the voices of their ancestors as valuable and important to the nation where they live and cannot negotiate their identities. This is a form of violence to the souls of our children, to the souls of all our people.

Bigler attempts to be objective in her treatment of these issues. Her dualistic portrayals allow us to view the Anglo-American elder perspective in Arnhem. She cites the statistics, the notion of meritocracy, the historical evidence, the Latino poets and writers, and she concludes, "*Only recently* have we begun to approach that understanding, and to explore the implications of the racial, ethnic, and class divisions that constitute the real forces threatening to 'disunite' America."

While it is probable that perhaps *only recently* some individuals have begun to explore these issues, it is also evident that our nation has had an ongoing struggle for our children's souls since the arrival of the European colonizers who were largely responsible for the initiation of the genocide of our Native American brothers and sisters. Perhaps *only recently* have these issues been explored by some while W.E.B. Du Bois (1903) reminded us of the problem of the color line. Perhaps *only recently* have these issues been explored while Ida B. Wells embarked on her anti-lynching campaign in 1892. Perhaps *only recently* have these issues been explored while Martin Luther King wrote his letter from the Birmingham jail (1963). Perhaps *only recently* have these issues been explored while Blaut (1993) documented how colonized people are ultimately perceived as children via concepts adopted from Piaget, Marx, Freud, and Jung. Perhaps *only recently* have these issues been explored while Loewen (1995) wrote *Lies My Teacher Told Me*, documenting historical flaws in widely used social studies textbooks. Cofer (1993) in one of her poems notes how

> Latin women pray in Spanish to an Anglo God/
> with a Jewish heritage,
> fervently hoping/
> that if not omnipotent/
> at least He be bilingual

(Cofer, 1993, p. 154)

The problem is one of historical amnesia coupled with racism, cultural invasion, domestication, language domination, and the imposition of an exclusionary curriculum. The introduction of a "superior" history and the establishment of otherness tear away at the sociocultural fabric of a people. The ultimate result is that diverse voices are silenced, unable to enter into dialogue and reflect on their daily realities and lived experiences. Ultimately this marginalization leads to multiple and complex issues for children, including issues of identity.

> "Cause and Effect" by Peter Spiro
> Cause you are poor
> you go to public school
> Cause public school is free
> you get a lousy education.
> Cause you get a lousy education
> you are undereducated.
> Cause you are undereducated
> you are treated with contempt. . . .

(Algarin & Homan, 1994, p. 146)

The result of the implementation of a colonial curriculum is a society that is virtually hypnotized, silenced, and unable to participate democratically in the political sphere. In the *Journal of Latinos and Education*, Enrique Murillo writes of defendants in the U.S., the detention of an undetermined number of people, and the willingness to listen to people's conversations. These conditions demonstrate that our democratic ideals are standing on fragile ground (Rethinking Schools, 2001–2002). Nancy Chang (2002) in her piece documents the "silencing of political dissent" that threatens our civil liberties. Is this the democracy we have all been dreaming about?

CURRICULAR MODELS

How do we move away from existing curricular models that can have a devastating effect on so many learners? There are no simple answers to the complexities we are examining, yet part of the equation includes a need for a continued critical understanding of issues of power, linguicism, racism, grand theories, and critical literacy. Also important is exploring how to move beyond existing multicultural curricular models. Steinberg and Kincheloe (2001) propose that multicultural educators study power and privilege within a critical multicultural perspective. Critical multiculturalism departs from (1) conservative (monocultural) multiculturalism, (2) liberal multiculturalism, (3) pluralistic multiculturalism, and (4) left-essentialist multiculturalism.

Critical multiculturalism draws upon the Frankfurt school of critical theory of the 1920s and focuses on issues of power and domination. This model presents a critical pedagogy that promotes a deep understanding and exposes the schools' function in sorting students. It identifies equity issues of race, social class, and gender; supports the elimination of human suffering; and examines issues of privilege. It is also committed to social justice and rejects notions of meritocracy (Steinberg & Kincheloe, 2001). This model opens up a space of possibility where dialogue, democratic participation, creativity, and reflection and action can take place. Freire's (1985) notion of "reading the word and the world" is well represented in a critical multicultural curriculum.

Indeed, Freire's notion remains a powerful tool for us in these times of uncertainty. Reading the word and the world means being able to critically analyze our experiences, our lives, our communities, and the political decisions of our leaders—crucial activities not only for ourselves but for future generations. Marcia Moraes's (1996) vision for a dialogic-critical pedagogy incorporates Baktin's and Freire's perspectives as we view ways of moving from the margins to the center and vice versa. It is difficult to see how the powerful ones have moved toward ameliorating the lives of the colonized. At the same time we need to move away from the same essentializing perspectives that come from an imperialist colonizing perspective.

McLaren (1995) describes the narrative's intersection with subjectivity, agency, and identity. He introduces us to "critical narratology" as an integral part of pedagogy. He describes the narrative's socializing function into particular ways of life through authorial voice: "Theories, ideologies, and social institutional practices—and our relationship to them—are all informed by narratives" (p. 91). McLaren sees the value of the dialectical by linking it to identity.

If narratives give our lives meaning we need to understand what those narratives are and how they have come to exert such an influence on us and our students. My position is that we need to be able to read critically the narratives that are already reading us. . . . I want to argue that identities are partly the result of narrativity of social life. (p. 89)

The notion of new meanings and identity is also captured by Homi Bhabha (1994, p. 190) in his theory of a "third space."

The possibilities of being somehow, *in between,* of occupying an interstitial space that was not fully governed by the recognizable traditions . . . often produces another *third space.* . . . [I]t opens up a space that is skeptical of cultural totalization, of notions of identity which depend for their authority on being "originary" . . . a space . . . cultural identification which subverted authority.

Bhabha's theory of a third space, Anzaldúa's (1987) border crossing project, critical multiculturalism, and critical narrative knowing can help us envision decolonizing perspectives in the curriculum and in the classroom. Kharem and Villaverde (in Soto, 2002b) offer teachers the notion of forging alliances. With this perspective teacher allies become coworkers with people of color to see and understand the daily lived realities of the oppressed populations while "tearing down the walls of oppression which will allow the human spirit to reach its potential" (p. 5). This type of curriculum signifies that the dialogic, the critical, the anti-racist, and the political are an integral part of the classroom. Forging alliances is a powerful weapon, as audre lorde's (1984) often-quoted advice reminds us: "The master's tools will never dismantle the master's house." The imperialist notion of rugged individualism, patriarchy, and competition can be challenged by acting in solidarity.

Only when our alliances are built with compassion and love will the internalized wounds of our learners and our nations heal. The painful stories of Golden Eagle, a Native American Latino child (Gutierrez-Gomez, 2002) entering kindergarten, of Irene Pabon (2002) growing up in Puerto Rico, and of Lynus Yamuna (2002) seeing students wearing dunce caps and signs around their necks for speaking their Melanesian home language remind us that these issues are prevalent not only in America but wherever the colonizers' imperialist eyes have gazed upon a people. "Imperialism still hurts, still destroys and is reforming itself constantly" (Smith, 1999).

SOUTH BRONX CHILDREN'S ASTHMA AND THE COMPLEXITIES OF POWER

"Dear President Clinton," the children from the South Bronx wrote. They contacted their president to describe how the dozens of nearby transfer stations, garbage dumps, junkyards, sewage treatment facility, garbage incineration plants, and junkyards and a fertilizer plant affect their daily health. President Clinton responded with "thanks so much for writing me about the environment." He then encouraged the children to recycle, ride bikes, use the mass transit, and consider a career in environmental technology. The children responded, "Dear Mr. Clinton, Thank you for your letter, but you didn't do anything about the pollution. We told you once and you didn't do anything. We're getting sick because of the pollution. Please close down the factory." In an NPR report (May 23, 1996), Melissa Block documented the asthma epidemic in the South Bronx from P.S. 48's Hunt's Point playground. The children in this neighborhood are mostly Latino/a, black, and poor. One-third to one-half of the 1,100 children suffer from asthma. The emergency room doctor at Lincoln Hospital treats 15,000 asthmatics every year. This story relates the complexities of power and education because children who are struggling to breath will have a difficult time learning.

Who cares about the children from the South Bronx? Several colleagues and I visited the South Bronx the year of 9/11. I was looking for P.S. 20 and 1024 Fox Street. My school, my apartment building. They were gone. The city eliminated all these buildings when fires gutted much of the neighborhood. It was a strange feeling to be told that your school records could be found in the basement of a different school building. We saw small townhouses in the place where the brick structures had stood. Who cares about the children from the South Bronx?

YOUNG LATINO/A CHILDREN

What do the children think about their contemporary situation? A recent study (Soto, 2002a; Soto & Lasta, 2005) conducted with Latino/a bilingual children indicates that they have a sense of altruism, a willingness to share their own wisdom and gifts with "the other." Young children's depictions of their own bilingualism move beyond dualisms and underscore how we can rid the world of oppression. Children's gifts of bilingualism are leading to an interpretation of agape love as opposed to a "burden of bilingualism/biliteracy." The children *help* to illuminate the needed new directions for a post–border crossing society *sin fronteras* (without borders). Anzaldúa (1987) captures the notion of a border crossing identity:

> To survive the Borderlands
> you must live sin fronteras
> be a crossroads (pp. 216–217)

The children very clearly explained to us that the main benefit of being bilingual (border crossing) subjects was being able to *help* others (classmates, family members, friends). This deliberate, voluntary behavior intended to benefit others was found in almost all the children. The children presented themselves as concerned about the well-being of others and having the will to *help* the other(s). Consider these examples of the conversations with the children:

> "I like to *help* people . . . I want them to feel good."
> "I tell her when you need *help*, tell me."

Their depictions express forms of socially desirable actions and behaviors such as teaching, translating, and helping in general, all instances of true altruism. Bicultural Latino/a children continue to reach out to "the other" with love and compassion (Soto, 2002a), exemplifying Freire's notion of pedagogy of hope.

SPACES OF HEALING

Our hearts as border crossers need to find that space for healing. This is no doubt difficult for those of us who are just beginning to retell, reconfigure, and reinvent our reinvented identities and our journeys. We welcome our theoretical allies like Joe Kincheloe, Shirley Steinberg, and Peter McLaren, who have walked the path with us. I dream about a day when peace and love will be the order of the day. Healing our inner wounds will someday lead us to reconciliation—a reconciliation preceded by compassion and forgiveness, a compassion and forgiveness preceded by understanding.

> When you understand, you cannot help but love. You cannot get angry. To develop understanding you have to practice looking at all living beings with the eyes of compassion.
>
> (Thick Nhat Hanh, 1991, pp. 79–80)

Our political leaders have scrambled to find experts who can speak particular languages or can understand particular cultures (e.g., during the Gulf War, after the World Trade Center tragedy, and during the war in Iraq). Yet these very linguistic and cultural gifts have been present in our classrooms. The monolingual, monocultural educational model has successfully wiped out possibilities for multilingual American children. We have relied on outdated teaching methods. Macedo and Bartolome (2000) note the irony of how America has dismantled bilingual education, a field with decades of research, while promoting foreign language education a field with well-documented failures. We have eliminated the very programs that can help our children and our nation (Soto, 1997b).

This form of language and cultural domination also establishes subordinate social relations whereby the possibility for critical literacy by bicultural, monocultural, and multicultural subjects is denied. Language domination by the "bilingual education abolitionists" constitutes hegemonic forces of class oppression and cultural invasion. This form of language conflict occurs when two languages compete for exclusive use of the same power-related function (e.g., schools or the government). This is one reason why bilingual education in the U.S. is constantly under attack by the English-only forces.

Linguistic domination is the work of the colonizer translating itself into a nightmarish slice of the American dream. Anzaldúa describes the linguistic terrorism of the "*deslenguados*":

Somos los del espanol deficiente.
We are your linguistic nightmare,
your linguistic aberration,
your linguistic mestizaje,
the subject of your burla.
Because we speak with tongues of fire
we are culturally crucified.
Racially, culturally and linguistically somos huerfanos—
we speak an orphan tongue.

(Anzaldúa, 1999, p. 80)

audre lorde (2003) provides a space for hope when she calls us to consider the following:

We need mass-based political movements calling citizens of this nation to uphold democracy and the rights of everyone to be educated, and to work on behalf of ending domination in all its forms—to work for justice, changing our educational system so that schooling is not the site where students are indoctrinated to support imperialist white-supremacist capitalist patriarchy or any ideology, but rather where they learn to open their minds, to engage in rigorous study and to think critically. (p. xiii)

The hope also lies in how children are immersed in altruistic behaviors.

CONCLUSION

In concluding this introduction I ask the reader to understand that there are personal reasons for writing such a work on behalf of Latino/a children just as there are larger societal implications in its creation. If the reader is able to grasp the complexities and the needed directions for implementing educational equity on behalf of Latino/a learners, then we will have accomplished our goals. The contributors to this handbook represent diverse experiences, diverse backgrounds, and diverse ideologies. One commonality brings us together, and that is the welfare of Latino/a learners in the U.S. educational context. Each contributor has highlighted the reader specific issues and knowledge that will help guide research, implement change, and advocate on behalf of an increasingly Latinized nation.

REFERENCES

Anzaldúa, G. (1987). *Borderlands/La Frontera: The New Mestiza*. San Francisco: Aunt Lute Books.

Bhabha, H. (1994). Between Identities. In R. Benmayor & A. Skotnes (Eds.), *Migration and Identity*. Oxford: Oxford University Press.

Bigler, E. (1999). *American Conversations: Puerto Ricans, White Ethnics, and Multicultural Education*. Philadelphia: Temple University Press.

Blaut, J. M. (1993). *The Colonizer's Model of the World*. New York: Guilford Press.

Carger, C. (1996). *Of Borders and Dreams: A Mexican-American Experience of Urban Education*. New York: Teachers College Press.

Carrasquillo, A. (1991). *Hispanic Children and Youth in the United States.* New York: Taylor & Francis.

Chang, N. (2002). *Silencing Political Dissent.* New York: Seven Stories Press.

Cofer, J. O. (1993). *The Latin Deli.* New York: W. W. Norton & Company.

Darder, A., Torres, R. D., & Gutiérrez, H. (Eds.). (1997). *Latinos and Education: A Critical Reader.* New York: Routledge.

DiSipio, L., & de la Garza, R. O. (1997). *Immigrants, Immigrant Policy, and Foundations of the Next Century's Latino Politics.* Latino civil rights conference, Washington, DC, December 5.

Du Bois, W.E.B. (1903). *The Souls of Black Folk.* Chicago: A. C. McClurg.

Frankenberg, R. (1993). *White Women, Race Matters: The Social Construction of Whiteness.* Minneapolis: University of Minnesota Press.

Freire, P. (1985). *The Politics of Education.* South Hadley, MA: Bergin & Garvey.

Garcia, E. (2001). *Hispanic Education in the United States.* New York: Rowman & Littlefield.

Gaston Report. (1999). *Latino Community Development and Public Policy* (Spring). Boston: Mauricio Gaston Institute.

Goldberg, D. T. (1993). *Racist Culture: Philosophy and the Politics of Meaning.* Cambridge: Blackwell.

Goldberg, D. T. (Ed.). (1990). *Anatomy of Racism.* Minneapolis: University of Minnesota Press.

Gutierrez-Gomez, C. (2002). Golden Eagle Enters Kindergarten. In L. D. Soto (Ed.), *Making a Difference in the Lives of Bilingual/Bicultural Children.* New York: Peter Lang.

Hanh, T. N. (1991). *Peace Is Every Step.* New York: Bantam Books.

Kharem, H., & Villaverde, L. (2002). Teacher Allies: The Problem of the Color Line. In L. D. Soto (Ed.), *Making a Difference in the Lives of Bilingual/Bicultural Children.* New York: Peter Lang.

King, M. L. (1963). *Letter from a Birmingham Jail.* New York: A. J. Muste Memorial Institute.

Loewen, J. (1995). *Lies My Teacher Told Me.* New York: Touchstone Books.

lorde, a. (1984). *Sister Outsider.* California: Crossing Press.

lorde, a. (2003). *Teaching Community: A Pedagogy of Hope.* New York: Routledge.

Macedo, D., & Bartolome, L. (2000). *Dancing with Bigotry.* New York: St. Martin's Press.

McLaren, P. (1995). *Critical Pedagogy and Predatory Culture.* New York: Routledge.

Mieir, K., & Stewart, L. (1991). *The Politics of Hispanic Education: Up paso pa'lante y dos p'atras.* Albany, NY: SUNY Press.

Moll, L., & Ruiz, R. (2002). The Schooling of Latino Children. In M. Suarez-Orosco & M. Paez (Eds.), *Latinos Remaking America* (pp. 362–374). Los Angeles: University of California Press.

Moraes, M. (1996). *Bilingual Education: A Dialogue with the Bakhtin Circle.* New York: SUNY Press.

Nieto, S. (Ed.). (2000). *Puerto Rican Students in U.S. Schools.* Hillsdale, NJ: Lawrence Erlbaum.

Pabon, I. (2002). A Life Span/Toda una vida: The Pain and the Struggle That Will Strike: El dolor y la lucha que embiste. In L. D. Soto (Ed.), *Making a Difference in the Lives of Bilingual/Bicultural Children.* New York: Peter Lang.

Pew Hispanic Center/Kaiser Family Foundation. (2002). *Survey of Latinos: Education.* Washington, DC. Available: www.pewhispanic.org.

Rand Corporation. (1994). *Educational Achievement of Generations: Executive Summary.* Los Angeles: Rand Corporation.

Rethinking Schools. (2001–2002). War, Terrorism, and Our Classrooms: Teaching in the Aftermath of the September 11th Tragedy. *Rethinking Schools* (Winter). Available: http://www.rethinkingschools.org/special_reports/sept11/index.shtml.

Silko, L. M. (1996). *Yellow Woman and a Beauty of the Spirit.* New York: Touchstone Books.

Smith, L. T. (1999). *Decolonizing Methodologies: Research and Indigenous Peoples.* London: Zed Books.

Sorensen, S., Brewer, D., Carroll, S., & Bryton, E. (1995). *Increasing Hispanic Participation in Higher Education: A Desirable Public Investment.* Washington, DC: Rand Rethinking Schools.

Soto, L. D. (1997a). Boricuas in America: The Struggle for Identity, Language, and Power. *Review of Education/Pedagogy/Cultural Studies* 19(4), 349–365.

Soto, L. D. (1997b). *Language, Culture and Power: Bilingual Families and the Struggle for Quality Education.* New York: SUNY Press.

Soto, L. D. (2002a). Latino Children's Perspectives of Bilingualism: Altruistic Possibilities. *Bilingual Research* Journal 26(3), 723–733.

Soto, L. D. (Ed.). (2002b). *Making a Difference in the Lives of Bilingual/Bicultural Children.* New York: Peter Lang.

Soto, L. D., & Lasta, J. (2005). Bilingual Border-Crossing. In L. D. Soto & B. B. Swadener (Eds.), *Power and Voice in Research with Children* (pp. 153–164). New York: Peter Lang.

Steinberg, S., & Kincheloe, J. (2001). Setting the Context for Critical/Interculturalism: The Power Blocs of Class Elitism, White Supremacy, and Patriarch. In S. Steinberg (Ed.), *Multi/Intercultural Conversations* (pp. 3–30). New York: Peter Lang.

Suro, R., & Passel, J. (2003). *The Rise of the Second Generation: Changing Patterns in Hispanic Population Growth.* Washington, DC: Pew Hispanic Center.

Tashakkori, A., & Ochoa, S. H. (1999). *Education of Hispanics in the United States: Politics, Policies, and Outcomes.* New York: AMS Press.

U.S. Census Bureau. Census 2002. Washington, DC: U.S. Department of Commerce.

Valdés, G. (1996). *Con respeto: Bridging the Distances between Culturally Diverse Families and Schools.* New York: Teachers College Press.

Valenzuela, A. (1999). *Subtractive Schooling: U.S.-Mexican Youth and the Politics of Caring.* Albany, NY: SUNY Press.

Walsh, C. (1996). *Pedagogy and the Struggle for Voice: Issues of Language, Power and Schooling for Puerto Ricans.* New York: Bergin & Garvey.

Wells-Barnett, I. (1969). *On Lynchings.* New York: Arno Press.

Yamuna, L. (2002). My Story and the Melanesian Knowledge. In L. D. Soto (Ed.), *Making a Difference in the Lives of Bilingual/Bicultural Children.* New York: Peter Lang.

Zentella, A. (1997). *Growing Up Bilingual: Puerto Rican Children in New York.* New York: Blackwell.

A

ACADEMIC ACHIEVEMENT AND LATINOS/AS

> In an additive school, one's language and ethnic identity are assets and figure precisely in what it means to be educated in U.S. society.
>
> Angela Valenzuela,
> *Subtractive Schooling*

Introduction

In March 1968, thousands of Chicano/a students walked out of classrooms in five East Los Angeles high schools in protest of miserable schooling conditions, demanding improvements in areas such as high dropout rates and the lack of Chicano curriculum and faculty. But whether the context of education for Latinos has improved since the Chicano blowouts of the 1960s is widely debated. Although more Chicanos/as and Latinos/as are eligible for community colleges and state universities and take the SAT, much research speaks to the formidable barriers that continue to exist for Latino/a students. Ryan (1971) believes that "despite years of marches, commissions, judicial decisions, and endless legislative remedies, we are confronted with unchanging or even widening racial differences in achievement." He refers to racial differences among ethnic and racial groups that exaggerate the social, political, and economic inequities found in society and position Latino/a students at the bottom levels of academic achievement.

Valencia (2002), author of *Chicano School Failure and Success,* equates school failure among Chicanos/as with a toothache that never goes away, a condition deeply rooted in the history of the U.S. His perception stems from personal research of the persistent and pervasive low academic achievement of Chicanos/as, as defined by low standardized test scores and high dropout rates. Sadly, Valencia reports that Chicano/a school failure pervades educational institutions across the nation, particularly those schools located in areas of low income. According to Valencia, "The results are alarmingly consistent: Chicano students, on the whole, tend to exhibit low academic achievement compared to their White peers" (p. 4). And yet, despite the need to reverse the desperate situation, little discussion surrounds or explains the forces that shape the educational attainment of those Latino/a students who are academically successful.

Why Is Research on Academically Successful Latino/a Students Necessary?

A catalyst in the quest to understand the forces behind academic achievement is the dramatic increase in the Latino/a population in the U.S. that has resulted in their presence as the largest minority group in the nation. It is a relatively young population with a median age of 26 or 27 years, seven years younger than other groups, and thus represents a significant portion of the nation's future workforce (Pérez & Salazar, 1997). Research suggests however, that "although Latinos represent a vibrant and sizable source of workers, their current social, education, and economic status must vastly improve if their demographic power is to be translated into economic strength, both for themselves and the United States" (Pérez & Salazar, 1997).

Despite the increase in their numbers, the gains in educational attainment for Latinos/as have not been proportionate to this growth. They are the least-educated major population group and the least likely to graduate from four-year universities (Gándara, 1995; Pérez & Salazar, 1997). Dropout rates for Latino/a students may exceed 50%, depending on the area of the country, surpassing those of any other major population group in the U.S. (Valencia, 2002). While students leave school for a myriad of reasons, family income and other aspects of family background are cited as the most common reasons (Gándara, 1995; Pérez & Salazar, 1997). Research also suggests that poor grades contribute to students' feelings of frustration and sense of disconnect with the school environment, particularly when coupled with issues such as limited English proficiency, acculturation, immigrant status, and poverty (Valencia, 2002).

The low level of Latino/a educational attainment must be linked to their poor representation in the U.S. labor force and economy. High numbers of Latinos/as are concentrated in low-skilled and unstable jobs and underrepresented in professional positions which require advanced degrees or well-developed math and literacy skills (Gándara 1995; Pérez & Salazar, 1997). An

analysis of the Latino/a participation in the labor force by Pérez and Salazar (1997) suggests that

reducing the inequality between Hispanics and the rest of society is an economic imperative and that increasing Hispanic educational attainment and other human capital characteristics is critical for the full integrations of Latinos into the future workforce. An undereducated, youthful, and growing Hispanic population has implications for labor force participation rates, earnings, socioeconomic stability and the nation's welfare. (p. 45)

This becomes even more problematic considering that the U.S. economy continues to evolve into a more competitive one where college degrees, much less a high school diploma, will become a prerequisite for most types of employment.

Deficit Thinking and Low Teacher Expectations

Critical to the discussions surrounding academic achievement among Latinos/as are research findings that may serve to inform school reform, teacher education, and public policy. If one adheres to the belief that schools are responsible for educating all children, then it follows that schools should seek to replicate the factors that ensure academic achievement for all students. This is especially important considering the obstacles Latinos/as face in obtaining an education, including ineffective and substandard schools, deficit thinking views, and low teacher expectations of them and their academic potential.

As a scholar who focuses on schools where low-income students of color achieve at or above national averages, Edmonds (1986) believes that "we must gain an understanding of how poor children of color are even now being properly educated in a number of public schools, and then ask the question: If this is so anywhere, then why not make it so everywhere?" (p. 110). His statement suggests that Latino/a students are routinely deprived of educational opportunities by schools that are not organized to facilitate their academic and personal growth. And yet, as part of the recent body of research on "effective schools," studies exist that document the effectiveness of several schools and teachers in meeting the needs of poor children of color. These schools share in common such characteristics as high expectations for students, teachers, and instructional programs; a positive attitude toward students and parents; competent leadership; and an emphasis on high achievement in academics (Lucas, Henze, & Donato, 1997). Such schools are devoid of the deficit views that compromise the educational experiences of Latino/a students.

As a result of misleading studies and widespread deficit views, grievous assumptions are made regarding the academic potential of Latino/a students in low-performing, low-income schools (*Coleman Report,* 1966; Fischer et al., 1996). Deficit thinking that draws from the culture of poverty paradigm presumes that because of defects in family background, poor students of color lack the intellectual ability and potential to succeed academically. These alleged defects may refer to parents' level of education, socioeconomic status, or English language abilities.

Whether related to success or failure, teacher expectations strongly influence students inside and outside the boundaries of the classroom. In one study, Entwisle, Alexander, and Olson (1997) report that "compared to children with the same test scores but of higher socioeconomic status . . . teachers held lower expectations for the future performance of students from low [socioeconomic] backgrounds and saw them as less active participants in class" (p. 214). Whether students participate less as a direct result of low expectations or whether teachers with low expectations perceive them as less active participants is unclear. Edmonds has observed that "professional personnel in less effective schools tended to attribute children's reading problems to non-school factors and . . . created an environment in which children failed because they were not expected to succeed" (p. 390). Thus, instead of acknowledging the shortcomings and ineffectiveness of many urban schools, a student's race, culture, and language are perceived as defects and used to explain low academic achievement. In addition, since a majority of Latino/a students experience school as English language learners, deficit views serve to exacerbate their already unmet language needs and relegate them to failure within the public school system.

What Makes for Academic Achievement?

Throughout the literature surrounding the topic, the definition of academic achievement varies according to different social and political circumstances. Some researchers deem individuals academically successful once they graduate from a prestigious university or attain an advanced degree. Others define achievement as matriculation at a four-year university or community college. For those who believe that in light of the many educational obstacles facing Latino/a students, such as high dropout rates, high school graduation embodies academic achievement. Many of the definitions rely on quantitative data and calculations, such as test scores, grades, and dropout rates.

Familial and Social Environments

In her introduction to *Over the Ivy Walls: The Educational Mobility of Low-Income Chicanos,* Gándara (1995) begins with the statement, "This is a study of high academic achievement found in the most unlikely of places: among low-income Mexican Americans from homes with little formal education" (p. 1). Few would disagree with her conclusion. Many studies have shown that high academic achievement correlates strongly with social class. In addition, much of the literature related to Latinos/as and education focuses on low academic achievement or the reported 35% to 50% of Latinos who leave school before their high school graduation (Romo & Falbo, 1996). In fact, *Over the Ivy Walls* is part of a shamefully limited body of research focusing solely on Latino/a students' success rather than failure.

In her unique study, Gándara (1995) explores why some Latino/a students from impoverished families surmounted extraordinary obstacles and achieved success among the educational elite. These academically ambitious individuals obtained a Ph.D., M.D., or J.D. from prestigious universities and chose to use education as a vehicle for social mobility. Gándara selected participants from backgrounds associated with school failure: poverty, low levels of parental education, large families, and limited exposure to English at home (Gándara, 1995). Through her qualitative study she sought to gain an understanding of how and why some low-income Chicanos/as find success in school. Based on the data derived from extensive interviews, Gándara divides the forces that shaped the participants' academic achievement into broad categories, including home influences, family stories as cultural capital, schools and neighborhoods, peers, and personal attributes and individual differences.

Gándara (1995), as well as Stanton-Salazar (2001), found that Mexican parents engaged in activities that the achievement literature reports as typical for engendering academic achievement among white middle-class students. The parents were supportive of their children's educational goals, encouraged literacy activities, and set high academic expectations. In Gándara's study, the major difference between the two sets of parents focused on parenting styles. The parents of the participants in her study were characterized as "authoritarians" who possessed sole decision-making power, a strategy oftentimes used to counteract the potential negative effects of their neighborhoods or slow the rapid acculturation of their children to American culture (Gándara, 1995; Stanton-Salazar, 2001). While the "authoritarian" parenting style is normally thought to discourage independence and motivation, Gándara believes that the participants learned self-reliance through other means. Many of the participants held positions of responsibility within their families, and many worked alongside their parents in fields and factories. Consequently, their parents engaged in difficult labor and communicated to their children the value of "hard work," which, in turn, permeated their children's academic endeavors.

Stanton-Salazar (2001) believes that Mexican immigrant parenting styles place a high premium on moral character, or *educación*. While the Spanish language definition encompasses much more personal and family responsibility than its English cognate, *educación* refers to a family's commitment to providing children with a sense of moral personal responsibility that they believe is essential to ensuring academic and personal success. This concept is oftentimes unfamiliar or easily dismissed by traditional schools, leading to further disconnect between Latino/a families and school staff.

In *Latino High School Graduation: Defying the Odds,* Romo and Falbo (1996) identified parenting strategies utilized by Latino/a or Mexican parents. Strategies that relate specifically to education include

1. Monitoring students in supportive ways;
2. Continuing to reinforce the "stay in school" message; and
3. Staying involved in school, which included participation in school activities, as well as maintaining ongoing communications with teachers and school administrators. (p. 126)

Thus, while parenting practices and school involvement may take on different forms among ethnic groups, the assumption that Latino/a parents are disinterested in or do not value the education of their children is unfounded. Parental involvement and support in educational attainment are present in the Latino/a community though poor parents may lack the time or resources to fully participate on-site. Furthermore, research suggests that poor, working-class parents are more involved in the education of their children when the schools implement programs to encourage their participation.

Another factor that Gándara (1995) found accounted for an intense desire for academic achievement was the transmission of family stories. In communicating their hopes and dreams for the future, many parents recounted stories of past wealth and prestige to their children. Gándara believes that

if one lives with stories about former exploits, about ancestors who owned their own lands and controlled their own destinies, it is probably

much easier to imagine that this is one's destiny. At the very least, the evidence exists that, by virtue of the family history, one is capable of a better life. (p. 112)

These parents created what she refers to as a "culture of possibility," one that encouraged their children to seek lives different from those they and their parents experienced in the past or present. For many of the participants, this manifested itself in intense academic achievement. Ultimately, Gándara (1995) noted that more than two-thirds of the participants cited their most important characteristic as persistence, not innate ability, and described their parents and themselves as "hard workers."

Inasmuch as the aforementioned characteristics played a role in creating a familial environment of academic achievement, Gándara noted that each of the participants also "met with opportunity" without which the other factors would have been inadequate (p. 113). She defined opportunity as the chance to participate in a college preparatory curriculum and also as access to the information and resources that would make a college education a feasible goal. Ultimately, this finding holds the greatest potential for informing educational policy concerning school reform and teacher education programs.

Academic and School Environment

In addition to the motivational factors inherent in the home environment, such as parents' level of education and economic status, it is also critical to examine the role of schools, particularly secondary schools, in potentially fostering academic achievement among Latino/a students. Oftentimes the familial and the academic environments are viewed as independent entities in the effort to promote academic achievement. Methodologically, it is almost impossible to separate the two and substantially easier to focus on the more controlled setting of the family environment. The perception that Latino/a students succeed "in spite" of their schools also exists. Thus, it is important to recognized the powerful influence exerted by schools on Latino/a students.

In *Subtractive Schooling,* Angela Valenzuela (1999) untangles the weave of familial and academic environments in order to help understand the patterns of academic achievement, and what she defines as underachievement, in U.S.-born Mexican students. Her study of students attending a large urban high school in Houston, Texas, comprised of a virtually all-Mexican student population, offers a glimpse into how one school "divests . . . youth of important social and cultural resources, leaving them progressively vulnerable to academic failure" (p. 3).

Instead of serving as "conduits for the American dream," Valenzuela (1999) argues, schools subtract resources from Mexican youth, including immigrant and first-, second-, and third-generation students. Schools like the one observed in her study are organized in ways that dismiss students' culturally based definition of education, or *educación,* and demean their culture and language. As a result of these practices, the skills, motivation, and social currency that students bring with them diminish over the course of their educational experiences. If subtractive schooling denies students opportunities for academic achievement, it then follows that schools that validate the cultural, linguistic, and social capital of students may serve to enhance their academic potential. Additive schooling, according to Valenzuela,

is about equalizing opportunity and assimilating Mexicans into the larger society, albeit

through a bicultural process. In this world, students do not have to choose between being Mexican or American; they can be both. This pluralistic model of schooling builds on students' bicultural experience—which all minority youth bring with them to school—to make them conversant, respectful and fluent in as many dialects and languages as they can master. (p. 269)

Valenzuela (1999) chose an ethnographic approach that utilized both qualitative and quantitative data. Her study began with a survey, focused on the correlation between generational status and academic achievement, of the entire student body. Using the information derived from the survey as a point of departure, the researcher then took on the role of participant observer and spent time talking with students in groups, individually, in class, during lunch, and at school and community functions. Over the course of three years, Valenzuela became intimately involved in the life of the school, and of some students, and subsequently gained a clear understanding of student attitudes toward education.

Valenzuela (1999) conducted informal interviews with students and teachers, and through those experiences she discovered the importance of human relations to students' motivations to succeed. Students often expressed their "affiliational needs in terms of caring" with regards to other students and teachers. Valenzuela found that productive relationships with teachers increased the likelihood that students felt positively toward school, thereby resulting in an educational environment students not only perceived as valuable but also believed they could navigate successfully. Students wish to be recognized as individuals, but their previous experiences with teachers temper their enthusiasm and place the responsibility of initiating a relationship upon the teacher (Valenzuela, 1999). Ultimately, positive social relations with teachers allow students to accumulate social capital, a form of trust that exists in the relationships between people (Coleman & Hoffer, 1997). Students may then transform social capital into resources or opportunities such as good grades.

Another important factor that influenced academic achievement among the students in Valenzuela's study was how the students grouped themselves and the types of activities they chose to participate in, before, during, and after school, through their affiliation with those groups. Valenzuela (1999) found that "students were invested in schooling if their friends were invested in it or if their teachers were invested in them" (p. 8). Not surprisingly, students defined their group associations according to English language fluency and generational status, dividing themselves even further based on recency of arrival. These misunderstandings may lead students to possess low levels of self-esteem and dismiss the worth of their culture and language, thereby decreasing the possibility of academic success.

With regards to the attrition of academic achievement among generations of Mexican immigrant families, Valenzuela (1999) parallels her notion of subtractive schooling with what is referred to as a "generational decline in academic achievement" (p. 6). The academic experiences of the students in her study parallel those of other first-generation Mexican immigrants and U.S.-born Mexican American students, which indicate that the academic achievement, as defined by grades, test scores, and dropout rates, of immigrant students is greater than of those generations who follow them. While immigrant, first- and often second-generation students tend to achieve higher academic success than their third- and fourth-gener-

ation counterparts, Valenzuela suggests that schools bear the brunt of the responsibility for the decline. She points out that the differences in achievement are found only in students placed in academic programs or tracks that do not presume college attendance. Students placed in college-bound tracks do not conform to the generational expectations, thus accentuating the importance of track placement in fostering academic achievement among Latinos/as.

Summary and Implications

The dearth of research surrounding Latino/a students and academic achievement, particularly those from low-income backgrounds, can be misleading. Simply because little research focuses exclusively on the topic does not mean that students with the potential to join the educational elite do not exist in high numbers throughout the U.S. This is particularly important considering the growing numbers of Latinos/as in the U.S. and their potential impact on the U.S. economy. Research such as that of Gándara, Valencia, and Valenzuela should be interwoven throughout the curriculum of schools and teacher education programs in order to provide successful representations of Latinos/as and raze the deficit views that permeate many classrooms. However, even more high-quality longitudinal research into the topic is needed to create positive educational experiences and opportunities for Latino/a students. Unfortunately, without more research regarding the forces that propel successful students to academic achievement, educational policy will be shaped by the prevalent views of Latino/a failure.

References

Coleman, J. et al. (1966). The Coleman Report. In R. Arum & I. Beattie (Eds.), *The Structure of Schooling: Readings in the Sociology of Education.* Mountain View, CA: Mayfield.

Coleman, J., & Hoffer, T. (1997). Schools, Families and Communities. In R. Arum & I. Beattie (Eds.), *The Structure of Schooling: Readings in the Sociology of Education* (pp. 69–77). Mountain View, CA: Mayfield.

Edmonds, R. (1986). *Characteristics of Effective Schools.* Hillsdale, NJ: Lawrence Erlbaum.

Entwisle, D., Alexander, K., & Olson, L. (1997). The Nature of Schooling. In R. Arum & I. Beattie (Eds.), *The Structure of Schooling: Readings in the Sociology of Education* (pp. 207–217). Mountain View, CA: Mayfield.

Fischer, C., et al. (1996). *Inequality by Design: Cracking the Bell Curve Myth.* Princeton, NJ: Princeton University Press.

Gándara, P. (1995). *Over the Ivy Walls: The Educational Mobility of Low-Income Chicanos.* Albany, NY: SUNY Press.

Lucas, T., Henze, R., & Donato, R. (1997). Promoting the Success of Latino Language–Minority Students: An Exploratory Study of Six High Schools. In A. Darder, R. D. Torres, & H. Gutiérrez (Eds.), *Latinos and Education: A Critical Reader* (pp. 373–397). New York: Routledge.

Pérez, S., & Salazar, D. (1997). Economic, Labor Force and Social Implications of Latino Educational and Population Trends. In A. Darder, R. D. Torres, & H. Gutiérrez (Eds.), *Latinos and Education: A Critical Reader* (pp. 45–79). New York: Routledge.

Rist, R. (1970). Student Social Class and Teacher Expectations: The Self-Fulfilling Prophecy in Ghetto Education. *Harvard Educational Review* 40(3), 411–451.

Romo, H. D., & Falbo, T. (1996). *Latino High School Graduation: Defying the Odds.* Austin: University of Texas Press.

Ryan, W. (1971). *Blaming the Victim.* New York: Pantheon Books.

Stanton-Salazar, R. (2001). *Manufacturing Hope and Despair: The School and Kin Support Networks of U.S.-Mexican Youth.* New York: Teachers College Press.

Valencia, R. (2002). The Plight of Chicano Students: An Overview of Schooling Conditions and Outcomes. In R. Valencia (Ed.), *Chicano School Failure and Success* (pp. 3–49). New York: Routledge.

Valenzuela, A. (1999). *Subtractive Schooling: U.S.-Mexican Youth and the Politics of Caring.* Albany, NY: SUNY Press.

Recommended Reading

Darder, A., Torres, R. D., & Gutiérrez, H. (Eds.). (1996). *Latinos and Education: A Critical Reader.* New York: Routledge.

Gándara, P. (1995). *Over the Ivy Walls: The Educational Mobility of Low-Income Chicanos.* Albany, NY: SUNY Press.

Valenzuela, A. (1999). *Subtractive Schooling: U.S.-Mexican Youth and the Politics of Caring.* Albany, NY: SUNY Press.

Alejandra Velasco

ACADEMIC MODELS: EXPLAINING ACHIEVEMENT

During the twentieth century and until the present, U.S. policymakers, researchers, and educators have used different educational explanations derived from anthropological, sociological, and psychological studies to characterize the academic achievement of Latino students in elementary and secondary schools (Foley, 1991; Montero-Sieburth, in press; Montero-Sieburth & Batt, 2001). These explanations, which have been characterized by social scientists for use by policymakers and other researchers, have emerged during different time periods, situated in specific social and cultural contexts, with different research foci and agendas (Bernstein, 1975; Bourdieu & Passeron, 1977; Bowles & Gintis, 1976; Cazden, Vera, & Steiner, 1972; Cook-Gumperz & Gumperz, 1982; Erickson, 1994; Fine, 1989; Fordham & Ogbu,

1986; Gibson & Ogbu, 1991; Mehan, Villanueva, & Lintz, 1996; Ogbu, 1978; Ogbu & Davis, 2003; Ogbu & Matute-Bianchi, 1986; Philips, 1983; Suarez-Orozco, 1989; Suarez-Orozco, C., & Suarez-Orozco, M., 2002; Trueba, 1987).

Their purpose has been to provide data on how different ethnic groups achieve academically in U.S. schools and to seek answers to the questions that are raised about why some ethnic group students succeed while others fail in their educational advancement. In this regard, they contribute to our understanding of Latinos and education by situating their progress over time and by identifying the types of research that have been conducted in the past and into the future.

These explanations have provided some degree of characterization of an ethnic group's advancement in education, particularly African Americans, Latinos, Asians, and Native Americans. They have identified areas in need of attention, such as the impact of testing and assessment on Latino students, and what needs to be done to help students advance. Yet they have also inadvertently contributed to the creation of negative perceptions and assessments of underrepresented groups, and in this case, Latino students, their families, and communities (Montero-Sieburth & Batt, 2001).

In general, the research of social scientists and policymakers interested in quantitative large-group analysis and qualitative case, school, or classroom studies and from studies conducted (1) between groups, (2) within groups, and (3) on the educational achievement of U.S.-born versus immigrant students in U.S. schools has given rise to these explanations. The between-group research has focused primarily on how well Latino students fare in terms of their educational advancement compared to white

Anglo middle-class students and in contrast to African American and Asian students (Darder, Torres, & Gutiérrez, 1997; Ogbu & Matute-Bianchi, 1986). These studies have tended to be longitudinal, using statistical large data analysis over time, such as that presented by the High School and Beyond research. This has been extended by research on closing the achievement gap between diverse groups (Portes, 2005). The within-group research has grown from studies conducted on the educational status of Cubans, Mexicans, and Puerto Ricans over the past few decades, but it now includes the research on Central Americans, South Americans, and diverse Caribbean groups (Chapa, 1996; Darder et al., 1997; Garcia, 2001). The seminal research of John Ogbu, Margaret Gibson, Henry T. Trueba, Marcelo Suarez-Orozco, and Carola Suarez-Orozco (Ogbu, 1991; Ogbu & Matute-Bianchi, 1986; Trueba, 1987; Suarez-Orozco, 1989; Suarez-Orozco, C., & Suarez-Orozco, M., 1995), among many others, characterizes the research that has been conducted on identifying differences between U.S.-born and foreign-born Latinos.

To date, a wealth of research has accumulated on Latino students and the types of explanations used to identify causes or reasons for their educational achievement in the past 40 years (Montero-Sieburth, in press). Yet the focus on Latino student achievement scores, testing, elementary and high school completion rates, graduation rates, and postsecondary opportunities, as well as dropout rates and studies on the achievement gap has targeted Latino students as one of the groups most in need of attention.

Many of the studies on Latino students show they lag behind not only their white counterparts but also other ethnic minorities; they have limited educational opportunities, have one of the highest dropout rates in the U.S., and are fast becoming part of a growing underclass—a two-tiered generation of those who "make it" and those who are lost to society (Calderon, 1997, 1998; Carter & Segura, 1979). Such results portray Latinos as being dismally disadvantaged compared to other groups, failing to advance academically, and being condemned to a limited and irrevocably poor education (*The Condition of Education*, 2002). Furthermore, some results from these studies are interpreted through explanations taken at face value to be true for all Latinos, creating biases, generalizations, and limited understanding of the underlying issues that affect the education of Latino students and their families. Some explanations have correlated Latino students' failure to pathological causes, stipulating that Latinos are unable to learn because they lack motivation, their use of Spanish rather than English detracts from their learning in academic contexts, and their culture and home environments are unconducive to preparing them for schools. Given such cultural deprivation and cultural deficit explanations, Latino students are either blamed for their status or victimized—roles difficult to overcome because some of these explanations are accepted as totally "scientifically based." Fortunately, researchers today have disproved such allegations, but the underlying assumptions remain evident in some current policies that advocate for active Latino participation in education and Latino students pulling themselves up by their bootstraps.

Accepting these explanations as science also raises certain issues and considerations: (1) the lack of understanding about the research paradigms and perspectives of researchers used at different times for studying Latino students and the consequences of their use; (2) the use of certain data sets over others and their implications; (3) the types of policies that have been generated as a consequence of such research; (4) the significance of the community perspectives of Latinos in relation to their education; and (5) the lack of shared faith in the inherent success that these Latino students and their families may have.

Understanding how such explanations have gained explanatory power, legitimization, and acceptance in academic and policy circles requires us to conceptualize theories and methodologies for explaining ethnic failure, their scientific contributions, and the historical grounding of such theories and methodologies.

This entry presents a brief overview of the most salient explanations for the academic achievement of Latino students by identifying the early research of Latinos and education evident in the thinking that persisted during the latter part of the nineteenth century into the early twentieth century; the research conducted during the 1960s and 1970s that gave rise to explanations on issues of poverty, social needs, and language differences; the research of the 1980s and 1990s that gives way to ecological and macro structural analysis including differential patterns of schooling; and the explanations that have arisen from the research being conducted from the 1990s to the first years of this millennium that focuses concretely on peer social relations and transnational and immigrant experiences and adaptation.

This cursory overview and critique builds upon previous literature reviews published by Montero-Sieburth & Batt (2001) in "An Overview of the Educational Models Used to Explain the Academic

Achievement of Latino Students: Implications for Research and Policies into the New Millennium" and by Montero-Sieburth (in press) in "Explanatory Models of Latino Education during the Reform Movement of the 1980s." Because each explanation requires greater presentation than can possibly be made through this entry, only those explanations that directly intersect with the lives of Latino elementary and secondary students in terms of their cultural backgrounds, language use, social class, economic background, immigrant and non-immigrant experiences, social relationships, and identity have been clustered together in the typology presented herein. A general critique of the basic contributions and limitations of these explanations is presented.

The presentation of the explanations in chronological order does not imply that each has a beginning or end, since some explanations have been dismissed, reified, expanded upon, or revived and some are current today.

Segregationist Educational Explanations: The 1860s to the 1920s and 1930s

The basis for some of the early educational explanations later applied to Latino students can be traced to the theories of social science advanced during the latter part of the nineteenth century into the early twentieth century. According to Menchaca and Valencia (1990), Charles Darwin's *The Origin of the Species* in (1859) gave rise to the debates about racial superiority and inferiority. Their rationale was fueled by Herbert Spencer's theory of the "survival of the fittest"; by ideas about selective intragroup breeding to maintain a pure race and culture; by the eugenics movement founded by Sir Francis Galton, which advocated for sterilization of racial minorities

and poor immigrant whites; and by the "Teutonic origins theory," which fostered the biological superiority of Anglo-Saxons. They contend that these academic theories, along with religious beliefs that Anglo-Saxons were "Chosen People," with governmental policies of expansionism and imperialism—as manifested in the Mexican and Spanish Wars, in the Mexican-American War of 1846–1848, and under the banner of Manifest Destiny—served to sustain the dominance of Anglo-Saxons over other groups.

This thinking, according to Menchaca and Valencia (1990), carried over into the passage of the "separate but equal" education code of 1874 and *Plessy v. Ferguson* in 1896, which sanctioned segregation legislation and created racist and discriminatory educational practices into the 1920s and 1930s.

Menchaca and Valencia (1990) point out that even though anthropologist Franz Boas demonstrated that social characteristics were not genetically hereditary, during this time social segregation increased based on IQ testing as well as cultural deprivation theories. Under this thinking, Latinos were presumed intellectually inferior (Stein, 1985). They note that "Mexicans were initially involuntarily segregated in the 19th century and the structure evolved into a pattern of residential ethnic isolation" (p. 229).

Even by 1947, when the *Mendez v. Westminster* case ended de jure segregation in California, segregation of school districts did not end. In fact, rather than diminishing, resegregation of school districts has continued to grow and has become rampant in many parts of the U.S. (Orfield & Yung, 1999). According to Orfield, Frankenberg, and Lee (2003), it is not surprising to find school districts with concentrations of 70%

low-income students in their student body, with limited human and material resources, evident discriminatory practices, inadequate curriculum, and poorly prepared teachers who have low expectations of students.

In fact, in some urban cities segregated schools for Latinos have become the norm. Redistricting and finding greater distributive equity may be structural solutions to segregated schools, although the role of parents and their participation in schools is another solution often underestimated in the case of Latino parents.

Several revisionist history researchers, including Ruben Donato (1999), David Montejano (1992), and Guadalupe San Miguel (1987), have documented the activism of Latino parents through factual and contextually bound data, which has been omitted in the educational history of Latinos. They have made evident the involvement of Latino parents during segregation, pointing out that these parents did not stand by passively but acted strongly in favor of the education of their children.

Today, given the demands of the No Child Left Behind Federal Act of 2001, the issue of equity and excellence, as well as of closing the achievement gap, looms high in the education of Latino students. Latino families are being asked to participate as partners in education; they are being asked to assume leadership roles in schools, yet for many that partnership requires that they have not only more voice in of choice to schooling but also leadership within their children's schools in terms of the policies and practices that affect their learning.

Critique. Viewed through our twenty-first-century lenses, these segregationist theories of the past century, though in disuse today, still carry over much of their institutionalized racism and discrimination in the ways that Latinos are served by schools. If Latinos are to succeed in schools, the way they are perceived, acknowledged, and recognized are as critical as the way they can be supported in their learning. Yet such learning needs to be regarded as an educational right. This demands having access to good schools that are not segregated, not of poor quality, not limited by lack of professional staff and curriculum that is irrelevant. Only then can we consider segregated schools a thing of the past.

The Cultural Explanations of the 1960s–1970s: Cultural Deficit, Cultural Deprivation, and Cultural Differences

During the 1960s and through the 1970s, explanations that presented the cultural deficits and disadvantages of underrepresented students prevailed. Problems in learning were located in the culture of the home, where underrepresented students were at a disadvantage compared to their middle-class Anglo counterparts because they lacked the reading resources, activities, and programs needed in becoming educated. Policies and programs were fostered first under President Lyndon B. Johnson's "Great Society" model and later under educational legislation that presumed that by re-educating the families and creating remedial programs, the so-called deficits would be offset, thereby creating a foothold for the education of underrepresented students.

Although the initial focus was on African American students, Latinos were also considered to be failing because they did not have the access to reading, writing, computing, and ways of speaking that mainstream white students had. Moreover, they did not speak English, and their standards were such that they could not achieve in schools. The way to offset such deficits was either through emphasizing behavioral changes that would lead to effective learning, preparing students at home with specialized instruction particularly targeted at parents, or receiving compensatory or remedial education in schools that would allow them to compete at the same level as their white counterparts.

Using the lens of the culture-of-poverty theory, explanations about the encapsulation of Latinos within their cultures, caught within a vice of poverty from which they could not rise, became a common characterization, linking Latinos to the cultural deprivation and cultural deficit models.

For many Latinos, the creation of Headstart became a vehicle for early childhood learning; yet for others, the sink-or-swim programs of English learning became their primary means of advancement (Stein, 1985). As Foley (1991) points out, another explanation emerged to shift the studies of classroom to student-teacher communication and to understanding the cultural background of students. This was the cultural differences explanation, which demonstrated that differences in speaking, and communication that appeared inappropriate in classroom settings for underrepresented students and their teachers, contributed to low academic achievement. Theories of mismatch and miscommunication between teachers and students as well as differences in learning styles and values were often proffered as examples of poor achievement. Studies conducted by Dell Hymes (1974), Courtney Cazden, John Vera, and Susan Steiner (1972), and Susan Philips (1983), among many others, did much to highlight conflict differences in speech patterns, in the linguistic and cultural codes and the values attached to these. Moreover, these microethnographic studies focused on how power dynamics between teachers and students were being played out.

Critique. The cultural deficit and cultural deprivation theories fell into misuse because they tended to place the blame on the families and students and presented a passive picture of the agency of these parents and students to act on their behalf. Latino parents are engaged in the education of their children, yet accessing that education requires understanding the infrastructure of educational policies as well as practices. In this regard, identifying the culture of the home as static and nonadaptive is in itself problematic.

The cultural difference model, while appealing and helpful in identifying sensitivities of teachers and school administrators with students and inequalities within teacher and student interactions, was limited in its scope. As John Ogbu (1978) pointed out, these studies were often decontextualized, devoid of historical and structural analysis, and presented solutions that could not explain why some students succeeded while others failed.

Language Explanations during the 1970s–1990s and into the Present

Spurred by the work of sociolinguists, psychologists, and anthropologists of the 1970s, the use of language functions, first and second language acquisition, differential code switching, and bilingualism took center stage in the education of Latinos (August & Hakuta, 1997; Christian & Genesse, 2001; Cummins, 1989; Hakuta, Butler, & Witt, 2000; Krashen, 1999). It is during this period, spanning to the present, that research on language patterns between students and teachers in elementary grades, ESL and bilingual learning strategies, longitudinal community studies, and code-switching linguistic patterns are emphasized. Not only did bilingual programs proliferate during the 1970s into the initial years of this century, but also English as a Second Language, early and late exit, and dual-language programs were expanded. The 1968 Bilingual Education Act, under the Elementary and Secondary Education Act, pushed through the initiatives of using native language instruction as a vehicle for acquiring English language proficiency. This was followed by the *Lau v. Nichols* initiatives, which allowed Chinese-speaking students as well as other to have special instruction to help them transition into English-speaking mainstream programs using different classes in their native languages and in English (Crawford, 1999).

But just as the research ranging from early studies of the 1980s with Dutcher (1982), Skutnabb-Kangas (1981), McLaughlin (1984), and Cummins (1989) to later studies conducted by Willig (1985), Kathryn J. Lindholm (1995), and Wayne Thomas and Virginia Collier (1999) became known, the debate about the effectiveness of bilingual education raged as a political battle. On the one hand, proponents of bilingual education supported the use of second language learning along with the maintenance of first language and cultural maintenance; on the other hand, opponents of bilingual education decried bilingual education as a denial of English language learning opportunities for students and as anti-American (Crawford, 1999).

The explanations that have followed have paralleled such a debate, and in this regard, Latino students have been caught in this political crossfire between the "English plus" proponents and the "English only" opponents (Baker & de Kanter, 1983; Padilla et al., 1991; Rossell & Baker, 1996). The passage of Proposition 227 in California, based on the proposal made in Arizona by Ronald Unz to diminish bilingual educational programs in favor of English immersion, and Chapter 386 of the Massachusetts Acts of 2002 requiring public schools to identify, assess, and place English language learners in sheltered English instruction classes typify the current trend occurring throughout American schools in favor of English immersion. In many school districts, sheltered English immersion (SEI), whereby teachers use physical activities, visual aids, and the environment to teach English vocabulary for concept development in mathematics, science, social studies, and other subjects to English language learners, has become the medium of instruction. Only in a few Massachusetts school districts—as, for example, in the Framingham schools—is bilingual education still in use.

In fact, this millennium has witnessed the dramatic decrease and elimination of bilingual education in favor of English immersion and the belief that by using a monolingual system, Latino students will succeed. The studies on high-stakes testing and its impact, on subtractive rather than additive bilingualism, and on the types of assessments Latino students are facing point altogether to the contrary (Valenzuela, 1999).

Critique. The research in language development has been extensive and supportive of many of the educational needs of Latino students, since language use is not only a cognitive achievement, as Catherine Snow (1992) has argued, but also a sociocultural phenomenon. Language research has contributed to the education of Latino students in several ways: First, it has provided greater understanding and knowledge of the complexities of language learning: in first and second language acquisition; of time needed for learning a second language; and of the consequences of language learning, use, and frequency.

Second, it acknowledges the importance of considering language status in second language acquisition. Third, it shows the learning of languages from generation to generation, with research indicating that by the third generation, Latinos use English more than Spanish, for example. Fourth, it demonstrates the interconnectedness of language to beliefs, attitudes, and identity. Fifth, it considers the role of language learning in community contexts. Finally, it makes clear the importance of policy initiatives around first and second language learning.

Yet as much as language research has generated such knowledge, the explanations for language learning for Latino students have become mired within the political debates attributed to bilingual education. The ground gained by bilingual education efforts of the 1970s and 1980s has been diminished by the institutionalization of English immersion. The issue of how Latino students are integrated in schools through English immersion, as English language learners, tested primarily using English and can be said to succeed remains a major unresolved concern.

Cultural and Ecological Explanations during the 1980s and into the Present

During the 1980s into the 1990s and even now, cultural and ecological explanations arose primarily from the research of John Ogbu (1978), Margaret Gibson and Ogbu (1991), Signithia Fordham and John Ogbu (1986), John Ogbu and Maria Matute-Bianchi (1986), and Michelle Fine and Lois Weis (2003), to name just a few. While Ogbu's research has to do with the interplay between the institution and an individual's economic opportunities, earlier studies had already begun to identify the role of the individual in the interplay between social and economic meanings. These were the contributions of research by Pierre Bourdieu and Jean Passeron (1977) on cultural capital, Samuel Bowles and Herbert Gintis's (1976) correspondence theory, and Paul Willis's (1972) resistance theory.

Using a macroeconomic stratification model that attempts to explain why underrepresented students see themselves as "not making it," Ogbu defines the ceiling of opportunities that the educational structure makes available to such students. He introduces the concepts of immigrant and involuntary minorities to distinguish the different gains achieved by each group. Immigrants arrive in the U.S. for economic and educational advantage, and they may do so because they are also serving their own communities. Such immigrants see their gains concretely, whereas the non-immigrant or involuntary groups, who have had a history of subjugation by conquest, colonization, or domination, see their educational opportunities as limited and constrained. Given these limitations, these non-immigrants or involuntary groups fail.

Ogbu attempts to study such phenomena in other contexts, and he develops a universalistic theory about the cultural ecological model of success and failure in school based on the students' sense of survival, of "making it," being able to be academically supported or by creating oppositional counterreactions. Signithia Fordham and John Ogbu (1986) identify such opposition for African American students as the burden of "acting white," that is, exhibiting behavior that hides one's academic abilities and in which one "dumbs down" in order to be accepted and included by white peer groups.

In more recent ethnographic studies of structural influences, Michelle Fine and

Lois Weis (2003) demonstrate through a historically grounded ethnography how urban students confront non-transformative educational practices. They show through their work how schools silence students and reproduce oppression. They also indicate the ways students create avenues for expressing their own discourse or conversations. Fine and Weis's focus is in describing the lived experiences of underrepresented students in the ways they engage in schooling, or counterresist, and in identifying the ways in which they can reconstruct their sense of self to meaningful knowledge and skills. In so doing, they show that even when schools create "cultures of failure," some students are resilient despite such odds.

Critique. The explanations fostered by Ogbu have been widely critiqued for their value-ladened distinctions that reify culture, for overemphasizing racial oppression and negative historical legacy, for not accounting for the variability found within groups, and for testing a theory at the student level and situating groups within a "self-fulfilling prophecy" (Foley, 1991; Foster, 2004). Yet, Ogbu's legacy in attempting to present a universal theory of cross-cultural analysis, in underlining the importance of economic structures along with institutional racism, and in presenting oppositional cultures is impressive and challenging.

Whereas Ogbu contributes methodologically and theoretically to understanding and explaining success and failure in schools, the research of his associates and most recent studies is directed to understanding schooling from the level of the individual student as manifested in Fine and Weis's research. In this regard, research on Latinos as that advanced by Gibson, Gándara, and Koyama (2004) and Stanton-Salazar (1997) on the significance of social

capital are an example of how peer culture is being internally studied rather than subsumed.

Psychological Explanations from the 1970s to the Present

Using the backdrop of many of the psychological and anthropological studies of the 1970s and 1980s on the culture-of-poverty theory and national character studies, the realm of psychological explanations directed at Latino students has been influenced among many concepts by the dual frames of reference, the peer coexistence model, and the notion of segmented assimilation. The dual frame of reference presented in the research of Marcelo Suarez-Orozco (1987) refers to the duality that is lived by some of the "new immigrants," such as Central Americans who live in the U.S., who make constant reference to how things are back home and in so doing show the borderlessness of their existence. Similarly, the peer coexistence model researched by Rumbaut and Portes (2001) and others shows that for Latinos the influence of peer associations often determines their chances for learning. Under this model, depending on the evident leadership, the color, and location of individuals within Eurocentric contexts, Latino students may experience downward or upward assimilation (Portes & Rumbaut, 2001; Portes & Zhou, 1993).

Current Research on Second-Generation Status of Latino Students, the Effects of Transnationalism, and Global Perspectives, 2000 to the Present

Current research has expanded upon this research to focus on adaptability of immigrants into the second generation. Reports following and tracking Latinos from one generation to another indicate that the educational profile of Latino immigrants is improving (Lowell & Suro, 2002). Current research by Marcelo and Carola Suarez-Orozco (1995, 2001) and Marcelo Suarez-Orozco and Paez (2002) indicates how many Latino students adapt in schools through resilience. The studies also show how motivation and achievement strategies are employed.

Transnational and comparative studies of Latinos are being used to help situate the schooling of such students in their countries of origin and identify what they bring to the U.S. This type of explanation has been growing steadily through case study analysis and quantitative research (Foner, 2003). Discussions of multiple identities, of diasporas, and of migration patterns have become commonplace articulations of Latino students and their lives (Wortham, Murillo, & Hamann, 2002). As Alejandro Portes and Rumbaut (2001) indicate, even understanding that different levels of accommodation and integration are achievable for these students allows us to analyze which educational models best fit their needs.

Critique. The early psychological contributions to the understanding of Latino students created generalizations that have been difficult to overcome. Only in the recent past has research on Latino students isolated the complexities of their adaptation to schooling as U.S.-born and foreign-born Latinos.

The generation of comparative and contrastive transnational studies, along with longitudinal studies of Latinos (Foner, 2003; Portes & Rumbaut, 2001; Rumbaut & Portes, 2001), has begun to shed light on the complexities and unique situations faced by these students. Moreover, studies of immigrants now into their second and third generation are also providing the intricacies of language-learning adaptations, social and cultural grounding, and identity formations. Given this trend, the ways in which Latino students are succeeding in schools will become more evident (Gándara, 1995; Stanton-Salazar, 1997; Trueba, 2004).

Major Contributions and Limitations of Explanations

In analyzing the value of these explanations to understanding Latino education, it is clear that they serve several purposes: They (1) bring attention to the educational status of groups that have been historically marginalized; (2) create longitudinal and case study research opportunities of such groups; (3) enable social scientists to follow through educational agendas over time; (4) test models that may work with diverse groups and begin to shed light on specific differences; (5) provide documentation of a group's advances during diverse policy initiative periods; and (6) provide a historical record of the research that has been conducted and the perspectives or paradigms held.

Along with several of these advantages, however, also come limitations created by these explanations, found mostly in the early models, yet lingering in their theoretical dimensions into the explanations used in this century. Among these limitations consider these: (1) The comparisons between groups and for Latinos has often been conducted from a Eurocentric white perspective using middle-class norms applied to U.S.-born and foreign-born Latinos without recognition of their status in the U.S. (2) Many of the studies have used national data sets that were not disaggregated by ethnic groups; thus Latinos have been qualified in quantitative and normative ways that do not represent the differences within groups and their particularities.

(3) Studies of one single group, such as Mexicans, have been used indiscriminately as explanations for the outcomes of other Latino groups, such as Puerto Ricans or Cubans, without differentiation of group or context, contributing to a monolithic categorization of Latinos. (4) Many of the early explanations of Latino students, and in particular Mexicans, were conducted mostly by non-Latinos who did not have the contextual or community understanding of the students they studied. (5) Unaccounted in some of the research is the role that Latinos and their communities share in common—the connectedness to community issues, their holism, political embeddedness, and problematization of issues.

Such limitations have given way, from the 1980s to the present, to explanations derived from studies and research undertaken from the perspective of Latinos and non-Latinos working within such communities and able to penetrate the academic and research circles using different approaches and paradigms (Montero-Sieburth & Villarruel, 2000; Pedraza & Rivera, in press). Moreover, these recent studies use perspectives that identify Latinos within their own subgroups; thus they include not only the traditional research of Cubans, Mexicans, and Puerto Ricans but also new studies of Colombians, Central Americans, and Dominicans. Focusing on revisionist theories, researchers have revived the historical background of Latinos in education and also re-examined the activism of parents in these communities (Donato, 1999; Montejano, 1992; San Miguel, 1987). Studies of Latino families and the significance of education in their lives, as well as the complexities of parental engagement, are also part of the growing research on Latinos (Delgado-Gaitan, 1991). Even the studies on language development, second language acquisition, and language immersion have become more targeted in terms of their effects on English language learners. Studies that focus on the resilience and resistance of Latino students have begun to proliferate, and a greater understanding of the role of peer and youth culture and social and cultural capital is challenging former explanatory models (Gibson, Gándara, & Koyama, 2004; Mehan, Hubbard, & Villanueva, 1994). In fact, studies of how Latinos succeed despite the normalization of school failure have begun to emerge, and some of these attend to issues that include the importance of afterschool programs for Latino students (Trueba, 2004; Villarruel, Montero-Sieburth, Wilson Outlay, & Dunbar, 2005) and effective programs for Latinos (Slavin & Calderon, 2000). They also expand upon the use of community funds of knowledge (Moll, 1992; Moll, Amnti, Neff, & Gonzalez, 1992).

We can expect to see developed future explanations that will also need to be analyzed in terms of the growing global, comparative, and transnational implications of Latino migration and Latino students throughout the world.

References

August, D., & Hakuta, K. (1997). *Improving Schooling for Language Minority Children: A Research Agenda.* Washington, DC: National Academy Press.

Baker, K., & de Kanter, A. (1983). Federal Policy and the Effectiveness of Bilingual Education. In K. Baker & A. de Kanter (Eds.), *Bilingual Education: A Reappraisal of Federal Policy* (pp. 33–86). Lexington, MA: Lexington Books.

Bernstein, B. (1975). *Class, Codes and Control.* London: Routledge & Kegan Paul.

Bourdieu, P., & Passeron, J. C. (1977). *Reproduction in Education, Society and Culture.* Beverly Hills, CA: Sage.

Bowles, S., & Gintis, H. (1976). *Schooling in a Capitalist America*. New York: Basic Books.

Calderon, M. (1997). Improving Latino Education: Preparing Teachers and Administrators to Serve the Needs of Latino Students. *ETS Policy Notes* 8(1), 1–3.

Calderon, M. (1998). Adolescent Sons and Daughters of Immigrants: How Schools Can Respond. In K. Borman & B. Schnieder (Eds.), *Yearbook of the National Society for the Study of Education* (pp. 65–87). Chicago: University of Chicago Press.

Carter, T., & Segura, R. (1979). *Mexican Americans in School: Decade of Change*. New York: College Entrance Examination Record.

Cazden, C., Vera, J., & Steiner, S. (Eds.). (1972). *Functions of Language*. Rowley, MA: Newbury Press.

Chapa, J. (1996). Mexican American Education: First, Second and Third Generation Adaptations. *Current Issues in Educational Research Workshops*. Cambridge, MA: Harvard University Graduate School of Education.

Christian, D., & Genesee, F. (Eds.). (2001). *Bilingual Education*. Alexandria, VA: TESOL.

The Condition of Education. (2002). Washington, DC: U.S. Government Printing Office.

Cook-Gumperz, J., & Gumperz, J. (1982). Communicative Competence in Educational Perspective. In C. L. Wilkinson (Ed.), *Communicating in the Classroom* (pp. 13–24). New York: Academic Press.

Crawford, J. (1999). *Bilingual Education: History, Politics, Theory and Practice* (4th ed.). Los Angeles: Bilingual Education Services.

Cummins, J. (1989). *Empowering Minority Students*. Los Angeles: California Association for Bilingual Education.

Cummins, J. (2000). *Language, Power, and Pedagogy: Bilingual Children in the Crossfire*. Clevedon, UK: Multilingual Matters.

Darder, A., Torres, R. D., & Gutiérrez, H. (Eds.). (1997). *Latinos and Education: A Critical Reader*. New York: Routledge.

Delgado-Gaitan, C. (1991). Involving Parents in the Schools: A Process of Empowerment. *American Journal of Education* 100, 20–46.

Donato, R. (1999). Hispano Education and the Implications of Autonomy: Four School Systems in Southern Colorado, 1920–1963. *Harvard Educational Review* 69(2), 117–148.

Dutcher, N. (1982). The Use of First and Second Languages in Primary Education: Selected Case Studies. *World Bank Staff Working Paper*, no. 504. Washington, DC: World Bank.

Erickson, F. (1994). Transformation and School Success: The Politics and Culture of Educational Achievement. In J. Kretovics & E. J. Nussel (Eds.), *Transforming Urban Education* (pp. 375–395) Boston: Allyn & Bacon.

Fine, M. (1989). *Framing Dropouts: Notes on the Politics of an Urban High School*. Albany, NY: SUNY Press.

Fine, M., & Weis, L. (2003). *Silenced Voices and Extraordinary Conversations: Re-Imagining Schools*. New York: Teachers College Press.

Foley, D. (1991). Reconsidering Anthropological Explanations of Ethnic School Failure. *Anthropology and Education Quarterly* 22, 60–86.

Foner, N. (Ed.). (2003). *American Arrivals: Anthropology Engages the New Immigration*. Santa Fe, NM, and Oxford: School of American Research Press & James Currey.

Fordham, S., & Ogbu, J. (1986). Black Students' School Success: Coping with the Burden of "Acting White." *Urban Review* 18, 176–206.

Foster, K. M. (2004). Coming to Terms: A Discussion of John Ogbu's Cultural-Ecological Theory of Minority Academic Achievement. *Intercultural Education* 15(4), 369–384.

Gándara, P. (1995). *Over the Ivory Walls: The Educational Mobility of Low-Income Chicanos*. Albany, NY: SUNY Press.

Garcia, E. (2001). *Hispanic Education in the United States: Raíces y alas*. New York: Rowman & Littlefield.

Gibson, M. (1988). *Accomodation without Assimilation: Punjabi Sikh Immigrants in an American High School and Community.* Ithaca, NY: Cornell University Press.

Gibson, M., Gándara, P., & Koyama, J. (2004). *School Connections: U.S. Mexican Youth, Peers, and School Achievement.* New York: Teachers College Press.

Gibson, M. A., & Ogbu, J. (1991). *Minority Status in Schooling: A Comparative Study of Immigrant and Involuntary Minorities.* New York: Garland.

Hakuta, K., Butler, Y. G., & Witt, D. (2000). *How Long Does It Take English Learners to Attain Proficiency? Policy Report.* University of California: Linguistic Minority Research Institute.

Hymes, D. (1974). *Foundations in Sociolinguistics: An Ethnographic Approach.* Philadelphia: University of Pennsylvania Press.

Krashen, S. (1999). *Bilingual Education: Arguments For and (Bogus) Arguments Against.* Washington, DC: Georgetown University Roundtable on Languages and Linguistics, May 6.

Lindholm, K. J. (1995). Theoretical Assumptions and Empirical Evidence for Academic Achievement in Two Languages. In Amado Padilla (Ed.), *Hispanic Psychology: Critical Issues in Theory and Research* (pp. 273–287). Thousand Oaks, CA: Sage Publications.

Lowell, B. L., & Suro, R. (2002). *The Improving Educational Profile of Latino Immigrants.* A Project of the Pew Charitable Trust and USC Annenberg School for Communication. Washington, DC: Pew Hispanic Center.

McLaughlin, B. (1984). *Second Language Acquisition in Childhood: Vol. 1, Preschool Children* (2nd ed.). Hillsdale, NJ: Lawrence Erlbaum.

Mehan, H., Hubbard, L., & Villanueva, I. (1994). Forming Academic Identities: Accommodation without Assimilation among Involuntary Minorities. *Anthropology and Education Quarterly* 25(2), 91–117.

Mehan, H., Villanueva, I., & Lintz, A. (1996). *Constructing School Success: The Conse-quences of Untracking Low Achieving Students.* Cambridge: Cambridge University Press.

Menchaca, M., & Valencia, R. (1990). Anglo-Saxon Ideologies in the 1920s–1930s: Their Impact on the Segregation of Mexican Students in California. *Anthropology and Education Quarterly* 21, 222–249.

Moll, L. C. (1992). Bilingual Classroom Studies and Community Analysis: Some Recent Trends. *Educational Research* 21(2), 20–24.

Moll, L. C., Amnti, C., Neff, D., & Gonzalez, N. (1992). Funds of Knowledge: Using a Qualitative Approach to Connect Homes and Classrooms. *Theory into Practice* 31(2), 132–141.

Montejano, D. (1992). *Anglos and Mexicans in the 21st Century.* Julian Samora Institute Occasional Paper, no. 3. East Lansing: Michigan State University.

Montero-Sieburth, M. (2005). Explanatory Models of Latino Education in the Reform Movement of the 1980s. In P. Pedraza & M. Rivera (Eds.), *Latino Education: An Agenda for Community Action Research* (pp. 99–156). A Volume of the National Latino/a Education Research and Policy Project. New York: Erlbaum Press.

Montero-Sieburth, M., & Batt, M. C. (2001). An Overview of Educational Models Used to Explain the Academic Achievement of Latino Students: Implications for Policy and Research into the New Millennium. In R. Slavin & M. Calderon (Eds.), *Effective Programs for Latino Students* (pp. 331–368). Hillsdale, NJ: Erlbaum.

Montero-Sieburth, M., & Villarruel, F. A. (Eds.). (2000). *Making Invisible Latino Adolescents Visible: A Critical Approach Building upon Latino Diversity.* New York: Garland Press.

Ogbu, J. (1978). *Minority Education and Caste: The American System in Cross-Cultural Perspective.* New York: Academic Press.

Ogbu, J. (1991). Immigrant and Involuntary Minorities in Comparative Perspective. In M. Gibson & J. Ogbu (Eds.), *Minority Status and*

Schooling (pp. 3–36). New York: Garland Press.

Ogbu, J., & Davis, A. (2003). *Black American Students in an Affluent Suburb: A Study of Academic Disengagement*. Mahwah, NJ: Lawrence Erlbaum.

Ogbu, J., & Matute-Bianchi, M. (1986). Understanding Sociocultural Factors: Knowledge, Identity, and School Adjustment. In *Beyond Language: Social and Cultural Factors in Schooling Language Minority Students* (pp. 73–142). Sacramento: California State Department of Education, Bilingual Education Office.

Orfield, G., Frankenberg, E. D., & Lee, C. (2003). The Resurgence of School Segregation. *Educational Leadership* 60(4), 16–20.

Orfield, G., & Yung, J. (1999). *Resegregation in American Schools*. Cambridge, MA: The Civil Rights Project, Harvard University.

Padilla, A., et al. (1991). The English Only Movement; Myths, Reality and Implications for Psychology. *American Psychologist* 46(2), 120–130.

Pedraza, P., & Rivera, M. (Eds.). (In press). *Latino Education: An Agenda for Community Action Research*. A Volume of the National Latino/a Education Research and Policy Project. New York: Erlbaum Press.

Philips, S. (1983). *The Invisible Culture: Communication in Classroom and Community on the Warm Springs Indian Reservation*. New York: Longman.

Portes, A., & Rumbaut, R. B. (2001). *Legacies: The Story of the Immigrant Second Generation*. Berkeley: University of California Press.

Portes, A., & Zhou, M. (1993). The Second Generation: Segmented Assimilation and Its Variants. *Annals* 530, 75–96.

Portes, P. R. (2005). *Dismantling Educational Inequality: A Cultural-Historical Approach to Closing the Achievement Gap*. New York: Peter Lang.

Reyes, P., Scribner, J. D., & Scribner, A. P. (Eds.). (1999). *Lessons from High-Performing Hispanic Schools: Creating Learning Communities*. New York: Teachers College Press.

Rossell, C., & Baker, K. (1996). The Educational Effectiveness of Bilingual Education. *Research in the Teaching of English* 30(1), 7–74.

Rumbaut, R., & Portes, A. (Eds.). (2001). *Ethnicities: Children of Immigrants in America*. New York: Russell Sage Foundation.

San Miguel, G. (1987). The Status of Historical Research on Chicano Education. *Review of Educational Research* 57(4), 467–480.

Skutnabb-Kangas, T. (1981). *Bilingualism or Not: The Education of Minorities*. Clevedon, UK: Multilingual Matters.

Slavin, R., & Calderon, M. (Eds.). (2000). *Effective Programs for Latino Students*. New York: Erlbaum.

Snow, Catherine E. (1992). Perspectives on Second-Language Development: Implications for Bilingual Education. *Educational Researcher* (Washington, DC), 16–19.

Stanton-Salazar, R. (1997). A Social Capital Framework for Understanding the Socialization of Racial Minority Children and Youths. *Harvard Educational Review* 67(1), 1–40.

Stein, C. B. (1985). Hispanic Students in the Sink or Swim Era, 1900–1960. *Urban Education* 20(2), 189–198.

Suarez-Orozco, C., & Suarez-Orozco, M. (1995). *Transformations: Migration, Family Life and Achievement Motivation among Latino Adolescents*. Stanford, CA: Stanford University Press.

Suarez-Orozco, C., & Suarez-Orozco, M. (2001). *Children of Immigration*. Cambridge, MA: Harvard University Press.

Suarez-Orozco, M. (1989). *Central American Refugees and U.S. High Schools: A Psychosocial Study of Motivation and Achievement*. Stanford, CA: Stanford University Press.

Suarez-Orozco, M., & Paez, M. M. (Eds.). (2002). *Latinos Remaking America*. Berkeley: University of California Press; Cambridge, MA: David Rockefeller Center for Latin American Studies.

Tharp, R. G. (1997). *From At-Risk to Excellence: Research, Theory and Principles for*

Practice. Santa Cruz: University of California, Center for Research on Education, Diversity and Excellence.

Thomas, W., & Collier, V. (1999). Evaluation That Informs School Reform: Study, Design and Findings from the Thomas and Collier (1998). National School-Based Collaborative Research on School Effectiveness for Language Minority Students. Paper presented at the American Educational Research Association meeting, Montreal, April.

Trueba, E. (2004). *The New Americans: Immigrants and Transnationals at Work*. New York: Rowman & Littlefield.

Trueba, H. T. (Ed.). (1987). *Success or Failure? Learning and the Language Minority Student*. Cambridge, MA: Newbury House.

U.S. Congress. (2001). *No Child Left Behind Act of 2001*. Public Law 107–110. 107th Congress. Washington, DC: U.S. GPO.

Valenzuela, A. (1999). *Subtractive Bilingualism: U.S. Mexican Youth and the Politics of Caring*. Albany, NY: SUNY Press.

Villarruel, F., Montero-Sieburth, M., Wilson Outlay, C., & Dunbar, C. (2005). "Dorothy, There Is No Yellow Brick Road": The Paradox of Community Youth Development Approaches for Latino and African American Urban Youth. In J. L. Mahoney, R. W. Larson, & J. Eccles (Eds.), *After-School Activities: Contests of Development* (pp. 111–130). Thousand Oaks, CA: Sage.

Willig, A. (1985). A Meta-analysis of Selected Studies on the Effectiveness of Bilingual Education. *Review of Educational Research* 55, 269–317.

Willis, P. (1972). *Learning to Labour: How Working Class Kids Get Working Class Jobs*. Westmead, Farmborough, Hants., UK: Saxon House.

Wortham, S., Murillo, E. G., & Hamann, E. T. (Eds.). (2002.) *Education in the New Latino Diaspora*. Westport, CT: Ablex.

Recommended Reading

Calderon, M. (1998). Adolescent Sons and Daughters of Immigrants: How Schools Can Respond. In K. Borman & B. Schnieder (Eds.), *Yearbook of the National Society for the Study of Education* (pp. 65–87). Chicago: University of Chicago Press.

Conchas, G. Q. (2001). Structuring Failure and Success: Understanding the Variability in Latino School Engagement. *Harvard Educational Review* 71(3), 475–504.

Foley, D. E. (1991). Reconsidering Anthropological Explanations of Ethnic School Failure. *Anthropology and Education Quarterly* 22, 60–86.

Foner, N. (Ed.). (2003). *American Arrivals: Anthropology Engages the New Immigration*. Santa Fe, NM, and Oxford: School of American Research Press and James Currey.

Fordham, S., & Ogbu, J. (1986). Black Students' School Success: Coping with the Burden of "Acting White." *Urban Review* 18, 176–206.

Garcia, E. (2001). *Hispanic Education in the United States: Raíces y alas*. New York: Rowman & Littlefield.

Gibson, M. (Ed.). (1997). Theme Issue: Ethnicity and School Performance: Complicating the Immigrant/Involuntary Minority Typology. *Anthropology and Education Quarterly* 28(3).

Gibson, M. (1988). *Accommodation without Assimilation: Punjabi Sikh Immigrants in an American High School and Community*. Ithaca, NY: Cornell University Press.

Gibson, M., Gandara, P., & Koyama, J. (2004). *School Connections: U.S. Mexican Youth, Peers, and School Achievement*. New York: Teachers College Press.

Gibson, M. A., & Ogbu, J. (1991). *Minority Status in Schooling: A Comparative Study of Immigrant and Involuntary Minorities*. New York: Garland Publishing.

Mehan, H., Hubbard, L., & Villanueva, I. (1994). Forming Academic Identities: Accommodation without Assimilation among Involuntary Minorities. *Anthropology and Education Quarterly* 25(2), 91–117.

Mehan, H., Villanueva, I., & Lintz, A. (1996). *Constructing School Success: The Conse-*

quences of Untracking Low Achieving Students. Cambridge: Cambridge University Press.

Montero-Sieburth, M. (In press). Explanatory Models of Latino Education in the Reform Movement of the 1980s. In P. Pedraza & M. Rivera (Eds.), Latino Education: An Agenda for Community Action Research. A Volume of the National Latino/a Education Research and Policy Project. New York: Erlbaum.

Montero-Sieburth, M., & Batt, M. C. (2001). An Overview of Educational Models Used to Explain the Academic Achievement of Latino Students: Implications for Policy and Research into the New Millennium. In R. Slavin & M. Calderon (Eds.), Effective Programs for Latino Students (pp. 331–368). Hillsdale, NJ: Erlbaum.

Montero-Sieburth, M., & Villarruel, F. A. (Eds.). (2000). Making Invisible Latino Adolescents Visible: A Critical Approach Building upon Latino Diversity. New York: Garland Press.

Ogbu, J. (1991). Immigrant and Involuntary Minorities in Comparative Perspective. In M. Gibson & J. Ogbu (Eds.), Minority Status and Schooling (pp. 3–36). New York: Garland Press.

Orfield, G., Frankenberg, E. D., & Lee, C. (2003). The Resurgence of School Segregation. Educational Leadership 60(4), 16–20.

Pedraza, P., & Rivera, M. (Eds.). (In press). Latino Education: An Agenda for Community Action Research. A Volume of the National Latino/a Education Research and Policy Project. New York: Erlbaum.

Portes, A., & Rumbaut, R. B. (2001). Legacies: The Story of the Immigrant Second Generation. Berkeley: University of California Press.

Portes, P. R. (2005). Dismantling Educational Inequality: A Cultural-Historical Approach to Closing the Achievement Gap. New York: Peter Lang.

Rumbaut, R., & Portes, A. (Eds.). (2001). Ethnicities: Children of Immigrants in America. New York: Russell Sage Foundation.

Slavin, R., & Calderon, M. (Eds.). (2000). Effective Programs for Latino Students. New York: Erlbaum.

Suarez-Orozco, C., & Suarez-Orozco, M. (1995). Transformations: Migration, Family Life and Achievement Motivation among Latino Adolescents. Stanford, CA: Stanford University Press.

Suarez-Orozco, C., & Suarez-Orozco, M. (2001). Children of Immigration. Cambridge, MA: Harvard University Press.

Trueba, E. (2004). The New Americans: Immigrants and Transnationals at Work. New York: Rowman & Littlefield.

Valenzuela, A. (1999). Subtractive Bilingualism: U.S. Mexican Youth and the Politics of Caring. Albany, NY: SUNY Press.

Villarruel, F., Montero-Sieburth, M., Wilson Outlay, C., & Dunbar, C. (2005). "Dorothy, There Is No Yellow Brick Road": The Paradox of Community Youth Development Approaches for Latino and African American Urban Youth. In J. L. Mahoney, R. W. Larson, & J. Eccles (Eds.), After-School Activities: Contests of Development (pp. 111–130). Thousand Oaks, CA: Sage.

Wortham, S., Murillo, E. G., & Hamann, E. T. (Eds.). (2002). Education in the New Latino Diaspora. Westport, CT: Ablex Publishing.

Martha Montero-Sieburth

ADDITIVE SCHOOLING

The term *subtractive schooling* as advanced by Chicana sociologist Angela Valenzuela draws attention to the role of schools in the American assimilation project by subtracting important cultural and linguistic resources from Latino students through formal and informal teaching and curricular practices that systematically devalue these resources and thereby contribute to the academic failure of students who do not possess the dominant culture taught within U.S. schools. Conversely, *additive schooling* practices reinforce immigrant and

U.S.-born Latino students' cultural and linguistic resources as a foundation for learning the dominant U.S. Anglo curriculum, with the goal of developing in students a bicultural network orientation (Stanton-Salazar, 1997), a situation where students are academically prepared to function at high levels within two or more cultures.

Building upon the concept of subtractive assimilation articulated by Cummins (1984, 1986) and Gibson (1988, 1993), which views assimilation as a non-neutral process that has a negative impact on the economic and political integration of minorities, Valenzuela argues that "the problem" of Latino/a student achievement is located "squarely in school-based relationships and organizational structures designed to erase students' culture" (p. 10). Further, she suggests, "schools may be subtractive in ways that go beyond the concept of subtractive cultural assimilation to include the content and organization of the curriculum" (p. 27), a notion supported by San Miguel (1999), who in reviewing the history of schooling in the Southwest describes subtractive Americanization—a process that occurred "when schools devalued particular minority groups and their specific cultural heritages, when they sought to replace the identities of these groups with an idealized American one, or when they sought to remove minority communities, languages, and cultures from the curriculum and educational structures" (p. 38).

In her book *Subtractive Schooling: U.S.-Mexican Youth and the Politics of Caring*, Valenzuela describes the day-to-day, ground-level experiences of Latino students at Seguín High School (a pseudonym), a large high school in Houston, and the often-poisonous interactions formed within a school structured in ways that create linguistic and cultural divisions between students and adults. Stagnant organizational dynamics and lack of administrative support isolate teachers, who in turn fail to form meaningful relationships with Latino students. The students, in turn, believe that most non-Latino teachers hold them in low regard. As Valenzuela observes, "The feeling that 'no one cares' is pervasive and corrosive" (p. 5). This description is highly evocative of the experiences of large numbers of Latino and other cultural and linguistic minority students in U.S. schools.

The prevalence of non-caring as a theme is linked to Noddings's (1984) feminist framework of caring in education and suggests that conflict at Seguín High School emerges as a result of competing notions of caring among teachers and students—notions rooted in differential cultural and class-based expectations about the nature of schooling. These expectations inevitably clash and, subsequently, fuel conflict and power struggles between teachers and students, who see each other as *not caring*. As a result non-Latino teaching staff see Latino students as *not caring about* school (aesthetic caring) while students see teachers as not *caring for* them (authentic caring). Teachers privilege the technical over the expressive, valuing impersonal and objective language, "including such terms as goals, strategies, and standardized curricula, that is used in decisions made by one group for another" (p. 22). Alternatively, Latino students experience the cultural and social distance between themselves and their teachers as depersonalizing and insincere. Latino students subscribe to an ethic of *educación,* a Mexican and Latino value of schooling based on caring, respectful relations that closely resembles Noddings's articulation of authentic caring and views sustained reciprocal relationships between teachers and students as the basis for all learning. As Valenzuela observes, "Students' precondition to caring about school is that they be engaged in a caring relationship with an adult at school" (p. 79).

Subtractive schooling also includes English-centered policies, practices, and curriculums at the school, district, state, and federal level that serve systematically to divest Latino students of their identities and "impede their prospects for fully vested bilingualism and biculturalism" (p. 172). In addition to creating tensions between students and teachers, these practices facilitate deep divisions between Mexican or Latino immigrants and U.S.-born youth, inserting a wedge between students and discouraging relationships that could result in the development of complementary bilingual-bicultural identities. This possibility is stifled by the established "pecking order, based on the privileging of English as both the medium of instruction and the ticket to participation in faculty sponsored school activities" (p. 186). Consistent with a deficit orientation, English as a Second Language (ESL) students are, for example, categorized as "limited English proficient" rather than "Spanish dominant" or "English language learners." The belief that English is superior pervades the school culture and manifests in myriad ways. One example is the subtle revision of students' Spanish names by teachers: "Loreto" becomes "Laredo"; "Azucena" is transformed into "Suzy." Even names that are common throughout the Southwest, like Martínez and Pérez are pronounced as MART-I-nez and Pe-REZ (instead of Mart-I-nez and PE-rez) (p. 173).

Implicit in the concept of subtractive schooling is its antonym, *additive schooling*, a process fundamentally "about equalizing opportunity and assimilating Mexicans into the larger society, albeit through a bicultural process" (p. 269). This is accomplished by an emphasis on teachers forging respectful and reciprocal relationships that nourish students on multiple levels. Such forms of practice affirm and include students' social, linguistic, cultural, and familial resources, and engage Latino students' participation and investment in learning rather than their resistance. While Valenzuela focuses on Mexican immigrant and Mexican American youth, the concepts of subtractive and additive schooling are relevant to a deeper understanding of the schooling success and failure of other Latino and marginalized groups in the U.S., including, but not limited to Native Americans, Puerto Ricans, Dominicans, and African Americans.

References

Cummins, J. (1984). *Bilingualism and Special Education: Issues in Assessment and Pedagogy*. Clevedon, UK: Multilingual Matters.

Cummins, J. (1986). Empowering Minority Students: A Framework for Intervention. *Harvard Educational Review* 56, 18–36.

Gibson, M. (1988). *Accommodation without Assimilation: Sikh Immigrants in an American High School*. Ithaca, NY: Cornell University Press.

Gibson, M. (1993). The School Performance of Immigrant Minorities: A Comparative View. In E. Jacob & C. Jordan (Eds.), *Minority Education: Anthropological Perspectives*. Norwood, NJ: Ablex.

Noddings, N. (1984). *Caring: A Feminine Approach to Ethics and Moral Education*. Berkeley: University of California Press.

San Miguel Jr., G. (1999). The Schooling of Mexicanos in the Southwest, 1848–1891. In J. F. Moreno (Ed.), *The Elusive Quest for Equality: 150 Years of Chicano/a Education*. Cambridge, MA: President and Fellows of Harvard College.

Stanton-Salazar, R. D. (1997). A Social Capital Framework for Understanding the Socialization of Racial Minority Children and Youths. *Harvard Educational Review* (Spring), 140.

Valenzuela, A. (1999). *Subtractive Schooling: U.S.-Mexican Youth and the Politics of Caring*. Albany, NY: SUNY Press.

Recommended Reading

Valenzuela, A. (1999). *Subtractive Schooling: U.S.-Mexican Youth and the Politics of Caring*. Albany, NY: SUNY Press.

Anthony de Jesús

ALTRUISM

We can learn more about altruism with examples rather than with books, although a book can help us better understand what altruism is about.

In a world characterized by vertiginous, violent, and selfish behaviors, the concept of altruism appears to be old fashioned and out of place. A look at today's newspaper headlines or the latest magazine articles reveals that success has become the ultimate value, leaving no space for other fundamental ideals. For instance, it has become increasingly hard to find articles that address the importance of helping the other(s), caring for the other(s), and assisting in the building of a society that cares for the well-being of its members.

Furthermore, the level of violence and intolerance peaked after the 9/11 events: the Middle East is increasingly at unrest, Europe has suffered its cruelest terrorist attack, at the same time East Asian countries have been awakened by the same threat. In Latin America political turmoil, with riots and aggression, has once again become the rule and not the exception. In short, our children are being raised in a world where taking care of the other(s) and trusting the other(s) are fading away as fundamental values. It is in this context that the relevance of a fundamental ideal of helping appears crucial

for the well-being of the current and future generations.

Latino Families as an Altruistic Source of Change

Values and beliefs motivate and promote aspirations and actions in our lives. Hispanic parents care deeply about their children's education and believe that moral values should be embedded in what they understand as education (Valdes, 1996). Furthermore, Hispanic parents believe that morality is more important than social status and intellectual achievements (Valdes). Since children are shaped (ideological becoming) by the values of certain adults, particularly parents, it is important to understand how the beliefs of Latino parents influence and shape their bilingual/bicultural children's identities.

Our Research

This entry shares spontaneous conversations with young bilingual/bicultural children living on the East Coast. This cohort consists of 5–6-year-olds from Latino origins attending a bilingual program (Spanish-English) in a public kindergarten. These youngsters are from predominantly working-class middle-lower- and lower-income households. In most cases these children had only one parent who spoke English, generally the father.

This entry portrays young children's perspectives and conceptions of themselves as bilingual subjects. Similar to a previous cohort (Soto, 2002b), these children demonstrate the daily-lived realities faced by young bilingual children. As a methodology, we used conversational interviewing and drawings, which allowed the bilingual/bicultural children to show us their feelings and thoughts. These combined methodologies enabled us to listen carefully to their words and to understand their perspectives on the multiple contexts and multiple layers of their families, themselves, and their community (Soto, 2002a).

The children's altruistic personalities emerged in their words and drawings. These bilingual/biliterate children very clearly explained to us that the main benefit of being bilingual and bicultural was being able to help their fellows. This intentional and voluntary behavior intended to benefit others was found in almost all the children. During our time with them we were immersed in powerful examples of the altruistic behaviors these children adopt in their daily lives.

We understand altruism as an intentional behavior carried out and intended to benefit or help another with or without contemplation for internal personal gain (Batson, 1991; Eisenberg, 1990; Hoffman, 1981) and for no other purpose than the desire to improve a recipient's welfare (Staub, 1986). Altruism understood in this way involves a socially desirable behavior that leads to a society that cares for the well-being of its members.

Discussion

The issue of altruism surfaced in the conversations and drawings exemplifying the presence of moral education in bilingual/bicultural children. Emphatic and helpful behavior in children was promoted and nurtured by the children's observing adults manifesting altruistic behaviors at different levels toward the child and sometimes toward other people in distress.

I help my mom sometimes and she helps me sometimes, she helps me clean my room... when I can't find the soap, she finds it for me so I can wash my hands... when I go to the park and fall she helps me walk and she puts me band-aids... she makes me feel comfort-

able, she makes me feel good and she makes me feel happy... my father helps me by making me coffee. (Rosa, 5 years old, when playing with her grandfather)

Cuando alguién habla en inglés y mi mamá no habla en inglés, yo les digo lo que dice mi mamá. (When somebody speaks in English, and my mother does not speak English, I tell them what my mother says.) Le, le, le digo en inglés lo que dice mi mamá dice en español, se lo repito en inglés. (I repeat in English what my mother says in Spanish.) Cuando pedimos algo de comer y él no sabe como se dice, yo lo le digo que me dé el teléfono y yo lo digo. (When we ask for something to eat and he doesn't know how to say it, I tell him to give me the phone and I will say it.) (Miguel, 4 years old, when helping his parents that speak Spanish)

"I help her with the dates, carry this, or pick up my brother on the bus." I tell her that... how to speak English. Como que hace mal la tarea, entonces yo lo ayudo para que él ya lo haga, entonces él la hizo conmigo. (He does not know how to do his homework so I help him to do it, he does it with me.) Lo ayudo porque quiero... y cuando él lo hace mal yo todavía lo ayudo (I help him because I want to do so... and when he does it wrong I still help him.) (Maria, 5 years old, helping her brother)

These are some of the many examples of altruistic behaviors that emerged from conversations with the children. Bilingual/bicultural children present themselves as concerned for the well-being of others and demonstrate the will to help the other(s). As two 5-year-olds expressed it: "I help them when they need my help." Their depictions express forms of socially desirable actions and behaviors such as teaching, translating, and helping in general, all examples of true altruism. Soto (in Soto & Lasta, in press) presents their altruistic behaviors as somehow paradoxical, for "in spite of their colonized existence, [the children] express love-altruism for the other[s]."

Bilingual/bicultural children face daily challenges in their homes and communities. Issues of language, power, and culture are intertwined in their existence and mark their lives (Soto, 1997). Despite the particular difficulties these children face, their "gift of bilingualism" leads them to prosocial behaviors. In a time when society is inundated and characterized by examples of extreme violence and intolerance, bilingual/bicultural children's commitment to others and thoughtfulness about the well-being of others should be followed and promoted.

Final Thoughts

Helping and sharing are both altruistic behaviors that society should prize and encourage in children. The interpretations of these bilingual/bicultural children help explain those areas of a child's moral development that are linked to comprehension of moral issues and principles. As the philosopher Kant said, moral behavior comes not from reason but from the heart.

These bilingual/bicultural children provide us with a model to be followed by societies faced with multiple linguistic and cultural changes. The children's deep commitment and concern for the well-being of others emerge as crucial wisdom to be followed and promoted. It is time to recognize the important contribution that this minority population can offer to society, as they hold much strength that, up to now, society has failed to acknowledge.

No space is free from large inequalities, but it is only under a deliberate commitment that fixed ways of oppression can be confronted (Fine, Weiss, & Powell, 1997). Bilingual/bicultural children continue to lead an oppressed existence while continually reaching out to "the other" with love and care (Soto, 2002b). Perhaps when we ac-

knowledge the wisdom that different and diverse communities have to offer we will be able to gather the courage, dedication, and commitment needed to initiate a real transformation and enable our children to inherit a better world.

References

Batson, C. D. (1991). *The Altruism Question: Toward a Social-Psychological Answer.* Hillsdale, NJ: Erlbaum.

Eisenberg, N. (1990). Prosocial Development in Early and Mid-Adolescence. In R. Montemayor, G. Adams, & T. Gullota (Eds.), *From Childhood to Adolescence: A Transitional Period?* Newbury Park, CA: Sage.

Fine, M., Weis, L, & Powell, L. (1997). Communities of Difference: A Critical Look at Desegregated Spaces Created for and by Youth. *Harvard Educational Review* 67(2), 247–284.

Hoffman, M. L. (1981). The Development of Empathy. In J. Rushton & R. Sorrentino (Eds.), *Altruism and Helping Behavior* (pp. 41–63). Hillsdale, NJ: Erlbaum.

Soto, L. D. (1997). *Language, Culture, and Power: Bilingual Families Struggle for Quality Education.* Albany, NY: SUNY Press.

Soto, L. D. (Ed.). (2002a). *Making a Difference in the Lives of Bilingual/Bicultural Children.* New York: Peter Lang.

Soto, L. D. (2002b). Young Bilingual Children's Perceptions of Bilingualism and Biliteracy: Altruistic Possibilities. *Bilingual Research Journal* 26, 599–609.

Soto, L. D., & Lasta, J. (2005). Bilingual Border Crossing Children's Ideological Becoming. In L. D. Soto & B. Swadener (Eds.), *Power and Voice in Research with Children.* New York: Peter Lang.

Staub, E. (1986). *A Conception of the Determinants and Developments of Altruism and Aggression: Social and Biological Origins.* Cambridge, MA: Cambridge University Press.

Valdes, G. (1996). *Con respeto: Bridging the Distances between Culturally Diverse Fami-*

lies and Schools: An Ethnographic Portrait. New York: Teachers College Press.

Recommended Reading

Soto, L. D., & Swadener, B. (Eds.). (2005). *Power and Voice in Research with Children.* New York: Peter Lang.

Juliana Lasta

THE AMERICAN GI FORUM

It is hard to imagine that discrimination was openly practiced when our troops came marching home after World War II. Socioeconomic, political, and educational conditions for Mexican Americans (and many others) were very dismal in those days. Some store fronts and restaurants still displayed signs that read "No Dogs or Mexicans Allowed" (Midobuche, 1999). Segregation was still the rule in Texas schools and many other establishments. Sink-or-swim educational approaches were still the norm in our public schools. The opportunities for higher education were at best severely limited. It appeared that our returning veterans would have to engage in another war. This battle would be at home. This time, however, the tools of war would be American law, books, and words instead of bullets and bombs (Benavides, 2003).

The initial battle in Texas began after the war ended, when Dr. Hector Pérez García, a noted Corpus Christi physician and himself a World War II veteran army doctor, noticed that the Veterans' Administration of Texas was neglecting many of his patients. These veterans were often denied the benefits due them, and this often proved a hardship in terms of their physical health and their providing for their families. They were also routinely denied hospital beds at the Corpus Christi Naval Air Station (Allsup, 1982). As a humanitarian, Dr.

García became directly involved in many of these cases. However, when a chapel in the town of Three Rivers, Texas, refused to bury Private Felix Longoria, a casualty from the war, he decided to take a very serious approach to the type of open discrimination practiced in Texas at the time. Although Longoria had lost his life in June 1945, it had taken the U.S. Army three years to recover his body. The refusal to bury this decorated *American* soldier led to the direct involvement of the American GI Forum and Dr. Hector Pérez García.

Dr. García had founded the American GI Forum on March 26, 1948, in Corpus Christi, Texas, as a civil rights organization aimed at improving the conditions of many returning war veterans and their families. This was just the type of case that would bring much-needed publicity to a cause that Dr. García felt very strongly about. After the initial bad press that the chapel received, they continued to refuse the burial of Pvt. Longoria. Because the Three Rivers chapel continued to refuse the reburial, Lyndon B. Johnson, the newly elected senator from Texas, intervened and Pvt. Longoria was eventually buried in Arlington National Cemetery on February 16, 1949, with full military honors (Allsup, 1982). This incident helped to galvanize Mexican American resolve to become more involved in civil rights and other pressing issues such as education. It provided a boost to the fledgling American GI Forum and helped to spread its appeal beyond Texas. New chapters of the Forum began to appear not only in Texas but also in several other southwestern states. Dues were relatively inexpensive (25 cents per member per year), thus establishing the forum as a genuine grassroots organization. Later, the Forum would expand to include a national organization.

Most of the returning veterans went about their private business of working and raising families. Although conditions for Mexican Americans were not that much improved in the late 1940s and 1950s these "ordinary" citizens remained for the most part fairly quiet. The age of protest had not yet permeated life as many Americans would know it in the 1960s. For the most part, these veterans were content to work hard and quietly and to send their children to school in numbers that were historically unseen and unheard of before then. They were, of course, part of the producers of the baby-boom generation that would eventually fill our nation's schools. Again in an indirect way the American GI Forum was responsible for giving voice and hope to a new generation of participants in the American dream.

Although many veterans agreed with the civil rights efforts of the American GI Forum, they were often reluctant to participate actively or openly in activities for fear of economic reprisals on the job (Felts, 2002). Therefore, the burden of activism often fell on the shoulders of their wives. Thus began a more active participation in civil matters—including schools. The dogged determination of these parents working very quietly, mostly anonymously, and usually alone, helped to form the first significant wave of Mexican American college students in the 1960s. Much of the credit for this success can be at least partially attributed to the American GI Forum and the thousands of dedicated veterans who wanted a better life for their children.

The American GI Forum persisted throughout the 1950s, growing in numbers and expanding to other states. Forumeers took on issues beyond those of needy veterans. They began to look into cases of discrimination in schools as well as cases of equal access to public amenities such as restaurants. The Forum also began to make inroads in the political arena. During Senator John F. Kennedy's second term, Carlos McCormick (a forumeer from Arizona), was given a position on his staff. According to Ramos (1998), it was McCormick who initiated the "Viva Kennedy" clubs during the president's 1960 campaign. This involvement at a national level brought the Forum clearly into the national limelight as a legitimate civil rights organization.

However, for all its fervor and acts of kindness toward the politicos of the moment, the American GI Forum was basically ignored by the Kennedy administration. The GI Forum was still basically a conservative organization, and the younger and more militant "Chicano" activists of the 1960s began to view the Forum as too accommodating and not radical enough in its approaches to problems. The lack of attention by first the Kennedy and later the Johnson administration seemed only to make their point—that their approach was definitely too accepting of the status quo and hardly militant enough to suit the younger generation. Their opposing attitudes toward the Vietnam War served only to deepen the differences on both sides. These differences created a schism within the "Hispanic" political community. One example of this is the very names employed by the organizations. The older and more conservative (mild-mannered) American GI Forum preferred the use of "Latin American" or later "Mexican American" as compared to the more radical groups that preferred the term "Chicano." Both groups viewed each other suspiciously. These "Chicanos" went on to form a third political party in Texas known as "La Raza Unida," thus creating an even deeper distrust.

Political differences aside, the American GI Forum was always a steadfast defender of Hispanic civil rights in every major way. Whether the issues were veterans' benefits, unequal school facilities, or matters of injustice within the judicial system, the American GI Forum was always ready to represent the interests of *the people*. There are many cases in which the Forum volunteered itself and its leaders to represent people who often had no representation. The American GI Forum has spread its work nationally in order to serve not only the veterans and families that need its assistance but also the many other families and individuals that need an ally in their struggle for equality and justice.

Today the American GI Forum serves many people. It continues to assist veterans and many others. It even provides college scholarships to deserving youth. It is this unselfish and relentless sacrifice that is indeed worthy of remembrance by people who love freedom, justice, and equality of opportunity. Ultimately, these are the same values they brought home with them after World War II—the values espoused by the American GI Forum.

References

Allsup, C. (1982). *The American G.I. Forum: Origins and Evolution*. Austin: University of Texas.

Benavides, A. H. (2003). Remembering the Voices of Heroes. *Bilingual Research Journal* 27(2), iii–iv.

Felts, J. (Producer). (2002). *Justice for My People: The Hector P. García Story* [TV broadcast]. Corpus Christi, TX: Corporation for Public Broadcasting.

Midobuche, E. (1999). Respect in the Classroom: Reflections of a Mexican-American Educator. *Educational Leadership* 56(7), 80–82.

Ramos, H.A.J. (1998). *The American G.I. Forum: In Pursuit of the Dream, 1948–1983*. Houston, TX: Arte Publico Press.

Recommended Reading

Benavides, A. H. (2003). Remembering the Voices of Heroes. *Bilingual Research Journal* 27(2), iii–vi.

*Alfredo H. Benavides and
Eva Midobuche*

AMERICANIZATION

"Americanization" has been a central tenet of programs for immigrant and non-white populations in the U.S. throughout the twentieth century. Characterized by political and patriotic intent, "Americanization" programs attempt to assimilate subordinate groups into the dominant social order. Sanctioned by state-driven policies, they strive to integrate non-dominant populations into the nation-state by emphasizing a "common language," history, faith, and tradition. Historically, this had had the simultaneous effect of suppressing class-consciousness and self-guided political action among oppressed groups.

Not surprisingly, the ethos of "Americanization" is connected to segregation, class inequality and violations of civil liberties. A variety of practices including Native American boarding schools, Japanese internment camps, and censorship under McCarthyism, immigrant labor programs and forced repatriation have been justified under the rhetoric of "Americanization." Such efforts, moreover, have involved schools as a primary site for reproducing "Americanization" ideals.

The "Americanization" movement of the early twentieth century profoundly shaped the experiences of Latinos and other immigrant communities. These efforts can be linked to isolationist policies of the U.S. during both World War I and II when protecting national borders and reducing the possibility of national disintegration became a general concern among legislators.

The progressive reform movement of the 1920s further enforced the "Americanization" ethic. Like assimilationists, progressives reinforced the idea that the culture of non-English speakers was a serious detriment to the social order. The Latino student, they argued, had to be "Americanized."

"Americanization" courses were held primarily in segregated schools. By 1928, for example, 64 schools in eight Southern California counties had almost 100% Mexican student enrollment (Frankenburg, Lee, & Orfield, 2003). Students in these programs were expected to learn English as well as "proper" manners and hygiene. As a consequence, they were subject to routine hygiene inspections and punished for speaking Spanish in school.

Psychometrics testing, endorsed by progressive thinkers in education at the time, further aggravated the unequal schooling of Latino students. They argued such tests made schools more efficient by enabling them to rank students according to their scores. The education psychologist Louis Turman, for example, designed intelligence tests used to match student scores with ability levels in the job market. Students could then be ranked (1) professionals (2) semi-professionals (3) ordinary skilled workers (4) semi-skilled workers or (5) unskilled laborers (Gonzalez, 1974). Not surprisingly, low classifications were commonly given to students of color. As a result, numerous education reports during the 1920s claimed that the "intellectual inferiority" of Latino students could now be scientifically proven (Wollenberg, 1974).

Another influential psychologist in education was Kimball Young. Young believed the education of Latino students should be "practical." Schools, in other words, should prepare these students for the kinds of jobs available to them. His ideas were so well received that districts with a high Latino population (such as Los Angeles, El Monte, San Bernardino, Denver, San Antonio, and El Paso) institutionalized vocational education programs for Latinos in high schools (Gonzalez, 1974). Females, for example, were taught sewing, homemaking, childcare, or knitting while males were taught carpentry, auto repair, or agriculture.

Latino students were thus tracked within particular industries. Few were allowed to take the academic courses offered Anglo children. Yet very few Latinos stayed in school long enough to reach the ninth grade. Too often, they were held back because they did not speak English. In Orange County, for example, 70% of Latino students in 1934 were labeled "retarded" because they were older than most students in the same grade (Wollenberg, 1974). In fact, it was not rare to find a Latino eighth grader in California who was 16 years old!

The kind of unequal education made available to Latino students under "Americanization" is inseparable from the economic needs of the country. Between 1899 and 1923, for example, the value of manufacturing goods in Los Angeles alone rose from $15 million to $417 million (Gonzalez, 1974). Substantial growth was also taking place in areas such as agriculture, construction, and transportation. Accordingly, American businesses demanded low-wage workers and schools responded with a ready supply of poor and Latino students trained for exploitative labor.

By the end of World War II, however, the Latino community started to show resistance to the "Americanization" process. No longer willing to tolerate second-class citizenship, Latinos began to move toward a politics that demanded equal access to the nation's institutions and improved economic opportunities.

Latino parents in particular began to take action against the unequal education their children were receiving. Many of these protests took place in California. Cities like Riverside, Mendota, San Bernardino, Santa Ana, and Ontario began to deal with increasing demands by Latinos for integrated schools (Wollenberg, 1974).

Several of these community struggles were waged in court. In the case of *Alvarez v. Owen* (1931), or *The Lemon Grove Incident*, as it is best known, 75 Mexicano students gained the legal right to attend school with 95 Anglo students in the Lemon Grove School District near the San Diego–Mexico border. In 1947, the *Mendez v. Westminster School District* decision challenged the segregation of Latino students in Westminster, Garden Grove, El Modeno, and Santa Ana. The ruling not only ended legal segregation in California but also proved valuable to desegregation cases in Texas (*Delgado v. Bastrop Independent School District*, 1948) and Arizona (*Gonzalez v. Sheely*, 1951). In addition, much of Judge McCormick's ideas were reflected several years later in Judge Earl Warren's 1954 landmark *Brown v. Board of Education* decision.

Nevertheless, large urban districts like Los Angeles continued to circumvent the law and operate separate schools. The situation intensified in the years after the *Mendez* decision as the Latino population grew and became increasingly urbanized. Consequently, the number of Latino children attending de facto segregated schools steadily increased.

By 1960, Latinos continued to encounter dismal educational and economic opportunities. Only 13% of all Latinos in 1960 had a high school education and less than 6% attended college (Ramirez, 1997). The majority of schools attended by Latinos, moreover, were poor with inadequate facilities and an inferior curriculum that continued to lock them into a rigid tracking system away from college prep courses and toward vocational training or military enrollment.

With the rise of the civil rights movement, however, Latino communities in the U.S. began to challenge the assimilative politics of "Americanization" directly. No longer willing to adopt the litigation and protest strategies of previous generations, the emerging militancy of Chicano/a youth emphasized self-determination and empowerment through working-class community struggle. They exposed the limits of "Americanization" ideals by voicing their collective experiences as an internally colonized population. Thus, Chicano/a youth challenged notions of equal access, freedom, and democracy with direct demands for cultural freedom, integrity, and equal educational rights.

In Denver, for example, Corky Gonzalez's Crusade for Justice organization called on schools to teach Mexican American history, culture, and language. School boycotts (or "blowouts," as they came to be known) took place across the Southwest in states like California, Texas, Colorado, and New Mexico. Student demands ranged from the firing of culturally biased teachers, an end to punitive measures for speaking Spanish in schools, bilingual education, culturally relevant courses, college preparatory classes, and control of local school boards (Ramirez, 1997).

Still, "Americanization" continues to affect Latinos. Title III of the No Child Left

Behind Act (NCLB), for example, eliminates continuing primary language support for bilingual students by imposing a three-year limit for English proficiency—a move that completely disregards the overwhelming research in favor of late-exit transitional programs. The result has destroyed bilingual education and their emphasis on the bicultural development of English language learners (ELL) (Krashen, 2001). It has also emboldened rising anti-immigrant sentiment particularly in states already affected by English-Only movements like California, Arizona, and Colorado.

NCLB also imposes norm-referenced, high-stakes standardized exams in reading and math for students in grades 3–8 and at least once in high school. Such exams have worsened the educational opportunities for poor students by promoting tracking, narrowing the curriculum, and increasing dropout rates (Miner, 2001). Moreover, NCLB imposes annual punitive measures on schools that fail to meet unrealistic achievement standards, thus worsening the situation for poor schools with diverse populations. The result has artificially inflated the demand for voucher schemes and begun to re-mobilize forces in support of the privatization of public schools. Behind NCLB's rhetoric of "high standards" and "academic achievement," therefore, lies the ever-present business ethos of "Americanization" ideology (Karp, 2003).

The consequences for poor and Latino students are serious. At a time when more and more jobs pay less than a living wage despite the enormous rise in corporate profit, attending poor schools has consequences far worse than those a mere generation ago (Orfield, 2001). Latino dropout rates exceed those of any other group, and Latino youth are subject to increasing rates of incarceration. In addition, they constitute the most segregated population in schools today and are most concentrated in states with dismantled affirmative action and bilingual education programs. The result has already intensified the subordination of Latinos within the logic of advanced capitalism and its hierarchical class structure.

References

Frankenburg, E., Lee, C., & Orfield, G. (2003). *A Multiracial Society with Segregated Schools: Are We Losing the Dream?* Cambridge, MA: Harvard Civil Rights Project.

Gonzalez, G. (1974). Racism, Education, and the Mexican Community in Los Angeles, 1920–30. *Societas—A Review of Social History 4*, 287–302.

Karp, S. (2003). The No Child Left Behind Hoax. *Rethinking Schools* (November). Available: http://www.rethinkingschools .org/special_reports/bushplan/hoax.shtml.

Krashen, S. (2001). Bush's Bad Idea for Bilingual Ed. *Rethinking Schools* (Summer). Available: http://www.rethinkingschools.org/ special_reports/bushplan/Bied154.shtml.

Millan, D. (1998). Historical Development of Capitalist Norms in Education and the Emergence of the New "Americanization" Ideology: Implications for Social Policy. In A. Darder (Ed.), *Cultural Studies in Education: Schooling as a Contested Terrain* (pp. 1–23). Claremont, CA: Claremont Graduate University.

Miner, B. (2001). Bush's Plan Is Shallow and Ignores Critical Details. *Rethinking Schools* (February). Available: http://www.rethinking schools.org/special_reports/bushplan/bush .shtml.

Orfield, G. (2001). *Schools More Separate: Consequences of a Decade of Resegregation.* Cambridge, MA: Harvard Civil Rights Project.

Ramirez, I. (1997). *Chicanismo: The Forging of a Militant Ethos among Mexican-Americans.* Tucson: University of Arizona.

Wollenberg, C. (1974). Race, Nationality and Segregation in California Schools. *California Historical Quarterly* 53(4), 317–332.

Recommended Web Site

Rethinking Schools. http://www.rethinking schools.org/.

Recommended Reading

Moreno, J. (Ed.). (1999). *The Elusive Quest for Equality: 150 Years of Chicano/Chicana Education*. Cambridge, MA: Harvard Educational Review.

Orfield, G., Losen, D., Wald, J., & Swanson, C. (2004). *Losing Our Future: How Minority Youth Are Being Left Behind by the Graduation Rate Crisis*. Cambridge, MA: Harvard Civil Rights Project.

Romo, R. (1986). George I. Sanchez and the Civil Rights Movement: 1940–1960. *La Raza Law Journal* 1(3), 342–362.

Laura Galicia

ANTI-BIAS EDUCATION

One of the most contested issues in contemporary education policy and practice concerns optimal strategies for educating English learners, Spanish speakers in particular. While a growing literature has sought to document the outcomes of various language instruction approaches, relatively little research has documented the experiences and perspective of children in these programs, particularly at the preschool level. Federally funded preschool programs such as Head Start strongly emphasize the acquisition of English, based on the belief that English proficiency is far more important to children's academic success and well-being in this country than proficiency in any native minority language. While the overall goals and successes of such programs as Head Start have proven extremely helpful in meeting many of the needs of children and families, we deplore the implicit message that English-only programs convey to children, their families, and communities—namely, that securing profi-

ciency in Spanish, and in Spanish literacy, is essentially irrelevant to Spanish-speaking children's education and academic success.

In contrast to an educational model that seeks to transition children away from their native language into English-only proficiency and literacy, strong or maintenance bilingual education programs (those that foster bilingualism and biliteracy) embody fundamentally different implicit assumptions about English and the minority language, as well as about the value of family participation in education. Bilingual education may prevent or slow native language loss at the same time it facilitates full academic and intellectual engagement among English-learning children, who would otherwise fall behind academically during the years it takes them to fully develop English.

Dual immersion (DI), also called two-way immersion, constitutes a form of strong, developmental bilingual education that capitalizes on the presence of English-speaking peers to aid English learners in developing English while at the same time provides English speakers the opportunity to learn a second language from their language minority peers. In DI, English-speaking students learn Spanish together with Spanish-speaking students, while Spanish speakers learn English; both groups of children become bilingual and biliterate in an atmosphere of mutual support and respect with the crucial benefit of peer language modeling and feedback.

Of the many forms of bilingual education, it has been proposed that DI is the model most likely to succeed in times of heightened opposition to bilingual education. DI, with its ability to provide real bilingualism to English-speaking children, appeals to a constituency that is historically more powerful, politically and financially, than the traditional, Spanish-speaking clients of bilingual education. No one, not even opponents of bilingual education, disputes the primary importance of providing meaningful education to English learners over any form of enrichment education for English-speaking children. Yet, the ability of DI to promote bilingualism and biliteracy in Spanish-speaking children may exceed levels of bilingualism achieved through other models. The fact that DI promotes bilingualism in English-speaking children is an added benefit, and the participation of English-speaking families has been found to provide much-needed support when bilingual education comes under attack.

In true immersion programs, teachers remain conscious of the needs of second language learners at all times in order to ensure all children's participation. The teacher may attempt to speak in a way that is comprehensible to those acquiring the second language, may employ a greater use of visuals and realia to provide sufficient context, and so forth. Such methods are known to benefit not only language learners, but all students. However, concern is occasionally expressed regarding the level of language development, the linguistic sophistication, that can be attained by Spanish-speaking students in such contexts, since a teacher may be perceived as "talking down" to students who already know that language, using only simplified language and concepts.

Fears of oversimplification are largely unjustified, however, for teachers trained in immersion methods learn to "shelter" content, which entails engaging students in sophisticated content without relying solely on linguistic means (Faltis, 2001). In DI, content is reinforced through lessons undertaken in both languages, in one language one day, for example, and in the other language on the next (Christian, Montone, Lindholm, & Carranza, 1997). This enables students to develop and strengthen their understandings, reinforcing previous lessons, without linguistic or content simplification. Linguistic sophistication stems from interaction with texts much more than with teachers, and good DI programs provide access to increasingly sophisticated texts as students move through the grades, just as other good programs do.

It is clear from research studies (Cazabon, Lambert, & Hall, 1993; Holobow, Genesee, & Lambert, 1991; Lindholm & Fairchild, 1990; Rolstad, 1999) that social integration of children is strengthened significantly in DI programs. Instead of entering a classroom in which the anticipated hegemony (and privileging) of English is the norm, children and teachers in DI programs find that the minority language at least temporarily assumes the more privileged position. As the language and power tables are turned, children are immediately confronted by the altered power dynamics and can quickly come to view each other as potential friends and language role models in a way that contrasts sharply with the linguistic and social devaluing that routinely occurs in English-only settings.

In Arizona State University's College of Education (COE) Preschool, the TWIST (Two-Way Immersion Spanish Time) program was implemented in fall 2002 to provide a cross-cultural, counter-hegemonic preschool experience while documenting some of the complex issues in young children's language-learning experiences, identity development, and attitudes toward peers.[1] The project was developed in collaboration with a local Head Start program; the children attending this Head Start are predominantly native Spanish speakers.

The goals of the TWIST program are to integrate Spanish-speaking children from Head Start and English-speaking children from the COE preschool for instruction and play facilitated in Spanish as a way of developing Spanish language skills in both groups of children while promoting social interaction and concepts of social justice through an anti-bias curriculum. Two-way immersion in elementary school has been found to successfully promote interaction between students who differ not only by the language they speak but also by their socioeconomic status (Lindholm & Fairchild, 1990). A fundamental goal of the TWIST program is to promote mutual respect and friendships among the primarily middle-class English-speaking children and the Spanish-speaking students in the Head Start program, an income-eligible program serving families.

The Head Start program, located on the Arizona State University campus, uses English for instruction with approximately 20 Spanish-speaking children Monday through Friday mornings. When Head Start children come to TWIST Monday, Wednesday, and Friday afternoons (1:00 PM to 3:30 PM), they join a second group of approximately 25 children. This group consists of primarily English speakers, but it often includes a few children who are bilingual in English and another language or, occasionally, monolingual in another language, such as Korean or Turkish.

These two groups of children, those from Head Start and those from the COE preschool, come together three afternoons per week to participate in TWIST's Spanish immersion in the COE preschool site. One of the three lead teachers is a native speaker of Spanish who leads instruction in her classroom during TWIST. In the other two rooms, native Spanish-speaking language enrichment teachers assume the instructional lead, supported by the two lead teachers who are learning Spanish. In addition, each classroom is assigned a native Spanish-speaking language reflector, whose role is to reflect Spanish back to individuals or the group, depending on the type of activity. The center director also began studying Spanish prior to the start of the program and occasionally interacts with children and adults during TWIST. All materials for parents are bilingual, and parent meetings and education are facilitated in both Spanish and English in collaboration with the Head Start staff.

TWIST was developed against a backdrop of national and state opposition to bilingual education, associated with a growing policy discourse of standards and accountability (Wiley & Wright, 2004). Proposition 203, an Arizona ballot initiative, became law in fall 2000 and mandates structured English immersion (SEI) for all language minority children in the state who have been designated as limited in their English proficiency. Many K–12 bilingual education programs in Arizona have survived under a waiver provision that permits bilingual education for those who request it. However, under recent related changes in language policies of the State Department of Education (ADE) following the election of a superintendent of public instruction who ran in part on an English-only campaign, bilingual education programs have become far more severely threatened. As the political and social climate continues to have an increasingly chilling effect on language minority children and communities, educational programs that support bilingualism and biliteracy create opportunities for counter-hegemonic praxis.

Little is known of how young children fare in language education programs, linguistically, psychologically, or socially. The TWIST project explores the linguistic and social effects on preschool children of a two-way Spanish-English immersion program, with the aim of addressing these gaps in the research literature.

Research on English immersion has established the dangers of English immersion to children's academic performance (Ramirez, Yuen, & Ramey, 1991) and emotiona well-being (Hernandez-Chavez, 1984; Soto, 2002; Wong Fillmore, 1991). Early advocates of English-only instruction insisted that it could be as effective as foreign language immersion in Canada but stipulated that SEI teachers must possess two critical characteristics: (1) the ability to understand the language of the children and (2) special training in immersion techniques (Baker & deKanter, 1981). When teachers do not understand the language of the children, children may feel silenced and be less likely to participate and therefore less likely to engage in learning opportunities. Teachers who are not adequately trained in immersion methods tend to marginalize English learners. While SEI, properly conducted by a qualified teacher, may sometimes be the most viable option in a given context, a lack of infrastructure in Arizona has undermined the enactment of an authentic SEI experience for the majority of English language learning (ELL) students. Although some nominal provisions for SEI methods instruction have been discussed in Arizona, and may eventually be made available to SEI teachers, there has been no recognition of SEI's requirement that teachers understand the language of the children they teach. Thus, a very threatening, often effacing atmosphere is created for ELL children, whose language and cultural resources are ignored or marginalized.

A threatening sociolinguistic atmosphere can be effectively countered with the authentic, valued use of the minority language and culture, such as that provided by DI to Spanish-speaking children. At the same time, English-speaking children in DI learn to value a second language and its speakers through a direct relationship with language minority children (Cazabon et al., 1993). The opportunity to interact with linguistically and culturally diverse peers also contributes to an anti-bias learning environment for young children (Derman-Sparks, 1989; Marsh, 1992; Soto, 2002; Swadener, 1988; Swadener & Lubeck, 1995). Spanish-speaking children's fluency in their native language may be valued in important ways by their Spanish-learning peers and contributes to Spanish-speaking children's self-esteem and confidence.

This integrative rather than isolating experience can lead to the development of cross-cultural skills and improved attitudes toward the other group on the part of both language minority and majority children, and it can positively affect self-esteem (Cazabon et al., 1993; Lambert, 1987; Lindholm, 1990; Rolstad, 1997). Such authentic interaction is encouraged by two-way programs such as the TWIST program. While not in itself sufficient to provide children with an anti-bias education, DI provides a unique experience and an excellent opportunity that teachers can use to help children explore a multitude of anti-bias themes.

An initial concern when starting the project was that two of the three lead teachers in the preschool were not proficient in Spanish. The stricture that only Spanish was to be spoken by adults during TWIST meant that any adults, whether teachers, teaching interns, students workers, or visitors who were not proficient in Spanish, would effectively be silenced; no English was to be spoken by adults. The hope was that this experience of language restriction would have two outcomes: to encourage these adults to learn Spanish and to provide them with an intense, deeply meaningful experience in difficult communication through a language they do not know well or at all. The difficulty and frustration faced by these adults is the usual daily experience of many English learners placed in English-only settings. Placing the burden of productive communication on the adults would help them to empathize and identify with the children they served.

An important question, of course, was how some adults' lack of Spanish proficiency would affect the program and children's valuing of Spanish and Spanish speakers. What effects might adults' flawed Spanish have on children, Spanish speakers, and English speakers alike? It seemed likely that instances of flawed Spanish production would be more than balanced by the children's access to accurate Spanish models provided by the native Spanish-speaking teachers who were always present in the room and by the children's parents and family members.[2] Moreover, the adults who were less proficient in Spanish were demonstrably eager to learn from the children, and in no way posed as if, or implied that, their Spanish production was in any way on a par with that already possessed by the Spanish-speaking children.

It was further assumed that Spanish-learning children would be relatively unaffected by adults' Spanish errors, not only because the errors would be balanced by the authentic Spanish of native speaking adults, but also because such errors are likely to escape the notice of children at this very

early stage of second language acquisition. Further, it is clear that children learn language usage to a far greater extent from their peers than they might learn from adults, and these children had daily access to their Spanish-speaking peers as appropriate linguistic models. It was predicted that these aspects of language acquisition would have no negative effects.

At the end of the first two years of the program, however, it was striking to see an overwhelmingly positive effect of that lack of Spanish proficiency on the part of some of the adults; namely, that children daily witness teachers making overt attempts to use Spanish and learning from the native Spanish-speaking children. While this has varied between teachers and not been present in all adults in these classrooms, data have provided striking and consistent examples of the shift in power dynamics created by the teachers' need to draw on the children's linguistic expertise.

One important change from the first year of TWIST to the second involved having the English-speaking children visit the Spanish-speaking children in the Head Start site before the TWIST program began. Because of site constraints, TWIST occurs in the COE preschool, placing it in the typical position of "integration" always happening on the dominant group's turf. It is difficult to counter the message that the language minority children appear to be the supplicants who are transported from a supposedly inferior place and position to a superior one. TWIST's approach was to transport the language majority children to the highly-appealing Head Start setting to strengthen the Head Start children's status upon introducing the children to each other. This introduction on the Spanish-speaking children's "territory" had a noticeably positive impact on how the two groups of children viewed each other from the outset, according to the COE preschool director and to TWIST teachers.

Just a few days into the first year of the program, a fundamental lack in the Spanish language environment was noted. Whereas children and one teacher suffice for DI in typical K–12 classrooms, the tender age and inexperience of preschoolers in school settings resulted in a heavy burden of language production falling on the lone Spanish-speaking teacher. Children were linguistically unresponsive, Spanish speakers and English speakers alike. Additional Spanish-speaking adults were clearly necessary to sustain full and engaging linguistic interactions—hence the addition of language reflectors, typically undergraduate native Spanish-speaking students, who play the critical role of reflecting Spanish back to teachers and children, ensuring a back-and-forth model of interaction for children to follow. The program has succeeded and become extremely popular with both groups of parents, even receiving an award from a national parents' organization. Yet, unlike in K–12 settings, its success depends on the presence of more than one engaged teacher.

The traditional model of DI consists of two groups of monolingual children who learn each others' languages together over the course of the elementary grades. In states where bilingual education has been legally curtailed or banned for children who do not already know English, DI programs have come to consist of children monolingual in English when they entered the program and children who were already bilingual when they entered the program. The benefits for children of this variation of the DI model have not been established, but we can expect that all the children will be-

come bilingual and biliterate. In one-way immersion, such as French immersion received by English-speaking children in Quebec, no peer language models are present in the classroom, yet monolingual English speakers attain high levels of bilingualism and biliteracy. At worst, DI programs that include only children who already know English may result in language outcomes similar to those in one-way immersion. Opportunities for anti-bias education remain greatest in DI, however, because two groups of children work together and play together in an environment that strongly reinforces the target minority language and culture.

Children's native languages belong in schools. While policymakers and educators may dispute variations in how children can best be educated within an English educational framework, opportunities to develop full bilingualism ought never be jeopardized, certainly not when there are viable alternatives. Despite the weight of evidence supporting this country's highly successful bilingual education programs, they face undeserved, negative political pressure in many areas. Despite DI's well-established success in educating English language learners to the highest levels, often over and above levels attained by monolingual English-speaking children, the broad sweep of anti-bilingual education reform undermines DI at the same time. When schools face the restriction that only children who already speak English be allowed to participate in DI, the challenge to educators becomes helping children prepare to pass English language assessments at a level that will satisfy bureaucratic demands. In such contexts, preschool programs that support both children's native language and English can prove an invaluable asset to communities that seek to maintain and develop bilingualism and biliteracy in their children. Which preschool models can best serve English language learners?

Native language proficiency appears to be most vulnerable, and subject to loss, in the youngest children, those aged 6 and below (Wong Fillmore, 1991). What role can preschool DI play in slowing or preventing native language loss? Or is the introduction of English in preschool already too early if parents desire bilingualism for their children? In the case of TWIST, the alternative for the Spanish-speaking Head Start children was to receive no preschool instruction in Spanish at all, such that TWIST provided native language support that would not have been available otherwise. We can imagine an ideal world where parents who desired bilingualism for their children could choose long-term native language instruction, with the gradual introduction of English. Would a DI preschool meet their needs? Perhaps not. However, in states like Arizona, where parents have no choices whatsoever regarding the language development of their children, DI remains the one window of opportunity for children to attain bilingualism and biliteracy, provided that these children can be equipped with sufficient English skills to qualify for the provisional waiver that exempts them from English-only instruction. In this setting, preschool DI programs can prove a crucial asset by supporting native language development in very young children while introducing English and providing interaction with English-speaking peers in a way that allows Spanish-speaking children to develop the English proficiency necessary to meet the kindergarten DI program requirements.

Many questions remain to be addressed regarding DI, not only in preschool but also in K–12 settings. One of the key questions about DI is how it facilitates English language learning for ELL students in comparison to English-only classes. Also, does a DI classroom better support an ELL child in school, irrespective of language acquisition? Academic success depends on far more than English proficiency, and other factors, such as parents' ability to support their children's learning, may be as important as any. Yet, an English-only program effectively blocks participation of parents who lack proficiency in English. We face a need for increased support of bilingual programs and for studies of variables often overlooked in traditional educational research.

A generation ago, even during the heyday of bilingual education, relatively few children (a maximum of 30% of English learners who might have benefited from bilingual education) were provided with opportunities to develop bilingualism and biliteracy in school. Today, DI may be the only form of bilingual education to survive the increased anti-bilingual campaigns, as has happened in California, Arizona, and Massachusetts. It is perhaps ironic that DI happens to be the most subversive of bilingual education approaches, presenting English-only advocates with the greatest threat of all—that of language minority students who attain the highest levels of achievement while retaining their native language abilities and of politically powerful language majority students who have come to value minority languages and communities through personal experience.

Dual immersion is possible only through grassroots organization and must by necessity involve parents and communities to help both create DI programs and sustain them. Historically, DI has struggled to involve parents from both constituent groups equally, with middle-class English-speaking parents typically enjoying the advantages of more time and resources to contribute to the success of these programs; but DI is gradually making strides in this direction. In Arizona, for example, the statewide Dual Immersion Association (DIA) was recently established in an attempt to organize parents from both language groups across districts in support of DI programs. Schools should and do include parents in their decision making, especially when groups of parents come together to clamor for successful programs. One of the major charges of the DIA organization is to develop strong linkages among both language majority and language minority parents. The alliance of these two populations, cemented through their years of DI integration in schools and bolstered by concerted efforts toward unity, could serve to twist English-only school policies inside out. Dual immersion presents a truly counter-hegemonic approach to education, one that can provide children with a solid foundation for future understandings of language difference and shifting power dynamics.

Notes

1. Many thanks are due to my friend and research partner Beth Blue Swadener for her invaluable help in facilitating the collaboration with Head Start that led to the implementation of the TWIST program and for our ongoing collaboration.

2. Although the variety of Spanish spoken in these communities is sometimes socially stigmatized, parents and other native speakers are nonetheless perfectly competent and proficient language users, providing a perfect model of language for their children. For more discussion of this point, see MacSwan and Rolstad (2003).

References

Baker, K., & deKanter, A. (1981). *Effectiveness of Bilingual Education: A Review of the Lit-*

erature. Final report to the U.S. Department of Education. Washington, DC: Office of Planning, Budget and Evaluation, U.S. Department of Education.

Cazabon, M., Lambert, W. E., & Hall, G. (1993). *Two-Way Bilingual Education: A Progress Report on the Amigos Program*. Santa Cruz, CA: National Center for Research on Cultural Diversity and Second Language Learning.

Christian, D., Montone, C., Lindholm, K. J., & Carranza, I. (1997). *Profiles in Two-Way Immersion*. Washington, DC: Center for Applied Linguistics.

Derman-Sparks, L. (1989). *Anti-bias Curriculum: Tools for Empowering Young Children*. Washington, DC: National Association for the Education of Young Children.

Faltis, C. J. (2001). *Joinfostering: Teaching and Learning in Multilingual Classrooms* (3rd ed.). Upper Saddle River, NJ: Prentice-Hall.

Hernandez-Chavez, E. (1984). Submersion of Language Minority Students. In *Studies on Immersion Education* (pp. 114–144). Los Angeles: California State Department of Education.

Holobow, N. E., Genesee, F., & Lambert, W. E. (1991). The Effectiveness of a Foreign Language Immersion Program for Children from Different Ethnic and Social Class Backgrounds: Report 2. *Applied Psycholinguistics* 12.

Lambert, W. E. (1987). The Effects of Bilingual and Bicultural Experiences on Children's Attitudes and Social Perspectives. In P. Homel, M. Palij, & D. Aaronson (Eds.), *Childhood Bilingualism: Aspects of Linguistic, Cognitive and Social Development*. Hillsdale, NJ: Lawrence Erlbaum.

Lindholm, K. J. (1990). Bilingual Immersion Education: Criteria for Program Development. In A. M. Padilla, H. H. Fairchild, & C. M. Valdez (Eds.), *Bilingual Education: Issues and Strategies*. Newbury Park, CA: Sage.

Lindholm, K. J., & Fairchild, H. H. (1990). Evaluation of an Elementary School Bilingual Immersion Program. In A. M. Padilla,

H. H. Fairchild, & C. M. Valadez (Eds.), *Bilingual Education: Issues and Strategies*. Newbury Park, CA: Sage.

MacSwan, J., & Rolstad, K. (2003). Linguistic Diversity, Schooling, and Social Class: Rethinking Our Conception of Language Proficiency in Language Minority Education. In C. B. Paulston & G. R. Tucker (Eds.), *Sociolinguistics: The Essential Readings*. Oxford: Blackwell.

Marsh, M. M. (1992). Implementing Antibias Curriculum in the Kindergarten Classroom. In S. Kessler & B. B. Swadener (Eds.), *Reconceptualizing the Early Childhood Curriculum: Beginning the Dialogue*. New York: Teachers College Press.

Ramirez, J. D., Yuen, S. D., & Ramey, D. R. (1991). *Longitudinal Study of Structured English Immersion Strategy, Early-Exit and Late-Exit Transitional Bilingual Programs for Language-Minority Children*. Final Report to the U.S. Department of Education. Executive Summary and Vols. 1 and 2. San Mateo, CA: Aguirre International.

Rolstad, K. (1997). Effects of Two-Way Immersion on the Ethnic Identification of Third Language Students. *Bilingual Research Journal* 21(1), 43–63.

Soto, L. D. (2002). *Making a Difference in the Lives of Young Bilingual Children*. New York: Peter Lang.

Swadener, B. B. (1988). Implementation of Education That Is Multicultural in Early Childhood Settings: A Case Study of Two Day-Care Programs. *Urban Review* 20(1), 8–27.

Swadener, B. B., & Lubeck, S. (1995). *Children and Families "At Promise": Deconstructing the Discourse of Risk*. Albany, NY: SUNY Press.

Wiley, T. G., & Wright, W. E. (2004). Against the Undertow: Language-Minority Education Policy and Politics in the "Age of Accountability." *Educational Policy* 18(1), 142–168.

Wong Fillmore, L. (1991). Language and Cultural Issues in Early Education. In L. Kagan (Ed.), *The Care and Education of America's Young Children*. The 90th Yearbook of the National Society for the Study of Education.

Recommended Reading

On English language education policy in the U.S.: Crawford, J. (2004). *Educating English Learners: Language Diversity in the Classroom* (5th ed.). Los Angeles: Bilingual Education Services.

On emotional well-being of young children in English language settings: Soto, L. D. (2002). *Making a Difference in the Lives of Young Bilingual Children*. New York: Peter Lang.

On dual or two-way immersion programs: Christian, D., Montone, C., Lindholm, K. J., & Carranza, I. (1997). *Profiles in Two-Way Immersion*. Washington, DC: Center for Applied Linguistics.

On key pedagogical benefits of dual immersion: Rolstad, K. (2000). Capitalizing on Diversity: Lessons from Dual Language Immersion. *NABE News* 23(5), 5–18.

On minority language death: Rolstad, K. (2002). Language Death in Central Mexico: The Decline of Spanish-Nahuatl Bilingualism and the New Bilingual Maintenance Programs. *Bilingual Review* 25(3), 1–14.

On class-based language prejudice and language deficit views: MacSwan, J., & Rolstad, K. (2003). Linguistic Diversity, Schooling, and Social Class: Rethinking Our Conception of Language Proficiency in Language Minority Education. In C. B. Paulston & G. R. Tucker (Eds.), *Sociolinguistics: The Essential Readings*. Oxford: Blackwell.

On preschool integration issues: Swadener, B. B. (1988). Implementation of Education That Is Multicultural in Early Childhood Settings: A Case Study of Two Day-Care Programs. *Urban Review* 20(1), 8–27.

Kellie Rolstad

B

THE BIENESTAR DIABETES PREVENTION PROGRAM

Recent studies are reporting an increasing number of low-income minority children being diagnosed with type 2 diabetes. Type 2 diabetes was once considered to be an adult onset disease, and it was estimated that less than 5% of all children with diabetes were type 2. In San Antonio, Texas, however, 18% of all diabetic youth seen in a pediatric endocrinology clinic were identified as having type 2 diabetes. A recent school-based study also found that of 987 low-income fourth grade students examined, 4.6% had abnormal fasting capillary glucose (FCG) levels (≥ 110 mg/dl). Common findings in diabetic youth are that most were minority, most were overweight, most were unaware of their disease, and all came from low-income households.

The Bienestar (*Well-being*) Health Program is a bilingual coordinated school-based diabetes prevention program. The Bienestar consists of creating a network of social support for children to decrease fatty foods, to increase fiber foods, to increase physical activity, and to control body weight. Systems selected to provide the social support are the home, the school, the school cafeteria, and the after-school care. The Bienestar, therefore, consists of the Bienestar Parent Fun Fiesta, the Bienestar Health and Physical Education Class, the Bienestar Health Club, and the Bienestar School Food Service.

When compared to non-participating students, Bienestar students have significantly decreased their fat intake, have increased their fiber intake, and have increased their physical fitness levels. For three consecutive years, the Bienestar has restored normoglycemia in children with abnormal FCG levels (see Table 1). These results suggest that early-age intervention may be the best approach to controlling diabetes in at-risk populations.

Presently, the Bienestar is being evaluated in a randomized clinical trial where children will be followed for four years. This study began in the fall of 2001 with near 700 students (72% response rate) in each arm (intervention and control) of the study. The National Institutes of Health–funded randomized controlled trial showed that children participating in the Bienestar were twice as likely to avoid the disease than children in the control (1.5% Bienestar vs. 3.1% control; $p < .05$). Type 2 diabetes in children is a rising medical problem, and the Bienestar is a program shown to reverse hyperglycemia in diabetic children and to prevent hyperglycemia in at-risk children. Because of similar diabetes risk factor levels in African American children, the Bienestar has now been translated to the African

Table 1
Mean FCG Levels for Three School Years

Students with Abnormal FCG ($\geq 110\,mg/dl$)	Baseline (August)	Follow-up (May)	p Value
1999–2000: n = 9	117 ± 5.2	93 ± 19.1	$p < .05$
2000–2001: n = 43	123 ± 17	99 ± 9	$p < .001$
2001–2002: n = 42	121 ± 16	91 ± 13	$p < .01$

American culture—the Neema (*Well-being in Swahili*) Health Program.

Roberto P. Treviño

BILINGUAL EDUCATION

Bilingual education refers to the use of two languages to teach a given population. The Office of Education, as cited in Ovando and Collier (1985), defines bilingual education as

the use of two languages, one of which is English, as mediums of instruction for the same pupil population in a well-organized program which encompasses all or part of the curriculum and includes the study of the history and culture associated with the mother tongue. A complete program that develops and maintains the children's self-esteem and a legitimate pride in both cultures. (p. 2)

Another definition of bilingual programs states that such programs in the U.S. have the following three characteristics: (1) continued development of the student's primary language; (2) acquisition of the second language, which for limited English proficient students is English; (3) instruction in the content areas using both the primary language and the second language (Ovando & Collier, 1985, p. 1).

Within bilingual programs there exists great variation in the two languages are used and what the programs aim to achieve. Mackey (1970) addresses this diversity in his identification of 90 varieties of such programs used on a global level. While a spectrum of bilingual programs exists throughout the U.S., three approaches, namely, the transitional model, the maintenance model, and the two-way bilingual model (also known as dual-language model), represent the most commonly used approaches in the education of language minority children in our nation.

Since Spanish speakers comprise the largest linguistic minority in the U.S., they are, not surprisingly, the population most affected by the implementation of the aforementioned bilingual programs.

Transitional Bilingual Programs

Transitional bilingual programs in the U.S. are the most numerous of the three aforementioned types of programs. Transitional programs consist of a course of study designed for children of limited English proficiency that provides structured English language instruction and native language instruction (Public Law 100–297, 1988). This approach centers on the main objective of achieving English competency. In such a model, students of limited English proficiency receive instruction in their native language in all subject areas as well as instruction in English as a second language. Native language instruction is provided to avoid loss of grade-level skills while mastery of a second language is taking place. When students have achieved proficiency in English, they are mainstreamed into monolingual classes with all-English-speaking students.

The two major problems that surround transitional programs consist of issues of perception about these programs and matters that deal with assessment. Transitional programs are problematic because they are perceived as remedial. This leads to their creation and implementation as segregated entities within a school. Such isolation limits the degree to which transitional program students interact with the rest of the school population, further contributing to the negative labeling of students enrolled in such classes. The insular nature of these programs does not facilitate the interaction of its students in language-centered activities with English speakers, thus depriving such students of opportunities that can help them achieve English competency through meaningful exchanges with English speakers. Even more important, another major flaw is their insistence in prematurely mainstreaming English language learners when research conducted on such children indicates that they have not attained the necessary skills to do academic work. Most transitional programs exit students into all-English classes after a maximum of two years despite research conducted on language acquisition that has shown that Cognitive Academic Language Proficiency (CALP, the ability to do academic work) is not attained for at least five to seven years. What is possibly attained in two years are Basic Interpersonal Communicative Skills (BICS), which do not provide students with the necessary skills to understand and succeed in the academic domain (Cummins, 1979, 1980). The subsequent consequences of such premature exiting from transitional classes oftentimes results in children who now find themselves in a monolingual English class without the necessary skills to meet the academic demands placed on them and facing the psychosocial and academic ramifications of being in that position. For young children who are forming their attitudes about school and learning, as well as developing self-concepts, such an experience can be life altering.

Maintenance of Bilingual Programs

Unlike transitional bilingual programs, maintenance programs emphasize the preservation of the ethnic language and culture and do not focus upon program completion. In maintenance models, content area instruction is conducted in both English and the native language with the goal of achieving competency in both languages while mastering subject matter skills. Implementation of such an approach allows students to increase their knowledge in content areas and their native language while developing their skills in English. Proponents of this method recognize that through such an approach, students do not fall behind in content areas. Furthermore, since the concepts, knowledge, and skills attained in their native language will eventually be transferred into English, this methodology ensures that students will not only become bilingual but also have grade-level knowledge in the content areas.

Bilingual maintenance programs in the U.S. are found in the childhood level and usually exist in demographic areas with a preponderance of linguistic minorities. Despite the benefits of becoming fluent in two languages and the empirical research to justify such an approach, the implementation of this model has prompted a controversy over how federal monies should be spent. Concerns include arguments that native language maintenance is not the task of the federal government.

Two-Way or Dual-Language Bilingual Programs

Two-way bilingual programs, also known as dual-language programs, employ an integrated model in which speakers of two languages are placed together in a bilingual classroom to learn each other's language and work academically in both languages (Snow, 1986). These classes are usually composed of equal numbers of language minority and language majority students. In the U.S., this would consist of classes with 50% of its students who are most likely English monolingual speakers and the remaining 50% of students who are English language learners and native speakers of the same non-English language. Both English and the selected non-English language are used as mediums of instruction. These schools were first created in the U.S. by the Cuban population in Dade County, Florida, during the 1960s when a large migration of Cubans took place in the state. These programs (Linholm, 1987, as cited in Baker, 1997, p. 187) have four characteristics:

1. A non-English language is used for at least 50% of instruction.
2. In each period of instruction, only one language is used.
3. Both English and non-English speakers are present in preferably balanced numbers.
4. The English and non-English speakers are integrated in all lessons.

Transitional, maintenance, and dual-language bilingual programs each embody a distinct approach with a particular aim. These models as cited in Baker (1997) represent programs that can be classified as being weak or strong in promoting bilingualism. For example, transitional programs are classified as weak in regard to facilitating bilingualism, whereas maintenance and dual-language programs are categorized as strong in the promotion of bilingualism and biliteracy (Baker, 1997). The aforementioned descriptions of bilingual education models, while helpful in explaining language use in the classroom, do not address the totality of philosophical, linguistic, political, historical, cultural, and cognitive issues regarding bilingual education.

The lack of consensus regarding what method should be used in the teaching of language minority children reflects the ever-changing nature of bilingual education in the U.S., which is driven by the political, social, and economic forces of this nation. Moreover, the widespread use of transitional programs is not only a byproduct of the aforementioned forces but also an indication of the little value placed on knowing more than one language in our country. The lack of importance given to learning a non-English language and the stress placed on cultural homogeneity despite our multicultural society are also driven by these forces. In essence, decisions regarding the education of linguistic minorities are being made and have historically been made based on political reasons rather than on pedagogical considerations.

The politicization of bilingual education has made it controversial and has thrown it into a very dangerous arena in which its future role in the education of English language learners is uncertain. Misguided opinions based on misinformation about bilingual education are affecting decisions about how children should be taught. It becomes the purpose of this document, therefore, to examine many of the false and inaccurate assumptions about bilingual education in order to have a more accurate account of such an approach.

In light of such a dismal account of how decisions are and have been made for language minority children, one should keep in mind that language is a fundamental right. The Declaration of Human Rights (1948) acknowledges that everyone is entitled to all the rights and freedoms set forth in it without distinction of any kind, such as language. Particular attention is given to article 26, which claims, "Education shall be directed to the full development of the human personality and to the strengthening of respect for human rights and fundamental freedoms. It shall promote understanding, tolerance and friendship among all nations, racial or religious groups, and shall further the activities of the United Nations for the maintenance of peace. Furthermore, parents are acknowledged as having a right to choose the kind of education that shall be given to their children."

There is historical evidence to show that the founding fathers of our country also recognized language as a human right. In the absence of such knowledge, many inaccurate and skewed perspectives regarding bilingual education emerge. For example, sentiments of patriotism and loyalty for our country are often misconstrued as being incompatible with bilingual education when in fact if one examines the early beginnings of our nation, one would conclude the opposite.

Some mistakenly deduce that it is unconstitutional or even un-American to conduct instruction in a non-English language because English is the official language of the U.S. In fact, the Constitution does not designate any language an official status, thus providing the citizens of this nation the right to be educated in the language of their choice. Such a very important omission in our national document is most likely a reflection of the language diversity that existed during this period and an attempt by our forefathers to unite rather than divide our nation. Moreover, it is recognition of the wrongfulness of imposing a language on a nation of immigrants who spoke different languages and thus a violation of their human rights.

Thinking that associates the speaking of English with patriotism or gives English an "official status," not surprisingly, also leads to mindsets that favor the sink-or-swim method of teaching linguistic minorities. Such an approach does not provide English language learners with any special accommodations in their education. Programs for linguistic minorities are often created (whether consciously or unconsciously) with one major concern, namely, the expedient mainstreaming of English language learners into English monolingual classrooms. This goal, not surprisingly, is also the goal of transitional programs. Such an approach is not the most pedagogically beneficial model for English language learners. Nonetheless, such a choice permits educators to make accommodations for language minorities and simultaneously feel comfortable because the approach may be closely aligned with their personal philosophical stances that favor cultural homogeneity. In making such decisions,

the proponents of "English only" also fail to raise two fundamental questions: First, if English is the most effective educational language, how can we explain over 60 million Americans being illiterate or functionally illiterate? Second, if education in "English only" can guarantee linguistic minorities a better future, as educators like William Bennett promise, why do the majority of Black Americans, whose ancestors have been speaking English for over two hundred years find themselves still relegated to ghettos? (Macedo, 1994, p. 126)

Another misconception regarding bilingual education that leads people to misguided thinking includes the belief that such an educational approach was first initiated by Hispanics to accommodate their needs and desires when in fact the creation of bilingual schools in the U.S. can be traced to the early beginnings of our nation when bilingual schools were created as a response to the linguistic diversity that existed during this early phase in our history. Thinking that bilingual education is a "Latino thing" because it is an accommodation for Hispanics paves the way for resentment from non-Latinos who are ready to remind you that their ancestors came to this country and they did not need bilingual education. Such arguments, although hollow because they do not address many of the racial, technological, educational, and socioeconomic realities of the twenty-first century in the U.S., do serve to convince many against bilingual education.

Nonetheless, education data of the eighteenth century demonstrate that bilingual education was first created in the U.S. for non-Latino groups. Instruction in non-English languages was fairly common throughout Pennsylvania, Maryland, Virginia, and the Carolinas during the 1700s. In these schools instruction was often carried out exclusively in non-English languages while English was taught as an academic subject. After independence, English emerged as a more often used medium of instruction. Nonetheless, bilingual education continued to emerge in the Southwest right up to the time of the U.S. annexation of this area after the Mexican-American War in 1848 (Keller & Van Hooft, 1982).

This climate of tolerance for cultural diversity soon come to an end, however, and was followed by a period of intolerance. The massive migration of persons from Europe to our shores during the latter part of the nineteenth century and the threat that such a vast change in the U.S. demographics represented, as well as the onset of World War I and the nationalism that emerged during this time, paved the way for a period that valued and promoted cultural homogeneity. During this period, as cited in Baker (1997), such legislation as the Nationality Act (1906), which required immigrants to know English, and a resolution by the U.S. Americanization Department recommending all states to prescribe that all students be educated in English reflected the philosophical change that had occurred in this nation, which had been a proponent of cultural pluralism. This thrust to "Americanize" also extended to American colonies like Hawaii and Puerto Rico, where language policy advocating the use of English was enforced and rightfully opposed by the citizens of these respective nations who were not Anglophones.

After World War II the climate of public opinion advocating linguistic homogeneity slowly began to change as a result of the experiences of Americans who while in Europe had witnessed the lack of most Americans' foreign language skills. Also, in response to the launching of Sputnik in 1958, the National Defense Education Act was passed. Such legislation provided not only for the study of mathematics and science but also financial incentives for the study of foreign languages.

This period was also characterized by the immigration of Cubans fleeing from Castro's newly established dictatorship. Settling predominantly in Dade County, Florida, this population mistakenly assumed that they would soon return to their native country thus, initiated the creation of a bilingual program in the Coral Way elementary school to prepare their children for that return. The success of this program became a model for programs soon to be established throughout the U.S.

Other major events in the form of judicial and legislative decisions during this time further paved the way for bilingual education. Although the Civil Rights Act (1964) did not directly address linguistic rights, it did speak to the equality of opportunity and educational opportunity for all. It laid the foundation for various movements that would follow this course grounded on a person's basic rights and freedom. In 1967 the Bilingual Education Act was passed. This legislation was created to help Spanish speakers who were not succeeding in the school system. This act indicated that bilingual programs were to be seen as part of federal educational policy (Baker, 1997, p. 169). It authorized the use of federal funds for the education of speakers of languages other than English. In 1974 the Supreme Court ruled in *Lau v. Nichols* that English submersion programs for language minority children were illegal. In essence, it recognized the educational rights of children who were not provided special programs to remedy the situation. During this same year *Aspira of New York v. Board of Education of the City of New York* mandated a system to identify Hispanic students in need of special instruction, set standards to teach in Spanish and English, and describe the necessary teacher qualifications. In essence, this was a period that witnessed great strides in favor of bilingual education. There was recognition that a population was not being educated and was in need of immediate attention.

With the swing of the pendulum, the course of bilingual education took still another turn during the late 1970s and throughout the next two decades. This was a period marked by efforts to curtail the role of bilingual education and the attempts to seriously weaken its role in the education of linguistic minorities. While these offensives have not totally ruined bilingual education,

they have made it difficult for a strong form to exist. These changes have come in the shape of changes and amendments to existing legislation and decisions that favored the use of bilingual education. The nonallocation of funds supporting strong bilingual programs has been the most effective way in leading to the weakening of these programs.

This assault on bilingual education has continued irrespective of information that supports the use of a child's mother tongue in the child's education. One of the first comprehensive studies to address language in education was conducted by the United Nations Educational, Scientific and Cultural Organization (UNESCO). Findings indicated that children educated in a language that was not their home language experienced difficulties in the classroom (UNESCO, 1953). According to this monograph conducted by international experts, the mother-tongue language (also known as the home language) is the best linguistic medium of instruction because it serves as the vehicle through which the cultural environment is absorbed. According to these authorities, the mother tongue should be used for as long as possible. The UNESCO report stipulates that competency of the second language can be attained if the mother tongue is the initial medium of instruction. The report also acknowledges that the use of one's home language facilitates literacy development, in addition to the learning of content areas, and helps to strengthen ties between the home and the school.

Arguments against bilingual education very often center on the detrimental effects that such an approach can have on the development of children when in fact research indicates that there are advantages to being bilingual. Numerous studies conducted in many countries indicate that being bilingual is cognitively advantageous. In international and cross-cultural studies conducted in Malaysia, Ireland, Eastern Europe, Singapore, the U.S., Mexico, and Canada, to mention a few, bilinguals were found superior to monolinguals on divergent thinking tests (see Ricciardelli, 1992, and Baker, 1988, for a review of these studies).

Other research attesting to the advantages of bilingualism have found that fluent bilinguals have greater metalinguistic awareness than their monolingual counterparts (Ben-Zeev, 1977a, 1977b; Bialystok, 1987a, 1987b; Bialystok & Ryan, 1985; Galambos & Hakuta, 1988; Ianco-Worrall, 1972). Such research addresses the ability to think about and reflect upon the nature and functions of language. This has been interpreted as the possibility that bilinguals may be ready slightly earlier than monolinguals in learning to read.

Additional findings have also found bilinguals to have greater communicative sensitivity than monolinguals (Ben-Zeev, 1977a; Genesee, Tucker, & Lambert, 1975). These studies have found that bilinguals have an increased sensitivity to the social nature and communicative functions of language. This can enhance one's communicative ability. Other research on bilingualism and its relationship to cognition found that bilinguals were more field independent than monolinguals. The importance of this is that field-independent individuals tend to achieve higher academically than those who are field dependent.

The future of bilingual education in the U.S. is not certain. However, one can safely conclude that the fate of this approach used for teaching English language learners will most likely be driven by external forces that have little to do with what is best for children. For regardless of official accounts that speak to the importance of being educated in the home language, the beneficial effects of being bilingual, and a constitution that does not reject such an approach, the assault against the implementation of such programs still continues. Only time will tell whether this attack is a momentary turn of the pendulum or a profoundly seeded disregard for bilingualism and a deep acceptance and narrow definition of what it is to be an American. In essence, are we truly a nation that values cultural diversity, or is such a perspective just a smoke screen to hide our desire to be truly culturally, racially, and linguistically homogeneous?

References

Baker, C. (1988). *Key Issues in Bilingualism and Bilingual Education.* Clevedon, UK: Multilingual Matters.

Baker, C. (1997). *Foundations of Bilingual Education and Bilingualism.* Clevedon, UK: Multilingual Matters.

Ben-Zeev, S. (1977a). The Effect of Bilingualism in Children from Spanish-English Low Economic Neighborhoods on Cognitive Development and Cognitive Strategy. *Working Papers on Bilingulasim* 14, 83–122.

Ben-Zeev, S. (1977b). The Influence of Bilingualism on Cognitive Strategy and Cognitive Development. *Child Development* 48, 1009–1018.

Bialystok, E. (1987a). Influences of Bilingualism on Metalinguistic Development. *Second Language Research* 3(2), 154–166.

Bialystok, E. (1987b). Words as Things: Development of Word Concept by Bilingual Children. *Studies in Second Language Learning* 9, 133–140.

Bialystok, E., & Ryan, E. B. (1985). Toward a Definition of Metalinguistic Skill. *Merrill-Palmer Quarterly* 31(3), 229–251.

Cummins, J. (1979). Cognitive/Academic Language Proficiency, Linguistic Interdependence, the Optimal Age Question, and Some Other Matters. *Working Papers on Bilingualism*, no. 19 (pp. 197–205). Toronto: Ontario Institute for Studies in Education.

Cummins, J. (1980). The Entry and Exit Fallacy in Bilingual Education. *NABE Journal* 4(3), 25–59.

Galambos, S. J., & Hakuta, K. (1988). Subject Specific and Task-Specific Characteristics of Metalinguistic Awareness in Bilingual Children. *Applied Psycholinguistics* 9, 141–162.

Genesee, F., Tucker, G. R., & Lambert, W. E. (1975). Communication Skills of Bilingual Children. *Child Development* 46, 110–114.

Ianco-Worral, A. (1972). Bilingualism and Cognitive Development. *Child Development* 43, 1390–1400.

Keller, G. D., & Van Hooft, K. S. (1982). A Chronology of Bilingualism and Bilingual Education in the United States. In J. A. Fishman & G. D. Keller (Eds.), *Bilingualism for Hispanic Students in the United States*. New York: Teachers College Press.

Macedo, D. (1994). *Literacies of Power*. Boulder, CO: Westview Press.

Mackey, W. F. (1970). A Typology of Bilingual Education. *Foreign Language Annals* 3, 596–608.

New York State. (2002). *A Profile of Latinos in the New York State Education System from Pre-K to Ph.D* (Report 655). Albany, NY.

Ovando, C. J., & Collier, V. (1985). *Bilingual and ESL Classrooms*. New York: McGraw-Hill.

Ricciardelli, L. A. (1992). Creativity and Bilingualism. *Journal of Creative Behavior* 26(4), 242–254.

Snow, M. (1986). *Common Terms in Second Language Education*. Education Los Angeles: University of California Press.

United Nations. (1948). *Declaration of Human Rights*.

United Nations Educational, Scientific and Cultural Organization (UNESCO). (1953) *The Use of Vernacular Language in Education*. Paris: UNESCO.

Recommended Reading

Soto, L. D. (2002). *Making a Difference in the Lives of Bilingual/Bicultural Children*. New York: Peter Lang.

Alma Rubal-Lopez

BORDER CROSSING

This entry highlights the wealth of diversity and multiplicity within the Latino group in contrast to the hegemonic assumption of Latino homogeneity. It specifically challenges the monolithic *María* assumption— where Latinas follow a simplistic, racially prejudiced image of what a Latina "should be" to the extent that at some point, Latinas are called and depicted as *María*, as "poor and working-class city dwellers... [who are] the reason for the rise on urban crime, [a] necessity for welfare reform, [embodying] moral decay" (Fine, 2000, p. 109).

A paradox occurs with the U.S. administration's social construction of the U.S.-Hispanic/Latino ethnic group.[1] This hegemonic device used to relegate Hispanics/Latinos as second-class citizens has been constantly reclaimed by the members of the Hispanic/Latino groups and transformed into a social amalgam that unifies and support the creation and re-creation of Latinoness and social success.

Based on an ethnographic research done in Lakeland,[2] four *Marías* were identified as successful Hispanics/Latinas by school officers and community leaders. Note that none of them has *María* as a first name, but they all, collectively, decided to use it as their pseudonym. They reclaimed *María* as their name to proudly cherish all Latinas who hold that name but also to challenge the simplistic assumptions that erased the multiplicity of Latino heritages, worldviews, names, accents, and "looks."

Meeting with the Latinas in this research project was illuminating. These women were diverse in their cultural, ethnic, and racial backgrounds, socioeconomic statuses, educational levels, languages, and lengths of residence in this country. Through their stories, I was able to touch a mythical image of strength that is the base for this entry. There is much sharing and learning in these stories. As Latinas, these *Marías* were engaged in the endless process of understanding U.S. mainstream culture, language, and schooling. As identified outsiders, the *Marías* were becoming aware of a multitude of non-spoken rules, such as their children's fitting into some fixed social category that—in the school—placed them under whites and Asians (Kondo, 1995, p. 63). The *Marías* promptly learned that social categories are theoretical, hypothetical groups but also entail meta-narratives by which people become socially defined, arranged, and conceived.

Nevertheless, all the *Marías* embraced the Latina label as their group membership, negotiating a multiplicity of roles and facets of their identities. Gloria Anzaldúa (1987) points out that the contradictions between awareness and social assumptions are determinant aspects of being Latino/a in the States. Anzaldúa goes further, defining Latinas—including herself—as *mestizas* who live in the borderlands of mixed heritages, languages, and social locations.

The best way to learn about the *Marías* as illustration of Latina multiplicity is through their own voices and tales. We begin with María C, followed by María D, María E, and María P.

María C was identified as a Latina role model by a community leader, a high-level university administrator, and a school principal who were eager to share stories of María C's endurance and persistence. At the time we met, María C—a Mexican immigrant, in her mid-30s—was married, a mother of five children—Jenny, Javier, David, Gabriel, and Julia—between college and elementary school age.

Being near María C felt as if a hurricane of energy has just arrived and taken over; she took care of her home, held a position as an aide at the local elementary school English as a Second Language (ESL) program, and was school-community liaison. It did not stop there; she was a college student herself pursuing her undergraduate degree and her Spanish-teaching license. María C's story can be read as a ratification of the mythical image of the immigrant who arrives in the land of abundance full of desires, few skills, and almost no means but who through hard work gets a better life. Her story, however, is one that can clarify the complex relation between hegemony, counter-hegemony, and the roles played by social agents (Gal, 1989; Gramsci, 1971; Mouffe, 1979). María C "couldn't have done it" without her strengths, but she would not have "made it" only with them. She needed the opportunities, the mentorship, the guidance, and the community support that became available to her and her family.

María C's story began with her difficult childhood in Mexico as a result of violence and abuse. From very young age, she worked and took care of her siblings but also followed her family's destructive path: she used to drink, smoke, and party.

Only a teenager, María C eloped with Ernesto to begin what she called "*vida de infierno*," her living hell. Short notes from those times in Mexico are their daughter Jenny's birth, their family conflicts, their struggles to find and maintain jobs and, their timely decision to head north to reconnect with María C's mother, who was in California. They sold the few things they owned and began their way north to Los Angeles.

We headed to the border and had to stay there for 15 days. We tried to get across but we kept failing ... the desert ... the quicksands ... the river, nothing worked ... the last thing were the tunnels and that worked out ... they made us walk as if we're animals and we made it ... at the end we were barefoot . . . dressed in rags . . . all wet . . . but we made it . . . we got to the damn Angeles.

Through María C's tale, there were two dramatic forces that sustained them, despair and poverty, and Los Angeles—the mythical land of opportunities and wealth waiting at the other side.

María C and her family were in Los Angeles, but the dreamed better life did not arrive. On the contrary, "Ernesto . . . hangout with my brothers and their gang. . . . He was drunk and stoned . . . a lot of abuse . . . no money, no support." At that point, María C made another drastic decision and moved to Chicago, where she had a sibling. They filled up "four paper bags with *nuestras pocas cosas*, our belongings" and left California. In Chicago things began to fall into place. María and Ernesto found jobs and were able to get an apartment for the now family of six. There for short time, Ernesto was called by his mother and left for Mexico. María C became the head of her family and found ways to support it. She got a break on her rent. To pay the basic bills and food, she worked in the local church, took care of people's children, and did household chores. When I asked María C where she found that much strength, she said,

I had to make it . . . for my children, they were so little, you know? I had to do it . . . regardless my lack of English and everything . . . I found ways to fight for my children . . . I did it all alone . . . it was . . . hard . . . but it helped me . . . helped me that I learned to trust myself.

Ernesto took almost six months to come back just to move again. This time, they chose a smaller city; they went to Lakeland because they had some relatives and had heard that jobs and "security" were available. Once more they were back to point

zero: no home, no jobs, and a family of six back as guests in María C's relative's apartment. Soon they found their own place in a subsidized building complex. Jenny and Javier began their schooling, kindergarten and Head Start, and María C began attending the community college to learn English and obtain her high school equivalence (GED).

María C made a decision to change her own and her children's lives. It was a conscious counter-hegemonic act of a strong social agent. Challenges were great, but María C's perseverance and determination were even bigger. This is one clear example of the complex relationship between hegemony and counter-hegemony and the role played by social agency. They constitute a unit whose primary elements are complementary but also opposites and on a continuum of change and adaptation. Paradoxical but feasible is the best way to describe it. María C counted on herself and her two older children—Jenny and Javier, who were less than 8 years old but had a definite role in supporting and helping their mother. As María C continued with her studies, she found a network that support and encouraged her. She found a job as an educational aide at the same school that her children were attending, and when she got her GED she became an ESL assistant.

I had many questions for María C. These questions were related to her commitment to the future and to the welfare of her family. She overcame colossal barriers. How had María C managed to change the way of her family's life? Where did she find the perseverance to maintain the commitment within herself? How, in the first place, did she choose the life path that would lead her family to a better life? María C's answers follow:

I don't know Miryam…the truth is that I wanted my children to have a different life, one that I didn't ever have…I didn't want to wait until someone, from the goodness of their heart, decide to give me a ride…or wait until someone wanted to translate for me, just to ask a thing…I was tired of all that.

María C's answers were simple and extremely wise. She had no plan to follow, just the inner desires to fulfill her children's basic needs (i.e., home, food, clothes). She saw formal education as a logical and reachable path. It was not easy; it was extremely difficult for her and her family to maintain themselves on that chosen path. María C shared that at times she had been frustrated, depressed, and overwhelmed, but it never lasted; she allowed herself to feel it, but she never stayed in those stages for long. I asked if the struggle got better or smoother over time. María C's answer surprised me. She is still struggling.

Our second voice comes from María D, a Nicaraguan immigrant woman who talked softly and had a way of blending into any room or any group of people with whom she socialized. María D was soft, elegant, with sad eyes, almost always with a cloud. She smiled, sometimes she laughed, but always she was alert and evaluating how much she would share. María D was invited to participate in this research on the basis of her own pride in her success. In a way, she invited herself; though, María D's participation was a great addition to our kaleidoscope of Latinas. I met María D at a Latina support group around the time we both arrived in Lakeland. As part of my research, for more than 2.5 years, I work and observed María D's children at school and at their home.

Always cordial, she made me feel welcome at her home, which she graciously opened for me to work with her children,

yet María D's boundaries were extremely clear and defined on what she identified as private. Throughout our many long, open-ended interviews and conversations, I learned that María D and two of her three boys were from Nicaragua's countryside; that their country was engaged in a bloody civil war; that three of them walked their way out to Mexico; that they had to swim across the Rio Grande to get into the States; and that the children's father was unreliable and never around.

María D wanted to be a stay-home mom—"as should be." For her, success was to spend time with her children; therefore her job at the school was perfect because they had similar schedules. She presented herself as a happy, successful person, but the reality of her life-situation somehow contradicted her statements. For example, when the family moved to a newer, better-located, ampler three-bedroom rental apartment, she presented as if she was living her dreams of homeowner and stay-at-home wife and mother: "Do you remember my old disgusting apartment…in that neglected building…stinky…weird people…look how beautiful is this condo…and Marcos he has bought me so many things…Marcos is a good man…he is a role model for my boys."

It sounded as if her dreams came true, yet her "condo" was a rental apartment in a state-subsidized building and Marcos, her recent husband—described as a "role model"—was in prison for dealing drugs. There were many contradictions in her stories. That afternoon María D compared the apartments, talked about Marcos as a role model, and shared pictures with accounts of prison visits, her homeowner experience, and an announcement of her wedding, which took place at Marco's detention center.

In our long interviews and conversations, María D showed me her new things, talked about her accomplishments, and told me the story of a life she wanted but seemed to clash with what I was observing. Nonetheless, on several occasions María D broke down crying, muttering broken phrases that made me think about her life in Central America, the long walk with two of her children, the stories of their border crossing, the betrayal of her former partner, and her unofficial status in the U.S. In those moments, her comments were limited to short phrases, almost utterances in which much was left out:

I don't want to remember . . . the only thing I want is peace . . . it comes back as nightmares . . . the war . . . houses burning down . . . people running . . . you know . . . one has to do things . . . for for the boys, you know . . . danger . . . all the time . . . what a life . . . my mother still is there . . .

Many silences followed this rosary of short, broken phrases. I was able to ask questions, but I never received direct answers. My role was to record, perhaps reflect on what María D shared, but nothing more. Her responses were cordial phrases to offer me something to drink, "*un juguito,*" or to eat.

It is very difficult for me to write about María D. On the one hand, I witnessed the external improvement in her life, her positive news, her pride and happiness. On the other hand, I also witnessed her discourse of success in which the pain of her recollections seemed to take over.

María D's tale can be read in several ways. It could be the story of many immigrants who arrived in the land of abundance full of desires for a better life and, through years of hard work, accomplished that. However, María D wanted more. For her, success included "a family as well as economic and social stability." At the point of the interviews, she had her children and a husband who was in jail. She had many belongings yet was not the homeowner she wanted to be. She had a low-skill job yet was working well with her children's schedule. Assertive, strong, and happy on the surface, María D seemed to appreciate life and the opportunities for her children. Her story is a different example of the complex relationship between hegemony and counter-hegemony and social agency.

Our third voice is María E, a Peruvian immigrant who had lived in Lakeland for more than 10 years. María E's experiences as a Latina woman, single mother, and second language learner were neither planned nor desired but developed as a consequence of her moving to the U.S.

María E's first social interchanges were marked by her lack of English proficiency, of any social network but her partner, and of experience with extremely low temperatures. Nor had she ever been in the Midwest.

María E learned about herself, language, and traditions but also about a new set of rules, language, and norms. María E remembered that it took her almost a week to get enough courage to leave the apartment, but only a "thank you" for a clerk to call her Hispanic and to discover that Hispanic was the translation of the unknown into a formal category within the social order. No one cared to know her heritage; the label erased her heritage, her self, and brought her into homogeneity, where she found herself addressed as Spaniard, despite her protests, and asked to prepare burritos—which she had never tried—and assumed to be part of the cleaning crew of her college building.

At the time of the interviews, María E had already been in the U.S. for several years, her English was impeccable, and she was pursuing her Ph.D. in a large research university. Interestingly, María E indicated that social images about Hispanics/Latinos were ethnic and racial clichés and stereotypes socially constructed that helped mainstream members to better understand "the other." María E was full of contradictions, for sometimes she could not see herself in the mirror created by these images. She was a newcomer who had been raised in a privileged environment where she was not a minority. Her daily life and practice informed her theoretical knowledge. As had María C and María D, María E made a concious decision to embrace Latino membership. Her quest was twofold: one goal was to understand and embrace her Latinness; the second was to understand and embrace the complex person who emerged from the paradoxical encounters with hegemonic discourses about Hispanics and the images she had of herself.

The following is the voice of María P, a non-immigrant, beautiful, slender, brown woman with a flame in her eyes that comes out as fire in her art and in her words. María P presented multiple facets of strength: she was a mother, a wife, an artist, a painter, and a ceramist. Her family was as central in her life as was her artwork; she weaved them together to bring the Torascans, her ancestors' heritage, back into their daily lives.

I'm a Chicana from Wisconsin . . . my ancestors from my father's side are from Michoacan, Mexico, and from my mother's side are from Texas, Northern Mexico . . . from the Chicano region. My mother was born in Wisconsin . . . she is the first Hispanic woman born in Racine.

María P was an example of the Mexican families that have been living in the Southwest longer than their memories; definitely before Texas was part of the U.S. Both sides of her family used to work in the agricultural fields until the 1940s; then they began moving north, following low-skilled, yet better-paid jobs that were open in the new industries. Without knowing each other, both families settled down in a small industrial town in Wisconsin, where they became the "Mexicans from Texas."

María P's parents raised their eight children in a predominantly Anglo working-class neighborhood where Spanish was not allowed at home nor at the Catholic private school they attended. María P indicates that she had to face many identity crises during her growing up:

My parents were raising us without Spanish . . . sent us to a Catholic school . . . a kind of two lives that I never really noticed 'til I got older . . . we played with those kids during the week . . . we were probably the only non white friends they had . . . and then Saturday . . . you play kick-the-can and all that stuff . . . a lot of fun . . . we all played in the neighborhood and was like that . . . but I never was invited to play with the kids from my school.

While María P identified herself as mainstream American, she was treated as a non-white, working-class child who felt as she were living two different lives. María P's search for her own identity continued through her early college years, when she discovered her indigenous heritage:

When I got into college . . . I took a Latin-American history class to learn about the Aztecs and the Mayas . . . I wrote to my grandmother . . . I wondered who we were connected to . . . 'cause on my father's side—and that's the thing with Chicano people—they'll say, we don't have an Indian connection we're Spaniards—my grandmother wrote me back . . . she explained to me that we were Torascan and should be very proud of it . . . I started to investigate and trying to find out about the Torascan . . . I could tell where I was coming from.

Also, she began participating in and learning more about the Chicano movement.

I grew up learning about Cesar Chavez and the United Farm Workers movement . . . we always paid attention on what was going on . . . during the strikes . . . I felt more clear about myself . . . a Chicana from Wisconsin . . . that gave me a stronger sense of belonging . . . that's why I say I'm a Chicana 'cause to me that makes a lot more sense.

At the time of the interviews María P was a political activist who used her art as expression of her mixed traditions (Chicana from Wisconsin, Torascan, and Spaniard), including those of her African American husband. For María P success was also a political act connected to her family and art:

I don't measure success in financial terms . . . I mean we have struggle all my life . . . I feel successful if I'm able to communicate with my children . . . and my art is my life . . . I never separate my family from my art or from myself . . . I'm in school because of my family . . . my family comes first because . . . but I don't want just survive . . . I wanna live . . . I wanna have something to say about life . . . be an active part of society . . . I believe we all have a responsibility . . . not everybody in the world recognizes their responsibility . . . leading your life and making a positive one not just for myself but for everybody . . . we're social beings . . . we're part of a whole . . . you have to communicate with each other in order to survive.

The choices María P made were different than the choices made by other interviewees. She delayed her studies to let her husband prepare for graduate work. She left a teaching job to stay a home. Yet María P was pretty successful, in her own words, "regardless of how much she owns or owes."

Summary

The Latinas portrayed here are an example of multiplicity, difference as well as harmony. They all embraced and reclaimed *María* as their name yet they proudly shared their diverse cultural, ethnic, and racial backgrounds, socioeconomic statuses, educational levels, languages, and lengths of residence in this country. There was much sharing and learning in the *Marías'* stories. The *Marías* were engaged in the endless process of understanding U.S. mainstream culture, language, and schooling, where they were identified outsiders. Nevertheless, all the *Marías* embraced the Latina/Hispanic label as their group membership where they negotiated a multiplicity of roles and facets of their identity/ies. As Gloria Anzaldúa points out, the contradictions between awareness and social assumptions are determinant aspects of being a Latina and a *mestiza* in the United States. Furthermore, enormous challenges are faced by Latinas/*mestizas* as their collective position is in the borderlands of mixed heritages, languages, and social locations.

> To live in the Borderlands means you
> are neither *hispana india negra española*
> *ni gabacha, eres mestiza, mulata*, half-
>   breed
> caught in the crossfire between camps
> while carrying all five races on your back
> not knowing which side to turn to, run
>   from;
> To survive the Borderlands
> you must live sin fronteras
> be a crossroads
>   (Anzaldúa, 1987, pp. 194–195)

Notes

1. The Hispanic ethnic group includes people originally from Latin America countries and the subsequent generations born and raised in the U.S. The term *Hispanic* was formally introduced in the 1980 U.S. National Census of Population and Housing. Before that year, people of Latin American ancestry were considered part of any previously defined racial group, such as white or black.

2. This longitudinal study was funded by the Spencer Foundation and the Wisconsin Center for Education Research.

References

Anzaldúa, G. (1987). *Borderlands/La Frontera: The New Mestiza*. San Francisco: Aunt Lute Books.

Fine, M., Weis, L., Weseen, S., & Wong, L. (2000). For Whom? Qualitative Research, Representations, and Social Responsibilities. In N. K. Denzin & Y. S. Lincoln (Eds.), *Handbook of Qualitative Research* (pp. 107–131). Thousand Oaks, CA: Sage.

Gal, S. (1989). Language and Political Economy. *Annual Review of Anthropology* 18, 345–367.

Gramsci, A. (1971). *Selections from the Prison Notebooks*. New York: International Publishing.

Kondo, D. (1995). Bad Girls: Theater, Women of Color, and the Politics of Representation. In R. Behar & D. A. Gordon (Eds.), *Women Writing Culture* (p. 63). Berkeley: University of California Press.

Mouffe, C. (Ed.) (1979). Introduction. In *Gramsci and Marxist Theory*. London: Routledge & Kegan Paul.

Recommended Reading

Behar, R. (1993). *Translated Woman: Crossing the Border with Esperanza's Story*. Boston: Beacon Press.

Delgado-Gaitan, C., & Trueba, H. (1990). *Crossing Cultural Borders: Education for Immigrant Families in America*. London: Falmer Press.

Haney Lopez, I. (1996). *White by Law: The Legal Construction of Race*. New York: New York University Press.

Oboler, S. (1995). *Ethnic Labels, Latino Lives: Identity and the Politics of (Re)Presentation in the United States*. Minneapolis: University of Minnesota Press.

Soto, L. (1997). *Language, Culture, and Power: Bilingual Families and the Struggle for Quality Education*. Albany, NY: SUNY Press.

Williams, P. (1991). *The Alchemy of Race and Rights: Diary of a Law Professor*. Cambridge, MA: Harvard University Press.

Miryam Espinosa-Dulanto

THE BORDER PEDAGOGY INITIATIVE

In order to increase the likelihood of student success in the border region, it is paramount that a concerted effort is launched to improve public schools on both sides of the border. Border pedagogy—defined as a complex and interactive set of instructional practices, curriculums, and knowledge bases that educators need to incorporate in order to be more effective with transnational students in the borderlands—is one such effort (Cline & Necochea, 2003). Border pedagogy has the potential to become an essential component that could catapult effective instructional practices along the U.S.-Mexico border, thus helping to transform education for the twenty-first century. As a heuristic tool that can help in the design and implementation of more effective strategies for transnational education, border pedagogy can help guide public schools in the borderlands toward instructional practices more congruent with the strengths and needs of the children being served (Cline & Necochea, 2003; Necochea & Cline, 2003; Reyes & Garza, 2005).

With this in mind, the Border Pedagogy Initiative was introduced in summer 2001 when a group of binational teachers were brought together to initiate a dialogue regarding the educational systems in both the U.S. and Mexico at California State University, San Marcos (Necochea & Cline, 2003). This initial dialogue was in response to the perceived need to address the academic and social concerns of transnational students within the public schools along the

San Diego–Tijuana border region. In an era of increased globalization and trade between Mexico and the U.S., collaboration and dialogue between teachers from both sides of the border is of vital importance if public education is to gain prominence in effectively teaching an increasingly transnational student population in the borderlands. Largely because of the implementation of the North American Free Trade Agreement (NAFTA) in 1993, the U.S.-Mexico border has become increasingly more porous, dynamic, and significant as people and goods go back and forth between the two nations (Fuentes, 1997; Martínez, 1994; Rouk, 1993; Urrea, 1996). Although many provisions were made under NAFTA for addressing environmental concerns, working conditions, and trade initiatives, few structures were put into place to deal with educational issues (Cline & Necochea, 2003; Fuentes, 1997; Quiocho et al., 2003).

When studying border regions, it is often difficult to discern the many influences that form the social, cultural, and economic landscape that go beyond the physical border and determine the invisible borders people create. The border between Mexico and the U.S. has been in turmoil since its inception, with increasing movement back and forth as individuals seek better economic conditions and greater ties with their counterparts across the border.

In the case of Tijuana and San Diego, the border region has been a robust economic area, with many individuals depending on the region to make a living and to provide for their families. Indeed, as a port of entry, this location has been witness to a constant flux of people, products, goods, and resources that make the trek from one country to another on a daily basis. It is a mutually beneficial relationship that allows both sides to have opportunities for economic and social activities. Indeed, in 2003 there were approximately 300 million crossings that provided ample opportunity for economic, social, and cultural development on both sides of the border (Cline & Necochea, 2003; Fuentes, 1997; Taylor, 2001).

A logical progression to this increased transnational activity is to develop a dialogue for teachers from both sides of the border, a dialogue that has not been realized because of its absence in the trade agreement, because of political barriers, and because educational issues have largely been ignored in border and regional studies. It is through education, however, that we will gain an understanding of one another and of our heritage, thus allowing for more equitable trade and prosperity between the regions. It is also through education that our children will learn to understand and appreciate the strengths that each nation has to offer through its language, culture, and traditions (Halcón, in press; Santamaría, 2003).

Against this backdrop, however, are school systems in turmoil as both countries try to instruct students whom educators do not understand, using methods at times incompatible, maybe even incomprehensible, to each other, and thus the need for transnational border dialogues for teachers (Cline, Necochea, Prado-Olmos, & Halcón, 2003; Quiocho et al., The 2003; Reyes & Garza, in press).

The Border Pedagogy Initiative

The Border Pedagogy Initiative was spearheaded to facilitate an exchange of ideas and best practices among educators to help transnational students achieve academic and social success. The targeted population was binational educators who work with children who live in the border region. The Initiative was designed to build the capacity of binational teachers to instruct transnational students to high levels of academic proficiency by implementing more effective strategies for the borderlands (Necochea & Cline, 2004; Quiocho et al., 2003; Reyes & Garza, in press).

Consequently, the Initiative has focused on a three-pronged approach: instructional strategies, knowledge of each system, and curricular adaptations deemed appropriate for transnational students. It is important that the Initiative take the social, linguistic, and academic needs of diverse students into account. In addition, social outcomes of the Initiative have included improved relationships between binational educators that have facilitated school visitations, development of a support structure for teachers, and enhanced communication between the two countries. An additional outcome has been improved instructional practices in the area of biliteracy in the border region as a major focus of the Initiative.

By far the ongoing face-to-face conversations between participants of both countries has been the most rewarding aspect of the dialogue, which has allowed for an exchange of educational ideas, resources, and knowledge that could enable transnational students to realize their full potential, whichever side of the border they reside on (Jeffries, 2003). These dialogues have enabled educators from each side to gain a deeper understanding of each country's educational system, share information on instructional practices, and learn teaching strategies that will help improve student achievement in the border region. Jeffries (2003) reflects about the Initiative:

The Border Pedagogy. Initiative is a new and hopeful intentional effort to interrupt the past ways of thinking about the border region. The creators of the Initiative have designed a container in which a rich *caldo* of conversation can take place on behalf of the thousands of students who are educated in the border regions and beyond. This "container" provides a "safe zone" in which educators and community leaders from the border regions can gather and exchange ideas that can advance the thinking and actions of adults involved in the education of children. This advancement will hopefully take the form of reducing the damaging myths, stereotypes, and actions that dog the interactions among and between individuals from the U.S. and Mexico border regions. (p. 72)

As this Initiative has progressed, conferences, seminars, institutes, research, and now a Center for the Study of Border Pedagogy have helped advance the goals of the Border Pedagogy Initiative, thus playing a role in transforming schools on both sides of the border.

The Center for the Study of Border Pedagogy

The Center for the Study of Border Pedagogy opened its doors in fall 2004 in support of the Border Pedagogy Initiative already underway in the College of Education at California State University, San Marcos. The Center's primary mission is to promote improved instructional practices, curriculum, and knowledge base in public schools on both sides of the border by engaging in dialogues among educators, conducting research in the border region, and disseminating information on schooling in the San Diego–Tijuana borderlands. The Center enhances the mutual understanding and cooperation in border communities by fostering collaboration between educational institutions in Mexico and the U.S. Through student and faculty exchange, regular dialogue and discussion, inter-institutional curricular development, and binational research projects, the center promotes the common interests of the borderland educational community.

The Center is driven by the belief *"que la educación no tiene fronteras."* Consequently, strong ties to the educational community in Tijuana through the Sistema Educativo Estatal (SEE), which is primarily responsible for public schools in Baja California, have been established. Working closely with SEE, the Center has been able to successfully build partnerships with public schools teachers and administrators on both sides of the border.

There is a strong commitment with both partners to transformational education, diversity, social justice, and equity on behalf of transnational students. The main goals of the Center include the following:

- Engage in continuous staff development in the area of biliteracy to help educators become aware of the best practices to teach reading and writing to a borderland population.
- Conduct research in the border region on the impact of border pedagogy on public schools on both sides of the border.
- Disseminate information to the schools along the border region regarding the unique linguistic, literacy, and educational needs of the students.
- Proactively promote biliteracy strategies that will enable the students to become proficient in both English and Spanish.
- Document student results with multiple measures that encourage the use and implementation of new strategies and instructional practices.

To this end the Center sponsors a series of events and activities designed to deepen the conversations and promote binational dialogues that will help improve schooling in the borderlands.

Conferences and Seminars

The primary goal of the conferences and seminars is to provide participants from both sides of the border with the tools, strategies, skills, and a knowledge base to implement a more just and equitable instructional program *para los estudiantes que compartimos*. These highly interactive sessions are designed to begin building bridges of understanding between the educational systems of the two countries as participants engage in face-to-face dialogues.

Institutes

The purpose of the Border Pedagogy Biliteracy Institutes is to promote the improvement of literacy instruction in the San Diego–Tijuana border region by providing schoolteachers from both sides of the border concrete strategies, techniques, tools, materials, and curriculums they can take back to their classrooms to improve student achievement. In addition, the Institute facilitates a deeper understanding of each country's educational systems and an opportunity to share information on biliteracy instructional practices.

Research

The Center is in the process of developing a research agenda for Border Pedagogy that to date has included two guest editorships, several published articles, focus group data collection, and the development of a conceptual model. The importance of research to place Border Pedagogy on the public agenda cannot be underestimated. It is imperative that research is conducted to help in framing the issues, defining the questions, evolving concepts on transnational educational concerns, and understanding the phenomenon of border pedagogy. The seeds of research on border pedagogy have been planted and are starting to germinate. From these beginnings, others will be able advance the study of borderlands education using a variety of research methods.

Conclusion

Yes, border pedagogy is a dream, but one grounded in the reality of those who educate in the borderlands between the U.S. and Mexico. Educators must speak with one collective voice, one regional truth, and one collegial culture. The "power of one voice" in the continuing binational dialogues among bicultural educators is the power that is amassed when shared work becomes the cornerstone of engaged conversations. The relationships among border people are critical to continuing the dialogue to include educational communities.

Since the mid nineteenth century, when the border between the United States and México became permanent, American and Mexican borderlanders have been engaged in forging a new society, building linkages that have thrived during the age of interdependence. Significantly, many cross-border bonds are rooted in the asymmetry that characterizes the binational relationship. . . . Symbiosis is most clearly evident in the binational trade, tourism, migration, and industrialization that bind the U.S. and Mexican border communities. (Martínez, 1994, p. 56)

Extending the symbiosis to education provides an opportunity for educational bonds to be strengthened and for public schools to forge a new social order—a society where biliteracy is a way of life rather than an aberration on the fringes, opportunities are equitable, and binational relationships are the norm. If education is to play its historic role of becoming the "great equalizer," then binational education needs to take center stage by binding U.S. and Mexican border communities into a coherent whole.

The Border Pedagogy Initiative is the first step in a long journey of transforming public schools on both sides of the border toward more just and equitable educational practices that respect the needs of both countries. The complexities of the two school systems compel educators to navigate the unchartered waters of borderlands education, fraught with challenges, dangers, and swells, but with the potential of transcending nationalistic borders and breaking down barriers to success.

Accordingly, it has become incumbent upon schools to ask the essential question: Can we transcend our own nationalistic borders on behalf of the children we share?

Let the dialogue begin and time will tell.
Jeffries, 2003, p. 76

References

Cline, Z., & Necochea, J. (2003). Education in the Borderlands: A Border Pedagogy Conceptual Model. *El Bordo: Retos de Frontera* 6(11), 43–57.

Cline, Z., Necochea, J., Prado-Olmos, P., & Halcon, J. (2003). The Border Pedagogy Initiative. *Hispanic Outlook* 13(9), 10–13.

Fuentes, C. (1997). *A New Time for México.* Los Angeles: University of California Press.

González, J. (2000). *A History of Latinos in America: Harvest of Empire.* New York: Viking Penguin.

Halcón, J. J. (In press). Educating the Burrito King. *Journal of Latinos and Education* 4(3), 211–216.

Jeffries, J. (2003). The Borders of Our Minds: A Reflection on the Border Pedagogy Initiative. *El Bordo: Retos de Frontera* 6(11), 71–76.

Martínez, O. J. (1994). *Border People: Life and Society in the U.S.-México Borderlands.* Tucson: University of Arizona Press.

Necochea, J., & Cline, Z. (2003). El poder de la voz. *El Bordo: Retos de Frontera* 6(11), 15–38.

Necochea, J., & Cline, Z. (2004). Binational Bridges through Teacher Dialogue. *Hispanic Outlook*, 42–45.

Quiocho, A., Dantas, M. L., Masur, D., Santamaría, L. J., Halcón, J. J., & von Son, C. (2003). Education on the Border: The Myths and Realities of Teaching on La Nueva Frontera. *El Bordo: Retos de Frontera* 6(11), 77–92.

Reyes, M.D.L., & Garza, E. (2005). Teachers on the Border: In Their Own Words. *Journal of Latinos and Education* 4(3), 151–170.

Rouk, Ü. (1993). *Schools along the Border: Education in the Age of NAFTA*. Washington, DC: Council for Educational Development and Research.

Santamaría, L. J. (2003). Latina by Default: The Veracity of Racial Ambiguity along the United States–Mexico Border. *El Bordo: Retos de Frontera* 6(11), 99–104.

Taylor, R. G. (2001). *El nuevo norteamericano: Integración continental, cultura, e identidad nacional*. Tijuana, Mexico: El Colegio de la Frontera Norte.

Urrea, L. A. (1996). *By the Lake of Sleeping Children: The Secret Life of the Mexican Border*. New York: Anchor Books.

Zulmara Cline and Juan Necochea

BROWN BERETS

In April 1966, the Los Angeles County Human Relations Council and community leaders met with some 200 teenagers from various backgrounds in an effort to address such problems as gangs, school dropout rates, and access to college education among Mexican American youths. The genesis of the Los Angeles Brown Berets can be traced to these round table meetings, which took place at Camp Hess Kramer, a 400-acre spread in the rolling hills just east of Malibu, California. Some of these same young people attended a follow-up meeting at the camp the next year. David Sánchez, one of the young participants to be invited the second time, stood out. He served as a youth worker for the Episcopalian Church of the Epiphany under Father John Luce. His leadership qualities earned him a place on the Mayor's Youth Council, which elected him chairman. To Sánchez, a pressing issue was the tension existing between the police and Mexicans in Los Angeles. When the precocious teenager tried to bring up the issue to the youth council he was rebuffed. Working through the system it seemed was often cumbersome and ineffective.

Still working for Father Luce in summer 1967, 17-year old Sánchez wrote a successful proposal to the Southern California Council of Churches for funding to start the Piranya coffee house, a club Father Luce and the budding young leader hoped would keep teens out of trouble. Friends from Camp Hess Kramer joined Sánchez at the center and they decided to form the Young Citizens for Community Action (YCCA). Initially, no other signs existed but that these clean-cut young Chicanos would work within the system. But young people throughout the country and in East Los Angeles were undergoing a radical transformation, an influence the YCCA could not ignore. As Sánchez and his youthful Piranya cohorts chose political issues rather than wholesome recreation, the group criticized law enforcement tactics. As a consequence, Los Angeles police often harassed them because and the young Mexican Americans in turn became more alienated from the officials. The group started calling themselves the Young Chicanos for Community Action (YCCA). At this time in California there existed many militant black organizations that thoroughly impressed Sánchez and his followers. Many sported berets during this era, the most famous being the Black Panther Party, made up of Marx-spouting activists. Sánchez lost no time and purchased some brown berets from the

General Hat Company. He distributed them among the YCCA members, and as he remembers, "people started calling us the Brown Berets." In addition, the group began to wear a tan paramilitary uniform to complement the beret.

In late March 1968 the Brown Berets attracted national attention when they helped organize a walkout of East Los Angeles high school students protesting inadequate educational conditions. Then city law enforcement officials decided that the activity was unlawful, and in early June, Los Angeles County officers arrested 13 walk-out organizers (known as the LA Thirteen), some of them members of the YCCA. After much legal maneuvering the county dropped charges against the LA Thirteen. Erosion of the organization began to take its toll by 1971 as the inexperienced and somewhat immature Berets began to squabble among themselves and to challenge Sánchez's leadership. Later that year Sánchez attempted to bolster his standing by organizing La Caravana de le Reconquista, a tour of the Southwest designed to proliferate Brown Beret ideas. But their decline continued, and to dramatize their cause 26 Brown Berets occupied Santa Catalina Island in August 1972. By their reckoning the

Channel Islands were not ceded to the U.S. in the Treaty of Guadalupe Hidalgo. The sheriff's department ended a 24-hour occupation, forcing the Brown Berets back to the California mainland.

Sánchez disbanded the organization immediately after this event. At one point Brown Berets membership surpassed 5,000, but contributing to the organization's collapse was its inability to create an ideological base that resonated with the general Mexican American community. There can be no doubt that in the Brown Berets' short existence they young militants served as the quintessential "shock troopers" whose tactics did not win rank-and-file support but brought to the forefront issues, some for the first time, that present-day, less romantic civil right leaders are still tackling.

Recommended Reading

Escobar, E. J. (1993). The Dialectics of Repression: The Los Angeles Police Department and the Chicano Movement, 1968–1971. *Journal of American History* 79, 1495–1496.

Marín, M. V. (1991). *Social Protest in an Urban Barrio: A Study of the Chicano Movement, 1966–1974.* Lanham, MD: University Press of America.

F. Arturo Rosales

C

The Effects of High-Stakes Testing and Social Promotion on Latino Youth: A Policy Briefing

Friday, March 15, 2002
The U.S. Capitol, Washington, D.C.

Sponsored by the Center for Mexican American Studies, the University of
Texas at Austin

During the past two decades, the linguistic and cultural diversity of California's schools and the growth of Latino students have increased dramatically, and both are expected to increase even more in the next several decades.

The challenges that California faces today are the challenges that the nation as a whole will face in the not-so-distant future. In the face of this tremendous challenge, California educators have been working hard to develop innovative ways to reach language learners and improve the academic achievement of minority children. Yet the following three dramatic policy shifts have made their jobs even more difficult in recent years.

The first of these was Proposition 227, known at the "Unz Initiative," a voter-approved initiative in 1998. Its purpose was to eliminate Bilingual Education. While it did not do so outright, approximately one third of primary language programs in the state moved immediately to English Only instruction [Gándara, 2000]. Even schools whose parents signed waivers to keep their children in bilingual programs are finding themselves pressured to do less and less primary language instruction and spend more and more time teaching in English.

The second recent policy shift was California Governor Gray Davis's "Public Schools Accountability Act" in 1999, a single-measure English-Only system of accountability. Under this system every public school in the state is assigned a number, called the Academic Performance Index (API), based upon their students' scores on the California Standards Test. Students are tested annually beginning in second grade. Connected to this number is a system of rewards and sanctions similar to those outlined in the 2000 reauthorization of the Federal Elementary and Secondary Education Act, known as No Child Left Behind.

Finally, on the local level, we are seeing a massive increase in the use of district mandated scripted reading programs, programs such as SRA/McGraw Hill's Open Court. Districts justify this forced implementation with the desperate need to increase standardized test scores. Heavily phonics based and highly scripted, these programs are the wrong tool to use with English language learners. Teachers are not being offered programs such as Open Court to use in their classrooms; teachers are being ordered to use these programs, in some districts for as much as three hours per day, including rigid schedules and formal systematic reprimands for teachers who fall behind. And for the most part (although not entirely), the programs are English Only.

These three policy initiatives work together to determine the form and outcomes of language minority students' education in California. Together, they are having negative effects on language minority students as they are subtractive in nature, ignoring the linguistic resources students bring to the classroom. In 2000, we interviewed teachers, principals, and district-level administrators in a statified random sample of 40 school districts statewide serving 25% or more Limited English Proficient (LEP) children. Their statements almost unanimously echoed concern for the contradictory positions they were being placed in. In the words of one teacher, whose school eliminated bilingual education after the passage of Proposition 227:

This year, first graders are being tested on the language arts section of the SAT9. The rationale is now that students are being immersed in English, we can go ahead and test them in English. So, Proposition 227 in a way has legitimized the English-only testing of English language learners.

A principal whose bilingual program has thus far remained intact through parent waivers explains her frustration:

Proposition 227 allowed us to maintain bilingual education if parents approve, for us to instruct kids in their primary language in content while they're learning English. Parent waivers are a provision of the law. And our parents have requested bilingual programs. And then they turn around and make those kids take a test in English—it's wrong . . .

We know we're doing the right things, using best practices, helping the kids learn English and the content areas in the best possible way . . . yet when you're judged in the newspaper by that score, you can't help but feel badly [sic] about it.

A preponderance of research points to a long-term academic advantage for students who remain in primary language instruction for four years or more. This advantage diminishes dramatically as children transition earlier and earlier into English instruction. Yet bilingual educators in California are being ranked and judged based on the English test scores of their second and third grade children. These educators are being placed in the awkward dilemma of having to choose between the future academic success of their students and the present API (and AYP) ranking of their school and their own job security. The heavy handed policies of the state are sacrificing the education of our children, forcing trained, experienced bilingual educators to ignore the scientific research about what works for English Language Learners for the sake of a single, meaningless score on a standardized test.

Recommended Reading

Gándara, P. (2000). In the Aftermath of the Storm: English Language Learners in the Post-227 Era. *Bilingual Research Journal* 24(1, 2). Available: http://brj.asu.eduv2412/abstract.html.

Garcia, E. (2005). *Teaching and Learning in Two Languages: Bilingualism and Schooling in the United States*. New York: Teachers College Press.

Kohn, A. (2000). *The Case against Standardized Testing: Raising the Scores, Ruining the Schools*. Portsmouth, NH: Heinemann.

Ohanian, S. (1999). *One Size Fits Few: The Folly of Educational Standards*. Portsmouth, NH: Heinemann.

Palmer, D., & Garcia, E. (2000). Voices from the Field: Bilingual Educators Speak Candidly about Proposition 227. *Bilingual Research Journal* 24(1, 2). Available: http://brj.asu.edu/v2412/abstract.html.

Valenzuela, A. (Ed.). (2005). *Leaving Children Behind: How "Texas-Style" Accountability Fails Latino Youth*. NY: SUNY Press.

Deborah Palmer

CALIFORNIA'S PROPOSITION 227

Proposition 227, known by its proponents as the "English for the Children" initiative, passed with a 61% majority of California voters on June 2, 1998. The initiative was an example of "people making law," written in response to apparent widespread discontent with the state's policies regarding the education of English language learners (ELLs) in public schools. The passage of Proposition 227 marked a significant event in California's educational history. Never before had the voting public been asked to vote on a specific educational strategy. Curriculur and programmatic decisions for students have generally been the responsibility of the education community. Proposition 227 marked a reversal of this trend. Gándara et al. (2000) argue that because of this, the law was opposed by every major educational association in the state.

The intent of the proposition was to end bilingual education. Specifically, the law required that "all children in California public schools shall be taught English by being taught in English" (California Education Code, chapter 3, article I, section 305). The law represents the latest policy move in a long and often contentious debate surrounding bilingual education. California, one of the first states to enact a comprehensive bilingual education bill, has been at the center of that debate. Given that over 80% of all English learner students in California speak Spanish as a first language, the policy and practice implications of the bilingual debate are central to the education of Latino immigrants in California.

Background on Bilingual Education and Proposition 227

Following the historic *Lau v. Nichols* (1974) Supreme Court decision requiring schools to take affirmative steps to ensure the meaningful participation of English learners, the Chacon-Moscone Bilingual-Bicultural Act of 1976 was passed. It declared that "the primary goal of all programs under this article [was], as effectively and efficiently as possible, to develop in each child fluency in English" (California Education Code, 1976, section 52161) while at the same time ensuring that they had access to the core curriculum. The law established that the preferred manner for doing so was the primary-language instruction. Although the law sunsetted in 1987, there had been an increasing acceptance toward the substantial use of immigrant students' home language in instruction. Despite this increasing openness to bilingual education, only 30% of California's 1.4 million ELL students were in bilingual programs at the time of passage of Proposition 227. Gándara et al. (2000) stress this point as crucial in exposing some of the faulty logic behind Proposition 227:

Proponents of Proposition 227 contend that bilingual education had failed as a pedagogical strategy and should be abounded. Evidence for its failure was found in the continuing underachievement of English learners and the low rate that English learners were reclassified as Fluent English Proficient. Yet, the fact was, less than one-third of all English learners were enrolled in a bilingual program prior to the passage of Proposition 227, so their poor academic achievement could not be attributed to these programs. (Gándara et al., 2000, p. 5)

In summer 1997, when Ron Unz, a former Republican gubernatorial candidate and millionaire software developer, launched "English for the Children," the bilingual education debate occupied the center of public and political discourse. In the campaign against bilingual education, Ron Unz leveraged a considerable amount of his personal fortune to attempt to persuade California voters to support his initiative. Much of his media efforts were directed at discrediting and demeaning the scholarly work regarding the effectiveness of bilingual education. Ron Unz attempted to cast the restriction of native language instruction in terms of a benevolent pro-immigrant stance. Arguing that he represented the true will of immigrants across California, Unz maintained that he was merely assisting Latinos and other recent immigrants free themselves from bilingual education (Gándara et al., 2000).

Although Unz attempted to maintain a "pro-immigrant" stance during the campaign, the campaign proved to be very racially divisive. Inevitably, much of the public discourse supporting the passage of Proposition 227 took nativist and xenophobic positions (Kerper-Mora, 2000; Orellana, Ek, & Hernandez, 1999). California became the center of a national debate between "nativist" and "multiculturalist" visions of education. The nativist position represented by Proposition 227 assumed a benevolent view of Americanization and the role that rapid learning of English plays in the process (Kerper-Mora, 2000).

Despite being opposed by many major political figures in California, President Clinton, and nearly all statewide teaching and educational associations, in June 1998

Proposition 227 passed by a majority of 61% percent of the vote. Once passed by the voting public, the initiative immediately became law, and districts were given 90 days to be in full compliance with its provisions.

Upon its passage, Proposition 227 became a part of the California Education Code (300–340). As required within its text, districts throughout the state were given only 60 days for implementation. Under this new education code, children entering California Public Schools with very little English must be "observed" for a period of 30 calendar days. Generally this observation period occurs in an English language classroom (Gándara et al., 2000). After 30 days, school personnel must decide if children have enough fluency in English to manage in a mainstream English classroom. If not, they are eligible to receive one year of "Sheltered English Immersion," also referred to as "Structured English Immersion," a program of English language instruction not described in detail in the law except for the requirement that instruction be "nearly all" in English (with the definition for the term "nearly all" left up to the district's discretion).

After one year children are normally expected to integrate into mainstream English classrooms, where instruction is required to be "overwhelmingly" in English. If parents or legal guardians find that district or school personnel, including classroom teachers, "willfully and repeatedly refuse" to provide English instruction as required, they have the right to sue for damages. Thus, in order to avoid legal liability it was necessary for teachers and district personal to understand and to implement the law fully. Given the ambiguity of many of the law's provisions, the threat of legal sanction created a great sense of insecurity with many district and school personnel across the state (Stritikus & Garcia, 2003).

The only legal alternative to Sheltered English Immersion and/or mainstream English classrooms is the parental waiver process. According to the new law, children who have special language needs, or whose parents specifically request it, can be placed in "Alternative Programs," most likely some form of bilingual program that includes instruction in the child's primary language. In order for a child to be enrolled in an Alternative Program, the parent or guardian must visit the school annually and sign a waiver requesting the placement. Nonetheless, the first year a child enters California schools he or she must go through 30 days of "observation," generally conducted in English language classrooms, even if parents have a signed waiver. Once the 30 days' observation period is completed, the child can enroll in an Alternative Program.

Despite its attempt to prescribe a uniform solution for the education of linguistically and culturally diverse students across the state, the law's impact on educational services for language minority students has varied widely from district to district, school to school, and in some cases classroom to classroom. Garcia and Curry-Rodriguez (2000) and Stritikus (2002) report that some districts across the state have used the waiver clause of the law to pursue district-wide waivers, others have implemented the English-only provisions of the law, and a third group has left the primary decisions up to individual schools. Districts with long-standing histories of bilingual programs were more likely to pursue parental waivers in order to maintain their existing programs than were districts with weaker primary-language programs (Gándara et al., 2000; Garcia & Curry-Rodriguez, 2000). The re-

search by Eugene Garcia and his colleagues examining implementation in over 40 districts throughout California showed that in the two years immediately following the passage of Proposition 227, the overall number of students in bilingual programs in the districts did not dramatically change with the passage of Proposition 227.

The long-term impact of Proposition 227 on native language instruction has not been so positive. The move toward a restrictive language policy in California coincided with a move toward restrictive literacy policy. For example, the Gándara et al. study of the initial implementation of Proposition 227 in 22 schools in California found that the new law and the statewide emphasis on high-stakes assessment caused teachers to shift their focus from broader, meaning-based literacy activities such as storytelling and reading for meaning, to skill-based literacy activities to be tested on the statewide assessment. In classrooms observed in the study, literacy instruction became more reductive and narrow in scope. Language and literacy were rarely used as tools in overall academic development. Heavy emphasis was placed on decoding and oral development. In addition, schools and districts that might have considered taking the steps to maintain their bilingual program were often moved away from that direction high-stakes testing in English. In 2000–2001, California Department of Education data from the California Educational Data System indicated that only 10% of ELL students were still receiving substantial instruction in their first language.

Making Sense of Test Data

Several national newspapers including the *New York Times* and the *Los Angeles Times* ran stories in the days following the release of California's SAT-9 scores in the first year of Proposition 227 implementation. A headline on the front page of the *New York Times* read, "Increase in Test Scores Counters Dire Forecasts of Bilingual Ban" (*New York Times*, August 20, 2000). Bilingual education had taken a front and center position in national discourse. Student performance on the SAT-9, a test considered by many test experts to be an inaccurate and inappropriate measure of culturally and linguistically diverse students' academic achievement (Garcia & Curry-Rodriguez, 2000), has become the yardstick by which the success of Proposition 227 is being measured.

Further analysis of the test data raises some important critiques about the accuracy of such claims. Analysis of statewide scores by Hakuta (2000) revealed the following problems with the claim regarding the success of Proposition 227 based on test scores:

- SAT-9 scores increased just as much in some school districts that retained bilingual education.

- SAT-9 scores increased in school districts that never had bilingual education and therefore were not impacted by Proposition 227.

- SAT-9 scores rose for both LEP students and native English speakers. In fact, the rise for native English speakers from poor performing schools was dramatic and larger than for students with limited English proficiency.

The analysis of test scores and the influences that Proposition 227 had on teachers and classroom practice through the implementation of the law indicates that Proposition 227 is not the "magic bullet" for the education of students with limited English proficiency. The results of the Hakuta study (2000) were further supported by analysis in Thompson and others (2002), who, through an examination of test data, questioned the success of Proposition 227. Similar results

were reached in a five-year study of the impact of Proposition 227 commissioned by the California Department of Education. Merickel, Parrish, and Linquanti (2003) found that test performance for bilingual programs improved for all ELL students across program types. In their examination of SAT-9 and language-testing data, they conclude that achievement data in California does not make a case for one type of instructional model (bilingual, English-only, etc.) over another.

Proposition 227 and the Ideology of English Only

While the impact of Proposition 227 on student achievement continues to be an area of study, the effect of the new law on the language rights for Latino students has had a chilling impact. By imposing the view that learning English as quickly as possible is essential for immigrant students, the proposition positions all other languages as having a marginal status. By attempting to dictate language use in the classroom, the law enacts an ideology of monolingualism (Schmidt, 2000).

The nativist position advanced by Proposition 227 is contrasted by multiculturalist and multilingualist notions that English-only instruction is deeply problematic. Rather than view the home language and culture through a lens of deficit, multiculturalist and multilingualist perspectives urge schools to see these as valuable educational resources (Banks, 1995; Gutiérrez, Baquedano-Lopez, & Asato, 2000; Olneck, 1995). Proposition 227 presents a direct challenge to the notion that languages other than English have a legitimate and valuable place in the education of diverse students. Hence, the normative assumptions underlying Proposition 227 position the language and culture of diverse students in a subordinate and inferior role to English (Cummins, 2000; Kerper-Mora, 2000).

These normative assumptions have important consequence that extend beyond the classroom. The nature of the law works to position certain groups in a peripheral role in American society. Sekhon (1999), in an article assessing the legal and political implications of the proposition, argues that Proposition 227 positions immigrants on the outside of mainstream America:

Proposition 227 positions English as "our" language by constructing it as our unlearned capacity: It is our birthright. The proposition differentiates "us" from "them" by denominating them in terms of an essential inability to call English their own. They must learn it. Proposition 227 not only demands that they learn out language, it demands that they forget their own. In so demanding, the proposition not only unleashes a salvo in the bilingual education debate, but is a moment in the broader debate over assimilation and acculturation. (p. 1445)

Thus, in its scope, focus, and ideological implications, Proposition 227 differs markedly from past educational reforms. The ideological implications of Proposition 227 have had a deleterious impact on the manner in which Latino students have seen their primary language (Gutiérrez et al., 2000; Stritikus & Garcia, 2003). Proposition 227, and related attempts to end bilingual education Arizona and Massachusetts, have severely limited schools' ability to draw upon the cultural and linguistic resources that Latino students bring to the schoolhouse door.

References

Banks, J. A. (1995). Multicultural Education: Historical Development, Dimensions, and Practice. In J. A. Banks & C. A. McGee-Banks (Eds.), *Handbook of Research on Multicultural Education* (pp. 3–34). New York: Macmillan.

Cummins, J. (2000). *Language, Power, and Pedagogy: Bilingual Children in the Crossfire*. Clevedon, UK: Multilingual Matters.

Gándara, P., Maxwell-Jolly, J., Garcia, E., Asato, J., Gutiérrez, K., Stritikus, T., & Curry, J. (2000). *The Initial Impact of Proposition 227 on the Instruction of English Learners*. Santa Barbara, CA: Linguistic Minority Research Institute. Available: www.uclmrinet.ucsb.edu.

Garcia, E. (1999). *Understanding and Meeting the Challenge of Cultural Diversity*. Boston: Houghton Mifflin.

Garcia, E., and Curry-Rodriguez, J. (2000). The Education of Limited English Proficient Students in California Schools: An Assessment of the Influence of Proposition 227 on Selected Districts and Schools. *Bilingual Research Journal* 24 (1, 2), 15–35.

Gutiérrez, K., Baquedano-Lopez, P., & Asato, J. (2000). "English for the Children": The New Literacy of the Old World Order, Language Policy and Educational Reform. *Bilingual Research Journal* 24 (1, 2), 87–105.

Hakuta, K., Goto Butler, Y., & Witt, D. (2000). How Long Does It Take English Learners to Attain Proficiency? University of California Linguistic Minority Research Institute, Policy Report 2000–2002.

Kerper-Mora, J. (2000). Policy Shifts in Language-minority Education: A Misma between Politics and Pedagogy. *Educational Forum* 64, 204–214.

Merickel, A., Linquanti, R., & Parrish, T. (2003). *Effects of the Implementation of Proposition 227 on the Education of English Learners, K–12*. Palo Alto, CA: American Institutes for Research.

Olneck, M. R. (1995). Immigrants and Education. In J. A. Banks & C. A. McGee-Banks (Eds.), *Handbook of Research on Multicultural Education* (pp. 310–327). New York: Macmillan.

Orellana, M. F., Ek, L., & Hernandez, A. (1999). Bilingual Education in an Immigrant

Community: Proposition 227 in California. *International Journal of Bilingual Education and Bilingualism* 2(2), 114–130.

Schmidt, R. (2000). *Language Policy and Identity Politics in the United States.* Philadelphia: Temple University Press.

Sekhon, N. (1999). A Birthright Rearticulated: The Politics of Bilingual Education. *New York University Law Review* 74 (5), 1407–1445.

Stritikus, T. (2002). *Immigrant Children and the Politics of English-Only: Views from the Classroom.* C. Suarez-Orozco & M. Suarez-Orozco (Eds.). New Americans Series. New York: LFB Scholarly Publishing.

Stritikus, T., & García, E. E. (2003). The Role of Theory, Policy and Educational Treatment of Language Minority Students: Competitive Structures in California. *Educational Policy Analysis Archives* 11 (26). Available: http://epaa.asu.edu/epaa/v11n26.

Thompson, M., DiCerbo, K., Mahoney, K., & McSwan, J. (2002). ¿Éxito en California? A Validity Critique of Language Program Evaluations and Analysis of English Learner Test Scores. *Educational Policy Analysis Archives* 10 (7). Available: http://epaa.asu.edu/epaa/v10n7.

Recommended Reading

Cummins, J. (2000). *Language, Power, and Pedagogy: Bilingual Children in the Crossfire.* Clevedon, UK: Multilingual Matters.

Gutiérrez, K., Baquedano-Lopez, P., & Asato, J. (2000). "English for the Children": The New Literacy of the Old World Order, Language Policy and Educational Reform. *Bilingual Research Journal* 24 (1, 2), 87–105.

Merickel, A., Linquanti, R., & Parrish, T. (2003). *Effects of the Implementation of Proposition 227 on the Education of English Learners, K–12.* Palo Alto, CA: American Institutes for Research.

Stritikus, T., & García, E. E. (2003). The Role of Theory, Policy and Educational Treatment of Language Minority Students: Competitive Structures in California. *Educational Policy Analysis Archives* 11 (26). Available: http://epaa.asu.edu/epaa/v11n26.

Tom T. Stritikus

CHICANO EDUCATION AND THE PROGRESSIVE TRADITION

The "progressive tradition" in the U.S. had many proponents, "reforms," successes, and failures. Yet, not much has been written on the impact progressive education had on communities of color in the U.S. Although many of the progressive schools opened during this time were directed toward white middle-class students and families, some of these same curricular reforms made their way into public schools that had pronounced effects on *Mexicano* immigrants as well as the *Mexicano*/Chicano population conquered through the 1848 Treaty of Guadalupe Hidalgo.

The history and representation of progressive education itself deserves further problematization. Many historians in the last 40 years have defined and redefined what this tradition meant. According to Cremin (as cited in Kliebard, 1995):

No capsule definition of progressive education exists, and none ever will; for throughout its history progressive education meant different things to different people, and these differences were only compounded by the remarkable diversity of American education. (p. 233)

To Chicanos in the Southwest, progressive education took the form of Americanization, assimilation, English-only, and tracking into domestic service and manual labor. All this came under the guise of social efficiency, child-centeredness, and vocationalism. What (white) progressive educators believed to be innovative and progressive at the time ultimately proved to be regressive for the Chicano community. However, one particular program that utilized the "progressive" model for alternative Chicano schools in the 1950s—The Little Schools of the 400—actually found some measure of success.

History of "Progressive" Chicano Education in the Southwest

After the Mexican-American War, the Southwest became a site of Anglo-American capitalism decimating the pre-capitalist, self-subsistent Mexican system (González, 1999). Agriculture and advanced industrial technology merged and dominated the area's economy. Throughout this transformation process the *Mexicano* community—though a major participant in the new economy through its supply of cheap and hard-working labor—was often viewed as a "problem" within the realm of education.

Mexicanos were believed to be far too distinct culturally, intellectually inferior, predisposed to hard labor, and a burden because of their use of Spanish. Under the guise of social efficiency, this population was considered to be a broken cog in the wheel of efficient, systemic progress:

In practice, efficiency meant that schools (and society) were to be managed by the same principles governing the large-scale business enterprise and employ the conveyor-belt system used in factories for processing students through their courses. Further, immigrants were a drag upon progress until Americanized and able to integrate into the bureaucratic social system. (González, 1999, p. 74)

Further substantiating the notion of the broken cog was the scientific administrators' use of intelligence testing. This wave in progressive education found that the Chicano child purportedly scored well below the average white student on IQ tests. Other areas where Chicanos were deemed inferior

included the notions of child-centeredness and adapting the curriculum to fit the needs of the child: according to scientific measurements, Mexican-origin students were not expected to receive the same curriculum as their counterparts nor were they expected to learn at the same pace. Instead, they were to be segregated and provided with different instruction: "Educators and academicians claimed that segregation provided a fitting environment in which to meet the educational needs of the culturally distinctive Mexican child" (González, 1999, p. 56). But the segregated schools Chicanos attended were radically different from those of their white counterparts. The same inferiority ascribed to their intelligence was ascribed to their schooling.

In Texas, Mexican-origin students faced cramped, dilapidated wooden frames for schools as well as inferior supplies and equipment. Because conditions were purposefully neglected and impoverished, several Mexican American communities in South Texas raised money to purchase playground equipment for their children's segregated schools, and families in San Antonio organized for more space and better facilities in their district in the 1930s:

The Anglo schools had a total of eighty-two acres of land for recreational purposes but there were only twenty-three acres for the Mexican American schools. The school district spent a total of $439,636 or $35.96 per Anglo child, but only $302,224 or $24.50 per Mexican-American child. Finally, the Anglo neighborhoods had air-conditioned "palaces" while the Mexican-American community only had deteriorating wooden frame buildings. (San Miguel, 1997, pp. 137, 146)

In California, where Chicano schools were not financially deprived, they were curricularly deprived. Segregated schools in these districts were known as the "industrial schools" (González, 1999). Again, through more "progressive" testing, Mexican-origin students were found to be able to master the demands of manual labor. Girls were tracked to enter the world of domestic service in Los Angeles City Schools in the 1920s, while boys were tracked into animal husbandry, auto shop, and basket weaving (González, 1999). Vocationalism in this context met the "needs" of the student and provided real-life experiences—connecting school to work—while it fit the "backward," un-Americanized Chicano into the fabric of capitalist American society.

LULAC

While progressive educators made their own attempts to address the Mexican "problem" and incorporate *Mexicanos* and Mexican Americans into U.S. society, the League of United Latin American Citizens (LULAC) launched its efforts in 1929 to turn around the negative perception of Mexican-origin communities. Founded in Corpus Christi, Texas, LULAC strongly saw its mission as incorporating the Mexican community into the political and social institutions of this country. The organization hoped to do this by utilizing assimilative strategies in all facets of their organizational efforts, including membership qualifications:

Unlike the *mutualista* organizations which welcomed both Mexican immigrants and Mexican American citizens, LULAC limited its membership to those who were U.S. citizens of Latin ancestry, eighteen years or over, male, and, to a large extent, registered voters. (San Miguel, 1997, p. 141)

The spread of Americanization, of assimilation, in many ways paralleled the frenzy of efficiency and progress. For Chicanos, this meant they had to prove their American-ness or, rather, become even more American looking and sounding in order to gain access to the arenas from which they were constantly barred.

Thus, it was not difficult for LULAC to see the need to adopt "progressive" strategies in the fight for better Chicano education. They knew that Anglo students received better facilities, better materials, and better instruction in the white schools. If Chicano students were to begin having access to these opportunities, their English skills needed to be developed before they entered the schooling process. In 1957 LULAC made this one of its educational goals in the form of "The Little School of the 400."

The Little Schools of the 400

The first "Little School of the 400" was opened in summer 1957 in Ganado, Texas, near the port city of Houston. Félix Tijerina, a member of LULAC, established the organization's goal of helping Chicano students pass the first grade. He and two other educators developed a list of 400 words in English that students would learn the summer before their first grade year. Through advertisements in LULAC's newsletter, they secured a recent high school graduate, Isabel Verver, to teach the first three students of the Little School of the 400 (Quintanilla, 1979).

In school districts across Texas, Chicano students were failing the first grade in disproportionate numbers. Many were spending two to three years trying to be promoted to second grade. To school administrators and to LULAC, the reason for the students' failure rested in their lack of English oral skills. By developing a basic English vocabulary before they entered the first grade, the Little Schools of the 400 hoped to give Chicanos a head start in their schooling.

After two years of operation and the spread of 13 Little Schools, LULAC proudly and nationally announced its success, hoping to encourage other LULAC chapters and school districts to adopt or develop similar programs. Students who enrolled in their summer schools were passing on to the second grade at a rate of almost 100% (Tijerina, 1962). According to Quintanilla (1976), this was a result of the program's commitment of "not only teaching a basic English vocabulary but of dealing with the whole child" (p. 9), resonating the progressive notion of a child-centered curriculum and whole instruction.

In 1962 Tijerina drafted a report in support of national funding for the program (expanded for the children of migrant farm workers). Prior to that, in 1959, the state of Texas had adopted the Little Schools concept under the title "Preschool Instructional Classes for Non-English-Speaking Children," in which over 18,000 students were served (Tijerina, 1962). The Little Schools subsequently became the core of Lyndon Baines Johnson's Head Start Program, which served preschool children of all ethnicities from low-income households nationwide under the "War on Poverty" campaign.

Although LULAC's Little Schools were a success for the Chicano community and later a model for other schooling instruction, the basis of this success alludes to something much larger. George I. Sánchez, a New Mexico school reformer and education historian during this time, critiqued the context of the program's success:

There must be something radically wrong with the regular first grade operation if the [LULAC] schools can do in eight weeks (summer) plus nine months (regular year) what, otherwise, takes eighteen or more months of regular school instruction. (Sánchez, 1997, p. 128)

Thus, fundamentally, the progressive model of instruction utilized by Chicano reformers did not serve to radically alter the schooling circumstances of the U.S. Chicano population. Although the Little Schools did help to ameliorate much of what was happening with English language learners and instruction, they did not bring significant change to all facets of Chicano education. Today many of us continue the struggle (within the legacy of the progressive tradition) to better the schooling of Chicano youth.

References

González, Gi. G. (1999). Segregation and the Education of Mexican Children, 1900–1940. In J. F. Moreno (Ed.), *The Elusive Quest for Equality* (pp. 53–76). Cambridge, MA: Harvard Educational Review.

Kliebard, H. M. (1995). *The Struggle for the American Curriculum, 1893–1958* (2nd ed.). New York: Routledge.

Quintanilla, G. (1979). The Little School of the 400 and Its Influence on Education for the Spanish Dominant Bilingual Children of Texas. In O. A. Ballesteros (Ed.), *Preparing Teachers for Bilingual Education: Basic Readings* (pp. 59–66). ERIC Document 172992. Houston, TX.

Sánchez, G. I. (1997). History, Culture, and Education. In A. Darder, R. D. Torres, & H. Gutiérrez (Eds.), *Latinos and Education* (pp. 117–134). New York: Routledge.

San Miguel, G., Jr. (1997). Roused from Our Slumbers. In A. Darder, R. D. Torres, & H. Gutiérrez (Eds.), *Latinos and Education* (pp. 135–157). New York: Routledge.

Tijerina, F. (1962). What Price Education? What Is It Worth? Where Does It Begin? Who Does It Benefit? What Can We Do about It? *1962 Report of the Little School of the 400* (League of United Latin American Citizens). ERIC Document 124311. Houston, TX.

Recommended Reading

Quintanilla, G. (1976). *The Little School of the 400.* ERIC Document 158905. Houston, TX.

San Miguel, G., Jr. (1999). The Schooling of *Mexicanos* in the Southwest, 1848–1891. In J. F. Moreno (Ed.), *The Elusive Quest for Equality* (pp. 31–52). Cambridge, MA: Harvard Educational Review.

Patricia Sánchez

CHICANO/LATINO STUDENT PRESENCE IN HIGHER EDUCATION

The successful attainment of upward mobility for Chicano/Latino communities rests in large part on their participation in higher education. Because this group continues to grow in significant proportions (e.g., 35% of the Latino population is under 18 years of age), this has implications in several areas, particularly for this population's college-going rates. Most often, it is in impoverished neighborhoods where the lack of advanced pedagogical practices and resources put students at a disadvantage. Findings indicate that those who succeed in graduating from underserved high schools oftentimes are underprepared to meet the challenges of a college education. Specifically, targeted study skills and exposure to advanced courses have not been a part of their schooling, and thus many fall behind during their transition from high school to college. This can have serious economical, social, and political implications for the advancement of this group.

The collective community embedded within this population allows entire communities to benefit from the educational achievement of those from their neighborhoods. Given the shortage of educators, doctors, lawyers, and engineers, among other professionals and intellectuals, in the less-serviced and impoverished vicinities in the country, a way to stimulate the local economy and promote growth in Latino underdeveloped regions is to encourage those who come from these communities to return, in order to teach, to lead, and to transform their neighborhoods. However, one must look at the historical context that has led to the development of Chicano/Latino students in higher education.

Chicano/Latino Higher Education in Historical Context

For example, over the past 40 years the U.S. has experienced a shift in the representation of Chicanos/Latinos in higher education participation, although the increase in enrollment, retention, and graduation figures has not been substantial. What is troubling is that most of the major challenges faced in the 1960s and 1970s continue to exist today. Historically, one sees that during the heyday of Chicano/Latino enrollment in postsecondary education, funding was provided to implement outreach initiatives such as Educational Opportunities Programs (EOPs) to increase enrollment levels. Programs such as these did more than simply motivate students. They assisted students to own their knowledge and to realize that they had just as much right as other students to enroll, participate, and graduate from college.

From 1968 to 1973, Chicanos were recruited in large numbers by accessible institutions open to diversity. Hence, between 1973 and 1977 more Chicano/Latino students entered graduate and professional schools than ever before (Acuña, 1988). After this period of advancement and progress, enrollment became stagnant, and it has continued to remain this way over the past two decades. Much of what was put in place in response to the demands of students, faculty, and communities is being compromised with the elimination of support programming and funding allocations. Although the number of potential Chicano/Latino university students is rapidly increasing, the reality is that low-income Latino students are still finding it difficult to achieve college admission.

Institutions of higher learning are driven by economic interests, which have proven disastrous for the recruitment and retention of Chicano/Latino students. The latter 1970s saw provisions of fellowship and grant awards for students to pursue postsecondary education; but with the Reaganomics of the early 1980s, reductions in federal grants and fellowships provoked a significant decrease in enrollment, especially affecting women, ethnic minorities, and low-income populations. One of the major concerns educators confront today is the budgetary reduction in outreach and recruitment efforts resulting in a decrease in Chicano/Latino enrollment at four-year colleges and universities. The budgetary cuts in K–16 outreach programming across the country, particularly in states such as California, have compromised the effectiveness of recruitment in the latter years of the 1990s through the present (see Table 1).

Although federal policies often drive enrollment and retention, state policies have had a negative impact on enrollment, as illustrated by Proposition 209 in California. In 1998, one year after the implementation of Proposition 209, 53% fewer Latinos were admitted to UC Berkeley's incoming freshman class, and 33% fewer at UCLA. This is a harsh contrast to the enrollment figures at these two main campuses prior to Proposition 209, where combined, they enrolled the highest number of underrepresented students within the University of California system (Gándara, 2002). Currently, this is a pattern that continues across college campuses nationally.

On another note, financial aid provisions continue to be a major factor in assisting students and parents with their college planning and selection; socioeconomic status plays a major factor in the completion of postsecondary education. More institutions recognize the importance of providing pertinent financial assistance information to families, especially after the solicitor scams that have transpired in the past 10 years, where parents have fallen victims to extortion. To better illustrate this case in point, it is important to highlight the discrepancies in annual earnings between non-Hispanic whites and Hispanics. Currently, the median annual income for non-Hispanic whites is $61,251 in comparison to Hispanics, which is a low $38,718 (U.S. Census Bureau, 2004b).[1] Overall, Hispanics are overrepresented in statistics of people living below

Table 1
Educational Attainment of the Population 25 Years and Over by Race, Hispanic Origin, and Age, 2003 (in percent)

Level of Education	Hispanic	Non-Hispanic White
Bachelor's degree or higher	11.4	30
Some college or higher	29.6	56.4
High school graduate or higher	57	89.4

Source: U.S. Census Bureau, Current Population Survey, 2003, Annual Social and Economic Supplement.

poverty levels, in contrast to their non-Hispanic white counterparts.

How are postsecondary institutions addressing these discrepancies? A substantial percentage of four-year colleges and universities depend heavily on foundation funding to increase their enrollment of Chicano/Latino students at their respective campuses. While this partnership is positive and provides pre-college program funding, faculty-of-color hiring, and more active recruitment of students, what is troubling is that institutions rely heavily on this funding to achieve these objectives. While budgetary cuts are a main reason for such action, this also may reflect an unwillingness to make full institutional commitment to access for students of color, who continue to remain in the periphery. Nevertheless, it is important to note that the progress made through these partnerships has been important during the years.

Recommendations

What is being done to prepare today's Chicano/Latino youth for postsecondary education? With budgetary cuts on the rise, how will the commitment of education to all be accomplished? When more jails than colleges and universities are being constructed, what message is this sending to our communities? There are those who argue that Chicanos/Latinos are unmotivated and lack ambition to pursue a college education. Latino youth continue to be discouraged from pursuing their fullest potential because of the preconceived notions and assumptions made by those in positions of power, including politicians, teachers, administrators, and other educators about students' aptitude.

The proposed recommendations are ones identified in other research, but it is imperative to understand that these continue to be areas that need further exploration, in order to identify alternatives to the challenges previously exposed.

Parental Involvement. Recent immigrant, first-generation families tend to not be well informed about how the K–12 public school system functions. Schools and university partnerships must assure that parents are provided the most updated information as to their children's choices. The U.S. pedagogical model tends to differentiate from parents' countries of origin. Parents need to be included in policy discussions that directly affect their children, as well as be informed of the different academic tracking and their right to demand an invigorating curriculum for their children.

Community Asset Building. Much of the research focuses on the deficit model of communities, on what individuals or groups lack in terms of resources or access to higher education. More needs to be done in the area of asset mapping. One cannot go into communities adopting the role of missionaries; instead, a way of respecting and honoring multiple communities is by learning how they generate their own social and cultural capital. It is important to acknowledge what resources and knowledge these communities bring with them.

Partnership. It is important to establish deeper levels of communication, collaboration, and partnership between K–12, postsecondary institutions, grassroots community organizations, and families (e.g., building on parent liaisons, where parent leaders from communities are informed about critical college information that can be shared in their communities). Alternative outreach efforts can be identified, including the coordination of scheduled barbeques and evening sessions or meetings to accommodate working parents.

Note

1. Category: People in Households— Households, by Total Money Income in 2003, Age, Race, and Hispanic Origin of Householder.

References

Acuña, R. (1988). *Occupied America: A History of Chicanos* (3rd ed.). New York: Harper & Row.

Gándara, P. (2002). Meeting Common Goals: Linking K–12 and College Interventions. In W. G. Tierney & L. S. Hagedorn (Eds.), *Increasing Access to College: Extending Possibilities for All Students* (pp. 81–103). Albany, NY: SUNY Press.

Tierney, W. G., & Hagedorn, L. S. (Eds.). (2002). *Increasing Access to College: Extending Possibilities for All Students.* Albany, NY: SUNY Press.

U.S. Census Bureau. (2004a). *Current Population Survey, 2004.* Annual Social and Economic Supplement. Available: http://pubdb3 .census.gov/macro/032004/hhinc/new03_000 .htm (accessed May 1, 2005).

U.S. Census Bureau. (2004b). *Educational Attainment in the United States: 2004.* Available: http://www.census.gov/prod/2004pubs/ p20-550.pdf (accessed May 1, 2005).

Recommended Reading

Acuña, R. (2004). *Occupied America: A History of Chicanos* (5th ed.). New York: Pearson Longman.

Darder, A., Torres, R. T., & Gutiérrez, H. (Eds.). (1997). *Latinos and Education: A Critical Reader.* New York: Routledge.

Tierney, W. G., & Hagedorn, L. S. (Eds.). (2002). *Increasing Access to College: Extending Possibilities for All Students.* Albany, NY: SUNY Press.

Valdes, G. (1996). *Con respeto: Bridging the Distance between Culturally Diverse Families and Schools.* New York: Teachers College, Columbia University.

Valencia, R. (Ed.). (1991). *Chicano School Failure and Success.* London: Falmer Press.

Valenzuela, A. (1999). *Subtractive Schooling: U.S.-Mexican Youth and the Politics of Caring.* Albany, NY: SUNY Press.

Rufina Cortez

CHILDREN'S LITERATURE: CRITICAL PERSPECTIVES

Latino/a children's literature constitutes a body of literary works written for young audiences by and about the experiences of Latinos/as in the U.S. Parallel to the proliferation of Latino/a literature in the U.S., the body of children's literature has also increased in the last 20 years. It represents diverse genres and themes with unique literary qualities.

In the literature available, the reader gets a sense of the heterogeneous characteristics of Latino/a identity, making this body of literary work rich and diverse in nature. Based on previous research (Medina & Enciso, 2002) various sociopolitical perspectives have been identified as prevalent or significant in Latino/a children's literature. These perspectives work as inspiration to craft rich literary images that communicate to readers the complex locations where Latino/a writers create texts. Nevertheless, it is important to mention that these perspectives are not static nor do they play out in the same way across all the literature.

Borderlands

As in the works of Latino/a writers for adult audiences, such as Anzaldúa (1987), and others, notions of borderlands and border crossing are at the center of many writings. The borderland is particularly significant in being a literary image that is poetic and rich. The images of borderland crafted by Latino/a authors represent the ideological, psychological, and physical consequences of being an outsider to mainstream U.S. culture. Many times based on an author's life experiences, the border is represented as an aspect of a complex Latino/a identity where multiple geographical, language, and cultural negotiations take place (Anzaldúa, 1987). One example is Gloria Anzaldúa's book *Friends from the Other Side* (1993), where, based on her experiences living in the U.S.-Mexico border region, she narrates the story of recent immigrants coming from Mexico to Texas. The story explores issues such as discrimination and persecution from the border patrol authorities. Similarly, a more recent and very interesting example is the newly published picture book *Super Cilantro Girl/La superniña del cilantro* (Herrera, 2003), a text where elements of Mexican popular culture—such as the wrestling figure of the El Santo—and Mexican comic book illustrations are used to convey a strong political and cultural message about border dynamics. When Esperanza's mother is kept prisoner at the border, the daughter turns into Super Cilantro Girl to save her from the border patrol. This text demands a different kind of reading that considers ways of knowing that are not the mainstream ways of reading a picture book. As Medina and Enciso (2002) noted:

Latino/a artists show us that when characters live "on the other side" they inhabit a space in which they are visible and invisible, hopeful and afraid, necessary and expedient, self-determining and dependent, willing and exhausted. And they are in the midst of remaking and redefining the border in their own lives. (pp. 37–38)

It is on these dynamic relationships of identity construction, making and remaking of their lives through writing, that many Latino/a authors find powerful inspiration to share their experiences with young audiences. The reader finds images of borderlands in realistic fiction picture books (Hanson, 1995; Perez, 2002), poetry (Argueta, 2003; Medina, 1999) and novels (Jiménez, 1997; Martínez, 1996). It is a theme that in many ways plays out as overarching in multiple literary texts written by Latinos/as.

Feminist Perspectives

Embedded in this notion of borderlands, another significant literary perspective on Latino/a children's literature is brought by Latina feminist writers who make visible and speak of the reality of being a woman within the Latino/a culture. One of the pioneer writers of this literature is Nicholasa Mohr, whose narratives focus on being first-generation Puerto Rican born and raised in New York City. Her books *Felita* (1990) and *Going Home* (1989)—also based on her personal experiences—center on how Puerto Rican adolescent girls negotiate a hybridity of identities and cultural values, such as the family's expectation to behave like a "traditional" Puerto Rican woman. At the core of these texts is a negotiation between expectations from the family and the larger U.S. social structure such as influences of popular culture. Similar issues are explored by writers such as Judith Ortiz-Cofer in her books *An Island like You: Stories from El Barrio* (1995) and *The Meaning of Consuelo* (2003); Chicana writer Sandra Cisneros in *The House on Mango Street* (1983); and Nancy Osa in *Cuba 15* (2003), written from a Cuban perspective. This composition of authors makes available for children diverse critical perspectives on the explorations of being Latina. Other Latinas who have also contributed include field pioneer Alma Flor Ada (1993), author-artist Lulu Delacre (2000), and writer Amada Irma Pérez with picture books such as *My Very Own Room/Mi propio cuartito* (2000).

Migrant Workers and Other Political Perspectives

The migrant worker's experience and other social and political realities constitute another perspective in the literature written by Latino/a authors, such as in the work of Juan Felipe Herrera (1995, 2003) Francisco Jiménez (2000, 2001) and Pam Muñoz-Ryan (2000). In these texts the authors craft narratives with powerful images that explore the social realities and struggles of the life of migrant farm workers. In *The Circuit,* for example, Jiménez tells his autobiography from the moment his family crosses the Mexico-U.S. border. He recounts their lives as migrant workers and the threat and injustices the face for not having citizenship. Through his story young readers have access to a present reality that is many times marginalized in school curriculums. In an interview (Barrera et al., 2003) Jiménez shared that writing his personal story is a form of catharsis where he discovers new aspects of his identity and the importance of his work as a writer: "They [his experiences] were not necessarily unique to me, but common to many, many people in the past and the present. As I reflected on and began to write about them, I learned this was a deeper purpose for having gone through these experiences" (p. 2).

In the literature one also finds texts that commemorate migrant farm workers' fight for rights and justice, or *la causa*, mostly through the figure Cesar Chávez. Gary Soto's recent book *Cesar Chavez: A Hero for Everyone* (2003) and Krull's *Harvesting Hope: The Story of Cesar Chavez* (2003) are good examples of this variety of texts. However, here it is important to mention that there has been overproduction of books that look at Cesar Chávez as the key figure of the migrant farm workers' fight for rights, giving the impression sometimes that this was a one-man struggle. Figure such as female activist Dolores Huerta and other key members tend to be situated at the margins of texts.

The sociopolitical context of Latin American and Caribbean countries, including the circumstances that forced many Latinos/as to leave their countries, are also part of the rich selection of literature available. There are numerous examples in the literature from the Caribbean, such as Julia Alvarez's recent novel *Before We Were Free* (2002), which narrates the story of Anita, a young girl living in the Dominican Republic. Her family has been fighting to liberate the Dominican Republic from Trujillo's dictatorship, and through her diary she tells the reader about the struggles and the fatal consequences of the family's actions. There are also authors Frances Temple (1995) and Edwidge Danticat (2002), whose literary work focuses on the social and political turbulence in Haiti. These novels capture the strength of their citizens, including the many circumstances which propel many people to leave their country. Other authors write about the life and politics in Latin American countries (Becerra de Jenkins, 1996).

Language and Literacy

In the creation of literary images, Latino/a authors use interesting combinations of English and Spanish language. Through these diverse and creative language representations the reader gets a sense of how authors use the richness of English and Spanish to craft their literary images. Among the most relevant ways in which language is used are bilingual texts form with English and Spanish versions side by side. There are also texts that integrate both languages in culturally authentic ways that disrupt notions of either Standard English or Standard Spanish and that represent language in hybrid ways. Relevant to this last category are studies (Barrera, Quiroa, & Valdivia, 2003) that point out that the use of Spanish words in literary texts needs to be carefully crafted: "Otherwise, Spanish elements will not be integral to a text, but merely token or superficial" (p. 164).

Reflections on schooling and language experiences are also present in the literature. *Tomás and Library Lady* (Mora, 1997) is a fictional text based on Tomás Rivera's reading experiences as a child of migrant farm workers. In this text the author represents Rivera's early passion for literary texts and the support his immediate family provides for his love for stories.

Poet Jane Medina creates a rich set of bilingual poems in her book *My Name Is Jorge on Both Sides of the River* (1999). Jorge is a recent immigrant from Mexico who struggles with his identity at school and his experiences with learning a second language. Each poem tells a piece of his life at school. Other poets create engaging celebrations of language, culture, and identity, such as in Francisco Alarcón's series of poetry on the seasons. The four books— *Laughing Tomatoes and Other Spring Poems/Jitomates risueños y otros poemas de primavera* (1997), *Angels Ride Bikes and Other Fall Poems/Los ángeles andan en bicicletas y otros poemas de otoño* (1999), *From the Belly Button of the Moon and Other Summer Poems/Del ombligo de la luna y otros poemas de verano* (1998), and *Iguanas in the Snow and Other Winter Poems/Iguanas en la nieve y otros poemas de invierno* (2001)—demonstrate the richness and complexity of writing bilingual

texts. The same is true of other poets such as Jorge Argueta (2001).

Artistas: Visual Representations

The field of Latino/a children's literature is also influenced by graphic artists whose illustrations in picture books add visual richness to the representations of Latino/a identity. Among the most influential illustrators are Carmen Lomas Garza, Consuelo Mendez, Yuyi Morales, Maya Christina González, George Ancona, Lulu Delacre, Raúl Colón, and David Diaz. Through a variety of mediums these artists convey images that include icons, traditions, and social realities. As artist Lomas Garza (1991) described it, "If you see my heart and humanity through my art then hopefully you will not exclude me from rightfully participating in this society" (p. 13).

Accessibility and Visibility

New authors and themes are always emerging to bring new perspectives to the rich body of Latino/a children's literature. Examples of new voices are Jorge Argueta (2001), who writes about his experiences coming from El Salvador to the Mission District in San Francisco, and Nancy Osa's (2003) literary work on being a second-generation Cuban American, including critical explorations of the cultural and political negotiations with Cuba by previous and younger generations. The excellent literary qualities of the work of these new authors bring much hope to the evolution of the field. Also, it is important to consider the rich selection of literature on folktales, traditional tales, famous Latinos/as, and rhymes and poetry that celebrate diverse cultural aspects of Latino/a identity (a selection of these texts has been included in the references).

There are other factors that support the growth and presence of Latino/a children's literature. The creation of publishing companies that recognize the value of this literature, such as Children's Books Press and Arte Público Press, as well as some mainstream publishers, has been fundamental to the evolution of the field. The establishment of national awards that recognize excellence in Latino/a children's literature has also provided exposure and access to larger audiences. The most significant awards are the Pura Belpré established by the American Library Association and the Américas Award established by the Consortium of Caribbean and Latin American Studies at the University of Wisconsin, Milwaukee. Both awards recognize excellence and set up standards to begin analyzing the cultural authenticity of these books.

From the point of view of literary criticism, it is important to mention that few critics have been committed to the analysis of images and themes among Latino/a writers (see references for a list of published works). Nevertheless, the works of literary critics have resulted in a better contextualization and theorizing of the literature. Particularly critics' work aids in disrupting notions that suggest a homogenous identity for Latinos/as, providing richness to the ways in which we read and interpret the literature. Their work has been particularly committed to helping teachers and educators develop ways to facilitate the literature with young readers.

Challenges and New Directions

While the field of Latino/a children's literature has grown and evolved, many interrelated challenges remain to be overcome. One big challenge is the extremely small amount of literature published each year compared to the rapid growth of the Latino/a community is the U.S. Connected to this first challenge is publishers' and bookstores' limited support, particularly from the mainstream, for authors and illustrators who bring critical perspectives on Latino/a children's literature. Most of the books published and distributed still represent narrow and stereotypical perceptions of being Latino/a. While some publishers support authors who write in authentic ways, fiestas and celebrations still dominate the market creating superficial representations of Latino/a identity.

The literature also lacks texts that explore issues of race and sexuality. Topics such as racial dynamics and gay and lesbian issues (topics now visible in other children's literature) remain almost invisible, giving the impression these irrelevant perspectives within Latino/a communities. Recently Judith Ortiz-Cofer addressed issues related to sexuality and identity in her book *The Meaning of Consuelo* (2003), but this seems to be a rare case.

Finally there is only a limited body of research that looks at young people's response to this literature. Some questions remain unanswered: How accessible is Latino/a literature in classrooms? What are the multiple identities readers bring to their interpretations of Latino/a literature? What kinds of lenses are being used in the interpretation of the literature?

References

Literary Criticism

Barrera, R., & Garza de Cortes, O. (1997). Mexican American Children's Literature in the 1990's: Toward Authenticity. In V. Harris (Ed.), *Using Multiethnic Literature in the K–8 Classroom* (2nd ed., pp. 129–154). Boston: Christopher Gordon.

Barrera, R., Quiroa, R., & Valdivia, R. (2003). Spanish in Latino Picture Storybooks in English: Its Use and Textual Effects. In A. Ingram Willis, G. E. García, R. Barrera & V. J.

Harris (Eds.), *Multicultural Issues in Literacy Research and Practice*. Hillsdale, NJ: Lawrence Erlbaum.

Barrera, R., Quiroa, R., & West-William, C. (1999). Poco a poco: The Continuing Development of Mexican American Children's Literature in the 1990's. *The New Advocate* 12(4), 315–330.

Medina, C., & Enciso, P. (2002). "Some Words Are Messengers/Hay palabras mensajeras": Interpreting Sociopolitical Themes in Latino/a Children's Literature. *The New Advocate* 15(1), 35–47.

Mohr, N. (1992). A Journey towards a Common Ground: The Struggle and Identity of Hispanics in the U.S.A. In A. Manna & C. S. Brodie (Eds.), *Many Faces, Many Voices: Multicultural Literary Experiences for Youth* (pp. 61–68). Fort Atkinson, WI: Highsmith Press.

Nieto, S. (1997). We Have Stories to Tell Puerto Ricans in Children's Books. In V. Harris (Ed.), *Using Multiethnic Literature in the K–8 Classroom* (pp. 59–94). Boston: Cristopher Gordon.

Quiroa, R. E. (2001). The Use and Role of Multiethnic Children's Literature in Family Literacy Programs: Realities and Possibilities. *The New Advocate* 14(1), 43–52.

Web Sites

Américas Award, http://www.uwm.edu/Dept/CLACS/outreach_americas.html.

Pura Belpré Award, http:www.ala.org/alsc/belpre.html.

Selected Bibliography on Latino/a Children's Books

These categories are not fixed, and several of the books could fit in more than one.

Contemporary Perspectives

Ancona, G. (1998). *Barrio: Jose's Neighborhood*. San Diego, CA: Harcourt Brace. (Mexican American)

Anzaldúa, G. (1987). *Borderlands/La Frontera: The New Mestiza*. San Francisco: Aunt Lute Books.

Anzaldúa, G. (1993). *Friends from the Other Side/Amigos del otro vado*. Illus. C. Méndez. San Francisco: Children's Books Press. (Mexican American)

Argueta, J. (2003). *Xochitl and the Flowers*. Illus. C. Angel. San Francisco: Children's Book Press. (Salvadorian)

Atkin, S. B. (1993). *Voices from the Fields: Children of Migrant Farmworkers tell Their Stories*. Boston: Little, Brown. (Latino/a)

Bunting, E. (1996). *Going Home*. Illus. D. Diaz. New York: HarperCollins. (Mexican American)

Cisneros, S. (1983). *The House on Mango Street*. Houston, TX: Arte Público Press. (Mexican American)

Hanson, R. (1995). *The Tangerine Tree*. Illus. H. Stevenson. New York: Clarion Books. (Jamaican)

Herrera, J. F. (1995). *Calling the Doves/El canto de las palomas*. Illus. E. Simmons. San Francisco: Children's Book Press, 1995. (Mexican American)

Herrera, J. F. (2003). *Super Cilantro Girl/La niña del supercilantro*. Illus. H. Robledo Tapia. San Francisco: Children's Books Press. (Mexican American)

Jiménez, F. (1997). *The Circuit: Stories from the Life of a Migrant Child*. Albuquerque: University of New Mexico Press. (Mexican American)

Jiménez, F. (2000). *The Christmas Gift/El regalo de navidad*. Illus. C. B. Cotts. Boston: Houghton Mifflin. (Mexican American)

Jiménez, F. (2001). *Breaking Through*. Boston: Houghton Mifflin. (Mexican American)

Martínez, V. (1996). *Parrot in the Oven: Mi Vida*. New York: HarperCollins. (Mexican American)

Mohr, N. (1989). *Going Home* (2nd ed.). New York: Bantam. (Original work published 1986.) (Puerto Rican)

Mohr, N. (1990). *Felita* (2nd ed.). New York: Bantam. (Original work published 1979.) (Puerto Rican)

Ortiz-Cofer, J. (1995). *An Island like You: Stories from El Barrio*. New York: Orchard. (Puerto Rican)

Osa, N. (2003). *Cuba 15*. New York: Delacorte Press. (Cuban American)

Pérez, A. I. (2002). *My Diary from Here to There/Mi diario de aquí hasta allá*. Illus. M. C. González. San Francisco: Children's Books Press. (Mexican American)

Soto, G. (2003). *The Afterlife*. Florida: Harcourt. (Mexican American)

Historical and Political Perspectives

Alvarez, J. (2002). *Before We Were Free*. New York: Knopf. (Dominican)

Ancona, G. (1997). *Mayeros: A Yucatec Family*. New York: William Morrow. (Mexican)

Andrew-Goebel, N. (2002). *The Pot That Juan Built*. Illus. D. Diaz. New York: Lee & Low. (Southwest)

Becerra de Jenkins, L. (1996). *So Loud a Silence*. New York: Lodestar. (Colombia).

Cohn, D. (2002). *¡Sí se puede!/Yes We Can!* Houston, TX: Cinco Punto Press. (Latino/a)

Dandicat, E. (2002). *Behind the Mountains*. New York: Orchard. (Haitian)

Joseph, L. (2000). *The Color of My Words*. New York: HarperCollins. (Dominican)

Krull, K. (2003). *Harvesting Hope: The Story of Cesar Chavez*. Illus. Y. Morales. San Diego: Harcourt. (Mexican American)

Mora, P. (2002). *A Library for Juana*. Illus. B. Vidal. New York: Knopf. (Mexican American)

Muñoz-Ryan, P. (2000). *Esperanza Rising*. New York: Scholastic Press. (Mexican)

Myers, W. D. (1996). *Toussant L'Overture: The Fight for Haiti's Freedom*. Paintings by J. Lawrence. New York: Simon & Schuster. (Haitian)

Ortiz-Cofer, J. (2003). *The Meaning of Consuelo*. New York: Farrar, Straus & Giroux. (Puerto Rican)

Temple, F. (1995). *Tonight by the Sea*. New York: Orchard Books. (Haitian)

Winter, J. (2002). *Frida*. Illus. A. Juan. New York: Scholastic. (Mexican)

Language, Literacy, and Identity

Ada, A. (1993). *My Name Is María Isabel*. New York: Simon & Schuster. (Puerto Rican)

Jiménez, F. (1998). *La mariposa*. Illus. S. Silva. Boston: Houghton Mifflin. (Mexican American)

Lumas-Latchman, O. (1995). *Pepita Talks Twice/Pepita habla dos veces*. Houston, TX: Arte Público Press. (Mexican American)

Mora, P. (1997). *Tomás and the Library Lady*. New York: Knopf. (Mexican American)

Medina, J. (1999). *My Name Is Jorge on Both Sides of the River: Poems in English and Spanish*. Honesdale, PA: Wordsong/Boyds Mills Press. (Mexican American)

Folktales, Rhymes, and Poetry

Alarcón, F. (1997). *Laughing Tomatoes and Other Spring Poems/Jitomates risueños y otros poemas de primavera*. Illus. by M. C. Gonzalez. San Francisco: Children's Books Press. (Mexican American)

Alarcón, F. (1998). *From the Belly Button of the Moon and Other Summer Poems/Del ombligo de la luna y otros poemas de verano*. Illus. M. C. Gonzalez. San Francisco: Children's Books Press. (Mexican American)

Alarcón, F. (1999). *Angels Ride Bikes and Other Fall Poems/Los ángeles andan en bicicletas y otros poemas de otoño*. Illus. M. C. Gonzalez. San Francisco: Children's Books Press. (Mexican American)

Alarcón, F. (2001). *Iguanas in the Snow and Other Winter Poems/Iguanas en la nieve y otros poemas de invierno*. Illus. M. C. Gonzalez. San Francisco: Children's Books Press. (Mexican American)

Anaya, R. (1997). *Maya's Children: The Story of La Llorona*. Illus. M. Baca. New York: Hyperon. (Mexican American)

Argueta, J. (2001). *A Movie in My Pillow/Una película en mi almohada*. Illus. E. Gómez. San Francisco: Children's Books Press. (Salvadorian)

Carlson, L. (1994). *Cool Salsa: Bilingual Poems on Growing Up Latino in the United States*. Intro. O. Hijuelos. New York: Holt. (Latino/a)

Castillo, A. (2000). *Mi hija, mi hijo, el águila, la paloma: Un canto azteca/My Daughter, My Son, the Eagle, the Dove: An Aztec Chant*.

Illus. S. Guevara. New York: Dutton. (Mexican American)

Cruz-Martínez, A. (1987). *The Woman Who Outshone the Sun/La mujer que brillaba aún más que el sol*. Illus. F. Oliviera. San Francisco: Children's Books Press. (Mexican)

Delacre, L. (1996). *Golden Tales: Myths, Legends and Folktales from Latin America*. New York: Scholastic. (Puerto Rican)

Endredy, J. (2003). *The Jouney of Tunuri and the Blue Deer*. Illus. M. Hernández de la Cruz & C. de la Cruz López. New York: Bear Cub Books.

Herrera, J. F. (1995). *Calling the Doves/El canto de las palomas*. Illus. E. Simmons. San Francisco: Children's Books Press. (Mexican American)

Mora, P. (1996). *Confetti*. Illus. E. Sanchez. New York: Lee & Low Books. (Mexican American)

Morales, Y. (2003). *Just a Minute: A Trickster Tale and Counting Book*. San Francisco: Chronicle Books. (Mexican American)

Nye-Shihab, N. (1995). *The Tree Is Older Than You Are: A Bilingual Gathering of Poems and Stories from Mexico with Paintings by Mexican Artists*. New York: Simon & Schuster. (Mexican)

Soto, G. (1992). *Neighborhood Odes*. Illus. D. Diaz. New York: Harcourt Brace. (Mexican American)

Soto, G. (1995). *Canto familiar*. Illus. A. Nelson. New York: Harcourt Brace. (Mexican American)

Celebrations of Culture

Ada, A. F. (2002). *I Love Saturdays y Domingos*. Illus. by E. Savadier. New York: Atheneum. (Latino/a–bicultural)

Ancona, G. (1998). *Barrio: Jose's Neighborhood*. San Diego: Harcourt Brace. (Mexican American)

Delacre, L. (1993). *Vejigante/Masquerader*. New York: Scholastic. (Puerto Rican)

Delacre, L. (2000). *Salsa Stories*. New York: Scholastic. (Puerto Rican)

Herrera, J. F. (1999). *Crashboomlove: A Novel in Verse*. New Mexico: University of New Mexico Press. (Mexican American)

Lomas Garza, C. (1990). *Family Pictures/Cuadros de familia*. Emeryville, CA: Children's Books Press. (Mexican American)

Lomas Garza, C. (1991). *A Piece of My Heart/Pedacito de mi corazón: The Art of Carmen Lomas Garza*. New York: New Press. (Mexican American)

Lomas Garza, C. (1996). *In My Family/En mi familia*. Emeryville, CA: Children's Books Press. (Mexican American)

Pérez, A. I. (2000). *My Very Own Room/Mi propio cuartito*. Illus. M. C. Gonzalez. San Francisco: Children's Books Press. (Mexican American)

Soto, G. (1995). *Chato's Kitchen*. Illus. Susan Guevara. New York: Putnam. (Mexican American)

Soto, G. (1997). *Snapshots from the Wedding*. Illus. Stephanie Garcia. New York: Putnam. (Mexican American)

Carmen Medina

THE COLOR OF MY SKIN

This piece by Luz Valenzuela Zamora reminds us of how children's voices can guide us in learning about the complexities involved in the education of Latinos/as. Luz's insights help us to understand how she has experienced the world. Luz's entry reminds us of Leslie Marmon Silko's (1996) words, "Where I come from the words most highly valued are those spoken from the heart" (p. 48).

Hi my name is Luz Valenzuela Zamora I'm a Mexican girl from Austin, Texas I use to live in Houston when I was four. I am now nine. I had a pretty not too bad life as a Mexican.

In Pre–K I was told by a young girl by the name of Kate that I couldn't go on the tire swing because I was Mexican I started to cry. I hid in the back of the playground looking at my dark skin I thought that the color of my skin wouldn't make a difference. Boy was I wrong I wish I wasn't. I look back now and think, what was she thinking maybe I was wrong maybe she wasn't thinking any thing. Where did she learn this from her mother her father or maybe siblings. I was surprised if this was how it was when I was only in Pre-K how was it goanna be when I was forty. My mother and father assured me I was some day to be told something that was very racist and since I was a girl that would be worse for me and, my sister Clara. But they told me to keep my chin up. My parents supported me all of the way and I thank them. When my father heard what Kate said to me he felt like going to my little school and giving Kate a piece actually the whole thing of his mind. My dad was a professor at the University of Texas he taught Mexican American history so I learned some interesting facts about Indians and Mexicans I learned that all those thanksgiving stories were not true the pinche pilgrims killed all the innocent Indians. I didn't hear any giving in that story.

References

Silko, L. M. (1996). *Yellow Woman and a Beauty of Spirit*. New York: Touchstone Books.

Soto, L. D., & Swadener, B. B. (Eds.). (2005). *Power and Voice in Research with Children*. New York: Peter Lang.

Luz Valenzuela Zamora

COURT STRUGGLES AND LATINO EDUCATION

Although public education is a vital component of the equality, prosperity, and opportunity enjoyed in America, the courts have historically refused to recognize education as a basic right. Desegregation court battles that have raged across the Southwest since the 1920s, have largely failed to address the educational needs of Latino children. Instead, the courts have given deference to school boards and state officials in efforts to take the needed steps they felt were in the best interest of Latino students.

Historically, Latinos have turned to the courts to find relief from social, governmental, and political injustices. By granting greater jurisdiction to state officials over educational matters or policies, the courts have relegated the Latino community to a position of lesser status and hindered their political involvement over educational matters. In this respect legal reform to education has given little agency to the Latino community, hampering efforts to improve an educational system that continues to be separate and unequal for many Latino students.

Selected Court Outcomes

The following court outcomes briefly document the few accomplishments of legal reform through the community's efforts to desegregate and bring greater equity to American public schooling across the Southwest. Of particular importance in this brief chronology of court outcomes are the two types of segregation, one being *de facto* (by social practice) and the other *de jure* (by law or policy).

Adolpho Romo v. Laird (1925). The courts held that Tempe School District No. 3 had failed to provide qualified teachers (state certified) for Mexican children. In consequence the Supreme Court ordered the district to hire certified teachers and allowed "limited integration" of the Romo children to Tenth Street School. Despite this victory the Arizona court along with the education code continued to allow segregation of students for teaching purposes so long as educational opportunities remained equal.

Independent School District v. Salvatierra (1930). The Texas Court of Appeals held that school authorities could not arbitrarily segregate Mexican children based on ethnic background. Despite the ruling the court said the district was not "subjectively" segregating children and was doing so only to accommodate students' linguistic difficulties or their late start if they entered school late because of migrant labor patterns. Ironically the court continued to allow segregation based on linguistic difficulty despite there being no testing instrument used to show that Latino children were less proficient in English.

Alvarez v. Owen (1931). The Supreme Court issued the first mandate ordering school desegregation for Latinos. In this respect Latinos where protected by due process under the Fourteenth Amendment of the U.S. Constitution.

Mendez et al. v. Westminster School District (1946). The Supreme Court sided in favor of Mendez by stating that segregation based on race (Mexican descent) violated Fourteenth Amendment rights of students. In this respect the court ruled that segregation of the Mexican child delayed the acquisition of English and denied them the opportunity to develop the cultural attitude necessary to function in American institutions. This case served as a trial run for arguments later used in the famous *Brown v. Board of Education* (1954) case.

Delgado v. Bastrop ISD (1948). The Supreme Court ruled that placing Latino students in segregated schools was arbitrary and discriminatory and in violation of the Fourteenth Amendment. Despite this ruling, the courts continued to allowed segregation of students after evaluating language proficiency of students through school testing.

Gonzalez v. Sheely (1951). The Arizona court stated that segregating Latino children labeled them inferior, injured their capacity to learn English, and stripped them of the opportunity to develop a common cultural attitude essential to American public life. The court ruling protected students' Fourteenth Amendment rights, which

had been violated by school officials. Despite this outcome, the courts continued to allow segregating Latinos for linguistic purposes.

Hernandez v. Texas (1954). The Supreme Court declared Latino segregation an indicator of their social or de facto created difference. As a result, the Court declared Latinos protected under the Fourteenth Amendment, since they where deemed a "class or group" whose rights had been violated by Jim Crow practices or discriminatory de facto behavior. Thus protection under the Fourteenth Amendment was limited to the facts of the case and failed to reach the "broader" question of whether the group comprised an "identifiable ethnic minority." The ruling would become important because Latinos represented an ethnic minority that needed judicial protection from the majority, in a similar way to African Americans.

Brown v. Board of Education (1954). After the Supreme Court delivered its decision declaring racial segregation to be unconstitutional, Latinos would have a difficult time arguing under the *Brown* ruling. Since *Salvatierra* (1930) the approach used by Latino attorneys was to argue from the "other white" perspective, making it difficult to argue that there was segregation based on racial grounds. Also the Court failed to distinguish de facto from de jure, yet in later decisions it would narrowly read *Brown* to declare de jure and not de facto segregation unconstitutional. Because Latinos were largely segregated not by policy but by social practice, de facto segregation was left unaddressed by the courts. Latinos could not continue litigation as the "other white" because of the *Hernandez* decision.

Crawford v. Board of Education of Los Angeles (1963). The California court found the Los Angeles public schools to be unlawfully segregated and ordered the board to desegregate them. The court decisions continued to allow segregating Latinos based on language "deficiency" and concluded that segregating based on the language factor was justifiable. In this respect the courts relied on stagnant court precedent to continue segregating based on language despite school evidence that "language" was used as a pretext for separating Latinos from Anglos.

Cisneros v. Corpus Christi Independent School District (ISD) (1970). The district court found the district's "dual" school system, which segregated Anglos on a few campuses and blacks and Latinos on the other, was illegal. At this time the Corpus Christi ISD had intentionally drawn attendance maps to suit segregated residential patterns that distorted de facto from de jure segregation. The courts at this time declared Mexican Americans an identifiable ethnic minority that deserved but had been denied equal protection under the Fourteenth Amendment, similar to the *Brown* ruling. This recognition gave legal protection to Mexican Americans under *Brown* for desegregation efforts.

Serrano v. Priest I (1971). At this time the California Supreme Court found the state's public school finance system to be in violation of the equal protection clause of both federal and state constitutions. At this time the court held that education was a "basic right" that could not be "conditioned" by parental wealth or the location of taxable private-commercial industry.

Keyes v. School District No. 1 (1973). The U.S. Supreme Court stated that blacks and Latinos suffered "identical" discrimination in treatment in comparison with Anglos. The Court declared that despite the variations of local custom and statutes, both groups on occasion suffered from identical discrimination and should benefit from the same remedies.

San Antonio Independent School District v. Rodriguez (1973). The Supreme Court stated that Constitution's guarantee of equal protection was not violated by the property tax system used to finance public education in Texas and most U.S. states. In this fashion the Court refused to look at the system under "strict scrutiny," since it declared that education was not a "fundamental right" explicitly or implicitly protected by the U.S. Constitution.

Lau v. Nichols (1974). The Supreme Court held that school programs conducted only in English

denied equal access to education to students who spoke other languages. In this respect the Supreme Court ordered school districts to help non-English speakers overcome their language disadvantage through meaningful teaching practices. At this time the Court stopped short of declaring bilingual education an absolute mandate.

Serrano v. Priest II (1976). The California Supreme Court stated that the system of financing schools was unconstitutional under the equal protection clause of the state constitution. The court ruled that property tax rates and per-pupil spending should be equalized and that the difference in base revenue limit spending to fewer than $100 per student. At this time the state court ruled that education was a fundamental right under the California constitution, declaring it as "those individual rights and liberties, which lie at the core of our democratic government."

Serrano v. Priest III (1986). The appellate court held that the state had complied with the 1976 Supreme Court mandate in overcoming disparities in educational spending to the point that a difference was not significant. This decision overturned the 1976 mandate that spending differences had to be cut to $100.

Williams v. State of California (2000). The state court ruled that California was reneging its constitutional obligation to provide students with the "bare essentials" needed to secure a "basic education." At this time the court ordered the state to ensure that students receive the proper instructional materials, adequate learning facilities, and qualified teachers essential for a basic education.

Conclusion

This chronological review of Latino litigation efforts to desegregate and bring greater fiscal equity to public schools throughout Arizona, Texas, Colorado, and California from 1925 through 2003 suggests that educational inequalities have historically hindered the educational advancement of the Latinos, given court dissent that has largely permitted segregation of Latinos because of language difficulties and migrant farming patterns. Until the *Cisneros* (1970) ruling, which rejected these "benign" reasons to segregate, the courts focused on addressing the de jure–de facto distinction to further justify segregation practices. In this respect, most courts took the position that de facto segregation did not violate the federal Constitution. Following segregation under de facto circumstances, litigation struggles turned their attention to equity (language and fiscal), starting with the *Serrano* (1971, 1976, 1986) and *Lau* (1974) rulings and capitalizing on the *Williams* (2000) outcome, which served to expose persisting inequalities in learning facilities, proper learning materials, and qualified teachers.

References

Adolpho Romo v. William E. Laird et al., No. 21617 (Maricopa County Sup. Ct. 1925).

ACLU Online. (2005). S.F. Judge Finalizes Historic Education Settlement. Available: http://www.aclu-sc.org/News/Releases/100841/.

Alvarez v. Owen, slip. op. At 5 (San Diego Country Sup. Ct. March 30 1931).

Alvarez Jr., Robert, R. (1986). The Lemon Grove Incident: The Nation's First Successful Desegregation Court Case. *Journal of San Diego History* 32(2). Available: http://www.sandiegohistory.org/journal/86springlemongrove.htm.

Brown v. Board of Education, 347 U.S. 483, 495 (1954).

Castellanos, David. (1985). *The Best of Two Worlds: Bilingual-Bicultural Education in the U.S.* Trenton, NJ: New Jersey State Department of Education.

Cisneros v. Corpus Christi Independent School District, 324 F. Supp. 599, 606 (S.D. Tex. 1970).

Crawford v. Board of Education of Los Angeles, No. 822854 (Cal. Sup. Ct. 1963).

Delgado v. Bastrop ISD, Civ. No. 388 (unreported: W.D. Tex. June 15 1948).

Gonzales v. Sheely, 96 F. Supp. 1004 (D. Ariz. 1951).

Hernandez v. Texas, 347 U.S. 475 (1954).

Independent School District v. Salvatierra, 33 S.W. 2d 790, 791 (Tex. Civ. App. 1930).

Keyes v. School District No. 1, 413 U.S. 189 (1973).

Lau v. Nichols, 414 U.S. 563 (1974).

Martinez, George, A. (1994). *Legal Indeterminacy, Judicial Discretion and the Mexican Litigation Experience, 1930–1980*. University of California, *Davis Law Review* 27(3): 555–618.

Méndez et al. v. Westminster School District. (1946). The Méndez Case: *Brown v. Board of Education* for Mexican Americans [Digital history]. Available: http://www.digitalhistory.uh.edu/mexican_voices/voices_display.cfm?id=106.

Muñoz, L. K. (2005). Separate but Equal? A Case Study of *Romo v. Laird* and Mexican American Education. Available: http://www.oah.org/pubs/magazine/deseg/munoz.html (last visited May 1, 2005).

San Antonio Independent School District v. Rodriguez, 411 U.S. 1 (1973).

Serrano v. Priest I, 487 P. No. 822854 (Cal. Sup. Ct. 1971).

Serrano v. Priest II, 557 P. 2d 929 (Cal. Sup. Ct. 1976).

Serrano v. Priest III, 226 Cal. Rptr. 584 (Cal. Ct. App. 1986).

Williams v. State of California, No. 312236 (Cal. Sup. Ct. 2000).

Recommended Reading

Camarillo, Albert. (1984). *Chicanos in California: A History of Mexican Americans in California*. San Francisco: Boyd & Fraser.

Gonzalez, Gilbert G. (1990). *Chicano Education in the Era of Segregation*. Philadelphia: Balch Institute Press.

Menchaca, Martha. (1995). *The Mexican Outsiders: A Community History of Marginalization and Discrimination in California*. Austin: University of Texas Press.

San Miguel, Guadalupe. (2001). *Brown, Not White: School Integration and the Chicano*

Movement in Houston. College Station: Texas A&M University Press.

Spring, Joel H. (1997). *Deculturalization and the Struggle for Equality: A Brief History of the Education of Dominated Cultures in the United States* (2nd ed.). New York: McGraw-Hill.

Wollenberg, Charles. (1976). *All Deliberate Speed: Segregation and Exclusion in California Schools, 1855–1975*. Berkeley: University of California Press.

Video

Robbie, S. (Writer/producer). (2002). *Mendez v. Westminster: For All the Children/Para todo los niños*. KOCE-TV Presentation. Huntington Beach, CA: KOCE Foundation.

Gerardo Diaz

CRITICAL DIGITAL EDUCATION

Critical Digital Education focuses on developing methodologies that make it possible for people to develop an autonomous and daily use of the Information and Communication Technologies (ICT), according to the characteristics of the twenty-first century. Critical Digital Education embraces the theory and practice of teaching ICT, drawing from authors in critical theory such as Freire and Habermas, and practices that have been carried out for decades in numerous community development projects in neighborhoods, villages, and cities by using ICT as a means for empowerment. Many of these are Latino communities around the world. One of their common features are the principles of dialogic learning (Flecha, 2000), which set the ground for the majority of these educational practices.

Challenges of the Information Society

During the 1970s and 1980s, the advent of ICT, among other technological advances introduced in industrial production, created socioeconomic changes that have affected many people: we shifted from a society with an economy based on industry to one increasingly centered on information and knowledge flows and the technologies that make these happen. This change generated a significant social rift between the few people who had access to ICT and those who could access these resources. Some authors like Jürgen Habermas called this exclusionary phenomenon *social Darwinism*; others talked of a Matthew effect to describe social a situation in which the people who already have resources will have more social opportunities, and those who do not will have even less. Those who can access information and technology (by means of education and high qualifications) will have the best jobs; those who do not have access will be left to unemployment and marginalization. This social polarization associated with technology is popularly known as the *digital divide*.

In the mid-1990s, after the exclusionary processes generated by the technological revolution, a second phase of the information society began, in which social groups and institutions began to work toward extending ICT to the maximum number of people, reaching out to the formerly marginalized. Today social and economic development of society no longer depends on the access of one sector or experts, but instead on the widespread use of the ICT in a society that is becoming increasingly dialogic. In fact, the democratization and widespread use of technology is in the interest of both software or technology companies and social movements, though perhaps for different reasons. People use the technologies because they provide the opportunity to carry out our personal and collective projects. This includes communicating with family members and friends, looking for an apartment or a job, and buying or reading the newspaper. This has been described as a second phase toward the *information society for all*. In this second phase the Internet initiates a process of universalization. Its very structures are the basis of communication and information exchange, the promotion of non-hierarchical dynamics and flexibility. The Internet thus opens up opportunities between people. These characteristics are precisely the basis of most projects focused on digital education today.

Benefits of Digital Education in the Information Age

New projects are emerging around the world propelled by people from socially excluded neighborhoods and areas and by populations that have been silenced in mainstream education. To mention some, there are the "somos@telecentros" in Latin America and the Caribbean; the Committee for the Democratization of Informatics (CDI) in Latin America; the Agora Spot in Barcelona, Spain; and the Plugged-in project in East Palo Alto, California. These are just a few examples of projects that promote technology access and empower children and adults through the critical use of media. They have been defined as *telecenters*.

In general terms, telecenters are public and community spaces of learning and public use of ICT. Their objective is to bring ICT closer to the people who have less possibilities of accessing them. Thus, they take people's needs into account and offer classes and activities that show ICT as a tool for social participation and inclusion of these people. Telecenters share basic methodological features for what is understood as "critical education" and "education for social change" in the digital world. Some of these shared features are these:

Taking a teaching approach that is people centered—especially focused on those who have never touched a computer, providing them with protagonism and leadership in both the daily learning dynamics of the telecenter and the decision making of the project.

Providing a direct link between technologies and the daily life of users. The digital world is understood as a means or a tool rather than as an end; the objective of providing everyone with "connectivity" helps people to empower themselves through ICT.

Reinforcing aspects of socialization and communication among people (for instance, email, forums, and the possibility of creating personal web pages).

Having high expectations about the possibilities for everyone to learn ICT.

Working in "interactive groups," a methodology grounded in dialogic learning that enhances collaboration and competencies' exchange.

In "interactive groups," learners of different ages, cultures, backgrounds, and digital proficiencies work together in multimedia creation around a common interest: creating a journal; designing a CD-ROM with information about National Natural Parks; reviewing the art of the city, neighborhood, or village where the telecenter is located; and so on. These working groups serve as a way to take full advantage of the technology, bringing together learning different tools (i.e., ofimatics, Internet, web design, CD and DVD use, digitalization and scanner use, etc.) with the process of creating a final multimedia product. People who join working groups leave them with a multimedia creation they have coauthored with peer learners. Critical Digital Education implies a dialogic approach to learning. We can explain dialogic learning through seven principles: egalitarian dialogue, cultural intelligence, solidarity, instrumental dimension, equality of differences, creation of meaning, and transformation. When telecenters take a dialogic orientation, we can identify these principles in the organization of the activities and the learning process. Working-class people, who may not have an academic background, find themselves in a space that does not question their capacity to learn or to use ICT. Far from that, educators clearly recognize that everyone can learn. In the dialogic telecenter, prior experiences are taken into account as a contribution rather than as a barrier (cultural intelligence). Taking on the challenge of learning ICT brings these tools closer to the daily lives of ordinary people. These ways help to bridge the digital divide mentioned before. Some individuals may want to learn a specific program, technicque, or tool; others may simply want to enjoy ICT. Whatever their reason, all find meaning in this learning by feeling they were not mistaken in approaching the telecenter. The moment their capacities are taken into account, a door opens for people to be able to participate according to their own interests and share them with others (creation of meaning and instrumental dimension of learning). Differences in these spaces are not reasons to exclude or label people; rather, they are reasons for dialogue, for understanding, and for enrichment. All people, whatever their identity and culture, have an equal right to a quality education (equality of differences). From the standpoint of equality and mutual respect, it is possible to reach understanding and agreements and to become all both learners and teachers (egalitarian dialogue).

Telecenters cannot be conceived of without the principle of solidarity. People most excluded from ICT, for socioeconomic reasons or because of barriers based on age, gender, or culture, find in telecenters the possibility to overcome these barriers. An il-literate woman able to prepare a presentation about the functioning of the telecenter by using Power Point later enrolled in a digital literacy program; a school-dropout adolescent discovered he could be a good student, he felt he was good at managing ICT, and now thinks of possibly preparing for university; some people who did not participate socially became catalysts in a local associations and use ICT to further citizens' participation and increase presence in spaces of decision making (transformation). They did not do this alone, of course, but in collaboration with other learners in the telecenter. Critical education in the digital space implies all these dimensions of dialogic learning.

These projects can take place only in an open and democratic atmosphere in which the participants become protagonists in the day-to-day running of the telecenter. As an example we quote the definition of the project somos@telecentros in Latin America and the Caribbean: "We are a human network of community telecenters and initiatives that work with the information and communication technologies for development. We participate in a learning process and exchange of knowledge and experiences based on respect and collaborative work" (see http://www.tele-centros.org).

The digital divide does not disappear merely through the provision of infrastructure, nor by guaranteeing access. It is necessary to consider people's needs and interests, and to focus the project on answering to them, by offering ICT as a tool that can be used to reach this goal. If the objective is to achieve an information society for all, we cannot just say we have to "access" or "learn" ICT; instead, we must promote a dialogic learning process that serves as real and direct participation for all people. As Paulo Freire (1998) said, education needs both professional and technical development and dreams and utopia. Critical digital education combines technology with human communication and dreams for social change.

References

Buckingham, D. (2003). *Media Education: Literacy, Learning and Contemporary Culture.* Cambridge: Polity Press.

Castells, M., Freire, P., Flecha, R., Giroux, H., Macedo, D., & Willis, P. (1999). *Critical Education in the New Information Age.* Lanham, MD: Rowman & Littlefield.

Flecha, R. (2000). *Sharing Words: Theory and Practice of Dialogic Learning.* Lanham, MD: Rowman & Littlefield.

Freire, P. (1998). *Pedagogy of Freedom: Ethics, Democracy, and Civic Courage.* Lanham, MD: Rowman & Littlefield.

Hammer, R., & Kellner, D. (1999). Multimedia Pedagogy for the New Millennium. *Journal of Adolescent & Adult Literacy* 42 (7), 522–526.

Tyner, K. (1998). *Literacy in a Digital World: Teaching and Learning in the Age of Information.* Mahwah, NJ: Lawrence Erlbaum.

Miquel Ángel Pulido

CRITICAL PEDAGOGY AND LIBERATION THEOLOGY

Liberation theology possesses great possibility as grounding for a critical system of educational ethics. As it attacks the modernist cult of objectivism, liberation theology lays the groundwork for an emancipatory system of meaning on which a critical pedagogy can be built. In its refusal to accept history as a record of what has prevailed—the record of the established and successful—liberation theology exposes the fact that the conquered and defeated have received the short end of the historical stick, that the unfulfilled dreams of the commoners have not found their way into the "official story." Pedagogically, this

exclusion contributes to oppression when students from subjugated groups are taught the science and culture of the dominant society without this knowledge passing through a filter constructed by a historically grounded self-consciousness. Brazillian educator Paulo Freire is known as education's leading liberation theologist. His "Pedagogy of the Oppressed," based upon the Frankfurt school's notion of critical theory, and the liberatory nature of theology are studied by educators. Especially affected by liberation theology and Freire's critical pedagogy are citizens and teachers from Latin and Central America, Spain, and Portugal. In fact, Spanish- and Portuguese-speaking nations have schools and private institutes based on Freire's teaching and liberation theology. Following is a description and discussion of liberation theology.

Liberation theology demands that all participants are exposed to the understandings that emanate from the critical interpretations of the oppressed. These critical interpretations often serve to "correct" the socially constructed blind spots in our sociocultural experience. Scholars, teachers, or curriculum developers from privileged backgrounds may learn from this epistemological insurrection; they may come to accept the pre-theoretical commitment that alternative voices and the knowledges of the oppressed should be heard. Indeed this pre-theoretical commitment to the value of subjugated knowledges is a compass for our journey into the unexplored outback of curriculum theory.

Foucault has taught us that while truth is not relative, it is relational. Relational truth means that constructions considered true are contingent upon the power relations and the historical context in which they are formulated and acted upon. The question that grounds our attempt to formulate a system of meaning on which to base our curriculum theory and practice asks: If what we designate as truth is relational and not certain, then what set of assumptions can we use to guide our activities as professionals, to inform our questions as teachers, learners, and researchers?

This is why critical pedagogy needs an emancipatory system of meaning so badly. This is why liberation theology is so important to our attempt to develop an emancipatory system of meaning. With its roots deep in the Latin American struggle against poverty and colonialism, liberation theology morally situates our attempt to formulate an explicit set of assumptions, an ethical starting line from which to begin our formulation of educational questions.

Revealing their solidarities, critical teachers operate on the anti-Cartesian assumption that knower and known are inseparable. Learning from the liberation theologian, critical researchers embrace subjugated knowledges, in the process disallowing an objectivist subject-object dualism. When teachers respect subjugated knowledge and the unique perspective of the oppressed, as a matter of course they begin to subvert the relationship of domination that permeates traditional objectivist education. It is a relationship of domination that allows both the manipulation of natural processes to serve the logic of capital (the needs of profit-making) and the manipulation of human beings as the passive objects of social engineering. This separation of knower (the individual who seeks knowledge/insight) and known (the knowledge/insight she seeks), this epistemological distancing, produces a tacit logic of domination between teacher and learner, researcher and researched, and knower and known. Indeed, it is the logic of hierarchy and authoritarianism, not democracy—it is the logic of bad work.

Operating within this domain of Cartesian logic, educational activity has often served the interests of power elites. Critical teaching, with its commitment to the perspective of the oppressed, seeks to confront such consequences. The view from above of the traditional paradigm gives way to views from below.

Emerging from the understanding and research for subjugated knowledge, such a way of knowing not only boasts of ethical assets but holds scientific benefits as well. The scientific dimension revolves around the hierarchical relationship of researcher and researched; much of the information gathered by traditional methods is irrelevant because the subordinate researched, realizing their inferior position, often develop a profound distrust of the researchers interrogating them. Oppressed groups interviewed by researchers from a higher social stratum often provide expected information rather than authentic data. Respect for subjugated knowledge helps researchers construct a research situation where the experience of the marginalized is viewed as an important way of seeing the socioeducational whole, not simply as a curiosity to be reported. Such a research perspective is counter-hegemonic and radically democratic as it uses the voice of the subjugated to formulate a reconstruction of the dominant educational structure. It is a radical reconstruction in the sense that it attempts to empower those who are presently powerless.

With this reconstructive imperative mind, a critical teacher must, as a central task, formulate questions that expose the conditions that promote social and educational advantage and disadvantage. It is obvious to many, for example, that when the methods of evaluation of advocates of the competitive, basics curriculum are employed, non-white and working-class students do not generally do well—their performance is interpreted as a manifestation of slowness, of inferior ability. Researchers devise tests to evaluate school, student, and teacher performance, forgetting throughout the process that evaluation is based on uncritically grounded definitions of intelligence and performance. The definitions of intelligence and performance employed are not generated by the marginalized. When liberals attempt, for example, to develop curricula or initiate research based on recognition of marginalized experiences, they miss the lessons provided by an understanding of subjugated knowledges. Subjugated knowledges are knowledges possessed by groups and individuals with low sociocultural and economic status that are ridiculed and dismissed by schools and other institutions of the dominant culture. A common liberal reform involves including women or blacks in a history curriculum that has traditionally emphasized committing famous facts (especially military facts) to memory. Such inclusion is a tokenism that perpetuates the power relations of the status quo. Another such reform might involve making sure that survey respondents include a percentage of women and minorities.

When teachers are grounded in an emancipatory system of meaning based on liberation theology, they develop a view from below—the double consciousness of the oppressed. If they are to survive, subjugated groups develop an understanding of those who control them (e.g., slaves' insight into the manners, eccentricities, and fears of their masters); at the same time they are cognizant of the everyday mechanisms of oppression, seeing the way such technologies shape their consciousness, their lived realities. Because of their class, race, and gender, many educators are insulated from the benefits of the double consciousness of

the subjugated and are estranged from a visceral appreciation of suffering. Contemporary social organization, thus, is viewed from a lens that portrays it as acceptable. Why would such teachers challenge research methods and modes of interpretation that justify the prevailing system of education? Which lived experience would create in the minds of such teachers an ethical dissonance that would make them uncomfortable with status quo?

This points us to an appreciation of liberation theology's notion of difference. Liberation theologian Sharon Welch (1985) maintains the pedagogical, political, and ethical value of heterogeneous communities. A homogeneous community too often is unable to criticize the injustice and the exclusionary practices that affect a social system. Criticism and reform of cultural pathology often comes from the recognition of difference—from interaction with communities who do not suffer the same injustices or have dealt with them in different ways.

Liberation theology sophisticates our system of meaning, inducing us to appreciate that we always profit in some way from a confrontation with another system of defining what is important. Consciousness itself is spawned by difference. In other words, we gain our first awareness of who we are when we understand that we exist independent of others. Critical postmodern teaching, therefore, values difference—but it is a difference grounded on solidarity. Solidarity is to be distinguished from consensus. Solidarity is based on two main points: (1) The first is that an ethic of solidarity grants social groups enough respect to listen to their ideas and to use them to consider or reconsider existing social values. (2) The second is that the ethic of solidarity realizes that the lives of individuals in differing groups are interconnected to the point that everyone is accountable to everyone else. No assumption of consensus or uniformity exists with this ethic—just a commitment to work together to bring about mutually beneficial social change.

In the classroom, this valuing of difference brings political and cognitive benefits. We see these benefits, for example, in a dialogical sharing of perspectives. In this process, students slowly come to see their own points of view as one particular socially and historically constructed way of perceiving. As the inclusive classroom develops, students are exposed to more and more diverse voices in various texts and discussions—a process that engages them in other ways of seeing and knowing. Thus, their cognitive circle is widened as difference expands their social imagination or, in other words, as their vision of what could be expands.

This liberationist theological valuing of difference holds a synergistic relationship with feminist notions of personal knowing—this is the passionate participation of the knower in the act of knowing. The emancipatory system of meaning is grounded on the interaction of these notions, as critical postmodern teachers embrace a passionate scholarship, a reconceptualized pedagogy that is grounded upon and motivated by our values and solidarities.

Søren Kierkegaard anticipated this notion of feminist passion, arguing in the first half of the nineteenth century that there is an intimate connection between commitment and knowing (see Anderson, 2000). Subjectivity, he maintained, is not simply arbitrary—instead, it reflects the most profound connection between an individual thinker and the world. As inquirers grow passionate about what they know, they develop a deeper relationship with themselves. Such a relationship produces a self-knowledge that

initiates a synergistic cycle, a cycle that grants them more insight into the issue being investigated. Soon, Kierkegaard argued, a form of personal knowledge is developed that orients the mind to see social life as more than a set of fixed laws. Social life is better characterized as a process of being, a dialectic where the knower's personal participation in events and the emotional insight gained from such participation moves us to a new dimension of knowing.

Another precursor of the feminist notion of passionate scholarship that shapes our system of meaning (and should serve to humble Eurocentric academicians) concerns the ways indigenous peoples have defined knowing. Note the similarities of Afrocentric and American Indian ways of knowing with anti-Cartesian perspectives of Kierkegaard, Polanyi, and modern feminists. To such peoples reality has never been dichotomized into spiritual and material segments. Self-knowledge lays the foundation for all knowledge in the African and Native American epistemologies. Great importance has traditionally been placed on interpersonal relationships (solidarity), and diunital logic has moved these traditions to appreciate the continuum of spirit and matter, individual and world. Indeed, indigenous ways of knowing the European Cartesian tradition come into direct conflict over the epistemological issues of mind and body, individuals and nature, self and other, spirit and matter, and knower and known—a conflict that has generated serious historical consequences. It is only in the last 30 years that some Eurocentric people have come to recognize the epistemological sophistication of the indigenous paradigm that recognizes a unity of all things and a connected spiritual energy embedded in both human and natural elements. Thus, that deemed primitive by traditional Western scholars becomes, from the perspective of critical postmodern teachers, a valuable source of insight into our attempt to reconceptualize an emancipatory system of meaning grounded on liberation theology's epistemological identification with the perspective of the oppressed.

Antonio Gramsci well understood some of these same epistemological concepts as he wrote from Mussolini's prisons. The eclectic base of our emancipating system of meaning grows more obvious as we combine liberation theology's ethical base with feminist analysis, Faucault's poststructuralism, anti-Cartesian notions of personal knowledge, the Frankfurt school, and Gramscian critical theory. Gramscian critical theory fits the emancipatory jigsaw puzzle because it argued that the intellectual's error consists of believing that one can know without "feeling and being impassioned." The role of intellectuals and teachers from Gramsci's (1988) perspective revolved around their attempt to connect logic and emotions in order for them to "feel" the elementary passions of the people. Such an emotional connection would allow the cultural worker to facilitate the struggle of men and women to locate their lived worlds in history. Finding themselves in history, they would be empowered by a consciousness constructed by a critically distanced view of the ways that the structural forces of history shape lives. One cannot make history without this passion, without this connection of feeling and knowing, since without it the relationship between the people and intellectuals is reduced to a hierarchial formality. Without passion the logic of bureaucracy prevails as intellectuals move to the higher rungs of the organizational ladder, assuming the privileges of a superior caste, a modern Egyptian priesthood. From the ethical starting point

provided by liberation theology, critical pedagogy builds its eclectic system of meaning, thus extending our ability to critique the so-called knowledge base of education and to formulate methods and questions for our work as teachers and researchers. We are better equipped to monitor our movement into another socioeducational dimension, a land of uncertainty where the traditional rules of knowing no longer apply. On the postmodern terrain we find a world where the distortions of the Cartesian dualism are exposed, where multiple ways of knowing are sought and valued. In this land where the rational voice is no longer a universal one, we are provided a vantage point from which to watch the evolution of critical pedagogy. Liberation theology is central to that evolution. It is central to our attempt to bring meaning to our lives and our work.

References

Anderson, S. (2000). *On Kierkegaard*. Belmont, CA: Wadsworth/Thomson Learning.

Freire, P. (1970). *Pedagogy of the Oppressed*. New York: Herder and Herder.

Gramsci, A. (1988). *An Antonio Gramsci Reader*. D. Forgacs (Ed.). New York: Schocken Books.

Welch, S. (1985). *Communities of Resistance and Solidarity*. Maryknoll, NY: Orbis Books.

Shirley R. Steinberg

CUBAN STUDENTS IN U.S. SCHOOLS

Although Cubans have lived in the U.S. for over a century and a half, they were a very small number of the Latino population until after the Cuban revolution of 1959. Beginning in the early 1960s, Cubans began arriving, especially in South Florida, and settling there or in other parts of the U.S. The 2000 census showed that there were more than 1.2 million living in the U.S.

(Boswell, 2002, p. 5). This represents 3.7% of the Latino population and makes Cuban Americans the third largest Latino group in this nation. (Ramirez & de la Cruz, 2002, p. 1). The Cuban population is heavily concentrated in Miami–Ft. Lauderdale (56%), followed by New York–New Jersey (11%), Greater Los Angeles (4%), and the Tampa, Florida, metropolitan area (3%) (Boswell, 2002, p. 5).

Cuban Americans have higher educational levels than other Latino groups in the U.S. They are more likely to have graduated from high school (74%) than Central Americans (70.8%), South Americans (66.8%), Puerto Ricans (64.7%) or Mexicans (50.6%). They are also more likely (18.6%) to have graduated from college than Central or South Americans (17.3%) or Mexicans (7.6%) (Ramirez & de la Cruz, 2002, p. 5). What accounts for the academic and subsequently higher socioeconomic position of Cuban Americans? Although higher than other Latino groups, both are slightly below the overall median for the U.S.

Some have suggested that Cubans in the U.S. represent a "model Latino minority." This label is not a fair description of Cubans in the U.S., nor is it a fair comparison with other Latino groups. Among the reasons for the educational achievement of Cuban Americans is that the Cuban migration to the U.S. contained a disproportionate number of immigrants with higher levels of education than most other immigrant groups have. This is especially true for immigrants in the decade of the 1960s, but later Cuban immigrants have tended to be more representative of the overall Cuban population. When well-educated immigrants settle in another country, they bring with them substantial "human capital" (education as well as success in business and the professions) even if they do not speak the language of their new nation. With time these immigrants learn the new language and are able to give greater academic and more economic support to their children than are immigrant parents who lack similar levels of education. One study of immigrant children in San Diego and Miami found that immigrant students who retained a strong family and cultural identity tended to outpace others in school, including their native-born Euro-American peers (Zhou, 1997, p. 80). These findings suggest that that maintaining fluency in Spanish and identity with Cuban culture have been educational assets, not detriments, to Cuban American students.

Another variable that sheds some light on Cuban American educational achievement concerns reverse migration. Nearly all Cubans who immigrated to the U.S. do not see reverse migration to Cuba as a viable possibility while the Castro government is in power. Even if political and economic circumstances were to change, one study found that 74% would not return to reside in Cuba (Gomez & Rothe, 2004, p. 60). Therefore, the imperative to achieve educationally may be a little greater for Cuban Americans than for other immigrant groups who see reverse migration to their country of origin at least as a realistic possibility.

One study of Hispanic youth in Miami looked at the use of English and Spanish among high schools seniors. This sample was composed of mostly Cuban American youth. The study found that they used English far more frequently in formal settings and Spanish was more prevalent in informal settings. However, one unexpected finding was that English was the preferred language among siblings. This suggests that although the study subjects were bilingual at the time of the study, English used in the personal domain could signal a shift, in time, toward English monolingualism (Garcia & Diaz, 1992, p. 24). Most Cubans in the U.S. would like to see their children become bilingual and biliterate in Spanish and English. Although Cuban Americans have a good educational track record among Hispanic Americans, time will tell whether this goal of Cuban parents will be achieved or will remain as elusive as it has been for many other immigrant groups.

References

Boswell, T. (2002). *A Demographic Profile of Cuban Americans*. Miami: Cuban American National Council.

Garcia, R. L., & Diaz, C. F. (1992). The Status and Use of Spanish and English among Hispanic Youths in Dade County (Miami), Florida. *Language and Education* 6(1), 13–32.

Gomez, A. S., & Rothe, E. M. (2004). *Value Orientations and Opinions of Recently Arrived Cubans in Miami*. Miami: University of Miami Institute for Cuban American Studies.

Ramirez, R. R., & de la Cruz, G. P. (2002). *The Hispanic Population of the United States: March 2002, Current Population Reports* (P20-545). Washington, DC: U.S. Census Bureau.

Zhou, M. (1997). Growing Up American: the Challenge Confronting Immigrant Children and the Children of Immigrants. *Annual Review of Sociology* 23, 63–95.

Recommended Reading

Diaz, C. F. (2003). Cuban Americans: Concepts, Strategies and Materials. In J. A. Banks. (Ed.), *Teaching Strategies for Ethnic Studies*. Boston: Allyn & Bacon.

Carlos F. Diaz

D

DEFICIT PERSPECTIVES: TRANSCENDING DEFICIT THINKING ABOUT LATINO/A PARENTS

To transcend is to rise above oppressive frameworks that misrepresent Latinos/as and perpetuate mistaken assumptions with dire consequences for the education of Latinos/as. Deficit thinking about Latino/a parents is about misperceptions of Latinos/as and the construction of difference as deficiency. Deficit thinking about Latino/a parents includes perspectives that attribute academic underachievement to cultural deficit theories, to a culture of poverty, and to social capital ideas. Deficit views mistake cause for effect. Such thinking is trait-based, for it categorizes Latinos/as. Whereas many oppose overt deficit thinking, covert deficit thinking, or what have become naturalized ways of thinking about Latinos/as, is present when a dominant group's behavior, thinking, or ways of doing are considered the norm. Deficit thinking is about the naturalization of categories that separate groups of people within hierarchies. As the classifications become enfolded into educational institutions and political infrastructures, they become firmly entrenched. Deficit thinking about Latino/a parents, for example, is pervasive in parenting literature that utilizes as normative, notions or conceptions of parenting, parenting styles, and parental involvement, based on middle-class monolingual Standard English speakers. In addition, to group all Latino/a parents within the same set is to make invisible their heterogeneity.

Parenting Styles

Deficit thinking is based on the construction of difference as deficiency (Cole, 1996; Rogoff, 2003). For an overview of the evolution of deficit thinking and its characteristics, beyond the purposes of this entry, consult Valencia (1997). In brief, however, Valencia identifies several characteristics of deficit thinking, including blaming the victim, oppression, pseudoscience (false persuasion by scientific pretense), and educability, Following is an example of how some of the characteristics of deficit thinking proposed by Valencia exist in conceptualizations of Latino/a parenting style.

Authoritarian parenting, high in parental control and low in parental responsiveness, prevails in Latino/a homes (Arzubiaga, Ceja, & Artiles, 2000). This style of parenting has been associated with lower scholastic achievement even when the association of authoritarian parenting and achievement appears weak in relationship to school grades for Latino/a males. In contrast, *authoritative parenting,* defined as high both in parental control and in parental responsiveness, prevails in middle-class Anglo Standard English speakers' homes. At the same time, authoritative parenting style has been associated with higher competence and achievement.

The imposition of the parenting style classification leads to blaming Latino/a parents for the lower scholastic achievement of their children. Regardless of the findings that the association between parenting styles and achievement does not hold true for Latino males, the negative implications of the authoritarian parenting label is entrenched in the ways of understanding parenting and associated with Latinos/as as a group. In this manner, Latino/a parents, as authoritarian, are conceived as guilty of providing parenting unconducive to achievement. Furthermore, the parenting classification itself reflects the hegemony or dominance of the middle-class English speakers' parenting because it is this population, and not Latinos/as or other groups, that establishes the reference norm for good parenting. The authoritarian label that has become associated with Latino/a parents is based on false assumptions, in a sense part of a process of false persuasion by scientific pretense, because the association between authoritarian parenting and achievement did not hold true for Latino boys. Nonetheless, the assumption, that authoritarian parenting, which is less adequate, prevails in Latino/a homes. From this perspective, Latino/a parenting is in need of change— and the change needed is toward the authoritative parenting that is the norm. The implication is that Latino/a parents need education and training for what they lack, which in this case is understood as parenting skills conducive to school achievement.

Latino Values/Beliefs

Cultural deficit theories about Latino/a parents misrepresent Latino/a values or beliefs. Among cultural deficit theories is the misconception that Latino/a parents do not value education. To the contrary, Latino/a parents, regardless of income level, hold high regard for the education of their children and can actively participate in their education (e.g., Delgado-Gaitán, 1990, 1992, 1993; Gándara, 1995). Latino/a parents' involvement in schools is misunderstood, however, and this has dire consequences for children's education because parental involvement in school is associated with children's academic success (Eccles & Harold, 1996; Epstein, 1986). Latino/a parents' school involvement is misunderstood because it may not include the behaviors or practices associated with parental involvement, such as active participation in parent association meetings. The problem is further confounded because immigrant Latino/a parents have limited understandings about how schools function in the U.S. (Delgado-Gaitán, 1992, 1993; Gándara, 1995; Lareau, 1996; Valdés, 1996), but not limited understandings about their children's education. Their limited understandings about schools, however, can lead school personnel to confirm or form the misconception that Latino/a families lack the ability and knowledge to help their children. In fact, educators continue to blame Latino/a parents for their children's school failure (e.g., Moles, 1993). They also fail to include and build on the cultural resources of Latino/a families.

Deficit theories based on a culture-of-poverty perspective make the assumption that parents are unable to provide their children with the environments they need to develop skills for success. The argument is that because parents do not socialize their children in the dominant culture, educational institutions need to compensate for all the skills children fail to receive at home. Like deficit theories, social capital theories also construct deficit views of parents (Rueda, Monzó, & Arzubiaga, 2003). Social capital is generally defined as the social networks that allow access to cultural capital or ability to secure benefits by virtue of access to social networks (Portes, 1998). In this sense, social capital affords opportunities to access cultural capital. The deficit view is that Latino/a parents do not have social capital and therefore also lack cultural capital. This deficit thinking has flaws. Latino/a parents do have social capital as well as cultural capital. In fact, when teachers approached Latino/a households to learn from them, they found that parents used networks, resources, and skills that would otherwise have gone unnoticed (e.g., Moll, Amanti, Neff, & Gonzales 1992, 1997). This line of research is referred to as "funds of knowledge" research. Recent studies intended to identify funds of mathematical skills within homes have also revealed a host of mathematical skills (Gonzales, Andrade, Civil, & Moll, 2001).

The deficit view surrounding social capital theories prevails, however, because the networks of underrepresented groups such as Latino/a parents are not recognized. In the same manner, Latino/a families' funds of knowledge are not part of what counts as "scientific" or legitimate knowledge or skills. In addition, understanding social capital or cultural knowledge as static or fixed ignores how social capital and cultural capital are dynamic and socially constructed in everyday activities.

Trait-Based Thinking

Deficit thinking is trait based and categorical thinking about Latina/o parents. Trait-based thinking, or attributing characteristics to a group of people, such as describing Latino/a parents as collectivistic or family, oriented, leads to deficit thinking. For example, collectivism is considered detrimental to children's achievement because unlike individualism, which is associated with competitiveness, individuals do not seek to stand out but, rather, seek the benefit of the group. However, although collectivistic behaviors served Latino/a parents well within certain circumstances, these behaviors do not make these parents collectivistic. As Gutiérrez and Rogoff (2003) argue, in this case the collectivistic practices are merely part of the repertoire of practices available to parents. A different set of circumstances may call for other behaviors or practices.

Transcending deficit thinking about Latino/a parents is about refusing to construct difference as deficit and about questioning and challenging cultural, culture-of-poverty, and social capital deficit views. It is about re-imagining parenting, parental involvement, and conceptions, such as parenting style, that perpetuate deficit views about Latino/a parents. The quest for equity in the education of Latino/a learners calls for research that emerges from studies that do not cluster Latinos/as as one monolithic group but, rather, considers their heterogeneity. More important, however, is to transcend deficit thinking about Latino/a parents to account for multiple ways of parenting as well as acknowledge the diverse ways parents provide their children with knowledge and skills.

References

Arzubiaga, Angela, Ceja, Miguel, & Artiles, Alfredo. (2000). Transcending Deficit Thinking about Latinos' Parenting Styles: Toward an Ecocultural View of Family Life. In Carlos Tejeda, Corinne Martinez, & Zeus Leonardo (Eds.), *Charting New Terrains of Chicana(o)/Latina(o) Education* (pp. 93–106). Cresskill, NY: Hampton Press.

Cole, Michael. (1996). *Cultural Psychology: A Once and Future Discipline*. Cambridge, MA: Harvard University Press.

Delgado-Gaitán, Concha. (1990). *Literacy for Empowerment: The Role of Parents in Children's Education*. New York: Falmer Press.

Delgado-Gaitán, Concha. (1992). School Matters in the Mexican-American Home: Socializing Children to Education. *American Educational Research* 29(3), 495–513.

Delgado-Gaitán, Concha. (1993). Parenting in Two Generations of Mexican-American Families. *International Journal of Behavioral Development* 16(3), 409–427.

Eccles, Jacquelynne S., & Harold, Rena D. (1996). Family Involvement in Children's and Adolescents' Schooling. In Allen Booth & Judith F. Dunn (Eds.), *Family School Links: How Do They Affect Educational Outcomes?* (pp. 3–34). Mahwah, NJ: Lawrence Erlbaum.

Epstein, Joyce L. (1986). Parents' Reactions to Teacher Practices of Parent Involvement. *Elementary School Journal* 86, 277–294.

Gándara, Patricia. C. (1995). *Over the Ivy Walls: The Educational Mobility of Low-Income Chicanos*. Albany, NY: SUNY Press.

Gonzales, Norma, Andrade, Rosi, Civil, Mata, & Moll, Lewis. (2001). Bridging Funds of Distributed Knowledge: Creating Zones of Practices in Mathematics. *Journal of Education for Students Placed At-Risk* 6(1, 2), 115–132.

Gutiérrez, Kris, & Rogoff, Babara. (2003). Cultural Ways of Learning: Individual Traits or Repertoires of Practice. *Educational Researcher* 32, 19–25.

Lareau, Annette. (1996). Assessing Parental Involvement in Schooling: A Critical Analysis. In Allen Booth Judith F. Dunn (Eds.), *Family School Links: How do They Affect Educational Outcomes?* (pp. 57–64). Mahwah, NJ: Lawrence Erlbaum.

Moles, Oliver C. (1993). Collaboration between Schools and Disadvantaged Parents: Obstacles and Openings. In Nancy F. Chavkin (Eds.), *Families and Schools in a Pluralistic Society* (pp. 21–49). Albany, NY: SUNY Press.

Moll, Luis, Amanti, Cathy, Neff, Deborah, & Gonzales, Norma. (1992). Funds of Knowledge for Teaching: Using a Qualitative Approach to Developing Strategic Connections between Homes and Classrooms. *Theory into Practice* 31, 132–141.

Moll, Luis, & Gonzales, Norma. (1997). Teachers as Social Scientists: Learning about Culture from Household Research. In Peter M. Hall (Ed.), *Race, Ethnicity and Multiculturalism: Policy and Practice* (pp. 89–114). New York: Garland.

Portes, Alejandro. (1998). Social Capital: Its Origins and Applications in Modern Sociology. *Annual Review of Sociology* 24, 1–24.

Rogoff, Barabara. (2003). *The Cultural Nature of Human Development*. New York: Oxford University Press.

Rueda, Robert, Monzó, Lilia D., & Arzubiaga, Angela. (2003). Academic Instrumental Knowledge: Deconstructing Cultural Capital Theory for Strategic Intervention Approaches. *Current Issues in Education* 6(14). Available: http://cie.ed.asu.edu/volume6/number14/(Accessed April 25, 2005).

Valdes, Guadalupe. (1996). *Con respeto: Bridging the Distances between Culturally Diverse Families and Schools: An Ethnographic Portrait*. New York: Teachers College Press.

Valencia, Richard (Ed.). (1997). *The Evolution of Deficit Thinking: Educational Thought and Practice*. London: Falmer Press.

Angela E. Arzubiaga

DROPOUT RATES

The Latino dropout—comprising about half of the Latino secondary school population—is usually male in an urban setting. He typically leaves high school early in his experience, finding the transition from eighth to ninth grade very difficult. He fails courses quickly, and with little chance for recovery finds himself rapidly submerged in a downward spiral of lost credits with restricted opportunities for extracurricular activities such as sports, an area that might have motivated him not to give up on the classes he finds so difficult. His academic English language skills are weak, making content area reading and writing very challenging. English language learners' (ELLs) needs went largely unaddressed in his elementary school years, where a pull-out English as a Second Language (ESL) program was all that was reluctantly offered. He frequently deals with bona fide learning disabilities that fester unremediated as well. His parents do not speak, read, or write much English and have had little formal schooling in their country of origin, which is usually Mexico, from where two-thirds of the Latino U.S. population originates (Rumberger, 1991). Therefore, they cannot help their son with his homework and often do not understand the types of academic support he desperately needs. Even if they did comprehend his challenges in schooling, they could not afford private professional tutoring for him nor could they finance a computer and tutorial software. They also do not know of their rights to demand diagnostic testing in their son's dominant language and the free and appropriate remediation he needs to succeed in school. In fact, they would find it very difficult to question *la maestra,* the teacher, whom they have been raised to trust to do the best thing for their child in the arena of schooling. Parent-teacher conferences also baffle them because in their experience with schooling in Mexico, meetings for parents were warm, friendly events that filled an entire evening. A 5–10 minute slot to talk to their son's teacher makes no sense to them, for properly greeting someone of the stature of a teacher would itself take 15 minutes. Because Latino dropouts' parents often work shifts and usually accept all the overtime they can handle because their income is at the poverty level, it is also difficult for them to justify losing a day or an evening of work for the sake of a 10-minute meeting in a language they do not fully comprehend, particularly when it includes educational jargon. Bosses in factories do not take kindly to absences, and, as is often the case, with four younger children at various school levels, parents' meetings mount up quickly. Latino parents would never jeopardize their chance to work, for unskilled labor is hard to find in this economy, and their family's economic survival depends on their employment.

Latino dropouts often report feeling that no one cared about them in their frequently large, minority concentration, urban high school. In fact, because Low-achieving Latinos pull down the school's standardized testing scores, so important to the Bush administration's No Child Left Behind (NCLB) program operating in all U.S. school districts, it makes sense to push out low-achieving Latino secondary students who jeopardize their school's chances for funding. Further, because of loopholes in NCLB, dropouts can now be reported as transfer students and thus no longer have any negative impact at all on school achievement or student attrition records (Midwest Conference on the Dropout Crisis, 2004).

In lieu of turning to a supportive network of teachers and leisure activities directed by inner-city schools or urban community organizations, which have lost much of their funding under the Bush government, the Latino dropout may find security and solace in joining a neighborhood gang. It is easy to hide this affiliation from parents who work long hours and have many children's mouths to feed. In their naïveté, often coming from small, rural towns in central Mexico, the dropout's parents frequently care unaware of the signs of urban gang activity. Their deep cultural belief in *la familia,* the centrality of family in one's life, called "familism" in sociological jargon (Cauce & Domenech-Rodríguez, 2002) makes it hard for them to comprehend their child's desire to belong to a gang.

The Latino dropout has difficulty finding legitimate employment that pays above the minimum wage; so when, for example, a gang buddy asks him to deliver an unopened package to a specific address and promises to pay well for doing so, it is done, no questions asked. Although the dropout quickly realizes that these deliveries must involve drugs, being a drug courier is better than eking out an existence as the working poor. For his entire life he has witnessed his parents and relatives doing just that, expending their energy, health, and joy with little to show for their labor.

Eventually, the Latino dropout can become part of yet another statistic, one of the 75% of jailed minority youth that did not go beyond the tenth grade (Wold & Losen, 2004) as he becomes more and more entangled in gang activities and, for example, gets arrested for possession of cocaine. The dropout's parents are ashamed and, at a time when the dropout's siblings are finishing school and the parents' lives are a bit less hectic, they are now saddled with raising the dropout's 4-year-old daughter, born out of wedlock. But they accept her with open arms and absorb her lovingly into their large family, the beloved granddaughter bequeathed to them by the lost sheep of their fold, their son who dropped out and left a gaping hole in the fabric of their American dream.

Latino dropouts, products of a school system that often fails to acknowledge their cultural strengths, ignores their native language, and offers a curriculum that is meaningless in their lived experiences, are victims of the tragic unresponsiveness of a society that does not value them. Yet those Latino dropouts who do not succumb to the unemployment-to-prison pipeline often become the backbone of the blue-collar and service economy of many U.S. cities. They mow lawns, wash the dishes, sew the clothing, mop the floors, pour the concrete, and work on assembly lines in a myriad of small factories. Others return to the border towns and pick the crops that make their way to our nation's tables. They believe in close family ties, follow organized religion, and have hope for the higher education of the next generation, despite their own dismal school experiences. And they often have a broader sense of what it means to have a well-educated child, one who not only attends to school work but is also respectful and responsible. Their lives and those of their families resemble, in many ways, the lives of the great waves of European immigrants that built modern America at the turn of the twentieth century. But their ardent retention of their native language and cultural ties, their refusal to be completely absorbed into the American melting pot philosophy, sets them apart from mainstream western European origin of America and keeps them "down" in the eyes of many. The Latino dropout, a uniquely American story, begs sentient pedagogical attention; begs culturally responsive resolution.

References

Cauce, A. M., & Domenech-Rodríguez, M. (2002). Latino Families: Myth and Realities. In J. M. Contreras, K. A. Kerns, & A. M. Neal-Barnett (Eds.), *Latino Children and Families in the United States: Current Research and Future Directions* (pp. 3–26). Westport, CT: Praeger.

Recommended Reading

Midwest Conference on the Dropout Crisis: Assessing the Problem and Confronting the Challenge. (2004). Chicago, IL, March 19.

Rumberger, R. W. (1991). Chicano Dropouts: A Review of Research and Policy Issues. In R. R. Valencia (Ed.), *Chicano School Failure and Success: Research and Policy Agendas for the 1990s* (pp. 64–90). London: Falmer Press.

Wold, J., & Losen, D. (2004). *Defining and Redirecting a School-to-Prison Pipeline*. Cambridge, MA: Harvard Civil Rights Project.

Chris Liska Carger

DUAL-LANGUAGE PROGRAMS

Public schools throughout the country are grappling with the academic achievement of children who enter school speaking a language other than English. In this era of accountability and consequent requirement that all students are academically successful, schools must pay closer attention to meeting the educational needs of their linguistically and ethnically diverse student populations if they are to make adequate progress toward reaching national and state academic targets. As educators seek solutions to this issue by reviewing the body of effective school research and best practices, they are looking with tremendous interest to the success of students in Two-Way Bilingual Immersion (TWBI) education programs throughout the country.

TWBI programs have become increasingly popular throughout the country as educators utilize second language learning for all students as a catalyst to propel their reform efforts. The analysis of longitudinal data from programs that have successfully implemented their TWBI models indicate that students participating in these program are in fact "closing the achievement gap." Students graduate from TWBI programs with high levels of bilingualism and biliteracy as well as grade-level and above-grade-level performance in other academic areas. This entry describes the TWBI program design and implementation issues and program outcomes for secondary students who participated in TWBI programs throughout elementary school. Because the focus here is on Latino students, discuss the model evaluation outcomes with particular respect to Latino students—both immigrant Spanish speakers and later-generation English speakers.

What Is Two-Way Bilingual Immersion Education?

Two-way bilingual immersion, or TWBI, education goes by many different names: Two-way bilingual immersion, dual-language immersion, dual-language education, bilingual immersion, or even Spanish immersion. There are approximately 260 TWBI programs in public schools throughout the US, though most of them are Spanish/English programs that primarily serve Latino and Anglo students.

TWBI programs combine features of full bilingual education for native Spanish speakers and early total immersion education for English-speaking students. Native Spanish and native English speakers are integrated for academic instruction that is presented separately through two languages. For both groups of students, one of the languages is their native language and one is a second language. The definition of TWBI education encompasses four critical features: (1) The program essentially involves some form of two-way bilingual instruction, where Spanish is used for a significant portion of the students' instructional day; (2) the program involves periods of instruction during which only one language is used; (3) both native English speakers and Spanish speakers are participants in a fairly balanced proportion; and (4) the students are integrated for most content instruction.

The major goals of the program are that (1) students will develop high levels of proficiency in both Spanish and English; (2) academic performance will be at or above grade level as measured in both languages, and (3) students will have high levels of psychosocial competence and positive cross-cultural attitudes. Traits characterizing TWBI programs are well documented (see Christian, Montone, Lindholm, & Carranza, 1997; Lindholm-Leary & Molina, 2000; Lindholm-Leary, 2001).

There are two common instructional designs in TWBI programs. In California, most programs follow the 90:10 model, whereas outside of California the majority of programs use the 50:50 model. The distribution of languages for instruction varies across the grade levels in the 90:10, but not 50:50, design. In the 90:10 model, in kindergarten and first grade, 90% of the instructional day is devoted to content instruction in Spanish and 10% to English. Thus, all content instruction occurs in Spanish, and English time is used to develop oral language proficiency. Reading instruction begins in Spanish for both Spanish- and English-speaking students. In grades 2–3, students receive 80% of their day in Spanish and 20% in English. As in the previous grade levels, most content is taught in Spanish. In second grade, English time is still largely spent in developing preliteracy skills and academic language proficiency. Students begin formal English reading in third grade. By fourth and fifth grades, the students' instructional time is balanced between English and Spanish. In the 50:50 model, instructional time is evenly divided between the two languages across all grade levels, as it is in grades 4–5 for the 90:10 model. However, reading instruction begins in both languages at some 50:50 sites; at other 50:50 sites, reading instruction initially occurs in the student's native language and reading instruction in the second language is added in grade 2 or 3.

For both the 90:10 and 50:50 models, the content areas taught in each language depend on the available curriculur materials and supporting resource materials and on particular needs at each school site. However, an attempt is made to assure that students are given opportunities to develop academic language in each of the major curricular areas.

Effective Program Features

Over the past several years a large body of literature has emerged on effective schools. There are several critical characteristics of effective schools that have implications for the success of implementing language education programs in general, but two-way bilingual immersion programs in particular (see Lindholm-Leary, 2001; Lindholm-Leary & Borsato, 2006).

School Environment. Research on effective programs clearly demonstrates that an effective program is integrated within the total school program, is supported by the school district administration and local board of education, and has a principal who is very supportive of and knowledgeable about the program. Studies of effective schools consistently and conclusively demonstrate that high-quality programs exist when schools have a cohesive schoolwide shared vision and a set of goals that define their expectations for achievement, as well as an instructional focus and commitment to achievement and high expectations that are shared by students, parents, teachers, and administrators (e.g., Corallo & McDonald, 2002; Marzano, 2003; Montecel & Cortez, 2002; Reyes, Scribner, & Paredes Scribner, 1999). At effective two-way schools, there is also a shared vision and goals focused on bilingualism, biliteracy, and multiculturalism. Establishing a vision of bilingualism and multicultural competence requires a clear understanding of and equitable treatment directed toward the needs of culturally and linguistically diverse students, as well as integrating multicultural themes into instruction (Lindholm-Leary, 2001; Lindholm-Leary & Molina, 2000). While important in other schools, equity is crucial in the two-way program model with its emphasis on integrating students of different ethnic, language, and social-class backgrounds.

Curriculum and Instruction. Studies show that more successful schools and programs have a curriculum that has been developed so that it establishes a clear alignment to standards and assessment; is meaningful and academically challenging and incorporates higher-order thinking; is thematically integrated; and is enriched, rather than remedial in nature (Cloud, Genesee, & Hamayan, 2000; Doherty, Hilberg, Pinal, & Tharp, 2003; Montecel & Cortez, 2002). Further, students in the two-way program receive the same high-quality and enriched curriculum as students in the English mainstream program.

Because of the vision and goals associated with bilingualism and biliteracy, language instruction is integrated within the curriculum. However, language objectives should be incorporated into the curriculum planning, and language and literature should be developed across the curriculum (Doherty et al., 2003) to ensure that students learn the content as well as the academic language associated with the content. Further, since the vision and goals also include multicultural competence and equity, the curriculum needs to reflect and value the students' culture(s) (Berman et al., 1995; Corallo & McDonald, 2002).

A number of strategies under the rubric of cooperative learning have been developed that appear to optimize student interactions and shared work experiences. Studies suggest that when ethnically and linguistically diverse students work interdependently on school tasks with common objectives, students' expectations and attitudes toward each other become more positive, their academic achievement improves, and their development of the second language is enhanced (Berman et al., 1995; Cohen & Lotan, 1995; Slavin & Calderón, 2001).

Promoting highly proficient oral language skills necessitates providing both structured and unstructured opportunities for oral production (Saunders, 2006). It also necessitates establishing and enforcing a strong language policy in the classroom that encourages students to use the instructional language and discourages students from speaking the non-instructional language (Lindholm-Leary & Molina, 2000).

Language Distribution and Use. In TWBI programs the two languages are kept distinct and never mixed during instruction. There are several reasons for keeping the languages separate: include (1) It improves the quantity and quality of teacher delivery, particularly the teacher's preparation (e.g., vocabulary, materials) for lesson delivery in Spanish. (2) Students need sustained exposure to Spanish in a variety of contexts to obtain native speaker levels. (3) Spanish needs sociocultural and political protection to assure that English does not encroach in the domains of language use because of its dominant status. (4) Avoidance of language mixing and switching allows for more reliance on comprehensible input, negotiation of meaning, and comprehension checks in both languages.

In most school sites at the early grade levels, teachers may team together so that they are models of only one language. The most common strategy for both the 90:10 and the 50:50 designs is to separate the languages by time of day, so that students study in one language in the morning and another language in the afternoon.

Balancing the Needs of Both Language Groups during Instruction. There is considerable variation in how the English time is used in 90:10 two-way education programs. Unfortunately, not enough attention has been paid to English time in many school sites where English time has been used for assemblies, physical education, or other activities that do not provide a good basis for the development of academic language proficiency in English. It is important that teachers understand what language skills they need to cultivate at each grade level so they develop the academic English language skills necessary for literacy, particularly for students who may not receive literacy training in the home.

Heterogeneous or homogeneous grouping also becomes a major consideration in TWBI programs, where ELL and language majority students can be at very different levels of English language proficiency. The argument in favor of heterogeneous grouping is that it is consistent with the remainder of the day, wherein students receive all their instruction in heterogeneous groups, including language arts in the non-English language. The counterargument, in favor of homogeneous grouping by language background, is that each group's needs can be better met, particularly providing second language learning activities and approaches for the non-English language speakers. There is no research suggesting that one grouping strategy is more effective than another for English language development. However, in successful TWBI programs, there is often a combination of the two strategies. For portions of the week, non-English language speakers receive English Language Development (ELD) instruction and the English speakers work on further English language development. For other portions of the week, the students are kept together and given English oral input through content areas.

Program Planning. The amount of planning within and across grade levels varies by school site, but a higher level of planning and articulation is associated with more successful programs (Corallo & McDonald, 2002; Montecel & Cortez, 2002). Strong planning processes should be in place that focus on meeting the goals of the program (in TWBI, this means promoting the students' bilingualism, biliteracy, and multicultural competence) as well as improving all students' achievement. While programs need to be flexible in understanding how the model can be adapted to their community and students, decisions about modifications should be based on student outcomes, research, and best practices. That is, there should be a clear rationale for modifications, rather than dabbling with whatever new and unproven curricular or instructional approach bandwagon emerges.

Program articulation should be both vertical across grade levels and horizontal within grade levels and should include proper scope, sequence, and alignment with developmentally appropriate practices and language proficiency levels in both languages. If the TWBI program is a strand within the school, then the program planning should be schoolwide and not include only the TWBI program teachers.

Assessment. Most research on effective schools, including effective bilingual and TWBI programs, discusses the important role of assessment and accountability. A substantial number of studies have converged on the significance of using student achievement data to shape and/or monitor their instructional program (see August & Hakuta, 1997). Effective schools use assessment measures that are aligned with the school's vision and goals and appropriate curriculum and related standards. TWBI programs require the use of multiple measures in both languages to assess students' progress toward meeting bilingual and biliteracy goals along with the curricular and content-related goals. Further, it is important to disaggregate the data for identifying and solving issues of curriculum, assessment, and instructional alignment and for accountability purposes (No Child Left Behind Act of 2001, 2002).

Staff Quality and Professional Development. Teachers in language education programs, as in mainstream classrooms, should possess the typical teacher qualities associated with high levels of knowledge relating to the subject matter, curriculum and technology, instructional strategies, assessment, and the importance and ability to reflect on their own teaching (Darling-Hammond, 1998). Effective two-way programs require additional teaching and staff characteristics. Teachers in language education programs need appropriate teaching certificates or credentials, good content knowledge and classroom management

skills, and training with respect to the language education model and appropriate instructional strategies. Teachers in TWBI education programs need native or native-like ability in either or both of the language(s) in which they are instructing—in speaking, listening, reading, and writing skills.

Teachers, although bilingual, may assume monolingual roles when interacting with students. In reality, because of the shortage of bilingual teachers, some English model teachers (providing English instruction only) are English monolinguals. It is important that these teachers be able to at least understand the child's mother tongue in the initial stages of language learning. If the teacher does not understand the native language, then he or she cannot respond appropriately in the second language to the children's utterances in their native language. In this case, comprehensible input, as well as linguistic equity in the classroom, may be severely impaired.

Effective professional development programs tend to align the professional development needs of faculty to the goals and strategies of the instructional program. Researchers and educators have discussed the importance of specialized training in language education pedagogy and curriculum, materials and resources, and assessment (Cloud et al., 2000; Lindholm-Leary & Molina, 2000). Essential training, which is important for any teacher, includes educational pedagogy, standards-based teaching, literacy instruction, sheltered instruction, high standards for all students, and parental and community involvement. To effectively administer and teach in a TWBI program, administrators and teachers also need professional development related to the definition of the TWBI education model and to the theories and philosophies underlying the model. Teachers must be trained in second language and biliteracy development so they understand and incorporate into their teaching knowledge of how languages are learned. To support the acquisition of language and literacy, teachers need to use content pedagogy methods and choose strategies that fit with the goals and needs of TWBI students. If teachers are not trained and do not understand the philosophy behind TWBI education, the program cannot succeed. Likewise, if any of the teachers within a TWBI program are strongly opposed to the model, the program cannot succeed. In addition, Guerrero & Sloan (2001) report that teachers need professional development in Spanish to develop higher levels of proficiency.

Family and Community Involvement. Another important feature of effective programs is the incorporation of parent and community involvement and collaboration with the school (Berman et al., 1995; Marzano, 2003). Effective programs tend to incorporate a variety of home-school collaboration activities. The general outcomes on the part of students are heightened interest in schoolwork and improved achievement and behavior (Berman et al., 1995; Lindholm-Leary, 2001).

Effective TWBI programs make the school environment a welcoming and warm one for parents of all language and cultural groups, where bilingualism is valued and there is a sense of belonging for students and their families. Latino, especially Spanish-speaking, parents are treated equitably, and English-speaking non-Latino parents do not dominate the advisory committees to the exclusion of the non-English-speaking or Latino parents (Lindholm-Leary & Molina, 2000). In addition, when parents come to the school, they must see a reflection of the vision and goals associated with bilingualism and biliteracy—for example, signs are in both languages and front office staff members are bilingual. Another way of providing a warm and welcoming environment is to provide a parent liaison who speaks Spanish and understands the needs of the Latino parents in the community. A parent liaison plans for parent education based on the parents' needs and the model, so they can become advocates for the program and school.

Evaluation Outcomes for Latino Students

Evaluation data were collected from 304 middle school and 116 high school Latino students who had attended a TWBI program at the elementary level and who were currently enrolled in a secondary-level program. In both samples, three-fourths of the students were native Spanish speakers (Spanish bilinguals, or SBs, who started school as English language learners), and one-quarter were native English speakers (English bilinguals, or EBs, who entered school proficient in English). Most of these students came from intact low-income families. About two-thirds of SB and 43% of EB students participated in the free lunch program. Half the mothers of SB students had received only an elementary or junior high education compared to 20% of EB students, and 15% of SBs but 37% of EBs had moms with at least some college background.

Language Proficiency. By grade 6 both SB and EB students who had attended a TWBI program since kindergarten or first grade were rated as proficient in both languages (see, e.g., Lindholm-Leary, 2001). In addition, at two school sites almost all the students who took the Spanish Advanced Placement test received the Advanced Placement credit.

Academic Achievement. Overall, by the eighth grade, both SB and EB students scored at or above grade level in reading achievement according to a norm-refer-enced standardized achievement test given in English (NCE = 48 for SB, and NCE = 65 for EB, where 50 is the average of the norming group at each grade level). Thus, the SB students performed at a similar level and the EB students at a higher level, compared to English monolingual students taught in English-only classrooms. In ad-dition, SB and EB students scored well above average on standardized achieve-ment tests in reading given in Spanish (NCE = 69–71). (Students also scored av-erage to above average in mathematics as measured in both English and Spanish as well.)

Attitudes toward School, Bilingualism, and the Two-Way Program

Students' attitudes toward school are generally very positive and show few dif-ferences among program participants—comparing Latino SB, Latino EB, and Euro EB students (for further information, see Lindholm-Leary & Borsato, 2001; Lind-holm-Leary & Ferrante, 2003). Most stu-dents possess fairly high academic competence and are motivated to do well in school. They believe in the value of edu-cation and strongly believe that getting a good education is the best way to have a better life. Almost all students want a col-lege degree, although Latino students more strongly so than Euro students. They also understand that it is important to get good grades to get into college. Thus, with re-spect to their own academic competence and attitudes toward college, the students have very positive attitudes.

In terms of college preparation, most students engage to some extent in behaviors that are conducive to doing well in college: taking part in classroom discussions, going back over work they do not understand, taking time to figure out schoolwork, and doing their homework on time. In addition, most TWBI students know the entrance re-quirements for various colleges and have attended college presentations at their high school.

The national rate for school dropout for Latino students, especially Latino ELLs, is higher than for any other ethnic group, having risen while that for other groups has fallen (Riley, 2000). Among the TWBI students, most agree that they are not in-clined to drop out of school. Obviously, this is a sample of students who have so far stayed in school. However, even 87% of ninth and tenth graders, together with 93% of eleventh and twelfth graders, say they will *not* drop out of school. Of those who have at least considered dropping out, most say they will stay in school because they need an education. Only a very small per-centage of Euro students, but one-third of EB and almost one-half of SB students, felt that the TWBI program kept them from dropping out of school.

Students' attitudes toward the TWBI program were very positive. Most believed that learning through two languages helped them learn to think better, made them smarter, and helped them do better in school. Students, especially Latinos, felt valued in the TWBI program, were glad they partici-pated in it, and would recommend it to other students. Although most students were in agreement, Latino students felt more strongly that the TWBI program challenged them to do better in school, gave them more confidence to do well in school, and gave them a better education.

Most students rate their school and classroom environments as conducive to learning: they feel safe; discipline is fair; there are few fights among different ethnic groups; there is not much gang activity; they do not feel discriminated against; they perceive that there are teachers who will help them if they need it; and they feel that teachers generally think they are smart.

Students also perceive that their parents expect them to do well in school, expect them to go to college, monitor their homework and friendships, and are supportive of and involved with them. Consistent with other research, even the lowest-educated Latino immigrant parents want to see their children succeed in school and, according to students, monitor the students to try to assure that they do.

Conclusion

The TWBI program has been carefully developed according to the theoretical and empirically based literatures on effective schools and language development to more adequately address the cultural, ethnic, and linguistic diversity represented in TWBI classrooms. It is important to note, however, that not all TWBI program coordinators and staff are aware of all these program features. Thus, the quality and effectiveness of the TWBI model implementation varies tremendously from school to school. Results demonstrate that the TWBI model can be successful: students demonstrated bilingual proficiency, biliteracy, achievement at or above grade level, and positive attitudes. However, variations in outcomes among schools demonstrate the importance of carefully designing the program to meet the educational needs of *both* groups of students—both English learners and English speakers. Only then will we ultimately demonstrate the power of TWBI bilingual immersion programs in promoting educa-

tional success for all Latino student participants.

References

August, D., & Hakuta, K. (1997). *Improving Schooling for Language-Minority Children: A Research Agenda*. Washington, DC: National Academy Press.

Berman, P., Minicucci, C., McLaughlin, B., Nelson, B., & Woodworth, K. (1995). *School Reform and Student Diversity: Case Studies of Exemplary Practices for English Language Learner Students*. Santa Cruz, CA: National Center for Research on Cultural Diversity and Second Language Learning and B. W. Associates.

Christian, D., Montone, C., Lindholm, K., & Carranza, I. (1997). *Profiles in Two-Way Bilingual Education*. Washington, DC: ERIC Clearinghouse Book Series.

Cloud, N., Genesee, F., & Hamayan, E. (2000). *Dual Language Instruction*. Boston: Heinle & Heinle.

Cohen, E. G., & Lotan, R. A. (1995). Producing Equal-Status Interaction in the Heterogeneous Classroom. *American Educational Research Journal* 32(1), 99–120.

Corallo, C., & McDonald, D. H. (2002). *What Works with Low-performing Schools: A Review of Research*. Charleston, WV: AEL, Regional Educational Laboratory, Region IV Comprehensive Center.

Darling-Hammond, L. (1998). Teacher Learning That Supports Student Learning. *Educational Leadership* 55, 6–11.

Doherty, R. W., Hilberg, R. S., Pinal, A., & Tharp, R. G. (2003). Five Standards and Student Achievement. *NABE Journal of Research and Practice* 1, 1–24.

Genesee, F., Lindholm-Leary, K. J., Saunders, W., & Christian, D. (2006). *Educating English Language Learners: A Synthesis of Empirical Evidence*. New York: Cambridge University Press.

Guerrero, M., & Sloan, K. (2001). A Descriptive Analysis of Four Exemplary K–3 Spanish Reading Programs in Texas: Are They

Really Exemplary? *Bilingual Research Journal* 25, 253–280.

Lindholm, K. J. (1997). Two-Way Bilingual Education Programs in the United States. In J. Cummins & D. Corson (Eds.), *Encyclopedia of Language and Education: Vol. 5, Bilingual Education* (pp. 271–280). Boston: Kluwer Academic Publishers.

Lindholm-Leary, K. J. (2001). *Dual Language Education*. Avon, UK: Multilingual Matters.

Lindholm-Leary, K. J. (2003). Guidelines in Evaluating Two-Way Bilingual Immersion Programs. In *Handbook of Two-Way Bilingual Immersion Education*. Sacramento: California Department of Education.

Lindholm-Leary, K. J., & Borsato, G. (2001). *Impact of Two-Way Bilingual Elementary Programs on Students' Attitudes toward School and College* (Research Report 10). Santa Cruz: University of California, Center for Research on Education, Diversity & Excellence.

Lindholm-Leary, K. J., & Borsato, G. (2006). Academic Achievement. In F. Genesee, K. Lindholm-Leary, W. Saunders, & D. Christian (Eds.), *Educating English Language Learners: A Synthesis of Empirical Evidence*. New York: Cambridge University Press.

Lindholm-Leary, K. J., & Ferrante, A. (2003). *Middle School Students' Attitudes toward School and College: Influence of Two-Way Immersion* (Final Report). Santa Cruz: University of California, Center for Applied Linguistics and Center for Research on Education, Diversity & Excellence.

Lindholm-Leary, K. J., & Molina, R. (2000). Two-Way Bilingual Education: The Power of Two Languages in Promoting Educational Success. In J. V. Tinajero & R. A. DeVillar (Eds.), *The Power of Two Languages 2000: Effective Dual-language Use across the Curriculum* (pp. 163–174). New York: McGraw-Hill.

Marzano, R. J. (2003). *What Works in Schools: Translating Research into Action*. Alexan-

dria, VA: Association for Supervision and Curriculum Development.

Montecel, M. R., & Cortez, J. D. (2002). Successful Bilingual Education Programs: Development and the Dissemination of Criteria to Identify Promising and Exemplary Practices in Bilingual Education at the National Level. *Bilingual Research Journal* 26. Available: http://brj.asu.edu.

No Child Left Behind Act of 2001. (2002). Pub. L. No. 107–110, 115 Stat. 1425.

Reyes, P., Scribner, J. D., & Paredes Scribner, A. (Eds.). (1999). *Lessons from High-performing Hispanic Schools: Creating Learning Communities*. New York: Teachers College Press.

Riley, R. (2000). Excelencia para todos— Excellence for All. The Progress of Hispanic Education and the Challenges of a New Century. Remarks as prepared for delivery by the U.S. Secretary of Education.

Saunders, W. (2006). Oral language. In F. Genesee, K. Lindholm-Leary, W. Saunders, & D. Christian (Eds.), *Educating English Language Learners: A Synthesis of Research Evidence*. New York: Cambridge University Press.

Slavin, R. E., & Calderón, M. (2001). *Effective Programs for Latino Students*. Mahwah, NJ: Lawrence Erlbaum Associates.

Web Sites for Two-Way Bilingual Immersion

California Department of Education, http://www.cde.ca.gov/sp/el/ip.

Centre for Applied Linguistics, http://cal.org/twi.

Kathryn Lindholm-Leary, http://lindholm-leary.com.

National Clearinghouse for English Language Acquisition, http://www.ncela.gwu.edu/res about/index.html/twoway.htm.

*Kathryn J. Lindholm-Leary
and Rosa Molina*

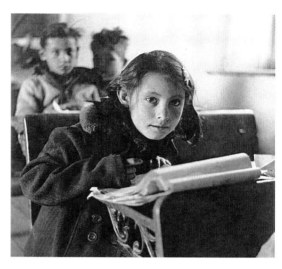

(*Left*) Ignacia Zuniga Saavedra was naturalized as a U.S. citizen in 1997, when she was 90 years old. UT Institute of Texan Cultures at San Antonio, No. 097-0201. Courtesy of Ignacia Saavedra. (*Above*) This young Mexican American student is from the Sarco family. Her photograph reminds us of the hopes, fears, and struggles of Latino children. Courtesy of the Library of Congress.

Young learners posing for a series of photographs entitled "American Education," Yonkers, N.Y. Courtesy of the Library of Congress.

(*Left*) This photo, entitled "Mexican American Children," was taken for Hemisfair 1968. UT Institute of Texan Cultures at San Antonio, No. 068-0615#14. (*Right*) Johnny Hernandez salutes the American flag, 1940s. The San Antonio Light Collection, UT Institute of Texan Cultures at San Antonio, No. L-298-I. Courtesy of the Hearst Corporation.

In this photo entitled "Migrant Farm Workers," children are working alongside their families. The San Antonio Light Collection, UT Institute of Texan Cultures at San Antonio, No. L-7090-71-36a. Courtesy of the Hearst Corporation.

A schoolhouse in Puerto Rico. Courtesy of the Library of Congress.

The entry on the Carlisle Indian School documents how Puerto Rican children were a part of an assimilationist and often genocidal experience. Courtesy of the Library of Congress.

This child is part of the "Mexican American children" series for the 1968 Mexican Texan exhibit at the Institute of Texan Cultures, Hemisfair 1968. UT Institute of Texan Cultures at San Antonio, No. 068-0615-E.

Arthur Campa, a professor at the University of Denver, Dr. George I Sanchez, a professor at the University of Texas at Austin, Joe Castanuela president of a local LULACS, and Ramon Galindo, president of a local Mexican-American Chamber of Commerce, were the principals in the *Delgado v. Bastrop ISD* desegregation case. The San Antonio Light Collection, UT Institute of Texan Cultures at San Antonio, No. L-3594-A Courtesy of the Hearst Corporation.

The depiction of children at the Aibonito, Puerto Rico, school is reminiscent of the complexity of issues faced by Puerto Rican learners. Courtesy of the Library of Congress.

Children in Las Monjas, Puerto Rico, experienced devastating poverty in the 1940s. Courtesy of the Library of Congress.

Puerto Rican children coming home from school in the 1940s. Courtesy of the Library of Congress.

Cantaloupe farmers in Puerto Rico, when a rural life was more prominent. Courtesy of the Library of Congress.

These Puerto Rican children walk through fertile and lush grounds that have been replaced by a commercial landscape. Courtesy of the Library of Congress.

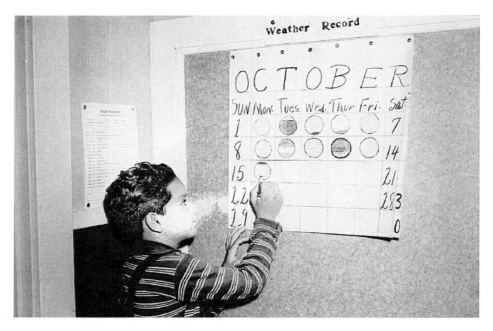

Rudolpho Jimenez, Jr. places information on a classroom weather chart. The San Antonio Light Collection, UT Institute of Texan Cultures at San Antonio, No. L-2271-H. Courtesy of the Hearst Corporation.

This photo depicts the interview process for migratory farm workers in the 1940s. The San Antonio Light Collection, UT Institute of Texan Cultures at San Antonio, No. L-3225-A. Courtesy of the Hearst Corporation.

A farmer's daughter in Puerto Rico during the Depression. Courtesy of the Library of Congress.

A migrant farm worker kisses her child. The San Antonio Light Collection, UT Institute of Texan Cultures at San Antonio, No. L-7090-71. Courtesy of the Hearst Corporation.

(*Left*) Lucas Alvarado, a member of the arts and crafts class at Lanier Junior-Senior School, learns weaving on a small loom, Texas, 1930s. The San Antonio Light Collection, UT Institute of Texan Cultures at San Antonio, No. L-1403-G. Courtesy of the Hearst Corporation. (*Right*) Three elementary school girls, Tivoli Texas, 1956. UT Institute of Texan Cultures at San Antonio, No. 096-0037.

A historically significant photograph of the League of United Latin American Citizens (LULAC). The General Libraries Benson Latin American Collection, University of Texas, Austin, Sid Richardson Hall 1.109.

E

EARLY CHILDHOOD EDUCATION

The period from birth through the end of the primary grades is extremely important educationally. The academic performance patterns that most children will have throughout their educational careers are established by the end of the primary grades. This also is the case for groups, that is, differences in academic achievement among racial and ethnic groups are substantial by the end of the primary grades and change little in size thereafter. Moreover, these differences in achievement at the end of the primary grades are presaged by differences in various measures of school readiness at the start of kindergarten and have antecedents prior to the start of traditional preschool (i.e., prior to age 3).

Hispanics are rapidly becoming a substantial majority of the nation's disadvantaged student population. For example, Georges Vernez and Richard Krop of the Rand Corporation have projected that, by 2015, Hispanics will constitute about 59% of the under-18 population with no parents with a high school degree (1999). They also project that, among the entire under-18 population, about 11% will be from homes in which no parent has completed high school, while about 30% of all Hispanics in this age group will be in that position. Complicating the situation further is the fact that most Hispanic youngsters with no parents with a high school degree are from immigrant families. This means that a substantial share of these low-socioeconomic-status (SES) youngsters have parents who do not speak English fluently and also who are not fully literate in Spanish. Vernez and Krop have projected that, by 2015, about 79% of Hispanics under age 18 with no parents who have completed high school will be from immigrant families. Indeed, both they and Garcia (2001) have projected that, by 2015, they will make up nearly half of the individuals under age 18 in the U.S. without parents with a high school diploma.

Data from the Early Childhood Longitudinal Study (ECLS) have made clear the pressing need to improve early childhood education for low-SES Hispanic children. In an analysis of that data set, Coley (2002) found that although 71% of all whites and 50% of all Hispanics could recognize letters of the alphabet when they started kindergarten, only 30% of the lowest-SES quintile of Hispanics could do so. Moreover, since 29% of all the Hispanic children in the ECLS were excluded from the reading tests at the start of kindergarten because they were from Spanish-speaking homes and did not score at a certain level on an English-screening assessment, the reading readiness skills of low-SES Hispanic children at the start of kindergarten may be much more limited than the 30% figure calculated by Coley (2002).

Other analyses of ECLS data by Sean Reardon (2003) suggest that other SES segments of Hispanic children could benefit from improvements in their early childhood education, including those growing up in high-SES circumstances. For example, among children in the highest-SES quintile, 52% of the whites could understand the beginning sounds of words when they started kindergarten, whereas only 41% of the Hispanics in that SES segment could do so. Similarly, whereas 41% of the whites in the highest-SES quintile could understand ordinal sequence of numbers, only 25% of their Hispanic counterparts could do so. It is very important that these "within-class" differences in the early childhood years be taken seriously because other data sets at the elementary and secondary levels (NAEP, SAT, Prospects, etc.) show significant within-class achievement differences between whites and Hispanics (and Asians and Hispanics) at all SES levels during the K–12 years, whether in the first grade or the twelfth grade. The importance of doing so is underlined by the reality that the number of Hispanic children growing up in middle-class families is growing rapidly. For instance, Vernez and Krop have projected that, in 2015, there will be about 2 million Latinos under age 18 with at least one parent with a bachelor's degree. Clearly, the needs of a segment this large should not be ignored.

Lastly, there is a growing body of data suggesting the importance of learning more about how the need for higher-quality early childhood education may vary among Hispanics of different national origins, especially owing to differences in their SES patterns. For instance, Roberto Suro and

B. Lindsay Lowell have shown that the education levels of recent Hispanic immigrants vary enormously by country of origin (Suro & Lowell, 2002). Notably, they have found that a high percentage of Mexican American immigrants have not completed high school and a low percentage have graduated from college, whereas the reverse is true for immigrants from several nation's in South America. Paying attention to the need for higher-quality early education for Mexican American children, of course, is very important not only because so many are from low-SES circumstances, but because they constitute a majority of Hispanic youngsters. Learning more about how the need for improvements in early childhood education for Hispanics varies by region of the country also is increasingly important owing to regional variations in Hispanic presence. Currently over four-fifths of the Hispanic population lives in just nine states: California, Texas, Florida, New York, Illinois, Arizona, New Jersey, New Mexico, and Colorado (Chapa & De La Rosa, 2004). However, the fastest growing Hispanic population growth is in the South and Southeast.

With regard to early education participation, the largest preschool program for Hispanic children, Head Start, is actually a funding program, which means that the substance of local Head Start programs varies considerably—including what is being done to prepare children academically for school. There is a press for greater uniformity of Head Start programs with regard to school preparation, especially in the area of reading readiness. This is proving to be very controversial. Debates in this area are likely to persist for many, both because students from underrepresented minority groups continue to start school well behind their white and Asian peers and because there are still no large-scale, rigorous evaluations that can provide strong evidence of long-term academic achievement benefits in school owing to Head Start. Among programs for children from infancy until they enter preschool, Early Head Start provides some of the most extensive evaluation evidence of benefits for low-SES youngsters from each racial and ethnic group, including Hispanics. Meaningful gains have been documented in cognitive, language, and social-emotional development, but gaps remain with middle- and high-SES children. Such findings raise questions about how to provide the benefits of the most promising approaches to low-SES Hispanic children and what improvements need to be mounted and tested for them. There also is the question of whether programs for these very early years need to be developed for middle- and high-SES Hispanic youngsters, given the previously mentioned within-class gaps that exist at the time of entry to kindergarten and thereafter.

Given the large number of low-SES Hispanic homes in which parents do not speak English, the question of what could be done to increase the percentage of early childhood educators who speak Spanish well enough to communicate effectively with the parents and the children in their native language is a major funding issue for government and a serious education program issue for colleges and universities that train early childhood professionals. Evidence continues to accumulate that having well-educated teachers contributes to higher levels of achievement in the primary grades, but that schools serving high concentrations of disadvantaged children are less likely to have such teachers. This is one of the most important challenges for school districts, state policymakers, and colleges and universities (which educate new teachers), including in parts of the country with high concentrations of Hispanic students.

References

Chapa, J., & De La Rosa, B. (2004). Latino Population Growth, Socioeconomic and Demographic Characteristics, and Implications for Educational Attainment. *Education and Urban Society* 36(2), 130–149.

Coley, R. (2002). Helping Underachieving Boys Read Well and Often. *ERIC Digest*, ED 467687. Available: http://www.ericdigests.org/2003-2/boys.html.

Garcia, E. (2001). *Hispanic Education in the United States: Raíces y alas*. Lanham, MD: Rowman & Littlefield.

Reardon, F. (2003). *Sources of Educational Inequality: The Growth of Racial/Ethnic and Socioeconomic Test Score Gaps in Kindergarten and First Grade*. University Park: Population Research Institute, Pennsylvania State University.

Suro, R., & Lowell, B. L. (2002). *New Lows from New Highs: Latino Economic Losses in the Current Recession*. Philadelphia: Pew Hispanic Center.

Vernez, G., Krop, R., & Rydell, P. (1999). *Closing the Education Gap: Benefits and Costs*. Lanham, MD: National Book Network.

Recommended Reading

Anyon, J. (1995). Inner City School Reform: Towards Useful Theory. *Urban Education* 30(1), 56–70.

August, D., & Hakuta, K. (1997). *Improving Schooling for Language-Minority Children: A Research Agenda*. Washington, DC: National Council Research.

Burns, M. S., Griffin, P., & Snow, C. E. (1999). *Starting Outright: A Guide to Promoting Children's Reading Success*. Washington DC: National Academy Press.

Clored, N., Beneree, F., & Hamayau, E. (2000). *Dual Language Instruction: A Handbook for Enriched Education*. Boston: Heinle & Heinle.

Cooper, C. R., Azmitia, M., Garcia, E., Ittel, A., Lopez, E., Rivera, L., & Martinez-Chavez, R. (1994). Aspirations of Low Income Mexican Americans and European American Parents for the Children and Adolescents. In F. Villaruel & R. M. Lerner (Eds.), *Directions in Children Development* (vol. 68, pp. 65–81). San Francisco: Jossey-Bass.

Crawford, J. (1999). *Bilingual Education: History, Politics, Theory, and Practice.* Trenton, NJ: Crane.

Darder, A., Torres, R. D., & Gutiérrez, H. (Eds.). (1997). *Latinos and Education: A Critical Reader.* New York: Routledge.

Figueroa, R., & Garcia, E. (1994). Issues in Testing Students from Culturally and Linguistically Diverse Backgrounds. *Multicultural Education* 2(1), 10–24.

Freeman, Y. S., & Freeman, D. E. (1998). *ESL/ EFL Teaching: Principles for Success.* Portsmouth, NH: Heineman.

Gándara, P., Maxwell-Jolly, J., Garcia, E., Striticus, T., Curry, J., Gutierrez, K., & Asato, J. (2000). *The Initial Impact of Proposition 227 on the Instruction of English Learners.* Santa Barbara: University of California. Language Minority Research Institute.

Garcia, E. (1997). The Education of Hispanics in Early Childhood: Of Roots and Wings. *Young Children* 52(3), 5–14.

Garcia, E. (2001). *Understanding and Meeting the Challenge of Student Diversity* (3rd ed.). Boston: Houghton Mifflin.

Garcia, E. (2002). Bilingualism and Schooling in the United States. *International Journal of the Sociology of Language*, 134(1), 1–123.

Garcia, E. (2004). *The Schooling Bilingual Students in the United States.* New York: Teachers College Press.

Garcia, E., Bravo, M., Dickey, L., Chun, K., & Sun, X. (2002). Rethinking School Reform in the Context of Cultural and Linguistic Diversity. In L. Minaya-Rowe (Ed.), *Research in Bilingual Education.* Greenwich, CT: Information Age Publishing.

Garcia, E., & Gonzalez, R. (1995). Issues in Systemic Reform for Culturally and Linguistically Diverse Students. *College Record* 96(3), 418–431.

Garcia, E., & McLaughlin, B. (1995). *Meeting the Challenges of Linguistic and Cultural Diversity in Early Childhood.* New York: Teachers College Press.

Gonzalez, J., Brusca-Vega, R., & Yawker, T. (1999). *Assessment and Instruction of Culturally and Linguistically Diverse Students: From Research to Practice.* Boston: Allyn & Bacon.

Gordon, E. W. (1999). *Educational Justice: A View from the Back of the Bus.* New York: Teachers College Press.

Gregory, S. (2000). *The Academic Achievement of Minority Students.* Memphis: University of America Press.

Lukas, T. (1997). *Into, Through and Beyond Secondary School: Critical Transitions for Immigrant Youth.* Washington, DC: Center for Applied Linguistics.

Mace-Matluck, B. J., Alexander-Kaspavik, R., & Queen, R. M. (1998). *Through the Golden Door: Educational Approaches for Immigrant Adolescents with Limited Schooling.* Washington, DC: Center for Applied Linguistics.

Mehan, H., Villanueva, I., Hubbard, L., & Lintz, A. (1996). *Constructing School Success: The Consequences of Untracking Low-Achieving Students.* New York: Cambridge University Press.

Miramontes, O., Nadeau, A., & Cummins, N. (1997). *Linguistic Diversity and Effective School Reform: A Process for Decision Making.* New York: Teachers College Press.

Nieto, S. (1999). *The Light in Their Eyes.* New York: Teachers College Press.

Oakes, J., & Lipton, M. (1999). *Teaching to Save the World.* Boston: McGraw-Hill.

Olson, L. (1997). *Made in America: Immigrant Students in Our Public Schools.* New York: New Press.

Ovando, C. J., & McLaren, P. (1999). *The Politics of Multiculturalism and Bilingual Education.* Boston: McGraw-Hill.

Slavin, R. E. (2003). *Effective Reading Programs for English Language Learners: A Best Evidence Analysis.* Baltimore: Center for Research on the Education of Students Placed at Risk.

Rivera, C., & Stausfield, C. W. (2000). *An Analysis of State Policies for the Inclusion and Accommodation of English Language Learners in State Assessment Programs During 1998–1999.* Washington, DC: The George Washington University Center for Equity and Excellence in Education.

Romo, H. (1999). *Reaching Out: Best Practices for Educating Mexican-Origin Children and Youth.* Charleston, WVA: Clearinghouse on Rural Education and Small Schools.

Romo, H. D., & Falbo, T. (1996). *Latino High School Graduation: Defying the Odds.* Austin: University of Texas Press.

Rumburger, R., & Gandara, P. (2000). *Crucial Issues in California Education 2000: Are the Reform Pieces Fitting Together.* Berkeley: University of California, Berkeley. Policy Analysis for California Education.

Soto, L. D. (1997). *Language, Culture and Power: Bilingual Families and the Struggle for Quality Education.* Albany, NY: SUNY Press.

U.S. Department of Education. (1998). *The Hispanic Drop-out Project Report.* Washington, DC: U.S. Department of Education.

Valdes, G. *Con respeto: Bridging the Distances between Culturally Diverse Families and Schools,* New York: Teachers College Press, (1996).

Vernez, G., Krop, R., & Rydell, P. (1999). *Closing the Education Gap: Costs and Benefits.* Santa Monica, CA: Rand Corporation.

Zentella, A. C. (1997). *Growing Up Bilingual,* New York: Blackwell.

Web Sites

ERIC Clearinghouse on Urban & Minority Education, http://eric.ed.gov.

National Clearinghouse for Bilingual Education (NCBE), http:www.gwu.edu./gshed/.

Eugene E. Garcia

EARLY CHILDHOOD EDUCATION IN THE BORDER REGIONS

The border between the U.S. and Mexico is an interesting region of binational, bicultural, and bilingual communities. This region is one of the fastest-growing in the U.S. The border extends from San Diego, California, to Brownsville, Texas, and covers a distance of 1,952 miles. The Rio Grande River separates the two nations in the region of Texas and the four Mexican states of Chihuahua, Coahuila, Nuevo Leon, and Tamaulipas. An estimated 500,000–600,000 Mexican nationals living in the border areas possess permits that allow them regular entry into the U.S. border area. Clearly, each border region varies considerably from county to county in terms of resources, economics, and characteristics. This entry focuses on the challenges facing young children, birth through age 8, in the border region of the lower Rio Grande Valley of Texas.

Brownsville is a city located in Cameron County, Texas, with an estimated population of 142,000, and is the county seat of Cameron County. According to the U.S. census, the racial makeup of the city is over 92% Hispanic or Latino. Of approximately 39,000 households, 51% have children under the age of 18 living in them, with specifically 35% under the age of 18 years of age. Census data show that over 34% of the families are below the poverty line; over 48% are under 18 years of age. There is a growing concern with the migration of agricultural workers, as well as with the apparent increase of children immigrating. This entry addresses five critical considerations with respect to this border region: culture, parent involvement, community involvement, and instructional strategies.

Cultural Considerations

If we ask people about culture, we receive a wide range of answers. Some say that culture refers to values or beliefs; others argue that it means the customs of a particular group. According to Spolsky (1978), "Culture is language, values, beliefs, and behaviors that pervade every aspect of every person's life, and is continually undergoing minor and occasionally major alternations." Still others (Gollnick & Chinn, 1994) point out that a person learns how to become a functioning adult within a specific society through culture.

Two similar processes interact as one learns how to act in society: enculturation and socialization. Enculturation is the process of acquiring the characteristics of a given culture and generally becoming competent in the language (Abercrombie, Hill, & Turner, 1984). We see examples of this as children from regions in Mexico enter our classrooms and begin to explore their new language, using English more frequently in their play. The second process, socialization, is the general one of learning the social norms of the culture (Abercrombie et al., 1984). Through this process we internalize the social and cultural rules of the family and community. We learn what is expected in different roles such as mother, child, student, and teacher. This is frequently observed in classrooms where the children have opportunities for dramatic play or in environments that offer diverse opportunities for problem solving and fantasy play.

Language Considerations

Over 97% of the children in Brownsville, Texas, are reported to be of Latino or Mexican American descent and speak Spanish as their home language. Although many immigrant and migrant families desire their young children to learn English, in reality many families are fluent only in Spanish and are challenged to model and interact with their young children in English. Of the numerous private and federal early childhood programs exist in the Rio Grande Valley, many lack clear language policies or practices of how best to foster dual language, or build the child's home language. Given the stress for academic assessment, many families are selecting infant, toddler, and preschool programs that foster English, believing this to be the best decision for their child. Here is an important area of needed advocacy where families require additional support and guidance in building and maintaining the home language as their children acquire the second language.

Frequently, many families choose English-only programs for their preschool children not realizing the critical stages of language acquisitions. These same children return home to parents who are usually monolingual Spanish speakers. Many other children attend early childhood programs where there is no clear language policy or guidance for them. Consequently, many youngsters face language disruptions in their development of the first language. Few language studies have focused on the social and emotional aspects of children in the border regions of the U.S. and Mexico. As educators, we are faced with many children who enter our public schools with unique challenges, and this is complicated when their language development is neither consistent nor supported instructionally. Clearly, early childhood community programs and public schools programs need to forge effective collaboration and communication to address diversity and provide quality approaches to language and literacy development. Community coalitions and projects will help support the important development of both languages: Spanish and English.

Involving Parents

Parental involvement is the participation within the school, the home, and the community for the purpose of formal and informal learning. Indeed, the three most important influences in the child's life are the school, the home, and the community. Extensive research (Seplocha, 2004) has shown that for children to benefit emotionally and academically, parents and schools need to collaborate through shared visions and communication. Goal setting is critical for parents and schools to work more effectively together to help children. As Epstein (2001) has pointed out, there needs to be a clear understanding of parent cooperation and effective parent involvement. Parent involvement needs to empower parents, giving them a clear voice regarding the welfare, growth, and learning of their children.

Three major goals have been identified as important in building home-school relationships. These include (1) a communication system in the family's home language; (2) effective, meaningful opportunities for parent involvement; and (3) diverse opportunities for involvement. These goals become a particular challenge when the school culture and language differ from that of the population of children. Communication becomes more complex when the parents and school do not share a common vision or if the parents are confused by the changing messages of the school culture.

In regions where there exist high levels of migration and immigration, communities are increasingly challenged to reach out to parents in more diverse ways. In southern Texas, for example, the migrant community represents thousands of families who move based on crops, weather, and opportunities for employment. These families travel through several ports of entry, and their children enter and then leave the community schools. This lack of permanence creates a unique challenge for the child, parent, and teacher. This high level of mobility gives a new level of importance to the social and emotional factors in schooling. Similarly, many parents report feeling uncomfortable in the school setting. They do not feel empowered.

Why Is It Important to Connect the Home, the School, and the Community?

Research has shown that the children are socially and academically better adjusted when the school has more communication and contact with the home. Clearly, children grow and develop in communities that have tremendous impact on development and learning. It is important for the home, school, and community to build systems of communication and collaboration for numerous reasons. The experiences and relationships of the child and family will become more enriched and diverse in family and community interactions.

A strong sense of community, will, determination, and expectation for students to succeed academically and socially will lead the new generations to prepare to make a living in our present and rapidly changing world. A school learning community collaborates, plans, and works together as a team or in partnership to increase learning opportunities and experiences for all students. Activities to increase and enrich all children's skills and talents may, for example, be done during lunch or after school. Certainly it is an exciting challenge to ensure that the school, family, and community partner in meaningful, yet diverse ways to ensure participation.

Strengthening school learning communities is a continuous benefit to children, families, schools, and communities. National initiatives such as the No Child Left Behind demand more accountability, and in doing so they increase the importance of schools and families working together to help students acquire proficiency in reading and the content areas.

Two Countries, One Community

Brownsville, Texas, and Matamoras, Mexico, reside in two distinct countries, divided by the Rio Grande River. Nonetheless, the two communities share family, language, culture, customs, and traditions. Such connections reflect the ongoing traffic between the two communities, which share values and history, as well as traditions and families. What we do know about our community is that communication, consistency, and collaboration are key elements for successful and prosperous environments for learning and well-being. Educators are more effective when they utilize instructional materials that build on themes relevant to the cultures and languages of the families that make up communities. Certainly the spoken language of the home environment must be carefully embraced throughout the curriculum.

Effective Teaching Strategies. Effective teaching strategies are based on numerous criteria, among them the key areas discussed here: (1) building on what children know, (2) making connections to culture, (3) making connections to language, (4) making connections to community, and (5) making connections to the large community

Building on What the Children Know. Best practice in early childhood education is based on knowledge of how children learn and develop (Bredekamp & Rosegrant, 1992) Developmentally appropriate teaching means that we approach children where they are and not where we think they ought to be (Bredekamp & Rosegrant, 1992). Doing so provides an exciting opportunity to work with children, who develop and learn in a rich binational environment, by building on understanding the children's backgrounds, abilities, and interests. Even in the border community, we are faced with tremendous diversity within the dominant culture and must deal with the circumstances of migration and immigration. Building on what children know also means understanding the impact of social trends in testing and how this influences parents' decisions for early childhood programs, as well as its effects on public school programs, which frequently exit children out of their home language too early. Building on what children know is important to how we teach and work with young children and families. There is no one-shoe-fits-all philosophy for young children, but rather a philosophical framework based on sound child development principles (Bredekamp & Rosegrant, 1992; Hyson, 2002).

Connections to Language

In all cultures there is a relationship between thought and language. As children begin learning the language of their parents, they also start to become socialized into their parents' culture. This important connection to home language strongly argues for increased parent and school communication and inter-involvement. Early childhood research clearly shows that children need to be supported in their home language, but extensive research consistently shows how children critically benefit from exposure to two languages. Although the potential advantages of being bilingual in our world are enormous, it is a challenge for many parents and teachers to foster bilingualism because it needs to be fostered and supported both at home and in school. We live in a world where English is a dominate language, but annual statistics show us that the home culture and language are important factors in children's cultural identity and socialization.

Early childhood professionals are in a strategic position to help children and families maintain their home language, yet in meaningful ways acquire English. Providing time for exploratory play and free play provides children with numerous opportunities to extend their home language, as well as build on their second language. Research by Dickenson and Tabors (2002) indicates that the teacher-child relationship, as well as the kinds of conversations that teachers and children have, makes the biggest difference to early language and literacy development. A shared vision for families and schools is to help a child become a bilingual, biliterate citizen.

Connections to Culture

Teachers are effective practitioners when they explore and support the cultures of their young students as the enter the formal educational system. By carefully designing the classroom environment, teachers have a keen opportunity to respond sensitively to the social, cultural, and developmental needs of the young child (Clayton & Forton, 2001; Duarte & Rafanello, 2001). As children begin learning the language of their parents, they become socialized into their parent's culture. Part of the enculturation of children involves learning the dialect of their parents and peers. In order to be effective teachers of the language arts, it is important

to understand the relationship between language and culture and to see how the two interact" (Clearly & Linn, 1993).

When an environment reflects the values, artifacts, and familiar aspects of the home, children explore, respond, and interact in more positive ways. Classrooms that support more than academic activities but promote more social and emotional interaction will help children develop independence as well as learn problem-solving and risk-taking behaviors. Equally important are environments where teachers understand and respect the diverse cultures the children bring into the classroom setting. Activities, attitude, and socioemotional climate all need to consistently support the home culture. As we internalize the social and cultural rules of the family and community, we learn what is expected in different roles such as mother, father, child, student, and teacher. This process is frequently observed in classrooms where children have opportunities for dramatic play or in environments that offer diverse opportunities for problem solving and fantasy play.

Connections to Community

Teachers have important opportunities to utilize community resources where families and schools reside. A community can involve the parents and other family members. Certainly active and effective learning is enhanced when the classroom teacher use the outreach services of the zoo, public library, or museums to connect with the children. Guest speakers, outreach services, materials, books, and products have been found to be very effective in the Brownsville community, which has a nationally recognized zoo, an innovative public library, and a newly built children's museum. To educate young children is no easy task without the help of parents and family. A child develops best through the integration of parents, family, and community. This connection enables us to see and consider what children do, how they think, and what they know. Such a connection is required for children to reach a level of learning that will be significant for them.

Connections to the Larger Community

Since the border region represents a diverse binational climate, teachers there have excellent opportunities to explore and utilize the richness of the two cultures, of the two national communities. The month of the young child, community festivals, and El Día de los Niños are excellent examples of how the community comes together to celebrate the importance of young children. The community's resources can serve as important building blocks for many instructional projects as well as serve as important language and literacy sources for young children. Integrating guest speakers with authentic cultural materials, information, and community events creates in the ongoing curriculum an important base of relevant language opportunities for young children.

Summary

The Rio Grande Valley in southern Texas is one border community among many that dot the landscape from San Diego, California, to Brownsville, Texas. It is a community that is bilingual, bicultural, and binational. This interesting community represents one of the fastest-growing regions of young children in the country. Educationally, the region is also challenged by the increasing number of migrant and immigrant children. This critical increase of children brings numerous opportunities for

educators to respond with more child-centered and family-centered strategies that build on child, family, and community. Educational leader and classroom teachers have important opportunities and responsibilities to embrace, foster, and help children maintain their home language and culture through communication, collaboration, and community initiatives.

References

Abercrombie, N., Hill, S., & Hill, Turner, B. S. (1984). *Dictionary of Sociology*. New York: Penguin Books.

Banks, J. A., & Banks, C.A.M. (Eds.). (1995). *Handbook of Research on Multicultural Education*. New York: Macmillan.

Bennett, C. I. (1990). *Comprehensive Multicultural Education: Theory and Practice* (2nd ed.). Boston: Allyn & Bacon.

Blank, Martin, J. (2003). How Community Schools Make a Difference. *Educational Leadership* 61, 12–18.

Bredekamp, S., & Rosegrant, T. (1992). Reaching Potentials: Guidelines for Appropriate Curriculum Content and Assessment. Available: http://www.ncrel.org/sdrs/areas/issues/students/earlycld/ea7refer.htm.

Burnett, G. (1994). *Varieties of Multicultural Education: An Introduction*. ERIC Digest 98, ED372146. New York: ERIC Clearinghouse on Urban Education.

Clayton, M., & Forton, M. B. (2001). *Classroom Spaces That Work*. Greenfield, MA: Northeastern Foundation for Children.

Cushner, K., McClelland, A., & Safford, P. (1996). *Human Diversity in Education: An Integrative Approach* (2nd ed.). New York: McGraw-Hill.

Derman-Sparks, D., & the A.B.C. Task Force. (1989). *Anti-bias Curriculum: Tools for Empowering Young Children*. Washington, DC: National Association for the Education of Young Children.

Dickinson, D., & Tabors, P. (2002). Fostering Language and Literacy in Classrooms and Homes. *Young Children* 57(2), 10–8.

Duarte, G., & Rafanello, D. (2001). The Migrant Child: A Special Place in the Field. *Young Children* 56(2), 26–34.

DuFour, Richard. (2004). "Schools as Learning Communities." *Educational Leadership* 61(8), 6–11.

Epstein, J. L. (2001). *School, Family, and Community Partnerships: Preparing Educators and Improving Schools.* Boulder, CO: Westview Press.

Gollnick, D., & Chinn, P. (1994). *Multicultural Edition in a Pluralistic Society* (4th ed.). New York: MacMillan.

Grant, C., & Sleeter, C. (2003). *Turning on Learning: Five Approaches for Multicultural Teaching Plans for Race, Class, Gender, and Disability.* Trenton, NJ: Wiley.

Henderson, A. T., & Mapp, K. L. (2002). *A New Wave of Evidence: The Impact of School, Family, and Community Connections on Student Achievement.* Austin, TX: Southwest Educational Development Laboratory.

Hyson, M. (2002). Professional Development: Emotional Development and School Readiness. *Young Children* 57(6), 76–78.

Sanders, M. G., & Harvey, A. (2002). Partnering with Families and Communities. *Educational Leadership* 61, 16–17.

Segura Velez, C. A. (2002). La relación padres-alumnos y escuela. *Difusión* 12(33). Matamoros, Mexico: Universidad Pedagógica Nacional en Tamaulipas, Publicación UBN.

Seplocha, H. (2004). Partnerships for Learning: Conferencing with Families. *Young Children* (59)5, 28–32.

Recommended Reading

Cleary, L. M., & Linn, M. (1993). *Linguistics for Teachers.* New York: McGraw-Hill.

Seplocha, H. (2004). Partnerships for Learning: Conferencing with Families. *Young Children* (59)5, 28–32.

Spolky, B. (1978). *Approaches to Language Testing.* Arlington, VA: Center for Applied Linguistics.

Georgianna Duarte, Elva Cerda Pérez,
and Graciela Rosenberg

EDUCATIONAL REFORM AND POLICY

In this entry we discuss the historical nature of challenges affecting the education of English language learners (ELLs), immigrant, Latino/a students within the mainstream reality of the U.S. public schools. Our purpose is to discuss American education reform from a historical perspective to provide an analysis of past and contemporary education policy, such as the No Child Left Behind (NCLB) Act of 2001. We discuss continuities and discontinuities of American education reform and policy since the early 1900s until the early twenty-first century, in relation to the academic achievement of English as Second Language (ESL) immigrant students in the U.S. public schools. Our analysis centers on the historical impact of educational reform and policies for providing genuine equal educational opportunities for Latino/a students, reducing the high dropout rates among Latino/a students, and reducing the academic achievement gap between majority and minority students (see also Gonzalez, 2001a).

More specifically, in this entry we provide a historical overview of solutions responding to the educational challenge of meeting the needs of culturally and linguistically diverse students. An overview of this entry is provided here for the reader as a synthesis of later discussions. This entry encompasses two main sections: (1) an analysis of the historical nature of educational challenges, providing a discussion of the education crisis and reform years, with an emphasis on equality and standards during the 1980s, 1990s, and early 2000s; and (2) conclusions with a synthesis of historical patterns on education reform for Latino/a students.

Historically solutions have been created for over 100 years in the form of educational reforms since the early 1900s until the early twenty-first century. During the early 1900s, the culturally and linguistically diverse students were southern and eastern European students who came, like contemporary Latino/a students, from ESL backgrounds. The demographic shifts since the 1980s have brought millions of Latino students who also represent an ESL immigrant group. In response, school reform of the 1980s called for improvement of education quality for *all* students in comparison to international competition, under the publication of *A Nation at Risk*, as the product of social and economic problems. For the first time in history, there was recognition of a relationship between underachievement and dropout rates to low-socioeconomic (SES, or *poverty*) conditions among minority *at-risk* students, such as Latino/a immigrant ELLs.

During the early 1990s, the America 2000 movement enforced the need for the U.S. public school system to undergo school reform. The policy of the early 1990s held schools accountable for all students' learning and achievement through developing communities of critical learners who could compete in the U.S. and global modern economy. Thus, the movement of national standards across core subject matters started in the early 1990s and became more critical during the early twenty-first century under the No Child Left Behind (NCLB) Act of 2001 for Title III. The NCLB comes as the product of 30 years of policy started under the civil rights movement of the late 1960s with the Bilingual Education Act, as a comprehensive, complete, and pervasive system that meets the needs of ELLs. The main section of this entry, presented next, provides a historical analysis of American education reform and its policies in relation to high-stakes standards and reducing the academic achievement gap of ELLs.

The Historical Nature of Educational Challenges

The historical nature of the need to restructure education is tied to meeting the contemporary challenges of the diverse students of the U.S. public schools, including the demographic shift of Latino/a ELLs during the 1980s, 1990s, and 2000s. But the educational challenge precedes the contemporary waves of Latino/a ELLs and goes back to a centuries-old problem. Consider the following critical evaluation of the status of contemporary education.

Today American elementary and secondary education is under active attack for alleged failures or shortcomings of various kinds. In the minds of those responsible for running the schools, much, if not most, of the criticism is distinctly ill-founded and irresponsible. School personnel have long been decrying outmoded practices and promoting new ones, many of the latter bearing the brunt of current condemnations. But present lay criticism seems to have caught a large segment of school personnel quite unprepared to meet it; hence responses are often unconvincing, recriminatory, or yielding. If the education profession is to maintain past and present gains and to achieve new ones, it must know what has been done in the past, what has proven unsatisfactory and what satisfactory, what innovations have been tried and what has come of them, and why we have come to do what we are doing. (Bayles, 1961, p. 43)

Even though Bayles's assessment fits the situation of schooling now, and especially the educational reality of ELLs today, this criticism was published in 1961. It shows that the history of U.S. education has always faced the challenges of keeping up with the social, cultural, and linguistic needs of diverse students. The criticism to educational problems and its solution is obviously a historical problem, even a centuries-old problem.

More recently Hampel, Johnson, Plank, Ravitch, Tyach, and Cuban (1996) recognized that the solution to educational challenges depended not on technical knowledge but on cultural value systems about the purpose and goals of education for mainstream as well as for minority and language minority students. They stated that

the improvement of American education depends not on a technocratic solution, not on getting the right laws written, not even on recognizing the school's bureaucratic structures. The missing ingredient continues to be widespread agreement on the value of a challenging and rigorous education for everyone. (p. 502)

Furthermore, Hampel and colleagues (1996) identified patterns of "school reform" since early in the twentieth century until the present, with similar mandated philosophies and educational practices. They recognized that "some familiarity with the history of public schooling would make it clear that many of the 'radical' policy reforms now being peddled as solutions to the system's problems were already shopworn in 1910" (p. 484). Public education in the U.S. also provides grounds for the affirmation of economic and political opportunities of its citizens. As Hampel and colleagues (1996) note,

Public education in the U.S. involves not only 'helping students to learn better' but also the allocation of billions of dollars, the distribution of opportunities and rewards across individuals and groups, the respective 'rights' of parents and professionals, and the definition and affirmation of legitimate knowledge. (p. 486)

Hampel and colleagues (1996) recommended analyzing the history of U.S. education in order to look at the impressive continuities of educational policy and school reform over long periods of time, on what they called "the grammar of schooling—the institutional regularities that govern practice in teaching and learning" (p. 492). Studying the continuities of educational history is key for developing solutions for the major challenges of the contemporary educational system. They recognized that "after all, the present and future can only emerge from the past" (p. 492). They identified many parallels between the early 1900s and the 1990s: despite social, economic, and political differences, these periods share major issues, such as "social dislocation, political realignments in constituencies, and fears of foreign competition due to industrialization, immigration, and urban turbulence" (p. 499). They found similarities between "administrative progressives during the early 1900s and neo-progressive policy elites who seek federal and state initiatives in national goals, curricular standardization, and high-stakes testing" (p. 499). These parallels in historical events also continue today with the continuities present between the Bilingual Education Act of the late 1960s and NCLB as the product of 30 years of policy started under the civil rights movement.

Bilingual Education: Equal Educational Opportunity for ELLs

The Bilingual Education Act of 1968 started the legitimization of the need to provide language instruction for ESL learners in order to provide equal educational opportunities for them. In *Lau v. Nichols* the Supreme Court ruled the support of bilingual education for ELLs. This suit

validated the case of unequal educational opportunities suffered by Chinese American
students in a San Francisco public school
district that offered English-only instruction. This social problem persists, with the
hot political debate of offering non-English
language instruction for new immigrant
ESL students in public schools. Mainstream
educational views still see schooling as the
traditional social institution to "Americanize" or assimilate new immigrants. Minority
leaders, however, supported by contemporary educational data–based studies, believe
in maintaining the cultural and linguistic
diversity in new immigrant and minority
students as part of the rich multicultural,
multilingual, multiracial "new mainstream
America." Thus, the educational challenge
of reducing the achievement gap among
ELLs mandated by NCLB legislation is
also tinted with a social and political debate.

The Reform Years

During the decade of the 1980s and 1990s
and in the early 2000s the federal government started to recognize the education
crisis. The 1983 publication of *A Nation at
Risk: The Imperative Education Reform*, a
report by The National Commission on
Excellence in Education, received public
attention on the need to improve the quality of education for all students. The report compared U.S. students' test scores
on international measures of educational
achievement in important subject areas
(i.e., mathematics, science, and technology)
with their counterparts in Korea, Germany,
and Japan. These politically allied nations
were U.S. competitors in economic and
industrial areas. However, the most important fact raised by the report was the connection between low test scores and dropout
rates, low-quality curriculums and aca-

demic requirements, and low teachers' salaries and expectations. The recognition of a
saturated and overburdened public school
system raised awareness about its lack of
political and economic support. For the first
time the education system was identified
as the product of society's social and economic problems, instead of the cause of
them.

Once again, in 1991, the America 2000
movement, supported by President George
Bush's administration, proclaimed the need
for schools to undergo an educational reform. That is, schools were to be held
accountable for their students' learning and
achievement and for developing "communities of learning," thereby enabling the
U.S. to become economically competitive
at the international level. The educational
goals stipulated by America 2000 were focused on schools facilitating *all* students to
become literate critical thinkers, so they
would be prepared for further learning,
becoming productive citizens in the modern
U.S. economy and competing effectively in
a global economy. The America 2000 goals
started the development of national standards in core subject matters as the central piece of a school reform movement in
which schools were held accountable for all
students to meet basic national standards.
Accountability was implemented through
standardized testing measuring how well or
poorly all students had mastered standards
across core subject areas.

Again, following the first recognition of
increased numbers of poor minority populations during the 1950s, in the 1980s the
economic gap increased. Again, the disparity on students' socioeconomic backgrounds
increased the achievement gap between
mainstream and minority students. Urban
and Wagoner (1996) believe the resulting
achievement gap "is a problem that stems

from changes in our economy rather than from deficiencies in our educational system. . . . Poor nutrition, atypical learning styles, and lack of a literate home environments are some of the conditions that impede poor children's school performance" (p. 345). One way in which poverty can be overcome is by developing preventive social programs that improve the home and schooling conditions of young children, such as Head Start. According to Urban and Wagoner (1996), "Some programs, such as Head Start, have shown consistent progress, but their lessons are ignored because of their costs. In spite of their substantial operating costs, preschool programs for the poor, at-risk children appear to be necessary if these children are to negotiate the school system successfully" (p. 345).

Hampel and colleagues (1996) criticized the school reform movement of the 1980s and 1990s because it was based "on the false assumption that you could fix the schools, so that the schools [in turn] can fix the kids" (p. 474) independently of their family and external social, economic, and cultural environments. They also recognized that "usually a student [of education] at some point proclaims that school reform is just like a pendulum, swinging back and forth, going nowhere" (p. 477).

Furthermore, the school reform movement of the 1980s and 1990s recommended comprehensive or systemic changes, including pedagogical improvements and professional development in teachers. These changes were to be initiated by educators and adapted at the local level. They recommended participation of teachers in a democratic debate about the purposes of schooling, such as engaging in discussions of the values and knowledge that they want to pass onto students, and the promotion of the best work environment that stimulates

individual and collective participation. However, there was some criticism centered on "the remnants of the hierarchical command structure instilled in school by the administrative progressives early in the century [that] still undermine teacher autonomy" (Hampel et al., 1996, p. 494). Criticism was also directed toward the heavy bureaucratic side of educational reform, including "federal and state regulations that have mushroomed in the last decade [of the 1980s, that is], often giving mixed signals to practitioners. Facing reams of forms to fill out, overworked educators often feel more like professional accountants than like accountable professionals" (p. 494). They proposed that recent models of Professional Development Schools, in which university faculty and public school teachers collaborate and engage in action research and reflective practice toward reforming the schools, from the inside out, may be successful approaches. A variation of this model are Professional Development Networks, which allow teachers to collaborate across schools in order to participate in workshops to analyze their classrooms problems and solutions together.

The No Child Left Behind Act of 2001

Our analysis of NCLB centers on its historical connection to the civil rights and educational reform movement in American public schools. The core of the civil right movement and school reform, represented through NCLB mandates, is related to the use of the public school system as a social institution for giving equal access to education for ELLs to become productive adults and members of society. Then, the large-scale problems of underachievement and high dropout rates for Hispanic students at the national level are not a direct effect of lack of English academic language proficiency but are compounded with mediational factors of low-SES and at-risk sociocultural factors resulting from poverty levels (for an extended discussion of this topic see, e.g., Garcia, 1994, 2001; Gonzalez, 2001b; Gonzalez, Yawkey, & Minaya-Rowe, in press; McLoyd, 1998).

Thus, providing ELLs access to high-quality education can be achieved by immersing them in bilingual education classrooms that can nurture their learning potential. For bilingual education programs to be successful, educators (including administrators, teachers, and supportive school personnel at both state education agencies (SEAs) and local education agencies (LEAs) need to become committed and competent professionals (1) to develop positive attitudes toward linguistic and cultural diversity, (2) to create effective networks with parents and community partnerships, (3) to become knowledgeable about research and its applications to pedagogy and assessment through participation in continuous and high-quality professional development activities, (4) to gain competency about policy mandates, and (5) to foster moral responsibility ("feeling morally accountable") or develop advocacy and commitment to become a mentor and role model for providing support for the academic achievement of all students.

More specifically, the four basic principles of NCLB Act of 2001 for Title III legislation are (1) stronger accountability for results, (2) increased flexibility and local control, (3) expanded options for parents, and (4) emphasis on teaching methods that are research data based and have been proven to work. Overall the objectives of Title III are, to (1) improve the education of ELLs by helping them learn English and to meet challenging state academic content

and high-stakes achievement standards, (2) enhance the instructional opportunities for immigrant students, and (3) provide highly qualified teachers and paraprofessionals knowledgeable in state-of-the-art and research-based educational practices for ELLs.

Whether English-only, ESL, or bilingual education programs are available for ELLs is a state decision. Presently some states are bilingual, others are ESL, but most are both; and others have chosen to enforce an English-only policy. An important point is that parents can request any education program of their choosing, a key point for school districts and states marketing and sustaining two-way bilingual programs across the nation. Most important, native language instruction and assessment can be used when necessary because the NCLB enforces the proper use of valid and reliable assessments for all. The NCLB mandates schools to use appropriate instructional programs aligned with assessments showing that ELLs are successful in learning English and another language, and in using English as an academic tool for learning content. Thus, Title III offers a framework of school reform with mandated federal policy that supports the civil rights of ELLs. Thus teachers must meet the educational needs of ELLs, not vice versa, with children meeting the instructional needs of teachers; and SEAs and LEAs must provide support for the professional development of teachers serving ELLs.

Conclusions: Historical Patterns on Education Reform for Latino/a Students

This entry has presented a synthesis of the history of U.S. educational policy aimed at meeting the culturally and linguistically diverse educational needs of Latino students at risk of underachievement, needs compounded by low-SES factors associated with historical and recent ESL immigration groups. Patterns of school reform since early in the twentieth century until the present are clear in the parallels between the early 1900s and the 1980s, 1990s, and 2000s as evident in policies calling for equity and equal educational opportunities for all students. These parallels correspond to waves of ESL immigrants (i.e., eastern and southern European ESLs during the early 1900s and Hispanics since the 1980s until the present) that required changes in the social and educational paradigms within mainstream America and called for school reform to meet the diverse needs of ELLs.

Moreover, historical pendulums of school reform have gone from (1) "blaming the tests and the curriculum" to (2) "blaming the victim" and taking a "fix the child" approach, and more recently to (3) a "fix the teacher" approach, with high-stakes accountability and standards for measuring teachers' effectiveness in reducing the academic achievement gap between ELLs and mainstream students. A major shift of educational paradigms happened during 1983 with the publication of *A Nation At Risk*. For the first time in educational history, the school system was identified as the product of social and economic problems, instead of the cause of them. Thus, for example, the high incidence of underachievement and dropout rates were recognized as the consequence of low SES among Latino students. Another milestone was marked by the onset of the America 2000 movement in 1991, when American schools were held accountable for students' learning and academic achievement. This movement called for school reform and national standards in core subject matters to enable the U.S. to become economically competitive at the international level; it declared that all students needed to become critical thinkers and members of communities of learners. Presently the message disseminated by the NCLB Act of 2001 calls for mandated massive professional development for both mainstream and ESL teachers, who must be informed by state-of-the-art research knowledge and practice, so they can positively influence academic achievement progress in at-risk language minority, low-income, students (such as Latino, immigrant, and ESL students). Depending on how resources and funding are allocated and used in SEAs and LEAs, ESL and mainstream educators, administrators, and researchers and educators in higher education have a mandated challenge to become advocates of ELLs and can lead change mandated by school reform policy through effective practice. This is not an easy educational endeavor, and the high-stakes national standards and accountability movement has become the center of a hot debate across the country. This challenge for mainstream and ESL educators can be an opportunity for engaging in a collaborative dialogue with colleagues and becoming knowledgeable about the cultural values, policies, and best research-based instructional and assessment practices for ESL students. They can collaborate at their SEAs and LEAs, as well as in their professional organizations at the national level.

References

Bayles, E. E. (1961). Sketch for a Study of the Growth of American Educational Thought and Practice. *History of Education Quarterly* 1(3), 43–49.

Gándara, P., & Maxwell-Jolly, J. (1998). Priming the Pump: A Review of Programs That Aim to Increase the Achievement of Underrepresented Minority Undergraduates. *Report to the Task Force on Minority High*

Achievement of the College Board. New York: The College Board.

Garcia, E. (1994). *Understanding and Meeting the Challenge of Student Cultural Diversity.* Boston: Houghton Mifflin.

Garcia, E. (2001). *Hispanic Education in the United States: Raíces y alas.* Lanham, MA: Rowman & Littlefield.

Gonzalez, V. (2001a). Immigration: Education's Story Past, Present, and Future. *College Board Review* 193, 24–31.

Gonzalez, V. (2001b). The Role of Socioeconomic and Sociocultural Factors in Language Minority Children's Development: An Ecological Research View. *Bilingual Research Journal* 25(1, 2), 1–30.

Gonzalez, V., Yawkey, T., & Minaya-Rowe, L. (In press). *English-as-a-Second-Language (ESL) Teaching and Learning: Classroom Applications for Pre–K Through 12th Grade Students' Academic Achievement & Development.* Needham Heights, MA: Allyn & Bacon.

Hampel, R. L., Johnson, W. R., Plank, D. N., Ravitch, D., Tyach, D., & Cuban, L. (1996). Forum: History and Education Reform. *History of Education Quarterly* 36(4), 473–502.

McLoyd, V. C. (1998). Socioeconomic Disadvantage and Child Development. *American Psychologist* 53(2), 185–204.

No Child Left Behind (NCLB) Act. *Official Federal Government Web Site.* www.ed.gov/nclb/landing.html.

Urban, W., & Wagoner, J. (1996). *American Education: A History.* New York: McGraw-Hill.

Recommended Reading

Abbott, E. (1969). *Immigration: Select Documents and Case Records.* 1924. Reprint, New York: Arno Press.

Abbott, E. (1936). *The Tenements of Chicago, 1908–1935.* Chicago: University of Chicago Press.

American Federationist. (1916). *American Foreign Workers* 23, 690.

Bayles, E. E. (1961). Sketch for a Study of the Growth of American Educational Thought and Practice. *History of Education Quarterly* 1(3), 43–49.

Bureau of Citizenship and Immigration Services. (2003). Available: www.immigration.gov/graphics/services/natz/natzsamp.htm.

Carlson, R. A. (1970). Americanization as an Early Twentieth-Century Adult Education Movement. *History of Education Quarterly* 10(4), 440–464.

Cohen, D. K. (1970). Immigrants and the Schools. *Review of Educational Research* 40, 13–27.

Cole, D. B. (1963). *Immigrant City: Lawrence, Massachusetts, 1845–1921.* Chapel Hill: University of North Carolina Press.

Coleman, J. S., Campbell, E. Q., Hobson, C. J., McPortland, J., Mood, A. M., Weinfeld, F. D., & York, R. L. (1966). *Equality of Educational Opportunity.* Washington, DC: U.S. Government Printing Office.

Conant, J. B. (1959). *The American High School Today: A First Report to Interested Citizens.* New York: McGraw-Hill.

Conant, J. B. (1961). *Slums and Suburbs: A Commentary on Schools in Metropolitan Areas.* New York: McGraw-Hill.

Cubberley, E. P. (1919). *Public Education in the United States.* Boston: Houghton Mifflin.

Daniels, R. (1990). *Coming to America: A History of Immigrants and Ethnicity in American Life.* New York: HarperCollins.

Drake, W. E. (1961). Some Implications of the Institutionalization of American Education. *History of Education Quarterly* 1(1), 41–47.

Ellwood, C. A. (1913). *Sociology and Modern Social Problems.* New York: American Book Company.

Ernst, R. (1965). *Immigrant Life in New York City: 1825–1863.* 1949. Reprint, Port Washington, NY: Ira J. Friedman.

Ferrie, J. P. (1994). The Wealth Accumulation of Antebellum European Immigrants to the US: 1840–1860. *Journal of Economic History* 54(12), 145–167.

Galenson, D. W. (1995). Determinants of the School Attendance of Boys in Early Chicago.

History of Education Quarterly 35(4), 371–400.

Gans, H. (1962). *The Urban Villagers*. New York: Random House.

Gonzalez, V. (2001a). Immigration: Education's Story: Past, Present, and Future. *College Board Review* 193, 24–31.

Gonzalez, V. (2001b). The Role of Socioeconomic and Sociocultural Factors in Language-Minority Children's Development: An Ecological Research View. *Bilingual Research Journal* 25(1, 2), 1–30. Adapted and reprinted by the College Board. Available: http://www.collegeboard.com/about/association/academic/2000_2001_scholars.html#gonzalez.

Gonzalez, V. (2004). *Second Language Learning and Cultural Adaptation Processes in Graduate International Students in U.S. Universities*. New York: University Press of America.

Hampel, R. L., Johnson, W. R., Plank, D. N., Ravitch, D., Tyach, D., & Cuban, L. (1996). Forum: History and Education Reform. *History of Education Quarterly* 36(4), 473–502.

Handling, O. (1951). *The Uprooted*. New York: Grosset & Dunlap.

Harrington, M. (1963). *The Other America: Poverty in the United States*. Baltimore: Penguin Books.

Heffron, J. M. (1991). Intelligence Testing and Its Pitfalls: The Making of an American Tradition. *History of Education Quarterly* 31(1), 81–88.

Hodge, G. B. (1912). *Association Educational Work for Men and Boys*. New York: Association Press.

Hughes, G. S. (1925). *Mothers in Industry: Wage Earning by Mothers in Philadelphia*. New York: New Republic.

Kellor, F. A. (1914). Who Is Responsible for the Immigrant? *The Outlook* 106, 912–913.

Kohn, M. (1969). *Class and Conformity: A Study in Values*. Homewood, IL: Dorsey Press.

Moore, L. B. (1907). *Wage Earners' Budgets: A Study of Standards and Costs of Living in New York City*. New York: Henry Holt.

National Research Council. (1999b). *Improving Student Learning*. Washington, DC: National Academy Press.

Odencrantz, L. C. (1919). *Italian Women in Industry*. New York: Russell Sage Foundation.

Olneck, M. R., & Lazerson, M. (1974). The School Achievement of Immigrant Children: 1900–1930. *History of Education Quarterly* 14(4), 453–482.

Perlmann, J. (1988). *Ethnic Differences and Social Structure among Irish, Italians, Jews, and Blacks in an American City, 1880–1935*. New York: Cambridge University Press.

Piper, Terry. (1998). *Language and Learning: The Home and School Years*. Upper Saddle River, NJ: Prentice-Hall.

Pope, C. L. (1989). Household on the American Frontier: The Distribution of Income and Wealth in Utah: 1850–1900. In D. W. Galenson (Ed.), *Markets in History: Economics Studies of the Past* (pp. 168–172). Cambridge: Cambridge University Press.

Psathas, G. (1957). Ethnicity, Social Class, and Adolescent Independence. *American Sociological Review* 22(3), 415–423.

Rosen, B. (1956). The Achievement Syndrome: A Psychocultural Dimension of Social Stratification. *American Psychological Review* 21(1), 123–137.

Safford, V. (1925). *Immigration Problems: Personal Experiences of an Official*. New York: Dodd, Mead.

Senate Documents. (1912a). *History of Women in Trade Unions*, vol. 10.

Senate Documents (1912b). *Infant Mortality and Its Relation to the Employment of Mothers* (vol. 12, p. 645).

Thomas, W. I., & Znaniecki, F. (1958). *The Polish Peasant in Europe and America*. 1918. Reprint, New York: Dover Publications.

Urban, W., & Wagoner, J. (1996). *American Education: A History*. New York: McGraw-Hill.

U.S. Immigration Commission. (1911). *Reports* (vol. 1, p. 761); *Reports* (vol. 26, pp. 226, 318, 404, 423, 577).

Weatherford, D. (1995). *Foreign and Female: Immigrant Women in America (1840–1939).* New York: Facts on File.

Whyte, W. F. (1943). *Street-Corner Society.* Chicago: Chicago University Press.

Virginia Gonzalez, Josefina Villamil Tinajero, and Pauline Dow

EDUCATIONAL TECHNOLOGY FOR LATINO/A LEARNERS

The application of technology to learning experiences, in particular the use of computers has reached all facets of organized education; however, the infiltration has been differential as evidenced by the digital divide. Latinos/as are technologically disadvantaged in this country because of economic, social, and political issues. In addition, power and distance issues reduce opportunities for Latinos/as to wield political power regarding their rights of having computers in schools. Many parents of Latino/a students find that they have little power inside the school walls and feel a certain distance from the mainstream school system. These issues can be exacerbated by economic difficulty, which can increase feelings of powerlessness among Latino/a parents and learners.

Economic challenges have led Latinos to see significant disadvantage in their allocation of computer technologies in classrooms today. This is so, "Given that 40 percent of Hispanic children are living in poverty, that Hispanics are the most undereducated major segment of the U.S. population" (Morton, 1992, p. 1).

It is essential to understand that having computers in the home and being internet connected are less important and less pressing needs than having human necessities such as food, shelter, and health. The U.S. Census Bureau has told us that 22.5% of Latinos/as live below poverty level and 32.7% do not have health insurance, it thus becomes highly unlikely that Latino/a populations would have up-to-date computer technologies available at home and even less likely that appropriate connectivity to the Internet would be present at home. Latino/a children are far less likely than the general school-aged population to have a computer and Internet access than other children. In fact, Latino/a children are four years behind the general population in terms of computer use and access (Becker, 2000). In 2001, only 40% of Latinos had computer access at home compared to the national average of 54%. And Internet access is no better, with only 32% among Latinos compared to the national average of 51% (Valdez, 2002).

There is also a cultural component to this digital divide. Many Latino/a learners come from homes founded on cultural elements that emphasize face-to-face communication, and this cultural predilection may tend to decrease the likelihood of rapid rate of adoption and diffusion of new technologies. In some cases, the sterile computer environment can be off-putting to Latino cultures. Milheim (1997) indicates that Latino/a parents may be hesitant to purchase computers for their children for fear they will become anti-social. Milheim also points to parents' concerns over the distracting nature of technology and the potential for children to see pornographic or other negative content on the Web. These concerns are common for all parents, yet most parents are not dissuaded from introducing technology into the household, nor are they aggressively making demands on the schools for acceptable technology solutions.

Compounding these cultural issues may be specific racial demographics such as those pointed out by Ponicki (1989), who shows a steady increase in the segregation of Latino/a learners over a period of 20 years. Nicolau and Ramos (1990) have specifically shown that many low-income Latino/a parents view the school as "a bureaucracy governed by educated non-Hispanics whom they have no right to question" (p. 13). This power distance may contribute to Latino/a disadvantage within schools in terms of current technology resources.

Several steps can be taken to begin to redress the challenges for Latino/a learners and technology, including

- Teacher training (cultural sensitivity)
- Parental involvement/empowerment
- Whole-family technology programs
- Parental technology education
- Direct assistance for home technology and connectivity needs
- Neighborhood computer clubs

Training teachers to be culturally sensitive and involving parents in school learning are standard potential solutions. Tailoring those solutions to technology issues is important so parents feel able to become involved in schools. Solutions must specifically redress any discomforts parents may feel not only culturally but in terms of their own technological skill levels and their abilities to appropriately requests or demands access to technologies for their children. Many technology instructors are reluctant to get involved in contextual and cultural issues, and many parents are even more reluctant to assert themselves where technology issues are concerned. Technology tends to engender a high degree of specialized knowledge, so both teachers and parents may be reluctant to do what we already know can help. There are some

promising programs, however, that have recently been giving hope to Latinos/as interested in advancing their learning through technology. For example, Carrillo (2004) outlines an National Science Foundation (NSF)–funded program called the Migrant Educational Technology, or MET, program. This afterschool program helps families in Detroit learn basic computing skills. Similar to Head Start programs in that the entire family is invited to join in learning, the program extends into the home to help with home computer connectivity. Another example highlights a Chicago low-income Latino/a community learning about computers through parent education and a neighborhood computer club (Chen & Dym, 2003). These small starts are excellent models for local, contextualized solutions that each community must find for itself in the quest for better solutions for Latino/a learners who are disenfranchised from computer technologies.

References

Becker, H. (2000). Who's Wired and Who's Not: Children's Access to Computer Use and Technology. *Children and Computer Technology* 10(2), 57.

Carrillo, R. (2004). *Making Connections: Building Family Literacy through Technology.* Report to the National Science Foundation, Washington, DC.

Chen, J. Q. & Dym, W. (2003). Using Computer Technology to Bridge School and Community. *Phi Delta Kappan* 85(3), 232–234.

Milheim, A. (1997). Buying into the Computer Age. A Look at Hispanic Families. Available: http://www.cgu.edu/inst/aw1-1.html (accessed January 28, 2005).

Morton, I. (1992). *Increasing the School Involvement of Hispanic Parents.* ERIC ED350380. New York: Urban Education.

Nicolau, S., & Ramos, C. L. (1990). *Together Is Better: Building Strong Relationships between Schools and Hispanic Parents.* Washington, DC: Hispanic Policy Development Project.

Ponicki, W. (1989). *School Segregation in Metropolitan Houston.* Chicago: Metropolitan Opportunity Project, University of Chicago.

Valdez, L. (2002). Latinos, Computers and the Internet. Available: http://www.lif.org/technology/fact_sheet.html (accessed February 22, 2005).

Recommended Reading

Espinoza-Herold, M. (2003). *Issues in Latino Education: Race, School, Culture and the Politics of Academic Success.* Boston: Allyn & Bacon.

Farber, B. (1991). *Crisis in Education: Stress and Burnout in the American Teacher.* San Francisco: Jossey-Bass.

Gross, B., & Gross, R. (1985). *The Great School Debate.* New York: Simon & Schuster.

Kozol, J. (1991). *Savage Inequalities: Children in America's Schools.* New York: Crown.

Latino Technology Network (LTN). (2005). Available: http://www.aamainc.com/tech_ltn.htm (accessed February 22, 2005).

U.S. Census Bureau, Income, Poverty and Health Insurance Coverage in the United States. Available: http://www.census.gov/prod/2004pubs/p60-226.pdf (accessed February 22, 2005).

Alison A. Carr-Chellman
and Luis Almeida

ELEMENTARY STUDENTS AND NATIVE LANGUAGE INSTRUCTION

According to the 2000 U.S. Census, language minority students will comprise a total of 40% of the school-aged population by 2030. A significant proportion of these students, moreover, are expected to be Latino/a. Currently there is an estimated 6.18 million Latinos/as between the ages of 5 and 13 who constitute the current Latino/a English language learner (ELL) population in U.S. schools. Such data require that state and federal governments enact policy measures consistent with the most effective practices for second language learners in schools. Nevertheless, the current No Child Left Behind legislation requires structural changes that run counter to second language acquisition theory. This raises serious questions about the education of Latino/a students.

Research on ELLs shows that native language plays a vastly important role in advancing both English proficiency and academic success (Collier, 1992; Cummins, 1979). Both educators and experts in the field of bilingual education recommend that ELL students between the ages of 4 and 7 continue to develop native language communication and literacy skills while simultaneously learning English. This enables the transfer of literacy-based knowledge across two languages. That is, as ELL students acquire basic concepts and skills in their native language, they transfer these skills and strategies to English as they acquire second language proficiency (Cummins, 1979). Furthermore, research in the field of bilingual education supports the use of native language at the elementary level of instruction because it aids a child's social, cognitive, and overall academic achievement at an early age. Education at the elementary level is thus a critical time for Latino/a students to develop a foundation to become successful biliterate, bilingual, and bicultural individuals. Furthermore, ELL students during the elementary school age have the dual task of acquiring language and literacy skills simultaneously in order to maintain academic competency in schools. To do this, ELL students require academic settings that enhance both their native language skills and English proficiency.

Given the importance of native language support at the elementary school level, the current No Child Left Behind legislation includes important mandates about the education that ELL students receive. A significant feature of the No Child Left Behind legislation is the dramatic change to bilingual education requirements and guidelines. The No Child Left Behind (NCLB) legislation replaced Title VII, also known as the Bilingual Education Act of the Elementary and Secondary Education Act (ESEA) with Title III, Language Instruction for Limited English Proficient. The ESEA act is the federal act of 1965, which is reauthorized by the current NCLB. It is important to note that the term *limited English proficient* as a government label for language minority students has surfaced again with No Child Left Behind, replacing the widely used term *English language learner*. The use of the label *limited English proficient* was previously rejected, with *English language learner* used in its place because the former classification implies both a major deficit and significant limitations in what language minority students bring to education and the process they go through in acquiring English. The basic goals in Title III of the No Child Left Behind legislation are similar to those of the former Bilingual Education Act in including English proficiency and high levels of academic attainment in English in order to meet the academic standards each state has set for all its students (section 3102, subsection 1). However, their basic approaches to reaching these goals are very different. Whereas the Bilingual Education Act focused on the role of native language instruction in attaining English proficiency, No Child Left Behind's Title III mainly focuses on English proficiency and aims to monitor the progress of ELL students,

stipulating a specific timeline for transfer into mainstream English classrooms.

While studies show that ELL students require 7–10 years to acquire English proficiency at a level equal to that of their native English-speaking peers, Title III of No Child Left Behind requires ELL students to transfer from bilingual education classrooms to mainstream English classrooms within three years of their placement in bilingual education. The No Child Left Behind legislation's focus is primarily on English proficiency for ELL students. It outlines a specific type of transitional bilingual program that is focused entirely on immersing ELL students into all English classrooms. In comparison with transitional, maintenance, and dual-language bilingual education programs, the type of immersion program mandated by No Child Left Behind has been considered to be the least successful for attainment of English proficiency. In addition, according to the U.S. Department of Education's Biennial Evaluation Report to Congress on the Implementation of Title III, Part A, of the ESEA for 2002–2004, "Title III is a formula grant program to States whereas Title VII provided funding for projects and services at the state, district, and school levels" (pp. 3–4). The National Association for Bilingual Education (NABE) goes on to report that the Bush administration's FY2006 budget provides no increase in spending on ELL students, leaving Title III for the third subsequent year without adequate funding. Given that No Child Left Behind focuses on testing as a primary means of holding schools accountable to meeting state standards and closing the achievement gap across student populations, it is imperative to understand the relationship between funding, standardized testing, and the academic success of ELL students.

The lack of native language support for Latino/a students has important implications for the overall quality of education they receive at the elementary level. This also has serious consequences for the academic success and development of Latino/a students. Jay Greene (1998) states that "a systematic statistical review of the literature on the effectiveness of bilingual education [finds] that children with limited English-proficiency who are taught using at least some of their language perform significantly better on standardized tests than similar children who are taught only in English" (http://ourworld.compuserve.com/homepages/JWCRAWFORD/greene/html). Further studies, including one by the Center for Research on Education, Diversity, and Excellence (CREDE), entitled *A National Study of School Effectiveness for Language Minority Students' Long-Term Academic Achievement* shows that the longer ELL students receive native language support, the higher they score on standardized tests. For example, the Center for Research on Education, Diversity, and Excellence's study focuses on comparing bilingual programs through analysis of ELLs' long-term achievement on nationally standardized tests, including ITBS, Stanford 9, Terra Nova, and CTBS. These national tests each measure academic problems in a variety of different subject areas. The study reports that ELL students immersed in mainstream English classrooms receiving no bilingual or English as a Second Language services showed the largest decreases in reading and math achievement by grade 5. Furthermore, two-way bilingual immersion students performed above grade level in English in grades 1–5, completing fifth grade at the 51st percentile and significantly outperforming their comparison groups in both transitional and developmental bilingual ed-

ucation programs. These reports show that there is a significant relationship between achievement on standardized test scores for ELL students and an increase in the amount of native language support these students receive. This relationship is important, given the current federal legislation guidelines for educational policy and practice for bilingual education and ELL students.

The guidelines set by No Child Left Behind for bilingual education and native language instruction show that the extensive research conducted on bilingual education and the importance of native language instruction is given little to no attention in federal policy. Consequently, questions are raised regarding Latinos/as and the quality of education they receive in the U.S. as well as issues such as language loss, language rights, cultural integrity, and consequences for U.S. society. Lucy Tse (2001) argues that language loss is one of the main implications of limiting native language instruction in the U.S., which ultimately affects individuals, communities, and society as a whole. Tse makes the argument that society benefits from bilingual and biliterate citizens, for there are biological advantages to a culturally and linguistically diverse population. The human race benefits from its extensive biodiversity. Tove Skutnabb-Kangas (2000) at the University of Roskilde argues that linguistic diversity has an important relationship to biodiversity, where subtractive bilingual education programs, such as Title III of No Child Left Behind, have serious consequences for richness in biodiversity. With the focus of federal educational policy entirely on English attainment and immersion of ELL students in mainstream all-English classrooms, the current legislation does not reflect the research on the role of native language instruction for elementary-level instruction of

ELL students. This suggests that the No Child Left Behind legislation may not be the answer for enhancing the quality of education for Latino/a students, the most rapidly growing sector of public school enrollment.

References

Collier, V. (1992). A Synthesis of Studies Examining Long-term Language-minority Student Data on Academic Achievement. *Bilingual Research Journal* 16, 187–212.

Cummins, J. (1979). Linguistic Interdependence and the Educational Development of Bilingual Children. *Review of Educational Research* 49(2), 222–251.

Department of Education (2005). Biennial Evaluation Report to Congress on the Implementation of Title III, Part A of ESEA, 2002–2004. Available: http://www.ncela.gwu.edu/oela/biennial05/summary.pfd.

Skutnabb-Kangas, T. (2000). *Linguistic Genocide in Education, or Worldwide Diversity and Human Rights?* Mahwah, NJ: Lawrence Erlbaum.

Tse, L. (2001). *"Why Don't They Learn English?" Separating Fact from Fallacy in the U.S. Language Debate*. New York: Teachers College Press.

Recommended Reading

Center for Research on Education, Diversity, and Excellence (CREDE), http://www.crede.org/index.html.

Cummins, J. (1981). *Bilingualism and Minority Language Children*. Toronto: Ontario Institute for Studies in Education.

Greene, J. (1997). "A Meta-analysis of the Russell and Baker Review of Bilingual Education Research." *Bilingual Research Journal* 21(2, 3), 103–122.

Krashen, S. (2001). Bush's bad idea for bilingual education. Available: http://www.rethinkingschools.org.

National Association for Bilingual Education (NABE). http://www.nabe.org/advocacy/nc16html.

No Child Left Behind Act (2002). Available: http://www.nabe.org/documents/policy legislation/NCLBAct.pdf.

Soto, L. D. (1993). Native Language for School Success. *Bilingual Research Journal* 17(1, 2), 88–97.

Laura C. Engel

EL PUENTE ACADEMY FOR PEACE AND JUSTICE

El Puente Academy for Peace and Justice is a small, innovative high school in New York City that emerged from, and is part of, El Puente, a community-based organization in Brooklyn, New York. Founded in 1982 by Latino/a activists who sought to stem the tide of violence among young people in this predominately poor and working-class Latino/a community, El Puente today is a vibrant institution that incorporates the a public high school, three youth development centers (afterschool programs), and a number of other community development initiatives. The organization was initially founded as an afterschool cultural development center in response to a protracted period of youth violence during the late 1970s and early 1980s and the inability of existing social service agencies and schools to address these problems. Luis Garden Acosta, El Puente's principal founder and executive director, refers to the streets of North Brooklyn in 1981 as the "killing fields," where one Latino/a young person was killed every week that year as the result of gang violence. In response to this crisis, the founders of El Puente sought to create a holistic afterschool learning community that affirmed the language, culture, and identities of Latino/a students and linked the individual development of students to a broader vision of community development. This philosophy, embodied by 12 principles of peace, justice, and human rights sought to counteract a deficit-oriented service provider ideology with a new vision of youth development and schooling grounded in commitments to self-determination and community development.

In 1993 El Puente Academy for Peace and Justice opened as a New York City public high school under the auspices of New Visions for Education, a non-profit initiative founded "to create a critical mass of small, effective schools that equitably serve the full range of children in New York City" (Rivera & Pedraza, 2000, p. 227). Now in its eleventh year, El Puente Academy serves 150 students in grades 9 through 12, 87% of which are Latino/a and 11% African American. The majority of students are residents of North Brooklyn and come from low-income backgrounds. Although El Puente is a New York City public school, the fact that it was founded by Latino/a community activists who explicitly sought to create a school whose purpose is linked to community development (for the community, by the community) creates organizational conditions that are more reflective of the interests and values of local Latino/a residents than those of professional school district administrators or school planners. These conditions have led to improved educational outcomes for Latino students.

Reference

Rivera, Melissa, & Pedraza, Pedro. (2000). The Spirit of Transformation: An Education Reform Movement in a New York City Latino/a Community. In S. Nieto (Ed.), *Puerto Rican Students in U.S. Schools*. Mahwah, NJ: Lawrence Erlbaum.

Recommended Reading

De Jesús, Anthony. (2003). Here It's More like Your House": The Proliferation of Authentic Caring as School Reform at El Puente Academy for Peace and Justice. In B. Rubin & E. Silva (Eds.), *Critical Voices: Students Living School Reform* (pp. 132–151). London: Routledge Falmer.

Anthony de Jesús

EMERGENT LITERACY

Possibly the single greatest service schools may offer their kindergartners are print-rich environments with a multitude of books, shelving, stuffed animals, and cushions. For Latino students whose print exposure at home may be confined to the labels on food packages, the access to reading materials in English and Spanish that kindergarten classrooms provide is crucial to students' emergent literacy development.

Latino students are the most rapidly growing student population group in the U.S. (U.S. Census Bureau, 2000; U.S. Department of Commerce, 1991), and at-risk Latino children, in particular, have been identified as being in need of early educational interventions at preschools and daycare centers (U.S. Department of Education, 1992). Faced with a variety of economic and language barriers, many young Latino children have become overwhelmed. Consequently, these students often find themselves behind their peers early in elementary school, forcing them to constantly play "catch up" (Stanovich, 1986). A disproportionate number of these students suffer later academic failure (De La Rosa & Maw, 1990; National Center for Educational Statistics, 1996), forcing researchers to examine interventions and assessments that may help prevent future educational difficulties.

Literacy Resources

The literacy resources schools provide children are obviously important in considering children's emergent literacy development. The relationship between access to books and student reading achievement and attitude (or, interest in books) has been analyzed in numerous studies (Elley, 1984; Gaver, 1963; Krashen, 1993). In several studies of students in developing countries (see reviews in Elley, 1998; Greaney, 1996), for example, it was shown that increased access to books at school increases the literacy capabilities of students with low socioeconomic status (SES). Here in the U.S. the increased availability of books to students has translated into better knowledge of vocabulary, comprehension, spelling, and general knowledge (Anderson, Wilson, & Fielding, 1988; Stanovich & Cunningham, 1992). "Book floods," programs that inundate educational facilities with increased book caches, have been shown to promote increased reading, which leads to greater improvements in literacy development (Elley, 1992; Morrow & Weinstein, 1986; Neuman, 1999). Improved literacy ability, in turn, has been shown to lead to improved attitude toward reading and enhanced language acquisition.

A growing number of researchers have examined how increased access to books affects Latino students' reading (see Madrigal et al., 1999; Yaden & Brassell, 2002; and reviews in Dowhower & Beagle, 1998; Neuman, 1999). However, a major dilemma for researchers of these young students lay in how best to assess these students' abilities. One of the most widely used measures of young children's concepts and understandings of the functions of literacy has been the Concepts About Print (CAP) test, which Clay (1993) describes thoroughly in *An Observation Survey of Early Literacy Achievement*. Since the CAP began to be used by educators in New Zealand in the early 1970s, it has been administered widely throughout the U.S. Yaden and Brassell (2002) observed that preschool Latino students significantly improved their early reading conceptualizations as a result of a comprehensive emergent literacy program, and Wells (1986) found that the CAP could be used as a major predictor of one's future academic success.

The CAP has been one of the most widely used standardized measures of students' early reading conceptualizations that goes beyond students' reading readiness skills and looks more closely at students' general understanding of print and its functions. Since it has been standardized in Spanish (Escamilla et al., 1996) as well as English, it has been seen as particularly useful in examining linguistically diverse students' early reading conceptualizations (Teale, 1990).

Conclusion

While studies have examined the effectiveness of various early reading interventions, the research on young Latino students is growing, but limited. Many have questioned the developmental appropriateness of formalized reading routines and assessments for young children, but a few researchers (Clay, 1979, 1993; Ferreiro & Teberosky, 1982; Paris & Paris, 2003) have shown the value of measuring students' early reading conceptualizations in unconventional ways. For that reason, formalized reading inventories conducted in English and Spanish are encouraged (Clay, 1979, 1993; Escamilla et al., 1996). Further analysis is required to examine how increased access to books in English and Spanish affects Latino kindergartners' first and second language development.

References

Anderson, R. C., Wilson, P. T., & Fielding, L. G. (1988). Growth in Reading and How Children Spend Their Time Outside of School. *Reading Research Quarterly* 23, 285–303.

Clay, M. M. (1979). *Early Detections of Reading Disabilities*. Portsmouth, NH: Heinemann.

Clay, M. M. (1993). *An Observation Survey of Early Literacy Achievement*. Portsmouth, NH: Heinemann.

De La Rosa, D., & Maw, C. (1990). *Hispanic Education: A Statistical Portrait 1990*. Washington, DC: Policy Analysis Center, Office of Research Advocacy and Legislation, National Council of La Raza (NCLR).

Dowhower, S. L., & Beagle, K. G. (1998). The Print Environment in Kindergartens: A Study of Conventional and Holistic Teachers and Their Classrooms in Three Settings. *Reading Research and Instruction* 37(3), 161–190.

Elley, W. (1984). Exploring the Reading Difficulties of Second Language Learners in Fiji. In J. C. Alderson & A. Urquart (Eds.), *Reading in a Second Language* (pp. 281–301). New York: Longman.

Elley, W. (1992). *How in the World Do Students Read?* Hamburg: International Association for the Evaluation of Educational Achievement.

Elley, W. (1998). *Raising Literacy Levels in Third World Countries: A Method That Works*. Culver City, CA: Language Education Associates.

Escamilla, K., Andrade, A. M., Basurto, A.G.M., Ruiz, O. A., & Clay, M. M. (1996). *Instrumento de observación de los logros de la lecto—escritura inicial*. Portsmouth, NH: Heinemann.

Ferreiro, E., & Teberosky, A. (1982). *Literacy before Schooling*. Portsmouth, NH: Heinemann.

Gaver, M. (1963). *Effectiveness of Centralized Library Service in Elementary Schools*. New Brunswick, NJ: Rutgers University Press.

Greaney, V. (1996). *Promoting Reading in Developing Countries*. Newark, DE: International Reading Association.

Krashen, S. D. (1993). *The Power of Reading*. Englewood, CO: Libraries Unlimited.

Madrigal, P., Cubillas, C., Yaden Jr., D. B., Tam, A., & Brassell, D. (1999). *Creating a Book Loan Program for Inner-City Latino Families* (CIERA Rep. No. 2–003). Ann Arbor, MI: Center for the Improvement of Early Reading Achievement.

Morrow, L. M., & Weinstein, C. (1986). Encouraging Voluntary Reading: The Impact of a Literature Program on Children's Use of Library Centers. *Reading Research Quarterly* 21, 330–346.

National Center for Education Statistics. (1996). *NAEP 1994 Reading: A First Look*. Washington, DC: U.S. Department of Education, Office of Educational Research and Improvement, National Center for Educational Statistics.

Neuman, S. B. (1999). Books Make a Difference: A Study of Access to Literacy. *Reading Research Quarterly* 34(3), 286–311.

Paris, A. H., & Paris, S. G. (2003). Assessing Narrative Comprehension in Young Children. *Reading Research Quarterly* 38(1), 36–76.

Stanovich, K. E. (1986). Matthew Effects in Reading: Some Consequences of Individual Differences in the Acquisition of Literacy. *Reading Research Quarterly* 21, 360–407.

Stanovich, K. E., & Cunningham, A. E. (1992). Studying the Consequences of Literacy within a Literate Society: The Cognitive Correlates of Print Exposure. *Memory & Cognition* 20, 51–68.

Teale, W. H. (1990). The Promise and Challenge of Informal Assessment in Early Literacy. In L. Morrow & J. Smith (Eds.), *Assessment for Instruction in Early Literacy* (pp. 45–61). Englewood Cliffs, NJ: Prentice Hall.

U.S. Census Bureau. (2000). *Current Population Survey: The Latino Population in the United States*. Washington, DC: U.S. Government Printing Office.

U.S. Department of Commerce, Bureau of the Census. (1991). *The Hispanic Population of the United States: March 1990*. (Current Population Reports, series P–25, no 995). Washington, DC: U.S. Government Printing Office.

U.S. Department of Education (1992). *Fourth Annual Dropout Report to Congress*. Washington, DC: U.S. Department of Education.

Wells, G. (1986). *The Meaning Makers: Children Learning Language and Using Language to Learn*. Portsmouth, NH: Heinemann.

Yaden Jr., D. B., & Brassell, D. (2002). Enhancing Emergent Literacy with Spanish-Speaking Preschoolers in the Inner City: Overcoming the Odds. In C. M. Roller (Ed.), *Comprehensive Reading Instruction across the Grade Levels: A Collection of Papers from the Reading Research 2001 Conference* (pp. 20–39). Wilmington, DE: International Reading Association.

Danny Brassell

ENGLISH LANGUAGE ACQUISITION MODELS

The primary difference between the various methods used in teaching English to students is the amount of instruction delivered in the students' native language. The two extremes on the spectrum are English immersion programs, with no help from the native language, and Transitional Bilingual Education (TBE), with the native language acting as the primary language of instruction as students slowly grow in English proficiency. Each method has its strengths and weaknesses, and by weighing these, a school district can make an informed decision on which to use.

English Immersion

In an English immersion classroom, as the name suggests, instruction is entirely in English. The assumption is that maximum exposure to the language maximizes the speed of the learning process. Teachers may strive to deliver lessons in simplified English so that students learn English and academic subjects. Most often, however, students are put in mainstream classrooms with no language assistance. This is often termed the sink-or-swim method by critics because students are expected to learn quickly and succeed by "swimming" or not adapt quickly enough, fail miserably, and "skin."

English as a Second Language

While English as a Second Language (ESL) classrooms are similar to immersion in that English is the primary language of instruction, some support is given to individuals in their native tongue. Typically, classes comprise students who speak many different languages but are not fluent in English, making it an efficient way to teach English to students from various backgrounds at the same time. Students may attend ESL classes for only a period a day, so they may work only on English skills, or for a full day to focus on academics in addition to English.

Transitional Bilingual Education

Although instruction for some subjects is in the students' native language in a transitional bilingual education classroom, contrary to what many critics claim, a certain amount of each day is spent on developing English skills. The amount of English used is increased steadily every year until students are proficient enough to be put in mainstream classrooms, typically within five to seven years. These classes are made up of students who share the same native language, which presents some difficulty when a student arrives speaking a less common language.

Recommended Reading

Antunez, Beth, & Nancy Zelasko. (2001). What Program Models Exist to Serve English

Language Learners? *OELA's National Clearinghouse for English Language Acquisition & Language Instruction Educational Programs.* Available: http://www.ncela.gwu.edu/expert/faq/22models.htm (accessed August 2, 2004).

Brock-Utne, Birgit. (2000). Education for All—In Whose Language? In Robert Phillipson (Ed.), *Rights to Language: Equity, Power and Education.* Mahwah, NJ: Lawrence Erlbaum Associates.

Crawford, James. (1995). *Bilingual Education: History, Politics, Theory, and Practice.* Los Angeles: Bilingual Educational Services.

Duigman, Peter. (1998). *Bilingual Education: A Critique.* Stanford, CA: Board of Trustees of the Leland Stanford Junior University.

Instructional Methods and Program Models for Serving English Language Learners: An Overview for the Mainstream Teacher. (2003). *NW Regional Educational Laboratory.* Available: http://www.nwrel.org/request/2003may/instructional.html (accessed August 2, 2004).

Porter, Rosalie Pedalino. (1996). *Forked Tongue: The Politics of Bilingual Education* (2nd ed.). New Brunswick, NJ: Transaction Publishers.

Marcela A. K. Movit and Regina Deil-Amen

ENGLISH LANGUAGE LEARNERS AND EQUITY

Equity for young children with disabilities who are culturally and linguistically diverse rests on understanding the role that the beliefs, attitudes, and behaviors of early childhood educators plays in the creation of environments in early childhood settings. This is critical because how these settings are organized, the content of the visible and hidden curriculum, and the language use patterns of the adults will have a significant impact on the development and learning of young children with developmental delays whose home language is not English. Equity in early childhood special education environments is premised on equitable relationships among all children, families, and educators and optimal sociocultural and linguistic support for learning and development. These criteria ensure that young culturally and linguistically diverse children with developmental delays are provided ample opportunities to develop and grow to their fullest potential without placing their cultural heritage in jeopardy. Equity also entails adherence to the normalization and multicultural principles espoused by the Division for Early Childhood (DEC) of the Council for Exceptional Children (CEC) as it identified recommended practices for early childhood special education programs (Odom & McLean, 1996).

Normalization is related to the least-restrictive setting requirement of the Individuals with Disabilities Education Act (IDEA), which promotes the use of inclusive educational settings for young children. According to Odom and McLean (1996), multicultural practices are important to ensure that the differences in cultural background between the practitioners and the children and families they serve do not contribute to cultural clashes but instead promote the cultural competence of professionals (p. 10). Ultimately, providing an equitable education requires dedication and commitment to eliminating barriers (biases and stereotypes) that impede the educational progress of diverse young children and access for families to the special education system and schooling in general.

In our increasingly diverse society, this task is made more difficult by the many questions that remain unanswered regarding preschool children with developmental delays whose home language is other than English (August & Hakuta, 1997; Baca, 1990). These include questions regarding appropriate assessment tools and approaches that can provide a true picture of the abilities and skills of preschool children who are culturally and linguistically diverse. And questions remain regarding the identification and placement of young children who are culturally, linguistically, and ability diverse (CLAD). Thus, the issue of whether young children whose home language is not English are overrepresented in early childhood special education programs continues to plague educators as they struggle to resolve problematic referrals. Additionally, once CLAD children are placed in preschool special education settings, educators must face the inevitable challenge of finding appropriate ways to ensure that the socioemotional, cognitive, language, and physical needs of culturally, linguistically, and ability diverse children are met in ways that validate who they are.

As a result, learning how to support the development and learning of preschool children with developmental delays who speak a home language other than English continues to be a formidable task for early childhood special educators. At issue is what constitutes an equitable and optimal learning environment in early childhood special education settings. The research supports settings that help linguistically and culturally diverse children develop their home language while they acquire English and learn in both their home language and in English. Unfortunately, current practices in many self-contained preschool special education settings fail to reflect the culture and language of the young diverse children they are designed to serve.

Current Practice

Frequently, young children whose home language is other than English are identified for special education services on the basis of "poor" or "limited" language skills as well as "poor" social skills. The standardized tests that are used to determine eligibility for these young children typically indicate that culturally and linguistically diverse children have weak cognitive skills as well. Use of norm-referenced tests persists despite the fact that examiners and consumers are aware that standardized tests not normed on young culturally diverse children do not represent their true range of abilities (Baca, 1990; Cummins, 2001; Ortiz & Yates, 1992). In reporting test scores, examiners are beginning to include the caveat that test results may not be truly representative of a child's knowledge and skills stemming from the bilingual nature of the child (Gosnell, 2003). Despite many reservations among early educators regarding standardized testing and young children whose culture and language differ from those in the mainstream on whom the tests are normed, diverse young children continue to be tested using traditional methods and placed in self-contained early childhood special education settings. This is not to say that there are no young children with special needs in the universe of diverse children; however, more work needs to be carried out regarding the best practice in assessing what diverse young children know and can do.

Once young children of diverse language and cultural backgrounds are placed in self-contained preschool special education programs, early childhood special educators are left to grapple with how to provide them with equitable education and services. There are two immediate issues that need to be addressed. One relates to the attitudes and beliefs of educators around working with immigrant children and their families who may also be low income. Educators' attitudes toward the use of languages other than

English for instruction and social purposes in early educational settings also play an important role in the linguistic support that culturally and linguistically diverse preschool children receive. When educators believe that their role is to teach young children English as quickly as possible because they are in America and English is the standard, they deny the richness of the experiences that immigrant children bring to the learning process. Failing to recognize and respect young children's culture and language by banning them from the curriculum and the classroom sends a clear message, unspoken or not, about what is valued and what is not.

The second issue relates to the types of language used by the adults (input) in early childhood special education classroom. Research has shown that how teachers use language directly influences young children's own use of language. Thus, providing input in English only and not varying the strategies used to get children to talk has the effect of restricting not only speaking opportunities for young children but also the quality of the young children's output. In other words, young linguistically diverse children with delays in speech and/or language who are in need of many opportunities to use language for a variety of purposes have few occasions to do so and no possibility of using their home language.

The issue then becomes how do teacher practices in self-contained preschool special education settings support the development of the home language, the acquisition of the second language (English), and the overall learning and development of culturally, linguistically, and ability diverse young children. The key to providing recommended practices for young children whose home language is not English lies in a teacher's knowledge of the important role that a well-developed home language plays in the acquisition of English and in learning in the second language. When a young children's home language is fully developed, they have an easier time acquiring the second language because what they know in one language and about language use transfers to the other. Supporting the development of the home language is essential to providing diverse young children with equitable and appropriate instruction regardless of the setting. Contrary to popular belief, linguistically diverse children with disabilities are not confused by the use of their home language nor does its use impede their learning. This means that administrators and teachers must understand and be able to use second language acquisition research, the role of culture or family stories and funds of knowledge, and practices that facilitate language development and learning for young diverse learners.

The Culture of the Classroom

When the home language of the children is not the language of instruction in early childhood special education settings, it is important to understand how the various features of classroom culture scaffold the development of the first language, the acquisition of English, and learning in general for young diverse children. The progress that linguistically and culturally diverse preschool children with developmental delays make will be affected by the organization of the physical space, how time is used for activities, how materials are used, and the social interactions between teacher and a child and children and their peers. Ultimately, aspects of classroom culture such as the content of the curriculum, instructional activities, materials, and teachers' language use patterns act to either advance or obstruct the learning of culturally diverse children. To facilitate optimal academic outcomes for children with developmental delays whose home language is not English, classroom structures must respect and reflect values and practices that are familiar to young culturally diverse children and build on what they know and can do. A critical issue is the failure of early childhood special educators to recognize and address the interdependent relationship between strong home language skills and the acquisition of a second language and learning in the second language as they organize the classroom and plan for instruction. Oftentimes special educators feel that the Individualized Education Plan (IEP) precludes the incorporation of culturally and linguistically relevant curriculum and instruction.

Attitudes and beliefs regarding diversity held by schools influence practices and policies that ultimately determine whether linguistically diverse children maintain their first language, attain high levels of proficiency in their second language, and succeed academically to their highest potential. The messages diverse children receive regarding the cultural and linguistic experiences they bring to their classrooms also influence children's concept of self and their acceptance of their families' cultural traditions and linguistic expression. In these self-contained contexts, the perspective of the adults determines whether and how diverse young children see themselves and their families represented in the day-to-day activities of the classroom. Making English the sole medium of instruction and providing activities that are significantly different from those experiences diverse children bring with them sends a clear message about what is important and valued in early educational settings. When young diverse children are exposed early to attitudes, values, and practices that disrupt home-school

continuity, they quickly fail to value their cultural roots and lose their ability to speak the home language, thereby weakening their socioemotional and sociocultural ties with their families (Sánchez, 1999; Sánchez & Thorp, 1998; Wong Fillmore, 1991).

The Role of Language and Significance of Teacher Talk

Although language is only one component of classroom culture, it plays an overarching role in the early childhood special education classroom because it permeates all activities and interactions. As a key component of classroom culture, the language use patterns promoted by the adults have a major impact on the language performance and learning of young children. They serve as the umbrella under which the progress and growth of young culturally, linguistically, and ability diverse children can either be promoted or hindered in all domains of development.

Classroom environments that are teacher directed have been found to provide young children with few opportunities to select or determine the outcome of activities or to initiate play because the setting and play materials are predetermined by the adults. Under these conditions, teacher talk predominates and has been shown to limit children's opportunities to use language in meaningful ways (Gosnell, 2003; Kim, 2004; Petti-Frontczak, Wheedon, & Janas, 1998). When teachers rely on a limited repertoire of strategies and techniques to elicit language across all activities in self-contained early childhood special education settings, language development and language acquisition for children whose home language is not English is hindered. Specific language types that inhibit language development and acquisition opportunities are the prompt-and-say model, leading or control questions (factual or known answer, questions with answer, forced choice), oral cloze, and a high use of directives. All these types of adult language use result in shortened responses (one or two words), nonverbal responses, or no response at all. Oftentimes when linguistically diverse children do not respond, they are given a model to repeat. Young children learning English as a second language encounter difficulty repeating the models not necessarily because there are speech impairment issues but often because they are in the beginning stages of acquiring a second language. Since they are not familiar with the sounds of English, it is not uncommon for sound combinations in English to create pronunciation problems for young English language learners. Teachers should provide models of language for linguistically diverse learners through expansion, repetition, and rephrasing, but they should not require children to repeat phrases or sentences on demand.

When questions and models are presented in rapid-fire succession, they shorten the window for children's responses and oftentimes prevent them from responding altogether. In fact, young diverse children's talk is disrupted when teachers, in an effort to engage them in conversation, use factual or known-answer questions, questions with answers, and forced-choice questions when children are engaged in play or during a teacher-directed activity. This happens because the teachers are testing children's knowledge of such things as colors, names of objects, and the like rather than asking open-ended questions and following a child's conversational lead. Teachers also miss opportunities to provide children who are learning English with key vocabulary and models of natural or "real-life" language use by not describing children's ac-

tions as they engage in play or by not asking children to talk about what they are doing and scaffolding what they say.

Some teachers use differentiated talk with different groups of children. When addressing native English-speaking children, a more natural conversational style is used. This conversational style can serve as a model for linguistically diverse children of real, turn-taking conversation. However, when talking to linguistically diverse children teachers tend to rely on the prompt-say model, control questions, and the oral cloze technique. It is not surprising, then, to find culturally and linguistically diverse children with developmental delays being silenced by classroom discourse structures.

Some activity periods in self-contained preschool special education classrooms lend themselves to the use of real conversational styles. One of these is snack time, when teachers and children prepare snacks from scratch. In these situations, teachers engage in more turn-taking conversations with the children and there are more instances of child-initiated talk. In addition, there is greater child interest and involvement, with more opportunities for incidental learning.

It is clear that adult language use patterns do influence and limit young children's communication to one- and two-word phrases, attempts at imitating the say model, and gesturing or pointing or not responding altogether. Moreover, teacher-directed classrooms minimize child-initiated talk and social conversations around topics of interest to children. When teacher talk during play is heavily dependent on testlike questions, the flow of child-initiated talk and activities is changed to the point of impeding children's talk. Under these conditions, many children ignore the adult or walk away from the play area. Teachers who follow the children's lead in play conversation or ask open-ended questions tend to observe more child initiations and more talking, including the use of self-talk. Conversely, when adults fail to expand on children's comments or to describe what diverse young children are doing, they miss those oft-promoted teachable moments. For diverse young children with delays in speech and/or language, teachable moments include opportunities to provide the much-needed language in natural ways that are meaningful for the child because the language is embedded within the context of an activity of the child's own making.

Implications for Practice

A diagnosis of speech and/or language delay is significant because bringing young culturally and linguistically diverse children into English-medium environments at age $2\frac{1}{2}$ or 3, when their home language is in the early stages of development, is problematic for a number of reasons. First, educators need to understand the research on early brain development. This research has shown the importance for parents and early caregivers in providing enriching experiences because these help young children make important conceptual connections as they explore and attempt to understand their world. The high quality of these early sensory and motor experiences and social interactions accounts for the complexity of the neural network connections established in the brain. These neurological connections lay the groundwork for later learning and language development (Begley, 1996; Shonkoff & Phillips, 2000).

Second, the brain research relates to experiences mediated in children's home language and, clearly, for many immigrant children English is not their home language.

Thus, for children facing the dual challenge of developmental delay and acquiring a second language, early experiences must be in the language of their parents and other significant caregivers to be meaningful and to maintain continuity in the development of these neural networks. The development of language and early conceptual development depends on these early building blocks of sociocultural experiences and sociolinguistic understandings. This early cognitive development is critical in particular for children who may be identified as having speech and/or language delays in the home language. The consequences of limiting input to an unfamiliar language at this early critical stage of development require more intensive and long-term study. Nonetheless, common sense dictates that providing input and experiences through a familiar language will facilitate learning and have more positive outcomes over the long term. This notion becomes critical in light of research that indicates that the development of a sound foundation in the home language of culturally and linguistically diverse children supports their acquisition of English and learning in that language (Cummins, 1996).

A third important reason that makes using and developing only the second language problematic for children whose home language is not English is the sociocultural and socioemotional disconnect that will occur between culturally and linguistically diverse parents and their children. When young diverse children very quickly lose their ability to speak their home language, the families are unable to continue the development of close emotional ties and relationships with their children (Sánchez, 1999; Valdés, 1996; Wong Fillmore, 1991). This means as well that parents are unable to instill important cultural values and beliefs in their young children. Furthermore, loss of the first language at an early age has been found to affect the level of proficiency in English that a child will be able to attain (Schiff-Myers, 1992), with serious consequences for a child attempting to reach grade-level achievement targets.

Finally, promoting the use of a child's home language for social and instructional purposes will help to offset the negative impact of adult language use patterns in the second language only. By relying on limited strategies in English to promote language development and acquisition in English only, teachers contribute to a rapid loss of the home language, including the loss of receptive skills. The serious consequences of language shift for young culturally and linguistically diverse children with developmental delays in the areas of English language proficiency, overall learning, and sociocultural relationships with their families were discussed earlier. But there are also serious repercussions when the culture of the classroom and curriculum and instructional activities ignore the rich cultural and home experiences that diverse children bring with them to formal early educational or intervention settings. When young diverse children are away from home and fail to see their cultural experiences and hear their home language on a daily basis, they receive a clear message of what is considered worthwhile, meaningful, and favored. Many well-meaning early childhood education settings work hard to bring CLAD children into the mainstream while separating them, intentionally or not, from their heritage language and experiences. This type of adult-directed environment is subtractive rather than additive because it minimizes or ignores the experiences and language that young children with developmental delays bring to

their new surroundings. By failing to use young CLAD children's sociocultural and sociolinguistic experiences as building blocks for the acquisition of English and learning in general, subtractive environments make the learning process more difficult by overlooking what is meaningful and familiar for young diverse children. Given the nature of a subtractive early educational setting, it is not uncommon for young diverse children to be labeled as learning disabled by the time they enter kindergarten. Scholars in the field of bilingual special education submit that such a disability could be caused by the educational experiences offered in self-contained special education settings (Baca & Cervantes, 1998; Ortiz & Artiles, 2000). It is also worth noting that at the end of their preschool special education program, a growing number of Spanish-speaking preschool children are officially labeled as learning disabled.

Equity for Culturally, Linguistically, and Ability Diverse Children

How can teachers create equitable environments that will support young children with developmental delays whose home language is not English? Educational professionals who are concerned about meeting the native language, acquisition of English, and other learning needs of children who are culturally, linguistically, and ability diverse must create a new early childhood special education paradigm for educating diverse young children. They must work toward creating school and classroom cultures that validate the language and cultural experiences of diverse young children and instill pride in who they are. To this end and to meet the normalization and multicultural goals of the Division for Early Childhood (DEC), a new early childhood special education paradigm must be conceptualized so that the essential features of programs that promote optimal learning opportunities for CLAD children can be realized. A newly reconfigured preschool special education paradigm embraces language-rich and inclusive settings as additive environments that serve the interests and needs of diverse young children while fostering policies and practices that build strong partnerships between families and special education professionals.

In this new paradigm, early childhood special educators are trained to create inclusive and additive settings that ensure that diverse young children with disabilities feel comfortable about using their native language as they play and learn alongside their typically developing peers and the adults who facilitate their development and learning when they are away from home. Teachers and paraeducators working in language-rich and inclusive preschool special education settings believe in the benefits of using the home language with linguistically diverse children with developmental delays, thereby promoting native language conceptual development while facilitating the continuum of English acquisition that ranges from informal conversational skills to the more formal and complex language necessary for academic achievement. Within a new early childhood special education paradigm, curriculum and instructional activities tap into diverse families' funds of knowledge as early childhood educators embrace families as equal partners in the educational process. Finally, early childhood inclusive settings that provide optimal opportunities for the learning and growth of culturally, linguistically, and ability diverse children promote and facilitate the active involvement of children in early literacy skills development in both the native language and English. This means that culturally relevant books and materials are made available in a purposeful manner and that diverse young children with developmental delays are provided multiple opportunities to engage with a variety of writing materials and experiences in meaningful contexts. In such settings, children are encouraged and provided time to share their family stories as vehicles through which early literacy development is promoted.

Ultimately, to meet the challenges of serving young culturally, linguistically, and ability diverse children and their families, teachers, paraprofessionals, and administrators must have the appropriate knowledge, skills, and dispositions to bring about change in practices in early childhood special education settings. Training for early childhood special education practitioners should be conceptualized within a framework of cultural sensitivity and competence that will enable them to first understand themselves, their attitudes, beliefs, and values and how these affect their practice. Such a framework will facilitate critical reflection and dialogue as early childhood professionals examine the lens through which they view current practices and policies that can inhibit building partnerships with families and transforming curriculum and instructional and assessment practices to better serve diverse young children with special needs. Moreover, preservice teacher preparation programs and inservice training must empower special educators to engage in critical inquiry around issues of social justice that are reflected in the schools and in their classrooms. Equity for young children with disabilities whose home language and culture differ from the mainstream will be realized when early childhood educators make a commitment to challenge current preschool special education policies and practices that deny CLAD young children the optimal learning opportunities offered to their typically developing peers and that isolate or ignore families as contributors to their children's education. Thus, the forging of a new early childhood special education paradigm rests on the willingness of early childhood special educators and administrators to work as allies and advocates to transform the field so it can implement the multicultural and pluralistic principles advocated in the policy statements of the major early childhood organizations, the National Association for Bilingual Education, and the National Association for Multicultural Education.

References

August, Diane, & Hakuta, Kenji. (1997). *Improving Schooling for Language-minority Children*. Washington, DC: National Academy Press.

Baca, Leonard. (1990). Theory and Practice in Bilingual/Cross Cultural Special Education: Major Issues and Implications for Research, Practice and Policy. In Office of Bilingual Education & Minority Languages Affairs, *Proceedings of the first Research Symposium on Limited English Proficient Students' Issues* (pp. 247–280). Washington, DC: U.S. Department of Education.

Baca, Leonard M., & Cervantes, Hermes T. (1998). *The Bilingual Special Education Interface*. (3rd ed.). Upper Saddle River, NJ: Merrill.

Begley, Sharon. (1996). Your Child's Brain. *Newsweek*, February, 55–88.

Cummins, Jim. (1996). *Negotiating Identities: Education for Empowerment in a Diverse Society*. Ontario, CA: California Association for Bilingual Education.

Cummins, Jim. (2001). Tests, Achievement, and Bilingual Students. In Colin Baker & Nancy. H. Hornberger (Eds.). *An Introductory Reader to the Writings of Jim Cummins* (pp. 139–147). Buffalo, NY: Multilingual Matters.

Gosnell, Elaisa Sánchez. (2003). *Classroom Culture and English Language Learners: Negotiating Meaning in Preschool Special Education*. Ph.D. dissertation, George Mason University.

Kim, Kaeley. (2004). Teacher Action Research Project: Researching Effective Teaching Practices. Unpublished paper, George Mason University.

Odom, Samuel L., & McLean, Mary E. (Eds.). (1996). *Early Intervention/Early Childhood Special Education: Recommended Practices*. Austin, TX: PRO-ED.

Ortiz, Alba, & Artiles, Arturo. (Eds.). (2000). *English Language Learners with Special Education Needs: Identification, Assessment, and Instruction*. Washington, DC: Center for Applied Linguistics.

Ortiz, Alba, & Yates, James R. (1992). Characteristics of Learning Disabled, Mentally Retarded, and Speech-Language Handicapped Hispanic Students at Initial Evaluation and Reevaluation. In Alba A. Ortiz & Bruce A. Ramirez (Eds.), *Schools and the Culturally Diverse Exceptional Student: Promising Practices and Future Directions* (pp. 51–62). Reston, VA: Council for Exceptional Children.

Petti-Frontczak, Kristi, Wheedon, Abbie, & Janas, Debra. (1998). Descriptions and Implications of Daily Interactions, Activities and Events in ECSE Classrooms. Workshop presentation at the Division of Early Childhood annual conference, Chicago, IL.

Sánchez, Sylvia Y. (1999). Learning from the Stories of Culturally and Linguistically Diverse Families and Communities: A Sociohistorical Lens. *Remedial and Special Education* 20(6), 351–359.

Sánchez, Sylvia Y., & Thorp, Eva K. (1998). Policies on Linguistic Continuity: A Family's Right, a Practitioner's Choice, or an Opportunity to Create Shared Meaning and a More Equitable Relationship? *Zero to Three*, 12–20.

Schiff-Myers, Naomi B. (1992). Considering Arrested Language Development and Language Loss in the Assessment of Second Language Learners. *Language, Speech, and Hearing Services in Schools* 23, 25–33.

Shonkoff, Jack P., & Phillips, Deborah A. (2000). *From Neurons to Neighborhoods: The Science of Early Childhood Development.* Washington, DC: National Academy Press.

Valdes, Guadalupe. (1996). *Con respeto: Bridging the Distances Between Culturally Diverse Families and Schools.* New York: Teachers College Press.

Wong Fillmore, Lilly. (1991). When Learning a Second Language Means Losing the First. *Early Childhood Research Quarterly* 6, 323–346.

Recommended Reading

Artiles, Alfredo J., & Zamora-Duran, Grace. (Eds.). (1997). *Reducing Disproportinate Representation of Culturally Diverse Students in Special and Gifted Education.* Reston, VA: Council for Exceptional Children.

Brice, Alejandro, & Rosa-Lugo, Linda I. (2000). Code Switching: A Bridge or Barrier between Two Languages? *Multiple Voices* 4(1), 1–12.

Brice, Alejandro, & Roseberry-McKibbin, Celeste R. (2001). Choice of Languages in Instruction: One Language or Two? *Teaching Exceptional Children* 33(4), 10–16.

Kagan, Sharon L., & Garcia, Eugene E. (1991). Educating Culturally and Linguistically Diverse Preschoolers: Moving the Agenda. *Early Childhood Research Quarterly* 6, 427–443.

Katims, David S., & Pierce, Patsy L. (1995). Literacy-Rich Environments and the Transition of Young Children with Special Needs. *Topics in Early Childhood Special Education* 15(2), 219–234.

Kayser, Hortencia (Ed.). (1995). *Bilingual Speech-Language Pathology: An Hispanic Focus.* San Diego: Singular Publishing Group.

National Association for the Education of Young Children (NAEYC). (1996). NAEYC Position Statement: Responding to Linguistic and Cultural Diversity—Recommendations for Effective Early Childhood Education. *Young Children* 51(2).

Nissani, Helen. (1990). Early Childhood Programs for Language Minority Children. *FOCUS*, no. 2. Washington, DC: National Clearinghouse for Bilingual Education.

Sánchez, Sylvia. Y. (1999). Learning from the Stories of Culturally and Linguistically Diverse Families and Communities: A Sociohistorical Lens. *Remedial and Special Education* 20(6), 351–359.

Wong Fillmore, Lilly. (1991). A Question for Early Childhood Programs: English First or Families First? *Education Week* (June), 32–33.

Elaisa Sánchez Gosnell

"ENGLISH ONLY"

The "English Only" movement, as its name suggests, is concerned with the preservation of English as the only official language of the U.S. In a society in which so many cultures are represented, accommodations must be made within schools to incorporate the linguistic needs of all students as they learn the common language. Although several methods of instruction have been proposed, the one that has garnered the most attention recently is "English Only," a program in which students are completely immersed in the dominant culture and, as the name suggests, are given instruction only in English. Spearheaded by policy entrepreneur Ron Unz, "English Only" policies are gaining support in some states, with California, Arizona, and Massachusetts among the first to adopt such an approach.

Since 1981 at least one proposal for constitutional amendment that would make English the official language of the U.S. has been brought forth in Congress each session (Donegan, 1996). Proponents of the movement emphasize the need for a single, unifying language in the public and private spheres. Within schools this has translated into support for English immersion programs that provide only transitional and short-term native language assistance.

The U.S. has always been a nation of immigrants who have brought their cultures, heritages, and native languages with them on their voyage to this country. More than 18 languages were spoken on Manhattan Island when New Netherland became a British colony in 1664 (Crawford, 1995, p. 21). Since then, the number of languages spoken has increased greatly. For the 2000 Census, "380 categories of single languages or language families" (U.S. Census Bureau, 2003, p. 2) were coded. Despite this variety, as Senator S. I. Hayakawa of California pointed out in 1982 in his introduction of a proposal to make English the official language of the U.S., "the United States, a land of immigrants from every corner of the world, has been strengthened and unified because its newcomers have historically chosen ultimately to forgo their native language for the English language" (Legislative, 2004).

Although the observation made by linguist and anthropologist Rudolph Troike that "no dialect is inherently better or more adequate or more logical than another, just as no language is inherently superior to another" (Porter, 1996, p. 10), remains true, one must acknowledge that English is the most useful language in this country (Porter, 1996, p. 11). To teach this language to students from the wide variety of cultures, schools must adapt their programs to accommodate the linguistic needs of all children as these students strive to guarantee their success in this country by learning English (Porter, 1996, p. 11). Because several methods may be used to accomplish this goal, there is a lack of uniformity from

state to state and even from school to school. Supporters of each method claim that theirs is the most effective, but the lack of conclusive research in this area suggests that there is yet no definitive answer as to which is the best way to help students learn the language.

Although the recent attention the "English Only" movement has garnered from the media may lead some to believe that it is a relatively new movement, since the beginning of American history proponents of native language instruction have had to defend their ideas from those who support English immersion programs. "What distinguishes today's English Only phenomenon is the apocalyptic nature of its fears: that the American language is 'threatened' and, with it, the basis of American nationhood" (Crawford, 1992). The potential impact of these policies on the other 379 or more languages spoken in this country is very real, forcing the movement into the focus of language policy activists across the nation.

"English Only" Organizations

As a public good, education in general attracts the attention of its many consumers. Public interest groups have formed around some of the most pressing issues, and the "English Only" movement is no exception, with U.S. English, Inc., and English First as the most well known of these groups. To support the exclusive use of English in all public arenas including schools, these public interest groups use a mix of positive promotion of their own agenda and negative blocking techniques, endorsing the use of English immersion in classrooms while claiming that the use of languages other than English within the classroom will divide the country. With the widespread recognition that they have gained, these groups have grown into significant opponents of bilingual education in this country. While no amendment or act has legally declared it so, English has slowly become the unofficial "official language" of the U.S. because of the hard work these groups do and because immigrants view English as a higher-status language (Trueba, 1989, p. 84).

Founded in 1983 by Senator S. I. Hayakawa, U.S. English, Inc., claims to be "the nation's oldest, largest citizens' action group dedicated to preserving the unifying role of the English language in the United States" (About, 2003). With Mauro Mujica as chairman and CEO, the organization has grown in numbers and strength over the years, permitted, in part, by the strong sense of cohesion that its members feel. United by their mission to make English the official language of this country so that immigrants may have increased opportunities to speak and use the language—what members feel is the most essential tool for the success of these immigrants—members actively work with Congress to promote bills that would make English the official language (About, 2003).

As a more aggressive group, English First prides itself in being "the only pro-English group to testify against bilingual ballots in 1992 and the only pro-English group to lead the fight against bilingual education in 1994" (What, 2001). The organization attempts to influence the government's agenda, at least in part, by heavily backing candidates who support "English Only" legislation (What, 2001). These efforts bring the group's members a step closer to accomplishing their goals of "making English America's official language[, giving] every child the chance to learn English[, and eliminating] costly and ineffective multilingual policies" (What, 2001). While these are noble goals, the

group has been heavily criticized for the militant manner in which the organization presents itself.

"English Only" in Practice

Over the past few years the "English Only" movement has enjoyed a wave of success with three states having opted to bar the use of bilingual education in favor of programs that use only English as the language of instruction. This recent push, which has been the subject of much publicity, is led by policy entrepreneur Ron Unz, who is working with the movement to gain influence state by state. Among the first states to adopt "English Only" policies were California and Massachusetts.

California. Throughout the 1990s Californians became increasingly polarized along racial, ethnic, and lingual lines. The change in demographics throughout the decade caused the sentiments that had led to Proposition 63 to grow even stronger. In 1998, as one-quarter of all students enrolled in kindergarten through twelfth grade in California had limited English proficiency and white Californians were quickly approaching minority status, the threat of losing political power and disdain for having to pay for expensive language programs that only benefited others' children opened a policy window in which the white citizens, who comprise a minority of the population but a majority of the voters, would be likely to support an "English Only" law (Crawford, 1997).

After a failed campaign for governor of California, Ron Unz, a policy entrepreneur, turned his attention to the adoption of such "English Only" policies. He took advantage of the opportunity that arose and, using his claim to a hearing and political connections, managed to couple an "English Only" policy with the "set of fears and

beliefs of a voting California unrepresen-
tative of the state—white, older, only 15
percent with children in public schools"
(Crawford, 1997). Nonetheless, Unz realized the importance of not alienating immigrants or Hispanics in ensuring the success
of his proposition and intentionally distanced himself from the traditional "English Only" organization whose nativist
views could be harmful to his campaign
(Crawford, 1997); selected as his co-chair
Gloria Matta Tuchman, a former first grade
teacher who widely publicized her Hispanic heritage (Crawford, 1998); and titled
his initiative "English for the Children," a
neutral goal with which no one could find
fault (Crawford, 1997); yet the issue of
language rights was never addressed. The
success of his pretense as an advocate
against schools that were not filling the
needs of the public—once more taking a
neutral position—can be seen in the more
than 510,796 petitions for this policy, which
allowed Proposition 227 to be placed on the
June primary ballot and in its adoption, with
61% in favor and 39% against the policy
(Crawford, 1997, 1998).

Although Proposition 227 officially ended
the use of bilingual education in classrooms
across California, bilingual education advocates were not ready to accept defeat and
reacted immediately to the new law. Even
before the school year began, restraining
orders were requested for this policy that
was said to infringe on the civil rights of
students with limited English proficiency.
Using the small loophole that they could
find, entire school districts requested waivers for their students so that bilingual education classes could continue to run and
students' language rights could be maintained. At every turn, however, the legal
efforts of those who supported the maintenance of this program were thwarted by a

district court or the State Department of
Education (Moore, 1998).

Although critics claim that the immediate
effects of the adoption of Proposition 227
were minimal, five years of data and observations allow for the evaluation of the
long-term consequences of this policy. Despite the non-compliance of some school
districts, "the percentage of students receiving bilingual education . . . has declined
and the percentage receiving varieties of
English-only instruction . . . has increased"
(Crawford, 2003), with 8.8% of language
minority students enrolled in bilingual education classrooms and 43.4% enrolled in
English immersion classrooms during the
2002–2003 school year, as compared to the
29.1% in bilingual education and 21.9% in
immersion classrooms in the 1997–1998
school year. Nonetheless, there has not been
a significant change in the percentage of
students with limited English proficiency
whose knowledge of English has improved
to such a degree that they may be redesig-
nated as fluent English proficiency students.
One year of English immersion has been
enough language instruction for only one in
every thirteen English language learners. In
short, Proposition 227 has failed 92% of the
students it was supposed to help (Crawford,
2003).

Massachusetts. Having successfully
headed the campaign for "English Only"
instruction in his home state of California,
Ron Unz turned his attention outward to
other states that he felt might be equally
receptive to his ideas. When Lincoln Tamayo and his organization, "English for the
Children of Massachusetts" (Dalton, 2002),
requested Unz's help in dismantling bilingual education in Massachusetts—a goal
they had been trying unsuccessfully to
achieve for 17 years—Unz jumped at the
chance to repeat his accomplishment. Al-

though there were other states, such as Florida or Texas, with larger numbers of language minority students, the ballot initiative process of Massachusetts seemed to be the ideal forum for Unz to once again work his magic (Forman, 2002).

Despite Massachusetts's reputation for being liberal (dePass, 2003), Unz's initiative had widespread appeal. Although not as overt as in California, "the ever-present currents of racism, cultural chauvinism and family mythology swirled" throughout the state (dePass, 2003). Just as he cleverly concocted the name "English for the Children" so that no one could find fault with the organization's explicit goals, Unz formulated his policy so it seemed to emphasize second language instruction, multiculturalism, and liberlism—all impeccable goals that quickly made the issue of language rights quite forgettable (dePass, 2003). The initiative was presented as "a choice between what they called 'a failed experiment,' and their tested 'common-sense' teaching approach" (dePass, 2003). With these clever marketing ploys, Unz was able to get Question 2 on the November ballot and have it pass with 68% in favor and only 32% against this initiative (Beardsley, 2003).

Although there was a huge margin in favor of the initiative as it stood, state legislators felt that it was too rigid to fill the needs of all students. Because of the indisputable success that has been shown in schools with two-way programs, these schools have been completely exempted from the provisions of the law. Legislators also broadened the eligibility requirements for waivers to allow students to remain in bilingual education classrooms, permitting more students to take advantage of this loophole in the policy. Much to the chagrin of "English for the Children" and the relief of those who wish to protect students' language rights, Question 2 has been weakened greatly (Vaishnav, 2003a).

Because Question 2 has been in place for only one school year, its long term effects have yet to be seen. While the policy may work well for students who immigrate to the United States from highly developed countries where they received an excellent education and may have had some previous exposure to English, one year in an English immersion program may not suffice for those from poorer countries with inadequate previous schooling. The way in which teachers interact with their classes also may be greatly affected as the law gives parents the right to take legal action to ensure that their child is being taught solely in English (Good, 2002). Quite to the contrary, however, many parents are taking advantage of the waivers that are being offered, which permit their child to remain in bilingual education classrooms (Vaishnav, 2003b). By the end of the school year, these issues will have been played out more fully, and the true effects of Questions 2 on students with limited English proficiency will be revealed.

California and Massachusetts: What the Future Holds

Despite the existence of well-established public interest groups that specialize in "English Only" policy, it was an individual policy entrepreneur that was able to understand and take advantage of the policy window when it presented itself. In California, Ron Unz realized that the cultural wars that were brewing could easily be coupled with his agenda to solve several problems at one time. Having gained national recognition for his achievements, his assistance was requested in Massachusetts to resolve similar existing problems with the same desired result. He quickly became invaluable to the "English Only" movement because he positioned himself to be in the right place at the right time and was able to identify the exact moment to act with little concern for the language rights of the students.

Because the main actor in both states was the same, it is not surprising that a side-by-side comparison of the two policies shows that they are very similar in their provisions. Both were meant to replace the bilingual education programs that existed in their respective states with English immersion programs in which students would be enrolled for only one year. The sentiment that being taught English in English is an inalienable right was so strong that both policies permit parents to take legal action to ensure that their children's rights were not violated. Although the intent is that the exemption only be used in extreme cases, both provide a small loophole—parents may sign waivers that allow their children to remain in bilingual education classrooms. Some of the details are slightly different, but the main stipulations are identical.

Even with the rash of requests for waivers that followed the adoption of Question 2, one can predict that students' language learning experience will suffer, as the same flood of appeals occurred immediately following the incorporation of Proposition 227. The similarity in the climate surrounding the adoption of these policies and in their terms suggest that Proposition 227 and Question 2 will have similar outcomes. While it is too soon to draw conclusions on the level of success of the latter, data from the former suggest that the outcome may be bleak. Proposition 227 has been shown to be a failure. Ironically, this policy that was meant to increase equity in schools by giving all students an equal opportunity to learn En-

glish has resulted in large numbers of immigrants who do not speak the language and have no hope of learning it because they have lost the language support they once enjoyed. Learning English has become more difficult for these students, yet they are being pushed into mainstream classrooms at faster rates. Any support that advocates of students' language rights may wish to provide must be done secretly as the dialogue about other programs, such as bilingual education, which have been proven to help students learn English while also preserving their native language, has been terminated. It is essential to heed the results of the California legislation in considering how to most effectively make our country's most necessary language accessible to all students.

References

About U.S. English. (2003). *U.S. English, Inc.* Available: http://www.us-english.org/inc/about/ (accessed April 3, 2004).

Beardsley, Elisabeth J. (2003). Polls Say Adiós to Bilingual Reform. *Boston Herald*, July 15.

Crawford, James. (1992). Preface. *Hold Your Tongue.* Available: http://ourworld.compuserve.com/homepages/JWCRAWFORD/HYTPREF.htm (accessed April 3, 2004).

Crawford, James. (1995). *Bilingual Education: History, Politics, Theory, and Practice.* Los Angeles: Bilingual Educational Services.

Crawford, James. (1997). The Campaign against Proposition 227: A Post Mortem. *Bilingual Research Journal.* 21(1), 1–29.

Crawford, James. (1998). Proposition 227: Antibilingual Education Initiative in California. Available: http://ourworld.compuserve.com/homepages/JWCRAWFORD/unz.htm (accessed April 3, 2004).

Crawford, James. (2003). A Few Things Ron Unz Would Prefer You Didn't Know About...English Learners in California. Available: http://ourworld.compuserve.com/homepages/JWCRAWFORD/castats.htm (accessed April 3, 2004).

Dalton, Tom. (2002). Cuban Immigrant Argues for Immersion. *Eagle Tribune*, October 20. Available: http://www.eagletribune.com/news/stories/20021020/FP_005.htm (accessed April 3, 2004).

Deil-Amen, Regina. (2003). Different Methods. EDTHP 597 Lecture, November 6.

dePass, Ty. (2003). Bay State Votes to Kill Bilingual Ed: Bilingual Vote Exposed Voter Biases on Language, Culture, and Race. *Resist, Inc.* Available: http://www.resistinc.org/newsletter/issues/2003/03/depass.html (accessed April 3, 2004).

Donegan, Craig. (1996). Debate over Bilingualism. *CO Researcher* 6(3), 51–64.

Forman, Ethan. (2002). Sunshine State Bachelor Battles for English-Only. *Eagle Tribune*, October 20. Available: http://www.eagletribune.com/news/stories/20021020/FP_004.htm (accessed April 3, 2004).

Good for Immigrants. (2002). *Providence Journal-Bulletin*, November 24. Editorial.

Legislative History: Sen. Hayakawa's Speech. (2003). *U.S. English, Inc.* Available: http://www.us-english.org/inc/legislation/history/speech.asp (accessed April 3, 2004).

Moore, Stephen. (1998). Bilingual Betrayal. *National Review* 50(19).

Porter, Rosalie Pedalino. (1996). *Forked Tongue: The Politics of Bilingual Education* (2nd ed.). New Brunswick, NJ: Transaction Publishers.

Trueba, Henry T. (1989). *Raising Silent Voices: Educating the Linguistic Minorities for the 21st Century*. Philadelphia: Newbury House.

U.S. Census Bureau. (2003). Language Use and English-Speaking Ability: Census 2000 Brief. *U.S. Census Bureau*. Available: http://www.census.gov/prod/2003pubs/c2kbr-29.pdf (accessed April 3, 2004).

Vaishnav, Anand. (2003a). Tamayo Targets Bilingual Changes Legislators Defy Voters, Says Backer of Language Plan. *Boston Globe*, June 12.

Vaishnav, Anand. (2003b). Immersion Waivers Granted Unevenly. *Boston Globe*, October 14.

What Is English First? (2001). *English First*. Available: http://www.englishfirst.org/whoef.htm (accessed April 3, 2004).

Recommended Reading

About U.S. English. (2003). *U.S. English, Inc.* Available: http://www.us-english.org/inc/about/ (accessed April 3, 2004).

Crawford, James. (1992). *Hold Your Tongue*. Available: http://ourworld.compuserve.com/homepages/JWCRAWFORD/HYTPREF.htm (accessed April 3, 2004).

Crawford, James. (1995). *Bilingual Education: History, Politics, Theory, and Practice*. Los Angeles: Bilingual Educational Services.

Crawford, James. (1997). The Campaign against Proposition 227: A Post Mortem. *Bilingual Research Journal* 21(1), 1–29.

Crawford, James. (1998). Proposition 227: Anti-bilingual Education Initiative in California. Available: http://ourworld.compuserve.com/homepages/JWCRAWFORD/unz.htm (accessed April 3, 2004).

Crawford, James. (2003). A Few Things Ron Unz Would Prefer You Didn't Know About . . . English Learners in California. Available: http://ourworld.compuserve.com/homepages/JWCRAWFORD/castats.htm (accessed April 3, 2004).

Donegan, Craig. (1996). "Debate over Bilingualism." *CO Researcher* 6(3), 51–64.

Porter, Rosalie Pedalino. (1996). *Forked Tongue: The Politics of Bilingual Education* (2nd ed.). New Brunswick, NJ: Transaction Publishers.

Trueba, Henry T. (1989). *Raising Silent Voices: Educating the Linguistic Minorities for the 21st Century*. Philadelphia: Newbury House.

What Is English First? (2001). *English First*. Available: http://www.englishfirst.org/whoef.htm (accessed April 3, 2004).

Marcela A. K. Movit and
Regina Deil-Amen

"ENGLISH PLUS"

Through its promotion of proficiency for all citizens in English as well as in another language, the "English Plus" movement is an acknowledgment of both the multilingual heritage of the U.S. and the current importance of English within this country. Advocates of this movement support the acquisition of English proficiency by nonnative speakers while encouraging the maintenance of their native language. In turn, there is strong encouragement for native English speakers to learn another language in addition to continually improving their own English proficiency. It is believed that rather than forcing the individual to lose his culture and heritage, "English Plus" allows the linguistic and cultural pluralism that define the U.S. to be fully embraced.

Although English is undeniably the primary language of the U.S. and will undoubtedly continue to be the most commonly used language within this country's borders, the 2000 U.S. Census found that almost 400 languages are spoken in the U.S. With the wide variety of languages and cultures represented by the citizens of this country, the "English Plus" movement has garnered increasing support as an alternative to "English Only" policies. Whereas the latter encourages the shedding of any previous identity as immigrants become "Americans," "English Plus" emphasizes the importance of embracing the heritage of students with limited English proficiency as an asset rather than as a flaw.

The history of the U.S. as a nation of immigrants makes this acceptance of those most recently arrived even more crucial, as the appreciation of their past will help us in understanding our own. More than 18 languages were spoken on Manhattan Island when New Netherland became a British colony in 1664. Today, this number has multiplied more than twentyfold. Although one language has grown indisputably in prominence through the years, it is a tribute to our nation's history to honor the languages of others.

To attain the goal of achieving proficiency in both English and another language, proponents of "English Plus" recommend changes that expand constitutional rights, enhance the effectiveness of federal employees who use a language that is not English in doing their jobs, and promote social unity. They support an increase in the educational opportunities available for English language instruction to all learners. They urge policymakers to pass laws that will allow those who have arrived most recently in this country to participate as fully as possible in society while demonstrating the commitment of the U.S. to pluralism, tolerance, and diversity once more. They suggest programs that will encourage those who speak a language other than English to maintain and further develop their mother tongue. They advocate language assistance for those who require such aid so they may have an equal opportunity to the rights guaranteed to all Americans. The advancement of our nation, supporters of "English Plus" claim, rests in the progression of multilingualism in this country.

Recommended Reading

English Plus Movement: Statement of Purpose & Core Beliefs. Available: http://www.mass englishplus.org/mep/engplus.html.

English Plus, Not English Only. (1996). IDRA Newsletter, January. Available: http://www .idra.org/Quotes/Quotes.htm#96jan.

English Plus versus English Only. *League of United Latin American Citizens*. Available: http://www.lulac.org/Issues/English/PlusOnly .html.

Lewelling, Vickie W. (1997). Official English and English Plus: An Update. *ERIC Digest*. Available: http://www.ericfacility.net/data bases/ERIC Digests/ed406849.html.

Online Resources. *Center for Applied Linguistics.* Available: http://www.cal.org/resources/update.html.

Position Statement: The National Language Policy. (1998). *The National Council of Teachers of English.* Available: http://www.ncte.org/about/over/positions/level/coll/107643.htm.

Marcela A. K. Movit

EQUITY AND ACCESS

This entry focuses on two-way bilingual programs as a means to obtain equity and access to education. It examines the demographic increase of English language learners (ELLs) in the country and relates it to the development and implementation of these programs. It provides a program definition, examines its benefits, and dispels myths about two-way programs by describing what the programs are not. It also discusses two complementary indicators for successful program development: access to and equity in education and educational innovation in the context of school reform.

The ranks of ELLs who need extra help learning English have burgeoned in recent decades in the U.S. Almost 4 million public school children—nearly one in twelve—received special assistance to learn English in 2001–2002 (NCES, 2003). An estimated 3.4 million ELLs ages 5 to 17 do not speak English or do not speak it well (U.S. Bureau of Census, 2003). Since the numbers of ELLs continue to rise steadily, schools will require instructional programs to prepare them not only to learn English but to compete academically and succeed in school.

Hispanics are the largest minority population at 37 million and 13% of the population (U.S. Bureau of Census, 2000). A 1996 White House report described Hispanics' overall school experiences as "a history of neglect, oppression, and periods

of wanton denial of opportunity ... [by a system that continues to] deny equitable educational opportunities to Hispanic Americans" (President's Advisory Commission on Educational Excellence for Hispanic Americans, 1996, cited in Osterling, 1998, p. 3). Since the 1960s, the dropout rate for Hispanics is regularly cited between 40% and 50% (Cummins & Fillmore, 2000), and as high as 90% for Puerto Ricans (Nieto, 2002/2003). August and Hakuta (1997) suggest that the educational status of Hispanics is problematic because this group is perceived as a threat to the status quo and scarce symbolic resources. Yet another dynamic contributing to differentiated academic achievement is the structure of schooling as an instrumental means of individualism and social mobility that advantages the dominant middle class (Ovando & McLaren, 2000).

The growth of ELLs in the nation's schools has created a greater gap between the program of instruction and the linguistic and academic needs of ELLs across the nation. Some of these students are in Transitional Bilingual Education (TBE) programs. These are subtractive programs and offer remedial or watered-down instruction to ELLs. They provide segregated, exclusive, and divisive education. Such programs result in the loss of native language literacy skills and limited bilingualism and in widening the achievement gap between ELLs and their English-speaking counterparts (Garcia, 2001). Evidence strongly suggests that in TBE programs, students exit at a critical point that does not allow them to develop more fully their native language literacy and higher cognitive skills that could translate into higher achievement in English-only classes (Calderón & Minaya-Rowe, 2003). Research suggests that programs require five to six years to bring

ELLs on par with average native English speakers in English proficiency and full mastery of the standards-based curriculum. Consequently, exiting ELLs at this critical moment limits their biliteracy skills, jeopardizes their cognitive growth, and lowers their academic achievement (August & McArthur, 1996).

The opportunities for ELLs to succeed academically depend on a solid program of instruction, like the two-way instruction. Two-Way Bilingual (TWB) programs offer all students equal access to quality education, its academic programs, and equal opportunity for academic achievement, bilingualism, and multiculturalism. All student groups benefit from meaningful, challenging, and accelerated—not remedial—instruction (Baker, 2001). Two-way instruction has the potential to offer long-term closure of the achievement gap and attainment of standards for ELLs (Thomas & Collier, 2003). Two-way programs can be construed as an equitable educational program where all students are treated with respect as equal members of the school community. It offers equitable instruction, and it welcomes and challenges all students and staff to do their best regarding race, national origin, education, language, and culture.

What Is a Two-Way Bilingual Program?

In TWB programs, English speakers and ELLs are students of a bilingual program where both languages and cultures are valued and used in instruction (Calderón & Minaya-Rowe, 2003). Schools transformed into TWB programs promote bilingualism, academic achievement, and cross-cultural understanding in all their students along with the other important curriculum goals of a regular school program. Such programs provide instruction for native English speakers and native speakers of another language, for example, Spanish and English, Chinese and English, French and English, Navajo and English, or Korean and English (Howard, Sugarman, & Christian, 2003). These programs are also known as two-way immersion, bilingual immersion, dual language immersion, developmental bilingual education, dual language, and two-way programs (Brisk, 1998).

TWB programs are developed using the same challenging academic and language development standards as basic K–12 education. They integrate ELLs and English-speaking students for instruction in and through two languages (Lindholm-Leary, 2001). The programs provide language, literacy, and content area instruction to all its students in both languages (Thomas & Collier, 2003). When properly implemented, TWB programs offer the following 16 indicators of success:

1. Instruction in the core academic curriculum rather than a watered-down version;
2. High-quality language arts instruction in both languages;
3. Separation of the two languages for instruction with no translations or repeated lessons in the other language;
4. Use of the non-English language for at least 50% of the instructional time and as much as 90% in the early grades;
5. Additive bilingualism at no cost to the students' first language;
6. An atmosphere of inclusiveness and integration for all students—ELLs and English speakers;
7. ELLs learn the mainstream curriculum in their first language while learning English;
8. Support of district and school administrators, teachers, students, parents, and the community;
9. Effective teachers who are proficient in the language of instruction;

10. Benefits from the other-language peers: ELLs help native English speakers learn through their second language, and native English speakers help ELLs acquire the curriculum through English;

11. Peer collaboration and learning together to improve student motivation and increase interest in the school and curriculum topics and activities;

12. Students expand their views, acknowledge and respect the many languages and cultures of the world;

13. Active parental involvement and parent/community–school partnerships;

14. Offered gradually to the whole school rather than on a one- or two-classroom basis;

15. Program implementation by adding more features each year; and,

16. Designed to offer a minimum of six years of two-way instruction.

An important goal of TWB programs is to eliminate the isolation of ELLs from English speakers by providing them with a rich English-language environment and by supporting their academic learning with no risk to their native language development, language maintenance, or their academic achievement (Howard et al., 2003; Thomas & Collier, 2003). On the other hand, English-speaking students are given the opportunity to learn a second language with native-speaking peer models (Cazabon, 2001).

A TWB program is an enrichment approach to bilingual education for all students, for the general population, and for the language minority and the language majority students. It can also be considered a bridge for all students to access and benefit from bilingual-bicultural education and general education programs. There is a valuing of and respect for the language and culture of the participants. It is a bilingual way for educating all students (Calderón & Carreón, 2000; Cloud, Genesee, & Hamayan, 2000).

TWB programs are effective when they are based on current scientific research and emphasize the standards-based curriculum domains while enriching the students' development in both their first and second languages (Calderón, 2004). These programs aim for full proficiency in two languages, understanding and appreciation of the cultures associated with those languages, and high levels of achievement in all core academic domains (Calderón & Minaya-Rowe, 2003; Cloud et al., 2000; Montague, 1997).

The Benefits of Two-Way Bilingual Programs

Research on TWB programs points to educational, cognitive, sociocultural, and economic benefits of bilingualism and instruction in two languages. A summary of these benefits follows.

- *Educational.* TWB programs benefit all students, whether they are minority or majority. All TWB students can acquire high levels of proficiency in their first language and in their second language (Calderón & Minaya-Rowe, 2003). Recent comparative studies have found substantial evidence in support of teaching strategies for students to read in both their first language—Spanish—and English used primarily in TWB programs and in support of expanding these programs (Slavin & Cheung, 2004).

- *Reform.* TWB programs are also potentially beneficial to *comprehensive school and/or district reform movements* as these reform efforts attempt to address the shortage of educational programs that meet educational needs of ELLs by providing them with a genuine schooling environment that sees to their language and academic competence, and social well-being (Lindholm-Leary,

2001). The goal is to have a balanced school and/or district's bilingual population of native English speakers and speakers of a non-English language who are both able to function effectively in two languages (Cazabon, 2001).

- *Cognitive.* Bilingual students demonstrate cognitive and linguistic benefits on academic tasks that call for divergent thinking, creativity, pattern recognition, and problem solving when compared to monolingual students. Furthermore, bilingual students possess enhanced levels of metalinguistic awareness. For example, they possess enhanced knowledge about the structural properties of language, including the sounds, words, and grammar of language. This knowledge is beneficial in the acquisition of reading because it facilitates decoding and in the development and use of academic language in school (Cloud et al., 2000).

- *Sociocultural.* Bilinguals are able to communicate with members of other cultural groups and to expand their world. They can understand and respect the values, social customs, and ways of viewing the world of other language communities. The global village is here and it confronts us with linguistic and cultural diversity that can be a source of conflict and misunderstanding or of celebration and enjoyment.

- *Economic.* TWB programs benefit students personally and their communities because they have the dual language and culture capabilities that are demanded in the global marketplace. There are plenty of jobs that call for bilingual or multilingual proficiency. Students who come to school speaking important languages, such as Spanish, Korean, Navajo, or Albanian, are valuable resources that can contribute to the nation's economic relations with other countries because they already know another world language.

- *Political.* Given the recent terrorist attacks to our nation and the current long-term war, our nation can benefit from bilingualism and bi-

culturalism as strategies and initiatives to bring peace to different parts of the world with non-English speaking communities. Our country would benefit from negotiations, protocols, and deliberations conducted using local languages to defend democracy and protect the general welfare of the citizens of the world.

What Two-Way Bilingual Programs Are Not

Research and practice have demonstrated during the past two decades that for TWB programs to be successful, they should do justice to both languages and cultures based on a strong program design and implementation (Calderón, 2001; Thomas & Collier, 2003). The following descriptors attempt to dispel misconceptions about the programs and list what effective TWB programs are not.

TWB programs are

- *NOT subtractive.* Their goal is to promote native language literacy skills and balanced bilingualism.

- *NOT remedial programs.* Their mission is to enrich with a quality program design for standards-based education while promoting bilingualism.

- *NOT compensatory programs.* Their mission is to educate first-class students who are able to achieve at the highest levels and who are bilingual. The programs need to be at the core of school and/or district efforts.

- *NOT superimposed on existing school or district structures.* They should not be superimposed on an infrastructure that was set up for a traditional bilingual program, like the TBE program. The structures need to be reorchestrated, redesigned, and integrated to make time for and do justice to the two languages.

- *NOT superimposed on existing mindsets.* The mindset of an "enrichment" versus "remedial" bilingual program needs to be clarified and addressed before and during program development and implementation.

Complementary Indicators for Successful TWB Programs

As schools contemplate restructuring, they have the opportunity to develop an innovative program that meets the particular school's needs. In this entry, we examine complementary indicators for successful TWB program development. They are considered conceptual building blocks and have been used in educational theory and effective practices of education. We link them to the education of ELLs, how to best meet their educational needs along with the needs of English speakers.

The two key indicators are these:

1. *Access to and equity in education.* This includes sociopolitical issues, attitudes toward bilingualism, and adequate education.
2. *Educational innovation.* This includes a research-based program of instruction, commitment, time, and perseverance to sustain change and professional development.

The two indicators can complement each other, occur simultaneously, and be used again and again as a rationale to refine and sustain a TWB program. They are the foundation for the initial steps in TWB program development, its rationale for planning the program, problem-solving, dissemination, and so forth.

While the basic philosophy of TWB remains constant, the components may vary depending on the school and student characteristics. For example, diverse ethnic backgrounds and linguistic needs as well as teachers' levels of expertise may vary and depend on the local needs. A TWB program design in one school may not exactly serve another school. However, as schools contemplate restructuring, they have the opportunity to develop an innovative program that meets the particular school's needs. Specifically, the planning process helps both mainstream and bilingual educators establish common goals and become more sensitive to students' needs. The program components are refined as educators gain a deeper understanding of the interplay of the two issues. Concomitantly, theory and practice are integrated into these issues.

The Two-Way Bilingual Program as an Opportunity for Access and Equity

A TWB program can embrace this indicator as a school goal to become more racially balanced and able to ensure equal opportunity for academic achievement, to decrease conflict, and involve parents and community members (Thomas & Collier, 2003). Creating an equitable TWB school environment is a complex and very demanding process. The schools or districts need to be committed to equal access to resources and social equity, and to narrowing the achievement gap between ELLs and non-ELLs. By designing and implementing TWB programs, they can accomplish substantial changes on behalf of ELLs.

TWB programs can help in the following ways:

- *Ensure equity in education.* ELLs have an equal chance to achieve their full potential in a program of instruction that guarantees the same standards-based curriculum offered to everyone in the school and the opportunity to take high-level and demanding courses.
- *Equal access to programs and activities.* TWB programs occupy the main building and the good classrooms; ELLs are no longer marginalized or segregated from the English speakers or allocated in the school's less desirable places.
- *Equal opportunity for academic achievement.* ELLs can learn and achieve to high levels,

and they are taught by qualified teachers who possess the attitudes and skills to be effective teachers of ELLs. They are not taught by inexperienced or ill-prepared, out-of-the-field teachers.

TWB program implementation can support principles of equity and access with respect to all its students so that these principles permeate all areas of schooling. TWB programs are grounded in theories concerning education, assessment, teacher growth, parental involvement, organizational structures, and social constructivism. Social constructivism recognizes that all students construct knowledge socially through meaningful interactions with parents, teachers, and peers regardless of ethnicity, class, and language background (Calderón & Minaya-Rowe, 2003).

The main benefit TWB program planners can derive from a theory in support of the equity and access to a quality education program is the guidance such a theory can provide in judging the soundness of the program designed to meet the needs of both ELLs and English speakers. For example, we can examine the relationship between the TWB program and community background factors (those social factors that go beyond the school and the program) and review the contextual interaction model proposed by Cummins (1979) and Cortes (1986) to fit the TWB model. Figure 1 illustrates this relationship.

The TWB program works as follows based on the contextual interaction model:

- *Community background factors* such as language use patterns in the home, and community attitudes toward the student's first language and the second language contribute to *student input factors*, which the student brings to the educational setting. The setting includes language majority and minority students or ELLs and English speakers. It also involves parental involvement patterns.

- *Student input factors* are first language proficiency, second language proficiency or no proficiency, self-esteem, levels of academic achievement, and motivation to acquire the second language and maintain the first language, literacy, and biliteracy development are in constant interaction with the *instructional program,* resulting in social integration, and various academic, cognitive, and affective student *outcomes.*

- *Educational input factors* lead us to an enrichment program where all students are treated equally. Pedagogy standards provide educators with guidelines for curriculum and teaching to ensure that ELLs have access to the knowledge necessary for their later success. Staff knowledge and application of effective teaching, curriculum innovations, and standards-based curriculum and assessment are crucial for the success of the TWB program. Equal school financing with fund allocations and resources comparable to other non-urban area is also important as are the expectations and attitudes toward the program.

- The *instructional program* gives high status to both groups of students and to their languages and cultures. The curriculum integrates language, literacy, and content, promotes the challenging standards-based curriculum offered to all students, and assesses students' progress continuously. It also has qualified bilingual and non-bilingual teachers and promotes team teaching, collegial working teams, or teachers' learning communities for action research opportunities and professional growth. It also educates and involves parents in their children's education and has partnerships with community organizations, universities, resource centers.

In conclusion, the contextual interaction model accounts for the interaction of the *community background factors* that ELLs and English speakers bring with them as

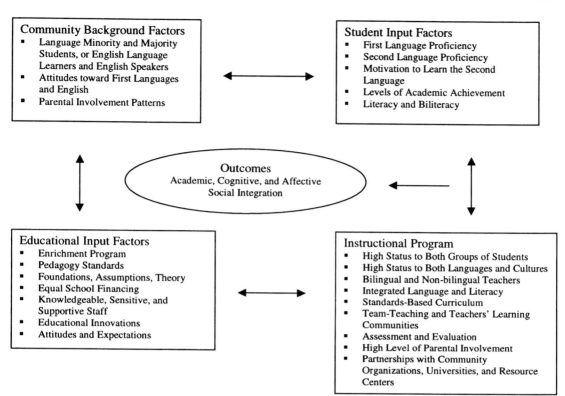

Figure 1
The Contextual Interaction Model for Two-Way Bilingual Programs

student input factors to the TWB instructional program to meet their immediate needs: first language proficiency, second language proficiency, academic achievement, and psychosocial adjustment. Proper implementation of TWB programs can yield positive academic, cognitive, affective, and social outcomes as described earlier.

The Two-Way Bilingual Program as an Educational Innovation

Educational reforms have raised the bar so that all students in the U.S. must finish school and participate in the economic and social world of the new century. These reforms place tremendous pressure on public schools across the nation; they are contin-

uously challenged to meet the needs of a widely diverse population. TWB programs are becoming more common as schools recognize their role to seriously make a difference and offer equal education to all their students.

TWB programs serve educational innovation efforts where ELLs receive enriched and sustained forms of instruction with support in their first language while learning a second language. We must caution schools with existing TBE programs in place who wish to switch to a TWB framework. TWB programs cannot be superimposed on the existing TBE structure or mindsets because they are not compensatory programs (Calderón, 2001). Since

TWB programs are not remedial or subtractive program, they require a whole school reform setting. TWB programs need a new structure; schools and/or districts need to start all over.

The following characteristics or premises of a TWB program need to be considered:

- Their goal is to promote native language literacy skills, balanced bilingualism, and multiculturalism. The atmosphere of inclusiveness in the TWB milieu meets the cultural needs of ELLs and also provides opportunities for ELLs and English speakers to experience the world of their peers.
- Their mission is to enrich with a quality program design for standards-based education while promoting bilingualism. Students have access to academically challenging courses and the opportunity to close the existing achievement gap between English speakers and ELLs.
- They need to be at the core of school and/or district efforts. Their mission is to educate first-class students who are able to achieve at the highest levels and who are bilingual.
- They should be built on a new infrastructure, well designed and integrated to make time for and do justice to the two languages and cultures.
- Their mission is to dispel the myth and mindset as "enrichment" versus "remedial" bilingual program before and during program implementation.

Policymakers and educators also point to education reform to change schools in order to correct perceived social and educational problems and to promote cognitive, academic, and linguistic development (Tse, 2001). The TWB program can be an innovative reform tool to be used to improve school performance. It can yield a procedural reform that introduces new and different socioeducational and linguistic contexts for equitable language and academic education with the goal to produce and sustain socioeducational change.

The implementation of a quality TWB program can make a difference in the school community (teachers, principals, parents, and students) with concrete short-term improvements such as the following:

- Support effective classroom teaching and learning with highly qualified teaching staff working in teachers' learning communities. This includes the development of the local TWB curriculum and instructional approach; the structuring and reinforcing of a TWB language and multicultural experience; specific roles of administrators, teachers, parents, and community and other stakeholders in the program; and building a school climate in the context of school improvement and systemic reform.
- Implement research-proven curriculum and program effectiveness to succeed in school. The implementation covers interactive training on features of the local TWB program: its instructional time, language distribution, student population proportion, implementation strategies, language teaching, curriculum model, assessment, literacy instruction, content instruction, staffing patterns, types and topics of staff development needed, parent education, and program evaluation.
- Design effective staff development with the potential of sustained long-term changes. The design includes detailed and extensive in-service training before and during the school year on instructional methods, materials, assessments and procedures, program evaluation, family support activities, and early intervention strategies. Teachers need succinct information to guide their daily instructional practice they need, for example, oral language development techniques for first and second languages to ensure vocabulary and discourse development, a framework for developing a range of reading skills, how to bridge reading and writing, effective teacher-student and student-student interaction strat-

egies, and ongoing classroom assessment and ways to incorporate them in daily instructional activities for oral, reading, and writing skill development.

- Improve racial relations by promoting positive interdependence among peers and between teachers and students. The program allows ELLs and English speakers to learn through a second language. Both instructional groups receive accelerated benefits (instructional, collaborative, and interactive) from their language peers and from their teachers' use of cooperative learning strategies to capitalize on this effect.

- Reduce dropout rates as students see the school as welcoming them as first-class citizens and where their language and culture are valued. Furthermore, effective pedagogy aims to address ELLs' needs. The program uses an array of techniques for teachers and adapts them to local conditions and to specific circumstances to promote the opportunity to intercalate social experience with academic content in an atmosphere that provides assisted learning and effective instruction.

- Strengthen community and parent participation in the education of children with parent education programs. Parent participation is maintained across the school's grade levels, not just the early grades, with strategies to help children at all grade levels also and with all types of families, regardless of the parent or family composition, with the premise that good results come from all parents. Bilingual volunteers, school-community liaisons, other parents, aides, or staff can form an important communication network to translate information to parents. Financial support is required to develop family-school contacts that support student progress (Delgado Gaitan, 2004).

TWB programs can be pursued through reform implementation, refinement, and sustainability in order to build a capacity for change in the system and to lead the school toward sustained educational improvement.

The TWB program as a reform tool can legitimize the overall performance of a school or district with a workable present and future of both structure and activity (Minaya-Rowe, 2002). The school requires time, focus, and the commitment of personnel who value student input factors. It may nurture school reform efforts with the goal to develop deep understandings of successful research-proven theories and applications for the improvement of teaching and learning (Calderón & Carreón, 2000). Integrating TWB program planning, implementation, and coordination in a multifaceted approach enables planners to alter instruction, curriculum, assessment, staff development, and other school organizational strategies.

Urban schools face many serious challenges in serving their students. With the proper implementation of a TWB program, progress can be made to meet these challenges and to sustain them. The TWB program can be the connection between instructional processes and student outcomes, integrated curriculum and instruction, models of staff development, and parental and community involvement. The program can also foster the organizational processes that sustain change. Existing urban schools' reform efforts have already demonstrated that it is possible for schools serving large numbers of students placed at risk to help these students to levels of education far above levels traditionally achieved by disadvantaged groups of students (Fashola, Slavin, Calderón, & Durán, 2000).

Conclusion

This entry has described TWB programs with the potential to promote an equitable school climate in the context of school improvement and systemic reform. It has provided a definition of TWB programs and illustrated their benefits. It has also described what well-implemented TWB programs are not. The entry has also examined two complementary indicators for successful program development: (1) access to and equity in education and (2) educational innovation in the context of school reform. A discussion of how these indicators can become tools to design an innovative program to stimulate policy changes at all levels and sustain them has also been provided.

TWB programs represent a significant development in the evolution of bilingual and bicultural education and systemic reform (Calderón, 2000). In a sense, TWB programs are the ultimate test of whether schools and districts can become meaningfully responsive to linguistic and culturally heterogeneity and can value students' languages and cultures and provide them with a successful schooling experience. Our challenge as educators, parents, students, policymakers, and researchers is to practice them and become part of the educational transformation.

References

August, D., & Hakuta, K. (Eds.). (1997). *Improving Schooling for Language-Minority Children: A Research Agenda.* Washington, DC: National Academy Press.

August, D., & McArthur, E. (1996). *Proceedings of the conference on inclusion guidelines and accommodations for limited English proficient students in the National Assessment of Educational Progress, December 5–6, 1994.* Washington, DC: U.S. Department of Education, Office of Educational Research and Improvement.

Baker, C. (2001). *Foundations of Bilingual Education and Bilingualism* (3rd ed.). Clevedon, UK: Multilingual Matters.

Brisk, M. E. (1998). *Bilingual Education: From Compensatory to Quality Schooling.* Mahwah, NJ: Lawrence Erlbaum Associates.

Calderón, M. (2001). *Teaching and Curriculum in Two-Way Bilingual Programs.* El Paso, TX: CRESPAR, Johns Hopkins University.

Calderón, M., & Carreón, A. (2000). *A Two-Way Bilingual Program: Promise, Practice, and Precautions.* Baltimore: Center for Research on the Education of Students Placed at Risk.

Calderón, M. E. (2004). Instructional Strategies for English Language Learners. Training delivered for the staff of the Lahaina Middle School, Maui, HI.

Calderón, M. E., & Minaya-Rowe, L. (2003). *Designing and Implementing Two-Way Bilingual Programs. A Step-by-Step Guide for Administrators, Teachers and Parents.* Thousand Oaks, CA: Corwin Press.

Cazabon, M. T. (2001). Coming Together in the Planning Team: Considering Seven Vital Focal Points in the Planning and Development of Two-Way Programs. *New England Equity Assistance Center.* Available: http://www.alliance.brown.edu/eac/coming_together.shtml.

Cloud, N., Genesee, F., & Hamayan, E. (2000). *Dual Language Instruction: A Handbook for Enriched Education.* Boston: Heinle & Heinle.

Cortes, C. (1986). The Education of Language Minority Students: A Contextual Interaction Model. In *Beyond Language: Social and Cultural Factors in Schooling Language Minority Students* (pp. 3–33). Los Angeles: Evaluation, Disemination and Assessment Center, California State University.

Cummins, J. (1979). Linguistic Interdependence and the Educational Development of Bilingual Children. *Review of Educational Research* 49, 222–251.

Cummins, J., & Fillmore, L. W. (2000). *Language and Education: What Every Teacher (and Administrator) Needs to Know.* (Casette Recording No. NABE00-FS10A). Dallas: CopyCats.

Delgado Gaitan, C. (2004). *Involving Latino Families in Schools: Raising Student Achieve-*

ment through Home-School Partnerships. Thousand Oaks, CA: Corwin Press.

Fashola, O. S., Slavin, R. E., Calderón, M, & Durán, R. (2000). Effective Programs for Latino Students in Elementary and Middle Schools. In R. E. Slavin & M. Calderón (Eds.), *Effective Programs for Latino Students* (pp. 1–66). Mahwah, NJ: Lawrence Erlbaum Associates.

Garcia, E. (2001). *The Education of Hispanics in the United States: Raíces y alas.* Boulder, CO: Rowan & Littlefield.

Howard, E. R., Sugarman, J., & Christian, D. (2003). *Two-Way Immersion Education: What We Know and What We Need to Know.* Baltimore: CRESPAR, Johns Hopkins University.

Lindholm-Leary, K. J. (2001). *Dual Language Education.* Clevedon, UK: Multilingual Matters.

Minaya-Rowe, L. (Ed.). (2002). *Teacher Training and Effective Pedagogy in the Context of Student Diversity.* Greenwich, CT: Information Age.

Montague, N. S. (1997). Critical Components for Dual Language Programs. *Bilingual Research Journal* 21(4), 1–9. Available: http://brj.asu.edu/articles/ar5.html.

National Center of Education Statistics. (2003). *Public Elementary/Secondary School Universe Survey 2001–2002 and Local Education Agency Universe Survey 2001–2002.* Washington, DC: U.S. Department of Education.

National Clearinghouse for Bilingual Education. (1999). *The Growing Numbers of Limited English Proficient Students.* Washington, DC: National Clearing House for Bilingual Education.

Nieto, S. M. (2002/2003). Profoundly Multicultural Questions. *Educational Leadership* 60(4), 6–10.

Osterling, J. P. (1998). Moving Beyond Invisibility: The Sociocultural Strengths of the Latino Community. The Case of Arlington's Salvadoran Families. Paper presented at the Annual Meeting of the American Educa-tional Research Association, San Diego, April 16.

Ovando, C. J., & McLaren, P. (2000). Multiculturalism: Beyond a Zero-Sum Game. In C. J. Ovando & P. McLaren (Eds.), *The Politics of Multiculturalism and Bilingual Education: Students and Teachers Caught in the Cross Fire* (pp. 225–227). Boston: McGraw-Hill.

Slavin, R. E., & Cheung, A. (2004). How Do English Language Learners Learn to Read? *Educational Leadership* 61(6), 52–57.

Tharp, R. G., Estrada, P., Dalton, S. S., & Yamauchi, L. A. (2000). *Teaching Transformed: Achieving Excellence, Fairness, Inclusion, and Harmony.* Boulder, CO: Westview Press.

Thomas, W. P., & Collier, V. P. (2003). The Multiple Benefits of Dual Language. *Educational Leadership* 61(2), 61–64.

Tse, L. (2001). *"Why Don't They Learn English?" Separating Fact from Fallacy in the U.S. Language Debate.* New York: Teachers College Press.

U.S. Census Bureau. (2000). *Age by Language Spoken at Home by Ability to Speak English for the Population 5 Years and Over.* Washington, DC: U.S. Census Bureau.

U.S. Census Bureau. (2003). *Language Use and English-Speaking Ability: 2000.* Washington, DC: U.S. Census Bureau.

Recommended Reading

Cazabon, M. T. (2001). Coming Together in the Planning Team: Considering Seven Vital Focal Points in the Planning and Development of Two-Way Programs. *New England Equity Assistance Center.* Available: http://www.alliance.brown.edu/eac/coming_together.shtml.

Cummins, J., & Fillmore, L. W. (2000). *Language and Education: What Every Teacher (and Administrator) Needs to Know.* (Cassette Recording No. NABE00–FS10A). Dallas: CopyCats.

Liliana Minaya-Rowe
and Margarita E. Calderón

F

FAMILY LITERACY IN LATINO COMMUNITIES

Literacy within the context of the Latino family has existed for hundreds of years. Today family literacy has emerged in the context of schooling, and what was the ordinary has now become the extraordinary. Foundational research (Anglum, Bell, & Roubinek, 1990; Bradly & Caldwell, 1987; Chaney, 1994; Purcell-Gates, 1998, 2000; Snow et al., 1991) in family literacy provides us with two suggestions. We are lead to think, first, that family literacy contributes to children's literacy learning and, second, that children's later literacy success in school is facilitated by home literacy practices. Purcell-Gates (2000) tell us that "today there seems to be a growing ideological difference in the field with some taking issue with the stance of family literacy programs that strive to change the behaviors of parents and family members" (p. 858), to change the deficit view of family literacy. Family literacy programs can no longer attempt to provide family education in a vacuum, divorcing the realities of the Latino community. Literacy program can no longer afford to look at Latino families as a "deficit" and claim that Latino families are illiterate and that Latino parents "just don't care." A fundamental epistemological shift inviting the field to retheorize family literacy is necessary for engaging with Latino communities. To begin retheorizing family literacy the author proposes a dialogical method mirroring the work of the Brazilian educator Paulo Freire.

Philosophical Underpinnings of Family Literacy in the Context of Latino Communities

A Freiren-based family literacy practice embraces the notion that knowledge as outlined in a family literacy program cannot be imposed, by family educators, on participants like empty vessels who are waiting to be filled. Instead, the family educator begins to critically engage the participant's distinctive experiences that they bring to the family literacy event and helps them to understand beyond those experiences. This is the essence of a Freiren-based family literacy practice.

Family educators must be seen as transformative intellectuals. Not only must they plan for the family literacy event and reflect with the participants about their ideas that inform their parenting but they also needs to learn about the communities in which the family educator works. Family educators need to create safe environments that appreciate participants' cultural and linguistic differences. The gap must be closed between what the family literacy curriculum and family literacy educator teaches and the real world in which participants live. This can happen only if family educators understand the need for power to shape the family literacy curriculum. Exercising this power creates a space in which the family educator can re-shape the curriculum that will in turn be suited to the interest of the participants.

Family educators spend many hours developing family literacy curricula based on principles of control and assessment. Thus, the focus of the family literacy curriculum then becomes that of teaching basic isolated knowledge and skills. Family literacy events must be seen as social sites with a dual purpose. The first is the imparting of "a knowledge" related to the family literacy training, and the second the "hidden curriculum" of the family literacy curriculums that segregate participants by race, social class, or gender and place value on the knowledge of the dominant culture and a single class (upper-middle).

In a Freiren-based family literacy practice the family educator is primarily concern with ways to educate participants to live responsibly in a democratic state. Family educators are cognizant that their work is political and their purpose is to teach family education such that participants think and act critically. This is done by encouraging participants to develop their own voices in interaction with the voices of the other participants during and after the family literacy event.

Components of a Freiren-Based Family Literacy Practice

A critical foundational characteristic of the Freiren's educational method is "Conscientization," the process in which people achieve a deepening awareness as participants come to understand the sociocultural reality that shapes their lives and their capacity to transform that reality. Components of a Freiren-based family literacy practice include five phases of engagement.

Phase 1: Critical Consciousness. In phase 1 problematic circumstances and conflicts that call for resolution are identified. Family literacy traditionally implores an attitude and model in which family educators enter a Latino community with the goal of providing families valuable information they can in turn used toward their goal of becoming self-sufficient. Usually this type of training is delivered through workshops that involve small and large group discussions and interactions related to the topic being presented.

Using a Freiren-based family literacy practice requires family educators to re-theorize their work and the intention of the family literacy curriculum and event. Although family educators continue to use traditional family literacy curriculum, they know the curriculum is only a means from which to launch the Freiren-based family literacy practice. In my work with family literacy projects in Latino communities, for example, the organization I am affiliated with sets forth requirements regarding the work I do in family literacy. Knowing this, I prepare to deliver the family literacy curriculum through workshops. In my planning, however, I add an additional aspect—that of understanding that the participants bring to the training topic their own lived experiences. To illustrate this point, supposed that the family literacy training is on stages of child development. Based on personal experiences, participants each have their own ideas of what the normal stages of child development are. My job, then, is to create an intentional space, during the training, in which the participants and I can explore their realities in relation to the topic under discussion.

When intentional spaces are created for participants to examine their realities in the context of the family literacy topic, what surfaces is a disconnection between the family literacy curriculum and the participants' realities. When this situation emerges, either the family literacy educator or a participant proposes that a *Convivencia* be held to closely examine the issue. This activity is conducted in phase 2 of the practice.

Phase 2: Family Literacy "Convivencias." In phase 2, concentric circles, situated in the family literacy project, enable participants to identify the obstacles that impede their full humanization. *Convivencias* are gatherings taking place outside of the family literacy event. In this phase of the Freiren-based family literacy practice participants further explore and examine those obstacles that impede their full humanization. *Convivencias* may be hosted at a group member's home, at a church, or in a public place like a park, library, or community center. Participants gather to dialogue and reflect on the identified issues. At the end of the session participants are asked to conduct *"Estudios,"* which are phase 3 of the Freiren-based family literacy practice.

Phase 3: "Estudios" (Study Engagements). Phase 3 engages participants in study of the local context or reality and their own perception of that reality—an integration of action and reflection. *Estudios* help group members understand the issues under investigation in deep and meaningful ways. An *Estudio* requires the participants to gather information about the community, home, or group's personal issues through interviews, photos, review of historical documents, and the like. Once this information is gathered, the participants bring what they have acquired to a subsequent planned *Convivencia* and enter into phase 4 of the Freiren-based family literacy practice.

Phase 4: "Decifrando Codificación" (Decodification). Phase 4 requires participants to ask questions about coded situations where the answers become new questions. During the *Convivencia* participants share their artifact or the documentation they compiled as a result of their investigation. The aim of this *Convivencia* is to codify and decode the information to discover meaning in emerging patterns and themes. This is done through dialogue and reflection. At the end of this process participants move into phase 5 of the Freiren-based family literacy practice either as a continuation of the same *Convivencia* or through another *Convivencia*.

Phase 5: Conscientization, Self-cognitive Development, and Liberation. Through this process participant become aware of the real issues they face and how these issues impede their humanization. In phase 5 the *Convivencia*'s main goal is to create a plan of action to resolve the identified issues. The action plan is implemented by assigning specific task to participants. The Freiren-based family literacy practice process is then repeated to ensure that the action taken creates the change necessary to resolve the identified issues.

Why Family Literacy Should Be Retheorized in the Context of Latino Communities

With the increasing rates of Latino student failure and dropout in the last decade, family literacy has come to the limelight as a promising program for parents' involvement in their children's ability to learn. At the same time the high influx of immigrant Spanish speakers in many areas of the U.S. is causing us to rethink how we educate non-dominant cultures. Although more culturally sensitive curriculums are being developed for Latino groups, most courses of study are simply translated from English to Spanish and are void of cultural responsivity. This lack of cultural responsivity in family literacy programs disconnects Latino families from the advantages a family literacy program can provide. Retheorizing family literacy in the context of Latino communities using a Freiren-based family literacy practice will yield results beneficial to children's learning.

References

Anglum, B. S., Bell, M. L., & Roubinek, D. L. (1990). Prediction of elementary student Reading Achievement from Specific Home Environment Variables. *Reading Improvement* 27, 173–183.

Bradley, R. H., & Caldwell, B. M. (1987). Early Environment and Cognitive Competence: The Little Rock Study. *Early Child Development and Care* 27, 307–341.

Chaney, C. (1994). Language Development, Metalinguistic Awareness, and Emergent Literacy Skills of Three Year Old Children in Relation to Social Class. *Applied Psycholinguistics* 15, 371–394.

Purcell-Gates, V. (1998). *Other People's Words: The Cycle of Low Literacy.* Cambridge, MA: Harvard University Press.

Purcell-Gates, V. (2000). Family Literacy. In *Handbook of Reading Research* (vol. 3). Mahwah, NJ: Lawrence Erlbaum.

Snow, C. E., Barnes, W. S., Chandler, J., Goodman, I. F., & Hemphill, L. (1991). *Unfulfilled Expectations: Home and School Influences on Literacy.* Cambridge, MA: Harvard University Press.

Recommended Reading

Davis, J., & Cooke, S. (1998). Parents as Partners for Educational Change: The Ashgrove Healthy School Environment Project. In B. Atweh, S. Kemmis, and P. Weeks (Eds.), *Action Research in Practice: Partnerships for Social Justice in Education.* London: Routledge.

Freire, P. (1975). *Cartas a Guinea Bissau: Apuntes de una experiencia pedagógica en proceso.* Mexico City: Siglo XXI.

Freire, P. (1992). *Pedagogy of the Oppressed.* New York: Continuum.

Freire, P. (1994). *Pedagogy of Hope.* New York: Continuum.

Horton, M., & Freire, P. (1990). *We Made the Road by Walking: Conversations on Education and Social Change.* Philadelphia: Temple University Press.

McCaleb, S. P. (1994). *Building Communities of Learners: A Collaboration among Teachers, Students, Families, and Community.* Hillsdale, NJ: Lawrence Erlbaum Associates.

McTaggart, R. (Ed.). (1997). *Participatory Action Research: International Contexts and Consequences.* Albany, NY: SUNY Press.

Purcell-Gates, V. (1996). Stories, Coupons, and the TV Guide: Relationships between Home Literacy Experiences and Emergent Literacy Knowledge. *Reading Research Quarterly* 31, 406–428.

Luis-Vicente Reyes

FUNDS OF KNOWLEDGE

The concept of funds of knowledge refers to the historically accumulated knowledge a household may possess resulting from the life experiences, schooling, and activities of family members. The term was coined by the anthropologists Carlos Vélez-Ibáñez and James Greenberg (e.g., 2005), building on Eric Wolf's (1966) analysis of non-market forms of exchange and household economies.

The educational research on funds of knowledge builds on the insight that all households possess a variety of accumulated knowledge (González, Moll, & Amanti, 2005). Thus, a family with rural origins may have developed knowledge about plants, animals, or the medicinal use of plants; a family from an urban area may have knowledge related to urban occupations, such as factory work and construction, or knowledge about particular institutions, such as government offices, hospitals, or city schools. The point is that all families, whatever their composition, origin, or social position within the economy, have accumulated knowledge through their collective experiences, and continue to do so given new life circumstances, that in great part come to define their particular households. As such, households, and the people or families who constitute such units, can be represented in terms of their funds of knowledge, their particular resources or assets for living.

A second insight stemming from the anthropological origins of the concept of funds of knowledge is equally important: how such knowledge is exchanged with other households or institutions. No household exists in isolation; they all form part of social networks with other family members, friends, or acquaintances, relations that also represent an important resource for their subsistence. Thus, the metaphor of "funds" also refers to the exchange of knowledge by household units; an example is when knowledge is activated to help a friend fix a car, knowing that the friend will later reciprocate, pay the favor, using his or her knowledge to help with a task or chore. These exchanges are mostly based on relations of trust, a central element in establishing and maintaining household social networks.

The research on funds of knowledge generally involves close collaboration between university researchers and classroom teachers, usually through the formation of study groups, in visiting local households.

The goal of these visits is to learn from the families and to establish trusting relationships that will allow documentation of their experiences and skills and the easy exchange of knowledge. A desired outcome of this work is for teachers to develop the necessary theoretical and methodological tools to approach local communities and households from a funds-of-knowledge perspective. This approach allows them to develop a representation of the families based, not on any form of deficit, but on the knowledge and resources the families possess. Another desired outcome is for teachers to work together in creating classroom lessons, often in the form of thematic units featuring student inquiry, that build on the funds of knowledge of the children's families as a way of connecting academic content to life experiences.

References

González, N., Moll, L. C., & Amanti, C. (Eds.). (2005). *Funds of Knowledge: Theorizing Practices in Households, Communities, and Classrooms*. Mahwah, NJ: Lawrence Erlbaum.

Vélez-Ibáñez, C., & Greenberg, J. (2005). Formation and Transformation of Funds of Knowledge. In N. González, L. C. Moll, & C. Amanti (Eds.), *Funds of Knowledge: Theorizing Practices in Households, Communities, and Classrooms* (pp. 47–69). Mahwah, NJ: Lawrence Erlbaum.

Wolf, E. (1966). *Peasants*. Englewood Cliffs, NJ: Prentice Hall.

Recommended Reading

González, N., Moll, L. C., & Amanti, C. (Eds.). (2005). *Funds of Knowledge: Theorizing Practices in Households, Communities, and Classrooms*. Mahwah, NJ: Lawrence Erlbaum.

Luis C. Moll

G

GENDER ISSUES

A 1991 study by the American Association of University Women (AAUW), *Short-changing Girls, Shortchanging America*, found that Latina girls report the greatest plunge in self-esteem of any girls surveyed, that

without the personal self-esteem of black girls or the academic opportunities enjoyed by many white girls, the consequences of silence and marginalization for Latinas are especially dire. . . .

In their teenage years, Latina girls are particularly vulnerable to gang membership and are twice as likely as white girls to become teenage mothers. In school . . . Latinas are less likely than other girls to speak out in class . . . [or be] recognized as gifted, and the least likely to believe they can achieve their dreams. (Orenstein, 1994, p. 199)

Passive and Weak?

However, a recent two-year study of Latina high school students participating in the internship program in a preschool in New York City seriously calls into question this image of high school-aged Latinas as passive, weak (Wilgus, 2002). Rather, these Latina adolescents demonstrated a healthy sense of self-esteem as they actively, intelligently critiqued the early childhood educational practices and beliefs promoted by the co-operating teachers who supervised them.

In her 1994 *School Girls: Young Women, Self-Esteem and the Confidence Gap*, a study of high school–aged girls in suburban and urban settings, Orenstein characterizes Latina high school–aged girls as having "a more negative body image" and being at greater risk for having "higher levels of emotional stress—anxiety, depression, nervousness, insecurity, or exhaustion—than any other group of children, male or female, or any race or ethnicity" (p. 199). One teacher in Orenstein's (1994) study commented:

As a teacher . . . with Latina girls you're combating some really entrenched sex roles: from the time they're little, they have to take care of their siblings and the boys don't have to do that. . . . Then you are combating the bias of people in the school . . . [and] if a girl mainly speaks Spanish, if her English isn't good, forget it. . . . She'll never be recognized as a leader . . . no matter how bright and interesting she is. . . . The Spanish-speaking girls are just pushed to the side and they end up leaving school, joining gangs, getting pregnant. (p. 201)

Orenstein's comment presents Latina high school girls as weak, passive, and easily victimized by the negative self-image the school—not to mention the society at large—attempts to impose upon them. In fact, Marta, the Latina high school girl described at length in Orenstein's study, appears to fit this profile with alarming accuracy. In what is probably an effort to extinguish expected behaviors and to assure she will not become one, her father calls her a *puta* (whore) and does not permit her to leave the house alone, although her brothers and male cousins are allowed to venture out at all hours. At the same time, she is expected to—and does—help her mother with the housework. Although Marta says she wants to become a lawyer, it is apparent in the interview data that she has little idea of the concrete tasks this involves and how to go about realizing her goal. In the absence of any encouragement or mentoring from her teachers or parents, Marta instead chooses to spend her time going for after-school car rides with boys from gangs who point guns in her direction for their own amusement. Marta's lack of self-esteem is evident in these choices—something Orenstein labels as "singularly, tragically female" and as efforts to "maintain self-esteem and seek alternative sources of self-worth" (p. 201).

Contemporary Changes

Observations of and interviews with the Latina high school students participating in the early childhood education internship program suggest that the situation of Latina adolescents is changing: These young women seemed highly self-confident and self-assertive as they actively *and* articulately critiqued the early childhood educational practices and beliefs promoted by the cooperating teachers who supervised them. Three Latina interns, Deirdre, Rona, and Ramona, described some of the cooperating teachers as rigidly, unbendingly committed to their beliefs about

early childhood education and as particularly unyielding with reference to how these should be implemented through classroom practice. In fact, several of the cooperating teachers supported this image of themselves through interview material. With reference to her interns, one teacher, Millicent, expounded, "High school interns come in thinking they know everything but I tell them, 'This is the way I do it.' It took a long time for me to realize that I could do this."

A second teacher, Richard, stated he has often found himself in the middle of "power struggles with new teachers who come in and think they know everything— but they don't." He says, "I know because I've been teaching so long...they try to make children be what they aren't...they try to tell you about the road you have already traveled 1,000 times. I try to tell them 'that's not a good street'...you don't understand...but I do!"

The above-named Latina interns, rather than simply allowing themselves to be oppressed and bullied by these teachers, critically evaluated the behaviors, ideas, and early childhood educational practices espoused by the cooperating teachers and made their own decisions about which beliefs and practices "made sense" to them, that is, which beliefs and practices were in the best interest of young children. One intern, Deirdre, who identified herself as Puerto Rican, actively critiqued the treatment she received from different cooperating teachers. She says:

I never felt disrespected by Gabrielle, my cooperating teacher in the morning, but I did feel disrespected by Jonna, the afternoon cooperating teacher....Gabrielle treats me as if I'm at the same level...she shows respect and consideration for the way I do things with the children and how I handle other classroom responsibilities.

Deirdre clearly believed that Gabrielle, the morning teacher, noticed and appreciated that she could "take care of business" on her own—that she didn't need to be told what needed to be done in the classroom next. But Jonna, the afternoon teacher, either didn't seem to notice this or chose to ignore it. She constantly instructed the Deirdre way in advance of the classroom routine; for example, she would tell her to start preparing the children's snack one-half hour before snack time. When left on her own, Deirdre was observed readily doing this in plenty of time for snack, without having to be reminded. Deirdre commented that as a result, she felt "disrespected" by Jonna: "She made me feel like 'you should know what to do and you're not doing it.' " After carefully assessing the situation, then discussing it with the morning cooperating teacher (Gabrielle) and the assistant teacher, Deirdre concluded, "It felt like there was something else going on," that Jonna, for some personal reason that had nothing to do with her, the intern, felt compelled to "put her in her place" and treat her as if she were a "step down" from the teachers. Deirdre then requested a special meeting with Jonna in which, she reports, she made particular efforts to assume a non-accusatory tone and simply make sure Jonna was aware of her own actions and how they made Deirdre feel. Although in the long run this did not to significantly alter Jonna's tendency to order interns around, Deirdre reports feeling better for having taken this initiative. Thus one would be hard pressed to characterize Deirdre as passive, weak, and easily victimized.

Deirdre's sense that she was entitled and competent to make judgments about early childhood educational ideologies and to then act on these judgments was evident in other situations. She expressed her annoyance with teachers who "just blast the radio or tapes and dance and sing at the top of their lungs." She found it disturbing that although "sometimes the teachers sing and dance with the kids, sometimes the babies just watch. They seem stunned and scared by the loud music and the sight of their teachers jumpin' up and down in their faces." Although Deirdre did not believe it was in her best interest to actively confront these teachers (interestingly, they were also Puerto Rican), she reports she attempted to "role model" by quietly turning the volume down as soon as there was an opportunity.

Deirdre was also critical of the practices of one of the assistant teachers in the lunchroom. At lunch one day the children at her table finished the bowl of mashed potatoes they had been served and wanted more. Deirdre saw that another table had a bowl, which was still quite full, so she encouraged a child to ask the teacher at that table if they would share their potatoes. When the child did so, the assistant teacher shouted at her, "No, and your table has already asked for more—don't come get our food—the rest of this food is for the children at *this* table, and stop staring at the food!" Deirdre found this reaction highly inappropriate if not cruel, especially since scarcity of food is an issue in this population of children, and she told the assistant teacher so.

Another intern, Ramona, who also identified herself as Puerto Rican and African American, critically engaged with the disciplinary ideologies and strategies utilized by her cooperating teacher. Her comments indicate that rather than passively adopting the disciplinary strategies espoused by her family and community, she instead carefully evaluated these strategies, particularly when her cooperating teacher, Gabrielle, presented her with new knowledge about child development. When asked if there was any difference between the way she was raised and the way children at the preschool are dealt with, Ramona drew on her experiences of taking care of her two-year-old nephew. She states:

At a certain age children should be able to understand the difference between right and wrong and the kids we teach (18 months to 2.5 years) fall within this age range. In my culture, kids get "popped" for doing things that are "wrong" since we believe they should understand what's right and wrong.

Ramona says she tried the preschool's disciplinary method of explaining to the child why he couldn't do certain things and he "stayed out of trouble much more than before." In general, she believed this approach "worked better and improved my relationship with my nephew." Ramona states she feels she has "learned things to take home."

In addition, Ramona states that Gabrielle explained that teachers do not make children in the class say "I'm sorry" when they have done something offensive to another child because in this age group children do not yet feel empathy for others. That is, according to developmental theory, these children are in an egocentric phase, a level of cognitive development in which they unable to put themselves in another's place or see things from anyone else's perspective. Accordingly, they are not capable of feeling "sorry" or remorseful for an act that has made another child unhappy or caused pain (e.g., grabbing a toy away from another child or biting another child). Thus in forcing a child at this "pre-empathic" level of development to say "I'm sorry," the teacher risks having a child learn to say "I'm sorry" in rote manner with no real

meaning for him. That is, the child is unable to make a connection between the emotion—a feeling of remorse—and the verbal convention, "I'm sorry." The ultimate danger of this practice is that children come to believe that saying "sorry" absolves them and exempts them from blame or responsibility when they have in some way harmed another. In the worst scenario, one sees children running about the classroom, grabbing and hitting, then mechanically spouting "sorry" when confronted for these offenses.

Ramona eagerly applied this developmental theory to her nephew. She says, "He obviously believes that saying 'sorry' will make things better." Thus she has stopped insisting that her nephew say "I'm sorry": She now attempts to help her nephew, as well as the children in the preschool, make connections between their own actions and another child's distress.

Another intern, Rona, commented, "Where I come from, parents usually do everything for their children, so the idea of getting a child to do as much as she can before helping in a task was new to me." When asked, "What is your attitude toward this idea?" Rona responded, "This way makes more sense . . . a child can learn to be independent. For example, my two year-old sister . . . she's still very . . . my parents do everything for her. She's not developing as quickly as these kids at the center." Thus Rona saw having children take responsibility for themselves in cleaning up and other activities as positively contributing to children's overall development.

The Latina interns have also demonstrated initiative, independent thinking, and critical abilities in their active and conscious rejection of certain of the beliefs and practices of the cooperating teachers in the early childhood center. Specifically, although many of the teachers at the center insist that it is important for children to become independent and autonomous as early as possible, several interns actively disagreed with this tenet and were able to clearly articulate why.

Several cooperating teachers noted that encouraging young children to clean up after themselves has been a "bone of contention" between themselves and the interns. One complained, "No matter how much you explain to them that it's important for the kids to clean up after themselves, they always want to clean up for them."

Cooperating teachers further reported having had particular difficulty getting Latina interns to "let children get as far as they can on their own" in performing a specific task, for example, climbing to the top of the slide. These teachers likewise complain that Latina interns sitting beside children who are drawing or painting frequently draw objects on the children's paper. Even when these teachers have explained that the child needs to be given total control over his or her artwork, many interns seem unable to resist adding to children's work. When questioned about these situations, Ramona, Deirdre, and Rona's responses were similar. Deirdre explained:

I know they think it's important for children to do as much as they can for themselves—to be, you know, like, independent—but in our culture, we like to do as much as we can for the children. We know they can do certain things for themselves—you know, pour their own juice, put on their own coats—but we like doin' stuff like that for them. We like it when they depend on us.

Ramona adds, "It's like when you do things for them, then they stay closer to you . . . we stay close to kids and they stay close to us. We like it that way . . . we're a real community." Finally, Rona states:

I know it's important for them to be independent—when they get older—but for right now, what's the rush? We want 'em to . . . when they grow up, when they're grown-ups . . . to be able to pay their own way . . . to be able to pay for a roof over their head and to pay for food . . . and to give some money back to the family—to be sure our parents are okay—but now . . . I mean, what's the rush?

The following is apparent: although the cooperating teachers believe their Latina interns are passively, obliviously conforming to the child-rearing ideals with which they have been raised (i.e., cleaning up after children and drawing or painting on their artwork), Deirdre, Ramona, and Rona have carefully considered what their cooperating teachers believe, namely, that it is of primary importance for children to be as independent and autonomous as possible, as early as possible. In the end, each of these Latina interns has actively, consciously decided not to "buy into" this idea. Rather, they believe that encouraging close relationships of dependence between themselves and children is of greater importance, that fostering a sense of community takes precedence over allowing a child to "get as far as she can on her own." In so doing, these Latina interns, rather than passively absorbing whatever ideas those in power over them espouse, once again actively evaluate and critique these ideas. They then accept some and reject others. Thus by any stretch of the imagination, these Latina high school students cannot be perceived as weak, submissive victims, lacking in self-esteem and always accepting of mainstream ideas.

Latinas Questioning Existing Ideologies

Lubeck and others support Ramona, Deirdre, and Rona in their decisions to question extent early education ideologies. Lubeck (1994) has discussed problems arising when teachers and administrators take for granted their positions as "experts in childrearing and early childhood education," then proceed to instruct parents, with little or no attention to the parents' individually, culturally, or ethnically based ideas about childrearing and early education. As Lubeck (1994) has pointed out, this position is premised on a belief that certain parents—usually parents of "disadvantaged" children—"will not or cannot provide children with what they need," that it is the responsibility of white middle-class professionals to train these parents in the "correct" child-rearing practices and provide their children with the "appropriate" preschool experiences (p. 33). The position implies a belief that "some cultural practices are preferable (and others, if not 'deficient', certainly less desirable)" (Lubeck, 1994, p. 20), resulting in a situation in which parents not versed in child development research are "expected to listen to those who make claims to greater knowledge and authority" (Lubeck, 1994, p. 33).

Gonazlez-Mena (2001) adds:

The ideal is that children benefit from learning new cultural systems and still keep their home culture; unfortunately that isn't always the case. More often, the dominant culture competes with the home culture and the home culture loses. This happens especially when the program's goals (whether conscious or unconscious) is to eradicate the home culture. When children encounter such "subtractive processes," they fail to grow up with bicultural skills and identities. (p. 11)

Fuller and Holloway (1999) likewise contribute to this discussion:

Many in the field of early childhood education (ECE) espouse a rather narrow view of childcare quality that largely represents the socialization and educational practices—the cultural models—of the white, American middle class.This representation of quality is often characterized by its proponents as "cultureless" by virtue of being rooted in universal norms of child development rather than socially constructed models of appropriate practices. We argue that all formulations about childrearing are constructed within a cultural context, including those that incorporate research findings and professional expertise. (p. 99)

All told, comments suggest that more in-depth investigations and accountings of young Latinas' lives are needed in order to better understand the way these young women navigate their lives outside the misunderstandings of others. Moreover, significantly more investigation need to be made into the nature of care giving as it is informed by culture.

References

AAUW Initiative for Educational Equity. (1991). *Shortchanging Girls, Shortchanging America*. Washington, DC: American Association of University Women.

Fuller, Bruce, & Holloway, Susan. (1999). Families and Childcare: Divergent Viewpoints, *Annals, AAPSS* 563, 98–115.

Gonzalez-Mena, Janet. (2001). *Multicultural Issues in Child Care*. Mountain View, CA: Mayfield.

Lubeck, Sally. (1994). The Politics of Developmentally Appropriate Practice: Exploring Issues of Culture, Class and Curriculum. In Bruce Mallory & Rebecca New (Eds.), *Diversity and Developmentally Appropriate Practices: Challenges for Early Childhood Education* (pp. 17–43). New York: Teachers College Press.

Orenstein, Peggy. (1994). *School Girls: Young Women, Self-Esteem and the Confidence Gap*. New York: Doubleday.

Wilgus, Gay. (2002). "Why Don't You Try Letting Her Do It Herself?" Ideological and

Practical Conflict in the Early Childhood Classroom. Unpublished Ph.D. dissertation, City University of New York Graduate Center.

Recommended Reading

McLaughlin, Milbrey. (2001). *Professional Communities and the Work of High School Teaching*. Chicago: University of Chicago Press.

Oquenda-Rodriguez, Aida. (1999). Latina Girls of Puerto Rican Origin Who Are Successful in Science and Mathematics High School Courses. Unpublished Ph.D. dissertation, University of Massachusetts at Amherst.

Romero, Mary, Hondragneu-Sotelo, Pierrette, & Ortiz, Vilma. (1997). *Changing Fronteras: Structuring Latino and Latina Lives in the U.S.: An Anthology of Readings*. New York: Routledge.

Gay Wilgus

GIFTED BILINGUAL CHILDREN

In the wake of a new millennium, more and more educators face a rich and inevitable diversity in their classrooms. Awareness of differences of culture, gender, ethnic background, and ability must permeate every curriculum and educational decision. Educators have the power to shape and constrain the lives of their students and must aim to meet each individual's needs.

Students with high academic potential and exceptional abilities, or gifts are part of this diversified reality. But who are these children with high academic potential? Who is a gifted student? Is giftedness inherited or acquired? Is it a rare characteristic in a chosen few, or is it present in all human beings? Is it a narrow concept, or does it encompass a multiplicity of abilities and skills? Although definitive answers to these questions have been the focus of considerable and controversial research and

reflection, I believe that there exists a hard-to-define quality (known as intelligence, potential, or talent) in gifted human beings that gives them the ability to acquire skills, become acclaimed performers, process information, and generate products within specific domains at a much higher level than those of the average population. I also believe that these abilities can be found in all ethnic, cultural, and linguistic groups and that socioeconomic stereotypes, ethnic prejudice, political climate, societal attitudes, and language can influence the identification and nurturance of this ability.

Historically speaking, Hispanics children have been disproportionately underrepresented in educational programs serving the gifted (Castellano, 2003). Reasons for their low representation vary, often reflecting a combination of factors related to the definition and conception of giftedness adopted and the identification procedure used. Depending on the criteria used, some children are classified as slightly above average; others are far above average. Some seem to have talent potential in a single area; others appear to have potential in a variety of areas. Some individuals with talent potential seem to have little or no motivation to develop or use that capacity; others are highly interested, motivated, committed, and involved. Some children manifest an unusual talent potential at a very early age; others show unusual performance much later in their development. Youngsters who are not identified and selected for inclusion in special programs are much less likely to be provided with the needed opportunities to nurture and develop their talent potential.

The gifted and talented are clearly a multifaceted and heterogeneous group of individuals, and so are the different definitions and conceptions of giftedness. When dealing with a population of bilingual students, the definition and conception of gift-edness is even more diverse and constitutes a complicated task, given that Hispanics in the U.S. do not constitute a homogeneous group. They represent a combination of people from different Spanish-speaking countries with distinctive characteristics. It is important to acknowledge the characteristics of the gifted bilingual population we are dealing with, since such characteristics will provide the foundation for a definition of giftedness, procedures for identification, and curriculum practices in a program for the gifted. Unfortunately, very few and varied data exist on the characteristics of gifted bilingual students. Until more information is available, care must be taken in generalizing from those few data that exist.

One of the most influential studies regarding gifted Hispanic children, specifically Mexican American, was developed by Bernal (1974). Interestingly enough, the characteristics attributed to gifted Mexican American children were of a behavioral nature, instead of the cognitive view of intelligence as reflected by IQ scores and other single standardized measures. Such characteristics as rapid acquisition of the English language once exposed to it, leadership ability, constant interactions with older playmates, engagement in risk-taking behavior, ability to keep oneself occupied and entertained, and being "street wise" were recognized by others as identifiers of a youngster who has the ability to "make it" in American society.

Based on research done by Maker and Schiever (1989) the following list of characteristics can be found in gifted bilingual students: (1) communicates fluently with peers and within community, even if using nonstandard English; (2) requires touching, eye contact, and feeling of support to achieve maximum academic productivity;

(3) uses personal initiative, independent thought, and verbal aggressiveness, often inhibited in females; (4) highly values nuclear and extended family closeness; (5) is able to function successfully in two cultures; and (6) accomplishes more, works better in small groups than individually.

In a survey conducted to assess the community's perceptions of characteristics of gifted Hispanic students, the following ten characteristics or indicators were associated with gifted Hispanic children: (1) finds many solutions to a problem, (2) likes to try new things, (3) is good at finding other uses for things, (4) is interested in a variety of things, (5) is observant, (6) is creative, (7) is curious, (8) likes to read, (9) is motivated to learn, and (10) asks questions (Bermúdez, Rakow, Márquez, Sawyer, & Ryan, 1991).

Not all gifted Hispanic students will exhibit the characteristics listed here. As previously stated, one cannot assume that all Hispanic students are alike. Each individual's characteristics, together with the cultural, social, economical, and political influences surrounding specific groups of Hispanics, vary. Educators most adopt a non-traditional definition of giftedness, one that view giftedness more broadly, composed of a variety of factors, more flexible, inclusive, and described within the context of a particular culture. The value of such a broad definition of giftedness lies in the potential of identifying a greater number of gifted children from bilingual populations.

Identification of Giftedness in Bilingual Children

There probably are as many different strategies and policies for identifying gifted and talented students as there are programs. Several assessment instruments are available that are well suited to gain reliable and comprehensive information about the gifted individual (see Castellano, 2002; Colangelo & Davis, 2003).

Identifying gifted bilingual students is a complex process because it involves students who are both gifted and from a language and cultural background different from that of middle-class, native English-speaking children. In addition, these children come to school with different levels of English proficiency. Ascertaining the child's language dominance (preferred language) and language proficiency (actual linguistic ability) is a complicated task. Some Hispanic children are fully proficient in English; others are Spanish-monolingual; yet others are in the process of developing a superficial mastery of English. In addition, one can mistakenly assume that all Hispanic children have Spanish language proficiency. Hispanic groups have different degrees of Spanish language exposure and usage.

When educators encounter the challenge of identifying gifted bilingual children, perceptions and judgments about the children's actual ability may be confounded by the children's cultural and language differences. Identification must then be based upon superior *potential* instead of superior performance. Therefore, it is recommended that the identification of Hispanic students for gifted programs should include a combination of qualitative (nomination forms, checklists, observations, interviews, questionnaires, performance-based products) and quantitative (student records, teacher-made and standardized tests, awards, accomplishments, achievements) data that embraces a multiple-criteria philosophy.

The Education of Gifted Bilingual Students

During the past two decades the debate about program development for gifted children has been in response to the general question, What type of curriculum is appropriate for gifted students? Certainly an organized curriculum is a key ingredient in the transformation of a gifted individual's high performance into a mature competence for academic and professional accomplishment. Although this quest generated multiple responses, reflecting the wide variety of definitions and conceptions of the term *gifted,* it showed little disagreement over the need for a differentiated curriculum for gifted children. According to Passow (1982), there are seven guiding principles of curriculum differentiation for gifted and talented students. Curricula for gifted and talented students should

1. Focus on and be organized to include more elaborate, complex, and in-depth study of major ideas, problems, and themes that integrate knowledge with and across systems of thought.

2. Allow for the development and application of productive thinking skills to enable students to reconceptualize existing knowledge and/or generate new knowledge.

3. Enable students to explore constantly changing knowledge and information and develop the attitude that knowledge is worth pursuing in an open world.

4. Encourage exposure to, selection, and use of appropriate and specialized resources.

5. Promote self-initiated and self-directed learning and growth.

6. Provide for the development of self-understandings and the understanding of one's relationship to persons, societal institutions, nature, and culture.

7. Be evaluated in accordance with prior stated principles, stressing higher-level thinking skills, creativity, and excellence in performance and products.

Passow's principles seem comprehensive, encompassing most of the curriculum modifications and adaptations suggested by other educators concerned with curriculum planning for gifted students (see Borland, 1989; Clark, 2002; Eliason & Jenkins, 1994; Gallagher, 1994; Maker, 1982; Tannenbaum, 1983; VanTassel-Baska, 1994).

Another aspect of curriculum planning for gifted children that has received vast attention is grouping arrangements. A wide variety of scheduling and grouping modifications exists in special instruction for gifted students: from modest changes in the program within the regular classroom, to part-time experiences during the school day, to separation from the regular program in special classes or special schools. Gifted bilingual education must take into account the language, cultural values, needs, and interests of the gifted children who are going to be served by the program. As Bernal (1976) stresses, "A gifted program suitable for bilingual children should utilize the cultural values represented and the various language or dialectical varieties found among its student members." It is very important, Bernal adds, that the diverse learning styles found in different individuals or cultural groups should also be incorporated into the curriculum design.

There is no one right way to teach gifted children. No single approach to meeting the needs of the gifted can possibly be right for all schools and all communities. Which scheduled or grouped strategies, or teaching-learning models, are most appropriate should be determined by the student's characteristics and special educational needs as well as upon the availability of specially trained staff, the number of gifted students identified, the physical facilities, provisions for transporting the children, and the general educational philosophy as re-

presented in the school district. Programs and practices for the gifted need to be carefully planned, designed, implemented, and evaluated in order to maximize their potential effect.

Conclusion

An integral part of the educational system requiring attention, gifted bilingual students must be appropriately identified and nurtured so their potential can be fully realized. These students are part of a social and cultural group, and teachers need to learn about it. Teachers need to become aware of how cultural differences may affect student learning and behaving and how to accommodate these differences in the classroom. Language diversity needs to be seen as an intellectual and cultural resource. Students can show potential for high academic achievement and yet be bilingual.

Note

This narrative is based on E. Kogan, *Gifted Bilingual Students. A Paradox?* (New York: Peter Lang, 2001).

References

Bermúdez, A. B., Rakow, S. J., Márquez, J. M., Sawyer, C., & Ryan, C. (1991). Meeting the Needs of the Gifted and Talented Limited English Proficient Student: The UHCL Prototype. *National Association of Bilingual Education: Annual Conference Journal, 1990–1991*, 115–133.

Bernal, E. M. (1974). Gifted Mexican American Children: An Ethno-Scientific Perspective. *California Journal of Educational Research* 25(5), 261–273.

Bernal, E. M. (1976). Gifted Programs for the Culturally Different. *National Association of Secondary School Principals (NASSP) Bulletin* 60(398), 67–76.

Borland, J. H. (1989). *Planning and Implementing Programs for the Gifted*. New York: Teachers College Press.

Castellano, J. A. (2002). Renavigating the Waters: The Identification and Assessment of Culturally and Linguistically Diverse Students for Gifted and Talented Education. In J. A. Castellano & E. I. Diaz (Eds.), *Reaching New Horizons: Gifted and Talented Education for Culturally and Linguistically Diverse Students* (pp. 94–116). Boston: Allyn & Bacon.

Castellano, J. A. (2003). The "Browning" of American Schools: Identifying and Educating Gifted Hispanic Students. In J. A. Castellano (Ed.), *Special Populations in Gifted Education: Working with Diverse Gifted Learners* (pp. 29–43). Boston: Allyn & Bacon.

Clark, B. (2002). *Growing Up Gifted: Developing the Potential of Children at Home and at School* (6th ed.). Columbus: Merrill.

Colangelo, N., & Davis, G. A. (2003). *Handbook of Gifted Education* (3rd ed.). Boston: Allyn & Bacon.

Eliason, C., & Jenkins, L. (1994). *A Practical Guide to Early Childhood Curriculum* (5th ed.). New York: Merrill.

Gallagher, J. J. (1994). *Teaching the Gifted Child* (4th ed.). Boston: Allyn & Bacon.

Maker, C. J. (1982). *Teaching Models in Education of the Gifted*. Rockville, MD: Aspen.

Maker, C. J., & Schiever, S. W. (1989). Summary of Hispanic Section. In C. J. Maker & S. W. Schiever (Eds.), *Critical Issues in Gifted Education: Vol. 2, Defensible Programs for Cultural and Ethnic Minorities* (pp. 69–74). Austin, TX: Pro-Ed.

Passow, A. H. (1982). Differentiated Curricula for the Gifted/Talented. A Point of View. Paper presented at the meeting of the National/State Leadership Training Institute on the Gifted and Talented, Ventura, CA.

Tannenbaum, A. J. (1983). *Gifted Children: Psychological and Educational Perspectives*. New York: Macmillan.

VanTassel-Baska, J. (1994). *Comprehensive Curriculum for Gifted Learners* (2nd ed.). Needham Heights, MA: Allyn & Bacon.

Esther Kogan

GROWING UP NUYORICAN

> Si no hubiera nacido en la tierra en que
> nací,
> Estuviera arrepentido de no haber nacido
> aquí.
> (If I had not been born in the land where I
> was born,
> I would lament not having been born here.)

For many years, this heartfelt refrain in *El buen borincano* (The Good Puerto Rican), by Rafael Hernández, left me feeling like I had missed out on an essential part of being Puerto Rican. But now I, and many thousands more, reinterpret those lines to mean that we celebrate having been born Puerto Rican in New York.[1] Personally, I consider it a privilege to have been raised in the New York Puerto Rican community during the defining period of its history, the World War II era. And I consider it my obligation to set the record straight for those who dismiss us as an immigrant group that went wrong because of a lack of significant social and structural assimilation by the third generation. Critics ignore the extent of our linguistic, cultural, educational, organizational, and economic achievements because our social workers, union leaders, *bodegueros* (*bodega* or grocery store owners), poets, musicians, teachers, garment workers, community activists, doctors, and so on, are missing from the history books. In spite of a colonized homeland that used our migration and sterilization as "escape valves," and inhospitable educational and socioeconomic policies in the new land that constructed us as semi-lingual pathological misfits, we left an indelible imprint on New York. The community that began at the end of the nineteenth century and grew from 60,000 in 1945 to 610,000 in 1960 shook up and reshaped Puerto Rico and New York and Spanish and English, creating strong but often disparaged blends of identities and languages. Today Puerto Ricans in New York are more than 800,000 strong, and a vibrant presence in *La Gran Manzana* (The Big Apple).

The Spanish and English labels—some imposed and some of our own making—that have identified us as a group reflect the linguistic and cultural transformations in which we have participated. At different periods and sometimes at one and the same time, we have been *puertorriqueños, antillanos, caribeños, Marín Taiguers, grinjornes, jíbaros, hispanos, latinos, boricuas, pororicans,* Spanish, Hispanics, Spiks, Puerto Ricans, and Nuyoricans.[2] Although Stavans defines "Nuyorican" as "Puerto Rican person in the mainland" in his *Spanglish* dictionary (2003, p. 181), mainlanders outside of New York do not identify with this term, nor does every Puerto Rican in New York. And many Nuyoricans have moved to Puerto Rico. Those who answer to the "Nuyorican" label with pride are primarily members of the second and third generations who remain bonded to each other and to Puerto Rico, New York, Spanish, and English by the linguistic inventions that took hold in the second half of the twentieth century and defined the "Nuyorican."

The contributions that Nuyoricans have made to the city's linguistic history have not been well received, in part because so many Puerto Ricans arrived during the period (1920s–1950s) identified as the most restrictive in language policies in the history of New York City (García, 1997). The xenophobia of the post–World War I era had given rise to many restrictions against immigrants and their languages, including national origin quotas and English-only laws. Negative attitudes persisted through the World War II era, perpetuated by the children of the immigrants of the first part

of the century. Sadly, they had internalized the pessimistic views of languages other than English and of bilingualism that their parents had been subjected to, and they formed and still form the bulk of the teachers of Puerto Rican children. In their view, Americans must speak English only (Pavlenko, 2002), and Puerto Rican Spanish is inferior. Even more sadly, many Nuyoricans learned those lessons well, but many today are challenging them.

The languages and language behaviors of Puerto Ricans, even those on the island, are attacked for reasons linked to linguistic as well as political, racial, and class prejudices. Some deem Puerto Rican Spanish unacceptable because it differs in pronunciation and some lexicon from that of Spain, although those very same critics would never expect the U.S. to speak the English of Great Britain. Our island's *puertorriqueñismos,* which reflect 500 years of cultural history, include antiquated Spanish terms (*prieto,* dark/black), Taíno words (*mimes,* no see'ums), Canary Island Spanish (*guagua,* bus), African loans (*ñangotarse,* to squat), and homegrown creations (*cur cur/cul cul,* to drink down quickly; *tostao,* crazy; *picao,* tipsy; *enfogonao,* angry), to name just a few.[3] But the cultural and economic power linked to the peninsular Spanish spoken in New York by those who had fled Franco's Spain in the 1930s contrasted with the working-class Spanish of Puerto Rican immigrants in the 1940s. Those invidious comparisons persist, exacerbated today by the negative attitudes of elite South Americans.

Evaluations of Puerto Rican English are no better; speakers are often ridiculed for their Spanish accent, second language errors, and African American influences, although European immigrants had transformed English before them, and new immigrants continue the process. Most misunderstood is the bilingualism of those who were born and/or educated in New York, particularly the ways in which we mix both languages to speak about new experiences, creating a truly Nuyorican *asopao* (stew). The roots of our bilingual style are located not in New York but in the colonial policies the U.S. imposed on Puerto Rico after occupying the island in 1898. For almost 50 years, school children were forced to study in a language they did not understand. The first sentence that my mother memorized, "I cannot tell a lie, I chop [sic] down the cherry tree," was taught as proof of George Washington's honesty and, by extension, proof of the decency and good will of his nation and the deserved supremacy of its government and language. Those benevolent views were put to the test in New York's garment district's *factorías* where *mami* worked hard days for 34 years— *"partáim," "fultáim," "haciendo pisuér"* (doing piecework), with little pay and frequent *"ley-of,"* despite the efforts of *la unión* (the ILGWU). Workers usually were laid off around Channukah and Christmas when *el boj o la bosa* (the boss), whom Italian coworkers often called *"sadamanbiches"* (sons of bitches), went to Florida. El *rosheo, trobol, taxes, la renta y los biles* were everyday worries, and those words laden with pain became integral to our Spanish.

In the garment district *mami* learned that the way you spoke English could stigmatize you forever, and she knew her accent made her a marked woman. Yet she could not speak her own language because it was considered impolite to speak Spanish in front of English speakers, even if you were not talking to them. Conflicted, she advised my sister and me not to yell *"mami"* in the street, but to imitate the English monolinguals who said, as she pronounced it, "moder." "Moder" remained a loving nickname for her as long as she lived, but we realized that giving up *"mami"* was too high a price to pay for trying to fit in. Growing up Nuyorican meant being raised with the message that Spanish was inferior to English, and Puerto Rican Spanish was particularly so, but instead of abandoning our ways of speaking we adapted them to our new reality.

The hard life in New York in the late 1940s and the new words that captured it are evident in Guillermo Cotto-Thurner's *Trópico en Manhattan* (1951). Cotto-Thurner ends his novel with a two-page glossary of the text's 80 *"Neoyorquismos"* (Newyorkisms), accompanied by a Spanish translation as well as the English words or expressions from which they were derived. It is among the earliest lists, to my knowledge, of the *anglicismos* (anglicisms) that pepper what is widely known today as "Spanglish," of the New York Puerto Rican (NYPR) variety.[4] Some of the borrowed words are no longer in style because the reality they captured has disappeared. For example, those were the days when it was common for single men to *"rentar un cuarto furnido"* (rent a furnished room) in a boarding house, or become *"bordantes"* (boarders) in the apartments of families who could not *"soportarse"* (support themselves) *con el "rilíf"* (the city's Home Relief supplement), and who lived in fear of *un "desposés"* (eviction). But the majority of the novel's *neoyorquismos* are still in everyday use, for example, *"lonchar"* (to lunch), *"londri"* (laundry), *"piquels"* (pickles), *"beibito"* (little baby), *"chequear"* (to check), *"liquear"* (to leak), *"chipe"* (a cheap person). And we have new terms for some of the same old problems, including *"guelfér"* or *"wilfrido"* for welfare, and *"cupones"* for food coupons.[5] Like most of the words that Puerto Ricans borrowed from English, they reflect the experience of living in New York.

Sometimes our inventions took the form of new meanings for old words (e.g., *"yarda"* became the schoolyard and back-alley in addition to the standard Spanish measurement), but English words with Spanish pronunciations are more genera-tive. Some of our adaptations of borrowed items are characteristic of the transforma-tions made by all Spanish speakers learning English. These include changing the soft <th>sounds to<t>, as in *"trifti"* (thrifty), the <sh>to<ch> as in *"chopin"* (shopping bag), the hard <j>to<y>as in *"los proyectos"* (the projects). In addition, by substituting the aspirated English <h>or Spanish<j>in place of<s> at the end of syllables, as is common in the Caribbean (e.g., *ejtoj* < *estos*), and changing the <r>at the end of syllables to<l>, as in *paltil* < *partir*, we Puertoricanized the words we borrowed, so that "to scratch" becomes *"ejcrachal."*

Because these creative combinations helped make me and the people I love most who and what we are, they remain identity markers that distinguish potential friend from stranger. When I hear them, I assume that person will laugh appreciatively at my jokes, sympathize with my problems, and agree with me as to who is *buena gente* (good people) or *un comemierda* (literally, a shit-eater). The loan words and ways of speaking that have come to be labeled "Spanglish" stir deep emotions in me be-cause they bond me to my fellow Nuyor-icans. After all, I grew up Nuyorican in Spanish, English, and Spanglish. For ex-ample:

My *"bildin"* (building) was in the middle of our *"bloque"* (block), across the street from *la "candistor"* (the candy store). It had *un "faya ejquéi"* (a fire escape), where we sat on steamy nights, and a four-stair *"estup"* (stoop), where we played stoop-ball, y *donde "jangueábamos"* (and where we used to hang out). We weren't allowed to *"janguear" en el "jol" o en el "rufo"* (to hang out in the hall or on the roof); only *títeres, putas y "bones"* (hooligans, whores and bums) did that. To the left of the stoop was *"el beijman"* (the basement), where *el "supel"* (the super, or superintendent), also known as *el "yánitol"* (the janitor) lived. That's where we went to complain *que no hay "ejtín" y nos estamos "frizando" aún con el "cou" puesto; dígale al "lánlol" que arregle la "boila"* (that there's no steam and we are freezing even with our coats on; tell the landlord to fix the boiler). In the summer, children yelled up to their win-dows: *"Mami, tírame un 'daim' "* (throw down a dime) or *una "cuora/cuara"* (a quarter), to buy *aijcrín* (ice cream).

In the 1940s and 1950s, Nuyoricans learned some Yiddish from Jewish neigh-bors, and co-workers in the garment district. Yiddish, and Yinglish, were very handy in the South Bronx in those days because of the yentes (gossips) who sat downstairs in their shmates (ragged housedresses), kvetching (complaining) about the me-shugenes (crazies) who passed by, and la-menting, "Oy gevalt," "Oy veh'z'mir" (Oh my goodness) over the tsuris (trouble) in their lives. "Gesundheit" competed with "Salud" in our vocabulary. Years later I learned that the deep blue numbers on some arms identified Holocaust survivors, and in their honor "Zei gezunt" (be of good health) remains one of my special blessings.

Jews, Catholics, *Pentecostales,* and many *"Negroes,"* including Colin Powell, the former secretary of state, studied to-gether in P.S. 39, on Longwood Avenue and

Beck Street. The massive influx of Puerto Rican students in the post–World War II period transformed that school and challenged the entire system. We brought a new language and a racially mixed group into schools controlled by teachers and administrators of European backgrounds who were unprepared for such diversity. Most of them no longer spoke the language of their immigrant parents or considered it a language worth speaking, particularly Yiddish, and they expected us to follow their example. Instead, our Spanish, English, and Spanglish grew to reflect all our influences, including the NYC standard spoken by teachers and *la principal* (the principal) and the popular varieties of English spoken by our Jewish, Irish, and African American playmates in *la yarda* (the yard).

My lifelong connection and identification with African Americans began in P.S. 39. The Puerto Rican migration was happening on the heels of a major black move from southern fields to northern factories between the wars, and neither group knew much about the other. Nor did we understand why we felt so battered or neglected in our classes that most of us did not graduate from high school. "Negroes" or "colored people," as they were called then, were still living under Jim Crow laws and being hunted and lynched like wild animals in the South. In the North, they were depicted as violent, lazy, and dirty, like their Puerto Rican neighbors. Newspapers that carried those stories also included reports on "crazy Puerto Rican Nationalists/terrorists" because of an armed revolt against U.S. domination on the island and the assassination of one of the president's guards in Washington, D.C., in 1950 and a shooting in Congress in 1954. I often wonder how those events shaped teachers' and other gatekeepers' views of Puerto Ricans

and "Negroes," and what impact their views had on our efforts to succeed. The liaisons forged between the children and parents who bore the brunt of racist prejudices deserve to be documented in full, including local collaborations like that of Mrs. Zentella and Mrs. Tyson in P.S. 39's PTA.[6] They helped lay the foundation for the mutual Puerto Rican and African American support that continues to this day, notwithstanding the rough spots. Puerto Ricans learned the hard way that the phenotypic complexities captured in their distinctions between *blanco, negro, grifo, jabao, indio, trigueño*, and *mulato* were lost on Americans of all races. Americans recognized only two color boxes, white and black, and respected only one. "Negro" did not have any positive connotations, as *negro* does in Puerto Rican Spanish, albeit alongside the negative. In the U.S. it easily became "nigger," an epithet even worse than the Spik label that Puerto Ricans endured. Soon "dirty Spiks and niggers" became a common refrain in the mouths of those who despised us.

During this period in our history "Puerto Rican" became synonymous with Spik, with gangs (*gangas*) like the Sharks depicted in West Side Story, who "rumbled" and ran from *la jara* (the police), with teenage killers like the demonized "Capeman," and with *joloperos* (muggers; literally, hold-uppers), *drogadictos* (drug addicts), alcoholics, whores, and welfare cheats who (supposedly) came to New York to sponge off the city. When they couldn't cut the mustard here, they returned to Puerto Rico and perpetuated a vicious cycle of social deviance and return migration, according to chronicles like Oscar Lewis's *La Vida* (1965). Dismay about the public perception of Puerto Ricans and the city's inability to deal with the community's problems prompted Antonia Pantoja and others to organize HYAA, the Hispanic Young Adult Association. As "Toni" poignantly recalls in her memoirs, they agonized, trying to find a way out:

During this period [1950–1953], the daily newspapers were carrying many articles about the problems that Puerto Ricans were bringing to the city. All the reports were negative.... Our discussions covered many issues: Why did our parents emigrate? Why do Americans hate us? Why do Americans accuse our women of being prostitutes and our men of being lazy? Why are we accused of coming to New York to get on welfare? Why? Why? Why? (Pantoja, 2002, pp. 73–74)

Even in scientific research, the primary reference to our presence denoted deviance: the "Puerto Rican syndrome" became the clinical label for hyperkinetic seizures of the type suffered by women who shook uncontrollably in response to a family tragedy. We got another label instead of a solution.

Puerto Rico's elites did not treat us much better. The Popular Democratic Party, which reigned between 1945 and 1965, fashioned a neocolonial Commonwealth designed to defuse nationalist sentiments for independence. An essential component of that design was the "escape valve" represented by the emigration of more than 50,000 Puerto Ricans annually in the post–World War II decade. After being encouraged to leave, Nuyoricans were viewed as adding fuel to the 50-year-old fire that raged around the political status of Puerto Rico and the U.S. impact on Puerto Rican culture. More than half a million Puerto Ricans who lived on the U.S. mainland instead of the island and spoke English or a despised Spanglish instead of a "pure" Spanish challenged the essentialist notions

of the Puerto Rican nation championed by traditional *hispanófilos* and worried *independentistas* (Duany, 2002). One solution was to exclude us from *la gran familia puertorriqueña,* as Seda Bonilla (1972) suggested.[7] A parallel move was to direct the Office of the Commonwealth in New York City to pursue an assimilation agenda without the advice or consent of the community, as Sánchez-Korrol (1994) and Pantoja (2002) document. Fortunately, the members of HYAA sought their own solutions through direct community activism. Beginning in the 1950s and extending into the 1970s, Antonia Pantoja and other members of HYAA helped create the most important Puerto Rican self-help institutions in the U.S.[8]

Given the hostility and pervasive images of immorality and inferiority that plagued Puerto Ricans in New York, how did we manage to get to the point where we eagerly lined Fifth Avenue by the thousands every first Sunday in June (beginning in 1959), making *La Parada* (the parade, El Desfile Puertorriqueño) New York's largest parade? And what source of inner strength produced all those Puerto Rican flags on cars and in windows, and the buttons and tee-shirts that said "I'm Puerto Rican and proud" or "Kiss me, I'm Puerto Rican"? Visionaries, including Antonia Pantoja, helped lead the way by highlighting our Puerto Rican ancestry in the names and programs of the organizations they established, for example, the Puerto Rican Forum, Universidad Boricua, and Aspira's Madrinas (godmothers) and its Areyto Initiation Ceremony. Since then we have demanded the right to identify as Puerto Ricans, in defiance of those Americans who want us to adopt a hyphenated-American label as well as those islanders who would prefer we drop any reference to "their" homeland. Why, then, do we also lay proud claim to "Nuyorican"? My answer: because "Nuyorican" makes a graphic statement—in a term that is emblematic of our mixing of Spanish and English—about our roots, our hybrid identities, and our complementary allegiances. *"De qué parte de Puerto Rico eres?"* (What part of Puerto Rico do you come from?), a caller was asked recently by a radio announcer on *La Mega.* *"Del Bronx,"* she answered. "Nuyorican" joins me to that caller, to the children of El Barrio whose bilingualism I documented (Zentella, 1997), and to all those who worked so hard for so long and so little, in defiance of demeaning labels and racist stereotypes. But not only those of us who were born in New York can be Nuyoricans; anyone who embraces our cause is welcome. Antonia Pantoja did not move to New York until she was in her twenties, but "I am a Nuyorican" is the triumphant last line of her memoir.

Conclusion

The voice of our imprint is "Spanglish," a misnomer if it gives the impression that a third language has been created. Instead, as Algarín noted in his introduction to the now-classic anthology *Nuyorican Poetry*, "the average Nuyorican has a working command of both [English and Spanish] and normally uses both languages simultaneously" (Algarín, 1975, p. 18). In fact, the majority of the poems in the anthology are primarily in English, with a few words and phrases in Spanish, or in Spanish. Basically, Spanglish is a colorful way of switching between varieties of English and Spanish, adopted because "newness in language grows as people do and learn things never done or learned before" (Algarín, p. 15). Principally it consists of borrowed words and meanings, constituting a New York

Spanish lexicon. Every Spanish-speaking country has its unique lexical items and features, and we have ours. Just as Costa Ricans cannot be accused of inventing a new and corrupted language when they say *"Se te deschocho'el colocho"* (Your curl has come undone), New Yorkers who say *"Tengo que vacunear la carpeta"* (I have to vacuum the carpet) are not destroying Spanish or hobbling their communication.[9] Instead, "the interchange between both [languages] yields new verbal possibilities" (Algarín, p. 15). The real problem isn't the number of English words that we have borrowed into Spanish, or switching from one language to the other, but the fact that our young people are losing Spanish altogether.

My generation asked to be recognized as Puerto Ricans with a Nuyorican style that blended two languages. Because we were rejected in both of our homelands and little was done to help us develop and pass on oral and literate skills in Spanish, the newest generations are claiming that it is not necessary to speak Spanish to be Puerto Rican. Not surprisingly, given the fact that they want to leave room for all members of their family *en la gran familia puertorriqueña,* even those who were born on the island support this view (Zentella, 2002). All Nuyoricans understand this claim to be a demand for respect for those who no longer can express themselves in Spanish but who still feel and act Puerto Rican, thereby challenging a narrow territorial and language based definition of who or what is a Puerto Rican. Have we learned enough from the high price we paid for dismissing the creative contributions of the Nuyoricans of the mid-twentieth century to help today's English-dominant youth affirm and strengthen the Spanish-speaking part of their identity? *Ojalá, bendito.*

Notes

An expanded version of this entry appears as "A Nuyorican's View of Our History and Language(s) in New York, 1945–1965," in Gabriel Haslip-Viera, Angelo Falcón, & Félix Matos Rodríguez, Eds., *Boricuas in Gotham: Puerto Ricans in the Making of Modern New York City* (Princeton, NJ: Markus Wiener, 2004), pp. 21–36.

1. Puerto Ricans in the U.S. surpassed the number of island Puerto Ricans early in 2004. New York City is home to more than 800,000, the largest concentration.

2. *Antillanos* (Antilleans), refers to the island chain of the Antilles, and *caribeños* recalls the surrounding Caribbean Sea. The *Marine Tiger* was one of the ships that brought emigrés from the island before direct air flights; newcomers were often dubbed *marín taiguers* or *grinjomes* (green horns), disparagingly. *Jíbaros* are the peasants from the countryside, but to be called a *jíbaro* meant you were a hick, not street smart. "Spiks" was the ethnic slur directed at all Spanish speakers, perhaps because they tended to say "espik" for "speak," in a typical confusion of the /I/ and /i/ phonemes. "Pororican" was based on the early U.S. name for the island, Porto Rico.

3. For lists of Puerto Rico's *criollismos*, *africanismos*, and *taínismos*, consult the work of Malaret (1937), Rubén del Rosario (1965), and Manuel Alvarez-Nazario (1961, 1977, 1990). Typical expressions have been collected by Núñez de Ortega and Delgado de Laborde (1999).

4. Puerto Rican essayist Salvador Tió claimed to have coined "Spanglish", which he lampooned mercilessly, in 1948 (1992, p. 5). But borrowing and mixing of Spanish and English had been occurring in Mexican communities in the Southwest for almost a century before Tió supposedly "named" it (McWilliams, 1948).

5. Other items in the *Glosario* were never widespread, or are apocryphal, for example, *"toquear"* (to talk), *"craca"* (cracker), *"flaua"* (flower), *"caque"* (cake). (See Cotto-Thurner, 1951, pp. 243–244.)

6. Mrs. Tyson's son Cyril became a prominent Democrat in NYC government in the 1980s; Colin Powell became the country's leading African American Republican.

7. Seda's experiences in the tumultuous early days of Puerto Rican Studies at Hunter College with students and colleagues (1970–1972), including *su servidora,* who challenged his elitist academic style and views, cemented his negative opinion of New York Puerto Ricans.

8. Aspira had offices in several cities, including one in Puerto Rico. Details about the founding of Aspira and the other organizations are in the chapter by Sánchez-Korrol (1994) and Pantoja's (2002) memoir.

9. For a description of the grammatical forms and discourse functions of Spanglish, see chapters 5 and 6 of Zentella (1997).

References

Algarín, Miguel. (1975). Introduction. In M. Algarín & M. Piñero (Eds.), *Nuyorican Poetry.* New York: William Morrow.

Alvarez-Nazario, Manuel. (1961). *El elemento afro-negroide en el español de Puerto Rico.* San Juan, PR: Instituto de Cultura Puertorriqueña.

Alvarez-Nazario, Manuel. (1977). *El Influjo Indígena en el Español de Puerto Rico.* Río Piedras, PR: Editorial Universitaria.

Alvarez-Nazario, Manuel. (1990). *El habla campesina del país.* Río Piedras, PR: Editorial Universitaria.

Cotto-Thurner, Guillermo. (1951). *Trópico en Manhattan: Novela.* San Juan, PR: Editorial Occidente.

Duany, Jorge. (2002). *The Puerto Rican Nation on the Move: Identities on the Island and in the United Status.* Chapel Hill: University of North Carolina Press.

García, Ofelia. (1997). In O. García & J. Fishman (Eds.). *The Multilingual Apple: Languages in New York City.* Berlin: Mouton de Gruyter.

Haslip-Viera, Gabriel, Angelo Falcón, & Félix Matos Rodríguez (Eds.). (2004). *Boricuas in Gotham: Puerto Ricans in the Making of*

Modern New York City. Princeton, NJ: Markus Wiener.

Lewis, Oscar. (1965). *La vida: A Puerto Rican Family in the Culture of Poverty—San Juan and New York*. New York: Random House.

Malaret, Augusto. (1937). *Vocabulario de Puerto Rico* (2nd ed.). New York: Las Américas Publishing.

McWilliams, Carey. (1948). *North from Mexico: The Spanish-speaking People of the United States* (2nd ed.). New York: Greenwood Press.

Núñez de Ortega, Rosario, & Delgado de Laborde, Isabel. (1999). *Los que dicen jay bendito! Dichos, modismos y expresiones del habla coloquial puertorriqueña*. San Juan, PR: Editorial Plaza Mayor.

Pantoja, Antonia. (2002). *Memoir of a Visionary*. Houston, TX: Arte Público Press.

Pavlenko, Aneta. (2002). "We Have Room for But One Language Here": Language and National Identity in the U.S. at the Turn of the 20th Century. *Multilingua* 21, 163–196.

Rosario, Rubén del. (1965). *Vocabulario puertorriqueño*. Sharon, CT: Troutman Press.

Sánchez-Korrol, Virginia. (1994). *From Colonia to Community: The History of Puerto Ricans in New York City*. Berkeley: University of California Press.

Seda-Bonilla, Eduardo. (1972). El problema de identidad de los niuyoricans. *Revista de Ciencias Sociales* 16(4), 453–462.

Stavans, Ilán. (2003). *Spanglish: The Making of a New American Language*. New York: Rayo/HarperCollins.

Tió, Salvador. (1992). *Desde el tuétano*. San Juan, PR: Editorial Cultural.

Zentella, Ana Celia. (1997). *Growing Up Bilingual*. Malden, MA: Blackwell.

Zentella, Ana Celia. (2000). Puerto Ricans in the U.S.: The Linguistic Repercussions of Colonialism. In Sandra Lee McKay & Sauling Cynthia Wong (Eds.), *New Immigrants in the United States: Background for Second Language Educators* (pp. 137–164). New York: Cambridge University Press.

Zentella, Ana Celia. (2002). Latin@ Languages and Identities. In M. Suárez-Orozco & M. Páez (Eds.), *Latinos: Remarking America* (pp. 321–338). Berkeley: University of California Press.

Zentella, Ana Celia. (2004). A Nuyorican's View of Our History and Language(s) in New York, 1945–1965. In Gabriel Haslip-Viera, Angelo Falcón, & Félix (Eds.), *Boricuas in Gotham: Puerto Ricans in the Making of Modern New York City* (pp. 21–36). Princeton, NJ: Marcus Weiner.

Recommended Reading

Zentella (1997) is an award-winning study of New York Puerto Rican children growing up with English, Spanish, and Spanglish in East Harlem in the 1980s and 1990s. Educational issues related to Puerto Ricans and their languages are addressed in Zentella (2000). The most extensive collection of research on the Puerto Rican experience is at the Centro for Puerto Rican Studies library at Hunter College, City University of New York.

Ana Celia Zentella

H

HEGEMONY

Hegemony is a concept used to describe the use of overt and subtle privilege within a social system to establish a dominant group's cultural and social norms as universal, thus affirming the social, cultural, political, and economic power status of the dominant group. One particular feature of hegemony as a concept describing power relations in a society is that the oppressed may be influenced to consent to their own oppression by accepting the taken-for-granted norms embedded in various social systems. Often, the oppressed groups of a society may be convinced that their acceptance of the universality of dominant cultural norms is actually in their best interest, which further solidifies their subordinate position within a social system. The concept of hegemony emerged from the field of sociology in the work of Antonio Gramsci, and it has been applied to a number of social systems to illuminate how domination and marginalization of groups occurs through various socialization processes. The field of education provides vivid examples of how social systems are used to facilitate cultural hegemony, as well as examples of efforts made to counter and eradicate it. For Hispanics/Latinos, one illustration of cultural hegemony is the treatment of English language learners in public schools that force students to replace, rather than build upon, their Spanish language skills in the interest of helping students to be more successful in educational settings that do not value linguistic diversity.

Several social science fields are devoted to the development of theories regarding the types of power that are wielded in different social contexts. There are many examples of tangible power in a society, such as in cases where legal or positional authority results in power and power relations that are relatively obvious. A variety of social theorists argue, however, that even within such legally sanctioned power structures there exists an embedded system of power and power relations that is often more subtle both in form and influence. Hegemony is the concept often used to describe overt as well as more subtle forms of power and power relations in a social system, and it relies on the acceptance of the social and cultural norms of a dominant group as universally applicable to all groups in a society. By privileging the social and cultural norms of one particular group, theorists argue, such norms begin to permeate all social systems within a society, thus thoroughly affirming the dominance of one group over others. Such social-cultural dominance not merely influences which forms of art or communications styles are valued but also extends to how various groups in a society are treated within common legal, educational, economic, and other social systems. In the U.S., for example, is history documents the differential treatment of women and people of color in laws governing voting rights, which were premised on the socially and culturally affirmed superiority of white men.

Hegemony, particularly cultural hegemony, has also been carried out by American public schools, according to various educational historians. There is, for example, documented use of public schools to socialize American Indians, Latinos, and other students of color by inculcating in them not only the dominant, white, middle-class, protestant social and cultural values but also the acceptance of their presumed inferiority by virtue of being different from the imposed norm. Educational theorists today argue that cultural hegemony is often carried out against increasingly diverse student populations by professionals who are not aware of how differential social status and power relations permeate the school's curriculum, organizational structure, and politics. Indeed, the contributions of researchers such as, Paulo Freire, Sonia Nieto, Guadalupe Valdés, Eugene Garcia, Richard Valencia, Daniel Solórzano, Henry Trueba, Angela Valenzuela, Harriet Romo, Toni Falbo, and Patricia Gándara have helped to demonstrate the various manifestations of social and cultural hegemony in schools serving Hispanic/Latino students throughout the U.S.

One vivid example of cultural hegemony facilitated by public schools serving Hispanic/Latino students is in the treatment of the needs of English language learners. Despite the tremendous growth in the English learner population in states with increasing Latino populations, school systems are slow to shift in their ability to adequately train teachers to adapt to these needs. As documented by Garcia (2001), Valdés (1996), Trueba (1993), and Gándara (1995), among others, teacher preparation in classroom practices and pedagogy that support the learning of Spanish speakers to maintain their native language while acquiring English language skills is a persistent weakness in most American public schools. Language policies, such as that required by the passage of Proposition 227 in California, are effective in assigning a subordinate status to languages other than English. In turn, to comply with policies that promote English language learning at the expense of native language maintenance, schools may be less inclined to embrace the diverse cultures, social norms, and community assets that English learners bring to the classroom. Moreover, as explained by Valencia and Garcia, as schools are increasingly held accountable for the academic achievement of subpopulations of students, English language learners confront assessments not only lacking in alignment with the curriculum they have been taught but also conducted entirely in English before students are fully proficient in the language. These overt practices arguably reflect a hegemonic stance; however, the subordinate status of the Spanish language (in this case) is further affirmed, social theorists argue, as English learner students and their parents themselves begin to reject instruction in Spanish because of the clear messages communicated through the curriculum, organization, and policies of schools that do not value linguistic diversity.

Efforts to enact "counter-hegemonic" practices and policies include support for certain forms of multicultural education. The counter-hegemonic aspects of multicultural education facilitate the recognition of privilege and its influence, and they produce collaborative learning processes that encourage the integration of diverse perspectives and sociocultural norms. Multicultural education experts assert that it is important for all participants in a social system to become aware of the impact of hegemony on their lives and interactions with others to enable them to construct alternative ways of conducting the social system. According to multicultural educators, whose work aims to eradicate hegemony in American society, there must also be a continual questioning of established systems, as well as the cultural and social norms that undergird them.

References

Gándara, P. (1995). *Over the Ivy Walls: The Educational Mobility of Low-Income Chicanos*. Albany, NY: SUNY Press.

Garcia, Eugene E. (2001). *Hispanic Education in the United States: Raíces y alas*. Lanham, MD: Rowman & Littlefield.

Trueba, H. (1993). Race and Ethnicity: The Role of America in Healing Multicultural America. *Educational Theory* 43(1), 41–54.

Valdés, Guadalupe. (1996). *Con respeto: Bridging the Distances between Culturally Diverse Families and Schools—an Ethnographic Portrait*. New York: Teachers College Press.

Recommended Reading

Adams, Maurianne, Blumenfeld, Warren J., Castañeda, Rosie, Hackman, Heather W., Peters, Madeline L., & Zúñiga Ximena. (Eds.). (2000). *Readings for Diversity and Social Justice: An Anthology on Racism, Anti-Semitism, Sexism, Heterosexism, Ableism, and Classism*. New York: Routledge.

Freire, Paulo. (1993). *Pedagogy of the Oppressed* (New rev. 20th anniv. ed.). New York: Continuum.

Nieto, Sonia. (1996). *Affirming Diversity: The Sociopolitical Context of Multicultural Education* (2nd ed.). White Plains, NY: Longman Press.

Omi, Michael, & Winant, Howard. (1994). Racial Formation. In *Racial Formation in the United States from the 1960s to the 1990s* (2nd ed., pp. 53–76). New York: Routledge.

Romo, H. D., & Falbo, T. (1996). *Latino High School Graduation: Defying the Odds*. Austin: University of Texas Press.

Solórzano, D. & Yosso, T. (2002). Critical Race Methodology. *Qualitative Inquiry* 8(1), 23–44.

Valencia, Richard (Ed.). (1997). *The Evolution of Deficit Thinking: Educational Thought and Practice*. Stanford Series on Education and Public Policy. London: Falmer Press.

Valencia, Richard (Ed.). (2002). *Chicano School Failure and Success: Past, Present, and Future* (2nd ed.). London: RoutledgeFalmer.

Valenzuela, Angela. (1999). *Subtractive Schooling: U.S.-Mexican Youth and the Politics of Caring*. Albany, NY: SUNY Press.

Gloria Rodriguez

HIGH-STAKES TESTING

Testimony in Support of HB 1612 and HB 1613

Hearings held before the Committee on Public Education in Austin, Texas, May 3, 2005, opened discussion on the use of standardized testing—the TAKS—as a single measure of sixth grade student achievement. This entry includes the testimony of Clara V. Zamora, a sixth grader at Austin's Barton Hills Elementary School. She raises questions about the fairness of the test and comes out in support of House Bills 1612 and 1613, which call for better ways to assess students. Also included here is the testimony of Angela Valenzuela of the Texas League of United Latin American Citizens.

Thank you for allowing me to testify today. First of all, I want to say that I am a sixth-grade student at Barton Hills Elementary in the Austin Independent School District. And also, I am refusing to take the TAKS test at my school because I do not agree with the way that the TAKS is being used. One of the ways that it is being used in a bad way is that it is being used to show the students' abilities, when if they want to see that information, they should look at the rest of the students' grades, not just ONE test. The student could be the brightest kid in the world, but have a low test score and be categorized in an incorrect way according to the test score. And this isn't fair.

Another reason why I do not agree with the TAKS test and think it is wrong is because it is taking up a bunch of the teachers' teaching time for preparation of the test. It's not fair to the students or the teachers. We have to spend SO much time to prepare for the test, that the teachers don't have enough time to make teaching fun! I remember for awhile we were late on learning some things in math, so we had to skim through the whole book, just so that we'd know something about what was in the book, before the test came along. It's not fair that it has to be a drag for the students to go to math or reading class anymore. I know that if the TAKS test is not emphasized so much that all the students will enjoy school a lot more, and all of the teachers, will like teaching more. The ratio of the hours of school for preparation of the TAKS to the hours of school total is overwhelming.

Another thing about the TAKS test that troubles me is that we have taken TAKS tests from the years before, and according to the grade on those, certain students get pulled out of class at certain times of the day for tutoring. I don't think there's anything really wrong about that, except for the fact that those students probably get embarrassed and they are missing out on important things that they might need to actually know for the TAKS test while they are in tutoring.

I am not protesting this for my own sake. I am doing this for all of the students in Texas that have to take the TAKS test every year. I hope that me doing this will have an effect on them, and show the students that they

don't have to put up with this, and they don't have to take it. Though their rights aren't shown, all of the students do have rights. I hope more and more students will protest the test and not take it, to the point that the government finally realizes that they do have to do something. The government can start by passing House Bills 1612 and 1613 since they call for a better way to determine students' abilities than the current way. Thank you very much.

Testimony in Support of HB 1612 and HB 1613 before the Committee on Public Education

Dr. Angela Valenzuela

Texas League of United Latin American Citizens

May 3, 2005

Thank you. Chairman Grusendorf. This is the third legislative session that we pursue this legislation. This legislation is not partisan. It's not for children of any particular race or ethnicity. It's for *all* children. It's not democrat. It's not republican. Nor does it weaken President Bush's national goals for improving education. Instead, it is pro-assessment—which is what I think we all want to be about. And it is pro-kid, honoring the many different ways that children can demonstrate their abilities. Indeed, it is our children's human right to be evaluated in a comprehensive manner when so much is personally at stake to them.

Although I do not want to go into this in my testimony, I do want to mention that current research—such as that contained in my recently published book, *Leaving Children Behind*, State University of New York Press—shows how the current system that we have in place is negatively correlated with outcomes that we care about, including SAT scores, ACT scores, TASP scores and high school completion rates. Instead of this focus, I feel that I need to underscore the following.

To fully understand and appreciate the Representative Olivo's legislation, legislators need to stop equating "testing" with "accountability." These are two separate concepts. Accountability is a much larger construct. It is a system with multiple components, including a school and district rating system and a system of information management that goes far beyond test scores to include myriad other forms of data. Moreover, as the Darling Hammond report from Stanford shows, to be anti-high-stakes-testing is not to be anti-accountability. In fact, the exact opposite is true when "states that use multiple measures assessments for graduation tend to have higher student test scores and higher graduation rates, and produce students who are better prepared for today's workforce and for higher education" (Darling Hammond, 2005). Isn't this what a good accountability system should be doing?

On behalf of my daughter, her protest is not a mindless exercise that she is engaged in. In fact, she has never received any grade lower than an A in school. Moreover, she has joined the ranks of several test resisters—one of them the highly publicized Macario Guajardo in the Valley who appeared on February 23, 2005, in the *New York Times*. To date, these are all privileged children and none of them are saying that they do not want rigor. The opposite is true. They want an educational experience that is fun, rigorous, and academically rich—something that the current test-centric system does not provide.

To conclude, I wonder why the burden has been on us in this legislature to demonstrate that *more* information should be used when judging children on decisions of such long-lasting consequence to them. The burden should not be on us, but rather on the state to demonstrate that *less* information is better and that our current dropout and failure rates are adequate, reasonable, and acceptable. Thank you.

Appendix

Multiple Measures Approaches to High School Graduation provides an in-depth examination of 27 states currently using multiple measures assessments to determine student eligibility for high school graduation. Multiple measures assessments differ from single-test assessments in that they consider a variety of student work, which may include student academic records, research papers, portfolios, essays, capstone projects, and oral exams. The report's key findings:

- States that use multiple measures assessments for graduation tend to have higher student test scores and higher graduation rates, and produce student who are better prepared for today's workforce and for higher education.

- Multiple measures approach allows for an in-depth, individualized assessment of the kinds of high-performance skills demanded by colleges, business, and employers.

- Problem-solving, research, writing, experimentation, leadership, collaboration, communication, presentation of ideas, and managing multiple and extensive project are among the essential indicators of college and work preparedness that cannot be assessed by a single standardized test with multiple-choice items, but can be demonstrated through a multiple-measure approach, using a range of performance assessments.

- Multiple measures assessments also provide more comprehensive and timely diagnostic feedback on student achievement for teachers, who can use the results of ongoing assessments throughout the academic year to inform their planning and instruction.

The report concludes that for states and districts, a multiple measures approach to high school graduation offers a more balanced and informative platform for holding students and schools accountable, one that stimulates discussion not only about how to improve curriculum and instruction, but also how to monitor a student's individual growth and progress, improve preparedness for college, and build readiness for work in the future.

Clara V. Zamora and Angela Valenzuela

HISPANIC/LATINO FAMILIES

Hispanic families have been considered a major factor in how well Hispanic students do in school. Hispanics, or Latinos,[1] are known for how they remain outside the mainstream. Aside from cultural elements, indicators of their difference lie in their high rates of dropout and poverty and low levels of college completion (Ramirez & de la Cruz, 2002; Suro, 1998; Trueba, 1999). Furthermore, the description of Latinos is often limited to their participation in various institutions (schools, health care, the labor market) or discussion of their ethnic and cultural difference (values and beliefs) with little to no consideration of their embeddedness in American social, political, and economic structures. In the end, these representations account for only partial or narrow views of the total lived experience of Latinos in the U.S. What is needed, therefore, is a more dynamic and complex understanding of the factors that interact and intersect to shape Latino family situations.

This narrow understanding of Hispanics extends to how families are perceived. Unlike more successful immigrant populations, Hispanics are continually perceived through their immigrant roots, and they remain in a perpetual state of assimilation or acculturation. Latino families are considered to be newly arrived immigrants, living in obscurity because they are immigrants, live in poverty, and struggle to find work and to acquire English. Very rarely is the heterogeneous nature of the community recognized (Ortiz, 1995; Suárez-Orozco & Páez, 2002). Latino families span recently arrived immigrants to well-established later-generation families (third generation or more); They live in the Southwest, South, and Northeast, but also in the Midwest and northern Pacific. The political, social, and economic circumstances of their countries of origin, like communism in Cuba for Cuban American families or the political turmoil in Central American countries for Honduran, Guatemalan, and El Salvadorian families, uniquely shape the way families operate in society. There are urban, suburban, and rural Hispanic families who may be two-parent, single-mother, single-father, or skip-generation families (grandparents raising grandchildren). Each of these variations colors the Hispanic family context, determining the resources and situations each family can provide for its members.

Unfortunately, where many institutions are concerned, Latino families have often been viewed as their own worst enemy: It is their "culture," their values, beliefs, and attitudes, that prevents them from experiencing the success achieved by other ethnic groups, such as European groups in the 1900s and Asian Americans. Latino students tend to reject the American value system in schools and therefore fail in schools (Trueba, 1991). The legacy of the cultural deficit and deprivation theories, which claim that Latino culture is inferior in its very essence, has given way to the theory of cultural difference, that Latino cultural values and orientations are different from the mainstream. It has been the deficit or difference theory that has explained their lack of academic success as a group. Although the latter may seem more innocuous than the former, with either perspective the onus for improving Latino student achievement falls squarely on the shoulders of the families themselves.

One example of Latino families' failure to help children succeed academically is the stereotypical myth that families do not value formal schooling and therefore do not encourage students to attend school or complete their schooling. Researchers like Valencia and Black (2002) acknowledge that scholarly works that identify parent and family involvement and support (Soto, 1998; Perez & Padilla, 2000; Romo & Falbo, 1996) and historical accounts of Chicano communities' fight for equality of education (Donato, 1997; San Miguel, 1987) demonstrate the opposite. One study (Delgado-Gaitan 2001) details how Mexican immigrant parents in a small coastal town in California formed a parent organization to contend with the school's reticence in addressing their children's heritage culture and language. Familiarity with the scholarship on Chicanos and Latinos fends against formulating and reinforcing overgeneralizations and stereotypes.

Another example of how Hispanic family culture is believed to interfere with academic success is the notion that Hispanic families are patriarchal, where women and girls are subordinate and submissive to men and boys: where women and girls' have only one role, as wives and mothers, and men and boys are authorities and providers. This cultural tendency has been used to explain why Latinas tend to do less well in school than Latinos. What needs to be understood is that like all other families, Hispanic families are adaptive to their circumstances and adjust to their environments.

Throughout the twentieth century, socioeconomic class has played a central role in the types of adjustments that Chicano families have made to gender roles (Griswold del

Castillo, 1984). To adapt to their unique economic circumstances, poor and working-class women entered the fields and labor market for family subsistence, whereas middle- and upper-class women stayed home to raise their children. In addition, as the statistics on Latinas in higher education (approximately equal to males at 10%) suggest, this perception of the family as strictly patriarchal is overgeneralized and oversimplified.

The field of education has also assumed these perspectives about the Hispanic family. While chiefly important, given that nearly 50% of Latinos are foreign born, many studies tend to focus on the needs and situations of immigrant parents and children (Portes & Rumbaut, 2001).[2] These Latino families are often characterized as requiring parent education, language instruction, and interpretation, since they have little access to mainstream life. At the same time, the distinction and needs of later-generation Hispanic families, who are largely U.S. born, English dominant, and U.S. educated, often go unrecognized and are subsumed in those of immigrant Latinos. As long as Hispanic families are viewed as homogeneous and uniform, schools and other social institutions will provide only marginally effective programs and services to the Latino community.

Perhaps the most pervasive and potentially detrimental perception of Latino families is that their culture is the root cause for Latino student failure. One such explanation for student failure is the heavy obligation the family places on its family members. Research (Chávez, 2001; Keefe & Padilla, 1990; Vega, 1995) claims that one of the stalwart and consistent elements of Chicano culture is *familism*. Defined as the strong connections and bonds to family, *familism* is generally seen as positive, regardless of generation, given the importance and persistence of family as an informational, social, and financial resource. However, when faced with the option to help family or to attend school, so the argument goes, Latino children will opt to help family members in order to fulfill their familial obligation, often thereby jeopardizing their academic performance.

While *familism* may be viewed as a possible cause for school failure, the overwhelming fact that Hispanic families are poor or working class (Gonzalez, 2001; Ortiz, 1996) suggests that other factors like parents' educational experience, the tendency for working-class students to be placed into general and vocational tracks, and family subsistence are also contributors. For example, Latino parents' working-class status influences the academic support they can offer to children. Research on parental involvement suggests that working-class parents' educational experience—largely high school graduation in general education—tends to make parents feel less capable in helping their children academically (Lareau, 2000, 2004); they are therefore less likely to help children with schoolwork at home. From this perspective, the U.S. school system, which has historically placed Latino students in general and vocational tracks (Gonzalez, 1999; San Miguel & Valencia, 1998), can be a factor in parents' academic competency or lack thereof. All this is to say that the view that a single cultural value is the leading cause for Latino academic failure (Suárez-Orozco & Suárez-Orozco, 1995) ignores the real and stalwart issues, namely, the historical legacy of economic and social restriction of opportunity based on race (Barrera, 1979) and class (Anyon, 1980), which has plagued the Latino population in all U.S. institutions.

Like all other families, Hispanic families are affected by their social class, since one's social position determines the resources one can expend. For poor families, parents' low level of education, low level of income, and environmental issues (Portes & Rumbaut, 2001) challenge the ways in which they can participate in their children's education. Whether the parents are native born or immigrant, their level of education and income determines whether they possess the academic knowledge and skills or the disposable income to address any difficulties their children may have in school. Often because they live at or below the poverty line, these families must put survival needs—their requirement for shelter, food, and safety—above all else.

Likewise, working-class Latino families, in which parents tend to be native born and high school graduates, face similar challenges to those of poor families. For working-class families—which still tend to be large, having, on average, three children—disposable income for additional tutoring or academic enrichment materials may be scarce. Although they may have command of English and a high school education, such parents, whose own education placed them on vocational or general tracks, lack the know-how to prepare their children for higher academic tracks.

Economic conditions of poor and working-class families often necessitate that members enter the workforce early to enable the family to subsist or maintain even a modest standard of living. Further, in regards to higher education Gonzalez (2001) suggests that low- or working-class families and students have to consider not only the direct costs of a college education, such as tuition and room and board, but also the indirect costs, "the income lost while being a full-time student, [and] the psychological costs of attending, such as being subjected to examinations or long and tedious courses"

(p. 72). The latter can be quite costly if the family requires the student family member's income to subsist, as is the case with poor families. The idea of a heavy loan burden is very threatening to a family whose household incomes are constrained by the hourly wage system of working-class jobs or to a family trying to stabilize savings and investments to leave even a modest inheritance for children.

In this light, both types of families face challenges not experienced by middle-class families, who have access to credit and loans, promotions, social networks, and greater disposable income. Thus their attempts at parental involvement should be understood within their socioeconomic context. The assumption that families have the disposable income and time for extra academic support is predicated on economic resources of the nuclear and individualistic family life of white middle-class Americans (Brantlinger, 2003), who do not have to contend with the precarious and unpredictable circumstances of the American poor and working class (Dohan, 2003; Rubin, 1994).

Schools perceive Hispanic culture, socialized in families, as an impediment to improving Hispanic student success. Many scholars claim that one problem that exists between Latino students and schools is the cultural mismatch. Schools promote the American mainstream values of individualism, competition, and independence, whereas Latinos students tend to be reared with values of social harmony, interdependence, and collectivism. The value of *ser educado* is rooted in Latino subgroups (Delgado-Gaitan, 2004; Zambrana, 1995) and persists across generations (Chávez, 2001; Martinez, 1999). Latino families socialize children to be *bien educado,* or to be respectable and respectful productive human beings. Valenzuela (1999) defines this concept as follows:

It refers to the family's role of inculcating in children a sense of moral, social, and personal responsibility and serves as the foundation for all other learning. Though inclusive of formal academic training, *educación* additionally refers to competence in the social world, wherein one respects the dignity and the individuality of others. (p. 23)

In a Latino household, a child is then raised with *una buena educación* if he or she has respectful and respectable relations with others. Children are taught to give mutual respect among family, to have *dignidad* (dignity), to give *respeto* (respect) to others, to be obedient and to have "firmness of character" (Griswold del Castillo, 1984, p. 74).

Coupled with the historical negligence and mistreatment of Hispanics in U.S. schools (Carter & Segura, 1979), this primary orientation to accommodate and respect others to create an atmosphere of mutual respect and cooperation starkly contrasts with the competitive drive promoted in school. This clash in values and practices, where parents likely may feel school officials and personnel are not appropriately (respectfully) attending to them and their children, can impede sincere commitment and communication in parent or family and school interaction.

Respeto is a concept integral to being *bien educado* and is at the heart of Latino children's orientation to the world. Mutual respect for family members and the goal of family interaction is gaining *respeto* for fulfilling one's role and giving *respeto* for those who do so. Accordingly, "Interactions between family members . . . [are] guided by respect for particular persons as well as respect for the obligations, rights, and privileges of the roles occupied by each individual" (Váldes, 1996, p. 131). From this perspective, family members are strongly defined by their social roles. For children this often amounts to being sub-servient and deferring to parents' and elders' authority. This characteristic, of course, is compatible with deferring to a teacher's authority, even when a child's academic interests are not being serviced well. As Soto (1997) suggests, however, this cultural value may play a role in the "silencing" of Latino families' voices in schools, since families believe being respectful to school officials is most appropriate. On the other hand, this value of *respeto*, in conjunction with *buena educación*, is also seen as a family resource: a student's ties to the family's goal of gaining respect can also motivate them to achieve academically (Buening, Tollefson, & Rodriguez, 1992; Chávez, in press; Moreno & Valencia, 2002).

Latino families see their role as fulfilling the need for children to be well behaved and the school's role as formally educating children in academic subjects (Martinez, 1999). This separation of duties could be construed as a lack of value for education, since parents or other family members do not assume the school's responsibility to educate children because they perceive teachers as the "authority" on school matters. As a result of the overwhelming push for parental involvement in schools, Hispanic parents and families are often harshly criticized for their lack of participation when in reality they are acting out of respect for teachers' specialized training. Later-generation parents, having been through the system and raised in the U.S., may invoke traditional parental involvement (i.e., monitoring children's progress, volunteering) but may experience mixed results, since these families may not understand the intricate connections between parental involvement and children's academic development (Chávez, in press).

This skewed perspective on Latino families, their lack of appropriate academic orientation in the home, lays the groundwork for "blaming" Latino families for their inability to help their children succeed in schools. The overemphasis on families as a socializer of school culture ignores what Latino families do in fact do well. Over generations, with the exception of the severely distressed, Hispanic families increase members' high school graduation rates and their standard of living (Garcia, 2001; Gonzalez, 2001). Added to the increase in Hispanic professionals over the last decade is the large percentages of Latinos who become part of the American working class, contributing productively to the social and economic life in the U.S. There are a greater number of Latinos in college than ever before as several universities have gained status as Hispanic-serving institutions. Hispanics families' emphasis on *familism* and *ser educado* has produced these results. If Latino families are to be criticized for their "failure," they must also receive credit for their success—raising socially responsible, respectable, and productive human beings.

In conclusion, policymakers, educators, and others concerned with the Latino community and improving Latino families' level of academic achievement must realize that simply transforming Hispanic families into their white middle-class counterparts undermines the families' sense of well-being and the very social system they have constructed to survive the harsh realities faced by America's poor and working class and of an American racial minority. In line with *educación* and *respeto*, families must be consulted about changes, and interventions on part of schools must resemble negotiations rather than mandates.

Hispanic families have developed strong and vital social, psychological, and financial support networks that have increased families' economic and social viability. Therefore, they must be viewed as adaptive and flexible, and they must be given the opportunity to decide in what ways they can maintain family cohesion while they work toward incorporating academic activity into their family context. Latino families view themselves as successful in many ways. In order to maximize quality long-term effects on Latino academic achievement, any changes in how they function must begin, not with their failure, but with their success.

Notes

1. This term recognizes that Mexicans and Mexican Americans are the largest subgroup, and, as a result much of the research represented here is based on their experience and circumstances.

2. Since acquiring English is a major factor in this population's social adjustment, and many studies and works focus on language issues (such as Zentella, 1997, or Valdés, 2001), this discussion will focus on other less recognized factors like socioeconomic class and the effects of racialization on Latinos.

References

Anyon, Jean. (1980). Social Class and the Hidden Curriculum. *Journal of Education* 162(1), 67–92.

Barrera, Mario. (1979). *Race and Class in the Southwest: A Theory of Racial Inequality*. Notre Dame, IN: University of Notre Dame Press.

Brantlinger, Ellen. (2003). *Dividing Classes: How the Middle Class Negotiates and Rationalizes School Advantage*. New York: RoutledgeFalmer.

Buening, Meredith, Tollefson, Nona, & Rodriguez, Fred. (1992). Hispanic Culture and the Schools. In Marvin J. Fine & Cindy Carlson (Eds.), *The Handbook of Family-School Intervention: A Systems Perspective* (pp. 86–101). Needham Heights, MA: Allyn & Bacon.

Carter, Thomas. P., & Segura, Roberto D. (1979). *Mexican Americans in School: A Decade of Change*. New York: College Entrance Examination Board.

Chávez, Christina. (2001). In Their Own Image: Five Generations of a Mexican American Working-Class Family in Los Angeles. Ph.D. dissertation, Stanford University.

Chávez, Christina. (In press). *In Their Words: Five Generations of a Mexican American Working-Class Family in Los Angeles* (Working title). Lanham, MD: Rowman & Littlefield.

Delgado-Gaitan, Concha. (2001). *The Power of Community*. Lanham, MD: Rowman & Littlefield.

Delgado-Gaitan, Concha. (2004). *Involving Latinos Families in Schools*. Thousand Oaks, CA: Corwin Press.

Dohan, Daniel. (2003). *The Price of Poverty: Money, Work, and Culture in the Mexican American Barrio*. Los Angeles: University of California Press.

Donato, Ruben. (1997). *The Other Struggle for Equal Schools: Mexican Americans during the Civil Rights Era*. Albany, NY: SUNY Press.

Garcia, Eugene. (2001). *Hispanic Education in the United States: Raíces y alas*. Lanham, MD: Rowman & Littlefield.

Gonzalez, Arturo. (2001). *Mexican Americans & the U.S. Economy: Quest for Buenos Días*. Tucson: University of Arizona Press.

Gonzalez, Gilbert G. (1999). Segregation and the Education of Mexican Children, 1900–1940. In José F. Moreno (Ed.), *The Elusive Request for Equality* (pp. 53–76). Cambridge, MA: Harvard Educational Review.

Griswold del Castillo, Richard. (1984). *La familia: Chicano Families in the Urban Southwest, 1848 to the Present*. Notre Dame, IN: University Notre Dame Press.

Keefe, Susan. E., & Padilla, Amado. (1990). *Chicano Ethnicity*. Albuquerque: University of New Mexico Press.

Lareau, Annette. (2000). *Home Advantage: Social Class and Parental Intervention in Elementary Education* (rev. ed.). Oxford: Rowman & Littlefield.

Lareau, Annette. (2004). *Unequal Childhoods: Class, Race, and Family Life*. Berkeley: University of California Press.

Martinez, Estela. A. (1999). Mexican American / Chicano Families: Parenting as Diverse as the Families Themselves. In Harriet P. McAdoo (Ed.), *Family Ethnicity: Strength in Diversity* (2nd ed., pp. 121–134). Thousand Oaks, CA: Sage.

Martinez, Fredda Gregg. (1992). Familism in Acculturated Mexican Americans: Patterns, Changes and Perceived Impact on Adjustment to U.S. Society. Master's thesis, Northern Arizona University.

Moreno, Robert P., & Valenica, Richard R. (2002). Chicano Families and Schools: Myths, Knowledge, and Future Direction for Understanding. In Richard R. Valencia (Ed.), *Chicano School Failure and Success: Past, Present and Future* (2nd ed., pp. 227–249). London: Falmer Press.

Ortiz, Vilma. (1995). The Diversity of Latino Families. In Ruth E. Zambrana (Ed.), *Understanding Latino Families* (pp. 18–39). Thousand Oaks, CA: Sage.

Ortiz, Vilma. (1996). The Mexican-Origin Population: Permanent Working Class or Emerging Middle Class. In Robert Waldinger & Medhi Bozorgmehr (Eds.), *Ethnic Los Angeles* (pp. 247–277). New York: Russell Sage.

Perez, William, & Padilla, Amado M. (2000). Cultural Orientation across Three Generations of Hispanic Adolescents. *Hispanic Journal of Behavioral Sciences* 22 (3), 390–398.

Portes, Alejandro, & Rumbaut, Ruben G. (2001). *Legacies: The Story of the Immigrant Generation*. New York: Russell Sage.

Ramirez, Roberto R., & de la Cruz, G. Patricia. (2002). The Hispanic Population in the United States: March 2002. *Current Population Reports* (pp. 520–545). Washington, DC: U.S. Census Bureau.

Romo, Harriet. D., & Falbo, Toni. (1996). *Latino High School Graduation*. Austin: University of Texas Press.

Rubin, Lillian B. (1994). *Families on the Fault Line: America's Working Class Speaks about the Family, Economy, Race, and Ethnicity*. New York: HarperCollins.

San Miguel Jr., Guadalupe. (1987). *"Let Them All Take Heed": Mexican Americans and the Campaign for Educational Equality in Texas, 1910–1981*. Austin: University of Texas Press.

San Miguel Jr., Guadalupe, & Valencia, Richard. (1998). From the Treaty of Guadalupe de Hidalgo to Hopwood: The Educational Plight and Struggle of Mexican Americans in the Southwest. *Harvard Educational Review* 68(3), 353–412.

Soto, Lourdes D. (1997). *Language, Culture, and Power: Bilingual Families and the Struggle for Quality Education*. Albany, NY: SUNY Press.

Soto, Lourdes D. (1998). The Home Environments of Higher and Lower Achieving Puerto Rican Children. *Hispanic Journal of Behavioral Sciences* 10, 161–167.

Suárez-Orozco, Carola, & Suárez-Orozco, Marcelo. (1995). *Transformations: Migration, Family Life and Achievement Motivation among Latino Adolescents*. Stanford, CA: Stanford University Press.

Suárez-Orozco, Marcelo M., & Páez, Mariela M. (2002). Introduction: The Research Agenda. In Marcelo M. Suárez-Orozco & Mariel M. Páez (Eds.), *Latinos: Remaking America* (pp. 1–37). Los Angeles: University of California Press.

Suro, Roberto. (1998). *Strangers among Us: Latinos Lives in a Changing America*. New York: Vintage Books.

Trueba, Henry. (1991). From Success to Failure: The Roles of Culture and Culture Conflict in the Academic Achievement of Chicano Students. In Richard Valencia (Ed.), *Chicano School Failure and Success* (pp. 151–163). New York: Falmer Press.

Trueba, Henry. (1999). *Latinos unidos: From Cultural Diversity to the Politics of Solidarity*. Lanham, MD: Rowman & Littlefield.

Valdés, Guadalupe. (1996). *Con respeto: Bridging the Distances between Culturally*

Diverse Families and Schools. New York: Teachers College Press.

Valdés, Guadalupe. (2001). *Learning and Not Learning English: Latino Students in American Schools.* New York: Teachers College Press.

Valencia, Richard R., & Black, Mary S. (2002). "Mexican Americans Don't Value Education!": On the Basis of the Myth, Mythmaking, and Debunking. *Journal of Latinos and Education* 1(2), 81–103.

Valenzuela, Angela. (1999). *Subtractive Schooling.* Albany, NY: SUNY Press.

Vega, William A. (1995). The Study of Latino Families: A Point of Departure. In R. E. Zambrana (Ed.), *Understanding Latino Families* (pp. 3–17). Thousand Oaks, CA: Sage.

Zambrana, R. E. (Ed.). (1995). *Understanding Latino Families: Scholarship, Policy, and Practice.* Thousand Oaks, CA: Sage.

Zentella, Ana Celia. (1997). *Growing Up Bilingual: Puerto Rican Children in New York.* New York: Blackwell.

Recommended Reading

Alvarez Jr., Robert R. (1987). *Familia: Migration and Adaptation in Baja and Alta California, 1800–1975.* Berkeley: University of California Press.

Chavez, C. (In press). *In Their Words: Five Generations of a Mexican American Working-Class Family in Los Angeles* (Working title). Lanham, MD: Rowman & Littlefield.

Diaz, Lourdes. (1988). The Home Environments of Higher and Lower Achieving Puerto Rican Children. *Hispanic Journal of Behavioral Sciences* 10, 161–167.

Gándara, Patricia. (1995). *Over the Ivy Walls: The Educational Mobility of Low-Income Chicanos.* Albany, NY: SUNY Press.

Gonzalez, Maria Luisa, Huertas-Macías, Ana, & Villamil Tinajero, Josefina. (1998). *Educating Latino Students: A Guide to Successful Practice.* Lancaster, PA: Technomic.

Hidalgo, Nitza M. (2000). *Puerto Rican Mothering Strategies: The Role of Mothers and Grandmothers in Promoting School Success.* In Sonia Nieto (Ed.), *Puerto Rican Students in U.S. Schools* (pp. 167–196). Mahwah, NJ: Erlbaum Associates.

Kanellos, Nicolás (Ed.). (1997). *The Hispanic-American Almanac.* Detroit: Gale Research.

Stanton-Salazar, Ricardo D. (2001). *Manufacturing Hope and Despair: The School and Kin Support Networks of U.S.-Mexican Youth.* New York: Teachers College Press.

Suárez-Orozco, Marcelo M. (1989). *Central American Refugees and U.S. High Schools: A Psychosocial Study of Motivation and Achievement.* Stanford, CA: Stanford University Press.

Trumbull, Elise, Rothstein-Fisch, Carrie, Greenfield, Patricia M., & Quiroz, Blanco. (2001). *Bridging Cultures between Home and School a Guide for Teachers (with a Special Focus on Immigrant Latino Families).* Mahwah, NJ: Lawrence Erlbaum.

Christina Chávez

I

IMMIGRATION TO THE U.S.

Immigration has always been one of the most entry defining features of the U.S. This essay traces the number of immigrants, their demographic characteristics, their migration and settlement patterns, and their educational attainment from the first great wave of immigration (1880 to 1930) to the present. Historical and legal aspects of immigration policy reflect the changes that shaped the social, political, and economic realities of the nation and continue to do so. Finally, immigration has important implications for education policy and funding as the children of immigrants, many of them non-speakers of English, enter United States schools to become effective and capable participants in the U.S. society and economy. Of increasing importance is the growing number of undocumented immigrants who because of their undocumented immigration status, are excluded from full incorporation into the society in which they work and whose schools their children attend. The essay concludes with research suggestions and a recommended reading list on immigration issues.

Numbers

The U.S.'s increasing ethnic and racial diversity is in part attributable to the largest wave of immigration since the influx of about 30 million immigrants between 1880 and 1930, the classic era of immigration with its first great wave of entrants (Gibson & Lennon, 1999). This classic era of immigration had a much higher immigration rate than the past decade, spiking at 10.4 per thousand U.S. population between 1901 and 1910 (U.S. Census Bureau, 2003). Although the decade of 1990 to 2000 alone saw a total influx of about 11 million immigrants, the immigration rate between 1992 and 2001 has hovered around 3.5 to 4 per thousand U.S. population, after a 1991 high of about 7.2, contradicting often raised fears about the U.S.'s dwindling capacity to absorb new immigrants.

Compared to immigration rates at the beginning of the twentieth century, the higher absolute numbers of immigrants to the U.S. also reflect a shift in national origin of legal immigrants. Between 1900 and 1920, Europe accounted for 86% of all immigrants, Latin America for 10%, and Asia for 4%. From 1980 to 2000, 50% of all immigrants hailed from Latin America, 34% from Asia, 13% from Europe, and 3% from Africa (U.S. INS, 2002). The new regional mix of immigrants has led to changes in the racial and ethnic mix of the U.S. population. Whereas during the first three decades of the twentieth century the U.S. population became "less black, more white, and more firmly European in culture and outlook" (Massey, 1995,

p. 633), the new immigrants are of unprecedented racial and ethnic diversity, leading to higher immigrant visibility and a shift in the ethnic and racial composition of the U.S. population. Moreover, contrary to European immigration, which peaked before World War I and practically ended in 1930, the new immigration from Latin America and Asia is ongoing. "Rather than being a one-time historical phenomenon, immigration has become a permanent structural feature of the postindustrial society of the United States" (Massey, 1995, p. 643).

What are the demographic characteristics of the foreign-born population? According to the U.S. Census Bureau's Current Population Survey (CPS) of March 2002, the foreign born (those who were not U.S. citizens at birth) make up 11.5% of the population; are more likely to live in urban areas, larger households, and in poverty; earn less and are more likely to be unemployed than natives (Schmidley, 2003). Areas of immigrant settlement tend to be more geographically concentrated than those of the native born. Roughly 40% of the foreign born live in the western U.S., with 31% in California alone. By 1990 California, New York, Texas, Florida, New Jersey, and Illinois hosted nearly 70% of the immigrant population in the U.S. (Borjas, 2000). Since the late 1990s this settlement pattern has been shifting to include non-traditional receiving states that have little previous experience with the integration of immigrants. The states with the greatest growth in their total Hispanic populations were North Carolina, Arkansas, and Georgia, leading to greater immigrant dispersal across the U.S. and making migration a nationwide phenomenon (Migration Policy Institute, 2002).

In 2000, according to the Census Bureau's CPS, the 10 source countries with the largest populations in the U.S. as percentages of the total foreign-born population (28,337,384) were Mexico (28%), Philippines (4%), India (4%), China (3%), Cuba (3%), Vietnam (3%), El Salvador (3%), the Dominican Republic (2%), Haiti (1%), and Nicaragua (1%). An economic downturn since 2000 and the attacks of September 11, 2001, have not significantly slowed the pace of immigration, even though the national unemployment rate increased from 4.1% in 2000 to 6.2% in 2003. Therefore, immigration cannot be considered a self-regulating process tied only to economic contexts (Camarota, 2003). Unless Congress enacts major changes in the nation's immigration policy or changes enforcement strategies, the U.S. will likely continue to experience immigration of more than 1 million annually (Martin & Midgley, 2003).

Historical and Legal Aspects of Immigration

The evolution of immigration to the U.S. mirrors the evolution of U.S. immigration policy as a response to social, political, and economic changes. The parallels between past and present are striking. Immigration legislation continues to be aimed at regulating the quality as well as the quantity of entrants while trying to curb the number of those entering illegally.

In 1882, at the beginning of the first great wave of mass immigration, ensuing fears of dwindling employment opportunities for Americans and rising racial and ethnic prejudice led to the passage of the Chinese Exclusion Act. The act suspended Chinese immigration and prevented Chinese immigrants from becoming U.S. citizens for 10 years (Hayes, 2001). Much like Mexican immigrants today, Asian immigrants were thought to take jobs away from white Americans while driving down wages to levels unacceptable to white workers. The act was extended three times, the last time in 1904 while immigration from Europe reached its peak.

In the course of a depression in 1891, restrictionist, nativist advocate groups gained political influence pushing, inter alia, for a literacy test to restrict immigration (LeMay, 2004). Congress did not successfully pass a native language literacy test for all immigrants over 16 years of age until 1917, when President Wilson's veto was overridden. National-origin quota laws, passed in 1921, 1924, and 1929, shifted immigration from mostly south, central, and eastern Europe back to the "more desirable" immigrants from northwestern Europe in response to increasing fears of allegedly unassimilable Greeks, Poles, Italians, Jews, and others. Apart from literacy requirements and the quota laws, World Wars I and II, as well as the Great Depression, reduced immigration from Europe. After World War II, Western Europe itself attracted large numbers of immigrants to rebuild war-shattered economies while communist Eastern Europe blocked emigration to the West (Massey, 1995). Because Latin America had not been affected by the quota laws of the 1920s, immigration from Mexico steadily increased, as did immigration from Cuba, the Dominican Republic, and Colombia. Agricultural labor shortages after World War II led Congress to sign the 1942 Bracero Accord, allowing Mexican workers to enter the U.S. as temporary workers. By 1964, when the Bracero program ended, Braceros had outnumbered legal immigrants during the period (Donato & Carter, 1999). The Immigration and Nationality Act of 1965 ended the national-origin quota systems, abolished the ban on Asian immigration, and encouraged family reunification for immigrants already in the U.S. (Green, 2003). In the wake of the 1965 legislation, immigration

shifted from predominantly European entry to Latin American and Asian immigration, establishing an immigration pattern that still exists today.

In response to refugee waves from Cuba, South Vietnam, Cambodia, and Laos and Haiti, Congress passed the Refugee Act of 1980, defining refugees "to include people from anywhere in the world, not just Communist countries or Middle Eastern nations" (LeMay, 2004, p. 6). In 1977 the Select Commission on Immigration and Refugee Policy had been created for the study of illegal immigration and refugee policy, leading to the Immigration Reform and Control Act (IRCA) of 1986 and the Immigration Act (IMMACT) of 1990. IRCA resulted in the legalization of 3 million undocumented immigrants; sanctions were imposed on those hiring or harboring undocumented immigrants; and border control was supposed to be stepped up through staff increases of up to 50%, which was not tackled seriously until the mid-1990s. IMMACT amended IRCA by adjusting admission categories; revising grounds for exclusion and deportation; revising non-immigrant admission categories; and redefining enforcement activities, employer sanctions, and criminal and deportation provisions (LeMay, 2004; Migration Policy Institute, 2002). The overall goal was to raise skill and education levels of legal entrants and discourage illegal entry. IRCA's effect in curbing the flow of illegal entrants from Mexico was temporary at best (Espenshade, 1995).

In 1994 Proposition 187 was passed as a ballot initiative in California, denying illegal immigrants education, health, and social service benefits in the wake of a resurging debate about increased illegal immigration. In response to the resurgence of the illegal immigration debate, Congress passed the Personal Responsibility and Work Opportunity

Act of 1996. Most of Proposition 187 had been ruled unconstitutional in 1995, but the 1996 legislation enacted many of the provisions of Proposition 187, such as prohibition of states from providing state or local benefits to most illegal aliens, restriction of federal benefits for illegal aliens and legal non-immigrants, and ineligibility of most legal immigrants for Supplemental Security Income and food stamps, inter alia (LeMay, 2004). Although the Clinton administration removed some of the more controversial denial-of-benefit propositions of the 1996 act in the wake of an improving economy, the easing of immigration policy ended with the September 11, 2001, terrorist attacks on the World Trade Center in New York and the Pentagon in Washington, DC. The attacks signaled the beginning of what LeMay (2004) calls the "era of 'Fortress America' in immigration policy" (p. 27) and led in 2001 to unanimous passing of the USA Patriot Act, which includes several immigration-related provisions such as denying entry to aliens suspected of terrorist activity or to those who publicly endorse such activities. In 2002, Congress passed the Homeland Security Act, which established the Department of Homeland Security (DHS). The Immigration and Naturalization Service (INS) was abolished on March 1, 2003, and reorganized into two bureaus under the auspices of the DHS: the Directorate of Border and Transportation Security (BTS) and the U.S. Citizenship and Immigration Services (USCIS). By tying immigration to national security, the act also permits and requires the attorney general to detain aliens whom he declares to be threats to national security, with habeas corpus suspended under certain conditions (USA Patriot Act, subtitle B, sections 411 and 412). The USA Patriot Act has been criticized as "legalizing the racial profiling of Middle Easterners"

(LeMay, 2004, p. 27) and raised concern with immigrant support and civil liberties groups because of the sweeping nature of the legislation. Immigration and national security debates will likely continue as the number of entrants, especially from Mexico, continues to increase, fueled by U.S.-Mexico talks about a proposed temporary worker program for new Mexican workers (Migration Policy Institute, 2002).

Implications of Immigration for Education and Schooling in the U.S.

Education has always been a key issue in immigration policy because the educational attainment of immigrants influences their future earning power and economic mobility and, consequently, their fiscal contributions. The higher the educational attainment of immigrants, the more taxes they will pay as a result of higher income levels; whereas those immigrants with less than a high school education will consume more in public services and benefits than they pay in taxes (National Academies Press Release, 1997). Therefore, immigrants' educational attainment is of great interest to immigrant-receiving states and to the nation as a whole.

What is the educational profile of today's immigrants? A comparison between the 2002 educational levels of U.S.-born Americans and foreign-born Americans who arrived in or after 1990 shows that 30% of the foreign born had an undergraduate degree or higher versus 24% of the U.S. born. However, 34% of the foreign born had less than a high school education, compared to 16% of the U.S. born (Sahlman, 2002). Immigrants are represented among the most-educated as well as the least-educated segments of the U.S. population. These numbers explain not only the growing inequality between the U.S. born and the foreign born but also the inequalities within the foreign-born population itself.

Of all foreign born, those from Mexico are the largest and most-disadvantaged group, with the highest level of child poverty at 32.9% in 2000 versus 25.4% for other Hispanic groups (Van Hook, 2003). This poverty rate correlates with low parental educational attainment: Approximately two-thirds of adult Mexican immigrants have not completed high school (Camarota, 2001) versus about only 13% from Asia and 16% from Europe who do not have a high school diploma (Schmidley, 2003). Although the child poverty rate increased for all children between 1970 and 1995 from 14.5% to 22%, it increased more rapidly for immigrant children, from 11.9% to 33%, within the same time span (Van Hook, 2003). The growing income inequality has important implications for education funding and policy as immigration continues to increase.

Regardless of educational attainment and income status, immigrant parents and children tend to have higher educational aspirations than their native counterparts. Hispanic aspirations, however, have declined over time (Vernez & Abrahamse, 1996). Parents realize that learning English is indispensable for educational and economic success. Thus the teaching of English language skills is a key issue for the nation's schools, which in the 2000–2001 school year provided services to 3.4 million students of limited English proficiency (Martin & Midgley, 2003). Teaching English as a second language (ESOL) poses many challenges for school systems. Many instructors have had little training in teaching non-English-speaking or limited English proficient (LEP) students. In the 1999–2000 school year, only 33% or fewer of high school students in math, science, social studies, English, arts and music, and physical education and health education classes had teachers who did not have a major and certification in the subject taught. However, 71% of high school students in English as a Second Language (ESL) or bilingual classes had teachers without a major and certification in ESL or bilingual education (McMillen Seastrom et al., 2002). This lack of qualified teachers for LEP students puts at risk an already vulnerable and rapidly growing segment of the student population. Not only is there a lack of qualified teachers for LEP students; LEP students also have only limited access to adequate educational resources in schools with high concentrations of poor children, since local school funding is generally property tax based.

Further complicating matters is a strong correlation between limited English proficiency and disadvantaged socioeconomic background, leading to increasing resegregation of Hispanic students. Poverty and housing patterns result in increasing isolation of Hispanic students from white students in almost every large school district. This isolation is almost always related to inequalities in curriculum, test scores, graduation, and college-going rates (Frankenberg & Lee, 2002). Hispanic students tend to go to schools with high concentrations of students of their own ethnic origin, resulting not only in ethnic segregation but also in linguistic isolation, which is especially problematic for those who are LEP immigrant students.

Given these problematic issues, the central question is how immigrant students fare in U.S. schools. Although immigrant and LEP students have higher attendance rates than U.S.-born children, the dropout rate of first-generation immigrant children is higher (17.6%) than the dropout rate of the second generation (11.2%) and the native born (13.5%). Dropout rates vary with ethnicity, though. First-generation Asian students have the lowest dropout rate at 4% and Mexicans the highest at 35%. Among first-generation students, LEP students are substantially less likely to complete high school, although those who stay in school seem to perform as well as non-LEP students with regard to grades and attendance. LEP status has the greatest effect on high school completion for Mexican students. Among LEP students, Mexicans are substantially more likely to drop out than are their non-LEP peers (37.9% versus 24.2%), whereas only 4.3% of LEP Asians are not enrolled in school versus 4.5% of non-LEP Asians (Ruiz-de-Velasco & Fix, 2000). These high dropout rates pose problems for schools with high proportions of LEP students.

How do schools deal with the generally higher dropout rates of LEP students? Under the No Child Left Behind Act (NCLB) of 2000, LEP status has taken on a new meaning for schools with a high proportion of these students, since the act requires racial and ethnic minorities, students with disabilities, and students from low-income families as well as English language learners (ELLs) to make "Adequate Yearly Progress" (AYP). If only one of these groups fails to meet these standards, the school in question has not achieved AYP. Thus LEP students might feel pressured to drop out under this accountability system, which relies on standardized test scores to determine school progress and sanctions schools with high proportions of ELLs (Orfield, Losen, Wald, & Swanson, 2004). Hispanic students face the greatest challenges under the accountability system of the NCLB Act, which further exacerbates Hispanics' already low high school completion rates and has social and economic implications for the future of the nation.

Implications for the Future

Of all immigrant ethnic groups, Hispanics students have the lowest completion rate while representing the largest proportion and fastest-growing segment of immigrant children to the U.S., a pattern that continues through second, third, and subsequent generations. A greatly undereducated, rapidly growing Hispanic population will have to support the aging and retiring white baby-boomers in a 65 and older population that is projected to triple by 2030 (Hayes-Bautista, Schink, & Chapa, 1988). At stake is not only the immigrants' welfare but also that of the states in which they reside, which will experience a major drain of public resources by undereducated, socioeconomically disadvantaged immigrants. Society has a major stake in addressing and understanding the educational attainment of immigrant youth, and researchers need to address specifically the educational needs of the Hispanic immigrant and LEP students, for "there may be no surer way to guarantee that any ethnic, racial, or religious group will reject integration into American society than to deny its members the tools and opportunities they need to achieve the American dream" (Lindsay & Singer, 2003, p. 252).

Undocumented Immigration

Although about 75% of immigrants enter the country legally (U.S. INS, 2000), substantial numbers of entrants either cross the border illegally or fall into undocumented status after having entered the country legally at some point. Undocumented, unauthorized, clandestine, or illegal entrants come from a variety of source countries for a variety of reasons. These entrants will be referred to as undocumented because most of the salient research uses this term and to de-emphasize the legal aspect of entry.

Immigration laws are rather complex and difficult to navigate; that is, an entrant might have come to the U.S. legally and with the proper documentation but subsequently fell outofstatusunwittingly. Alternatively, someone might have entered the country without the proper documentation and later made used of immigration law provisions allowing a switch to legal status. Some people enter legally but overstay their visas. Others enter legally with non-immigrant visas and illegally start working, thus violating their visa conditions. Then there are also those immigrants who fall under Temporary Protected Status (TPS) and asylum seekers who have legal authorization to live and work in the U.S. but who are nevertheless included in estimates of the undocumented population (Passel, Capps, & Fix, 2004). Common to all these cases is the eventual lack of proper documentation for the specific contexts in which the undocumented entrants find themselves.

The INS coined the term "unauthorized." The majority of what the INS calls "unauthorized immigrants" are "foreign born persons who entered without inspection or who violated the terms of temporary admission and who have not acquired LPR [Legal Permanent Resident] status or gained temporary protection against removal by applying for an immigration benefit" (U.S. INS, 2003). Thus "unauthorized" describes a bureaucratic conception of an entrant into the U.S., a legal status that can be subject to subsequent revision based on salient legal frameworks. These legal frameworks themselves depend on sociopolitical and economic contexts as well as the citizenship concept of not only the U.S. but any nation-state. Legal frameworks are subject to revision, as has been pointed out in the previous section on the evolution of immigration legislation. Therefore, "undocumented"

seems to be the most appropriate description for a rather heterogeneous group of people.

Whereas immigration policy evolves along with sociopolitical and economic conditions, the U.S.'s ambivalence about undocumented immigration and undocumented workers in a global capitalist economy has always manifested itself in the de jure regulation of legal entry and the de facto lack of "funding for the INS to evacuate the United States of undocumented migrants by means of deportations nor even for the Border Patrol to 'hold the line'" (De Genova, 2002, p. 438). The discrepancy between the de jure and de facto situations reflects not only ambivalence toward undocumented immigration but also the continuous mismatch between immigration law and the social and economic realities of the U.S.

Although undocumented immigrants are a heterogeneous group, Mexico is the leading source country for undocumented entry, accounting for 57%, or about 5.3 million, of the 9.3 million estimated undocumented immigrants residing in the U.S. in March 2002. Other Latin American countries account for 23%, Asia for 10%, Europe and Canada for 5%, and the rest of the world for another 5% of undocumented entrants (Passel et al., 2004). Estimates of the undocumented population are based on Border Patrol apprehensions. Espenshade (1995) assumes that "the estimated size of the illegal migrant flow is roughly 2.2 times the number of Border Patrol arrests" (p. 198). According to most recent estimates (Passel et al., 2004), undocumented immigrants were estimated to number about 9.3 million, or 26% of the total foreign-born population in 2002. Undocumented immigrants show the same geographic clustering as documented immigrants, although the largest increase in the undocumented population after the mid-1990s has been outside the traditional receiving states. Among the 10 states whose undocumented population makes up more than 40% of the foreign born are Arizona, Georgia, and North Carolina. According to Passel and others (2004), there are about 6 million undocumented workers, making up 5% of U.S. workers and leading to a 96% labor force participation rate for undocumented workers, two-thirds of whom earn less than twice the minimum wage (versus one-third of all workers). The manufacturing sector employs more than a million undocumented workers; a similar number works in the service industries, more than 600,000 in construction, and more than 700,000 in restaurants (Lowell & Suro, 2002). Contemporary Mexican undocumented immigration in particular has led to a considerable presence of women and entire families who settle and integrate into permanent communities (Hondagneu-Sotelo, 1994). According to Passel, Capps, and Fix's (2004) estimates, there were 1.6 million children under the age of 18 years in the U.S. who are undocumented immigrants themselves and approximately 3 million children who are U.S. citizens but whose parents are undocumented. These children face issues similar to those faced by other immigrant children but have to live with the additional problems that come with undocumented legal status: psychological stress from the illegal entry experience, which has become more dangerous because of stepped-up border surveillance; constant fear of deportation; limited access to health services; ineligibility to obtain a driver's license; inability to open a bank account without a social security number; ineligibility to work after high school graduation; and lack of access to scholarships and financial aid for higher education. All these obstacles add to the acculturative stress that all immigrants experience, leading to a sense of caution and mistrustfulness on the part of undocumented students, which in turn makes it more difficult for teachers and counselors to establish trusting relationships with these students (Smart & Smart, 1995). Under these circumstances the lack of research on undocumented students and their plight in the U.S. educational system is understandable. Given the number of undocumented immigrant children and the native-born children of undocumented parents, the acculturation and adaptation, or the lack thereof, of these children to their host country should be a key societal concern.

Conclusion

As documented and undocumented immigration, especially from Latin America and Asia, is likely to continue to shape the social and economic fabric of the U.S., policies dealing with documented and undocumented immigration need to move beyond cost-benefit analyses and partisan polemics about national identity and crime. An overview of the historic and legal aspects of immigration shows that immigration policies have traditionally been directed outward to control who is coming in without regard to what happens to immigrants once they are in the country. To become fully incorporated into U.S. society and culture, immigrant youth must have access to adequate and relevant education, to certified ESOL and bilingual teachers, to adequate educational materials and facilities, and to qualified counselors who can give immigrant students the guidance needed to successfully navigate the U.S. educational system.

Research with documented and undocumented immigrant students will require the building of trusting relationships between researchers and students, which requires prolonged and extensive community involvement of researchers and close collaboration between researchers and teachers who successfully teach immigrant students. Voters and legislators will have to decide how to deal with undocumented immigrant children who are not legal but definitely cultural and economic citizens of this country and who, according to the U.S. Supreme Court ruling of *Plyler v. Doe,* 1982, have the same right to a free public education as documented immigrant children and U.S. citizens. Policies of inclusion will ensure the survival of society and culture and help us "to open our eyes to the multicultural, transnational community we have always shared but seldom seen" (Petronicolos & New, 1999, p. 404).

References

Borjas, G. J. (2000). Introduction. In G. J. Borjas, *Issues in the Economics of Immigration* (pp. 1–14). Chicago: University of Chicago Press.

Camarota, S. A. (2001). *Immigration from Mexico: Assessing the Impact on the United States.* Washington, DC: Center for Immigration Studies.

Camarota, S. A. (2003). Immigration in a Time of Recession: An Examination of Trends since 2000. *Backgrounder.* Washington, DC: Center for Immigration Studies, November.

De Genova, N. P. (2002). Migrant "Illegality" and Deportability in Everyday Life. *Annual Review of Anthropology* 31, 419–447.

Donato, K. M., & Carter, R. S. (1999). Mexico and U.S. Policy on Illegal Immigration: A Fifty-Year Retrospective. In D. W. Haines, & K. E. Rosenblum (Eds.), *Illegal Immigration in America: A Reference Handbook* (pp. 112–132). Westport, CT: Greenwood Press.

Espenshade, T. J. (1995). Unauthorized Immigration to the United States. *Annual Review of Sociology* 21, 195–216.

Frankenberg, E., & Lee, C. (2002). *Race in American Public Schools: Rapidly Resegregating School Districts.* Cambridge, MA: The Civil Rights Project at Harvard University.

Gibson, C., & Lennon, E. (1999). *Historical Census Statistics on the Foreign-Born Population of the United States: 1850 to 1990.* U.S. Census Bureau Working Paper, no. 29. Washington, DC: U.S. GPO.

Green, P. (2003). The Undocumented: Educating the Children of Migrant Workers in America. *Bilingual Research Journal* 27 (1), 51–71.

Hayes, H. (2001). *U.S. Immigration Policy and the Undocumented: Ambivalent Laws, Furtive Lives.* Westport, CT: Praeger.

Hayes-Bautista, D., Schink, W., & Chapa, J. (1988). *The Burden of Support: Young Latinos in An Aging Society.* Stanford, CA: Stanford University Press.

Hondagneu-Sotelo, P. (1994). *Gendered Transitions: Mexican Experiences of Immigration.* Berkeley: University of California Press.

LeMay, M. C. (2004). *U.S. Immigration: A Reference Handbook.* Santa Barbara, CA: ABC-CLIO.

Lindsay, J. M., & Singer, A. (2003). Changing Faces: Immigrants and Diversity in the Twenty-first Century. In H. J. Aaron, J. M. Lindsay, & P. S. Nivola (Eds.), *Agenda for the Nation* (pp. 217–260). Washington, DC: Brookings Institution.

Lowell, B. L., & Suro, R. (2002). *How Many Undocumented: The Numbers behind the U.S.-Mexico Migration Talks.* Washington, DC: Pew Hispanic Center.

Martin, P., & Midgley, E. (2003). Immigration: Shaping and Reshaping America. *Population Bulletin* 58 (2). Washington, DC: Population Reference Bureau.

Massey, D. (1995). The New Immigration and Ethnicity in the United States. *Population and Development Review* 21 (3), 631–652.

McMillen Seastrom, M., Gruber, K. J., Henke, R., McGrath, D. J., & Cohen, B. A. (2002). Qualifications of the Public School Teacher Workforce: Prevalence of Out-of-Field Teaching, 1987–88 to 1999–2000. Available: http://nces.ed.gov/pubs2002/2002603.pdf.

Migration Policy Institute. (2002). A New Century: Immigration and the U.S. *Migration Information Source* (Washington, DC: Migration Policy Institute), May. Available: http://www.migrationinformation.org.

National Academies Press Release. (1997). Overall U.S. Economy Gains from Immigration, but It's Costly to Some States and Localities. May 17. Available: http://www4 .nationalacademies.org/news.nsf/isbn/030906 3566?OpenDocument.

Orfield, G., Losen, D., Wald, J., & Swanson, C. (2004). *Losing Our Future: How Minority Youth Are Being Left Behind by the Graduation Rate Crisis.* Cambridge, MA: Civil Rights Project at Harvard University.

Passel, J. S., Capps, R., & Fix, M. (2004). *Undocumented Immigrants: Facts and Figures.* Washington, DC: Urban Institute Press.

Petronicolos, L., & New, W. S. (1999). Anti-immigrant Legislation, Social Justice, and the Right to Equal Educational Opportunity. *American Educational Research Journal* 36, 373–408.

Ruiz-de-Velasco, J., & Fix, M. (2000). *Overlooked & Underserved: Immigrant Students in U.S. Secondary Schools.* Washington, DC: Urban Institute.

Sahlman, S. (2002). Executive Summary Insert: 2002 Demographic Characteristics of Immigrants. Available: http://www.prcdc .org/summariesinsert02/immigrationinsert02 .html.

Schmidley, D. (2003). The Foreign-born Population in the United States: March 2002. *U.S. Census Bureau, Current Population Reports.* Available: http://www.census.gov/prod/2003 pubs/p20-539.pdf.

Smart, J. F., & Smart, D. W. (1995). Acculturative Stress of Hispanics: Loss and Challenge. *Journal of Counseling & Development* 73, 390–396.

U.S. Census Bureau. (2003). *Statistical Abstracts.* Table HS-8. Immigration—Number and Rate: 1900 to 2001. Available: http:// www.census.gov/statab/hist/HS-08.pdf.

U.S. Immigration and Naturalization Service (INS). (2000). *Statistical Yearbook of the U.S. Immigration and Naturalization Service, 1998.* Washington, DC: U.S. Government Printing Office.

U.S. Immigration and Naturalization Service (INS). (2002). *Statistical Yearbook of the U.S. Immigration and Naturalization Service, 2000.* Washington, DC: U.S. Government Printing Office.

U.S. Immigration and Naturalization Service (INS). (2003). *Executive Summary: Estimates of the Unauthorized Immigrant Population Residing in the United States, 1990–2000.* Available: http://www.immigration.gov/gra phics/aboutus/Statistics/2000ExecSumm.pdf (accessed April 19, 2003).

Van Hook, J. (2003). Poverty Grows among Children of Immigrants in US. *Migration Information Source.* Washington, DC: Migration Policy Institute, December.

Vernez, G., & Abrahamse, A. (1996). *How Immigrants Fare in U.S. Education.* Santa Monica, CA: RAND.

Recommended Reading

Chávez, L. (1998). *Shadowed Lives: Undocumented Immigrants in American Society* (2nd ed.). Fort Worth, TX: Hartcourt Brace.

Díaz de Cossío, R. (1997). *Los mexicanos en Estados Unidos.* Mexico City: SITESA.

Nieto, S. (1999). *The Light in Their Eyes: Creating Multicultural Learning Communities.* New York: Teachers College Press.

Portes, A. (Ed.). (1996). *The New Second Generation.* New York: Russell Sage Foundation.

Portes, A. (2001). Immigration Theory for a New Century: Some Problems and Opportunities. In M. Suárez-Orozco, C. Suárez-Orozco, & D. Qin-Hilliard (Eds.), *Interdisciplinary Perspectives on the New Immigration* (pp. 275–289). New York: Routledge.

Rumbaut, R., & Portes, A. (Eds.). (2001). *Ethnicities: Children of Immigrants in America.* Berkeley: University of California Press.

Shorres, E. (1992). *Latinos: A Biography of the People*. New York: Norton.

Suárez-Orozco, C., & Suárez-Orozco, M. (1995). *Transformations: Immigration, Family Life, and Achievement Motivation among Latino Adolescents*. Stanford, CA: Stanford University Press.

Suárez-Orozco, C., & Suárez-Orozco, M. (2001). *Children of Immigration*. Cambridge, MA: Harvard University Press.

Suárez-Orozco, C., Suárez-Orozco, M., & Qin-Hilliard, D. (Eds.). (2001). *Interdisciplinary Perspectives on the New Immigration* (pp. 125–133). New York: Routledge.

Suro, R. (1998). *Strangers among Us*. New York: Knopf.

Recommended Web Sites

Center for Comparative Immigration Studies at the University of California at San Diego, http://www.ccis-ucsd.org/.

Center for Immigration Studies think tank devoted exclusively to research and policy analysis of the economic, social, demographic, fiscal, and other impacts of immigration on the U.S., http://www.cis.org.

Center for Research on Education, Diversity, and Excellence (CREDE) at the University of California at Santa Cruz, http://www.crede.ucsc.edu/.

Grantmakers Concerned with Immigrants and Refugees (GCIR), http://www.gcir.org.

The Harvard Immigration Projects at Harvard Graduate School of Education, http://www.gse.harvard.edu/~hip/.

Immigration Policy Center (IPC) of the American Immigration Law Foundation in Washington, DC, http://www.ailf.org/ipc/ipc_index.asp.

Migration Information Source at the Migration Policy Institute in Washington, DC, http://www.migrationpolicy.org/.

The National Immigration Forum in Washington, DC, http://www.immigrationforum.org.

The Pew Hispanic Center at the University of Southern California, Annenberg School for Communication, http://www.pewhispanic.org.

Public Policy Institute of California, http://www.ppic.org.

Sabine E. Teaver

INTERGENERATIONAL FAMILY LITERACY

Poet Francisco Alarcón (1997) writes, "My Mother's hands are as eloquent as the finest books . . . ¡sí se puede!" (p. 15). In a study of literacy teachers (Rummel & Quintero, 1997) we learned about the teachers' family histories and saw the importance of what families across cultures do best—care for, attend to, and love each other; regardless of conditions. The teachers in our study brought the effects of their own families to their relationships with their students and to their teaching. They showed us how positive it is when educators are informed by families' knowledge. Family knowledge and literacy are interwoven fabric of cultural practices. The art of using this family knowledge and related literacy practice promotes strength, encourages nurturance, and supports risk taking for students and teachers.

Many teachers, like many well-known writers and visionaries (Allen, 1992; Walker, 1990) talk about the importance of passing on stories by parents and grandparents. In our study (Rummel & Quintero, 1997) one teacher talked about the positive moments of working with his family members in the fields as migrant workers. He said, "Your mother's there, your father's there. Your brothers and sisters are there. Everyone is talking and sometimes joking" (p. 58). We were together. That was important.

The same man also talked about his confusion as a young elementary student realizing that the white, middle-class families in the elementary textbook illustrations did not look at all like his family. "My dad didn't wear a tie" (Quintanilla, 1997, p. 59). And he talked about being teased by his Mexican national cousins about the way he spoke Spanish and about being teased by the Anglo kids about the way he spoke English. Now as an activist teacher working with Latino and Hmong students and their families in Minnesota, he relentlessly stresses the importance of family history, cultural knowledge, and native language.

Another teacher in New York discusses the complexity of her own heritage as a point of departure for her work to learn from and work with the families of her students:

When I think of my ethnic identity, honestly I think of so many things I don't know where to start. My family come from all over the place actually, so I don't really know which ethnic group I identify myself with most. My mother is American by birth, as is her mother. But, my grandmother grew up in Mexico, as did my grandfather. My grandmother's family was from Mexico. My grandfather's father was from Greece, his mother from Mexico. My father, born in Mexico, is of European descent. His father was born in Stockholm, his mother in San Antonio, right next to the Alamo. My grandmother also has Swedish and German ancestry. And while he is not Latino, my father grew up in Venezuela.

She discussed neighborhood and language:

These are all of the things I think of when I think of my ethnic background. I tend to relate more to the Latino side of my family, because I grew up in San Antonio where there is such a large Latino population. I guess that would be the place my ethnic identity is tied to. Everyone in my family speaks Spanish; all my grandparents, aunts, uncles, etc. While the history of Mexican people has not played a large role in my upbringing, I know some of it, mostly what I learned in school and from my surroundings.

People in San Antonio are very aware of the Mexican culture and this is shown in various ways throughout the city. Even though I am American, I relate to the Mexican culture most out of all of my backgrounds because it plays such a vital role in my everyday life. There is not a large Swedish or Greek community in San Antonio.

And traditions:

The earliest things I remember about my cultural background and ethnicity are the traditions of my family. I did not know much about Swedish people, but I knew what they ate at Christmas time. I knew some of their manners from stories told to me by my father's parents. I knew about the Greeks and what kinds of things they did at Easter. My mother's parents would take us to the Greek Festival held each year at St. Sophia's Greek Orthodox Church downtown. This is how I was introduced to my ethnic background.

Learning from Families in Difficult Situations

Because my colleagues and I believe that we teachers must make an effort to learn from families in a variety of situations, we have begun qualitative research in Central America and Turkey that has further emphasized the cultural and political and historical effect a family situation has on children. The participants are Iranian and Iraqi refugee women in Ankara, Turkey, and the other groups of mothers in Guatemala. The interviews are framed by the following questions: In what ways are caregivers able to educate (talk to, read to, tell stories to, or sing with) your children within the context of refugee camps or other refugee contexts? How do you give important learning information to your children, through stories or activities? Are programs available to support the children's learning where you live now? The interview data are categorized and analyzed according to the theoretical perspectives framing the study, and then selections are used in lessons for the university students.

The information gleaned from the interviews with the refugees informs both educators and policymakers about the strengths and needs of refugee women and children in terms of critical literacy and learning. This information could be used around the world in creating pedagogy for literacy, using local knowledge of particular sites, and drawing on a range of strengths and histories for families and children to advocate for their rights to literacy and learning in difficult times.

We began the problem-posing activities that evening with information in poetry format that had been developed from the actual interview texts from Guatemala.

What Mothers Do

Listening

- Think and write about a mother figure in your life or your own mothering. What support did that person need from the community in order to mother? From the schools? From the government?

- Remember one strong experience related to mothering. What is some important thing that a mother figure did for you? What did that person do or make? Try to hear that person talking to you. What are some things that person says (or said). Write it down.

- Read the following poem.

"What Mothers Do" by Mary Kay Rummel

Call her not Noemi that is beautiful
But Mara that is bitter
For the Almighty hath quite
filled her with bitterness ... Catholic liturgy for
stations of the cross
In Guatemala red is Mary's color
At the side altar in La Iglesia de San
  Francisco

the Mayan Mary is a shepherdess with long
  curled hair
skin darkened by sun and time surrounded
  by three lambs.
Today her gown is plain red velvet, her
  straw hat embroidered
with bright flowers, the shepherdess before
  the sorrow,
before the child, and after when he is feeding
from her breast.

In front of her we chant, "Lamb, Lamb, Lamb."

I walk the cobbled courtyard outside the
  church
under the spell of Naomi, find her and
  Mara both
in a young girl who sits and weaves, loom
  in lap
her finished tapetes arranged carefully
  behind her.
Her blouse is blue embroidered with
  flowers
her arms strong with the push and pull of
  thread.
She fast talks with silences between words
  that I
can't hear to her son who sits on a basket
across from her, his brown eyes lost in the
  distance
or sometimes turned down as he is wound
  in her words.
She talks in the rhythm of the weave—her
  voice rising
with teaching, praying,
  complaining, working
the skeins of her words, the world she is.

"Lamb," we chant to her, "Lamb, Lamb, Lamb."

Dialogue

- What work is the mother in this poem doing? What could she be saying to her child as she works? What is she teaching? How is she keeping her child near?

- Discuss choices you make in your daily life that take a stand.
- Brainstorm with your group ways the different choices we all make influence teaching and learning.

Action

- Go to the web site for the Resource Center of the Americas, http://www.americas.org/. This is a Minneapolis-based non-profit publisher of AMERICAS.ORG, which is devoted to the notion that every person in this world is entitled to the same fundamental human rights. Their starting point for promoting these rights is learning and teaching about the peoples and countries of the Americas—their history, culture, and politics. Read one or more of the articles and relate the information to the poem.
- From your reading at the web site, describe the ways the women of Guatemala have organized to sell their reading. Read the article about Colibri and the organizing of Guatemalan weavers.

Read the following poem.

"A Dozen Reasons to Give Up Haggling over the Price of Weavings" by Roseann Lloyd (www.CyberPoet.com/Roseann-Lloyd.html)

1   For the weaver herself who takes the
        bus to market at 4 A.M.
1.5   for the buck and a half she brings
        home each day
2   for the discount rate *para dos* she
        offers too readily
3   for the 3 languages she speaks,
        working on the 4th
4   for her babies born after the war
        one for the cousin killed in the
        highlands
        one for uncle in Minnesota
        two for the brother and sister
        hiding in Mexico
5   for the age she started to weave
6   for her favorite colors: canario, rojo,
        verde, morado, indigo y café

7   for the quetzal/dollar exchange
8   for the animals that dance in her
        cloth: cat, quetzal, monarchs, deer,
        baby, chickens, dog, squirrel eating
        chamomile, dove
9   for the tortillas in her apron pocket
10   for ten fingers she says she's lucky to
        have
11   for the family she has to feed
12   for the men, the dozens of unmarked
        graves

- Write a poem based on this model: "A Dozen Reasons to . . ." Think about issues you could have your students write about related to the topic of taking a stand as educators (e.g., a dozen reasons to have children use their home language).
- Share ideas for applying problem posing to your teaching.

Conclusion

In this entry, I have elaborated on my strong stance about the importance of using family knowledge and strengths, cultural and linguistic, in education. I am currently working with Latino teachers who are interviewing parents and students about bringing family and community knowledge into the classroom as legitimate knowledge and as a valued part of the curriculum.

References

Alarcón, Francisco X. (1997). *Laughing Tomatoes and Other Spring Poems: Jitomates risueños y otras poems de primavera*. San Francisco: Children's Book Press.

Allen, Paula G. (1992). *Grandmothers of the Light*. Boston: Beacon Press.

Rummel, M. K., & Quintero, E. P. (1997). *Teachers' Reading/Teachers' Lives*. Albany, NY: SUNY Press.

Walker, A. (1990). *The Color Purple*. New York: Pocket Books.

Elizabeth Quintero

IQ COLONIZATION

The Latino community in the U.S. represents a lifelong pedagogical struggle against European American constructions of academic achievement in relation to the notion of intelligence quotients (IQ) a la Stanford-Simon (Binet & Simon, 1905) and, later, other combinations of knowledge standardization. Under the guise of the melting pot theory and with the predilectory call of *liberty and justice for all,* standardized tests have always been misused to stratify the social order by implementing a supposedly harmless and disarmed (neutral) academic foundationalism to select, sort, label, and place student populations. The Stanford-Binet (1916) intelligence scale is a direct descendent of the Binet-Simon scale, commonly known as the first intelligence scale created in 1905 by the French psychologist Alfred Binet and his assistant Dr. Theophilus Simon. Lewis Terman of Stanford University later designed the test to be used as an intelligence measurement in America and thus the name Stanford-Binet. In his initial research, Alfred Binet argued that high intelligence was tied to cerebral volume and supposedly produced a higher achievement performance. In his later research, however, Binet discredited this claim and turned to other forms of measurements but remained cautious that the tests could be misused quite easily and admitted of his trepidation regarding how someone could move in adverse directions with his findings (Gould, 1981). And so his fear came to pass time and again as European American educationists fell captive to the ideologies of superiority and the cast of hereditarianism and applied Binet's work to their pedagogical practice.

And is if that was not racist and destructive enough, Richard Herrnstein and Charles Murray reinstituted the role of callous stratification with their publication of *The Bell Curve: Intelligence and Class Structure in American Life* (1994). Several books responded to Herrnstein and Murray: *Measured Lies: The Bell Curve Examined,* edited by Joe L. Kincheloe, Shirley R. Steinberg, and Aaron D. Gresson III; *Inequality by Design: Cracking the Bell Curve Myth* (1996), by Claude S. Fischer et al.; and *The Bell Curve Wars: Race, Intelligence, and the Future of America* (1995), edited by Steven Fraser, to name a few.

IQ and Symbolic Power

The single number notion of IQ played a major role in the academic emplacement of multiethnic children in American schools. The use of physical science research placed an overemphasis on positivistic assumptions regarding achievement that strongly remains in our pedagogical repertoire today even as we realize how social science research cogently influences curriculum and instruction (social undertakings). Numbers alone cannot be used to consign children to the lower academic strata and thus to the social and economic margins. Numbers alone cannot interpret diverse cultural and linguistic meanings or be used to decide the academic performance of multiethnic children whose scholarly abilities are also interwoven into the edification of their everyday life. The power of numbers to industrialize the mind cannot be overlooked. Numbers are little more than symbolic codes used to interpret groups' cultural values. Numbers are callous and cannot take into consideration the feelings, beliefs, and personal desires of humans. Numbers have so often misrepresented the desires of humans in areas such as sheer will, personal power and desire of the heart, and a vision of the future, including thought and imagination. Numbers cannot express or measure personal passion, love, resistance, and the multiple qualities of human aspirations. The point here is that numbers have misguided the majority of educators, who, in turn, have applied them to undermine the climacteric human elements which move people to overcome their subordination and despair. Numbers cannot measure these human attributes.

Why, then, is there so much value placed on the numbers game? Stephen Jay Gould (1981) eloquently responded to this topic, indicating that

the urge to classify people, to rank them according to their supposed gifts and limits, is strong in us. It has been so, from prescientific times when the tools of classification were said to be divine, to our day when numbers are king. (*Mismeasure of Man*, back flap)

This courageous announcement (or denouncement) by Gould aided progressive educators in alerting a broad audience of social scientists even though his claims have remained tacit among most educators. In fact, most educators have virtually remained uninformed about Gould's research on the academic mismeasure of humans and have thus remained indifferent with regard to the deployment of standardized tests. Social scientists such as Renato Rosaldo (1989) have assisted educators, especially critical educators, in rethinking the standardizing analyses invoked in traditional notions and applications of academic performance measures.

For Latinos in American public education, bilingual education has served as a site of pedagogical respite given the mean-spirited undertakings of high-stakes testing and extreme curricular and instructional insensitivity. Although bilingual education in its multiple forms and practices has lacked in its overall praxis, it remains the pedagogy that has most sincerely served the Latino community without completely stripping it of its cultural and linguistic characteristics.

The Multiple Roles of Bilingual Education

The history of bilingual education is rooted in a struggle of resistance politics similar to the oppositional struggles of other pedagogical themes such as special education, multicultural education, and diversity. That history of struggle emanates from an even longer history of resistance within and among the various multilingual communities in the U.S. to maintain their distinctiveness against monolithic canons and narratives that have served to divide and conquer their cultural and linguistic legacy of diversity. The primary intention of those mainstream discourses addressing linguistic diversity have striven to truncate bilingual education from its cultural and pedagogical legacy and to infantilize it as a fatuous formula for supposedly wounding the academic performance of culturally and linguistically diverse students. Linda Chávez (1998), for example, frequently attempts, in almost everything she writes concerning bilingual education, to smudge it as an impediment to bilingual children's academic progress. In some cases it may well do that. It does that, however, not because the concept of educating children in two languages is debauched, but because bilingual education has been envenomed by mainstream edification. In other words, the common methodology for educating children in two languages has been more about trying to fit it into conventional practices of instruction than it is about flexibly implementing bilingual pedagogies. As such, bilingual education as it is practiced in schools today, especially under No Child Left Behind (NCLB), has become a pedagogical insurance for schools to secure bilingual children's grasp of mainstream schooling skills and thus society's rules and procedures for proper allegiance to American citizenship. Bilingual education has become, in a sense, a mainstream sociocultural practice for maintaining the proper transmission of dominant cultural politics and clinically assimilating them into American society.

Educating children can occur in any language or in any number of languages. What remains vacant for most children, whether in a monolingual or bilingual classroom, is the engagement of ideas and information more so than the challenge of learning a second language. There is little difference in what children learn in monolingual English classrooms from what they learn in bilingual classrooms, and that must become the leading concern of educators. What are children learning in classrooms? Pat Buchanan and other social conservatives are concerned about losing America to a "tide" of illegal immigrants who fail to assimilate. He should be more worried about completely losing America to a host of militia groups whose benign intent is to destroy America rather than share and reinvent her with new groups whom the militias deem menacing to their monopolous values. The content of ideologically constructed curriculum that children receive in monolingual and bilingual classrooms all offer assimilationists' views, so children who come from other countries and do not speak English can quickly gain the same reproductive eminence that American-born children have. By the time they acquire and learn English, the brainwashing mission eases the effort for schools to inject its ideology. The cultural content and context of school curricula by nature do not intellectually challenge students of any background. By the time bilingual children learn English, they have been socially and culturally produced in the image of the dominant culture and thus naturally and assuredly reject their own cultural and linguistic identities and family values. The symbolic violence inherent in the cultural politics of traditional curricula destroys any remnant of who they really are.

Approaching the debate of how to educate bilingual children must be conducted within a dialectical format that allows a variety of critical views and strategies to be considered. The pedagogical approach of the last 30 or more years among most bilingual educators has been to use conventional educational philosophies, with the exception of using bilingual students' native languages to impart knowledge. Little debate, if any, has transpired among scholars in relation to what is informing the pedagogical constructs bilingual teachers use. As a result, little attention is given to how bilingual students are socially produced by the curriculum. Most bilingual educators follow school district curricula with minimal regard for how bilingual children are emotionally and culturally affected by the curriculum. As well, most bilingual teachers have not been provided with an alternative language for referencing their teaching, which commonly results in unproblematized methodologies and practices. In other words, they remain socially and intellectually unengaged just as most of their training (preparation) calls for. In most colleges and schools of education the discussion about intellectual engagement is void in most materials and narratives regarding the formation of bilingual teachers. Little opportunity has been provided for bilingual teachers at any level to connect with critical perspectives while studying in teacher preparation programs.

The primary logic invoked in the preparation of bilingual teachers remains monolithic and traditional except for the provision of native language instruction in a language other than English. More importantly, the philosophical formation of bilingual teachers remains positivistic and non-analytical. It is within this configurational context that bilingual teachers are prevented from fully understanding their roles more broadly as public intellectuals and cultural workers. Most teacher preparation programs simply train teachers as classroom mechanics whose roles are reduced to technicians or clerks (Giroux, 1983). The call for teachers to become public and engaged intellectuals and cultural workers places the work of teachers at the forefront of a pedagogical politics that raises questions, subjectifies knowledge, and pushes classrooms toward a democratizing notion regarding schooling.

The life of a society generally projects itself into the life of a school. School policy plays out much of what is practiced in the larger society with regard to democracy or autocracy and the power of their cultural politics. What is seriously needed in the U.S. is a new way of thinking about schooling or, as Renato Rosaldo (1989) so aptly puts it, a remaking of social analyses applied to the ways in which we think about schools. Transformation and improvement of schools is not likely to occur with the utilization of a colonial language that refuses to acknowledge change as a natural and healthy phenomenon. Instead, it insists on drawing its language from the standardized knowledge industry and rejects any new discourses for remapping schools as sites of ongoing instigation regarding human agency and social and political dynamics.

Human agency among bilingual teachers is largely limited to the extent that most do not use theoretical and philosophical groundings for situating their practice. Most bilingual educators mistakenly place experience as the primary condition for justifying what they do and do not do as teachers. Much of the success students apperceive is to their credit as they struggle against an educational arrangement that perceives them as deficient in a number of ways. The diverse identities of poor and working-class children work against them in standardized learning school settings. Those school settings are socioculturally constructed and positioned for dominant-class children and youth whose gender, ethnicity, race, and everyday life are reflected in the school curricula more closely. The symbolic violence inherent in school curricula systematically attacks the identities of children who are not represented by conservative, anti-utopian conceptions of knowing and being.

In ideological terms, though, bilingual education has stood boldly against the European American conception of schooling. It has denounced a false American spirit of forgetting one's roots to become a full-fledged member of society. History is not discussed or used to inform the sociocultural position of numerous native-to-America multilingual populations. Any discussion of history is bereft of its role in promoting awareness of longtime injustices. But its original impetus for rupturing colonial hegemony has been, in a sense, swallowed up by the predatory cultural and pedagogical politics located in ideologically traditional educational discourses and narratives. In a slow but calculated move, the established and discursive theories and philosophies have devoured bilingual education's distinct features for educating bilingual children. In its initial stages, bilingual education's distinct features included a close association between language, culture, history, class, sociolinguistics, and multiethnic and racial commemoration. The empowering assets that bilingual education constituted at the outset promoted cultural and linguistic pride, avenues of hope for bilingual children to perform and complete school, and a determined sense that dreams can be realized. Bilingual education at one time contained its own agency for empowering bilingual teachers and for children to take pride in their identities and histories that naturally befitted the multicultural terrain inherent to America.

Over the last 30 or more years the relentless assault on bilingual education by traditional canons and conservative narratives has diminished the supportive stance of bilingual teachers and generally sympathetic school administrators. The asymmetrical relations of power between bilingual education and the established discourses to name the practice of bilingual education has increased. Bilingual education has increasingly been associated with remedial education and special education in the special needs sense of the term. The epistemology of bilingual education is associated with assisting second language learners to join and participate with cultural and linguistic distinctiveness within existing mainstream schooling activities. It is also associated with trying to make bilingual education a comprehensive practice for all children.

The Need for Bilingual Education

Bilingual education's most vicious and vile attacks came and continue to come from English-only advocates and, lately, immigration opponents. According to English-only proponents, bilingual education is un-American, divisive, and damaging to bilingual children's academic development. It also fosters welfare-type native language dependency. Never is it mentioned by English-only advocates that research on properly developed and implemented bilingual education renders bilingual children increased sociocultural fulfillment, improved intel-

lectual and academic aptness, broader appreciation of their cultural and historical heritage, and numerous other advantages. Unfortunately, the focus of today's bilingual education programs is English language development, mostly speaking and reading, with a strong push for improving standardized test performance (NCLB, 2001). The judgment laid out by opponents of bilingual education states that the faster bilingual children learn English and become monolingual English speakers, the more success they will experience. In other words, the more bilingual education becomes like mainstream and traditional education, the more it will be accepted as a transitioning practice for bilingual children. In its original design, bilingual education supported a dual-language education for all children through high school. Shortly after its inception as an educational practice for all children, the federal government moved swiftly to require it only for children who needed it according to the measurements of a variety of linguistic needs assessments. Of course, these were politically motivated actions imposed by federal policy, although they were never regarded as cultural politics necessarily.

For many educators today bilingual education represents a passive revolution, menacing in sound, but ineffective in action. For bilingual educators it represents a hegemonized position because it has been forced to consent to a second-class pedagogical stratum. In Gramscian terms, bilingual education at one point in its history constituted a "counter-hegemonic" force in education containing a sociocultural, political content and context. Gramsci's counter-hegemony called for taking a position against the ruling social bloc.[1] This counter-hegemony moved against the "common sense" logic of established notions of knowing and allowed for the formation of opportunities among disenfranchised groups to negotiate their plight in life. That is now a more difficult construct to pursue as bilingual education has been reduced to a mechanistic pedagogy that usually refrains from challenging dominant discourses and narratives.

Few educators have written or talked about bilingual education as a pedagogy of resistance, as a pedagogy of everyday life and struggle for agency. Antonia Darder's (1991) *Culture and Power in the Classroom,* Joan Wink's (1996) *Critical Pedagogy in the Real World,* and Marcia Moraes's (1996) *Bilingual Education: A Dialogue with the Bakhtin Circle,* are a few of the critical views one can find on bilingual education. That is not to suggest in any manner there are not others, but that critical views regarding bilingual education are few at this current juncture in its history. The language of critical theory and pedagogy offers an exciting new trek for rerouting and reinventing bilingual education as a viable and resistant pedagogy. Authoritarianism in educational institutions has long characterized the roles of teachers and schools. By virtue of its multidiglossic negotiating position, bilingual education has the potential to offer a broader democratic promise for engaging in sociopolitical, cultural, and pedagogical dialogues. That cannot and will not happen, however, without human intervention. That space has to be created, exercised, and negotiated by various groups. The promise of such a possibility, nonetheless, deserves pursuit and struggle.

The narrow and almost strict boundary in which bilingual education has been constructed and defined has restricted the notion of educating bilingual children to mostly linguistic treatises. Culture, everyday life, history, and other categories were addressed in dominant cultural terms indicating there

was little opportunity to politicize those concepts against the dominant cultural politics. Bilingual children's learning was reduced to language acquisition and learning the dominant curriculum with little regard for how cultural power and politics played a controlling role on pedagogical themes aside from language learning, as if language learning was the principle category for promoting academic achievement among bilingual children. Although bicultural concepts were initially introduced, bicultural themes and topics were introduced as cultural commodities or artifactual items rather than political entities through which cultural power and curricular issues could be negotiated.

Ideology and Education

At the risk of sounding pessimistic and unable to move beyond a pedagogical paralysis, this entry offers an analysis for a transformative pedagogy in which bilingual and monolingual teachers can work collectively through an agency of emancipation. Without a critique, however narrow and limited it may appear, it provides an opportunity for all educators, but especially bilingual educators, to rethink where and how bilingual education may be reconstituted as part of a broader pedagogical knowledge base in which consideration of a viable pedagogical practice could occur. The ideology from which the education of bilingual students needs to be considered must be open to critique and analyses. It is in this spirit of critique and possibility that these themes and issues are offered. Not to use a critiquing discourse would make no difference to the ways in which we now understand and practice bilingual education.

An issue that weakened bilingual education as a viable pedagogy for educating bilingual children was its promotion within and throughout a series of mainstream methods, strategies, and approaches constructed from the standardized knowledge industry in which lock-step, time-on-task, and back-to-basics assumptions are utilized to distribute, implement, and measure the learning abilities of *all* children regardless of their class, gender, ethnic, racial, and physical ability (Bartolomé, 1996). Teaching and learning are accomplished through curricular packages that see no need to acknowledge children as culturally and linguistically diverse from what the official school curriculum offers. Although educated as bilingual educators, teachers are reduced to technocrats whose role is to carry out their educator tasks borne of accountability and management schemes and theories (Giroux, 1991). In the overall picture of things, little difference is attributed to how children perceive and experience the world because in the classroom they will all be provided the same pedagogical prescription for learning, one is offered more as a recipe for proper socialization and assimilation into mainstream American life and service than as academic conceptualization, abstract development, and an understanding of democracy. It is also a great deal about ideologically indoctrinating children and youth to understand the world in traditional, dominant terms with regard to history, culture, and politics.

The struggle against this powerful ideology becomes a major challenge, since most teachers are unaware of its operating presence or underpinnings. Most teachers who understand long-established schooling ideologies rarely engage in ways to contest their operative dogma. In bilingual education theory and practice this has been the case, although one would think that the opposite effect would be true, since bilingual education originated from the civil rights movements and equality of educa-

tional opportunity struggles. In the initial inception of the Bilingual Education Act, federal and state laws and guidelines forced school districts to comply with meeting the diverse needs of learners; however, on the other side of that same coin, many sociocultural principles necessary for effective bilingual and multicultural curriculum and instruction were negotiated out of the ensuing bilingual education acts. For example, in its original configuration, bilingual instruction allowed children's social, economic, historical, and cultural content to be utilized and implemented through bilingual education programming. The spirit of creating culturally democratic educational environments (Ramírez & Castañeda, 1974) was quickly smothered when the focus of the act became the central theme for learning English as quickly as possible. No consideration for academic development, cultural diversity curricula, or a sociohistorical background was provided given the primary emphasis on learning English in as little time as possible.

The time spent learning English has always been a controversial issue in bilingual education programs. Most educators attribute learning English to academic success or academic achievement and mastery. Many educators do not distinguish between learning English and being academically successful. There is a common public belief, including among conventional educators, that once children learn English, the goal for educating bilingual learners has been accomplished. When this does not happen, bilingual children are indiscriminately pathologized as slow or incapable learners. Too many educators, including many bilingual educators, do not grasp that one does not necessarily need to know a language to understand a concept in that language. The real concern here is that language learning becomes a prerequisite for learning concepts, which, of course, is not the case. Learning occurs in a variety of ways, some of which do not require one to understand the language in which the concept is being presented or used. The psychologized versions of learning have provided educators, and the public at large, a one-dimensional view of learning as something that happens somewhere within the brain only.

The ideological constructions of learning have fastened many educators' beliefs to the notion that learning is an exclusively enterprise of brain activity. Although several ideas have been offered about the possibilities for learning outside of brain activity, it has not made its way into teacher preparation programs broadly. Bilingual education remains on the margins of language and linguistic themes. Current linguistic thought among many non-bilingual educators entertains the idea of official languages as a possible solution to bilingual education. Actually, there are more than 27 states that legally do not grant another language recognition. Bourdieu's publication *Language and Symbolic Power* (1991) helped clarify this discomfort: an official language can be considered "linguistic capital," which then allows its holders "symbolic power." When additional states join the English-only movement, it is not inconceivable that for utilitarian reasons there will be a move favoring exclusive institutional use of English in the long term (Loos, 2004).

Bilingual Education as Cultural Politics

Bilingual education was, in a sense, naïvely born out of a survival form of cultural politics. The initiators of bilingual education launched what they thought was a politically instinctive pedagogy to help non-English and bilingual students access learning through native language pedagogical constructs. Broadly unaware of their cultural-political location, pioneer bilingual educators genuinely believed they could assist bilingual children through the schooling process by providing them linguistic tools for mastering concepts school. Although aware that mainstream educators were uncomfortable and some deeply concerned about dual-language approaches to educating bilingual children, bilingual educators little realized at that point the vehement attacks bilingual education would undergo in the ensuing 30 years.

Traditional American models of learning psychology cogently reject the notion that learning in two languages is helpful or useful and, in fact, pungently allege that it damages children socially, academically, and emotionally. Learning is rarely presented as a problematized sphere in teacher education programs. Most of the time, learning theory and practice are presented as linear, uncomplicated commodities to be acquired and applied rather than questioned and negotiated. They are presented as part of a repository of cultural goods to be attained and implemented in classrooms regardless of children's needs and backgrounds. Traditional learning theory impels a reproductive agenda of learning and knowing. Knowledge in traditional educational domains is presented as predetermined status quo and is not negotiable. The socialization students experience comes from a curriculum that marginalizes them in society even though students frequently do not engage in it. The dominant cultural codes etched into the minds of all children are not negotiated between giver (schools) and receiver (children); rather, they are inserted into children's repertoires without their conscious consent. This approach remains a dominant practice. The children are provided with a world already named and constructed for them. They have little opportunity to engage the knowledge base offered by schools as curriculum.

Bilingual educators with all their hearts and best intentions try to make an advantageous difference for bilingual children in classrooms, but they remain unaware of what informs their pedagogy and so will most likely fall prey to the predatory cultural politics of dominant curriculum discourses and narratives. What is presented as legitimate knowledge is always constructed inside a dominant cultural politics that has the power to name, substantiate, and consider what students will study and how teachers will present it. Bilingual education, in this view, is a subordinate pedagogy whose agency to empower bilingual children is diminished by mainstream discourses and narratives. Although bilingual education comes to us by way of various civil rights initiatives and struggles, today's bilingual educators have little awareness of its original commitment to equality of educational opportunity. The history of bilingual education has been eroded to suggest it never had an oppositional posture toward mainstream educational constructs. The political anesthetization of bilingual education, through a predatory cultural politics, has in many cases turned bilingual educators against its practice easily and successfully, defeating its very advocates. If there was ever a border pedagogy, it was bilingual education. Bilingual education initially combined border-crossing efforts from history, sociology, political science, economics, and other disciplines to present a comprehensive view of bilingual children and their learning.

Bilingual education has endlessly been running from mainstream inventions of what it is, should be, and is not. It has also been running from itself in that its definitions convey a variety of pedagogical views and practices. For some, bilingual education connotes a model for mainstream education conducted temporarily in two languages until English is acquired; for others, it represents a process of always using two languages to pursue learning and living. In any event, bilinguals engage in the painstaking struggle to know which approach is taken, given various dominant renditions of who they should be. Many bilingual populations and individuals unknowingly embrace an outlaw status accorded them by dominant social construction and perception. Bilingualism in school settings has completely tarnished the immaculate notion of what America stood for, a notion that systematically rejected the use of two languages, ideologically censuring it as un-American. One's ethnic culture and experience are commonly regarded or dismissed as fugitive because they are not born of European or American canon or experience. Ethnic cultures and languages are frequently constructed by mainstream society as artifactual items to be nostalgically talked about or referred to as relics rather than real-life agencies to be studied.

The status of outlawry for diverse school children and youth extends beyond what schools deem un-American. Children whose culture, language, gender, ethnicity, race, and class diverge from the mainstream canon fall into outlaw status bestowed on them by traditional narratives from the pages of American pop culture à la John Wayne and Ozzie and Harriet. Many bilingual children in America have for generations given up their native languages and cultural identities associated with their heritage and history only to be inevitably denied access to full participation in America's social, cultural, and institutional spheres.

But for America, it is not enough for diverse groups to give up their identities. Bilingual learners must reject their linguistic and cultural heritage to prove their loyalty to America, displaying an incisive measure of patriotism that, in the long run, will only conditionally gain them acceptance as hyphenated Americans. Bilingual education will continue to exist, however, if its supporters are willing to move outside the dominant circles of wanting to re-create it as a viable pedagogy for linguistic minority learners and all learners. Bilingual education fell prey to the role of IQ colonization, yet it is a worthy pedagogy that can educate, liberate, and empower linguistically diverse communities. We must be willing to move it beyond its pedagogically colonized constructions. ¡Vale la pena!

Note

1. Gramsci, A. (1891–1937). Antonio Gramsci's political and social writings occured across two distinct periods; pre-prison (1910–1926) and prison (1929–1935). His pre-prison writings tended to be politically specific, whereas his prison writings tended to be more historical and theoretical.

References

Bartolomé, L. (1996). Beyond the Methods Fetish: Toward a Humanizing Pedagogy. In T. Beauboeuf-Lafontant & D. S. Augustine (Eds.), *Facing Racism in Education.* Boston: Harvard Educational Review.

Binet, A., & Simon, T. (1905). Méthodes nouvelles pour le diagnostic du niveau intellectuel des anormaux. *L'Année Psychologique* 11, 191–244.

Bourdieu, P. (1991). *Language and Symbolic Power.* Cambridge, MA: Harvard University Press.

Chávez, L. (1998). *Our Hispanic Predicament.* New York: Commentary Magazine.

Darder, A. (1991). *Culture and Power in the Classroom: A Critical Foundation for Bicultural Education.* Westport, CT: Bergin & Garvey.

Fischer, C. S., et al. (1996). *Inequality by Design: Cracking the Bell Curve Myth.* Princeton, NJ: Princeton University Press.

Fraser, Steven (Ed.). (1995). *The Bell Curve Wars: Race, Intelligence, and the Future of America.* New York: Basic Books.

Giroux, H. A. (1983). *Theory and Resistance in Education: Pedagogy for the Opposition.* South Hadley, MA: Bergin & Garvey.

Giroux, H. A. (1991). *Postmodernism, Feminism, and Cultural Politics: Redrawing Educational Boundaries.* Albany, NY: SUNY Press.

Gould, S. J. (1981). *The Mismeasure of Man.* New York: W.W. Norton.

Herrnstein, R. J., & Murray, C. (1994). *The Bell Curve: Intelligence and Class Structure in American Life.* New York: Free Press.

Kincheloe, J. L., Steinberg, S. R., & Gresson, A. D., III (Eds.). (1996). *Measured Lies: The Bell Curve Examined.* New York: St. Martin's Press.

Loos, E. (2004). Composing "Panacea" Texts at the European Parliament: An Intertextual Perspective on Text Production in a Multilingual Community. *Journal of Language and Politics* 3(1), 3–25.

Moraes, M. (1996). *Bilingual Education: A Dialogue with the Bakhtin Circle.* Albany, NY: SUNY Press.

No Child Left Behind (NCLB). (2001). U.S. Department of Education. Washington, DC: U.S. Government Printing Office.

Ramírez, M., & Castañeda, A. (1974). *Cultural Democracy, Bilicognitive Development and Education.* New York: Academic Press.

Rosaldo, R. (1989). *Culture and Truth: The Remaking of Social Analysis.* Boston: Beacon Press.

Stanford-Binet. (1916). Stanford-Binet Tests of Intelligence Measurements.

Wink, J. (1996). *Critical Pedagogy in the Real World.* New York: Allyn & Bacon–Longman.

Hermán S. García and Vivian G. López

J

JOURNAL OF LATINOS AND EDUCATION (JLE)

Journal of Latinos and Education (JLE), an academic journal published quarterly since 1992, provides a cross-, multi-, and interdisciplinary forum for scholars and writers from diverse disciplines who share a common interest in the analysis, discussion, critique, and dissemination of educational issues that affect Latinos. Education is defined in the broad cultural sense and not limited to just formal schooling. Particular attention is given to geographical equity to assure representation of all regions and "Latino" groups in the U.S.

JLE was first conceived when a group of scholar-activists from California State University, San Bernardino (CSUSB), presented a symposium on the effects of California's Proposition 227 at the American Educational Studies Association in 1999. During this conference a collaborative partnership was found with Lawrence Erlbaum Associates, Publishers, for the proposed creation of a new academic publication to specifically address issues surrounding the education, broadly defined, of Latinos in the U.S. The founding group, which now included members of the Center for Equity in Education at CSUSB, worked and met regularly over a full year to design and describe the editorial scope of the new publication.

While conducting a comprehensive and broad document review and analysis of the previously existing academic journals, it became apparent that academic articles on Latinos and education were being published sporadically, appearing singly, apart, or in isolated instances in highly specialized journals, or they were simply absent. This situation was produced by a compound of factors including but not limited to high competition for available publishing space, a lack of interest or concern in these issues, or lack of opportunity to publish at all.

Some of the critical factors most closely considered were the ongoing diversity and population increase of Latinos. The black-white social order had faded, long gone with the old century, and the new millennium inaugurated Latinos as the largest minority group in the U.S. In K–12 public schools, Latinos had also surpassed the number of African American students. As the numbers become larger and the population diverse, there was to be an accompanied step-up in the published articles on research, policy, and status related to Latinos. Therefore, demographics augured an increment in publications on Latinos and education, as well as an increase in the interest and consumption of those same publications.

The same increasing numbers and diversity of Latinos has generated the need to examine educational issues that affect Latinos using the lenses of many fields and disciplines. The result is the publication of a wide and broad range of formats for articles, including research articles, essay reviews and interviews, practitioner and community perspectives, book and media reviews, and other forms of creative critical writing. Four arenas encompass most issues of relevance: (1) policy, (2) research, (3) practice, and (4) creative and literary works. Policies and practices promoting equity and social justice for linguistically and culturally diverse groups are particularly encouraged and welcomed for publication consideration.

JLE emboldens novel ways of thinking about the ongoing and emerging questions around the unifying thread of Latinos and education. The quarterly publication supports exchange—for researchers, practitioners, authors, and other stakeholders working to further all levels of understanding—be it theoretical, conceptual, empirical, clinical, historical, methodological, or other in scope. It attempts to identify and stimulate more relevant research, practice, communication, and theory by providing a rich diverseness of information and a nurturing outlet for sharing. The audience for the JLE includes researchers, teaching professionals and educators, academics, scholars, administrators, independent writers and artists, policy and program specialists, students, parents, families, civic leaders, activists, and advocates— in short, individuals, groups, agencies, organizations, and institutions sharing a common interest in educational issues that affect Latinos.

Manifestations of the diverse frameworks and topic areas typically range from—but are not limited to—theoretical and empirical analyses to policy discussions, research reports, program recommendations, evaluation studies, finding and improving practical applications, carefully documenting the transition of theory into real-world practice, linking theory and research, new dissertation research, literature reviews, reflective discussions, cultural studies, and literary works.

Numerous scholars, practitioners, and community representatives at the forefront of their chosen fields and disciplines serve on a rotating basis on the Editorial Advisory Board. In addition, the members of the Center for Equity in Education at CSUSB serve as the Executive Council. An even larger pool regularly serve as blind peer reviewers during the submission and review process. Together the scholarship, learnedness, and expertise brought to this collaborative venture have established the JLE's reputation as a high-quality, credible academic journal. The announcement of the founding and creation of the JLE at numerous professional conferences and listservs has been met with much excitement, well wishes, support, encouragement, and numerous declarations of "It is about time!"

References

Center for Equity in Education, California State University San Bernardino (May 2000). Unpublished proposal for *Journal of Latinos and Education*, submitted to Lawrence Erlbaum Associates, Inc., and CSUSB College of Education, Dean's Office, University President's Office, University Provost and Vice-President's Office, and the University Budget Council.

Lawrence Erlbaum Associates (2004). LEA Journal Online Access. Available at http://www.leaonline.com/loi/jle.

Murillo E. G., Jr., Flores, S. Y., & Martinez, C. (2002). From the Editor's Desk, *Journal of Latinos and Education* 1(1), 1–5.

Enrique G. Murillo Jr.

L

LANGUAGE AND CULTURE INTEGRATION

The potential advantages of being multilingual and multicultural in today's world are enormous, and the acquisition of other languages should be fostered and supported wherever possible. Although we live in a multicultural, multilingual world, English is the dominant language in the U.S. As early childhood professionals we are in a key position to promote, advocate, and assertively argue for linguistic and cultural diversity through our interactions as professionals and in our personal relationships. There is no middle ground on the importance of children maintaining their home language and our supporting them in meaningful ways as they acquire English and succeed in life, thus becoming bilingual and biliterate individuals. It is the intent of this entry to carefully examine the importance of consistency, and integration in reaching those goals.

Key Considerations

Importance of Observation. Observation is critical in our efforts to better understand children's growth, development, and individual uniqueness (Billman & Sherman, 2002). Given the increasing diversity of our classrooms, teachers have an important role in investing time and attention to the task of observing children.

Best Practices

- Varied observational tools
- Consistent system of observation and documentation
- Varied locations for observations, inside and outside
- Collegial shared responsibility of observation

Importance of Listening. Many researchers believe that the process of acquiring two languages promotes higher cognitive and social levels of understanding (Cummins, 1979; Hakuta & Garcia, 1989). Teachers consistently point out that children require more time and more careful listening because they are frequently processing two or more languages. Tabors and Snow (1994) have pointed out that although children may pause or not communicate overtly for a period, they have not stopped communicating. They are busy collecting information about the new language, experimenting with sounds, and building their understanding of it (receptive language).

Best Practices

- Make efforts to learn the language background of your children and families.
- Practice, and reflect on the amount of time spent listening rather than talking.
- Use technology—videos, cameras, and audio equipment—in efforts to understand more

clearly the content and purposes of language in the classroom.

- Be sure to repeat or ask questions for clarification for better comprehension.
- Physically position yourself so the child has eye contact or physical proximity to the speaker. Be aware and sensitive of how different cultures respond to "eye contact."

Connecting with Parents. Parental involvement is the participation within the school, the home, and the community for the purpose of formal and informal learning. As Epstein (2001) has pointed out, there needs to be a clear understanding of what constitutes parent cooperation and effective parent involvement. Parents are empowered when they know they have a clear voice regarding the welfare, growth, and learning of their child. This fosters a high level of parental involvement. Research has shown that children are socially and academically more adjusted when there is more communication and contact between the home and school.

Best Practices

- Communication and school information in the languages of the families
- Diverse methods of communication
- Varied locations for contact and cooperation: home, school, community agencies, and social services
- Formal and informal communication
- No assumptions about language background and frequency of use
- Informal contacts to build respect and rapport

Integration of Culture, Language, and the Environment. Children learn extensively through hands-on interactions with children, adults, and the physical environment. Research has shown that children learn best through physical interaction with their worlds. Vertical and horizontal physical

environments have tremendous potential for children's growth, development, and learning in all developmental areas.

Best Practices

- The physical environment needs to reflect and validate the authentic and contemporary cultures of the children it serves. This can be reflected through materials, visuals, and instructional materials.
- Room arrangement can vary to embrace the variety of cultures and languages in the room.
- Organizing elements, containers, and shelving can and should reflect the variety of cultures that exist in the classroom.
- Posters, wording, signs, bulletin boards, and the like should firmly reflect a philosophy that promotes recognition and respect for diversity.
- A culturally responsive curriculum can be instituted to incorporate culturally relevant materials and activities.
- Verbal, visual, and textual references must strongly oppose derogatory stereotypes and materials.
- Cultural responsiveness can be promoted to oppose inappropriate curriculum, including holiday or touristic centered approaches.

Instructional Integration of Language and Culture. The overall goal of integration is to promote love and respect for language and culture.

- Plan a culturally responsive curriculum
- Avoid the stereotypical merry-go-round
- Model pride in use of the language
- Teach diverse ways of using language

Outreach to Parents. Parents can support children's learning by engaging in numerous shared activities. Our advice to parents:

1. Dedicate quality time to having *fun* with your child.
2. Talk—have real conversations. Ask specifics: "Tell me what you did during...?"

(retelling); "What do you *think* about...?" (metacognitive); "What would you do if...?" (problem solving).

3. Read, Read, Read to *and* with your children. Then talk about what you read.

4. Tell them stories about their own history (birth, family members, special events).

5. Play table games or other games that involve following instructions or rules.

6. Cook together. Model how to follow a recipe or how you measure ingredients.

7. Limit and supervise TV viewing *and* computer games.

8. Support self-reliance and autonomy.

9. Promote *respect* for self and others.

10. Do whatever you can to make school a positive and healthy experience. Get to know the teacher; ask questions; volunteer or visit; provide information about your child; give input into curriculum.

Summary

Children's cultures and languages need to be integrated with a clear understanding of and sensitivity to families. This requires careful listening and meaningful interactions between educators and families. Instructional practices must include intentional observation, planning, and reflection that goes beyond simply providing multicultural literature, music, or materials. The integration of culture and language must be articulated in instructional practices, communication systems, environmental changes (indoors and outdoors), and reflective dialogue.

Examples of Books to Read Together

Abuela

Adelita: A Mexican Cinderella Story

An Alphabet in Spanish & English

Arroz con leche

La carrera del sapo & el venado

Cinderella (U.S.)

Erandi's Braids

Gathering the Sun

A Gift from Papa Diego

Going Home

The Korean Cinderella

The Little Brown Roadrunner

Lupita's Papalote

La mariquita malhumorada

My Very Own Room (Mi propio cuartito)

Popular Songs & Rhymes from Latin America

Roadrunners Dance

Sip, Slurp, Soup, Soup, Caldo, Caldo, Caldo

Too Many Tamales

Tortillitas para mama

Los tres cerdos—Nacho, Tito y Miguel

References

Billman, J., & Sherman, S. (2002). *Observation and Participation in Early Childhood Settings*. Redwood City, CA: Addison-Wesley.

Cummins, J. (1979). BICS and CALP. Available: http://www.iteachilearn.com/cummins/biscalp.html.

Epstein, J. L. (Ed.). (2001). *School, Family, and Community Partnerships: Preparing Educators and Improving Schools*. Boulder, CO: Westview Press.

Hakuta, K., & Garcia, E. (1989). Bilingualism and Education. *American Psychologist* 44(2), 374–379.

Tabors, P. O., & Snow, C. (1994). English as a Second Language in Preschools. In F. Genessee (Ed.), *Educating Second Language Children* (pp. 103–125). New York: Cambridge University Press.

Georgianna Duarte and Cathy Gutierrez-Gomez

LANGUAGE POLICY

Language policy is a body of ideas, laws, regulations, rules, and practices enacted to promote systematic linguistic change in a community of speakers. These policies might be enacted through legislation, court decisions, executive action, or other means. In most instances, language policies are the result of language planning. In this process, officials determine the linguistic needs, wants, and desires of a community and then seek to establish policies that will fulfill those goals. Such goals might include cultivating language skills needed to meet national priorities; establishing the rights of individuals or groups to learn, use, and maintain languages; promoting the growth of a national lingua franca; and promoting or discouraging multilingualism.

Unfortunately, language policy in the U.S. has developed absent a consistent language ideology and with very little planning per se. Instead, it has evolved through a number of important court cases and some legislation. This has meant that instead of following a smooth path towards some goal, it has historically been a path laid out in fits, starts, and adhocracy shaped by various political, social, and economic forces. As regards language diversity, this inconsistency is seen in a history that moves through three distinct periods: a period of benign neglect in which language diversity was tolerated, to a period of severe restriction with an emphasis on assimilation, to a period of opportunism that saw a revived importance placed on language learning and maintenance (Ovando, 2003). Recent policy enactments indicate a return to a certain level of restrictionism.

When exercised, language planning can seek to achieve a variety of goals, including maintaining the status quo, reforming the language characteristics of a community of speakers, or transforming the language characteristics of a community of speakers (Weinstein, 1990). Within each of these three broad goals, language planning can occur at both micro and macro levels. The micro level involves corpus planning and the macro level involves status planning.

Corpus planning deals with "those aspects of language planning which are primarily linguistic and hence internal to language" (Kaplan & Baldauf, 1997, p. 38). One of the primary tasks in corpus planning is standardizing the language, especially in terms of its grammar, writing system, and vocabulary. In France and Spain, the Commissariat de la Langue Francaise and the Real Academia Española, respectively, take on the task of standardizing the French and Spanish languages and endeavor to eliminate or minimize the infiltration of foreign words and expressions. Another example of corpus planning would be the modernization of languages. Corpus planning also includes efforts to reform languages. Many Native American languages, for example, are being revitalized. This revitalization requires, among other things, modernization of the vocabulary. Indigenous translations for words such as "airplane," "computer," or "hard drive" must all be determined. This example demonstrates how status planning and corpus planning can become intertwined. The Northern Ute, Ute Mountain Ute, and Southern Ute all speak varieties of the Ute language. Whose variety should the standardization and modernization of the language reflect?

Despite the frequent need to consider corpus and status planning simultaneously to achieve a given language goal, the latter encompasses most of the language planning and policy issues that have arisen in the U.S., especially as concerns education. Status planning deals with "those aspects of language planning which reflect primarily social issues and concerns and hence are external to the language(s) being planned" (Kaplan &

Baldauf, 1997, p. 30). The determination of which language(s) should be used for official purposes is a focus of status planning, for example. In the U.S., federal legislative efforts to make English the official language exemplify status planning with the goal of maintaining the status quo. Even though the officialization of English would be a change to its current official status, it would serve to maintain the status quo since English is already the de facto lingua franca and language of power in the U.S.

Given the dominance of English in a multicultural society such as the U.S., some status planning to reform has taken place. One of the most significant examples of status planning to reform in the U.S. is the 1975 amendments to the Voting Rights Act (1965). The Voting Rights Act, as amended in 1975, requires states and political subdivisions to conduct elections and provide certain election materials in languages other than English. This Act is invoked whenever more than five percent of the voting-age citizens in the state or political subdivision are members of a single language minority group.

Our lack of any reasoned or systematic approach to language policy in the United States has direct ramifications for education. If we are to be a monolingual society, what is the best way to educate children? If we respect families' rights to their own language and culture, need we supply the resources to promote them? If we want to respect private bilingualism but promote societal monolingualism, how should we educate language minority children?

In the educational arena, the most significant actions toward status planning to reform have been the Bilingual Education Act (1968) and the Supreme Court case of *Lau v. Nichols* (1974). The Bilingual Education Act set out to reform education for language minority students. Even though

the act was explicitly compensatory, it left some ambiguity as to whether its goal was merely to speed the transition to English-only instruction or whether it could be interpreted as a way to promote bilingualism (Crawford, 2004). One of its early effects was that it gave license for schools to use children's first languages as languages of instruction at least part of the time. This has been a key, but contentious, idea in the struggle for equity in education for language minority students.

In the *Lau* case, a group of Chinese-speaking students in San Francisco sought relief against unequal educational opportunities created by English-only instruction. While lower courts absolved the school district of any responsibility, the Supreme Court, in a unanimous decision, disagreed. They found instead that the sink-or-swim mentality and practices of the school were a violation of the students' civil rights. Even though the Court declined to offer any specific remedy, the *Lau* decision, by requiring that the special needs of English language learners (ELLs) be attended to, represented a major shift in language policy in education and a major reform. At the end of its tenure, the Carter administration tried to take this reform a step further by issuing the "*Lau* Remedies." These remedies included the requirement that, at least in the elementary school, some instruction be provided in a student's stronger language.

While the *Lau* case was brought on behalf of a group of Chinese students, much of the debate around bilingual education has centered on the Hispanic community given that Spanish is, by far, the most widely spoken language in the U.S. after English. In fact, the Bilingual Education Act and the *Lau* decision were followed by a series of lawsuits brought by Hispanic communities across the country seeking equal educational opportunity for their children (e.g., *Cintron v. Brentwood* [New York, 1978]; *Rios v. Reed* [New York, 1978]; *Castañeda v. Pickard* [Texas, 1981]; *Gomez v. Illinois* [1987]).

A backlash against language minorities, especially Spanish speakers, rose in the wake of these somewhat progressive language policies in education. In 1983, two years after introducing a (failed) constitutional amendment that would make English the official language of the U.S., Senator S. I. Hayakawa founded "U.S. English." The organization quickly became, and remains, a tenacious political interest group lobbying for an amendment to make English the official language of the U.S. One of its other stated goals is to "reform" (read: eliminate) bilingual education. Similarly, anti-bilingual education policies became a cornerstone of the Department of Education under the leadership of Secretary William Bennett in the 1980s.

Hispanic leaders organized quickly against the English-only backlash. In 1985, the league of United Latin American Citizens (LULAC) and the Spanish American League Against Discrimination (SALAD) joined forces to launch a campaign known as English Plus (Crawford, 2004). Attracting more than 50 other organizations opposed to official English and the English-only movement, the English plus campaign resulted two years later in the formation of the English Plus Information Clearinghouse (EPIC). Two of the primary purposes of EPIC were (1) to foster the development of second or multiple language skills of everyone and, especially, (2) to promote the retention and development of a person's first language.

While the English Plus movement has served a very positive role in the fight against the English-only movement, it certainly has not been the success supporters hoped it would be. If successful, the English Plus movement would represent a significant shift in language planning and policy. It would move current language policy from its stagnation in the reforms from 30 years ago to a new level: language planning and policy to transform.

Historically, language planning to transform—changing identities, replacing one elite by another in the state apparatus, and altering patterns of access to reflect the replacement of a dominant class or ethnic group (Weinstein, 1990)—is most readily seen in policies designed to make languages disappear. Historical examples include France's policies toward Alsace, Spain's policies toward Cataluña, and the U.S.'s policies toward Native Americans. In educational policy, this kind of "negative language planning" (Kaplan & Baldauf, 1997) has often meant severe repression of the minority language in schools, including punishment for its use. Language policy actively seeking to promote bilingualism, as proposed by English Plus, would indeed be historical change. English Plus represents a policy position that would promote transformation by providing second language instructional programs throughout K–12, especially through effective approaches such as bilingual education for both language minority and language majority students. While the goal would not be to de-emphasize English, the transformation here would be an emphasis on individual bilingualism never before pursued in the U.S.

Unfortunately, recent changes in language policy in education portend a dire future. Policies that have severely curtailed bilingual education in favor of English immersion have passed in California (Proposition 227, 1998), Arizona (Proposition 203, 2000), and Massachusetts (Ballot Question 2, 2002). Hispanics in each of these states fought against these initiatives that have signaled a return to negative language planning and have limited the educational options available. In both California and Arizona, Hispanics voted two to one against the initiatives. Ninety-two percent of Massachusetts' Hispanic population voted against the measure there. In other words, negative language policy in education is supported most by people whose children are affected least. Those who promote negative language policies ignore historical record that demonstrates that "the endeavor to plan language behavior by forcing a rapid shift to English has often been a source of language problems that has resulted in the denial of language rights and hindered linguistic access to educational, social, economic, and political benefits even as the promoters of English immersion claim the opposite" (Wiley & Wright, 2004, p. 144).

Hispanics and other language minority groups in the states mentioned certainly have an uphill battle to reclaim their voices in educational policy, especially as concerns language. But the phenomenon of negative language planning is, unfortunately, not localized. Despite President George W. Bush's promise of smaller government, the passage of the No Child Left Behind (NCLB) Act in 2002 has ushered in unprecedented federal involvement in education policy. The term "bilingual" has been purged from federal vocabulary. For example, the Bilingual Education Act has been replaced with the "Language Instruction for Limited English Proficient and Immigrant Students" provision (Title III) of the act. Similarly, the Office of Bilingual Education and Language Minority Affairs has been replaced with the Office of English Language Acquisition, Language Enhancement, and Academic Achievement for Limited English Proficient Students. While the Act permits bilingual education, a number of schizophrenic provisions and requirements may make bilingual programs difficult to pursue. The requirements, for example, set a double standard that allows English language learners to pursue bilingualism as a legitimate goal only when sufficient numbers of English speaking students share this goal. In short, the new language policies in NCLB have moved us away from the language policies to reform represented by the Bilingual Education Act and *Lau* and back to negative language policies to maintain the status quo, maintaining unearned privileges for language majority students. It is perplexing, therefore, that not a single member of the Congressional Hispanic Caucus voted against the legislation. For without vigorous leadership—especially from the community that arguably has contributed most to the fight for progressive language policy—language policy and planning to transform a society handicapped by English monolingualism seem quite remote.

References

Crawford, James. (2004). *Educating English Language Learners: Language Diversity in the Classroom* (5th ed.). Los Angeles: Bilingual Education Services.

Kaplan, Robert B., & Baldauf Jr., Richard B. (1997). *Language Planning: From Practice to Theory*. Philadelphia: Multilingual Matters.

Ovando, Carlos. (2003). Bilingual Education in the United States: Historical Development and Current Issues. *Bilingual Research Journal* 27(1), 1–24.

Weinstein, Brian. (1990). Language Policy and Political Development: An Overview. In B. Weinstein (Ed.), *Language Policy and Political Development* (pp. 1–21). Norwood, NJ: Ablex.

Wiley, Terence, & Wright, Wayne. (2004). Against the Undertow: Language-Minority Education Policy and Politics in the "Age of

Accountability." *Educational Policy* 18(1), 142–168.

Web Sites

Crawford, James. Language Policy Website & Emporium. Available: http://ourworld.compu serve.com/homepages/JWCRAWFORD/.

Wiley, Terrence (Director). Language Policy Research Unit. Available: http://www.asu.edu/ educ/epsl/lpru.htm.

John Petrovic

LATINO CULTURAL LEADERS AND THEIR CONTRIBUTIONS

Latinos have made significant contributions to education over the centuries. These contributions are well known throughout the world. What follows describes some of the most famous Latinos and their contribution to world culture. Among these celebrities are Puerto Rican educator and writer Eugenio María de Hostos; Puerto Rican poet and politician José de Diego; Puerto Rican poet Julia de Burgos; Puerto Rican chemist, lawyer, writer, and revolutionary leader Pedro Albizu Campos; Puerto Rican physician and slave abolitionist Dr. Ramón Emeterio Betances; Mexican artist Frida Kahlo; Mexican muralist Diego Rivera; Mexican farmers' rights activist Cesar Chávez; and Bolivian teacher Jaime Escalante. These individuals were selected because of their extraordinary and far-reaching contributions, contributions that are significant not only because they are recognized by the world community but, more important, because they continue to transform and inspire lives. This entry is a tribute to them.

Eugenio María de Hostos

Eugenio María de Hostos was born in Mayagüez in 1839 and died in the Dominican Republic in 1903. He earned a B.A. in literature from the University of Bilbao in Spain. He also studied law at the Universidad Central in Madrid. While he studied in Spain he also fought for autonomy and the emancipation of slaves in Cuba and Puerto Rico. It was also during this time that he published *La peregrinación de Bayoán*, in which he critiqued the colonial regime in America and Spain through fiction.

From 1871 to 1874 he campaigned in favor of the independence of Cuba and Puerto Rico through various countries: Colombia, Peru, Chile, Argentina, and Brazil. In Chile he published *Juicio público de Hamlet*. He also fought for women's right to scientific instruction. In Argentina, he started the project that lead to the construction of train rails through the Andes. In Brazil he wrote about the unique beauty of the country. In 1877, while in Caracas, he published the biography of Cuban native Francisco Vicente Aguilera, and he started teaching at the college level.

In 1879 he moved to the Dominican Republic. He founded the Escuela Normal in 1880 and directed it as well. He also spent most of his time lecturing and teaching constitutional rights, international law, politics, and economy at the Professional Institute. During this time he also published his book *Moral social*.

In 1888 Hostos returned to Chile. In 1890 he was the director of El Liceo Miguel Luis Amunategui in Santiago. This institution was created with the purpose of implementing his education policy. He also lectured and taught constitutional rights courses and worked as a journalist and writer.

Hostos tried to convince the U.S. to let Puerto Ricans decide their political status after the American invasion in 1898. He wanted a referendum and with this in mind founded La Liga de Patriotas. The purpose of this organization was threefold: political, pedagogical, and cultural. Around this time Hostos went to Washington to establish a dialogue with President McKinley in order to convey the needs of Puerto Ricans at this particular point in time.

In 1899 he founded El Instituto Municipal de Mayagüez. He also realized Puerto Ricans could not unanimously agree on their political status. Disappointed, he returned to the Dominican Republic, where he directed El Colegio Central and La Inspección General de Instrucción Pública. He continued to write and pass laws related to educational issues. He also founded schools and institutions and collaborated with the culture of the Dominican Republic until his death in 1903.

1905 a volume was published in the Dominican Republic as a tribute to his legacy and his contribution to education. This volume included his biography and related articles.

In 1940 Hostos's contribution to education was recaptured in 20 volumes by the Puerto Rican government in one edition. This publication includes his diary and his memoirs, *La peregrinación de Bayoán*, and his *Tratado de derecho constitucional, moral, lógica, ciencia de la pedagogía, y geografía evolutiva,* among others.

José de Diego

José de Diego was born on April 16, 1866, in Aguadilla, Puerto Rico. He studied in the town of Mayagüez. He also studied in Spain at the Instituto Politécnico de Logroño. After he graduated, he enrolled at the University of Barcelona to study law. Health issues compelled him to return to Puerto Rico in 1990 to finish his studies.

In 1891 he continued to study in Cuba and earned a doctorate in law. He returned to Puerto Rico, where he worked at the firm of Rosendo Matienzo Cintron. He moved to Arecibo and married Petra Latorre. This marriage was later annulled by the Catholic Church. Politics was his public passion. Carmita Echevarría was the "la Laura" he wrote about in his poems. De Diego was profoundly affected by her tragic love story, and it became a major source of poetic inspiration.

De Diego was admired for his public speaking performances and for his dedicated efforts to gain independence for Puerto Rico. In 1897 he was appointed joint secretary and was also Magistrado de la Audiencia Territorial.

After the North American invasion in 1898, a military government established in Puerto Rico eliminated the possibility of an autonomous government. De Diego worked as attorney and as the president of the Audiencia de Mayagüez. He also worked as an executive advisor in 1900. Three years later he was elected by the country as a member of the Cámara de Delegados. He became its president in 1907. De Diego became the first president of the Cámara de Representantes under the Foraker Act. It was also at this time that he married Georgina Blanes.

An avid defender of Hispanic culture and language, he played a major role when the U.S. government tried to impose the English-only bill on the island and when Americans tried to Americanize the population. He was well-known as a poet and educator as well as an excellent public speaker. Among his poems are "Sor Ana" (1887), "Jovillos" (1887), "Pomarrosas" (1916), and "Cantos de Rebeldía" (1916). Among the poems published after his death are "Canto de Pitirre" and "Hojas y Flores."

A well-respected educator, de Diego was president of the Ateneo Puertorriqueño. He was also a member of La Real Academia Española, La Liga Cervantina Universal, La Sociedad de Escritores y Artistas, La Academia Internacional de Historia de Paris, and La Unión Iberoamericana de Madrid, among other prestigious institutions. He also believed in the Confederación de las Antillas, which granted independence to the Caribbean islands.

De Diego's public speaking performance facilitated the foundation of the Partido Unión de Puerto Rico. This political party was able to pass the Base Quinta, which opened the possibility of independence as an alternative for Puerto Ricans. He disputed the Foraker Act and demanded self-government for the island. He was also named Caballero de la Raza in Madrid because of his eloquent speeches.

De Diego died in 1918 after his right leg was amputated as a result of gangrene. However, his legacy situates him as one of the most famous Puerto Rican educators.

Julia de Burgos

Julia Constantina Burgos García was born in Carolina, Puerto Rico, on February 17, 1917, and died in New York on July, 1953. She spent her school year in Santa Cruz in Carolina and in Rio Grande. In 1928 her family moved to Río Piedras, where she graduated from high school. She continued to study at the University of Río Piedras and earned a teacher's certificate. She worked as a teacher for a year at Cedro Arriba in Naranjito.

The first decades of her life were tumultuous. Congress authorized and gave American citizenship to Puerto Ricans soon after World War I began. Puerto Rican men were then recruited as part of the mandatory military service. There were bloody encounters between the police and their North American chief Riggs. Beginning in 1934, she worked for the Puerto Rico Economic Reconstruction Administration (PRERA) in the city of Comerío. But in 1937 she was fired because of her political beliefs, made evident in her performance as a script writer

for the radio show *La Escuela del Aire*, which was part of the Public Instruction Department. It was during this time that her three-year marriage to Ruben Rodríguez Beauchamp ended in divorce.

In 1937 de Burgos delivered the speech "La mujer ante el dolor de la patria." The daily *El Imparcial* published her poems for the first time. It was also during this year that she finished her first book, *Poemas exactos a mi misma*. In 1938 she published *Poema en veinte surcos*. The following year she earned an award presented by the Puerto Rican Institute of Literature for her book *Canción de la verdad sencilla*. At the beginning of World War II she migrated to New York, where she suffered many economic and personal adversities.

In January 1940 de Burgos moved to Havana to live with political activist Dr. Juan Isidro Jiménez de Grullón. In Cuba, however, she was unable to earn a degree at Havana University because of economical hardship. Instead, she finished her book *El mar y tú* and socialized with writers and intellectuals. Among these was Pablo Neruda, who praised her writing. She also occasionally contributed to Puerto Rican newspapers. An example of such contributions was her poem "El campo."

In 1942 de Burgos ended her relationship with Jiménez and returned to New York. There she encountered new financial hardships and faced discrimination. She married Armando Marín in 1943. She also worked as a writer and editor for the weekly publication *Pueblos Hispanos* directed by Antonio Corretjier. In 1944 she worked as an office clerk in Washington, DC, and tried to study in the evenings at the same time.

De Burgos returned to New York and in 1946 received an award for her article "Ser o no ser es la divisa." Her health deteriorated during this time, for her problems with alcohol caused hepatic cirrhosis. She was admitted to the hospital on various occasions. In July 1953 she was found unconscious on 105 Street and died at the Harlem Hospital on August 4. The Puerto Rican Journalist Association requested that her remains be sent to Puerto Rico.

Julia de Burgos's contribution to literature and education transcended the *vanguardismo* that characterized the 1930s and the existentialism of the 1950s. She was influenced by great artists and writers of the twentieth century such as Neruda, Alfonsia Storni, Juan Ramon Jiménez, García Lorca, and Juana de Ibarbourou. Her poems reflect not only her personal struggles but also her political and social beliefs. She will forever be immortalized in her poem "Río Grande de Loíza."

Pedro Albizu Campos

Pedro Albizu Campos was a leader of the Puerto Rican revolution and the fight for the independence of Puerto Rico. He studied at Harvard and earned degrees in military sciences, chemical engineering, and law. He also actively participated in the fight for the independence of India and Northern Ireland. He also fought for the rights of African Americans, Native Americans, and Latin Americans. He was the president of the Cosmopolitan Club and the League to Enforce Peace. He was also an international member of the International Polity Club and belonged to the Chemical Club, the American Chemical Society, and the Speakers Club. He also directed the Capítulo de Reconocimiento de la República Irlandesa en Harvard.

Albizu spoke many languages, among them Greek, Latin, French, Italian, Portuguese, German, English, and Spanish, his native language. This vast knowledge enabled him to relate well to intellectuals and leaders around the world.

Because of his political beliefs he was incarcerated for 20 years. After his second incarceration, Albizu denounced agents of the U.S. armed forces, specifically the marines, charging them with burning him with atomic rays and exposing him to radiation from an unknown origin. This atomic radiation would kill him, he charged, and would lead to a cancer that would cause a heart attack. Albizu refused to be physically or mentally evaluated, stating that the only purpose of the government was propaganda.

Even though Albizu's followers were able to determine through scientific means that there was radiation in Albizu's body during his incarceration as well as after he served time in jail, the Department of Justice announced to the world that Albizu was crazy. This event took place on September 29, 1953. Soon after this claim, he was expulsed from jail and sent home.

After Albizu was expulsed from jail, the newspapers published pictures that showed his burned and swollen legs. On March 6, 1954, the then-governor of Puerto Rico, Luis Muñoz Marín, ordered the arrest and incarceration of Albizu, blaming him for the attack of the Nacionalistas against the U.S. Chamber of Representatives.

Albizu's brilliant erudition could have won him privileged positions and riches beyond his expectations, but the call to serve the need of his nation was stronger than the lure of luxury. Therefore, he became a militant activist of liberty like his Latin American predecessors, the liberator Simón Bolivar. Some people did not understand his rejection of wealth and materialism. His answer to these people was indicative of his resolve: "This is my duty for having been born in an enslaved country."

Albizu was a powerful orator. During the 1930s and 1950s, multitudes in Puerto Rico gathered around his podium in the public

squares to listen to his persuasive and articulate discourses of emancipation, to palpi-
tate with patriotic enthusiasm, and to learn
from his passionate message. Most of his
speeches dealt with the search for Puerto
Rican roots and the spiritual presence of the
heroes of the nineteenth-century rebellions
against Spain. Scholars who have studied
his works and thought consider him the
first great theoretician of anti-colonialism
and the first to describe the contradictions of
the colonized.

Ramón Emeterio Betances

Dr. Ramón Emeterio Betances occupies a
privileged place in the Puerto Rican history
of famous educators. Born in the city of
Cabo Rojo on April 8, 1927, he spent his
elementary school years in Cabo Rojo and
his high school years in Mayagüez. He
earned his M.D. in Paris, France. His parents were Don Felipe Betances and María
del Carmen Alacán.

Dr. Betances fell in love with Maria del
Carmen Henry, who died a few days before
the wedding. This tragedy caused him
enormous pain. He lived in Cabo Rojo and
worked as a physician as well as an abolitionist. He worked with other abolitionists
to free slave children and founded an abolitionist association to help his cause.

Dr. Betances fought for the independence of
Puerto Rico as well as for the independence of
Cuba and Dominican Republic. He played a
major role in "El Grito de Lares," a historical
event that took place on September 23, 1868.
He was also the precursor of the Antillean
Confederation and claimed as his motto,
"America is for the Americans and the Antilleans are for the Antilleans." This is why he is
also known as "the Antillean." He was also a
playwrite and among his most famous writings
is *La vírgen de Borinquen,* which he dedicated
to his late fiancée. As a physician he conducted

a research project, which he titled *Tratado
sobre elefantitis,* which was well known at the
different medical schools in Europe.

Dr. Betances died in Paris, France, in
1898 the same year the American invasion
took place in Puerto Rico. He was buried in
his hometown of Cabo Rojo in 1920. There
is a sculpture and a park named after him.
The Puerto Rican flag and the "Grito de
Lares" flag are also displayed in front of his
sculpture, made by Italian artist Diego
Montano. He is also called by Cabo Roje-
ños, the people of his hometown, as the
greatest son of Cabo Rojo.

Frida Kahlo

Frida Kahlo is the most famous Mexican
female artist known around the world. Her
art is very personal and also profoundly met-
aphoric. She was born in 1907 in Mexico and
died in 1954. When only 18 years old she
suffered a tragic accident that confined her to
bedrest for a long period of time. It is during
this time that she learned and started to paint.

She married Diego Rivera, also a very
famous artist. In 1932 she had a miscarriage.
This experience influenced her art and inspired two of her most valuable paintings,
Henry Ford Hospital and *Frida y el aborto.*
The complex symbolism of these paintings
was explained by Frida herself. Among her
most famous paintings with very complex
interpretations are *Autoretrato con monos*
and *Las dos Fridas.* Andre Breton saw her
art and subsequently invited her to give an
exhibition of her paintings in New York and
Paris. He declared that Frida was a spontaneous surrealist. Frida however, never felt
she was a surrealist, and at the end of her life
she decided that her art formed no part of the
surrealist tradition.

In her search for her aesthetic Mexican
roots, Frida Kahlo drew beautiful pictures of
children inspired in the Mexican iconogra-

phy that had existed prior to the *Conquista*. But it is her unique and sometimes tragic life that has made Frida Kahlo one of the most famous artists of the twentieth century.

Diego Rivera

Diego Rivera was born in 1886 in Guanajuato, Mexico. He died in 1957 in Mexico City. One of the most famous muralists of Mexico, a nation best known for its murals, he studied at the Academia de San Carlos in Mexico with Santiago Rebull and José María Velasco. In 1907 he studied in Madrid with Eduardo Chicharro. His formative years as an artist were spent in Europe, and his two initial phases as an artist reflect the influence of realists like Zuloaga and Chicharro, as well as the cubists Gris and Picasso.

Diego Rivera's affiliation with the communist movement led him to paint in the Indian tradition without forgetting European techniques. His art thus represents the synthesis of different cultural movements: the European technique, popular culture, and his social and political ideologies so evident in his art.

The founder of the Communist Party in his country, Rivera also visited the Soviet Union from 1927 to 1928. After he returned to Mexico, he married Mexican artist Frida Kahlo and in 1936 persuaded the government to give political asylum to Leon Trotsky, which caused Rivera to be expelled from his party.

Rivera lived in the U.S. from 1930 to 1934 and painted murals in San Francisco, Detroit, and New York City. His mural at the Rockefeller Center was later destroyed because it included a portrait of Lenin. In Mexico he decorated the Office of Education, the National School of Agriculture, the Cortes Palace in Cuernavaca, the National Palace, and the National Palace of Fine Arts in Mexico City.

Cesar Chávez

Cesar Estrada Chávez was born on March 31, 1927, near Yuma, Arizona. Chávez's father escaped slavery on a Mexican ranch and moved to Arizona in the 1880s. The second of six children, Chávez began his education at age 7 but found it very difficult because his family spoke only in Spanish. In the 1930s his father lost his job as a result of the Great Depression. The family then moved back to the ranch. Severe weather later caused them to lose the ranch, however, and after this lost they moved to California in search of work. In California Chávez's family became part of the immigrant community and were thus forced to move from farm to farm to pick fruits and vegetables during the harvest.

After Chávez completed the eighth grade, he quit school and worked full time in the vineyards. His family rented a small cottage in San Jose. Chávez married Helen Fabela in 1948 and began to fight to change the poor working conditions and the low wages of the farm workers. This motivated him to become a part of the Community Service Organization (CSO) in 1952 after meeting Fred Ross, who was also a member of this organization. Chávez traveled throughout California urging Mexican Americans to register to vote and also canvassing in support of workers' rights. In 1958 he became the general director of CSO.

Four years later he formed his own organization, called National Farm Workers Association (NFWA). The name was later changed to the United Farm Workers (UFW). In the early 1970s Chávez's organization arranged strikes and boycotts to get higher wages from grape and lettuce growers. During the 1980s the group boycotted to protest the use of toxic pesticides on grapes. Chávez died on April 27, 1993.

Jaime Escalante

Jaime Escalante, a native from La Paz, Bolivia, is one of the most famous Latino educators in the U.S. His accomplishments as a teacher were immortalized in the film *Stand and Deliver*. Escalante taught physics and mathematics for 14 years before he migrated to the U.S. in 1964. His first stop was at the University of Puerto Rico, where he took courses in science and mathematics. He moved to California but did not know how to speak English. He studied at nights at the Pasadena City College and earned a degree in electronics.

In 1976 he began teaching at Garfield High School in East Los Angeles, California. He was able to motivate a group of minority students considered low- or underachievers to take and pass the AP calculus exam in 1982. The Educational Testing Service, which administered the test, invalidated the scores because its evaluators believed the students had cheated on the exam. The students took and passed the exam one more time, making Escalante a hero to the Latino community.

In 1991 Escalante left Garfield High School and began working for the Sacramento School District. He is considered one of the most famous educators in the U.S. The film *Stand and Deliver*, based on his accomplishments at Garfield High School, has become one of the classic films about American education. He was awarded the U.S. Presidential Medal and the Andres Bello Award by the Organization of the American States.

Recommended Reading

Aponte Vazquez, P. *¿Quién fue Pedro Albizu Campos?* Available: http://goecities.com/maestropr/quien_fue_pac.html (accessed January 16, 2005).

Bustamante, R. (1995). Jaime Escalante: El maestro de todos los tiempos. *El Diario La Prensa*, December 2.

Cole, M. (1994). Escalante Tech. *Hispanic*, November.

Frida Kahlo. Available: http://www.biografiasy vidas.com/biografia/k/kahlo.htm (accessed January 14, 2005).

García-Leduc, J. M. *Ramón Emeterio Betances: Renovación historiográfica en los albores del centenario de su fallecimiento.* Available: http://cuhwww.upr.clu.edu/exegesis/ano9/v25/25_5.html (accessed January 16, 2005).

Libman, G. (1995). Success keeps multiplying for Jaime Escalante. *Los Angeles Times* (Home ed.), December 23.

Negrón-Hernández, L. R. *José de Diego.* Available: http://members.aol.com/visitantes preb/poetico/jdediego/htm.

Negrón-Hernández, L. R. *Julia de Burgos.* Available: http://www.preb.com/poetico/jburgos.html (accessed January 16, 2005).

Sahlman, R. *Cesar Chavez.* Available: http://www.iincwell.com/Biographies/Chavez.html (accessed January 14, 2005).

Torres-Santiago, J. M. *100 Years of Pedro Albizu Campos.* Available: http://www.hunter.cuny.edu/blpr.albizu.html (accessed January 15, 2005).

Velez, I. *Eugenio María de Hostos: Biografías.* Available: http://www.prtc.net-isavelez/host osbiog.html (accessed January 16, 2005).

Rosita L. Rivera

LATINO FAMILY AND SCHOOL INVOLVEMENT

Family or parental involvement has been a major focus in education since the conception of education in the U.S. (Ramirez, 1999a) and is still a focus internationally (Delors, 1996; Ramirez, 1999a). Family involvement is highly desired in education because many studies show student achievement increases when parents are actively involved. Although we have seen an increase in K–12 student success when parents are involved, we still need to take into consideration that (1) no one child is like another, (2) no family is like any other, (3) not all teachers support parental involvement, (4) not all schools support parental involvement, and (5) teacher education must review what is taught about parents and parental involvement. These points become more difficult when we address the issue of Latinos and parental involvement. In this case, we need to address stereotypes, diversity, communication, policy, and school attitudes and training.

Perceptions

Unfortunately we still live in a day where much of our perceptions are derived from the media, and often Latinos are portrayed negatively in such mediums (CNNfyi.com, September 26, 2000, http://cnnstudentnews.cnn.com/2001/fyi/lesson.plans/09/10/bel.hernandez/). Because of such stereotypes and political ideologies such as the English-only movement and political rhetoric of Latinos taking over the U.S. (CNNfyi.com, September 26, 2000, http://cnnstudentnews.cnn.com/2001/fyi/lesson.plans/09/10/bel.hernandez/) teachers and schools need to be aware that such perceptions may counteract positive school-home relations.

While cultivating our nature as human beings, we perceive our surroundings based on our previous experiences. Our perceptions are not based on passive, objective, or neutral processes. Rather, every perception is an active process. Human beings distinguish between important and unimportant items. As humans we tend to perceive certain situations and people actively and clearly, whereas other situations are perceived only partially or are fully ignored. This is important to understand if we are to research school-home relationships in ethnic communities. Often we fail to focus on the many perceptions teachers have of parents

(Ramirez, 1999a). In my experience with schools, perceptions toward families and students are predetermined before the student walks into the classroom on the first day of class (Ramirez, 1999a). Colleagues of mine would discuss students and their Latino parents in negative and often harsh tones within the faculty lounge. "You know, if those [Latino] parents would only listen, it would make my job easier" and "Don't they know this is America, they should learn English so I can speak to them" were common comments. These negative attitudes, though not characteristic of all teachers, have made working with Latino parents more difficult. They have also led many Latino parents to question how they can become more actively involved in their child's education and whether they can trust school personnel and officials.

Many Latino parents interviewed felt their children's teachers perceived them to be "uncaring" primarily as a result of previous relationships the teachers had with other Latino parents (Ramirez, 2003). Imelda, a Latina mother, stated, "Before I went to meet the teacher, her attitude toward me was so negative that I didn't want to go back and talk to her during Open House." Another parent commented, "I mean, why would I want to go to my child's school when all I hear is that Latino parents don't care about education?" Perceptions have caused parents and teachers to miscommunicate, as a result creating an atmosphere of antagonism. These perceptions could be altered, however, if teachers develop multicultural understanding and communication skills (Nieto, 1996).

When teachers are better able to understand the community in which they teach, their teaching may become more enjoyable. Steve, a high school science teacher who was working in an urban Latino school, made this clear:

When I finally found out how to say something in Spanish to my non-English speaking parents, their eyes widened and smiled, even when I said something wrong. The parents were very grateful that I was trying to speak in Spanish, and when I approached a mother and father to help me with learning their language they were very helpful. Today I am learning more and have parents translate the newsletters I send home as well as school information. My principal is impressed that the parents are willing to step forward and help. What she didn't understand, which I do now, is that all the parents want to help. We just need to reach out.

Steve went on to make the comment that his trying to communicate with his parents went further in creating stronger school-home connections then anything he has tried. He later commented that his perception of Spanish-speaking parents changed as a result of his simple effort in trying to communicate in the parents' language. He understood that his parents had the same concerns as he did regarding education. Steve later realized, however, he was stereotyping the parents by believing all Latino families spoke Spanish. He also rethought his position of English-only language policies regarding schools.

Language, Communication, and Culture

Language policies and language use by teachers and students are volatile subjects, especially in the state of California, where bilingual instruction is permitted only with a parent's written permission. School districts often fail, however, to tell Latino and other second language parents their children have the right to bilingual education. Assessments and standardized testing have contributed to making some teachers feel the need to teach toward the test they are administering, for many teachers, principals,

and superintendents, fear for their jobs if test scores are low. In some Spanish-speaking communities parents have been asked by schools to teach their children more English skills within the home. As we can see, doing this is problematic, for many Spanish-speaking families lack the resources or skills to help their children learn English (personal communication, Office of Bilingual Education, Los Angeles Unified School District, January 2000). Although schools want parents to teach their children English, many teachers lack the training to assess student fluency in English (personal communication, Office of Bilingual Education, Los Angeles Unified School District, January 2000).

Research in the school community found teachers and parents willing to address the topic of limited English proficient (LEP) students. Some of the information gathered was positive about working with English language learners (ELLs); other information was negative.

Amy, a first year teacher working in a high school, commented that before she went into teaching, she had no desire to teach ELLs and viewed bilingual education negatively. She felt she was "ignorant" as to what "this" community (Latinos) wanted from education. This young teacher fresh from a teacher education program was asked to teach a sheltered education course (traditionally, sheltered education involves teaching strategies for students who enter an English-only course after being enrolled in English as a Second Language courses). Reluctant at first, she soon witnessed her own transformation, for she noticed her sheltered students were more motivated to learn than were her English-speaking students. Amy became more involved in her students' lives and grew to become an advocate for ELLs. She began to recruit parents to assist her in translation, met with families off campus to discuss student progress, and generated grant monies to assist parents with furthering their own education. Contrary to Amy's experience is that of an elementary school teacher within the same district.

Grace, a fifth grade tenured teacher with six years' experience, said she demanded her students to speak only English while they were in school, for she wanted to know what they were saying about her. This reaction toward second language students created a negative reaction from parents. Because Grace felt parents needed to work with their children in the English language but were "not doing their part," she believed the parents did not want their children to learn English and did not care for them. She reported that many parents transferred their children to another school, where the administration "catered" to the desires of the Spanish-speaking community. When asked their reasons for transferring their children, parents were eager to tell their stories. Parents believed if their children could speak Spanish during recess and lunch, and then learn English during their classes, the children would become bilingual, which would give them more opportunities later in life. The school administrator whom Grace questioned was a bilingual educator and worked with students and parents in becoming academically fluent in both English and Spanish. Parents who become advocates for their children are often questioned and stigmatized by schools and administrators.

Mary, a Latina woman from Guatemala, commented that teachers "persuaded" her younger daughter to forgo bilingual education and be immersed in English-only classrooms. Although the woman's two older sons had a bilingual education and

succeeded at major universities, the daughter struggled to learn both English and Spanish by the time she was a sophomore in high school. The mother's insistence that the school provide bilingual education for her daughter, she felt, led the school district to label her "troublesome," for she was not being allowed to speak to any school administrators or officials.

Another teacher, Greg, who teaches at the elementary school, while discussing how he communicated with parents stated, "Yes, I write letters home in Spanish so my parents will have all the information regarding the school and my classroom." Upon further review, Greg confirmed he was not fluent in Spanish, nor did he obtain a translator to assist his letter writing. When asked what level of Spanish he had mastered, he commented, "Oh I just do my best [he had two years of high school Spanish]. I mean, they can't read anyway." Other teachers said that although they were willing to work in districts with large populations of Spanish speakers, they did not want to obtain a credential in second language learning, nor did they wish to learn a second language.

For K–12 students from bilingual homes, there are overall cognitive advantages to learning two languages (Baker, 1996). Should teachers acquire a second language in Spanish, their ability to communicate with Latino students and their families would create stronger school-home partnerships. Teachers would also be better able to assist students if they learned strategies to teach LEP students.

Cultural Conflicts and Schooling

Miscommunication between the school and home makes both families and schools unaware of each other's expectations. One such expectation from schools throughout the nation is for parents to attend Open

House or Back-to-School Nights. However, the idea of stepping foot onto school grounds is foreign for many cultures and families. Although teachers desire parents to attend Open House, obstacles may prevent parents from attending (Ramirez, 1999a). Consider this: in one predominately Latino community, Robert, a ninth grade teacher, desires to work in a district 30 miles from his home. His reason for working so far away is simple: "I love working in the city of Santa Lucia. The parents never show up for anything, and they never question my teaching." Parents in this community face a Catch-22: If you never show up to events such as Open House, then you are seen as "uncaring." If you do show up and start to ask questions, then you are looked upon with suspicion. When parents were interviewed regarding the reasons they did not attend functions such as Open House, a different picture emerged. They cited many obstacles:

- The inability to get off work, for most school functions are on weeknights and many Latino parents work late shifts
- The inability to find daycare
- Transportation difficulties
- Teachers not showing up for school functions
- Lack of respect from the teachers and school officials
- Children working to supplement family income and the parents wanting to be home in case of accidents
- Not knowing when functions were scheduled
- Feeling they would disrespect the teachers and school if they did attend

This last issue is compelling, for many immigrant Latino parents are unaware of the educational differences between their former country and the U.S. In many countries, teachers are regarded as experts in the education of children; therefore, parents feel

the teachers are in charge and not to be questioned. Schools need to consider this attitude when working with immigrant Latino families. Communicating consistently with immigrant populations would promote better school-home relationships.

In one study, the communication patterns among the teachers were such that only 5% of their students' families were contacted during the school year (Ramirez, 1999b). In a recent interview on the issue of Title I, national program that gives resources to low-income or low-achieving schools with high parental involvement, Sheneekra Williams, an administrator with a large school district in California, stated, "I am in contact with many of the principals and vice-principals in this district. I am honest to say that I would be surprised if Title I schools are in compliance regarding parents.... Rarely do the schools survey let alone communicate with parents in ways that Title I dictates" (personal communication, Jan. 2000). When asked about urban ethnic communities, she started to laugh. She stated, "Latino families need to push harder than other families just to see the teachers! Then when they do, the parent is labeled as being a troublemaker. I would like to see more schools communicate better with all of our families."

The interaction between families and schools is unique. Schools face the challenge of considering the many ethnicities and cultures within their schools. Families need to familiarize themselves with school expectations, namely, that they produce children who are ready to learn and are knowledgeable about the school culture. This combination can be highly volatile, especially when working with a group as diverse as Latinos. Although the current population of families is more educated than ever before, educators still need to reach out without creating divisions between the families and the school.

Excellent teachers have to be excellent communicators as well as fine technicians. This is why quality school-home communication is needed. The difficulty with examining quality communication is that teacher education programs seldom demand that students complete public speaking or other communication courses. The result is what Leary (1957) calls *dominance-submission*, where one person is controlling the communication. Often the teacher is the person who is controlling the communication within the classroom. Although Wubbels, Levy, and Brekelmans (1997) found that good teachers are dominant, which contributes to student achievement, Ramirez (1999a, 1999b) found that schools control the level of communication between the school and the home. Unfortunately, this develops into misunderstood or ineffective communication between parents and the school. Leary also suggests a *cooperation-opposition* dimension, where levels of cooperation are present between people. Wubbels and colleagues (1997) found that good teachers need to have both dominant and cooperative understandings of their students. They need to set standards, yet be able to understand the needs of their students in a controlled environment that allows for measures of freedom for students. Therefore, while working with Latinos and their families, teachers need to investigate not only the idea of dominance but also the idea of "educentrism" that may occur within schools.

"Educentrism" is a difficult issue to understand. Whereas "ethnocentrism" refers to the notion that one's own ethnicity is superior to that of others, in education, and especially in the relationship between parents and schools, teachers and administrators often believe that their way of educating is superior. They know better than students,

visitors, and especially parents. They are thus "educentric." Educentrism needs to be explored, especially in working with parents from a variety of backgrounds. In developing communication between the school and the home, teachers and administrators would need to understand that a person is made up of a variety of layers, like an onion. The outer layer is what is seen: language, food, clothing styles, and the like. The second layer consists of values the person shares with others, along with norms. These values represent a person's definition of what is good and bad, and the norms are what the person perceives as right and wrong among people. By looking at this definition, we can understand that communication between schools and Latino homes can be difficult if the senders of information (schools) do not clarify what their cultural communication entails.

Effective school-home communication is vital for the health of a school. Unfortunately, traditional communication between schools and parents consists of Open House, teacher-parent conferences, and sporting events. Often when communication is delivered, it is ineffective and deals with disciplinary circumstances (Ramirez, 1999b). To better facilitate communication between the school and Latino families, schools need to recognize communication may be a problem; they need to pursue a personal connection with the parents, communicating with them by making positive phone calls home, sending notes and letters in the families' native language, simply and clearly but not condescendingly, and engaging a translator on site. This demonstration by school personnel would empower parents. By questioning how they communicate with families, schools may recognize there are always ways to improve how they say things to families and the community.

Parents develop perceptions of the school and its role based on the reality of their specific historical-cultural experiences. Educators would better facilitate communication with Latinos if they understood that language barrier, difficulty adapting to a new society, and socioeconomic differences between teachers and parents all contribute to the lack of effective communication. Therefore, if educators wish to understand how messages are understood, they need to realize that different peoples communicate in different ways. By doing this, educators would promote parental self-efficacy and assist in bettering communication. In other words, empowerment is the key in communication with families.

Alvarez, Hofstetter, Donovan, and Huie (1994) suggests specific strategies to improving communication:

- Any assessment of problems or issues must seek input from the spectrum of racial-ethnic groups attending a school, recognizing that none of the groups are internally homogeneous, and that perceptions affecting communication vary widely within and between groups.

- Differences in perceptions of constraints demand a varied approach to programs designed to involve parents in schools. A blanket strategy will not be effective in most urban schools.

- Unbalanced participation among groups of parents should trigger a reassessment of a school's communication strategy, not a suggestion that one or more groups of parents are merely apathetic and therefore may be disregarded.

- University or communication facilitators, community opinion leaders, or teacher linkages to organize parents for securing more active, reflective public involvement should be considered.

My suggestion for schools is to engage a translator at Open House or other school-related functions to allow parents who are second language speakers to express themselves and become more active in their children's school. Also, asking for parent volunteers to translate school documents would empower parents. Schools need to recognize that parents may be more effective than computer translators, which often fail to translate documentation or colloquialisms properly. Communicating through technology is an issue many schools are exploring, but when working with diverse language populations like Latinos, we need to understand the limitations of technology.

Technology within Schools

Ramirez (1999a) found teachers were willing to improve communication if parents were able to respond to teachers' needs. Teachers in this study were concerned that teacher-parent relations were strained by the lack of communication, but they stated that Open House and a new voice mail system had made it easier for parents to communicate with teachers. During this same study one teacher commented that although communication needed improvement, the "Internet home pages would soon be available to allow parents access to homework, the curriculum, and the teachers' expectations." Teachers felt that this development would help reduce the fear and insecurity that both teachers and parents felt regarding communication. In contacting and communicating with parents teachers reported difficulties that included disconnected numbers, lack of phone numbers, and lack of teacher time. Other teachers stated that during the teacher preparatory period a teacher can make up to 10 calls to homes to relay information or make introductory phone calls that lasted no longer than a minute. Other teachers also shared that the main difficulty in communicating with parents are the teachers who are unwilling to make phone calls (Ramirez, 1999a). These same teachers verified that when a teacher phones home, it is mostly to report a negative situation that occurred at school, rather than give a supportive report on the child.

Parents usually hear of the Open House or Back-to-School Night and conferences through letters sent home, newsletters the school distributes, or a phone call. If a family member is unable to read the printed material—24% of the nation is functionally illiterate past the third grade level (U.S. Department of Commerce, 1991)—or a phone is disconnected, then the parents do not receive the information. This issue becomes more difficult when speaking of foreign language parents. Often teachers do not speak the language of the students' families, and some teachers feel it is unnecessary to learn the parents' first language (Ramirez, Autry, & Morton, 2001). To combat these issues, teachers can send home cards to collect information on parents (phone numbers) and call or write a letter to inform them of who they are. Repeating these steps ensures teachers will know their students and their students' parents.

Teachers in the Ramirez study (1999a) agreed that the new school voice mail system enhanced communication between school and parents. Along with this technology, the principal at one school suggested, each teacher should create Web pages to allow parents access to homework, curriculum, and tests. A social studies teacher acknowledged that the home pages would "assist in increasing school-home communication." Some teachers recognized that many parents do not have access to a phone and would therefore neither receive information from the school, nor have access to Web pages, nor be able to leave messages over voice mail. Also, immigrant Latino parents may be unable to read the material on the Web.

Although there may be reasons for the lack of communicative efforts on the part of the schools to reach all parents, researchers comment that communication is the key to successful parental involvement in schools (Burbules, 1993; Center on Families, Communities, Schools and Children's Learning, 1995; Epstein, 1995). Epstein (1995) reported that school-home and home-school communication is essential in developing an understanding of school programs and children's progress. So how can we as teachers use technology to develop stronger communication with parents? Here are a few suggestions.

- Never assume your students have access to technology while at home. If your student does not have access, it is a good bet your student's parents do not have access. Distribute a 3 × 5 card on which students indicate whether they have access.

- Ask the main office of your school for the most current telephone numbers for your students' families. However, the phone numbers may be outdated. Also pass around a 3 × 5 card to your students and get the information from them as well.

- Contact parents early in the school year. As a teacher I was encouraged to contact all 160 parents within the first two weeks of school. Although the task seemed daunting, it was done. Your first phone call is *always* positive.

- Parents wish to be involved in their child's education. If you wish to use the Web for assignments and information, tell the parents and share a time where you or someone else may be willing to train parents how to use a computer to access the information.

- Access to technology may be complicated. Do not assume parents will be able to travel to a destination to get online. Many parents have transportation and daycare issues. Also, some are single parents.

- Inform parents in advance about Open House nights. Also, try to arrange with administrators to provide teachers with two half days during the week so the Open House could be on a Saturday, when more parents may be able to attend.
- Involving technology, know that your students could be your biggest asset in training you and others. Use them!
- Establish bilingual hotlines for the parents.
- Develop phone trees for parents, manned by parents. Parent involvement practices do not mean teachers need to do everything. Recruit, recruit, and recruit parents to work with you.
- Use surveys (either written or over the Web) to ask parents what they think of the school.
- If you are in a population with families whose first language is not English, write some of the Web site information in the family's native language.

Teacher Education

Thus far this entry has concentrated on communication and cultural differences between the school and Latino families. Discussed next is how to inform teacher education programs and newly credentialed teachers regarding Latinos and their families to create stronger parental involvement opportunities.

What has been said in education regarding Latinos? To determine this, several colleagues were asked to send their syllabi for review. These colleagues have taught multicultural education, and some are teaching courses on families and schools. After a general investigation into the syllabi, it became evident that many educators foster stereotypes. Teacher candidates are led to believe that Latinos are Spanish speaking, gang involved, low socioeco-

nomic, immigrant, and urban living. They are predominantly single-parent families and adolescents who dropped out of school. Most surprising was that the literature included showed these commonalities as well.

In a multicultural course of a teacher education program in California, students were given a handout describing Latinos, whose characteristics included these:

Ethno-Hispanic (includes Cuban, Mexican, Puerto Rican, Argentinean, Chilean, etc.)

- Love of beauty: arts, crafts, churches, wedding, music, etc.
- Punctuality not important
- Strong sense of individual
- Close geographical area
- Honor and loyalty: maintain image of family and community
- Share, cooperate, work together, accountable for everyone's well-being and honor
- Generally a laboring people
- Less educated than whites
- Disabilities may be looked upon as an illness
- Extended family
- God and parents very important
- Family the center of an individual's life
- Intermarriage with whites
- Children included in all family gatherings
- Double standard (male and female)

How many cultures can identify with these traits? The difficulty with creating lists such as these pigeonhole families and maintain stereotypes differentiating one family from another. The issue regarding this list is not only the stereotypes that may be generated with students and their families but also the lack of room for individuals who are multiethnic. In society many people have married outside of their culture and ethnicity. If we agree that Hispanics marry with whites (as the list includes), then their offspring would be multiethnic. How, then, would the teacher communicate with a student's family if that student has one parent who is Latino but another who has French, Irish, or German ancestry?

What researchers and educators also minimize is the diversity within ethnic groups. A recent migrant from the city of Juárez, Mexico, is probably different than a recent migrant from a small town such as San Juan de los Lagos, in Jalisco, Mexico. Although they reside within the same country, they may communicate in different ways. Whether educated or not, northern Mexicans have regional biases often with one another. Likewise, Puerto Ricans and people from Honduras, Guatemala, and so on, all have differences among themselves. Perhaps the one commonality recent immigrants from Latin American countries share is the Spanish language, although in this there are also many regional differences. Given such diversity, we also need to recognize the ever-growing dependency on technology to communicate with others.

The stereotype that is being taught was not my experience as an adolescent. When we as educators investigate Latinos, we need to be aware that this group is as diverse as all other groups and individuals. We also need to recognize that within the Latino population there are prejudices toward those Latinos that do not speak Spanish, which may cause difficulty in researching diverse language populations. While investigating some common qualities teachers need to have while working with diverse populations, one characteristic Gordon (1977) describes as "withitness."

Gordon (1997) reports that beginning teachers need to develop a sense of "Social insight," as well as "withitness," to maximize classroom learning. Social insight involves learning about the students' (1) verbal language, (2) nonverbal communication, (3) culture, (4) worldview, (5) behavioral style, (6) values, (7) methods of reasoning, and (8) cultural and ethnic identification. "Withitness" takes what is learned by social insight and constructs learning that expresses a familiarity with the students' culture; through this framework mutual respect can be formed between the school and home. By constructing these within a teacher's learning, the teacher becomes aware of what is meaningful in the students' lives. The socially insightful and "withit" teacher uses cultural information effectively. Then, the teacher will be better able to communicate with parents about their students and their students' education.

Gordon proposes that teacher gain social insight and "withitness." To do this, teachers need to (1) expose themselves to adolescent culture, (2) affirm students' interests, (3) relate content to students' outside interests, (4) know their students and (5) share their humanity with their students. So how can we use this approach within the Latino communities? Communication is important when developing social insight and "withitness." Communicating with family members in a non-educational arena would give teachers more information to build the necessary blocks to provide for a less stressful teaching and learning environment for the teacher and the students. Some schools offer Back-to-School nights on Saturday's instead of during the week, and the atmosphere includes potlucks, skits, and presentations from teachers and students. Another way of gaining insight is through the use of home visits.

Home Visits

Home visits, although not new, contribute to the funds of knowledge from households for teachers and schools (Gonzalez et al., 1995; Nieto, 1996). With the information that home visits generate, schools would be better able to communicate with homes and families. Home visits would also establish reciprocity for the schools. Should a family be unable to attend school functions, the home visit would enable teachers to inform parents of school events, their children's progress, and other useful information. However, to produce home visits that would ensure the best for school personnel and families, the teachers would need to enter the Latino home as a learner.

As part of a teacher preparation course that I teach, students are asked to interview parents from a variety of Latino families who are from other countries, who are from the U.S., and who come from different socioeconomic backgrounds. The students are asked to make contacts with the parents and interview the parents in their homes and in pairs. Before interviewing the parents, students are asked about their attitudes toward parents and their experience. Most comments mirror this one from a preservice teacher: "I don't mind if parents wish to get involved. I would just hope that they don't back their children all the time if I phone home regarding a problem."

When asked about phoning home, the preservice teacher acknowledged that she would only have time to contact parents whose children were doing poorly or were in trouble. Most of preservice teachers felt apprehensive regarding the project. When asked why they felt apprehensive, many students said they thought it was "too obtrusive" to enter a parent's home. Others asked, "Why do we need to do this," and "What do you want us to ask?" Upon completion of their interviews, however, the preservice teachers had different assessments. Many said they learned from the

parents and desired to make home visits a part of their teaching. Although we discussed the difficulty of going to every student's home if teachers had over 150 students, we were able to generate ideas of how to incorporate such visits into their curriculum. One suggestion was to visit only those parents with whom they were unable to make some contact. From the visits the preservice teachers learned a great deal:

- Latino parents do care for their child's education (there were comments to the contrary, however, if parents did not attend Open House).
- Latino parents were knowledgeable about curriculum matters (preservice teachers had decided before the visits that parents should not be a part of curriculum decision making).
- Latino parents desired to be asked their opinions.
- Some Latino parents were unable to attend Open House because of work, childcare, or transportation issues and other related matters.
- Latino parents were inviting (some preservice teachers were asked back for dinner, others were fed, and one student returned to interview the mother for another project for the class).
- Some Latino parents were knowledgeable regarding second language acquisition policies.

The preservice teachers learned that ethnography could be used as a tool to learn about families and the lives of their students. Many were able to look within Latino families for the first time and realized that they shared experiences with Latino families. Some preservice teachers felt unable to address all the needs of the parents, but they felt comfortable asking where to obtain information to address the parents' needs.

This observation by the students in these multicultural courses parallels what Jones and Velez (1997) suggest regarding how to communicate with Latino families and the "sociocultural capital" that is apparent in Latino families, and what Nieto (1996) suggests in communicating with ethnic families. The preservice students in their observations recognized that in Latino families, many members of the family were concerned about the well-being of the child in school. Many of the students in my class felt that the schools were not meeting the needs of the parents interviewed. The parents felt that the educational system "took them [parents] for granted" for parents would do anything the school desired, but they were never asked; they were contacted only if their child was doing poorly academically or was disruptive. Parents whose children were doing well rarely received communication from the school. Harry (1992) mentions that many ethnic families defer trust to the schools unconditionally. This trust, if not respected by schools in communicating effectively with the home, may be lost from the parents. Like Harry in her observations of ethnic families, my students found parents who did not trust their schools, policies, and many of the faculty and staff. Often the parents cited "no communication" from the school as the reason for their lack of trust.

Information to Include in Teacher Education Programs

Today teacher education programs need to deliver information to future teachers that includes positive reflections upon Latinos and their families. These positive attributes should also be given regarding all families regardless of their ethnicity and socioeconomic status. Teacher education programs should minimally include these activities:

- Lessons on improving listening techniques
- Lessons on interpersonal and intercultural communication

- Lessons on how to create a positive classroom experience with parents by making positive phone calls and strategies on sending home positive notes
- Lessons on how to create a win-win situation during parent-teacher conferences
- Giving parents an opportunity to share their cultural capital within the class, or outside the class at school functions
- Giving parents an opportunity to share what positive attributes their children have
- Giving credential candidates research information on parent-family involvement programs
- Having students interact with families through interview projects
- Having students interact and survey schools on parent involvement practices, and
- Having students research their own culture and ethnicity to better appreciate their identity so they will appreciate the diversity of others

These are a few suggestions for teacher trainees, but one important strategy remains for the teacher educator. Often teacher educators have been teachers but lack the training to work with parents and families in positive ways. Therefore, teacher educators must rethink their definition of family involvement as well as their ideas regarding ethnic groups. Teacher educators have the responsibility to assist future teachers in developing non-stereotypical images of Latinos and their families within their classrooms. Should teacher education develop multicultural teachers, then all Latino families will feel welcomed within their children's schools.

References

Alvarez, D. S., Hofstetter, C. R., Donovan, M. C., & Huie, C. (1994). Patterns of Communication in Racial/Ethnic Context: The Case of an Urban Public High School. *Urban Education* 29(2), 134–149.

Baker, C. (1996). *Foundations of Bilingual Education and Bilingualism.* Bristol, PA: Multilingual Matters.

Burbules, N. C. (1993). *Dialogue in Teaching: Theory and Practice.* New York: Teachers College Press.

Center on Families, Communities, Schools, and Children's Learning. (1995). *Schools, Families, and Students Get Stronger When Parents and Teachers Take Collaboration into Their Own Hands.* Baltimore: Johns Hopkins University.

Delors, J. (1996). *Learning: The Treasure Within: Report to UNESCO of the International Commission on Education for the Twenty-first Century.* New York: UNESCO Publishing.

Epstein, J. (1995). Perspectives and Previews on Research and Policy for School, Family & Community Partnerships. In Booth and Dunn (Eds.), *Family-School Links: How Do They Affect Educational Outcomes?* Hillsdale, NJ: Lawrence Erlbaum Associates.

Gonzalez, N., Moll, L. C., Tenery, M. F., Rivera, A., Rendon, P., Gonzalez, R., & Amanti, C. (1995). Funds of Knowledge for Teaching in Latino Households. *Urban Education* 29(4), 443–470.

Gordon, R. L. (1997). How Novice Teachers Can Succeed with Adolescents. *Educational Leadership* (April), 56–58.

Harry, B. (1992). *Cultural Diversity, Families, and the Special Education System: Communication and Empowerment.* New York: Teachers College Press.

Jones, T. G., & Velez, W. (1997). Effects of Latino Parent Involvement on Academic Achievement. Paper presented at the annual meeting of the American Educational Research Association, Chicago, IL, March 24–28.

Leary, T. (1957). *An Interpersonal Diagnosis of Personality.* New York: Ronald Press.

Nieto, S. (1996). *Affirming Diversity: The Sociopolitical Context of Multicultural Education.* White Plains, NY: Longman.

Ramirez, A. Y. (1999a). Teachers' Attitudes toward Parents and Parental Involvement in High Schools. Ph.D. Dissertation, Indiana University.

Ramirez, A. Y. (1999b). Survey on Teachers' Attitudes regarding Parents and Parental Involvement. *School Community Journal* 9(2), 21–39.

Ramirez, A. Y. (2003). Ethnic Family Communications: The Triumphs and Tragedies of School-Home Communication with African-American and Latino Families. In Diana I. Rios (Ed.), *Brown and Black Communication.* Westport, CT: Greenwood Press.

Ramirez, A. Y., Autry, M., & Morton, M. L. (2001). Sociopedagogy: A Move beyond Multiculturalism to Stronger Community. In F. Schultz (Ed.), *Multicultural Education 01/02* (pp. 63–69). Guilford, CT: McGraw-Hill. Reproduced article.

U.S. Department of Commerce. Bureau of the Census. (1991). *Statistical Abstract of the United States.* Washington, DC: U.S. Government Printing Office.

Wubbels, T., Levy, J., & Brekelmans, M. (1997). Paying Attention to Relationships. *Educational Leadership* (April), 82–86.

Recommended Reading

Ramirez, A. Y. (2003). Ethnic Family Communications: The Triumphs and Tragedies of School-Home Communication with African-American and Latino Families. In Diana I. Rios (Ed.), *Brown and Black Communication.* Westport, CT: Greenwood Press.

A. Y. "Fred" Ramirez

LATINO/HISPANIC IMMIGRATION FROM LATIN AMERICA

Just as millions of European immigrants have had to leave their countries over the centuries to escape repressive rulers and poverty for a chance at a better life, immigrants from Central America have come to the U.S. for the same reasons and have worked hard to become productive and responsible citizens. But unlike European children who learn in U.S. public schools of the oppression their families fled from in Europe, Latin American children are forced to receive an education that erases the historical oppression their families have had to face. They are "systematically stripped of their integrity, independence, freedom and voice" (Soto, 2002, p. xxiv). Large numbers of Latinos in the U.S., especially illegal immigrants, are marginalized—punished— and left to low-skilled employment opportunities, their children pushed aside in schools, and whole families excluded from social services available to other poor immigrants (Chavez, 1998). These people are left with zero historical contexts and absolutely no acknowledgment of why they have had to abandon their homelands and their sense of self and the power inherent in communicating in their own language, all for life in the U.S.

This entry argues that the U.S. imperialist foreign policy of the Monroe Doctrine, including its military and covert interventions in Latin America, as well as the cold war policy of "containment" to halt the perceived spread of communism, have caused not only instability of government, economic atrocities, and tremendous poverty but also a mass exodus of millions of people trying to escape their war-torn, unstable countries for a better life in the U.S. In addition, this entry posits that the cause of the majority of the emigration from Latin America has been war, waged in the name of capitalism under the disguise of a communist threat. The last half of the entry addresses the unjust U.S. policies that continue to dictate the lives and opportunities of Latino people within the country.

U.S.–Latin America Relations

In 1823 the U.S. issued the Monroe Doctrine as a diplomatic decision, which greatly influenced the world and the way it has developed to the present day. It was a policy, initiated by President James Monroe, that aimed to limit European expansion into the Western Hemisphere. Monroe proclaimed, "The American continents, by the free and independent condition which they have assumed and maintain, are henceforth not to be considered as subjects for future colonization by any European powers" (Perkins, 1965). The U.S. accepted the responsibility of being the protector of independent Western nations and affirmed that it would steer clear of European affairs.

Nevertheless, like an abused child that then abuses its own, the U.S., while proclaiming itself the champion of the free world and democracy, proceeded, between 1798 and 1895, to intervene in the affairs of other nations over 100 times under the pretext that it was protecting American interests. The following century was marked with nearly as many "interventions" in Latin America alone, as well as the support of several dictators (Boot, 2002). This history, however, does not make it into our high school textbooks. Furthermore, when the U.S. sends the military to Latin America, the American people are always told, by way of the news, that our government has sent our troops to protect American interests. The question the American people, including the media, *never* asks is, "What interests do we have in Latin America that we need to protect?"—something an invested citizen and taxpayer would want to know, considering that sending hundreds of thousands of troops and equipment across the globe costs millions in tax dollars.

Had the history textbook writers been doing their jobs correctly, more Americans might know that American interests in Latin America are corporations that have taken over large tracts of land to grow products to be sold to Americans and other people around the world. Companies like United Fruit Company in Central America and the Caribbean, and the Dole family in Hawaii, for example, need protection from the local people whose lands have been taken over by American corporations (Zinn, 2003). In addition, these local people, so long as they remain poor and in need, provide a significant source of cheap labor either as migrant workers like the braceros during World War II or as employees of U.S. factories in their native lands, facilitated by contracts like the North American Free Trade Agreement (NAFTA) (Bigelow & Peterson, 2002).

What Americans generally *do* know is what the news chooses to convey. With regard to recent U.S.–Latin America relations, the American media have shown waves of illegal immigrants crossing the border between Mexico and the U.S. and claimed that most are petty criminals or drug dealers; that they receive free health care from our hard-earned tax dollars; and that theses illegal immigrants take jobs from Americans. As a result, it is not surprising that the mass immigration of Latinos from Central America in the early 1990s has given rise to concerns from the American public (Smith & Edmonston, 1997). On the other hand, there has been no public outcry that illegal Canadians compose a large segment of illegal aliens in the U.S. Nor does the media focus on the large Russian immigration and the crime this group has brought to the U.S. All the while, the Mexican border is the most heavily guarded part of the world (Andreas, 1998; Finckenauer, 1998).

Unfortunately for Latin America, these guards work to keep Latinos out of the U.S., but not Americans out of Mexico and the rest of the region, thereby allowing U.S. relations with Latin America, which have been marked by "intervention"—the U.S. invasion of Latin American nations—for land, labor, and resources (Smith, 1996), to persist. This policy began with the expansionism of the Monroe Doctrine, including the acquisition of more territory through both treaties and war with Mexico and Spain, as well as the acquisition of formal colonies throughout the region. Later, U.S.–Latin America relations also became characterized by economic dependence, first formally facilitated by Wilson's "dollar diplomacy" where the U.S. assumed the debts held previously by European banks for various Caribbean countries, thus allowing a strong U.S. presence in the region to handle taxes and other related transactions, and at times calling for a military presence to further support these efforts. After several failed U.S. interventions, an economic depression, and a change of U.S. administration, policy in the region entered a so-called golden age with the "Good Neighbor" edicts of FDR, including subtle tactics focused on free trade with the region, rather than military strength to secure a U.S. foothold (Boot, 2002). Nevertheless, the "good" neighbor soon moved on, leaving room for a very bad neighbor.

Despite U.S. efforts, spanning a century, to export a capitalist democracy throughout Latin America, by 1954 only four so-called democracies remained—Uruguay, Costa Rica, Chile, and Brazil. Latin America's dominant classes, including their military forces, had begun turning toward dictatorship and other oppressive regimes in response to progressive movements for social reform by the large majority of the various nations, the poor. Meanwhile U.S. policy supported these far-right governments, believing, as Secretary of State John Foster Dulles insisted, that "they are the only people we can depend on" in the throes of a worldwide communist rebellion (Smith, 1996, pp. 130–131).

Although the American people have not been given a context in which to understand why the people of Latin America have had to flee their homelands, one does undoubtedly exit. Primarily, that the region was caught up in the cold war. U.S. claims that it felt threatened by perceived Soviet encroachment into Latin America brought about policies and actions to eradicate any alleged Soviet influence, including support for Latin American dictators, who then waged war against the peasant population in places like El Salvador, Guatemala, and Nicaragua (Blum, 1995). These Central American dictators, along with their military and police, which were trained and supported by the U.S., committed human rights violations against their own people in the alleged war against Soviet communism, which then caused thousands of refugees from these Central American countries to seek asylum in the very country that waged war against them.

The U.S. had failed to recognize two crucial points: one, the effects of destabilizing a country in such close proximity to itself, which was and continues to be a politically stable and economically secure nation—effects, including the mass exodus of refugees and exiles (otherwise referred to as illegal immigrants and aliens); and two, that Latin American history prior to the cold war and since Spanish colonial rule was marked by revolution in response to a minority of aristocratic leaders who dominated land ownership and the masses of poor people who worked it.

U.S. Involvement in Latin America: A Brief History

Guatemala. In Guatemala American interests grew from profits that were hand-somely paid off to governments that turned the other way as corporations like the United Fruit Company made huge gains off the land. In 1899 the Boston Fruit Company and the United Fruit Company (UFCO) merged, thus forming the largest banana company in the world with plantations in Colombia, Costa Rica, Cuba, Jamaica, Nicaragua, Panama, and the Dominican Republic. The UFCO owned 11 steamships, known as the Great White Fleet, plus 30 other ships rented or leased. The company also owned 112 miles of railroad linking the plantations with ports.

In 1901, while the U.S. solidified its holdings in Cuba after the Spanish-American War and also expanded into the Philippines, the Virgin Islands, and Hawaii, U.S. business representatives were pushing into Guatemala. The Guatemalan dictator Manuel Estrada Cabrera granted to UFCO the exclusive right to transport postal mail between Guatemala, and the U.S. thus became UFCO's first entry into Guatemala. Cabrera, a right-wing dictator who did anything UFCO wanted, along with the company judged Guatemala to have "an ideal investment climate." The UFCO created a subsidiary of the company and called it the Guatemalan Railroad Company and capitalized it at $40 million. The UFCO contracted with Cabrera to build a railroad between Guatemala City and Puerto Barrios on the coast. It also obtained permission to purchase lots in Puerto Barrios at a nominal price and received a grant of land one mile long by 500 yards wide on either side of the municipal pier. The UFCO also negotiated the contract to build telegraph lines from the capital to Puerto Barrios (Dosal, 1993).

Other countries in Central and South America also fell under the thrall of the mighty UFCO, also called *yunai* or *La Frutera* or *El Pulpo* (The Octopus) in Latin America, but none were more under UFCO's thumb than Guatemala. United Fruit's Guatemalan operation generated about 25% of the company's total production. In Guatemala, United Fruit gained control of virtually all means of transportation and communications. United Fruit charged a tariff on every item of freight that moved in and out of the country through Puerto Barrios. For many years the coffee growers of Guatemala paid very high tariffs, and the price of Guatemalan coffee on the world market was high because of this (Kepner, 1967). Ironically, this is reminiscent of British policies regarding tea and other goods the Imperialist Grandfather had monopolized, and which eventually incited public unrest in the American colonies, thus driving their independence.

Furthermore, the capital of the United Fruit Company's empire was in Guatemala, where the company focused on infrastructure, but not fruit. From the town of Bananera, where its headquarters were located, it masterminded its empire and corrupted every level of government and politics in Guatemala. UFCO also managed to exempt itself from virtually all taxes for 99 years and had its fingers in almost every pie in Guatemala. The company had the unconditional support of right-wing dictators who maintained their power by terrorizing the people and arresting prominent citizens, who were either killed on the spot or tortured in prison to extract confessions. During one wave of repression under Jorge Ubico, hundreds were killed in just two days.

In 1944 the people of Guatemala overthrew Jorge Ubico and Guatemala held its first true elections in history. The people elected Dr. Juan José Arevalo Bermej to the presidency. A new constitution was drawn up, based on the U.S. Constitution. Arevalo was a socialist and an educator who built over 6,000 schools in Guatemala and made great progress in education and health care (Dosal, 1993).

Despite these efforts toward reform, real estate continued to govern the people. At this time in Guatemala just 2.2% of the population owned over 70% of the country's land. Only 10% of the land was available for 90% of the population, most of whom were *indígenas* (natives). The people dispossessed from the land were forced to move into the urban areas, and those who once made a living from farming now had to struggle to make ends meet in dilapidated urban housing and poverty. This led to unrest among the people who wanted land reform and relief from all the poverty that had engulfed their countries in Central America. Most of the land held by the large landowners was unused.

Arevalo was succeeded in another free election by Jacobo Arbenz, who continued the reform process begun under Arevalo. Arbenz proposed to redistribute some of the unused land and make it available for the 90% to farm. Here is where the problem arose: the UFCO was one of the big holders of unused land in Guatemala and complained to the many friends it had within the U.S. government, including President Eisenhower and Secretary of State John Foster Dulles, saying that Guatemala had turned communist (Cook, 1981; La Feber, 1993). The State Department and United Fruit embarked on a major public relations campaign to convince the American people and the rest of the U.S. government that Guatemala was a Soviet "satellite." The campaign succeeded, and in 1954 the Central Intelligence Agency (CIA) orchestrated a coup, invaded Guatemala with 150 men, and convinced the Guatemalan public and President Arbenz that a major invasion was underway. The CIA set up a clandestine radio station inside the U.S. embassy to carry propaganda, jammed all Guatemalan stations, and hired American pilots to bomb strategic points in Guatemala City, injuring and killing civilians. The U.S. replaced the freely elected government of Guatemala with another right-wing dictatorship that would again bend to UFCO's will (Blum, 1995). Howard Zinn says that Arbenz's government overthrown by the U.S. was "the most democratic Guatemala ever had" (Zinn, 2003, p. 430). UFCO later changed its name to United Brands and then ran into financial difficulties during the 1970s, when its lands were bought by the Del Monte Corporation, which now operates the former holdings of the UFCO.

By the 1960s the remnants of the Mayan people in Guatemala were reduced to conditions that resembled slave labor. Malnutrition claimed more than half the children before they reached 5 years of age; the leading cause of death was gastroenteritis, a disease from pesticides sprayed directly upon the people from planes; thousands were living in cardboard or tin houses with no running water or electricity; and men worked on coffee plantations for less than 50 cents a day. As people sought reform of their economic and living conditions, they were labeled communists not only by their own government but also by the U.S. The Guatemalan government with U.S. Special Forces advisors stationed in Panama set out on a program to eradicate all civil and political unrest through death squads, mass killings, and torture (Galeano, 1969; Langguth, 1978; Melville & Melville, 1971).

During the 1980s President Ronald Reagan's administration perpetuated this violent handling of supposed threats in Latin America, sending millions of dollars in military aid in support of right-wing governments in Central America, which led to continued atrocities that cost the untold lives of thousands of people in the region. Meanwhile, the American people have no

idea that their tax dollars have been used to train right-wing military officers, death squads, and dictators in American military schools and that these people have lived on CIA payrolls without any accountability to the American public.

El Salvador. U.S. support for right-wing dictators in El Salvador and Nicaragua under the Reagan and Bush administrations was also couched under the continuous slogan of communist infiltration and Soviet takeover of Latin America. Reagan waged war against a peasant population in El Salvador that killed thousands of people and displaced thousands more because he believed in the old domino theory that if Central America fell to the communists, then eventually so would all of the Western Hemisphere, including the U.S. El Salvador had always been controlled by one dictator after another and by 14 coffee and industrial families. A history of starvation and malnutrition, living in misery, social injustice, and educational and job opportunities given to the same privileged group left the frustrated Salvadoran people to public protest and rejection of a despotic government. The government's response, with the support of American aid over the years, has been systematic repression by security forces. American aid allocated for El Salvador was always used to train the military and the police and later to train death squads that killed tens of thousands of people (Dunkerley, 1982; McClintock, 1985).

In 1982 El Salvador's Atlacatl Battalion trained by U.S. Special Forces massacred nearly 1,000 people in the village of El Mozote, killing mostly women, children, and old men (Bonner, 1984; Danner, 1993, 1994). The *New York Times* (Jan. 11, 1982, p. 3) published interviews of Salvadorean army deserters who had been present during various torture sessions of teenagers by the

U.S. Special Forces advisors. As human rights organizations denounced the U.S. and El Salvadorean governments, President Reagan told Congress that the human rights organizations had joined the communists (Amnesty International, 1984; Arnson, 1993). Then, in 1988 the American Civil Liberties pressured the FBI to investigate the kidnapping, interrogation, and rape of a Salvadorean woman named Yaniri Corea in Los Angeles by a Salvadorean death squad right outside the Los Angeles office of the Committee in Solidarity with the People of El Salvador (CISPES), a grassroots labor and immigrant organization that fights for the rights of immigrants from Central America and is against neoliberal policies like the U.S.–Central American Free Trade Agreement (CAFTA), which supports corporate controlled globalization that does not guarantee any rights of the workers in Central America and causes the loss of thousands of jobs in the U.S. (like NAFTA, this agreement has cost 879,280 jobs in the U.S. in 2002 alone).

Nicaragua. The story of U.S. involvement in Nicaragua is no different. Starting in 1927, President Calvin Coolidge sent the U.S. Marines into Nicaragua to protect American corporate interests. By the 1980s President Ronald Reagan had invested millions of American tax dollars to topple the Sandinista government that had ousted the Somoza dynasty, which had raped and pillaged its own country. The *New York Times* (July 22, 1979) claimed that when Somoza landed in Miami, he was worth about $900 million, whereas the average Nicaraguan earned less than $300 a year. President Reagan authorized the CIA to conduct terrorist attacks upon the Nicaraguan economy, mine the Nicaraguan harbor, and use a paramilitary army called Contras in a guerrilla war, ultimately terrorizing the countryside, kill-

ing, and disrupting Nicaragua's infrastructure (Bradford, 1987; Cockburn, 1987). On October 5, 1986, Eugene Hasanfus, flying a plane carrying weapons and other lethal supplies, was shot down in Nicaragua. The Reagan administration denied Hasanfus worked for the CIA, but 12 days later Congress approved $100 million to the Contra army to wage war in Nicaragua and then in 1987 ceased all military aid when Oliver North of the National Security Council was discovered supplying the Contras through unofficial sources (Colhoun, 2003; Simpson, 2003; U.S. Congress, House Committee on Foreign Affairs, Subcommittee on Western Hemisphere Affairs, 1987).

As right-wing Central American dictators gained political refuge in the U.S., the thousands of poor people seeking political asylum from the oppressive dictators were blocked from entering the country legally. In response many churches in the Sanctuary Movement, started by John Fife at the Southside Presbyterian Church in Tucson, Arizona, assisted refugees to cross the borders illegally and transported them throughout the U.S. in defiance of the law (Gage, 2002; Silverstein, 2004). Relatively few Americans are aware of our ugly past in Latin America. A few groups have, like the Sanctuary Movement, taken a stand to defend the rights of Latinos who have fled to this country. Among them, some 300 churches across the U.S. during the 1980s became public sanctuaries for refuges from Central Americans fleeing death squads and oppression. The Sanctuary Movement pressed the U.S. government, which supported the oppressive regimes in Central America, to reform its foreign policies and stop blocking political asylum. By 1992 Rigoberta Menchú Tum, a Guatemalan woman, had published her accounts of the atrocities of the Guatemalan army against the people and was then forced to flee to Mexico. International actors acknowledged her work and awarded her the 1992 Nobel Peace Prize. Nevertheless, her cry for awareness and help was not taken as seriously in the region itself, for no reform action had been taken in her homeland and she still had to remain in hiding.

American intervention in Latin America has been a policy of "keeping the subordinates in line" by using oppressive neofascist regimes that terrorize its people so the U.S. can obtain a favorable investment climate. It has caused oppression and torture in Latin America. The result of this state terror has sent thousands of peasants into the U.S. to become the new cheap labor force. These Latin American immigrants are no different than the millions of European immigrants who ran to escape the terror of their own regimes. Yet the American public refuses to see itself in the faces of the Latin American immigrants who came just as many others have come to this nation. Time and assimilation will absorb the Latin American population, as they have done all the other groups in the U.S.

References

Amnesty International. (1984). *Torture in the Eighties: An Amnesty International Report*. London: Amnesty International Publications.

Andreas, Peter. (1998). The US Immigration Control Offensive: Constructing an Image of Order on the Southwest Border. In Marcelo M. Suárez-Orozco (Ed.), *Crossings: Mexican Immigration in Interdisciplinary Perspectives*. Cambridge, MA: Harvard University Press.

Arnson, Cynthia J. (1993). *Crossroads: Congress, the President, and Central America, 1976–1993* (2nd ed.). University Park: Pennsylvania State University Press.

Bigelow, Bill, & Peterson, Bob. (2002). *Rethinking Globalization: Teaching for Justice in an Unjust World*. Milwaukee: Rethinking Schools Press.

Blum, William. (1995). *Killing Hope: U.S. Military and CIA Interventions since World War II*. Monroe, ME: Common Courage Press.

Bonner, Raymond. (1984). *Weakness and Deceit: U.S. Policy and El Salvador*. New York: Times Books.

Boot, Max. (2002). *The Savage Wars of Peace—Small Wars and the Rise of American Power*. New York: Basic Books.

Bradford, Burns E. (1987). *At War in Nicaragua: The Reagan Doctrine and the Politics of Nostalgia*. New York: Harper & Row.

Chavez, Leo. (1998). *Shadowed Lives: Undocumented Immigrants in American Society* (2nd ed.). Fort Worth, TX: Harcourt Brace.

Cockburn, Leslie. (1987). *Out of Control: The Story of the Reagan Administration's Secret War in Nicaragua, the Illegal Arms Pipeline, and the Contra Drug Connection*. New York: Atlantic Monthly Press.

Colhoun, Jack. (2003). The Family That Preys Together. In Ellen Ray & William H. Schaap (Eds.), *Covert Action: The Roots of Terrorism*. Melbourne: Ocean Press.

Cook, Blanche Wiesen. (1981). *The Declassified Eisenhower*. New York: Doubleday & Co.

Danner, Mark. (1993). The Truth about El Mozote. *New Yorker*. December 6.

Danner, Mark. (1994). *The Massacre at El Mozote: A Parable of the Cold War*. New York: Vintage Books.

Dosal, Paul J. (1993). *Doing Business with the Dictators: A Political History of United Fruit Company in Guatemala, 1899–1944*. Wilmington, DE: SR Books.

Dunkerley, James. (1982). *The Long War: Dictatorship and Revolution in El Salvador*. London: Zed Books.

Finckenauer, James O. (1998). *Russian Mafia in America: Immigration, Culture, and Crime*. Boston: Northeastern University Press.

Gage, Julienne. (2002). Saints at the Border: A Salvadoran Refugee Shares Her Memories of the Sanctuary Movement. *Tucson Weekly*, March 21. Available: http://www.tucson weekly.com/gbase/Currents/Content?/oid= oid%3A45173.

Galeano, Eduardo. (1969). *Guatemala: An Occupied Country*. Trans. Cedric Belfrage. New York: Monthly Review Press.

Kepner, Charles David. (1967). *The Banana Empire: A Case Study of Economic Imperialism*. New York: Russell & Russell.

La Feber, Walter. (1993). *Inevitable Revolutions: The United States in Central America*. New York: W. W. Norton.

Langguth, A. J. (1978). *Hidden Terrors*. New York: Pantheon Books.

McClintock, Michael. (1985). *The American Connection: State Terror and Popular Resistance in El Salvador*. London: Zed Books.

Melville, Thomas, & Melville, Marjorie. (1971). *Guatemala: Another Vietnam?* Harmondsworth, UK: Penguin.

Perkins, Dexter. (1965). *The Monroe Doctrine, 1826–1867*. Gloucester, MA: P. Smith Publishers.

Silverstein, Evan. (2004). Sonoran Samaritans: Arizona Presbyterians Patrol Desert to Keep Migrants Alive. *Presbyterian News Service*, June 18. Available: http://www.pcusa.org/pcnews/2004/04295.htm.

Simpson, Christopher. (2003). The Use of Counterterrorism. In Ellen Ray & William H. Schaap (Eds.), *Covert Action: the Roots of Terrorism*. Melbourne: Ocean Press.

Smith, James P., & Edmonston, Barry (Eds.). (1997). *The New Americans: Economic, Demographic, and Fiscal Effects on Immigration*. Washington, DC: National Research Council, National Academy Press.

Smith, Peter H. (1996). *Talons of the Eagle—Dynamics of U.S.–Latin American Relations*. New York: Oxford University Press.

Soto, Lourdes Diaz. (2002). Introduction: The Political, the Dialogue, and the Critical. In Lourdes Diaz Soto (Ed.), *Making a Difference in the Lives of Bilingual/Bicultural Children*. New York: Peter Lang.

U.S. Congress, House Committee on Foreign Affairs, Subcommittee on Western Hemisphere Affairs. (1987). *The Downing of a United States Plane in Nicaragua and United States Involvement in the Contra War: Hearing before the Subcommittee on Western Hemisphere Affairs of the Committee on Foreign Affairs, House of Representatives, Ninety-ninth Congress, Second Session, October 15, 1986*. Washington, DC: U.S. Government Printing Office (microfiche no. 1017-A, 1017-B, Gov. doc. no. Y4.F76/1:N51/24).

Zinn, Howard. (2003). *A People's History of the United States, 1492–Present*. New York: HarperPerennial.

Recommended Reading

Bigelow, Bill, & Peterson, Bob. (2002). *Rethinking Globalization: Teaching for Justice in an Unjust World*. Milwaukee: Rethinking Schools Press.

Bouvier, Virginia M. (Ed.). (2002). *The Globalization of U.S.–Latin American Relations Democracy, Intervention and Human Rights*. Westport, CT: Praeger.

Castro, Fidel. (2000). *Capitalism in Crisis: Globalization and the New World Order*. Melbourne: Ocean Press.

Castro, Fidel. (2002). *War, Racism and Economic Injustice: The Global Ravages of Capitalism*. Melbourne: Ocean Press.

Chomsky, Noam, & Edwards, Herman. (1979). *The Washington Connection and Third World Fascism*. Boston: South End Press.

Chomsky, Noam. (1999). *Latin America: From Colonization to Globalization*. Melbourne: Ocean Press.

Danner, Mark. (1994). *The Massacre at El Mozote: A Parable of the Cold War*. New York: Vintage Books.

Pearce, Jenny. (1982). *Under the Eagle: U.S. Intervention in Central America and the Caribbean*. Boston: South End Press.

Ray, Ellen, & Schapp, William H. (Eds.). (2003). *Covert Action: The Roots of Terrorism*. Melbourne: Ocean Press.

Schoultz, Lars. (1987). *National Security and United States Policy toward Latin America*. Princeton, NJ: Princeton University Press.

Haroon Kharem and Sara Lippi

LATINO IDENTITY

The label "Hispanic" is an official category of ethnic identification that has been equally assigned to populations that have lived here for centuries and to newcomers from Spain, Latin America, and the Caribbean. Most supposedly Hispanic people feel uneasy under this Hispanic identity label, and many outrightly reject it, except as it applies to those individuals directly descendant from Spain. Both in the official and the mainstream discourse, "Hispanic" is a name applied to "the other," to those different from the "norm" represented by the Euro-American.

Another label also applied to so-called Hispanics is that of "minority," which is in itself disempowering and facilitates disingenuous people to stereotype and discriminate against Hispanics. In the U.S., being identified as Hispanic or Latino/a makes one vulnerable to discrimination, low expectations, and other mistreatments. This label has attached to it a certain index of vulnerability. Of course, not everybody has the same index of vulnerability. There are some Latinos/as whose vulnerability is exponentially increased as other factors besides race and ethnicity, combined or individually, become visible aspects of their identity. The factors are often gender, Spanish as the first language, Spanish accent in English, socioeconomic status, and reputation of the country of origin, among others. These factors can become visible aspects of Latino/a identity.

In some schools, we often hear school personnel referring to "Hispanic" students as "the bilingual kids," not as assets, but as sources of problem and concern. Individuals are all put into the same box regardless of their degree of bilingualism or their mastery of Standard English. There is little recognition of the diversity of "Hispanics" in educational level, socioeconomic status, country of origin, race, and other areas. However, a pattern is always present: the lighter their skin color, the less vulnerable Hispanic students are to being segregated within the school and in society at large. Lighter-skinned students have a greater possibility of being assimilated into the school culture, which tends to be that of white middle-class students and teachers.

Latino/a as a Pan-Ethnic Identity

The term *Latino/a* is increasingly used, instead of "Hispanic," by those whose roots are in Latin America, but it is usually accompanied by a more specific country identifier such as Dominican Latino or Venezuelan Latina. This act of renaming ourselves can be considered a way of resisting the official "Hispanic" label, although it does not in itself assure better treatment. Latino/a has become a pan-ethnic identity, connected but not strictly defined by home language (mostly Spanish), religion (mostly Catholic), a perceived socioeconomic position labeled third world, and shared experiences of immigration, discrimination, and colonization. This pan-ethnic identity can be better characterized using a more relational notion of identity.

Reframing Latino/a Identity

Defining Latino/a identity involves revising the characteristics imposed by adopting other characteristics Latinos/as themselves feel best describe them. It also involves reframing identity within another philosophical and conceptual framework. The self-contained identity and selfhood of the conventional psychology is based on the idea that the locus of control for defining and determining identity of a given person resides totally inside that person. Therefore, the ideal state of identity development occurs when the self shows integration, autonomy, coherence, and consistency. Accordingly, the approach to characterize one's own identity is through self-reflection, which often proves painful and elusive. It is painful because such a person may find it difficult to approach the ideals of self-identity. It is elusive, because it makes people believe that the locus of control resides inside themselves, when in reality that identity has been imposed and then internalized.

In contrast to the conventional individual-centered identity is a proposed *dialogical identity*. From the dialogical perspective, identity is conceived as socially constructed while individuals are engaged in their daily activities and interactions. Dialogical identity is relational, since it involves the notion of otherness as a defining characteristic, and not merely as a dim background against which a given individual operates. The relational character of identity is based on the notion that human beings are interdependent and interactive; that is, they are socially defined and constituted, and in continual change, hopefully for the better. Thus, identity is constructed in the boundary between the self and the other, in the dynamics of relations among people, not in the interior of their minds. Relations of power among people affects the way identity is constructed and reconstructed in each specific context. A group, community, or individuals are able to reach an authentic self-identity when they are able to voice their particular specificities on an equal footing with others able and willing to recognize those particular specificities. The possibility of co-constructing one's identity is the most distinctive meaning of dialogical identity.

Pan-ethnic Latino/a identity is really community based. It embodies the widely recognized commitment made by many Latinos and Latinas to give back to their re-spective communities. It also conveys the image of many Latino groups and communities who are formed because the members feel they fit in and can identify with the community. Being identified with the Latino community entails active participation in defining, negotiating, and enhancing the opportunities of life improvement for all Latinos despite their diversity in ethnicities, races, origins, and socioeconomic situations.

In *Latinos Unidos,* Trueba (1999) brings up the notion of *multiple identities* and multiple layers of our personality as an adapting mechanism while Latinos/as engage in negotiating their identities within the Latino community and also with people from other cultures, languages, and social strata. De Peuter (1998), based on the dialogical perspective, characterizes identity as dynamic and fluctuating between unity and fragmentation, synthesis and dispersion, coherence and incoherence, a kind of *transient identity*. Trueba and de Peuter are not referring to an undeveloped or abnormal identity. Both characterize identity from perspectives that contrast with the individualist and static notion of identity in conventional psychology. According to the explanation of transient identity, the common experiences of Latinos/as that require adaptation, adjustment, change, and negotiation of identity are actually the norm, not the abnormality. Of course, such transient identity is not exclusive to Latinos/as.

The Power of Communion

Communion among Latinos/as is often part of the process of cultural identification. The power emerges as stories of exclusion, misrepresentation, and mistreatment are shared and perceived as similar, despite the particular specificities of each person's situation. Power also emerges as Latinos/as share stories of reliance, courage, and success, which confirms the now famous lemma "*Sí se puede.*" As stories are told, the listeners and readers start connecting deeply and intensively with the teller. Indeed, this connection is a communion experienced with the whole being: cognition, affection, and hope.

The coming together of Latino communities, despite their great diversity of ethnicities, social strata, and race, facilitates both their empowerment and their healing the pain of the wounds of injustice. One can experience great relief in realizing that many of the problems and obstacles one has faced are not just one's own fault. In addition, a feeling of solidarity is a source of strength that helps many to move on with their lives. Similarly, diversity is itself a source of strength inasmuch as Latinos/as can see quite easily the threads that connect their shared stories, as well as their extraordinary resilience to extremely harsh conditions.

Another process that is part of this Latino/a communion is the construction of a collective interpretive discourse about specific Latino issues, which can be a venue for collective action toward achieving the Latino community's goals of fairer treatment and participation. Throughout history it has been repeatedly demonstrated, especially concerning Latino causes, that only through collective action are Latinos/as able to resist domination and segregation and improve their opportunities and participation in obtaining social goods.

Some authors (e.g., Trueba, 2002) have pointed out the strengths and assets of the Latino community, such as solidarity, community orientation, and resilience, which Trueba (2002) calls a "new cultural capital." In the same vein Moll (1992) identified and promote "funds of knowledge," the notion that some Latino communities organize and use as strategy for survival, often when their material resources are very limited. The idea is that the abilities, skills, and knowledge of members of a given community are put to the service of other members of the same community. Eventually every family gives and receives some type of service and help at their most basic level of need. Thus, the whole community or neighborhood becomes united and enabled to overcome critical harsh conditions. This is a clear example of community agency and self-empowerment.

Final Remarks

Latino/a identity is not precisely a fixed set of prototypical characteristics applied to a variety of groups united by certain cultural tools and symbols such as language. Latino identity involves, most of all, the stories of discrimination, segregation, and colonization that "weave" many Latinos/as together as a community. The uniqueness of this identity is not only the diversity within the Latino community but also the ongoing identity reinterpretation and redefinition as it is negotiated in dialogue with other members of the same culture and those of other cultures in ever-changing contexts and power relations.

Language is just a means to express the characteristics of one's identity; it is part of its construction, definition (criteria of inclusion and exclusion), and naming. The label "Hispanic" is a very good example of how language embodies the power that some people hold to name and characterize others according to their own worldview, not that of those named. Although Latinos/as are rapidly moving to claim the power to name themselves, their identity is in continual negotiation within the Latino community, with other minority groups, and especially with the dominant group. These negotiations often include educating people to understand what it means and how costly it is to be Latino/a in the U.S.

Although it may sound too pessimistic, Latino/a identity makes persons extremely vulnerable. Yet, awakening to this vulnerability and to the injustice it represents at the same time propels communion with other Latinos/as through cultural identification, commitment to working together for mutual betterment, and most of all to foster pride in their heritage, culture, and language. Many Latino/a scholars who have written extensively on these issues, especially on Latino identity, call on all Latinos/as to move from the rhetoric of oppression to the rhetoric of strength, possibility, and dignity. But most of all, the call should move us from the realm of discourse to unite and take action for a real improvement of educational and job opportunities, as well as to achieve the quality of life in what should be a genuine democratic, just, and peaceful society for all its members. Communion through the building of Latino/a identity is a powerful stepping stone in that pursuit.

References

De Peuter, J. (1998). The dialogics of narrative identity. In M. M. Bell & M. Gardiner (Eds.), *Bakhtin and the Human Sciences: No Last Words* (pp. 31–48). London: Thousand Oaks, CA: Sage.

Moll, L. C. (1992). Bilingual Classroom Studies and Community Analysis. *Educational Researcher* 21(2), 20–24.

Trueba, E. T. (1999). *Latinos Unidos: From Cultural Diversity to the Politics of Solidarity*. Lanham, MD: Rowman & Littlefield.

Trueba, H. T. (2002). Multiple Ethnic, Racial and Cultural Identities in Action: From Marginality to New Cultural Capital and Modern Society. *Journal of Latinos and Education* 1(1), 7–28.

Recommended Reading

Bruner, J. (1994.). Life as Narrative. In A. H. Dyson & C. Genishi (Eds.), *The Need for Story: Cultural Diversity in Classroom and Community*. Urbana, IL: National Council of Teachers of English.

Freire, P. (1992). *Pedagogy of the Oppressed*. New York: Continuum.

Freire, P. (1994). *Pedagogy of Hope*. New York: Continuum.

Genishi, C., & Dyson, A. H. (1994). Conclusion: Fulfilling the Need for Story. In A. H. Dyson & C. Genishi (Eds.), *The Need for Story: Cultural Diversity in Classroom and Community*. Urbana, IL: National Council of Teachers of English.

Torres, M. N. (2004). To the Margins and Back: The High Cost of Being *Latina* in "America." *Journal of Latinos and Education* 3(2), 123–141.

Myriam N. Torres

LATINO STUDENTS IN ADVANCED SPANISH CLASSROOMS

The recent population shift in the U.S. has involved a widespread increase in the number of students with diverse ethnic, cultural and linguistic backgrounds. The same can be said of the population of foreign language (FL) classrooms, where the subject taught by native and non-native instructors may also be the language of students from homes where languages other than English are spoken, or who have had in-depth exposure to another language— "heritage language" (HL) learners (Campbell, 1996). For the most part, FL courses are designed for monolingual speakers of English with little or no knowledge about the language or the people and the cultures involved (Campbell & Peyton, 1998), even in the case of less commonly taught language courses attended by a larger numbers of heritage learners (Brecht & Ingold, 1998). Lower-level FL courses in medium and large institutions are usually taught by teaching assistants (TAs), lecturers, or adjunct faculty. Courses at more advanced levels are generally conducted by tenure-track or tenured faculty members. In contrast to the lower-level classes, where TAs and other instructors generally work under the supervision of a language program coordinator, advanced-level classes tend to fall under the responsibility of the faculty member who has designed or has been asked to teach the course.

Research has already demonstrated that HL learners are different from the traditional FL student, especially with regard to their sociolinguistic background (Roca & Gutiérrez, 2000; Lynch, 2003). It is thus essential to explore the uniqueness of Latino learners in order to understand their interaction with native and non-native instructors in the advanced Spanish classroom. The social and cultural background of Latino learners may involve numerous questions: How well established is the student's heritage community? How strong is the contact between the heritage community and its country or countries of origin? What are the perceptions toward the specific ethnic group speaking the heritage language? What attitudes are there about particular dialects of the heritage language?

It is difficult to "match" heritage speakers' individual language abilities in every advanced Spanish course or to tailor courses to serve HL learners' needs, especially when some basic questions have not been answered. For example, it is crucial that teachers know how different language skills may transfer to ensure that pedagogical practices will suit the objectives of a course for such diverse group of students. Also, a heritage learner may be fluent in the prestige variety or in the colloquial (and often stigmatized) variety of the target language; he or she may be English-dominant with or without good academic skills; he or she may be a recent immigrant or may be a U.S.-born second- or third-generation bilingual (Valdés, 1997). Some students may resist enrolling in an academic course on their heritage language after having internalized that their language variety is defective andneeds to be "corrected." Other students are mostly receptive bilinguals conditioned not to "produce" anything in the target language or who may switch languages during a conversation.

In colleges and universities, the use of linguistic and cultural registers is compounded by the diverse backgrounds of instructors and students. Newly arrived learners generally have high levels of linguistic and cultural competency in Spanish, but they may lack second- and third-generation learners' familiarity with the linguistic and cultural characteristics of both English and the new HL community where they may have settled. Likewise, non-native instructors often know the language and how to talk about it, whereas native instructors often have a less-structured knowledge of their own language but are more familiar with the target culture(s). Another group of instructors consists of HL learners enrolled as graduate students of their own language. These teachers demonstrate linguistic and cultural competency in both English and the target language, but they may have difficulties with regard to the spoken and written variety they use in instruction.

An ongoing discussion about the perceived need to teach an educated, standard variety of the target language (Politzer, 1993), and about the notion of "standard variety" itself (Villa, 1996, 2002, 2004), affects linguistic interaction not only in bilingual settings but also in advanced Spanish classrooms. In this context, native and non-native teachers—usually speakers of a prestige variety with exposure to other varieties in their professional and social communities—have to maintain a careful balance between the needs and interests of multiple constituents: (1) monolingual Anglophone students who either have spent periods of time in a Spanish-speaking country where their education is (often) provided through a prestige variety of the target language or who have developed a close contact with heritage communities in this country; (2) newly arrived students, generally educated in what is considered the prestige variety in their country of origin; and (3) HL students with a wide range of attitudes toward the standard variety used in the textbook and other course materials and spoken in the classroom.

Affective dimensions of the relationship between HL learners and FL teachers should be viewed as interrelated. Furthermore, the exposure to and the interaction between the variety of backgrounds, motivations, attitudes, and beliefs that can be found in any FL classroom need to be considered. Besides general variables such as attitudes, anxiety, self-confidence, language aptitude, learning strategies, and measures of achievement in the language, HL learners may have different reasons for studying Spanish at an advanced level, among these:

- To seek greater understanding of their culture or seek to connect with members of their family (Mazzocco, 1996)
- To reinforce the development of their own identity as members of a group with specific cultural characteristics (Benjamin, 1997)
- To fulfill a foreign language requirement (Teschner, 1983)
- To take advantage of the demand for graduates with professional-level skills in FL (Brecht & Ingold, 1998)

HL students may have to address unreasonable expectations concerning their knowledge of the heritage language and their involvement in classroom pedagogic interaction. HL learners may display nega-

tive reactions to corrections in the classroom, particularly (1) when they make mistakes in their use of the standard variety usually required in a formal academic context, and (2) when they use certain lexical or syntactic forms common in their heritage community. In both cases, HL learners may perceive these situations as signs of disrespect or disregard for their cultural identity.

Another important affective dimension has to do with the interaction between monolingual Anglophone students and heritage students, especially in advanced-level Spanish courses. The former group tends to feel intimidated by the HL students' more native-like knowledge of the target language. Also, the Anglophone students may find that native instructors sometimes show some degree of favoritism toward HL learners, even if they differ culturally. HL students may feel that monolingual Anglophone students have a better grasp of standard grammatical structures of the Spanish language and a wider knowledge of specialized terminology. In other words, HL learners' level of self-esteem can be affected by apparent gaps in their formal knowledge of Spanish.

The three main components of this analysis of Spanish teacher–HL learner interaction—social and cultural background, pedagogical conditions, and affective dimensions—cannot be addressed separately; rather, they should be considered as interrelated factors within a dynamic community with its own culture defined by multiple identities, roles, attitudes, beliefs, and behaviors. Some recent recommendations and initiatives have captured the significance of such factors at a pedagogical and an administrative level. With regard to the pedagogical interaction between the classroom participants, the first major recommendation refers to the advantages that Spanish instructors may find in establishing connections with their students' heritage cultures and dialect varieties (Romero, 2000). Respect for and interest in the language and cultural experiences that students bring to the classroom may have a positive effect on the overall levels of motivation and attitudes among participants. Spanish teachers are also urged to get to know their students in terms of not only their linguistic and intellectual abilities but also their personal and academic interests (Ariza, 1998). This recommendation might even involve a paradigm shift from traditional FL instruction in which students would bring to class what they need to drive the curriculum, so that both curriculum and classroom interaction become more intrinsically interesting and personally relevant to heritage students (Romero, 2000). Keeping in mind the difficulties involved in such action, especially in institutions with many teachers or students, a possible pedagogical compromise could be to incorporate multicultural resources into the instruction (Rodríguez Pino, 1997). These resources could come from the different areas where the target language is spoken, including the heritage community. Students could be exposed to a range of materials so they could develop their receptive and productive skills while at the same time learning to appreciate some of the essential linguistic characteristics of different varieties. Students could also be asked to participate in the collection of information about their communities beyond what their textbook may offer. This process could involve the use of different ethnographic techniques, such as the development of unstructured and semi-structured interviews by which students could gather data on particular linguistic, social, cultural, historical, and political topics.

Another major recommendation for teaching HL students in advanced Spanish classrooms is to use the linguistic diversity of the participants as a learning tool for both teachers and students (Draper & Hicks, 2000). As Villa points out in his paper on varieties of Spanish (1996), the argument would now relate to the more specific question, What are the goals of the instructor or the academic institution with regard to mastery of the written language? since the issue of imposing any spoken variety is abandoned (p. 198). Further consideration should be given to the use of codeswitching in the Spanish classroom, especially in advanced-level courses where proficiency in both target and native language may be more balanced. Riegelhaupt (2000) reviews some possibilities for codeswitching as a pedagogical strategy in bilingual methodology. These include (1) presenting content in one language and then translating the material into the other language, (2) specifying one language for a given subject, and (3) using the two languages interchangeably.

A recent initiative in the field of Spanish for native speakers (SNS) has been the publication of a monograph by the American Association of Teachers of Spanish and Portuguese (AATSP, 2000) intended to assist teachers with the needs of HL speakers of Spanish who may enroll in their classes. This volume brings together several researchers in the field of Spanish language instruction in order to review its history and to examine some of the most current initiatives and considerations in areas like varieties of Spanish spoken in the U.S., teacher and student motivation, placement tests, assessment of linguistic skills, and instructional materials (see also Valdés, Lozano, & García-Moya, 1981; Merino, Trueba, & Samaniego, 1993; Colombi & Alarcón, 1997; Roca & Colombi, 2003; Fairclough, 2004).

At the administrative level, the goals of any Spanish program with a significant population of heritage learners need to be determined and the professional and material resources to achieve these goals selected. Recent large-scale projects carried out by teams of researchers, teachers, and administrators have begun to lay the foundations for programs specifically designed to prepare FL teachers to work more effectively with HL learners. For example, the Hunter College Project (Webb & Miller, 2000) gathered successful teaching practices and materials from many teachers who worked with HL learners. These materials were then examined and tested by a number of specialists in assessment, linguistics, and sociolinguistics. This project resulted in numerous recommendations concerning instructional practices, student attitudes toward FL learning, teacher knowledge and beliefs, and assessment and standards for HL learners. In addition, the Hunter College Project sought to establish a model for teacher education based on collaboration and practice, which eventually became a methods course specifically designed for the teaching of HL learners. The new course allows FL teachers to familiarize themselves with rather complex theoretical notions such as language use and variety, bilingualism, and language attitudes. At the same time, teachers have the opportunity not only to examine these notions within the classroom context but also

to come to their own understanding of issues identified by others and to problematize the assumptions underlying such identification. By allowing participants to reframe questions, to offer new definitions, and to produce a set of principles and goals to guide their practice, project leaders invited teachers to "own" both the challenges and the solutions. (Valdés, 2000, p. 246)

References

Ariza, E. (1998). Role Reversal: The Problems of a Spanish-Speaking Anglo Teaching Spanish to English Dominant Puerto Rican Children. *Foreign Language Annals* 31, 431–436.

American Association of Teachers of Spanish and Portuguese (AATSP). (2000). *Spanish for Native Speakers*. Professional Development Series Handbook for Teachers K–16. Fort Worth, TX: Harcourt College Publishers.

Benjamin, R. (1997). What Do Our Students Want? Some Reflections on Teaching Spanish as an Academic Subject to Bilingual Students. *ADFL Bulletin* 29(1), 44–47.

Brecht, R., & Ingold, C. (1998). Tapping a National Resource: Heritage Languages in the United States. ERIC Document No. EDO-FL-98–12.

Campbell, R. (1996). New Learners and New Environments: Challenges and Opportunities. In R. C. Lafayette (Ed.), *National Standards: A Catalyst for Reform* (pp. 97–117). Lincolnwood, IL: National Textbook Company.

Campbell, R., & Peyton, J. (1998). Heritage Language Students: A Valuable Language Resource. *The ERIC Review* 6(1), 38–39.

Colombi, M., & Alarcón, F. (Eds.). (1997). *La enseñanza del español a hispanohablantes: Praxis y teoría*. Boston: Houghton Mifflin.

Draper, J., & Hicks, J. (2000). Where We've Been; What We've Learned. In J. Webb & B. Miller (Eds.), *Teaching Heritage Language Learners: Voices from the Classroom.* (pp. 15–35). Yonkers, NY: ACTFL.

Fairclough, M. (2004). *Applied Sociolinguistics: U.S. Spanish and Heritage Language Education*. Madrid: Iberoamericana.

Lynch, A. (2003). Toward a Theory of Heritage Language Acquisition: Spanish in the United States. In A. Roca & M. Colombi (Eds.), *Mi lengua: Spanish as a Heritage Language in the United States* (pp. 25–50). Washington, DC: Georgetown University Press.

Mazzocco, E. (1996). The Heritage versus the Non-heritage Language Learner: The Five

College Self-Instructional Language Program Solutions to the Problem of Separation or Unification. *ADFL Bulletin* 28(1), 20–24.

Merino, B., Trueba, H., & Samaniego, F. (Eds.). (1993). *Language and Culture in Learning: Teaching Spanish to Native Speakers of Spanish.* London: Falmer Press.

Politzer, R. (1993). A Researcher's Reflections on Bridging Dialect and Second Language Learning: Discussion of Problems and Solutions. In B. Merino, H. Trueba, & F. Samaniego (Eds.), *Language and Culture in Learning: Teaching Spanish to Native Speakers of Spanish.* (pp. 45–57). London: Falmer.

Riegelhaupt, F. (2000). Codeswitching and Language Use in the Classroom. In A. Roca (Ed.), *Research on Spanish in the U.S.:* (pp. 204–217). Summerville, MA: Cascadilla Press.

Roca, A., & Colombi, M. C. (Eds.). (2003). *Mi lengua: Spanish as a Heritage Language in the United States.* Washington, DC: Georgetown University Press.

Roca, A., & Gutiérrez, J. (2000). Sociolinguistic Considerations. In American Association of Teachers of Spanish and Portuguese, *Spanish for Native Speakers.* (pp. 21–28). Professional Development Series Handbook for Teachers K–16. Fort Worth, TX: Harcourt College Publishers.

Rodriguez Pino, C. (1997). Teaching Spanish to Native Speakers: A New Perspective in the 1990s. *ERIC/CLL News Bulletin* 21 (1). Washington, DC: ERIC Clearinghouse for Language and Linguistics.

Romero, M. (2000). Instructional Practice in Heritage Language Classrooms. In J. Webb & B. Miller (Eds.), *Teaching Heritage Language Learners: Voices from the Classroom* (pp. 135–158). Yonkers, NY: ACTFL.

Teschner, R. (1983). Spanish Placement for Native Speakers, Nonnative Speakers, and Others. *ADFL Bulletin* 14 (3), 37–42.

Valdés, G. (1997). The Teaching of Spanish to Bilingual Spanish-Speaking Students: Outstanding Issues and Unanswered Questions. In M. Colombi & F. Alarcón (Eds.), *La en-*señanza del español a hispanohablantes (pp. 8–44). Boston: Houghton Mifflin.

Valdés, G. (2000). The ACTFL–Hunter College FIPSE Project and its Contributions to the Profession. In J. Webb & B. Miller (Eds.), *Teaching Heritage Language Learners: Voices from the Classroom.* (pp. 235–251). Yonkers, NY: ACTFL.

Valdés, G., Lozano, A., & García-Moya, R. (Eds.). (1981). *Teaching Spanish to the Hispanic Bilingual: Issues, Aims, and Methods.* New York: Teachers College Press.

Villa, D. (1996). Choosing a "Standard" Variety of Spanish for the Instruction of Native Spanish Speakers in the U.S. *Foreign Language Annals* 29 (2), 191–200.

Villa, D. (2002). The Sanitizing of U.S. Spanish in Academia. *Foreign Language Annals* 35 (2), 222–230.

Villa, D. (2004). Heritage Language Speakers and Upper-Division Language Instruction: Findings from a Spanish Linguistics Program. In H. Byrnes & H. Maxim (Eds.), *Advanced Foreign Language Learning: A Challenge to College Programs.* (pp. 88–98). Boston: Heinle & Heinle.

Webb, J., & Miller, B. (Eds.). (2000). *Teaching Heritage Language Learners: Voices from the Classroom.* Yonkers, NY: ACTFL.

Recommended Reading

Valdés, G., Lozano, A., & García-Moya, R. (Eds.). (1981). *Teaching Spanish to the Hispanic Bilingual: Issues, Aims, and Methods.* New York: Teachers College Press.

Manel Lacorte and Evelyn Canabal

LATINO STUDENTS STUDYING THEIR OWN HISTORY

Our cultural, human roots that we pass on to children are no longer neatly contained within borders. According to Clandinin and Connelly (1996), stories are the nearest we can get to experience, as we tell of our experiences. They say that the act of our telling our stories seems "inextricably linked with the act of making meaning, an inevitable part of life in a... postmodern world" and only becomes problematic "when its influence on thinking and perception goes unnoticed" or is ignored (Goldstein, 1997, p. 147). Brady (1995) points out that in identifying a politics of difference and identity, literacy is a central mechanism for discussing power, subjectivity, history, and experience. It becomes a way to translate these issues of politics into pedagogy.

I have used problem-posing activities based on Latino children's literature in teacher education classes. Several of my student teachers are adapting the activities for use with their students in the field. This entry is about what students' responses have been.

After going through a series of activities relating to family history, using the storybooks *Diego, Frida, El Barrio, I Love Saturdays y domingos*, a group of students wrote reflections in their journals. One excerpt is this:

When I think of my ethnic identity, honestly I think of so many things I don't know where to start. My family come from all over the place actually, so I don't really know which ethnic group I identify myself with most. My mother is American by birth, as is her mother. But, my grandmother grew up in Mexico, as did my grandfather. My grandmother's family was from Mexico. My grandfather's father was from Greece, his mother from Mexico. My father, born in Mexico, is of European descent. His father was born in Stockholm, his mother in San Antonio, right next to the Alamo. My grandmother also has Swedish and German ancestry. And while he is not Latino, my father grew up in Venezuela. These are all of the things I think of when I think of my ethnic background. I tend to relate more to the Latino side of my family, because I grew up in San Antonio where there is such a large Latino population. I guess that would be the place my ethnic identity is tied to.

Everyone in my family speaks Spanish; all my grandparents, aunts, uncles, etc. While the history of Mexican people has not played a large role in my upbringing, I know some of it, mostly what I learned in school and from my surroundings. People in San Antonio are very aware of the Mexican culture and this is shown in various ways throughout the city. Even though I am American, I relate to the Mexican culture most out of all of my backgrounds because it plays such a vital role in my everyday life. There is not a large Swedish or Greek community in San Antonio. The earliest things I remember about my cultural background and ethnicity are the traditions of my family. I did not know much about Swedish people, but I knew what they ate at Christmas time. I knew some of their manners from stories told to me by my father's parents. I knew about the Greeks and what kinds of things they did at Easter. My mother's parents would take us to the Greek Festival held each year at St. Sophia's Greek Orthodox Church downtown. This is how I was introduced to my ethnic background.

So What?

A trusted friend and literacy specialist working diligently with brilliant students in one of the poorest, most threatened schools in Brooklyn, New York, gave advice to educators:

Base your teaching on experience. Be passionate about what you do and bring that passion to the children and keep it going Be a lifelong learner and learn from the children. Take chances, take risks. Share. Bring the outside world into the classroom.... Be grounded in your skills, be grounded in your curriculum, but don't just stay with that one book—be open to other resources. (Russell, 1999)

Steinberg (2001) says that

great people, humanitarians, are ignored in favor of many, louder voices, or privilege of color or class. We demand a pedagogical revolution. Voices from teachers and students that will rise up and demand social justice and curricular inclusion of broad global perspectives. (p. xxiv)

I believe students and their teachers, who experience problem-posing curriculum with the use of personal story, can fuel this revolution.

References

Brady, J. (1995). *Schooling Young Children: A Feminist Pedagogy for Liberatory Learning.* Albany, NY: SUNY Press.

Clandinin, D. J., & Connelly, F. M. (1996). Teachers' Professional Knowledge Landscapes: Teacher Stories—Stories of Teachers—School Stories—Stories of Schools. *Educational Researcher* 25(3), 24–30.

Goldstein, L. S. (1997). *Teaching with Love: A Feminist Approach to Early Childhood Education.* New York: Peter Lang.

Russell, P. (1999). Personal interview, New York.

Steinberg, S. (2001). *Multi/intercultural Conversations: A Reader.* New York: Peter Lang.

Elizabeth Quintero

LATINO VERSUS HISPANIC

There is a panic over "Hispanic," as the Latina writer Himilce Novas says (1998, p. 8). A Hispanic comes from *España*, and those ties were severed long ago. It also comes from *español*, what was once, for some, the language of the enemy.

To make matters worse, once Spain became a mere image on a wall calendar, the warped word *Hispanic* was adopted by gray, naïve bureaucrats whose only concern was counting Hispanics. It also became a label "the preferred one in Madison Avenue boardrooms, Capitol Hill press conferences, and newsrooms across the nation. Between 1982 and 1984, advertisers increased their spending on what they call the Hispanic market…they invented targeted strategies…such as Mattel's Hispanic Barbie Doll" (Gomez, 1995, p. 665).

A well-received Latina writer, Sandra Cisneros, even refuses to let her work appear in anthologies that use the *H* word because she considers it to be a "repulsive slave name" (Novas, 1998, p. 4).

But does one dare say *Latina* or *Latino*? Enrique Fernández, the editor of *Más*, a Spanish language entertainment magazine, believes that *Latino* refers to an even older empire—the one that took over Spain. What's more, as Gustavo Perez-Firmat so rightfully puts it, "You can dance *rancheras*, but how do you dance Latino? And if you drink a rum and Coke, it's a *Cuba Libre*, not a *Latino Libre*" (Novas, 1998, p. 4).

By opting for *Latino*, one could also be grouping several ethnic or social groups and national origins as a single entity. What's more, it is possible that by the time this ethnic moment is over, the word *Latina* will sound as bad as her tactless stepsister, *Hispanic*.

But *Latino* could very well be the right word. First, it does not come from Rome. So let us forget *Latium*; no need to analyze roots. It does not come from the Spanish either, nor from the English. *Latino* is in fact a *Spanglish* word, "an English word with a Spanish pronunciation, and its signifier connotes and unites two linguistic and cultural referents" (Luis, 1997, p. 279). William Luis adds that the term *Latino* "refers to a specific yet changing reality. It has a specific origin but is often used and misused, sometimes to an extreme degree" (p. 279). William Luis subsequently explores the term's historical context in order to clarify some misconceptions and traces the word back to the late 1960s, when it first appeared in the Young Lords Party 13-point program and platform.

On the one hand, Moore and Pachón (1985) group all Hispanics together, simply because Hispanics "have become a *national* minority" (p. 2). William Luis, on the other hand, has brought dynamic proportions to the word *Latino*.

In an essay entitled "On the Nature of Latino Ethnicity," Felix Padilla (1995) attempts to understand Latinos as an ethnic group or "as a collective and emergent type of group form created out of the interethnic relations of at least two Spanish speaking groups" (p. 439). Much like William Luis, Padilla therefore analyzes *latinísmo* as a situational group identity and consciousness.

William Luis (1997) even takes it a step further when analyzing the issues of postmodernity and postcoloniality. The fact that the U.S. has one of the largest Hispanic populations in the world, and that its history includes histories of Hispanics, makes him come to the conclusion that the U.S. is in this respect also part of Spanish America. He defines *Latino* in his own way, so it reflects "the lives of those born or raised in the United States." He believes his definition greatly differs from the one used by other scholars and by politicians.

Whereas the general tendency is to use the terms Hispanic and Latino interchangeably, I prefer to be more specific about the words' referenciality. Latino is a re-appropriation of the nomenclature Latin, as in Latin American. The usage of Latin in the U.S. context is meant to distinguish those who reside in Latin America from those who live in the United States.

But Latins or Latinos growing up in North America inherit the culture of their parents and that of the U.S. Therefore the definition William Luis proposes for Latino "is different from the broader term Hispanic, which refers to those born or raised in their parents' country of origin" (Luis, 1997, p. x–xi).

William Luis then goes on to divide Hispanic and Latino literature into two categories. The first category, Hispanic, includes writers whose works were written in their native countries and who later emigrated to the U.S., where they continued to write in their vernacular. As to Latino literature, it includes writers born or raised in the U.S. who speak mostly English: "As a group, Latinos write an ethnic literature" (Luis, 1997, p. xi).

It is interesting to note that Moore and Pachón published their study of Hispanics in 1985, calling their subjects Hispanics, which was the term of predilection at the time. But several years earlier, Moraga and Anzaldúa (1983) were already calling Hispanic women by another name, *women of color*, a more radical name, the name that decides for a clean break. By this simple choice, the literature that cries from the heart, refuses to be erased, and demands an ear, a pen, and a place is way ahead of the serious studies backed with tables, U.S. Census figures, indexes, percentages, and more numbers.

The use of *white* and *non-white* for categories could have contributed to the difficulties in the coining of a correct name for Hispanics. Because of these color categories, the neurotic number gatherers could no longer grab hold of those Mexicans. Thus, the Mexicans went from being "Other" in 1930, to "persons of Spanish mother tongue" in 1940, to "white persons of Spanish surname" in 1950 and 1960, and to "persons of both Spanish surname and Spanish mother tongue" in 1970.

Then, in 1980, Mexican Americans, Puerto Ricans, and other Hispanics became a kind of "super" ethnic group: they are listed along with other national descent groups, and they are also in a separate category, sometimes as a race. . . . This confusion is a consequence of the bi-racialist assumption and a grudging and inconsistent acknowledgment that Chicanos, Puerto Ricans, and other Hispanics are something other than a simple ethnic group. (Moore & Pachón, 1985, p. 3)

That is precisely what happens when one tries to put race, ethnicity, and that all-encompassing "Other" in one bag.

Speaking of "Other," traditionally Latinos are divided into four groups: Chicanos, Puerto Ricans, Cubans, and Other Latinos. Lately, the Dominicans have managed to shed that word "Other" to don a real name.

The textbooks and other studies usually begin with Chicanos and Chicanas because they have been in the U.S. the longest. As a matter of fact, as Luis Valdez (1981) said, "some Mexicans didn't even come to the United States, the United States came to them" (p. 11).

References

Gómez, Laura. (1995). The Birth of the Hispanic Generation. In Antoinette Sedillo López (Ed.), *Latinos in the United States* (pp. 660–690). New York: Garland.

López, Antoinette Sedillo. (Ed.). (1995). *Latinos in the United States*. New York: Garland.

Luis, William. (1997). *Dance between Two Cultures*. Nashville: Vanderbilt University Press.

Moore, Joan, & Pachón, Harry. (1985). *Hispanics in the United States*. Englewood Cliffs, NJ: Prentice Hall.

Moraga, Cherrie, & Anzaldúa, Gloria. (Eds.). (1983). *This Bridge Called My Back: Radical Writings by Women of Color*. New York: Kitchen Table.

Novas, Himilce. (1998). *Everything You Need to Know about Latino History*. New York: Penguin Putnam.

Padilla, Felix. (1995). On the Nature of Latino Ethnicity. In Antoinette Sedillo López (Ed.), *Latinos in the United States* (pp. 430–467). New York: Garland.

Valdez, Luis. (1981). Introduction. In Toni Empringham (Ed.), *Fiesta in Aztlán*. Santa Barbara, CA: Capra Press.

Recommended Reading

Luis, William. (1997). *Dance between Two Cultures*. Nashville: Vanderbilt University Press.

Beatriz Rivera-Barnes

THE *LAU V. NICHOLS* SUPREME COURT DECISION

Critical aspects of the policy dynamics related to the education of Hispanics have depended, historically, on issues of language. The most important of these have been decided in state and federal courts. But the issues that have been raised tend to be generic rather than focused mainly on the Spanish language. Much of this history has been linked directly to language policy issues involving other language groups. In 1974 the U.S. Supreme Court handed down a landmark decision in the *Lau v. Nichols* case. After *Brown v. Board of Education* (1954), which ended segregation in schools, *Lau v. Nichols* (1974) is the most influential Supreme Court decision on the education for linguistic minorities because (1) it asserted that Chinese-speaking students had a right to a better education than they were receiving; (2) that the San Francisco Unified School District (SFUSD) was responsible for providing them a "meaningful" education; and (3) that the Office for Civil Rights (OCR) of the U.S. Department of Education had the authority to issue regulations compelling such education.

There is little argument that the decision by the Supreme Court to hear *Lau v. Nichols* (1974) on appeal from the Ninth Circuit in San Francisco was intended to resolve a civil rights question rather than a language policy issue. Nonetheless, over its 30-year history the *Lau* case has come to be viewed as an important statement of equity for millions of public school students who come to school speaking languages other than English. Although the case was not intended to be dispositive of the question of whether bilingual education is preferable to English as a second language (ESL) or vice versa, the case became inextricably embroiled in that debate. *Lau* was concerned with civil rights in education rather than language rights. This entry attempts to clarify the myth, legacy, and current status of *Lau v. Nichols* and its inseparable legal companion, Title VI of the Civil Rights Act (CRA) of 1964.

In preparing this entry we encountered several legal concepts that are important for the accurate portrayal of the current and future status of *Lau,* Title VI, and related topics. Among the most important of these are "disparate impact," "private right of action," "coextensiveness," and "proof of intent." We do not elaborate on these terms in the entry because they are somewhat arcane for our purposes. Furthermore, it is important to note that the future of Title VI and Title VI regulations may continue to evolve. For these reasons, we explain these critical concepts only briefly.

Methodologically, this entry relies chiefly on analyses of the case, both by us and by others; open-ended interviews with persons having a practical or theoretical expertise with the issues involved; and interviews with stakeholders who have had a continuing involvement with the case over its 30-year history. The narrative is organized according to the broad questions posed to the subjects we interviewed. In most cases, follow-up questions were used to develop the responses more fully. The interviews were tape-recorded and analyzed according to the major questions and themes. Where only one or two interviewees opined differently from the others, this fact is noted. Otherwise, and in all other cases, we integrated the responses into the narrative without attribution.

Background

Before beginning our discussion of *Lau v. Nichols,* its myth, legacy, and current status, it is helpful to give a brief summary of what was happening at the time and why this case was brought to the attention of the U.S. Supreme Court. In 1971, there were 2,856 Chinese students in the San Francisco Unified School District (SFUSD) who did not speak English. Instructional services such as supplemental courses in English were given only to 1,000 of those students in an attempt to meet their language needs. The other 1,856 received no special instruction. In this class suit, the plaintiffs argued that the SFUSD was not providing equal educational opportunities, thus violating the Equal Protection Clause of the Fourteenth Amendment and of §601 of the Civil Rights Act of 1964. They did not seek a specific remedy (e.g., bilingual education).

In the initial decision by the court of first instance, the federal district court in San Francisco, the court found in favor of the school district. The district court reasoned that the school district had not created the problem of language difference and should not be held liable for how it might contribute to children's poor progress in school. Furthermore, the Court of Appeals affirmed, reasoning that "every student brings to the starting line of his educational career different advantages and disadvantages caused in part by social, economic and cultural background, created and continued completely apart from any contribution by the school system" (*Lau v. Nichols,* 1974). However, the U.S. Supreme Court reversed that ruling on appeal. In its decision, the Supreme Court stated in part:

Under these state-imposed standards there is no equality of treatment merely by providing students with the same facilities, textbooks, teachers, and curriculum; for students who do not understand English are effectively foreclosed from any meaningful education. Basic English skills are at the very core of what these public schools teach. Imposition of a requirement that, before a child can effectively participate in the educational program, he must already have acquired those basic skills is to make a mockery of public education. We know that those who do not understand English are certain to find their classroom experiences wholly incomprehensible and in no way meaningful. (*Lau v. Nichols*, 1974)

Four years before *Lau v. Nichols* in 1974, Stanley Pottinger, then director of the OCR of Department of Health, Education, and Welfare (DHEW) had sent a policy memorandum on May 25, 1970, to school districts around the country with more than 5% national origin–minority group children. The principal audience for the May 25, 1970, Memorandum was the nation's school boards. It was the first of several attempts by the federal government to go beyond race in its efforts to assure quality education for minority children and youth. The document was short; it did not call for specific remedies, but it set out, in broad terms, the grounds for corrective action on the part of school districts in instances involving "national origin," a label that took little notice of language difficulties. In the May 25, 1970, Memorandum, Pottinger stated four major areas of concerned related to compliance with Title VI:

1. Where inability to speak and understand the English language excludes national origin–minority group children from effective participation in the educational program offered by a school district, the district must take affirmative steps to rectify the language deficiency in order to open its instructional program to these students;

2. School districts must not assign national origin–minority group students to classes for the mentally retarded on the basis of criteria which essentially measure or evaluate English language skills; nor may school districts deny national origin–minority group children access to college preparatory courses on a basis directly related to the failure of the school system to inculcate English language skills;

3. Any ability grouping or tracking system employed by the school system to deal with the special language skill needs of national origin–minority group children must be designed to meet such language skill needs as soon as possible and must not operate as an educational dead-end or permanent track;

4. School districts have the responsibility to adequately notify national origin–minority group parents of school activities which are called to the attention of other parents. Such notice in order to be adequate may have to be provided in a language other than English.

It should be noted that in *Lau v. Nichols*, the U.S. Supreme Court affirmed the responsibility of the OCR to provide operational definitions and interpretations to the schools. Specifically, the Supreme Court supported the May 25, 1970, Memorandum and gave it greater legal authority. The Supreme Court thought the memorandum was worthy enough that it quoted Pottinger's point 1 and point 3 in its ruling: "Where inability to speak and understand the English language..." and "Any ability grouping or tracking system...."

In addition to the Supreme Court's *Lau* decision and the May 25, 1970, Memorandum, there were two other key documents: the "*Lau* Remedies" (formally titled "Task Force Findings Specifying Remedies Available for Correcting Past Educational Practices Ruled Unlawful under *Lau v. Nichols*") and the "Notice of Proposed Rulemaking" (NPRM) pursuant to *Lau*, which later became more commonly referred to as the "*Lau* Regulations."

The "*Lau* Remedies" was formulated by OCR staff to provide guidelines to assess school districts' compliance in meeting the needs of non-English-speaking students. According to the "*Lau* Remedies," school districts found to be in noncompliance with Title VI under *Lau* were required to submit a plan that highlighted eight key areas of necessary compliance: identification of students' primary or home language; stipulation of diagnostic or prescriptive approach; selection of educational program; arrangement of required and elective courses; identification of instructional personnel requirements; elimination of racial/ethnic isolation and/or identifiability of schools and classes; notification to parents of students whose primary or home language is other than English; and evaluation. Although the "*Lau* Remedies" were originally envisaged as guidance for the OCR staff in conducting compliance reviews and evaluating district plans, the document was widely distributed and quickly took the place, operationally, of formal regulations, which were not available until 1980, more than six years after the decision. The "*Lau* Remedies" served both as a guide for government officials and as a template for school districts. However, critics of OCR's enforcement strategies complained that the unit was going beyond its legal functions and intervening excessively in curriculum matters.

It is important to note that the *Lau* Notice of Proposed Rulemaking, or NPRM (1980), was never adopted nor enforced and was withdrawn shortly after the inauguration of President Ronald Reagan. It has never been reissued. When the *Lau* NPRM was first announced, the U.S. Department of Education received thousands of letters objecting to it because many perceived it to be an intrusion into the prerogatives of state and local boards of education. Furthermore, the *Lau* NPRM went beyond the Supreme Court ruling by prescribing transitional bilingual education while the Supreme Court did not prescribe a remedy in its *Lau* decision.

Two less-known documents dealing with the *Lau* decision were the December 1985 and September 1991 policy memoranda. In the December 1985 Memorandum, then secretary of education Terrell Bell issued new guidelines. He advocated for a more flexible approach with low levels of interference into local planning. He took a more collaborative stance as compared to the *Lau* NPRM of 1980, but he did not cite specific legal authority or interpretations to support this new approach. He stated:

In viewing a school district's compliance with Title VI regarding effective participation of language minority students in the educational program, OCR does not require schools to follow any particular educational approach. The test for legal adequacy is whether the strategy adopted works—or promises to work—on the basis of past practice or in the judgment of experts in the field. (December 1985 Memorandum)

Further, compliance was judged on a case-by-case basis.

In the September 1991 Memorandum, the three-part test was introduced as a basis for assessing the adequacy of *Lau*/Title VI plans. There were flaws in the policy because there was a clear emphasis on English acquisition at the expense of a more comprehensive approach. Furthermore, certain decisions were left under local control. Finally, program flexibility and compliance assessments on a case-by-case basis tended to make the policies less stringent. In 1997 the U.S. Commission on Civil Rights concluded, upon reviewing the memorandum that (1) OCR's policies have not clearly defined "limited English proficiency," "national origin-minority," nor "students whose primary home language is other than English"; and (2) Title VI regulations also do not define terms and offer no criteria for establishing when a student's language needs place him or her in a position to benefit from *Lau*.

The *Lau* Decision and Its Legacy

What were the most important findings in the U.S. Supreme Court decision of *Lau v. Nichols*? Two fundamental issues went before the high court in *Lau*. The first of these was whether DHEW had the authority to issue regulations requiring schools receiving federal assistance to take special steps on behalf of non-English-speaking students. Title VII of the Elementary and Secondary Education Act of 1965, as amended in 1968, had provided funding for such programs but had not required them. The issue was decided affirmatively after the Supreme Court reviewed the legislative history of section 602 of the 1964 Civil Rights Act (CRA), which imposed on federal agencies the responsibility for ensuring nondiscrimination in programs and activities involving federal financial assistance. The second and arguably more important issue was whether the educational program of the SFUSD in the early 1970s violated section 601 of the 1964 CRA.

Perhaps the most important contribution of *Lau* was the ringing endorsement it provided for the idea that children who have different characteristics from those of the mainstream population must be educated with proper cognizance of those differences. The Supreme Court asserted that it is not enough to provide the same education to children who are different; opportunity for one group may mean a denial of opportunity for another. By contrast, in much of the litigation brought by African Americans against the schools after *Brown v. Board of Education* (1954), plaintiffs sought access to school programs already available to

white students. In the main, these cases sought access to the same curriculum and school activities available to majority group students. In *Lau,* the opposite was true; a remedy could be said to exist only if differentiated instruction were made available. *Lau v. Nichols* (1974) made clear that equality is not synonymous with uniformity.

Lau also recognized the right and responsibility of enforcement agencies in the executive branch to promulgate regulations to enforce Title VI of the CRA of 1964. In so doing, the Supreme Court accepted one of the bilingual requirements that had been promulgated by the OCR of the then DHEW as one of the requirements of the May 25, 1970, Memorandum. By acknowledging the appropriateness of previous enforcement efforts by the OCR, the U.S. Supreme Court, in effect, adopted an important provision of the May 25, 1970, Memorandum, namely, the requirement that in cases where parents do not speak English, communications sent by the school to the home should be in the parents' language. To our knowledge, that requirement has never been disputed in subsequent litigation, although it may not be a common practice today. Several experts and stakeholders interviewed for this entry believed that because of the high court's acknowledgment, the May 25, 1970, Memorandum is still entitled to great weight in planning school programs. Even in states that have passed anti-bilingual education measures, interviewees contend that the mandate for school-home communications in the child's home language remains valid and enforceable, since school-home communications were not a school practice abolished by the anti-bilingual initiatives in those states.

A third important message in *Lau* was that schools have a responsibility to teach those academic skills they require of their students before they can graduate from high school. At the time of *Lau*, high-stakes graduation tests were not as prevalent as they are today. California, however, required that high school students must acquire a strong command of the English language in order to graduate. The Supreme Court did not question California's right to require this:

This is a public school system of California, and §71 of the California Education Code states that "English shall be the basic language of instruction in all schools." That section permits a school district to determine "when and under what circumstances instruction may be given bilingually." (*Lau v. Nichols*, 1974)

This posture by the high court supports some of the concepts of school accountability that are current today. We can only speculate whether the use of high-stakes graduation tests in English would be viewed in a similar vein by the courts today if that requirement were in place without the existence of an effective program for teaching English. To our knowledge, no such case has yet been brought. Under the current interpretation of the No Child Left Behind Act (NCLB, 2002) legislation, the requirement of passing a test in English and other subjects appears to sit squarely on the shoulders of students rather than serve as a test of the viability of the instructional program and its promise to facilitate a good command of English.

Among scholars and long-term observers of the *Lau* decision who tend to view it in a wider context of educational change, there is concern about the focus on English embodied in *Lau*. Richard Ruiz, an expert on language policy and politics, asserts that the emphasis on language barriers and on the primacy of English over all other subjects underscores the widespread popular view

concerning the overarching importance of English. Ruiz asserts that suggesting that young people are, in some sense, less than complete until and unless they learn English is an ethnocentric view of the aims of education (Ruiz, personal communication, Feb. 23, 2004). Because the Supreme Court referred to this single aspect of education—teaching the *lingua franca*—and to no other, the decision gives no support to a broad mandate for making schools more sensitive to other needs of language minority children.

One of the myths of *Lau* has been that many educators and advocates believe that *Lau v. Nichols* was a mandate for, or at least a strong endorsement of, bilingual education in schools serving English language learners (ELLS). Strictly speaking, the *Lau v. Nichols* decision was never intended to clarify rules for the use of languages or of language policies in schools. The decision can and should be seen as a civil rights ruling rather than as a ruling on *language rights* of public school students. The belief that *Lau* was a language policy pronouncement is based on contextual factors. First, most cases of civil rights in education prior to 1974 had focused on the educational rights of African American students, principally on issues of desegregation and integration. There had been no landmark rulings focusing on the rights of language minority students. Several interviewees stated that in their opinion, equity for language minority students could not be achieved without a strong mandate for "understandable instruction," a term often used as an encapsulation of the instructional requirement intended in *Lau*. For this reason, they read the language of the decision as being strongly supportive of bilingual education. They argue that a principle of the *Lau* decision is that learning is precluded when students do not understand their teachers.

Furthermore, many question why *Lau* stopped short of requiring a specific educational remedy to the needs of ELLs, be it transitional bilingual education, ESL, or something totally new. The suit brought by the parents of Kinney Lau and other Chinese-speaking students was a civil rights complaint; it sought relief in the form of access to the curriculum but did not specify a curricular approach. Since the SFUSD and the state of California had a requirement that students must have a good command of English before graduating from high school, the Supreme Court reasoned that if the students were responsible for *learning* English, the district had a parallel responsibility for *teaching* it effectively. The court ruled that fashioning an instructional remedy was the responsibility of the enforcement units in the executive branch working in concert with school boards. According to the doctrine of judicial restraint of the U.S. Supreme Court, justices refrain from making law and seek only to interpret it. As an acknowledgment of this practice, Justice Douglas wrote that "a remedy is not urged upon us" as its reason for not dictating a particular remedy (*Lau v. Nichols*, 1974). It should be remembered that although the Supreme Court did not mandate bilingual education, it did not mandate anything else that could be construed as a more appropriate remedy. The Court limited itself to supporting the OCR position promulgated several years earlier in the "May 25, 1970, Memorandum" that "the district must take affirmative steps to rectify the language deficiency in order to open its instructional program to these students."

Lau's importance in raising awareness among school people of the importance of adapting school curricula to the needs of language minority students is immense. For language minority students and the schools they attend, there is no question that *Lau* was one of the most significant stimulants for policy change in the twentieth century. It served to turn public policy around 180 degrees and made it possible for parents and advocates to strengthen equity claims and demands for change in their interaction with the schools. Before *Lau*, the responsibility of adapting to the language of instruction rested squarely with students and their families. Children and youth who did not have a command of English were assumed to be disadvantaged, but for the schools this was an explanation of the failure of those students rather than a reason for changing the instructional program. *Lau* was explicit in placing the responsibility for change and adaptation on the schools and removing it, in large part, from the shoulders of students and families.

The impact of *Lau* in raising educators' awareness of the importance of adapting school curricula to the needs of language minority students was reinforced by enactment of the Equal Educational Opportunity Act (EEOA) in late 1974. Much of the relevant portions of EEOA was taken almost verbatim from the *Lau* decision. This progression from schools recognizing the need to adapt curricula to accommodate language minority students' language needs, to acknowledging that LEP students dropping out is a loss in "human resources," is an important one because it shows a change from the mentality of "blaming the victim." Historically, schools viewed students' failure to learn English and to stay in school as the problem of the students or their families, but *Lau* and the EEOA marked a clear policy shift toward another position: the recognition by schools that they share in this responsibility.

Lau's Current Status

Some advocates believe the anti-bilingual voter initiatives in Arizona, California, and

Massachusetts violate the spirit of *Lau* by precluding schools from choosing transitional bilingual education as an option for complying with *Lau*. Expert opinion on this point suggests that such a case would not be a strong one, at least under the aegis of *Lau* and Title VI of the CRA. To make possible such a scenario, the federal courts would have to outlaw voter-initiated initiatives—this is a doubtful prospect. The ultimate judgment, however, may rest with those charged with enforcing the decision. In the case of *Lau,* that would be the Office for Civil Rights of the U.S. Department of Education. There is one scenario under which the voter initiatives outlawing bilingual education could end up in a federal court, although the outcomes are far from predictable. For this to occur, it would be necessary for plaintiffs to show that a school district had been doing an effective job of educating ELL children *before* the initiative, and that it accomplished this through the use of bilingual education. Once the initiatives were implemented and bilingual education ended, the plaintiffs might be able to show that adverse effects were visited upon the ELL population because bilingual instruction was no longer available. In other words, it would be necessary to demonstrate that adverse effects resulted from the absence of bilingual education. To trace these effects to the loss of bilingual education and to no other factor(s) would be difficult. This strategy, however difficult, may be the only way to reverse restrictive voter initiatives that have sought to end bilingual education in U.S. schools.

Some experts believe that Title VI is no longer the best approach for seeking legal relief in the federal courts. Pursuant to *Alexander v. Sandoval* (2001), private right of action is no longer an option. *Sandoval* prevents individuals from suing under Title VI of the CRA; only government agencies like OCR can use Title VI and Title VI regulations as enforcement tools.

The impact of *Alexander v. Sandoval* on education civil rights litigation may be great. According to the Mexican American Legal Defense and Education Fund (MALDEF) and the Applied Research Center (ARC, 2001), the *Sandoval* case "erects a giant legal barrier" that "may leave many cases dead in the water because all too often, even in instances where discrimination is obvious, racist intent is nearly impossible to prove." The *Alexander* ruling was explicit in repudiating more than two decades of legal precedent when the high court ruled that "discriminatory effects cannot be challenged in court and that plaintiffs can only go to court when they can show deliberate discrimination" (MALDEF & ARC). Under Title VI relief is available to individuals only if they file a complaint with the appropriate agency, which is free to pursue or not pursue the matter. MALDEF and ARC state that "the ability to sue in court has been crucial because the federal government has lacked both the political will and the resources to enforce these regulations in each of the 50 states."

A corollary question that has not been examined in litigation is whether these initiatives deprive parents of choosing an educational option they consider important for their children: the choice to continue to use and study the home language. This position seems reasonable, given one of the features of NCLB that provides greater parental choice to all parents in the education of their children. According to NCLB, the parents of a language minority child (or any child) attending a school that fails to make adequate yearly progress could choose to send that child to a different school. In the three states named in this entry (i.e., Arizona, California, and Massachusetts), the choice of sending children to a bilingual school has been effectively foreclosed through the mechanism of voter initiatives.

Furthermore, some question if the promise and potential of *Lau* to leverage positive change in the schools has been eroded by other cases decided by the Supreme Court after *Lau*. The answer to this depends on whether one relies solely on Title VI of the CRA or on a sister statute, the Equal Educational Opportunities Act of 1974, the codification of *Lau* into law. To understand this better, some background is necessary. When the CRA of 1964 was enacted—the basis under which *Lau* was decided—it was meant to supplement the provisions of the U.S. Constitution known as the Equal Protection Clause, which is embedded in the Fourteenth Amendment to the Constitution. The Equal Protection Clause states that

no state shall make or enforce any law which shall abridge the privileges or immunities of citizens of the United States; nor shall any state deprive any person of life, liberty, or property, without due process of law; nor deny to any person within its jurisdiction the equal protection of the laws. (U.S. Constitution, Amendment 14, section 1)

One of the most important trends in civil rights litigation after *Lau* was the tendency of the high court to blur the distinction between the Equal Protection Clause, which requires proof of intentional discrimination, and Title VI of the CRA which, historically, has not had the same requirement of proof of intent. Simply put, to prevail in a case filed under the Equal Protection Clause, plaintiffs must show that the other party *intended to discriminate against them* and therefore intended to do them harm by virtue of differential treatment received. In most Title VI cases up to and including *Lau*, intentionality was not an issue. It was suf-

ficient for plaintiffs to show that a disparate impact had ensued without regard to the defendant's motives. The erosion suffered by Title VI after *Lau* was the gradual imposition of a coextensiveness concept, which had the effect of eliminating the distinction between the two provisions, the question of intentionality. However, under the Title VI Regulations, differential impact is still a violation, although only OCR can enforce the regulations. As Title VI and the Equal Protection Clause gradually became coextensive, their essential difference disappeared. The change in question began with *Regents of the University of California v. Bakke* (1978) but was driven home in *Alexander v. Sandoval* (2001), in which the Supreme Court in essence said it had changed its mind from the position it had taken in *Lau*. Coextensiveness appears to start in the context of *Bakke*. In that case, the high court ruled that a violation of Title VI turns on a showing of discriminatory intent and not just discriminatory impact. But while the legal force of *Lau*/Title VI was reduced substantially by a blurring of the distinction between Title VI of the CRA and the Equal Protection Clause in cases decided subsequent to *Lau*, it is quite likely that the spirit and intent of *Lau*/Title VI will live on in a reincarnation, the Equal Educational Opportunities Act of 1974 (EEOA, 1974). This legislation codified the findings of *Lau* into federal law and, in so doing, gave the decision new life and a greater potential for change than it now enjoys under Title VI of the CRA of 1964. In EEOA there is explicit reference to "language barriers" and to the schools' responsibility for helping students overcome them. This legislation was originally intended to reduce or eliminate cross-district busing in metropolitan areas as a remedy for segregation. But whatever its original intent, and for reasons that have now been forgotten, it included language that echoed the *Lau* decision:

No state shall deny equal educational opportunity to an individual on account of race, color, sex, or national origin by...the failure by an educational agency to take appropriate action to overcome language barriers that impede equal participation by its students in its instructional program. (EEOA, 1974)

It is important to note that EEOA specifies *a failure to act* as a violation of the statute. This makes moot the issue of whether there was intent to discriminate as required by the Equal Protection Clause and currently, pursuant to *Alexander v. Sandoval*, by Title VI of CRA. In short, by congressional action, EEOA now makes up for the diminished potency of Title VI. The stability of EEOA may be the best explanation for the fact that since the 1980s, OCR has relied almost exclusively on the *Castañeda* "three-part test" (*Castañeda v. Pickard*, 1981) to assess the appropriateness of programs in the schools that are offered as compliance efforts responsive to *Lau*. The three-part test has become a shorthand for a process defined in a circuit court decision in the *Castañeda v. Pickard* (1981) case in Texas. *Castañeda* was filed under EEOA and under Title VI of the CRA, although it was the EEOA legislation that carried the day, since it codified *Lau*. The *Castañeda* three-part test specifies that a program for limited English proficient (LEP) students is acceptable only when it meets the following conditions: (1) the program is based on educational theory that is recognized by experts in the field; (2) the programs or practices used are reasonably calculated to effectively implement the adopted theory; and (3) the program successfully produces results that

indicate the language barriers are being overcome.

Summary and Conclusions

In summarizing the myths, legacy, current status, and speculations on the future of the Supreme Court *Lau* decision, we were most impressed by aspects that occurred repeatedly in the interviews with the experts and stakeholders with whom we spoke:

1. While the decision was an unequivocal landmark for public education, it created or left unanswered a number of critical questions.

2. The choice by OCR to adopt an extremely flexible paper compliance approach during most of the intervening 30 years constitutes a failure to exploit the decision to its fullest, but this minimalist approach is probably sufficient in meeting agency responsibilities before the law.

3. One of the lasting impressions 30 years after the decision is that bilingual education is an appropriate remedy and that the Supreme Court erred in not promoting its use.

4. The unequivocal placement of responsibility on school districts to modify their curricula in order to serve ELLs more appropriately was the single most important policy gain for these children in the history of public education in the U.S.

5. While it answered an important question, that of responsibility of school districts, the decision contributed little or nothing to assist in the design of school reform efforts beyond those involved in being more efficient in teaching English, the *lingua franca*.

Few would argue with the assertion that *Lau*'s greatest legacy was that for the first time in the nation's history, the right of language minority students to an education that takes cognizance of their language needs was protected. However, through the course of our research one thread that seemed to continually run through the interviews is that perhaps advocates expected too much of *Lau*. Its immediate effects were far from dramatic. Perhaps this is the most prevalent myth of *Lau*—that the Supreme Court's ruling for the Chinese-speaking students raised hopes that bilingual education would get a much-needed legal boost. This was not the final outcome, and all our interviewees acknowledged it. A more optimistic view is that *Lau* was a means to leverage more substantial changes in the education of language minority students, including the use of home languages other than English for instruction. Schools were left free to use such techniques and to promote the added value of keeping children's home languages alive. Our interviewees saw nothing in *Lau* that could be read as denying that added benefit. As a nation, the U.S. has never encouraged immigrants to maintain their native tongues (Wiley, 1998). It was a myth of *Lau* that it gave students in the public schools language rights; this is untrue. This entry has shown that *Lau* was never about language rights, but about civil rights.

We asked our interviewees, Where are we in regards to meeting the needs of language minority students? Are we any better off in 2004 than we were 30 years ago in 1974? All our interviewees answered with a resounding yes. While *Lau* failed to meet the high expectations many advocates had, the pressure to improve American education for all children has continued unabated.

As to the current status of *Lau*, it appears that court cases such as *Bakke* (1978) and *Sandoval* (2001), the erosion of Title VI, and the federal government's more hands-off policy toward education civil rights have combined to take much of the bite out of

Lau/Title VI. At start of the millennium, a cloud of negativity has prevailed against immigrants since the events of September 11, 2001. This hostile climate, especially against Mexican undocumented immigrants, may have stymied additional progress in the policy arena. The pessimistic view that Title VI has been buried by *Alexander v. Sandoval* is offset by the optimistic view that the Equal Educational Opportunities Act will serve the purpose of individual right to sue equally well.

If *Lau v. Nichols* did not alter national language policy for schools, it seems equally doubtful that it could be regarded as an encouragement to redirect social policy. Having acknowledged that fact, it should not surprise us if the decision is someday regarded as a small indicator that there is an evolving view of how Americans regard the acculturation of immigrants. The traditional view of the immigrant transition to full-fledged citizenship in the U.S. is that they will abandon their cultural and linguistic baggage and replace them with those that prevail in the society. Historically, this is how immigrants have become American. Even when they agree that the country owes much to immigrants, members of the mainstream culture accept immigrants more readily when the newly arrived are willing to follow the assimilationist path followed by their own ancestors. It is interesting to note that *Lau* did not reify that view of how immigrants become American. With the exception of a minor aside by Justice Harry Blackmun, the decision was silent on the enduring expectation that immigrants should give up their native language and culture expeditiously. Only Justice Blackmun, in his concurring opinion, mentioned the assimilation process followed by immigrants:

We may only guess as to why they [plaintiff children] have had no exposure to English in their preschool years. Earlier generations of American ethnic groups have overcome the language barrier by earnest parental endeavor or by the hard fact of being pushed out of the family or community nest and into the realities of broader experience. (*Lau v. Nichols*, 1974)

Optimists might argue that as a society, the U.S., has begun to move away from assimilationist views such as those expressed by President Theodore Roosevelt in his "Square Deal" speech (1912): "We have room for but one language here, and that is the English language, for we intend to see that the crucible turns our people out as Americans, and not as dwellers in a polyglot boarding house." Was it the intention of the high court to challenge that view by placing part of the acculturation responsibility on schools? Given the close nexus between language and culture, was the Supreme Court also taking a position, however obliquely, on acculturation? Or was the collective silence of the justices another example of judicial restraint? There is little evidence one way or another concerning this question. At best, we could argue that the Court's silence on the issue of acculturation may reflect a growing sense of neutrality in the society toward that idea. Explicit in *Lau* is the idea that children should not be expected to go it alone in learning English and preparing to enter the cultural, linguistic, social, and economic mainstream of their new country. The public schools have a responsibility to help them get there. That is no longer a vague concept or a mere aspiration. Since *Lau*, it is a mandate by the highest court in the land. Thirty years after the decision, the Court's pronouncement that schools have an affirmative responsibility to help students learn English and, concurrently, to

"participate effectively" in school programs remains clear. This position has not been challenged by the schools or by their political representatives in Washington. The debate over approaches and methods will continue, but the final goal seems clear. It remains to be seen (a) whether the research will prove one approach to be uniformly superior to all others, or whether variations on the theme may be equally effective; and (b) the degree to which political antagonists to language diversity engendered by California's Proposition 227 will continue to stir up sentiments for and against the use of languages other than English in schools.

References

Alexander v. Sandoval, 532 U.S. 275 (2001).

Brown v. Board of Education, 347 U.S. 483 (1954).

Castaneda v. Pickard, 648 F.2d 989 (1981).

Civil Rights Act of 1964. PL 88–352 02JUL64.

December 3, 1985, Memorandum. Office for Civil Rights Title VI Language Minority Compliance Procedures.

Equal Educational Opportunity Act of 1974 (20 USC Sec. 1703).

Equal Protection Clause. U.S. Constitution, Amendment 14, section 1.

Kansas State Department of Education. (n.d.). *Lau* Remedies. Available: http://www.ksde.org/sfp/esol/lauremedies.htm (accessed March 31, 2004).

Lau v. Nichols, 414 U.S. 563 (1974).

May 25, 1970, Memorandum. Identification of Discrimination and Denial of Services on the Basis of National Origin, 35 Fed. Reg. 11,595.

Mexican American Legal Defense and Education Fund & the Applied Research Center. (2001). *Supreme Court blunts civil rights sword with Sandoval decision*. Retrieved Available: http://www.arc.org/C_Lines/CLA/story_web01_03.html (accessed February 24, 2004).

No Child Left Behind Act of 2001, Pub. L. No. 107–110, 115 Stat. 1425 (2002).

Regents of the University of California v. Bakke, 438 US 265 (1978).

September 27, 1991, Memorandum. Policy Update on Schools' Obligations toward National Origin Minority Students with Limited-English Proficiency.

Wiley, T. G. (1998). The Imposition of World War I Era English-Only Policies and the Fate of German in North America. In T. Ricento & B. Burnaby (Eds.), *Language Politics in the United States and Canada: Myths and Realities* (pp. 211–241). Philadelphia: Lawrence Erlbaum.

Recommended Reading

Lau v. Nichols, 414 U.S. 563 (1974).

Josué M. González and Ha Lam

M

MATHEMATICS

From a formal point of view *mathematics* is defined as the axioms and propositions of a deductive character that aim to describe or explain the world around us. Given its importance in all societies, it becomes indispensable to include mathematics in any educational project. It is a discipline with propositions that have at times been defined as self-evident—in other words, a science that is justified in itself—and as having a marked character of abstraction. A large number of the definitions assure that mathematics is the most general empirical science, and they highlight the analytical character of its propositions. However, from the science of logic, people like Kurt Gödel (1931) have formally demonstrated the internal inconsistency of the most fundamental mathematical principles. That is to say, it is openly questioned that mathematics is valid a priori; it is such for a series of prior social agreements of a universal nature and that look to empirical experience as a reference point, upon which mathematics is built. On the other hand, this reduced vision of mathematics has broadened thanks to the contributions of other, more ample definitions. These consider the social and cultural aspects in the definition of *mathematics* that permeate problem-solving methods and strategies. From this point of view the interest lies not only in the epistemological and formal character specific to mathematics but also in its quality, which is actually a part of the things that surround us. In this sense there are authors who find mathematics in the most picturesque places of daily life, such as in nature (sunflower seeds that dispose of a symmetrical form following a relationship with a ratio that has a proportion of the golden ratio; or the perfectly geometrical structure of honeycombs, which are always hexagonal, a natural form of maximizing space using the least amount of material), in cities (the geometrical forms that populate the architecture of our urban centers, the statistics that hide behind the numerous people who walk our streets), in the home (the household budget, the proportions of the ingredients for the birthday cake), and a long etcetera. Mathematics, therefore, is a complex concept that is difficult to define. It covers a great many dimensions in the daily lives of people and allows us to take control of and intervene in them. At the same time, the teaching and learning of mathematics is a complex issue fraught with differences based on a person's cultural background and socialization. There is not only one-way of teaching mathematics, and each culture, whether Hispanic, Anglo-Saxon, Asian, or Arab, has its own particularities.

Mathematics Literacy

Mathematics literacy is defined as the capacity to understand and use mathematics concepts and ideas. The Crockcroft Committee defined numerate as the possession of two attributes: (1) the capacity to use mathematics skills in different areas of daily life and (2) the skill of understanding information presented in mathematical form. Generally, as O'Rourke and O'Donoghue (1998) argue, the definitions of mathematics literacy can be grouped into three categories: (1) those that are based on the social perspective, (2) those that stress the relationship between numeracy and mathematics, and (3) those that relate numeracy with literacy. The majority of mathematics educators agree that numerical literacy is more that mathematics alone or "knowing mathematics" because it includes understanding mathematics reasoning, as well as the skills and procedures we apply in our daily lives that correspond with mathematics structures—addition, subtraction, multiplication, synthesis, symmetry, and so on—but are also part of daily popular culture. Therefore, mathematics literacy is understood as the creation of meaning in mathematics and also the development of a critical attitude toward it. Literacy is part of mathematics education.

Mathematics Education

To capture the complexities of what *mathematics education* means, we must not overlook its many nuances. If we attend to its solely instrumental dimension, mathematics education is a discipline whose exclusive objective is the transmission of mathematic knowledge. In any curriculum of mathematics education programs it is highly likely to find teaching methods, theories, strategies, and procedures that guide mathematics teachers in their teaching job. It is the approach to carrying out the task of teaching mathematics that is important.

Since the failure of so-called modern mathematics—unsuccessful because it proposed mathematics teaching from a very abstract and decontextualized perspective—the mathematics education community has carried out an enormous task in research in order to identify teaching methods and strategies that facilitate and overcome the obstacles to mathematics learning. There have been different educational models adopted. The main critique of modern mathematics was its excessive formalism. It was a form of mathematics teaching that was destined toward a very small group of students who sought a profession in mathematics. The mathematics manuals proposed activities that were completely artificial, without any relationship to students' daily lives. The focus was very formal, and a prior in-depth knowledge of mathematics structures was necessary. Many studies clearly demonstrated the lack of motivation this type of teaching produced. In the face of this perspective, which aimed to respond to the traditional model of the nineteenth century, models appeared that promoted meaning in mathematics. Not only the object of mathematics but also its teaching methods and strategies are questioned. The restricted idea of mathematics as a set of abstract axioms and propositions, regulated by strict systems of rules, opens up to a much broader concept.

Educational research projects demonstrate that mathematics are part of the world that surrounds us; they at times pass unperceived by us (the paradox of invisibility), but they are there and part of our lives, as Niss (1994) argues. Studies carried out in various parts of the world show another vision of mathematics that is distanced from textbooks. This is a daily mathematics based on procedures and ways of doing that are part of the popular culture, all transmitted from generation to generation orally or through practice. These do not have the degree of formalism of the axiomatic propositions of formal mathematics. Nevertheless, this does not mean that they are worse ways of resolving problematic situations. On the contrary, they are "recipes" that serve perfectly well for finding completely valid solutions in the contexts in which they are applied. One emblematic case is that of the children of da rua of Brazil, as Carraher, Carraher, and Schliemann (1982) explain. In the 1980s there appeared an important line of mathematics education, which included the cultural dimension in research. Teaching perspectives based on this line of work emerged, such as D'Ambrosio's (1985) ethnomathematics. The alternative that D'Ambrosio proposes is the recognition that the individual is an integral whole in whom cognitive and organizational practices, as well as historical, social, and cultural context in which the person lives come together. Therefore, mathematics education must integrate all these elements in an inclusive pedagogical practice. Bishop's (1991) works on mathematical enculturation, Gerdes's (1988) analysis of diverse cultural elements such as ethnomathematics and the contributions of Civil, and Andrade (2003) and Powell and Frankenstein (1997) about the connections between students' culture and real life that surrounds us can all be situated in this line.

The idea of context is also developed in Europe. Pólya (1957) proposes a form of mathematics teaching that leads to the perspective of problem solving and, currently, to the trend in *realistic mathematics*, developed mainly by members of the Freu-

denthal Institute, in Holland. Pólya highlights the idea of creation of meaning. He moves away from formal mathematics and presents a teaching method that seeks to motivate students to learn this subject. The members of the Freudenthal Institute present mathematics learning as a constructive activity that implies changing mathematics into something concrete; it is recognized as a discontinuous process that moves through various stages of complexity. Moving from one stage of "comprehension of mathematics" to another occurs abruptly; thus they propose models that stimulate reflection, which integrate elements from the students' context.

Currently another approach in mathematics education has emerged, from the field of adult education that emphasizes egalitarian dialogue. It is presented by Flecha as a form of developing mathematics abilities that we attain from living in a given social and cultural context. *Dialogic mathematics* seeks the creation of meaning within mathematics through the exchange of arguments between diverse people with different prior experiences, which enriches the debate and students' mathematics learning.

Mathematics Literacy in Hispanic Culture

In recent decades there has been profound change emerging in mathematics teaching in Hispanic culture. In Spain, for instance, during the 1970s the mathematics-teaching model was profoundly rooted in the modern mathematics perspective. During the 1980s the presence of subjects like geometry was reduced in the school curriculum, at the same time as the use of the *lenguaje de los conjuntos* (language of groupings) was promoted; functions were introduced from the concept of correspondence and, through the use of activities that were not very significative, on many occasions they were completely disconnected from reality. In general terms, the teaching model that was used was based on the transmission of ideas, illustrated with an example the teacher wrote on the blackboard. Routine tasks were prioritized for promoting the memorization of mathematics concepts and procedures. In the 1990s educational reform in Spain was based on the introduction of the constructivist paradigm. The mathematics curriculum was focused on aspects like significative learning and concepts like geometry, estimation, and the use of functions from a qualitative point of view, prioritizing resolution of systems of equations through graphs. This pedagogical theory is currently spreading in various Latin American countries, despite its failure in Spain. This reform failed because of the principle of diversity, which created profound inequalities between different schools and students. Presently educational innovation is centered on *learning communities* (University of Barcelona), a concept based on a curriculum of maximum expectations and the inclusion of all voices through egalitarian dialogue and argumentation in heterogeneous groups made up of students with diverse learning paces (interactive groups).

Research Related to U.S. Hispanic Groups

Traditionally the Latino community has been one of the groups with the lowest academic results in the U.S. Diverse authors have discovered that the relationship of language to mathematics learning is an element that is highly relevant, which explains the difficulties Hispanic students have in fully learning mathematics concepts, as Secada, Fennema, and Adajian (1995) point

out. Between the end of the 1990s and the beginning of the 2000s, some propositions were passed in several states (California, Arizona, Massachusetts) banning bilingualism in schools. It explicitly prohibited the use of languages other than English for teaching in elementary schools. These propositions have had terrible effects on the education of Hispanic students. Cummins (2000) has shown that bilingual education promotes learning and is also a form of fighting against the exclusion that Hispanic students face in North American classrooms. Over 150 empirical studies confirm the positive relationship between additive bilingualism and the linguistic, cognitive, and academic progress of students. In 2000 and 2004, MAPPS—Math And Parent Partnerships in the Southwest—directed by Dr. Civil, gave a significant push forward to the teaching of mathematics to Hispanic students and families in the U.S. Southwest. MAPPS has promoted the participation of families in their sons' and daughters' mathematics education. Workshops, minicourses, and leadership development programs have been introduced with the objective of involving fathers and mothers (largely Hispanic) in their children's mathematics classes. The activities are based on an innovative point of view, stressing the construction and discovery of mathematics meanings through egalitarian dialogue.

Mathematics gatherings are an example of a new form of teaching mathematics. An important movement has emerged regarding the idea of involving families in the education of their children on an international level. It reveals the future trend toward linking school with the familial context. Some examples of this are programs like The Smile program (Oregon State University), Face to Face (Boston, Massachusetts), the family literacy movement (available to everyone in the United States), Rosa Parks Elementary School (San Diego), and the project carried out by the Practical Parenting Partnerships (in Montana); all these are grouped in the framework of MAPPS, which has given rise to a center, recognized by the NSF, that does research on the relationships between culture, language, and mathematics learning (CEMELA), directed by Dr. Civil. In all these examples we see a trend in mathematics teaching and in research that is oriented toward practice, toward finding strategies and forms of overcoming the problems that impede mathematics learning. The most innovative contributions today toward mathematics education include aspects related to context, egalitarian dialogue, and the creation of learning communities. Everything seems to indicate that this is the direction that will be followed in the years to come.

References

Bishop, A. J. (1991). *Mathematical Encultura-tion—A Cultural Perspective on Mathematics Education*. Dordrecht, The Netherlands: Kluwer Academic Publishers.

Carraher, T. N., Carraher, D. W., & Schliemann, A. D. (1982). Na vida, dez, na escola, zero: Os contextos culturais da aprendizagem da matematica. *Cadernos de Pesquisa* 42, 79–86.

Civil, M., & Andrade, R. (2003). Collaborative Practice with Parents: The Role of Researcher as Mediator. In A. Peter-Koop, V. Santos-Wagner, C. Breen, & A. Begg (Eds.), *Collaboration in Teacher Education: Examples from the Context of Mathematics Education* (pp. 153–168). Boston: Kluwer Academic Publishers.

Cummins, J. (2000). *Language, Power and Pedagogy: Bilingual Children in the Crossfire*. Toronto: Multilingual Matters.

D'Ambrosio, U. (1985). Ethno Mathematics and Its Place in the History and Pedagogy of Mathematics. *For the Learning of Mathematics* 5, 44–48.

Gerdes, P. (1988). On Cultures, Geometrical Thinking and Mathematics Education. *Educational Studies in Mathematics* 12(2), 137–162.

Gödel, K. (1931). On Formally Undecidable Propositions of Principia Mathematica and Related Systems I. In K. Gödel (Ed.), *Collected Works*, vol. 1 (pp. 145–195). New York: Oxford University Press.

Niss, M. (1994). Mathematics in Society. In R. Biehler, R. W. Scholz, R. Sträber, & B. Winkelmann, (Eds.), *Didactics of Mathematics as a Scientific Discipline* (pp. 367–378). Dordrecht: Kluwer Academic Publishers.

O'Rourke, U., & O'Donoghue, J. (1998). Guidelines for the Development of Adult Numeracy Materials. Proceedings of ALM 4.

Pólya, G. (1957). *How to Solve It* (2nd ed.). Princeton, NJ: Princeton University Press.

Powell, A. B., & Frankenstein, M. (Eds.). (1997). *Ethnomathematics: Challenging Eurocentrism in Mathematics Education*. Albany, NY: SUNY Press.

Secada, W. G., Fennema, E., & Adajian, L. B. (Eds.). *New Directions for Equity in Mathematics Education*. New York: Cambridge University Press.

Javier Díez Palomar

MEXICAN AMERICAN FAMILIES: SOCIALIZING BILINGUALISM/ BICULTURALISM IN SOUTH CENTRAL LOS ANGELES

This entry contributes to the ways in which larger macro-sociopolitical contexts influence language socialization practices. Much of the work carried out by anthropologists (e.g., Ochs & Schieffelin, 1984) on language socialization have largely focused on monocultural systems that influence the ways in which caregivers speak to children. For example, anthropologists suggest that in some societies children may be treated as conversational partners and in others not. They argue that the use of clarifications and expansions (as opposed to directives) indexes an egalitarian relationship between parents and children. Bicultural and bilingual studies often give simplistic accounts of how two languages and two cultures may be incorporated into one system and do not always demonstrate how structural factors could play a major role in the home linguistic practices of poor communities of color. This entry study shows that macro-structural factors may play a significant role in the ways in which parents, children, and caregivers socialize their young children. As González (1999) suggests, by focusing on the cultural and linguistic mismatch between home and school anthropologists have overlooked the deeper, structural context of cultural production and school failure. This entry attempts to go beyond simply explaining the cultural values of children's home life to examine, on the one hand, the systemic inequalities children encounter and the ways these structural factors play out during interactions between young children and caregivers. In doing so, this entry contributes to an expanded understanding of bilingualism/biculturalism, where biculturalism can be understood not simply as a sum of two cultures or two languages but, rather, as sums of varying social forces where sociopolitical factors may play a significant role in the socialization of young children, especially in the case of poor immigrant families living in segregated neighborhoods.

The following paragraphs describe the families' living space and then briefly illustrate the ways in which larger systems influence their verbal practices.

The Families

The Rodríguez Family. The Rodríguez family migrated to the U.S. from rural Mexico, Morales, in the year 1989. Both parents received little formal education in Mexico. Jesús, the father, completed first grade, and the mother finished fourth grade. Jesús came to the U.S. alone and lived with some relatives at first. A year after finding a job, he arranged for his common-law wife and their 1-year-old daughter to join him. Since then, Jesús has held several jobs. When I met the family, Jesús was working at a Chinese restaurant in Monterry, Los Angeles, and continued to work there for two years. His wife, Carmen, a woman with a quiet temperament, occasionally works from home for sweat shops. On certain days she spends several hours trimming pants and shirts, earning five dollars at the end of the day. This family also receives assistance from WIC, AFDC, and Medi-Cal. The family is undocumented, and Carmen often describes her family with much chagrin as "wetbacks": *somos mojados* (we are wetbacks). Thus Dominga, the couple's daughter, had internalized the negative attitude of mainstream society toward undocumented immigrants to the extent that the denigrating term *mojados* forms an integral part of her identity (see Solis, 2002, for an excellent discussion on this topic).

The Rodríguez family now has seven children, Esmeralda being the youngest. At the time of my fieldwork she was 2 years old and was known in her family for her fiery temper. One of her older siblings told me at one point that Esmeralda knows how to play "rude" and "get real angry" because two of her brothers, ages 3 and 4, play "rude" with her. I was personally fascinated by Esmeralda's dancing ability. During family gatherings and parties she would join in with an older sibling and dance in perfect rhythm to *corrido* music and to *banda* music played by bands such as Los Tucanes de Tijuana.

The Hernández Family. The family of María and Mario Hernández have been in the U.S. since the year 1986. The father first arrived in the U.S. in 1979. After a few years Marío returned to Mexico and then came back to the U.S. with his wife and two children in 1989. Until the year 2003 the older children and his wife did not have legal residence. The oldest child, Carolina, determined to obtain a higher education and so did much of the paperwork on her own to obtain her work permit. This process was by no means easy, and she learned about the bureaucracies of the immigration process at an early age. Although very recently she did receive her work permit and was able to pay non-resident fees, she was denied financial aid on the grounds that she still had to obtain legal residency. Nevertheless, Carolina is very determined and continues to take science subjects in order to transfer to a four-year university, for she aspires to become an astronomer. Over several years I observed Carolina spending much time pouring over the Immigration Naturalization Service's (INS) Web site, writing letters, talking to various community lawyers, and keeping in close touch with her college counselor. These types of structural issues directly affect children's education; however, such tensions between individuals and social institutions (a common occurrence in poor immigrant communities) rarely enter the public discourse.

The Álvarez Family. Daniela, the mother of the Álvarez family arrived in the U.S. in 1980, when she was in her late teens. Daniela never attended school, however, and immediately began to work in sweatshops in Los Angeles. There she met her husband, José, who was also working for the factory as a truck driver. José and Daniela both have different jobs now. He works as a driver for an ice-vending company, and she, after staying at home for several years to care for her children, now works as a hotel maid. She says she enjoys her work even though she earns minimum wage because she gets to leave the house. Moreover, the job does not require much English. She has learned some English, though, and her husband jokingly says that she understands the English word "tip" very well.

Daniela is one of the few mothers whom I observed to be actively involved with her children's schoolwork and performance. Many of the other parents would remind their children of their *tarea* (homework), but Daniela would actually sit with her children and help them with their homework. She also participated in an after-school reading program for a few months. During this period she would meet her three young children and a neighbour's child at school, check out books from the school library, and then read to the children. However, as the children grew older and Daniela started to work full time, these literacy activities diminished and the children did their homework independently.

All four of the Álvarez children were born in the U.S. The Álvarez twins, Miguel and Rolando (age 8), have been diagnosed as dyslexic and are in special education programs. Until second grade they were in mainstream classes and their special needs status remained undiagnosed. Because of their reading difficulties, the teacher reported many behavioral problems, which culminated in major fights with other children. At this point Daniela requested that the twins be transferred to another school, where they were placed in a special education program. Hence, Daniela always participated actively in her children's education.

The Families' Living Space

The three Mexican families who form part of this study live in South-Central Los Angeles. Although the face of the inner city has changed and is being revitalized through micro-level entrepreneurship (with images of Virgin de Guadalupe painted on many of the storefronts), these efforts not only go un recognized but are persecuted. South-Central Los Angeles continues to be represented in monolithic, stereotypical ways as a gang-infested and high crime area. Although the area has many active gangs, there is little critique of structural factors that lead to gang activity, with most people shunning the neighborhood. Hence, South Los Angeles remains segregated in many respects.

These challenging circumstances substantially impact the children's language growth and worldview. Small wonder that poor Mexican American children's vocabulary does not always compare favorably with children growing up in middle-class families. The early educational experience of young children of poor Mexican immigrant families is, in the absence of supportive social structures, left largely to the struggling family members. Despite many structural constraints, the families live their everyday lives. Older children go to school, where they learn to be bicultural and bilingual, and in turn they socialize their younger siblings in bilingual and bicultural ways. Parents teach children to tease and talk in more traditional styles. Fictive kin tease young children, challenging them to defend themselves.

The next section briefly describes the language socialization process, through directives, evident in the three Mexican immigrant families.

Socializing Language to Young Children

In several instances, I noted interactions between caregivers and children that have been described by psychologists and anthropologists to occur typically in Mexican and Puerto Rican families. Young children in Latino families frequently serve as messengers functioning to tease members of the family (cf. Eisenberg, 1986; Zentella, 1997). Zentella notes that "in seeming contradiction to a community's *respeto* and gender norms, boys and girls are taught language routines that challenge the cultural taboo against disrespect, but serve to cement family ties in the process (Zentella, 1997, p. 236). By the time Esmeralda was 2 years old and was beginning to speak, she frequently played the role of a child messenger. Caregivers, through the use of overt directives such as *Dile* (Tell her) or *Di* (Say) frequently directed Esmeralda to repeat recitation of teases. Esmeralda did not passively listen to these directives but actually learned to recite these forms of teases, as shown in the following example:

1 Comadre: *(To Esmeralda)*
       Mocossa.
       Snot nose.

2 Carmen: →   *(To Esmeralda)*
       Cálmate, dile. La migra, dile.
       Calm down, tell her. The Immigration. Tell her.

3 Esmeralda: → *La miga.*
       The miga.

4 Carmen: →   *Dile. Te lleva la migra.*
       Tell her. The immigration will take you.

5   *Van a venir.*
       They are going to come.

6 Comadre: *(Stops teasing Esmeralda and begins to talk to her comadre on a different topic)*

While Esmeralda's godmother teases her, Esmeralda's mother directs her 2-year-old daughter to challenge her teases by directing Esmeralda to tell her godmother to calm down: *Cálmate. Dile* (Calm down. Tell her). Moreover, she directs Esmeralda to threaten her godmother with *La migra. Dile* (The immigration. Tell her). In her subsequent turn, in line 3, Esmeralda repeats the words *La miga* with a slight phonological alteration, as she omits the *r* in her use of the word *migra*. Carmen continues to give Esmeralda directives to threaten her godmother with the word *miga* until the godmother ceases to tease Esmeralda. Carmen employs the explicit prompt *dile* (say it) as she instructs Esmeralda to tease her godmother. In this context, the child is pushed into interaction in a triadic exchange. These imperatives, as Farr (2005) points out, index a *franqueza* (frank, direct) style where children are socialized to be strong and self- assertive individuals. What is particularly noteworthy in this segment, however, is the use of the term *migra*. It is apparent that the immigration police has replaced the *cuci* (the bogey man). For undocumented members of the family their (illegal) status becomes an inherent part of their everyday lives and is played out in various ways. In this particular segment, the mother who is undocumented considers the immigration police a greater threat than the bogey man and socializes her U.S.-born child into using this threat against her godmother, who, incidentally, has legal status. As Solis (2002) aptly argues, through the experience of undocumented parents even children who are born in the U.S. are drawn into the world of illegality. In this context, not only the child but also the *co-madre* (a naturalized citizen) shares the experience of the world of illegality. Hence, structural factors can play a significant role in the ways caregivers select to socialize their young children.

In the following segment, Carmen employs the explicit prompt *Dile* (Tell her) as she instructs Vanessa to tease her godmother.

(Two-year-old Vanessa's godmother is making faces at her in order to amuse her)

1	Comadre:	*Ay niña. Mensadas. Mensadas.* Ay little girl.
2	Esmeralda:	*Das.*
3	Comadre:	*Mocosa.*
4	Esmerelda:	*(xxxx)*
5		*(Puts her arms around Carmen, who is sitting on the table).*
6	Comadre:	*(Continues to wave her hands around at Vanessa)*
7	Esmerelda:	*Ia. Ia.*
8	Carmen: →	*POLICIA!* Police.
9	Esmerelda:	*IA!*
10	Carmen: →	*Venga por ella.* Come for her.
11		*(Carmen points to comadre)*
12	Comadre:	*Ira. Mucho miedo. Mucho miedo.* Look. Very scary. Very scary.
13		*(Continues to make faces and shake her hands)*
14	Esmerelda:	*IAA.*
15	Carmen:	*Dile. Policia venga por ella.* Say it. Police come for her.
16	Esmerelda:	*iaa xxx.*
17	Carmen:	Heh . . . heh.

Carmen implicitly instructs Esmeralda to challenge her godmother's teases. Carmen does not employ the explicit prompt *Dile* (Tell her) or *Di* (Say) but simply employs the word *policia.* Carmen conveys her meaning explicitly by indicating verbally and non-verbally whom the police are supposed to come for as she points to her *comadre*. Carmen makes her command extremely overt by employing the directive *Dile* (Tell her). Note that Esmeralda attempts to repeat her mother's words in each turn irrespective of the way in which her mother gives her the directive. Once again, what is interesting in this segment is that rather than using the term *cuci* (the bogey man), the mother urges Esmeralda to use the word *policia* (police) for the purpose of challenging her godmother. This is not very surprising, since the police are highly visible in South-Central Los Angeles. Helicopters constantly frequent the area, and young children often witness the constant presence of police in their neighborhood. Once again this segment illustrates that it is the families' immediate world that plays a strong role in the language socialization process of young children.

Drawing on an ethnographic and discourse analytic methodology, these segments illustrate that in low-income Mexican immigrant families there is much verbal interactions between caregivers of varying ages and young children. In many ways these verbal interactions reflect traditional cultural practices, since many scholars have documented that teasing and verbal challenges form an integral part of verbal practices in Latino families. What is significant here, however, is that caregivers employ terms from their larger sociocultural context as well as their own cultural systems. Thus Mexican American children living in South-Central Los Angeles are not socialized simply into the worlds of Spanish and English at home. Rather, they are socialized into the worlds they find themselves in—worlds where the language behaviors of these particular cases of poor undocumented working-class Mexican families very well reflect their social conditions.

References

Eisenberg, A. R. (1986). Teasing: Verbal Play in Two Mexican Homes. In B. Schieffelin & E. Ochs (Eds.), *Language Socialization across Cultures* (pp. 182–198). Cambridge: Cambridge University Press.

Farr, M. (2005). Mexicanos in Chicago: Language, Identity, and Education. In A. C. Zentella (Ed.), *Building on Strengths: Language and Literacy in Latino Families and Communities*. New York: Teachers College Press.

Gonzales, W. (1999). What Will We Do When Culture Does Not Exist Anymore? *Anthropology and Education Quarterly* 30(4), 431–435.

Ochs, E., & Schiffelin, B. B. (1984). Language Acquisition and Socialization: Three Developmental Stories. In R. A. Shweder & R. A. LeVine (Eds.), *Culture Theory: Essays on Mind, Self, and Emotion*. Cambridge: Cambridge University Press.

Solis, J. (2002). The (Trans)formation of Illegality as an Identity: A Study of the Organization of Undocumented Mexican Immigrants and Their Children in New York City. Ph.D. dissertation, City University of New York.

Zentella, A. C. (1997). *Growing Up Bilingual: Puerto Rican Children in New York*. Malden, MA: Blackwell.

Recommended Reading

Courtivan, I. (2003). *Lives in Translation: Bilingual Writers on Identity and Creativity*. New York: Palgrave Macmillan.

Darder, A. (Ed.). (1995). *Culture and Difference: Critical Perspectives on the Bicultural Experience in the United States*. Westport, CT: Bergin & Garvey.

Freeman, R. D. (2004). *Building on Community Bilingualism*. Philadelphia: Caslon Publications.

Hornberger, N. H. (Ed.). (2003). *Continua of Biliteracy: An Ecological Framework for Educational Policy, Research, and Practice*. Clevedon, UK: Multilingual Matters.

Howard, K. M. (2003). Language Socialization in a Northern Thai Bilingual Community. Ph.D. dissertation, University of California, Los Angeles.

Oller, D. K., & Eilers, R. E. (Eds.). (2002). *Language and Literacy in Bilingual Children*. Clevedon, UK: Multilingual Matters.

Valdés, G. (2003). *Expanding Definitions of Giftedness: The Case of Young Interpreters from Immigrant Communities*. Mahwah, NJ: Lawrence Erlbaum.

Wei, L., & Dewaele, J. M. (Eds.). (2002). *Opportunities and Challenges of Bilingualism*. Berlin: Mouton de Gruyter.

Fazila Bhimji

MEXICAN AMERICAN LEGAL DEFENSE FUND (MALDEF)

The Mexican American Legal Defense Fund, or MALDEF, was founded in 1968 in San Antonio, Texas. The organization is one of the oldest non-profit organizations that deals with multiple facets for Latino empowerment. It represents the first Latino-focused legal institution in the country. The organization achieves its mission by concentrating its efforts on employment, education, immigration, political access, language, and public resources.

Throughout its history MALDEF has been primarily funded by the Ford Foundation. "Modeled after the NAACP Legal Defense Fund, MALDEF, with an initial $2.2-million grant was formed with the mandate 'to assist Hispanics (legal or otherwise) in using legal means to secure their rights' " (Hymowitz, 2005, p. 6). It relies solely on the generosity of individuals, private foundations, and corporations.

MALDEF's growth altered the dynamics, numbers, and demographics of the board committee. Pete Tijerina, civil rights attorney, became the first executive director. The initial board members were also male Chicano attorneys, except for Jack Greenberg, from the NAACP Legal Defense Fund. Upon its inception, he Ford Foundation requested that the board become diversified in areas of membership, ethnicity, geography, and occupation. By 1971 MALDEF had added sixteen new board members, two of which were women. "In 1973 Vilma Martinez, who had worked with the organization since 1968, and who had previously served as a staff attorney for the NAACP Legal Defense Fund, assumed the position of president and general counsel of MALDEF" (*Stanford Legal Research Guide*, 2005, p. 8).

MALDEF's involvement with education has been highly visible over the years with a variety of legislations and court cases promoting language, culture, and identity. The organization has undoubtedly been one of the most influential advocates for bilingual education. "Building on the first federal bilingual education program in 1968, MALDEF won its first major victory on behalf of Hispanics in *Serra v. Portales* (1972), a case that won Spanish-speaking children in New Mexico the right to bilingual education" (Hymowitz, 2005, p. 6). MALDEF's investigative strength proofled significant to the Supreme Court case *Lau v. Nichols* (1974), "which forced school districts to remove language barriers that prohibited linguistic minorities from fully participating in public education" (Hymowitz, 2005, p. 6). MALDEF filed a petition similar to *Gutter v. Bolinger* (2002), which defended the affirmative action program in undergraduate admissions, in October 15, 2002.

MALDEF has also been a strong advocate for equitable worker rights, specifically among the Latino community. "In October 2002, the federal court approved the class settlement agreement in *Brionez v. United States Department of Agriculture*. The agreement, covering Region 5 (California) of the U.S. Forest Service, follows the Service's failure to make much progress, under a 1990 Administrative Agreement, in addressing Latino under-representation in employment" (MALDEF, 2003).

Currently two major components of MALDEF's education department are the Community Education and Leadership Development initiative (CELD), founded in 1975, and the Parent School Partnership (PSP) program. The PSP is a national program designed to train parents, school personnel, and community-based organizations to provide leadership and support for the educational attainment of Latino students.

MALDEF promotes higher education through scholarship programs. Scholarships are offered to first-, second- and third-year law students. Scholarships range from $3,000 to $7,000. In addition, MALDEF seeks to support Latino students who are committed to the Latino community, and to academic and professional achievement, and are in need of financial assistance.

The MALDEF headquarters is located in Los Angeles, with regional offices in Atlanta, Georgia; Los Angeles, California; San Antonio, Texas; Chicago, Illinois; and Washington, D.C. It also has satellite offices in Sacramento, California, and Houston, Texas.

References

Hymowitz, K. (2005). The Birth of a Nation: At the Ford Foundation Ethnicity Is Always Job 1. Available: http://www.americanpatrol.com/REFERENCE/MALDEF-LA_RAZA-Hymowitz.html.

MALDEF. (2003). MALDEF documents, Development Department, pp. 1–4.

Stanford Legal Research Guide. (2005). Available: http://www-sul.stanford.edu/depts/spc/guides/m673.html.

Judith Estrada

MIGRANT EDUCATION IN THE U.S.

This entry is synopses of a life history study about three academically successful Mexican American migrant students. It is about a long-ignored and yet well-researched group of people. The image of this group has been constructed in a way that locks them in a perpetuating cycle of failure. Consequently, many educators are convinced that these children will never be able to escape such a restrictive hold. Sadly, many of these students are led to believe that it is their fate to follow this path of hopelessness that has been imposed on them for generations.

Who Are These Children?

In many cases this group of students has been referred to as the "invisible children." Being invisible is not the worst of circumstances because it at least implies that they exist even if they cannot be seen. While this is certainly a concern, in other instances they are not even acknowledged. This mystery child is known as the "migrant student."

Not much emphasis has been given to Mexican American students who have overcome the obstacles and barriers impeding success. Little is known about the Mexican American student who is academically invulnerable (Alva & Padilla, 1995). If we know little about the successful Mexican American student, much less is known about academically successful Mexican American migrant children in our nation's schools. This study was conducted to address this void in the research literature; it is a study that probes into the lives of three academically invulnerable Mexican American migrant students. There are many stories of success that have not been told. The literature is rich with accounts about the plight and demise of the Mexican American migrant student. Many studies have been conducted to explain why so many Mexican American students are failing in schools. Their poor achievement has been consistently linked to a variety of sociocultural factors that compel Mexican American students to academic failure. The assumption of these findings is that the Mexican American child does not have the necessary competencies, values, and personal characteristics to succeed in America's schools.

By focusing on the reasons for failure of these students in a system designed for mainstream white upper- and middle- class children, these types of studies have failed to generate effective long-term solutions. These students have been placed in demeaning and stigmatizing remedial pullout programs that have served to perpetuate negative teacher attitudes and low expectations about Mexican American students in general.

Migrant Family Life

Most migrants live in poverty and in hunger, and they are always uncertain about the next place to go. Day after day the children watch their parents doing back-breaking work, always stooping and always picking. They move from field to field, often county to county or state to state. The children are hopelessly locked in the arms of this lifestyle of migrancy (Coles, 1971). The main reason why these families move from one job to another is to try to better their financial and economic situation. These families tend to migrate along well-established geographic routes. The three distinct streams are the East Coast Stream, the Mid-continent Stream, and the West Coast Stream (Shotland, 1989). The East Coast Stream consists of American blacks, Mexican Americans and Mexican nationals, Anglos, Jamaican and Haitian blacks, and Puerto Ricans. This route includes the

states along the eastern seaboard and the southern part of the U.S. The Mid-continent Stream primarily consists of Mexican Americans and Mexican nationals, with small numbers of American Indians. The route begins in southern Texas and moves north through the midwestern and western states. The Western Stream starts in California and moves up through Oregon and Washington. Although composed mostly of Mexican Americans and Mexican nationals, it has in recent years also included Southeast Asians (Shotland, 1989).

The Migrant Student Record Transfer System (MSRTS) identified 628,150 migrant farm worker's children in 1992 (MSRTS, 1992), and as many as 800,000 in 1994 (MSRTS, 1994). The number of migratory children rose by 17% during the 1980s. They range between 3 and 21 years of age, and most of these children travel with their migrant parents and do agricultural work. Texas is second only to California in the number of migrant students served (National Commission on Migrant Education, 1992). Many things that surround them and their families affect migrant children's lives. The circumstances of these children are particularly heartbreaking. They are the invisible children in our schools and our communities. Poverty and mobility are the two main factors that affect migrant children. They are the poorest, most-impoverished, and most poorly nourished children in our schools today. Although their parents play such a critical role in bringing food to our tables and labor in the midst of an abundance of food, ironically many of the children suffer from malnutrition and often go to bed hungry (Shotland, 1989). In addition to the problems associated with mobility and poverty, other impeding factors are language, culture, inconsistent record keeping, lack of academic skills, overage in grade placement, and the need to work or care for younger children. Migrant students and their families also face economic, cultural, and social discrimination (Chavkin, 1991). These children face many other hardships associated with their migrant lifestyle. Many still travel in tarp-covered trucks owned by labor contractors who transport them to their work destinations. They drive for long hours in pitiful, unsanitary conditions because they lack of bathroom facilities. Families stake claim to part of the truck bed and keep their belongings within this designated area. The trip in itself is an ordeal, and once the migrants reach their destinations, most of these children live in deplorable substandard housing if they can find it and afford it.

Constant mobility makes it hard for farm worker children to complete their education. These students average two to three schools a year and are usually behind grade level six to eighteen months. The median educational level for the head of a migrant family was six years in 1986 (Harrington, 1987). The research shows that high mobility lowers student achievement, especially when it is coupled with poverty and living in uneducated, illiterate families. Consequently, these students have the highest failure and dropout rates (Straits, 1987). Migrant students have the lowest graduation rate of any population group in the public schools. Five times as many migrant students are enrolled in the second grade as in the twelfth grade, and migrant educators place the dropout rate for migrant students anywhere from 50% to 90% (Interstate Migrant Education Council, 1987). The Migrant Attrition Project conducted a study that showed a 45% national dropout rate, whereas a study done 12 years earlier had reported a 90% dropout rate (Salerno, 1991).

It is not uncommon for a migrant child to be enrolled in school one week and gone the next. Many students leave school without making the proper withdrawal arrangements. Many parents of migrant students are forced to leave on a short notice from the labor contractors or growers. Efficient transfer of student records is a major problem because many times receiving schools may not ever get them or may have to wait three to five months for them. Without this information, very often these students are held back or given inappropriate placement (Ascher, 1991). In many instances school officials refuse to admit these children to their schools because they lack documentation. In spite of the *Plyler v. Doe* ruling in 1982 that specifically protected these children, schools continue to violate their civil rights (Hunter & Howley, 1990).

Why Families Migrate

The migrant family migrates to secure better job opportunities. Most families find themselves in dire financial stress just to meet basic survival needs. Consequently, education becomes a secondary priority. According to Prewitt-Diaz, Trotter, and Rivera (1989), the teenager who works in the fields gives 80% of his or her earnings to the family. The frequent change of environment keeps the migrant child in a continuous state of adjustment to school, friends, and language. School staff and classmates do not readily accept these children. The high percentage of dropouts among migrant students in many cases results from their feelings of isolation. Because of insufficient attendance and lack of effective coordination between home base and receiving schools, the child's education is interrupted and fragmented (Harrington, 1987). Educational strategies, curricula, and textbooks vary from school to school, and many times teachers are not willing to serve a student who will be in their classrooms only a few weeks. As these children fall further behind, their self-concept is damaged. As a consequence, migrant children usually have very low self-esteem. Many times they are mistreated, embarrassed, and humiliated for speaking Spanish, for the way they dress, and simply for being different.

Migrant Children in the Classroom

Migrant children present a challenging problem for our schools today. These children immediately earn the label of being disadvantaged and at risk. Because schools are not equipped to serve migrants, many times these children are made to feel as if they are a burden. In the recent past and probably in some instances today, many schools and teachers have placed these children in the back of the room and practically ignored them. In some cases, a teacher assistant may have been assigned to help them with their coloring and worksheets to keep them busy. Often, a common strategy has been to refer migrant children to special education programs. This is a conspicuous form of tracking. It denies these children equal access to learning. Tracking perpetuates inequity and contributes to the continuing gaps in achievement between disadvantaged and affluent students and between minorities and whites (Oakes, 1985).

Another widely used form of tracking with migrant students has been to group them according to their English language proficiency. According to Braddock (1990), ability grouping increases when a high number of black and Mexican American students are enrolled. "The failure of such children can be attributed to a lack of compatibility between the characteristics of minority children and the characteristics of a typical instructional program" (Cardenas & Carde-

nas, 1977, p. 22). To hear politicians and policymakers say that schools need to return to teaching the basics is disturbing. Obviously, those who will be taught the basics will be the migrant and other disadvantaged students. Thus, the achievement gap will continue to grow, and these students will continue to lag further behind. Migrant students must be challenged with higher expectations. "They need more from education than the basics. They need an education that can be related to everyday life, an education that will give them hope for a brighter future" (Dyson, 1983, p. 1). It is evident that migrant children have not been afforded equal and equitable opportunities to be successful in America's schools. Whatever the reasons and whether intentionally or not, the fact is that migrant children have been denied the privileges most mainstream American children enjoy as rights.

Until about 40 years ago, no programs existed to compensate for the special needs of children of migrant workers. As a result of the president's War on Poverty program, efforts to change this situation were initiated at the federal government level. Congress created the Migrant Education Program in the mid-1960s as a result of the Elementary and Secondary School Act. For almost 30 years it has provided essential instruction and support services for children of migrant farm workers whose education was interrupted or otherwise limited (National Commission on Migrant Education, 1992). For eligibility purposes, a migrant child or youth is one who moves across district lines for the purpose of seeking employment in agriculture or fishing. To qualify, the student must have moved within the preceding 36 months, although prior to the 1994 Illinois Association of School Administrators, students were eligible for six years.

Education Programs and Intervention Approaches

A variety of programs and intervention approaches have been implemented since the conceptualization of the Migrant Education Program.

Mid-1960s–early 1970s: Segregated Classrooms. One of the early approaches in many Texas schools with high numbers of migrant students during this period was to group all migrant children together. Migrant children were not only segregated through grouping, but in many cases they were physically detached from the rest of the school and excluded from activities. Finding and recruiting qualified and competent teachers to serve in this program was difficult. The children who needed the most help got the least-experienced and less competent teachers. In many cases migrant teaching positions were never filled, and uncertified substitute teachers were in and out of these classrooms year round.

Early and Mid-1970s: Segregated, six months' Extended Day. During this period schools created a special calendar for migrant students congruent with their patterns of migration. The school year lasted from November through April, and the school day lasted from 7:00 A.M. to 5:00 P.M. A typical day was 12 to 14 hours' long. Segregation seemed more defined. It had been hard for migrant students to participate in co-curricular activities before, but now it was almost impossible. They got to school before everyone else, ate lunch at different hours, went home after everyone else, and even rode different school buses.

Mid and Late 1970s: Return to Segregated Classrooms. The compacted six-month program did not last very long. Most schools returned to the initial segregated classroom model. This model was still in practice as late as 1976. This approach had not been adequate or effective before, yet it was implemented again without any attempts to improve it based on the previous lessons of failure.

Late 1970s–Late 1980s: Integrated and Remedial Pullout Programs. It took over 10 years for migrant students to be reintegrated to the regular classrooms. Migrant students and migrant program teachers seemed reluctant to join the system that had long ignored them and kept them in isolation. Likewise, the system was not prepared to accept migrant students back into the mainstream classrooms. Although students were integrated, most were still grouped by ability and tracked. Remedial reading labs were set up, and resource teachers pulled migrant students out of their classrooms for special instruction. The migrant label became even more negative and stigmatizing for those students who were being pulled out.

Early 1990s–Present: Pullout Accelerated Instruction. Some schools have genuinely shifted from remedial to accelerated instruction. Many, however, have simply changed terminology and continue to serve the migrant students through ineffective and demeaning pullout remedial programs. A true accelerated instructional model can facilitate detracking for the migrant student population. All students receive the enriched curriculum generally reserved for gifted and talented students. The curriculum not only is fast paced and engaging but also includes concepts, analyses, problem solving, and interesting applications (Levin, 1987).

Present-Day Approaches: Schoolwide Projects. Currently school districts with a high percentage of migrant students and/or students of low socioeconomic status are consolidating funds to serve all students in more heterogeneous settings. The IASA authorizes the combination of federal, state, and local funds for schoolwide programs that serve migrant children. This approach has its advantages and disadvantages. One obvious advantage is that the categorical restrictions are lifted. All children have access to all programs, and they do not have to be stigmatized by labels. On the other hand, migrant students who need the most services and generate the most funds may not access their equal share of these monies.

A Review of the Literature

The review of the literature about Mexican American migrant students was not very encouraging. The searches produced deficit-thinking literature that focused mostly on the failure of migrant students. Given the pervasive nature of these studies, it is not surprising why teachers have developed such low expectations of these students. In view of these findings, the main purpose of this study was to elucidate the amazingly successful life journeys of academically successful migrant students. The intention is to help change attitudes and raise expectations about the capabilities and competence of the Mexican American migrant student.

The study used a qualitative, life history approach to examine in depth the lives of three people who were migrant farm workers. Because few studies have focused on success stories of Mexican American migrant students, the participants chosen for this study were all deemed to have been successful in school.

The findings of this study are the result of an 18-month period of intensive fieldwork. The researcher spent countless hours with the participants, their families, friends, and others and had the opportunity to observe

them in diverse settings. Why did these three participants become academically invulnerable? As children of migrant farm workers they had all the attributes and qualities necessary to survive in any kind of environment, but a second question emerged. How and why did they develop these attributes in the first place? Their migrant lifestyle taught them the basic lessons for survival. These experiences helped them develop resiliency. Their lifestyle was a natural setting that served to develop their social competence, problem-solving skills, autonomy, and sense of purpose and hope.

This study focused on the effects of stressful life factors (sociocultural) and the personal and environmental resources that served to bridge the gap between success and failure. The participants all struggled through the adverse conditions prompted by sociocultural variables and the unique at-risk factors of their migrant lifestyle. The research subjects shared several common characteristics that match the profile of the academically invulnerable and resilient child.

According to Benard (1991), an academically invulnerable and resilient child is one who

- Has the ability to establish and keep meaningful relationships with others,
- Has developed problem-solving skills that enhance his or her ability to make wise choices,
- Has a strong sense of autonomy, and
- Has a strong sense of purpose and future.

They research subjects succeeded because they were able to develop extraordinary protective resources. The personal and environmental resources perpetuated each other. When they were young children, their parents provided the essential security that protected them while they formed support within the schools. As their support system evolved, their personal resources were enhanced. By the same token, as their pool of personal resources grew, their ability to form meaningful relationships increased accordingly. The level of interaction between the sociocultural, personal, and environmental factors determined the degree of invulnerability and success. This helped to mediate the mitigating effects of the stressful life events that resulted from the sociocultural factors.

It is not difficult to understand how the stressful effects connected to at-risk factors may create a sense of failure and hopelessness for many students. What is difficult to explain is how the migratory lifestyle that supposedly dooms these children to failure may also be why many migrant children succeed. On the one hand at-risk factors impede success, but on the other, the migrants' way of life also facilitates experiences that help migrants develop personal resources that make them resilient. Their lifestyle can be blamed for their academic failure, but it must also be given credit for their success. Students like Sonia, Belinda, and Benito survived the negative effects of these stressors because of lessons learned as members of a migrant farm worker family.

The migrant lifestyle is often blamed for the academic failure of migrant children, but it must also be given credit for their success. Many children of migrant farm workers have overcome the negative effects of the stress factors associated with the migrant lifestyle. They have "beat the system" precisely because of, not in spite of, lessons learned as members of a migrant farm worker family. The migrant lifestyle taught them the basic lessons for survival. These experiences helped them develop resiliency.

The participants shared an extensive core of values and beliefs. This core includes determination, persistence, a strong work ethic, responsibility, commitment, resourcefulness, cooperation, and a sense of hope. The migrant experience was like a survival-training session designed to help them develop the personal resources common to the resilient child. Their resilience, coupled with their intellectual potential, helped to mediate their reaction to stressful life events and conditions.

It is ironic that a lifestyle that deems migrant children "culturally disadvantaged and severely at risk" and bestows upon them the low expectations of a deficit-thinking society is also the lifestyle that enabled the research subjects to become resilient and invulnerable.

References

Alva, S. A., & Padilla, A. M. (1995). Academically Invulnerability among Mexican Americans: A Conceptual Framework. *Journal of Educational Issues of Language Minority Students.* Available: www.ncbe.gwu.edu/miscpubs/jeilms/vol15/academic.html.

Ascher, C. (1991). Highly Mobile Students: Educational Problems and Possible Solutions. New York: ERIC Clearinghouse on Urban Education (ERIC Digest ED 351 426).

Benard, B. (1991). *Fostering Resiliency in Kids: Protective Factors in the Family, School, and Community.* Portland, OR: Northwest Regional Educational Laboratory.

Braddock, J. H. (1990). *Tracking: Implications for Student Race Ethnic Groups.* (Report no. 1). Baltimore: Johns Hopkins University, Center for Research on Effective Schooling for Disadvantaged Students.

Cardenas, J. A., & Cardenas, B. (1977). *The Theory of Incompatibilities.* San Antonio, TX: Intercultural Development Research Association.

Chavkin, N. F. (1991). Family Lives and Parental Involvement in Migrant Students'

Education. Charleston, WV: ERIC Clearinghouse on Rural Education and Small Schools (ERIC Digest ED 335 174).

Coles, R. (1971). *Migrants, Sharecroppers, Mountaineers* (vol. 2). Boston: Little, Brown.

Dyson, D. S. (1983). Utilizing Available Resources at the Local Level. Fact sheet. Las Cruces, NM: ERIC Clearinghouse on Rural Education and Small Schools (ERIC Digest ED 286 702).

Harrington, S. (1987). How Educators Can Help Children of the Road. *Instructor* 97, 36–39.

Hunter, J., & Howley, C. B. (1990). Undocumented Children in the Schools: Successful Strategies and Policies. Charleston, WV: ERIC Clearinghouse on Rural Education and Small Schools (ERIC Digest ED 321 962).

Interstate Migrant Education Council. (1987). *Migrant Education: A Consolidated View.* Denver, CO: Interstate Migrant Education Council.

Levin, H. M. (1987). Accelerated Schools for Disadvantaged Students. *Educational Leadership* 44(6), 19–21.

Migrant Student Record Transfer System. (1992). *FTE and Student Distribution Summary, January 1–December 31, 1994.* Little Rock, AR: MSRTS.

Migrant Student Record Transfer System. (1994). *FTE and Student Distribution Summary*, January 1–December 31, 1994. Little Rock, AR: MSRTS.

National Commission on Migrant Education. (1992). *Invisible Children: A Portrait of Migrant Education in the United States* (Final Report). Washington, DC: U.S. Government Printing Office.

Oakes, J. (1985). *Keeping Track: How Schools Structure Inequality.* New Haven, CT: Yale University Press.

Oakes, J., Ormseth, T., Bell, R., & Camp, P. (1990). *Multiplying Inequalities: The effects of Race, Social Class, and Tracking on Opportunities to Learn Mathematics and Science.* Santa Monica, CA: Rand Corporation.

Prewitt-Diaz, J. O., Trotter, R., & Rivera, V. (1989). *The Effects of Migration on Children:* *An Ethnographic Study.* Harrisburg: Pennsylvania Department of Education, Division of Migrant Education.

Salerno, A. (1991). Migrant Students Who Leave School Early: Strategies for Retrieval. Charleston, WV: ERIC Clearinghouse on Rural Education and Small Schools (ERIC Digest ED 335 179).

Shotland, J. (1989). *Full Fields, Empty Cupboards: The Nutritional Status of Migrant Farmworkers in America.* Washington, DC: Public Voice for Food and Health Policy,

Straits, B. C. (1987). Residence Migration and School Progress. *Sociology of Education,* 60(1), 34–43.

Recommended Reading

Atkin, S. B. (1993). *Voices from the Fields: Children of Migrant Farmworkers Tell Their Stories.* Boston: Little, Brown.

Rivera, T. (1992). *And the Earth Did Not Devour Him* (2nd ed.). Houston, TX: Arte Publico Press.

Jimenez, F. (1997). *The Circuit: Stories from the Life of a Migrant Child.* Albuquerque: University of New Mexico Press.

Jimenez, F. (2000). *Cajas de carton: Relatos de la vida pergirina de un niño campesino.* Boston: Houghton Mifflin.

Encarnacion Garza

MINORITY EDUCATION IN THE U.S.: SOCIOCULTURAL AND SOCIOPOLITICAL CONTEXT

What I have been proposing is a profound respect
for the cultural identity of students—a
respect for the language of the other,
the color of the other, the gender of the
other, the class of the other,
the sexual orientation of the other,
the intellectual capacity of the other;
that implies the ability to stimulate the
creativity of the other.

Paulo Freire, *A Response*[1]

Unprecedented cultural, ethnic, and linguistic diversity in U.S. classrooms has presented a challenge to contemporary educators, school administrators, and policymakers alike (Acuña, 2003; Garcia, 1999; Moses, 2002; Ovando, Collier, & Combs, 2003; Seller & Weis, 1997; Suárez-Orozco & Suárez-Orozco, 1995, 2001; Weis & Fine, 1993; Wortham, Murillo, & Hamann, 2002). The ongoing debate on *how to educate* children from diverse ethnic, cultural, and linguistic backgrounds in the U.S. is intimately associated with ideological orientations in the greater political, economic, and social arenas. As such, the philosophical and practical question on how to educate diverse students will necessarily have as many answers as there are definitions what is meant by *to educate;* however, not all definitions hold the same sociopolitical power. Within today's neoliberal society and globalizing world, the most prominent and powerful definition guiding educational aims and practices is one that emerges from the correlation between the needs of a stratified and capitalist enterprise with the educational orientations that are thought to produce the individual inclinations and human workforce required (Aronowitz, 2004). Within the current conflicted sociopolitical climate of schooling driven by a Western, positivist ideology of standardization and accountability, to be "made in America" (Olsen, 1997) necessarily implies to adhere to this logic and conditions. Accordingly, education is necessarily a political and never a neutral endeavor (Apple, 2004). Within this scenario, the official knowledge (Apple, 1993) and privileged cultural capital (Bourdieu, 1977) becomes the most-desired and sought-after commodity. It is believed that in a democratic society, these valuable skills and knowledge should be distributed equally, or that

at least all students should have the equal opportunity to acquire such; nevertheless, unlike the view of schooling as a safe ladder to social and economic mobility, schools have been found to collude in the reproduction of the very social relations that permeate our capitalist societies (Bourdieu, 1977; Bowles & Gintis, 1976; Willis, 1977). As such, schools serve as agencies of the state and participate in the practice of sorting or tracking students (Oakes, 1985).

The education of cultural, ethnic, and linguistic minorities must be viewed from the varied dynamics that influence its outcomes. *Being all that we can be* is not a matter of equal opportunities. As noted by Kao, Tienda, and Schneider (1996), one of the most consistent research findings over the past decades is the influence income inequality and other social factors have in determining children's academic success in schools. Historically, the education of ethnic and linguistic minorities in the U.S. has been characterized by the often-violent outcomes of the inclusion versus exclusion, assimilation versus acculturation, and structure versus agency dynamics in schools. Current educational policies like the No Child Left Behind Act and those promulgating English-only (Stritikus, 2002) have clear ideas as to what is meant by "to educate." In following a linear, functionalist, and utilitarian logic, these policies are intended to alleviate the failure to achieve academically that many Latino and black children are experiencing. Within the current educational frenzy of assimilation, standardization, and accountability, ethnic and linguistic minorities are being set up to fail rather than to achieve.

Democratic ideals are just that—ideals. As shown by Smith (2003) educational policies developed during the past 30 years have not been based on democratic consensus; instead, these have been formulated to generate personal partisan gains. Recent neo-liberal educational policies have been issued in complete disregard of the research base developed over the past 30 years by educational researchers. In terms of the education of immigrants and minorities in the U.S., these policies disregard the important nexus between identity and schooling. As noted by Seller and Weis (1997), the impact of group identity on children's schooling has been shaped by at least four key factors: (1) the degree of difference between the cultures of children's home communities and the culture of their schools; (2) the meaning and value both communities assign to their difference; (3) the political and social relations between the two communities, including the degree to which one has the power to impose its will on the other; and (4) the agency of the home community, that is, the active efforts of community leaders, parents, and sometimes children to resist, change, supplement, or replace what is offered by the school.

As noted in Omi and Winant (1994, p. 10), Robert E. Park's race relations cycle, with its four stages of contact, conflict, accommodation, and assimilation, has been widely regarded as one of the most important contributions to the field of sociology. This interpretation of racial dynamics in the contemporary U.S. is challenged, however, by current and unapologetically resistant modes to traditional, Eurocentric ways of conceiving of assimilation and the melting pot ideology, as is generally the case of Latinos in the U.S. Moreover, as noted by Castles and Davidson (2000), the position of minorities within democratic nation-states today is marked by a fundamental contradiction: a failure to make them into full citizens undermines the inclusive principle of democracy and leads to divided

societies; but political inclusion without cultural assimilation may undermine cultural and national identity, which is a crucial factor of integration in nation-states. Minorities can no longer be assimilated because of the speed and volume of migration, the continual nature of population mobility, the cultural and social diversity of the migrants, the ease with which they remain in contact with the society of origin, and the situation of rapid economic and cultural change. As such, the notion of the immigrant who comes to stay and can be assimilated as an individual into a relatively homogeneous society is no longer viable (Castles & Davidson, 2000, pp. 153–154). Schooling in "democratic" and multicultural America remains a conflict between the powerful and the marginal, between contested ethnicities, cultures, languages, genders, and social classes.

The sociocultural and sociopolitical context of the education of ethnic and linguistic minorities in the U.S. and Latinos in particular is complex as a result of the oppositional and conflictual ideological positions guiding understandings regarding current pedagogical practices and guiding the issuing of anti-democratic educational policies. Nevertheless, and beyond the needs of our capitalist market economy and the retention of a Eurocentric cultural logic, we should not forget that immigrant children in our schools are human beings learning how to do life and how to do school in a conflicted country where students and their teachers are caught in the crossfire of ideological and political spectacles (Smith, 2003) disguised under the accountability of No Child Left Behind and English for the Children—or ironic and linguistic riddles of injustice.

If we are to call ourselves a democratic nation and to begin a trend of schooling for democracy (Fischman & McLaren, 2000)—guided by tenets of equity and social justice—we must begin to pay closer attention to the negative effects of current educational policies affecting ethnic and linguistic minorities. As for the Latino population in the U.S. and their unprecedented modes of adaptation, resiliency strategies, multiple memberships and affiliations, and identity formation, we urgently call for a realistic, radical shift in current neoliberal educational policies, given that these hinder, rather than foster, the actualization of effective pedagogical practices for the acquisition and further development of interdisciplinary, transcultural, multilingual, and critical thinking skills and orientations that Latino children in our public school system need to become productive and engaged social agents across nations, languages, and cultures, and beyond the needs of our market economy. Only then we may begin to rethink the current understanding of what it means to be a human being.

Note

1. In P. McLaren, *Che Guevara, Paulo Freire and the Pedagogy of Revolution* (Lanham, MD: Rowman & Littlefield, 2000).

References

Acuña, R. F. (2003). *U.S. Latino Issues*. Westport, CT: Greenwood Press.

Apple, M. (1993). *Official Knowledge: Democratic Education in a Conservative Age*. New York: Routledge.

Apple, M. (2004). *Ideology and Curriculum* (3rd ed.). New York: RoutledgeFalmer.

Aronowitz, S. (2004). Against Schooling: Education and Social Class. *Social Text* 22(2), 13–35.

Bourdieu, P. (1977). *Reproduction in Education, Society and Culture*. Beverly Hills, CA: Sage.

Bowles, S., & Gintis, H. (1976). *Schooling in Capitalist America*. New York: Basic Books.

Castles, S., & Davidson, A. (2000). *Citizenship and Migration: Globalization and the Politics of Belonging*. New York: Routledge.

Fischman, G. E., & McLaren, P. (2000). Schooling for Democracy: Towards a Critical Utopianism. *Contemporary Sociology* 29(1), 168–180.

Garcia, E. (1999). *Understanding and Meeting the Challenge of Student Cultural Diversity*. Boston: Houghton Mifflin.

Kao, G., Tienda, M., & Schneider, B. (1996). Race and Ethnic Variation in Academic Performance. *Research in Sociology of Education and Socialization* 11, 263–297.

Moses, M. (2002). *Embracing Race: Why We Need Race-Conscious Education Policy*. New York: Teachers College Press.

Oakes, J. (1985). *Keeping Track: How Schools Structure Inequality*. New Haven, CT: Yale University Press.

Olsen, L. (1997). *Made in America: Immigrant Students in Our Public Schools*. New York: New Press.

Omi, M., & Winant, H. (1994). *Racial Formation in the United States: From the 1960's to the 1990's* (2nd ed.). New York: Routledge.

Ovando, C. J., Collier, V. P., & Combs, M. C. (2003). *Bilingual and ESL Classrooms: Teaching in Multicultural Contexts* (3rd ed.). Boston: McGraw-Hill.

Seller, M., & Weis, L. (Eds.). (1997). *Beyond Black and White: New Faces and Voices in U.S. Schools*. Albany, NY: SUNY Press.

Smith, M. L. (2003). *Political Spectacle and the Fate of American Schools*. New York: Routledge.

Stritikus, T. (2002). *Immigrant Children and the Politics of English-Only: Views from the Classroom*. New York: LFB Scholarly Publishing.

Suárez-Orozco, C., & Suárez-Orozco, M. M. (1995). *Transformations: Immigration, Family Life, and Achievement among Latino Adolescents*. Stanford, CA: Stanford University Press.

Suárez-Orozco, C., & Suárez-Orozco, M. M. (2001). *Children of Immigration*. Cambridge, MA: Harvard University Press.

Weis, L., & Fine, M. (1993). *Beyond Silenced Voices: Class, Race, and Gender in U.S. Schools*. Albany, NY: SUNY Press.

Willis, P. (1977). *Learning to Labor: How Working Class Kids Get Working Class Jobs*. New York: Columbia University Press.

Wortham, S., Murillo, E. G., & Hamann, E. T. (Eds.). (2002). *Education in the New Latino Diaspora: Policy and the Politics of Identity*. Westport, CT: Ablex.

Cristian R. Aquino-Sterling

N

NAMING A LATINO/A CURRICULUM

The search for a name,
more than an act of classification,
is actually a process of historical imagi-
    nation
and a struggle over social meaning at
diverse levels of interpretation.
    Juan Flores on "The Latino Imaginary"[1]

Current debates over official knowledge and curricular understanding are about more than Spencer's question of what knowledge is of most worth.[2] The debates are fundamentally about establishing the borders of identifications and subjectivities, about what will be marked intelligence and, conversely, what will be deemed of little value. In short, the relationship between Latinos/as, education, and curriculum involves struggles over what will be everyday knowledge and what will be too difficult to think about on most days, if ever. This entry considers three concepts to understand and name the present-day curriculum for Latinos/as. It then outlines three critical lenses for re-examining race and curriculum.

First Concept: Post-Colonialism

In the first concept, post-colonialism, current educational knowledge of and about Latinos/as cannot be articulated outside discursive[3] understandings of colony building and its effects, the reaction to the imposition of Western culture on native peoples during efforts at European expansion. Accordingly, post-colonial theory, as a curricular lens, asks how knowledge is produced and circulated as a result of social relations created out of imperialist expansion. The knowledge deemed worthy enough to be passed on to the next generation, the knowledge that gets nullified, and the meaning given over to ideas that mark cultures are related to the ensuing sense of dispossession and displacement that many Latinos experienced (or currently experience) and the ways the ongoing legacy has been manifest in the political, economic, and educational communities that developed after World War II. From the first colonial settlements to more current understandings of sovereignty and freedom, settlement has meant a number of things for Latinos/as that are important to how we think of curriculum: (1) the displacement of Latinos by non-Latinos and Latinos alike and inculcation of a Western worldview that shapes knowledge of race and social relations; (2) the fracturing of personal, historical, and cultural understanding through slavery, servitude, and travel in ways that complicate knowledge, memory, and trauma; and (3) cascading levels of marginality and centrality (and perceptions of race, class, gender, and region) that operate at the formation of the very basic categories that give meaning to teaching and learning. For example, while many Spanish "settlers" might have felt some inferiority in relation to their homeland, they might have felt superior in the colonies they "settled," settings that had their own complicated divisions along the lines of race, class, and gender. Accounting for a Latino/a curriculum requires coming to terms with the forces of a colonial legacy that cannot be pared down into a static binary of the oppressor and oppressed.

Second Concept: Text

In the second concept, the relationship between Latinos/as and curriculum can be better understood through the notion of text. The idea of text is useful because it takes the idea of post-colonialism, that what we know and what we teach is shaped by European expansion and the clash and melding of cultures, and grounds it in specific experiences. In this way text can be as narrow as a specific written text or as broad as the individual "reading" of social reality. It helps us understand that race, in this case Latinas and Latinos, has its origins in the gap between the other and the self. In this gap we find that race is far more than an unchanging biological concept. Accordingly, Stuart Hall (1997, 2001), well-known scholar of cultural studies, responds to the question of how race gets signified (how the text takes on racial meaning) by examining the cultural processes that link visible differences in appearance—the differences of skin, hair, and bone that W.E.B. Du Bois (1903) noted shape all our lives—to natural, innate biological differences. The discursive character of race suggests that culture is used to fix visible differences through storylines that connect present circumstances (poverty, wealth, intelligence, ig-

norance, physical ability, language, and lifestyle) to that which is not easily observed (phenotype, genetic differences, brain power, and physical ability). Consequently, meaning making from reading various texts has changed over time. The racial category of black grew out of slavery just as Latino/a and Indian grew out of the conquest of their land. In each of these cases, diverse peoples of culturally rich and varied histories were collapsed into broad categories "by an ideology of exploitation based on racial logic—the establishment and maintenance of a color line" (Omni & Winant, 1989, p. 64). Because textual readings change and racial categories are contested and shift over time, those individuals deemed "non-white" have not been the same throughout history. As Ronald Takaki (1993) notes,

The Irish came here in greater numbers than most immigrant groups. Their history has been tied to America's past from the very beginning. Ireland represented the earliest English frontier: the conquest of Ireland occurred before colonization of America, and the Irish were the first group the English called "savages." ... [They came to the United States] about the same time as the Chinese, but they had a very distinct advantage: the Naturalization Law of 1790 had reserved citizenship for "whites" only. Their compatible complexion allowed them to assimilate by blending into American society. (pp. 11–12)

Racial categories for Latinos/as, among others, change as contact between the self and other shifts the terms for social, economic, political, and educational relations and, in accordance, curricular understanding. For example, the Irish were able to mobilize solidarity that allowed for the creation of political power and significantly increased control over blue-collar occupations. Through successively changing iterations of racial meaning over time, Irish identity shifted from one largely in opposition to dominant culture to one in accordance with it. Those who have experienced extremely limited mobility and fewer opportunities to assimilate, as is often the case for Latinos/as, particularly those of lower-socioeconomic standing, developed in opposition to, as opposed to assimilation into, dominant cultures. Beyond differentiating themselves from other social groups, a history of exclusion lends itself to the deployment of texts and textual readings that utilize distinction as a method of identifying self and social group by what dominant culture is not. For Latinos/as, the notion of symbolic and oppositional identities is appropriate for understanding the complex relations brought on by Spanish colonization, a legacy of conflicts between countries and regions, and struggles that involve other groups, including whites, over cultural and material relations, from language to land ownership.

Third Concept: Identity

Accordingly, as a last concept, in addition to post-colonialism and textual reading, identity is a key notion in the effort to understand the relationship between Latinos/as and curricular understanding. The very idea of individuals having an identity outside and apart from their community is not outside of history—is not beyond time and space—for many indigenous Latin communities, as well as Native American, have little sense of self apart from nature, earth, and community context. Who we are and how we see ourselves, as well as others, is not universal but situated by place and moment in history, as well as by race, class, gender, and sexuality. In this sense identities can be incommensurable, partly overlapping, but always with an

excess of understanding that in its difficulty is given over to difference.[4]

Contingent upon the immigration period, a symbolic or oppositional sense of self and community is not unlike rigid social orders reproduced through generations that necessitate (for protective purposes) identities woven out a collective experience of subjugation. In gaining a sense of identity collectively, historically oppressed people often find a sense of self and create alterative understandings that stand in contrast to dominant cultures. Within these "subaltern spaces,"[5] social relations often develop in ways that allow for the protection and maintenance of a shared symbolic reality. Teaching and learning in and out of the classroom involves the reproduction and transformation of identities; knowledge deemed of worth already enables and constrains the possibilities for transformative self-understanding. Relevant not only to Latinos/as, drawing identity into relation with post-colonialism and texts acts as a cogent reminder that how knowledge is produced, circulated, and put to work matters not only to minority and majority social groups but also to our national identity as a whole. Curriculum is fundamentally a question of what knowledge will be deemed worthy enough to pass on and what will be laid to rest in curriculum's burial ground.

As Toni Morrison (1989) so aptly reminds us, race has functioned historically, as in the present, as a metaphor central to our understanding of Americanness; in the creation of a national identity, as in a national curriculum, "Americanness" has been equal to "white." In this sense, knowledge is a reflection of truths that are not wholly self-evident, but are positioned and repositioned by what remains unknown or thought of, when attended to at all, as ignorance. If we take *currere*[6] seriously, then every time curriculum tells only part of a story—that among the knowledge claims there are absences, renunciations, and breaks—it speaks to a colonial history that has to be continually subjugated each time it rears its ugly head. The fragmented self that arises out of this subjugation brings with it the trauma of alienation, often in the form of white denials of privilege that are supported by a colonial past—Latino/a heritage that is washed over, muddled, and rendered of little consequence by dominant cultural, political, and economic institutions. In such a world, all racial selves experience a contorted public sphere, as in a fun house mirror, the images reflected back signify something other than what each of us knows of ourselves. The missing knowledge results in representations that are often beyond the control of social groups, even as they affect how they are thought of and portrayed. Self-alienation among subordinate and dominant groups ensues: whiteness becomes ubiquitous while brownness becomes a scarcity within broader public knowledge.

Failing to address a colonial history in curriculum gives over to generations that cannot access fuller self-understanding or understanding of the conditions of their own existence. Under these terms of subjugation, identities are not tied to legacies of symbolic and material inequities but conceived of as if they exist in an originary state, a sense of self and community severed from history and yet, most peculiar, linked to a dreamt up past.[7] Reduced in capacity, such selves lack the ability to make informed decisions built out of complex deliberations, and instead act in ways that maintain the present-day dreamscape, a decontextualized understanding of self and the world. To deal with curricula requires dealing with a racialized past that is also classed, gendered, and sexed. Curriculum is always a relationship between knowledge and power and the ability to produce, circulate, and regulate representations.

This entry is intended to illustrate that curricular knowledge is never solely "out there" in a myriad of facts and truths found in textbooks and worksheets. Our bodies of knowledge are imbricate with our bodily identifications, how we like to see ourselves and the social cultural significations that make such seeing possible. When we begin to comprehend these seemingly disparate elements of teaching and learning are actually in relationship, then multicultural education might not be about competencies alone but about examining the links between knowledge, ignorance, and our own sense of self. To do this work requires understanding that the dominant underpinnings of school curriculum operate in ways that negate a historical understanding of Latinos/as as a diverse group of people central to the building and maintaining of the U.S. While textbooks and media suggest otherwise, the cultural styles and intellects that constitute the foundation of the U.S. must be understood as racialized texts that belong primarily to people of color. Some might think the right of people of color to be placed central in U.S. history is the result of demographic shifts, such as the exponential growth of Latinos/as in the South, Southwest, and West; but as apartheid in South Africa so cogently illustrates, colonial legacies can remain intact, supporting minority group rule.

What is asserted here is that we must begin to come to terms with the realization that the U.S. was largely built out of the labor of Latinos/as, African Americans, and Asian Pacific Islanders, and that it is regular and systemic subjugation of this history in pursuit of a whitened America where national identity, Latinos/as, and curricular interests intersect. Coming to terms with a colonial legacy means becoming critically aware of how Latino/a styles, intellects, and material labor inform a broad range of American existences. For students privileged by race, class, gender, and sexuality to have a truer sense of self involves understanding the borderline that marks intelligibility and ignorance—to know oneself is to understand the process of identification often involves defining ourselves against that which we are not. We need not always search out "true" Latino/a culture, as often happens in multicultural education, as white identities are already predicated upon, imbricate with, and informed by relations with Latinos/as. Each of us is already born into a world where our lives have been shaped greatly by Latino/a cultures.

With this understanding, we can begin to grasp that changing mission statements or adding on a diversity day to the monthly calendar does not easily correct absences in the curriculum. Instead, the absences have the larger social effects of structuring the seeming neutrality and centrality of the curricular body, or as Deborah Britzman (1991), well-known curriculum scholar, describes it, empathetic approaches are a problem because they often focus on the other[8] while failing to trouble seemingly objective curricula and pedagogy. In a corresponding relationship, the denial of many rights to Latinos/as, including employment opportunities and protection from injury,[9] corresponds to the resistance to and downright hostility toward teaching Latino/a history in schools, and even in colleges and universities.[10] Resistance to understanding curriculum as racialized evokes an air of neutrality that makes it difficult to comprehend the raced, classed, gendered, and sexed dimensions of who we are and

how we like to see ourselves. Neutrality as an overlay on the absences in the curriculum brings into play a process of fragmentation, falsely separating out race from knowledge and text. To be unaware of racial dimensions of teaching and learning has origins in the reliance upon knowledge built out of half-truths and refusals to re-imagine a difficult past. Such denials are interlinked: racially coded thoughts play out in electoral politics, conceptions of appropriate school leadership, and forms of discourse that will be officially acknowledged.

Subjugated knowledge is evidenced in our lives in the most fascinating of ways. As we enter the new millennium we see the merger of government and big business as individuals like G. W. Bush and D. Cheney move back and forth almost seamlessly, representing the new American public leader: the advocate for government of and by big business. Rather than the slow and deliberate practices of a government past, represented by historical figures like Franklin Delano Roosevelt and Kennedy, the new government is hierarchical, quick to move, shrewd, and committed to cost-effectiveness at all costs. Its leaders are white, male, religious, and open to representational (but not ideological) diversity as long as the job gets done.[11] These men of instrumental reason can be compared to the representations of Latinos/as in American culture: humorous, artistic, athletically inclined, intuitive, and unpredictable. Between the two representations a synthesis can be grasp, that of the need for calculating, consistent, and reasoned white heterosexual male leaders and their compatriots to dominate and control the affectively motivated and emotionally inclined in ways that maintain conventional social orders. As Michael Apple (2001), a well-known curriculum scholar, warns us, while neoliberals and neoconservatives might differ on social policy, they just as importantly align on the desire to modernize the economy, effectively eliminating the viability of designating a liberal-conservative continuum, at least when it comes to economic policy. Similarly, in the shift in leadership, the diversity of representation has been permitted to grow while ideological diversity has shrunk considerably. While proponents call themselves passionate conservatives and reasoned liberals, these complex relationships mean that those outside of this vision of human relations find their knowledge is further undermined, the further fragmentation of progressive ideological solidarity and public sphere committed to the common good. In analyzing the complex dimensions of leadership lies the Latino/a curriculum, the teaching and learning that take place through transformative interpretations of intelligence.

Edgar González-Gaudiano, scholar at the National Autonomous University of Mexico, asserts that conservative curricular prescriptions can be better understood by looking at the discourse around issues of environmental protection and national security (McClaren & González-Gaudiano, 1995). In particular, his work suggests that sloganistic phrases like "Don't waste, recycle," "Put it here," and "Save the planet" draw little attention to the larger issues of consumption, capitalism, and social policy and how these impact all of us, but in particular countries and regions not capable of regulating and fending off big business. In this way, neoconservatives and neoliberals are much more closely aligned in presenting the problems of overconsumption and global warming as an individual problem of not recycling, not global classism and racism that would require significant changes in everyday business practices and government politics. Sure, it is significant that neoliberals have called for increased deliberation over issues that are raced and classed, suggesting slow and constant incorporation of new viewpoints that honor difference and allow for equality, but it is taken up in ways that typically favor dominant social groups. Questions of curricula are about more than purpose, scope, organization, and evaluation,[12] they are about the way social relations extend and constrain the meaning making that occurs; transformative Latino/a curriculum might begin with more effort put toward understanding the individual experience of the public. Rather than belittle or ignore race altogether, curriculum as racial text asserts that every dimension of U.S. culture is at its origins raced, classed, gendered, and sexed. Curricular understanding requires that, far from the assertion that U.S. Americans can move beyond race, we search out and explore the ways race shape perceptions and experiences. When the complexities of race are brought to the surface and explored critically and continuously, suppressed dimensions of being might begin to surface. Debates over what knowledge is of most worth can then be understood as fundamentally competing conceptions over how we would like to see ourselves, as well as what will be seen as representing intelligence.

Wendell Berry (1990) illustrates in "A Remarkable Man," a piece that speaks to cultural co-optation and indigenous knowledge, that people of color and white Americans live in an imbricate relationship, though one of frequent unequal relations. Without understanding the varied lived experiences of those living as racially different beings, those living as white and people of color will never know themselves. Although the life experiences might be very different, urban, suburban, and rural white individuals must come to understand that they are also Latino/a. As Berry points out in his critique of a white author's misquoting of a southern man of color (because of vernacular misunderstanding), intelligibility cannot exist without schema for knowing how to evaluate what is worth knowing; even as "the other" defines the self, it is the lack of understanding of the other in ourselves that is most troubling. Berry's cogent critique of a white author's misappropriation of southern African American culture and misconstrued comparisons of African Americans to whites, particularly his characterization of the southern man of color as the "Black William Faulkner," illustrates my point. Always and already in the relationships drawn between people of color and white people there is within the identity of each the intertwined cultural legacy of both. William Pinar, well-known scholar of curriculum, makes this point clear when he states that "all Americans are racialized beings; knowledge of who we have been, who we are, and who we will become is a text; curriculum—our construction and reconstruction of this knowledge—is indeed a racial text" (1993, p. 63).

A search of newspapers and magazines of the past decade showcases the crisis surrounding public education, heightened since the publication of *A Nation at Risk* (National Commission on Excellence in Education, 1983), while certainly detectable before. Within the nexus of debates regarding public education, concern over whether we should promote cultural understanding does not seem to be at the center of the controversy: students are asked to know more key historical events, significant dates, and document content. Indeed, it would be safe to say that there are common calls from conservatives and liberals for a return to the canon and outrage that students know so little about the past. What seems to bring out the controversy involves the composition of such cultural understanding. For example, what does it suggest when students do a critical exploration of Che Guevara and his significance for understanding labor relations and globalism, as opposed to a conventional study of the merits of Taylorism and mass production? In the former there is a heightened sense of possibility of engendering critical consciousness through a study of a countercultural worker while the latter might simply reinforce the benefits of Western, patriarchical systems of knowledge that are already prevalent in American society. The question is, how critically aware do we want our citizenry to be? It is not that students should avoid study of Taylorism, for such a suggestion would deny its massive impact on Latino/a American politics, culture, and education. Countercultural events, however, can be used as an entry point into studying larger social dynamics that include what are now the largely unquestioned assumptions regarding the production of material goods. By entering from a subjugated perspective, critical consciousness might be engendered; Taylorism was a necessary precursor for Che Guevara to come into existence. In a dialectical fashion, we can see how the conventions of social organizations—mass production, capitalism, globalism, and multinational corporations—set the context for victimization and rebellion. A curriculum that honors Latinos/as sets into motion the study of historical events that aim to engender critical consciousness in regards to social conventions. It is through the study of inspirational thinkers, such as Che Guevara, that Americans might come to terms with a racialized past.

Three Critical Lenses for Examining Race and Curriculum

The last section addressed several keys lenses helpful for naming and understanding the Latino/a curriculum. The next considers the symbolic and material origins of race and knowledge in the curriculum.

Symbolic. Those who argue that racial differences are matters of thought and culture note that the origins of discrimination and racism can be located in intellectual matter: the ways people think, and their language and perceptions of the world. Therefore, they attend to teaching and learning and its relationship to the social construction of reality. Those working in symbolism are often invested in the power of deconstruction, the idea that people can become more aware of oppression through critiquing individuals, institutions, and cultural practices to illustrate how these different dimensions contribute to oppression. To foster understanding of racial and ethnic differences, they hope to change the conventional network of words, representations, feelings, and scripts that in everyday practices incite denigrating myths and misunderstandings.

Material. Those who argue that racial differences are matters of tangible resources note that the origins of discrimination and racism can be located in matters of capital: the ways a society sorts privilege and status. Accordingly, they attend to ways that race is used to demonize a group of people so they can be exploited for material gain, often correlating the ways dominant groups circulate negative images and ideas when they desire laborers or want to occupy the land of another. They might point to the ways that southern ranchers and plantation owners have historically promoted ideas regarding the inferiority of Mexicans,

among other social groups, when they wanted to utilize Mexican land or engage in expansionist project that required increased amounts of manual labor. Taking a rather Darwinist approach, they note that historically different social groups have consistently looked for ways to take advantage of or exploit other groups. Curriculum is rarely an issue of marking altruistic events; historically groups act in their own self-interests.

Structures of the Past in the Present Curriculum

Take a look at a set of curriculum documents for most public schools and you will most likely find a series of subject area content sections along with instructional aids for how to teach the material, or descriptions of how it has been taught in the past. Imagine that little of this curriculum reflects an alternative conception or an innovative understanding of curriculum. In this situation, present curriculum documents and conventional understandings lead to dead ends; they are filled with solutions that have failed to work. What is required in the mix of teaching and learning involves innovation and change, not the reapplication of previous ways of thinking about curriculum. When Ralph Tyler wrote the *Basic Principles of Curriculum and Instruction* (1949), he laid down the foundations for curricular thought, a document that served as a template with which future generations of teachers and scholars have to contend. The change that came afterward was slow, and it was not until the 1970s that a paradigm shift occurred, of which an element of it was analyzing the intersections of race and curriculum. The reconceptualization of the field began with critical examinations of cultural difference and social inequality as they related to the reproduction and transformation of the status quo.

Understanding Latino/a curriculum requires methods for railing against the structure of the past that matter now because they affect the present.

Attending to Power in the Curriculum

Consider the ideas that are often invoked around curriculum and knowledge. For example, knowledge is often thought of as a tool for the pursuit of truth. If a problematic idea is presented, individuals who recognize it might be urged to seek out the correct information and use it to advance understanding and, therefore, society as a whole. In this sense, they are advised to take up a free market response: If Latinos/as or another often subjugated social group finds that their culture is being misinterpreted or they are not reaping the benefits of a democratic society, the solution is not to transform how representations are created and distributed or revolutionize the economy; rather, the free market response is to speak back, make your voices heard, and participate in democratic processes: "When democracy is in question the answer is more democracy."

The problem when such ideas are invoked is that they fail to attend to how power circulates though social relations and shapes the individual experience of the public. It might be dangerous to seek out and present more truthful information, just as it might be dangerous to speak out and attempt to engage democratic practices on a more meaningful level when the voice is not native to the dominant culture or ways of communicating are not perceived as signs of intelligence. When power is not acknowledged in the ways that we teach and learn, there is a failure to move to a level of critical conscious necessary to analyze that which is missing from the present-day curriculum. The historical representations of Latinos/as,

from "Frito Bandito," the thieving rascal Frito Lay chip character, to Carmen Miranda, the fun-loving Chiquita Banana Spitfire, were in their era thought of as cute or funny, or, in the worst case, truthful representations of Latinos and Latinas. How possible is it to correct problematic representations, even when the social group holds more truthful knowledge, when these very notions of Latino/a culture are threaded throughout the U.S. American psyche? The belief that individuals can invoke language in ways that will undo the meaning others have made with the same language is to be guilty of failing to attend to power relations—that somehow offering a better narrative will inherently lead to a change in a previous narrative are likely to end as thwarted attempts to engender empathy.

Conclusion

In the debates over official knowledge and curricular understanding, we must attend to the complexities of a colonial past, the excesses of textual readings, and the diverse ways in which individuals experience the public. Latino/a curriculum requires that we examine the boundaries of intelligence and ignorance in a search to understand the ways in which knowledge is a racialized text. As educators, we must refuse everyday practices that fail to interrogate the ways in which knowledge is assigned worth—this is the Latino/a curriculum of a post-reconceptualist era.

Notes

1. J. Flores, "The Latino Imaginary," in *From Bomba to Hip-Hop: Puerto Rican Culture and Latino Identity* (New York: Columbia University Press, 2000), pp. 191–203.

2. In Spencer's (1869) "What Knowledge Is of Most Worth?" he asserts that this question must be answered before the commencement of curriculum and instruction. As a Social Dar-

winist, he felt the curriculum should aid in advancing survival and progress and specified five essential curriculum activities: self-preservation, performance of occupations, child-rearing, social and political participation, and recreation and leisure.

3. Covering a wide range of topics; eclectic; rambling.

4. Ultimately in the space between the other and the self there are those things that individuals do not understand but attempt to give meaning to because the dissimilarity matters to them. Understanding how these disparate elements of our lives come to have meaning is a key aim of Hispanic curriculum.

5. The term is used to designate subjugated alternative spaces where historically oppressed groups gather to make meaning outside the dominant cultures of the conventional community spaces. For example, during the civil rights era, churches were key subaltern spaces for developing an different understanding of "blackness" than that of the dominant white culture.

6. *Currere,* the Latin root of curriculum, means "to run a course." In the field of curriculum, currere has been interpreted, particularly through the work of William Pinar (2004), as inquiry into the individual experience of the public. This theoretical perspective suggests that a cogent approach to teaching and learning will have to address how various people have divergent understandings of the public sphere.

7. As a part of the mythology surrounding the American dream, particularly the investment in rugged individualism, is a denial of how our identities are shaped by social and historical contexts. In this sense, who we are as people is always located and enabled and limited by our lived experiences and the legacies of those who came before us. The notion of a dreamt up past refers to appeals to a historical period when things were better by those who would use such pleas to silence historically oppressed groups who, particularly since the 1960s, have asserted their own voices.

8. The notion of the other encapsulates a wide range of social groups and identities that are out-side the mainstream. This includes gay, bisexual, lesbian, and transgender concerns, as well as race, gender, and class issues, among others.

9. Latinos run the highest risks of suffering injuries and job-related illnesses and also have a higher fatality rate than the rest of the country's workers. See La Raza, http://laraza.com/news.php?nid=22280.

10. There has been documented resistance to establishing academic programs and social services for Hispanics and Latinos in colleges and universities. See Rhoads (1998).

11. One of the most interesting dimensions of present-day politics involves the concurrent bodily diversification and ideological homogenization of government leadership. Such situations speak to the need to have more complex discussions of racial issues in the general public.

12. These four questions are drawn from the Tyler Rationale, arguably one of the most influential curriculum documents shaping how curriculum is thought about in the academy as well as schools. See Tyler (1949).

References

Apple, M. (2001). *Educating the "Right" Way: Market, Standards, God, and Inequality.* New York: RoutledgeFalmer.

Berry, W. (1990). "A Remarkable Man." In *What Are People For?* (pp. 17–29). San Francisco: North Point Press.

Britzman, D. (1991). *Practice Makes Practice: A Critical Study of Learning to Teach.* Albany, NY: SUNY Press.

Du Bois, W.E.B. (1903). *The Souls of Black Folk.* Chicago: A. C. McClurg.

Hall, S. (1997). *Representation: Cultural Representations and Signifying Practices.* Thousand Oaks, CA: Sage.

Hall, S. (2001). *Different.* New York: Phaidon.

McClaren, P., & González-Gaudiano, E. (1995). Education and Globalization: An Environmental Perspective—An Interview with Edgar González-Gaudiano. *International Journal of Educational Reform* 4(1), 72–78.

Morrison, T. (1989). Unspeakable Things Unspoken: The Afro-American Presence in

American Literature. *Michigan Quarterly* 28(1), 1–34.

National Commission on Excellence in Education. (1983). *A Nation at Risk: The Imperative for Educational Reform.* Washington, DC: U.S. Government Printing Office.

Omni, M., & Winant, H. (1989). *Racial Formation in the United States: From the 1960s to the 1980s.* New York: Routledge.

Pinar, W. (1993). Notes on Understanding Curriculum as Racial Text. In C. McCarthy & W. Crichlow (Eds.), *Race, Identity and Representation in Education* (pp. 60–70). New York: Routledge.

Pinar, W. (2004). *What Is Curriculum Theory?* Mahwah, NJ: Lawrence Erlbaum.

Rhoads, R. (1998). *Freedom's Web: Student Activism in an Age of Cultural Diversity.* Baltimore: Johns Hopkins University Press.

Spencer, H. (1859). What Knowledge Is of Most Worth? In H. Spencer (1861), *On Education.* London: Everyman Publishing.

Takaki, R. (1993). *A Different Mirror: A History of Multicultural America.* Boston: Back Bay Books.

Tyler, R. W. (1949). *Basic Principles of Curriculum and Instruction.* Chicago: University of Chicago Press.

Recommended Reading

Anzaldúa, G. (1999). *Borderlands/La Frontera: The New Mestiza.* San Francisco: Aunt Lute Books.

Britzman, D. (1998). *Lost Subjects, Contested Objects: Toward a Psychoanalytic Inquiry of Learning.* Albany, NY: SUNY Press.

Britzman, D. (2003). *After-Education: Anna Freud, Melanie Klein and Psychoanalytic Histories of Learning.* Albany, NY: SUNY Press.

De Alba, A., González-Gaudiano, E., Lankshear, C., & Peters, M. (1999). *Curriculum in the Postmodern Condition.* New York: Peter Lang.

De Genova, N., & Zayas, A. R. (2003). *Latino Crossings: Mexicans, Puerto Ricans, and the politics of Race and Citizenship.* New York: Routledge.

Delgado, R., & Stefancic, J. (2001). *Critical Race Theory: An Introduction.* New York: New York University Press.

Laclau, E. (2001). Democracy and the Question of Power. *Constellations* 8(1), 3–14.

Morrison, T. (1993). *Playing in the Dark: Whiteness and the Literary Imagination.* London: Vintage.

Pinar, W. (2004). *What Is Curriculum Theory?* Mahwah, NJ: Lawrence Erlbaum.

Erik Malewski

NATIONAL DROPOUT PREVENTION CENTER/NETWORK

The National Dropout Prevention Center/ Network (NDPC/N) at Clemson University was founded in 1986 to serve as a clearinghouse for information on issues related to school improvement and dropout prevention and to offer strategies that increase the graduation rate in America's schools.

The NDPC/N has learned that in "dropout prevention" you can never start too soon to ensure future success. Thus the strategies we have identified include approaches for the youngest of our nation's children as well as for those youth who have experienced years of difficulty in school. Within all school improvement initiatives are dropout prevention strategies that can be found at all grade levels and in community and family settings.

The NDPC/N is a well-established national and international resource for sharing solutions for student success. It does so through its clearinghouse function, through its active research projects and publications, and through a variety of professional development activities. In addition, the NDPC/N conducts a vast array of third-party evaluations of school-based and community-based dropout prevention projects.

An Added Dimension—Students with Disabilities

In January 2004 the NDPC/N became the home of the new National Dropout Prevention Center for Students with Disabilities (NDPC-SD). This federally funded initiative is a partnership with the Education Development Center, Inc. (EDC), and the Intercultural Development Research Association (IDRA) and will strengthen the NDPC/N work with state and local education agencies, educators, parents, and others working with this special population. Join a growing network of advocates and practitioners. Check our Web site, www.drop outprevention.org.

Marty Duckenfield

NATIONAL TASK FORCE ON EARLY CHILDHOOD EDUCATION FOR HISPANICS

During summer 2004 the National Task Force on Early Childhood Education for Hispanics was established to identify major issues in early childhood education for Hispanic children in the U.S. and to make recommendations for action. Launched with a grant from the Foundation for Child Development, the task force has as its focus the educational needs of Hispanic children from birth through the primary grades. The task force's chair is Dr. Eugene E. Garcia, Dean of the College of Education and Vice President for School-University Partnerships at Arizona State University (ASU). Members of the task force, housed at ASU, include policymakers, practitioners, corporate, community, strategic thinkers, researchers, and educators of early childhood educators and teachers. The task force has convened for an initial period of two years, at the end of which time it will issue a major report on its findings and recommendations for action. It is projected that the task force would meet once per year, with the initial meeting having taken place in fall 2004.

The task force has been created for several reasons. Available evidence indicates that the much lower levels of academic achievement in high school and college of Hispanic students compared to whites and Asian Americans are heavily related to the large differences in achievement that exist at the end of the primary grades. Moreover, the lower levels of achievement of Hispanics in the primary grades are related in part to substantial differences in school readiness at the beginning of kindergarten between Hispanics and their white and Asian counterparts. Thus, there is a pressing need to improve educational outcomes and share these outcomes with the greater community, including an emphasis in the Latino community.

Available evidence also indicates that Hispanic youngsters who have serious academic difficulties tend to be economically and educationally disadvantaged. Their parents tend to have little formal education and low incomes, and their schools typically serve high percentages of disadvantaged students. Their situation is complicated further by the fact that a majority of disadvantaged Hispanic youngsters are from immigrant families, which means that many are not proficient in English when they start kindergarten (and many of their parents are not proficient in English). Furthermore, finding ways to help much higher percentages of these children get off to a good start during the early childhood years is an increasingly pressing matter for the nation because Hispanics are rapidly becoming a large majority of disadvantaged youngsters in the U.S. Although less recognized, there also is a need to improve academic performance in the early child-hood years for middle-class Hispanics, who are not yet doing as well as middle-class white and Asian students.

There are three major challenges for the task force. The first challenge is to identify the most effective existing strategies for improving educational outcomes in the early childhood years for Hispanics, in-cluding the most effective approaches for promoting development of infants and toddlers, the most effective approaches for preschool education, and the most effective approaches for K–3 schooling. The second challenge is to lay out an agenda for de-veloping a larger set of proven strategies, because the existing body of strategies with strong evidence that they improve out-comes for Hispanics is expected to be rel-atively small. The third is to develop recommendations for policymakers, prac-titioners, National Latino organizations, and other key parties that can help ensure that effective strategies are disseminated among key local, state, and national groups, in-cluding key Latino groups.

Eugene E. Garcia

THE NEED FOR HIGHLY QUALIFIED LATINO TEACHERS

All children in the U.S. should have access to a high-quality education, which clearly requires having highly qualified teachers. For the Latino community, where a ma-jority of children struggle academically, discussions regarding what constitutes "highly qualified" may include conversa-tions regarding the possibility of having teachers who are also Latino. Although most educators agree that a highly qualified teacher should not be defined by whether or not he or she matches culturally, spe-cifically ethnically or linguistically, with a

classroom of students, that most educators do not is a concern in the Latino community for a number of reasons. The following are some major issues connected to the need to increase and maintain a strong cadre of highly qualified Latino teachers: (1) aca-demic performance of Latino students, (2) the potential benefits of having a Latino teacher, (3) the Latino teacher shortage and recommendations for the recruitment and retention of highly qualified Latino teachers.

Academic Performance of Latino Students

Latino students in our public schools are still performing as poorly today as they did 10 years ago (Espinoza-Herold, 2003). The difference from 10 years ago is that the number of Latino students has increased significantly. Unfortunately, most of these students are considered to be at risk of school failure; without intense intervention, this problem will only continue to worsen in the years to come. Factors typically used to define Latino students at risk include those living in a family headed by a single parent, having parents with limited educations and who depend on welfare (Espinoza-Herold, 2003), and being limited English proficient (Garcia, 2001). It is expected that the number of Latino students at risk will in-tensify at the same rate that student diver-sity in general will continue to flourish. Estimates predict that the minority student population, which was 39% in the year 2000 (NCES, 2003), will continue to increase and put white students in the minority in about 40 years (García, 2001). This is already the case in many school districts in California, where 34% of the Latino population resides (Brice, 2002). Many other states across the country, including Texas, Florida, and New York, are also coping with school districts where minorities are the majority and where often Latinos are the largest group (Brice, 2002). By the year 2000, Latinos made up 17% of the minority enrollment in public schools (NCES, 2003). Sadly, an alarming number of Latino students, approximately one-third, end up dropping out of school (Espinoza-Herold, 2003).

It is important to be mindful that the Latino, or Hispanic, population is quite heterogeneous, comprised of diverse subgroups, each with particular characteristics that require consideration whenever social factors are discussed. In the U.S. the Latino population is about 32 million, with Mexicans making up 58% of that total. Together with Puerto Ricans (13%) and Cubans (6%), these groups comprise 77% of the total Latino population (Brice, 2002). In the year 2000 there were approximately 3.4 million language minority children, between the ages of 5 and 14, in the U.S. (García, 2001). Today there are well over 3 million limited English students in public schools, 70% of which come from Spanish-speaking homes (Brice, 2002).

Why do Latinos drop out of school at such an alarming rate? Along with the significant increase of Latino students there is a wider disparity of educational experience. Whereas whites and blacks have seen an increase in the number of students graduating from high school, Latinos have remained stagnant. In the year 2000 almost three out of every ten Latinos dropped out of school in comparison to only 3.8% of Asian/Pacific Islanders, 6.9% of whites, and 13.1% of blacks (Espinoza-Herold, 2003). Surprisingly, immigrant Hispanics had lower dropout rates, 8.3%, than native-born students of Hispanic descent and were also more likely to pursue a college degree (García, 2001). While poor academic performance accounts for half of the reasons Latino students are unsuccessful in schools

(García, 2001), other reasons include feeling disconnected from the school, absence of caring adults to talk to, and racist attitudes from teachers (Espinoza-Herold, 2003).

Educators need to engage in critical dialogues to address other pertinent questions. Some questions to consider: What difference does it make if a student has a teacher from the same cultural and linguistic background as themselves? Can student performance differ significantly when their cultural and/or linguistic backgrounds match with that of their teacher's? Or, more specifically, Will Latino children perform better with a Latino teacher?

The Potential Benefits of Having Latino Teachers

Several underlying principles support the belief that Latino children would benefit from having Latino teachers. Latino teachers bring cultural and linguistic familiarity. They can help bridge the gap between home and school. They can also provide positive role models for Latino children. Being from the same community, the Latino teacher may understand differences in beliefs between the community and the school environment. For example, there is a distinct difference in how a Latino community and a typical public school define what it means to be educated or to have "educación" (CREDE, 2001; García, 2001). While being educated typically means academic achievement according to public school standards, to a Latino family it may mean that the individual is well mannered and respectful (García, 2001).

Knowledge of the culture and language can also facilitate the development of a meaningful social relationship between the student and teacher. Latino students may be more inclined to communicate with a

Latino teacher who speaks Spanish, especially if the students are recent immigrants or, beginning English language learners (ELLs). Having someone validates their culture and language may help counteract the negative experiences of Latino students, who are often surrounded by harmful messages about their ethnic group or language (Espinosa-Herold, 2003). Also, Latino students may be more open about sharing culturally relevant information when they are speaking to someone who has some understanding as opposed to someone totally unfamiliar with their culture and language.

In many bilingual or English as a Second Language (ESL) instructional settings, however, it is the paraprofessional and not the lead teacher who develops personal relationships with the students (CREDE, 2001). Often while the teacher is involved in formal academic instruction and monitoring entire classes, the paraprofessional is engaged in providing individualized social and emotional support (CREDE, 2001). Unquestionably, Latino students would benefit tremendously, as would any student, from having a Latino teacher able to invest individualized time in getting to know them and addressing their social and emotional needs.

Having teachers who provide culturally responsive instruction is also critical to Latino student achievement (Bennett, 2003; García, 2001). This is not to imply that simply because a teacher happens to come from the same ethnic, cultural, or linguistic group as the student that automatically the teacher will incorporate more culturally responsive curriculum. There is, however, the possibility that a Latino teacher may be more disposed to incorporate students' cultures and languages into the curriculum. Some Latino teachers, especially those who share similar backgrounds and school ex-

periences with their students, have acquired an understanding for the importance of culturally relevant pedagogy (García, 2001).

In addition, Latino children need Latino role models (Espinoza-Herold, 2003; Nieto, 2004), and non-Latino students would also benefit from having a Latino teacher (García, 2001). When teachers are from the same racial, ethnic, and cultural backgrounds as the students, there are significant positive results on the students' academic performance (Bracy & Molnar, 2003; Nieto, 2004; Zirkel, 2002). Having a teacher to identify with affords students a positive role model to emulate and also serves as concrete evidence of possible achievement levels for themselves. It is equally important for the non-Latino student to experience having a Latino teacher. Given the direction of this country's projected demographics, all students would benefit from having teachers from a diversity of racial, ethnic, and cultural backgrounds. Being afforded more opportunities to engage in educational or social experiences with teachers, and others, from diverse backgrounds can help prepare students to work more effectively among the culturally diverse workforce they will undoubtedly be a part of (Bennett, 2003; García, 2001).

The Latino Teacher Shortage

While concerns over the critical teacher shortage facing our country today have been in the forefront for some time, the alarming shortage of Latino teachers, currently between 3% to 4% of the total teaching force (García, 2001), has not received the serious attention and imperative action needed. The current status of Latino student academic performance, along with the projected Latino student growth, necessitates swift action. Educators need to ask tough questions: Why are Latino children doing so poorly in the public schools across the country? One possibility is that teachers are not adequately prepared to deal with the growing number of culturally and linguistically diverse children coming into their classrooms, most of whom are Latino. How is higher education addressing this problem? Or, what is higher education doing to recruit and prepare Latino students into teacher preparation programs? Although some gains have been made, it is not enough to keep up with the demands, given the trend in Latino student population growth.

Our country cannot afford to continue to ignore this problem at the expense of better futures for Latino children. To ignore this issue would be to ignore the impact this situation will have on the future of this country. Educators and politicians need to investigate this issue closely and reflect on the enormous burden that multitudes of uneducated and unskilled Latinos will have on our future welfare. As García (2001) so poignantly asks, "Can education rise to this challenge and accommodate students it has historically underserved but needs so desperately in the future?"

Highly Qualified Latino Teachers

Teachers are unquestionably the most influential factor affecting academic success or failure in the typical classrooms today (Bennett, 2003; García, 2001). Given that a diversity of students will come in with varying degrees of knowledge, skills, and abilities, it is the teacher who must orchestrate the delivery of the same curriculum to all of them. It is also the teacher who will be held accountable for assessing student performance that must adhere to the expected state or national standards. This enormous challenge becomes even more difficult when there is immense disequilibrium between the students' cultures and that of

the school. Consequently, it becomes even more essential that students be taught by the most highly qualified teachers possible.

Currently some professional organizations are attempting to define exactly what "highly qualified" means; others attribute specific characteristics to this type of teacher. According to the No Child Left Behind Act (Yell & Drasgow, 2005), highly qualified teachers must have (1) full state certification or licensure, (2) a bachelor's degree, and (3) proof that they know each subject they teach. Others, including educators and professional organizations, use a diversity of criteria to define what a quality teacher is and what constitutes quality teaching. Cruickshank and Haefele (2001) compiled the following list of 10 terms, used by a number of different entities since the mid-twentieth century, to define perceptions of a good teacher: ideal, analytic, effective, dutiful, competent, expert, reflective, satisfying, diversity-responsive, and respected. All these attributes are important and should be expected of individuals preparing to become teachers. Ideally, and in addition to being diversity-responsive, for those teaching Latino students, speaking Spanish would be another important attribute to possess. Also, research strongly supports the fact that high teacher expectations is an apparent indicator of student success (Bennett, 2003; García, 2001; Nieto, 2004).

Eugene García (2001), a highly respected educator and scholar, describes that while having a strong family infrastructure was also a critical factor, it was teacher expectations that dictated the academic path he followed. He relates how during his junior high years he learned not to work very hard because no one expected him to, and how he managed to make a C in Spanish without ever opening a book. He also excelled in sports, which he credits to brothers and cousins who had him playing basketball and baseball at a very young age. Had it not been for several coaches who noticed his athletic skills and abilities, one in particular who "cared" about him, and a Spanish teacher who pushed him academically, he may not have gone on to pursue a higher education. García acknowledges that "academic success became its own reward" and eloquently states, "Access to that success opened new worlds, created new visions and goals, and offered me resources that were not available to many of my family members." Today Dr. Eugene E. García is dean of and professor in the School of Education at the University of California, Berkeley, has published extensively, and has served in numerous high-level positions.

Recruiting and Maintaining More Latino Teachers

Although some efforts to recruit and maintain qualified Latino teachers in exist, they are limited and operating on scarce resources. One endeavor worth modeling is Project Alianza, which is currently being implemented by the Intercultural Development Research Association (IDRA) in response to the need for more bilingual education teachers (Rodriguez, 2003). Working in partnership with universities and communities in the U.S. and Mexico to implement this program, Project Alianza is committed to sharing a number critical lessons learned. These lessons merit reiterating here:

- Schools of education must place high value on teacher education for a diverse student population and support this work within their institutions.
- Schools must share successful approaches for recruiting and retaining Latino teachers in teacher preparation programs in states with emerging numbers of Latino students.
- We must expand the body of research and knowledge about preparing Latino educators with key stakeholders in education, community and policy.
- We must compile a comprehensive set of policies, practices and programs that enhance the preparation of educators who teach Latino students.
- Schools of education must prepare educators to serve Latino students and other students from culturally diverse backgrounds.
- Schools of education must identify and recruit teacher candidates from alternative and non-traditional pools, such as *normalistas,* instructional assistants or professionals in other fields.
- We must develop holistic assessment and support programs for educators that rely primarily on the demonstration of knowledge and performance in the classroom.
- Schools of education must provide consistent support for individuals when they enter a teacher education program to complete all requirements for certification and work in the classroom.
- Schools of education must disseminate innovative strategies that prepare teachers for Latino and other minority students for teacher educators, both in school districts and in universities.
- Schools of education must create meaningful partnerships between schools, communities and universities to support teacher recruitment, preparation, and placement, allowing prospective teachers to study theory and practice throughout their training while they apply prior experience.
- Schools of education must develop a corp faculty across disciplines with the primary responsibility for reshaping teacher preparation.
- Schools of education must hire faculty for their teacher education programs who are experienced, well prepared and knowledgeable about effective strategies for Latino and other minority students.

- Schools of education must work in conjunction with schools and communities to tap alternative pools of teacher candidates in order to develop a cadre of teachers who are more experienced, more culturally diverse, and more understanding of Latino and other minority students' needs.

- Schools of education must expose teacher candidates to K–12 classrooms with Latino and diverse student bodies early in their preparation.

- Teacher education programs should build competencies that emphasize all aspects for developing Latino student self-esteem and motivation.

- We must continue to foster strong alliances and networks with key institutions across borders dedicated to improving teacher recruitment, preparation, and placement for our changing demographics. (Rodriguez, 2003)

Conclusion

All students across the country, not only Latino students, could benefit from an increase in the number of highly qualified Latino teachers in their classrooms. The emphasis is on "highly qualified" to ascertain that simply being a Latino teacher is not regarded at the same level as being a "highly qualified" Latino teacher. Clearly, for Latino students as well as for other students, there are many benefits to having teachers who are Latino. Primarily, Latino teachers can serve as positive role models and cultural bridges between the communities and the schools. Having Latino teachers who are familiar with Latino culture and language and express an appreciation for both appears to affect students' academic performance positively. It is also clear that a more responsive school context that builds and supports bridges between home and school would contribute in invaluable ways by providing teach-

ers who reflect the population of students served.

References

Bennett, C. I. (2003). *Comprehensive Multicultural Education: Theory and Practice* (3rd ed.). Boston: Allyn & Bacon.

Bracy, G. W., & Molnar, A. (2003). *Recruiting, Preparing and Retaining High Quality Teachers: An Empirical Synthesis*. Tempe: Arizona State University, Education Policy Research Unit (EPSL-0302-102-EPRU).

Brice, A. E. (2002). *The Hispanic Child*. Boston: Allyn & Bacon.

Center for Research on Education, Diversity & Excellence (CREDE). (2001). *Sociocultural Factors in Social Relationships: Examining Latino Teachers' and Paraeducators' Interactions with Latino Students* (Research Report 9). Washington, DC: CREDE.

Cruickshank, D. R., & Haefele, D. (2001). Good Teachers, Plural. *Educational Leadership* (February), pp. 26–30.

Espinoza-Herold, M. (2003). *Issues in Latino Education: Race, School Culture, and the Politics of Academic Success*. Boston: Allyn & Bacon.

García, E. E. (2001). *Hispanic Education in the United States: Raíces y alas*. Lanham, MD: Rowman & Littlefield.

National Center for Education Statistics (NCES). (2003). *The Condition of Education*. Washington, DC: U.S. Department of Education.

Nieto, S. (2004). *Affirming Diversity; The Sociopolitical Context of Multicultural Education*. Boston: Allyn & Bacon.

Rodriguez, R. G. (2003). The Power of Partnerships: How Alianza Is Reshaping Bilingual Teacher Preparation. *IDRA (Intercultural Development Research Associates) Newsletter*, May.

Yell, L. Mitchell, & Drasgow, E. (2005). *No Child Left Behind: A Guide for Professionals*. Upper Saddle River, NJ: Pearson.

Zirkel, S. (2002). Is There a Place for Me? Role Models and Achievement among White

Students and Students of Color. *Teachers College Record* 104, 357–376.

Recommended Reading

Gibson, M. A., Gándara, P., & Koyama, J. P. (Eds.). (2004). *School Connections: U.S. Mexican Youth, Peers, and School Achievement.* New York: Teachers College Press.

McLaren, P. (2000). *Che Guevara, Paulo Freire, and the Pedagogy of Revolution.* Lanham, MD: Rowman & Littlefield.

Valdés, G. (2001). *Learning and Not Learning English: Latin Students in American Schools.* New York: Teachers College Press.

Cathy Gutierrez-Gomez

THE NEW LATINO DIASPORA AND EDUCATION

Over the last two decades of the twentieth century the Hispanic population of the U.S. more than doubled and now makes up 12.5% of the entire U.S. population (Hobbs & Stoops, 2002). This phenomenal growth is part of the "New Immigration," which began in 1965 when immigration laws changed, bringing newcomers primarily from Latin America, Africa, and Asia. The new Latino immigrants, who come especially from Mexico and Central America, have transformed the U.S. Hispanic population in traditional immigrant-receiving areas such as California and the Southwest, Texas and Florida, and the urban areas of New York and Chicago. They have also brought a new cultural presence to the Midwest, the Southeast, and the Rocky Mountains states, where there were previously few Hispanics. The 2000 U.S. Census shows that the Hispanic population in many counties throughout these latter regions grew more than 200% since 1990.

The Latino newcomers of the 1980s and 1990s affect communities of all sizes throughout the country, but they have had special impact on smaller towns and rural areas. This "New Latino Diaspora," as it has been called (Wortham, Murillo, & Hamann, 2002), created radical changes in longtime stable, relatively homogeneous communities very quickly. In more rural areas, predominantly European American towns that had experienced little diversity since they were founded changed dramatically, often in less than 10 years. In one midwestern county, for example, a meatpacking plant opened in 1992; the Latino population grew from 1,634 in 1990 to 6,003 in 2000—a growth of over 350%.

Reasons for the Latino Diaspora

At the root of these changes was the growing U.S. economy. Businesses needed workers in occupations requiring agricultural skills such as landscaping and groundskeeping, as well as in the tourist and hotel industry, construction, light manufacturing, and the meatpacking industry. The meatpacking industry is a key player throughout the Midwest and Southeast, whereas in the Rocky Mountain states the tourist industry is a primary employer. In many instances, however, immigrants found work not with one major employer but in a variety of smaller businesses throughout a locale. They provide needed workers, contribute to the U.S. economy, and pay taxes.

Some rural areas with new Hispanic populations were earlier stops on migrant workers' routes picking fruit and other crops, or working in other seasonal occupations. In these areas, some families settled out of the migrant stream when year-round jobs became available. Others, however, have come directly from Mexico and Central America to the U.S., sometimes joining family and friends in a new hometown or region, or have been recruited by a labor go-between for a particular company.

The current workers from Mexico and Central America continue a tradition of supplying labor to U.S. businesses. Mexican migrant labor has picked crops, built the U.S. railroads, and worked in industry since the U.S. took over the Mexican lands north of the Rio Grande. At times these workers have had official sanction, such as the "Braceros" program that brought Mexican workers into the U.S. from 1942 to the early 1960s. In 2004, building on this tradition, President George W. Bush and President Vicente Fox of Mexico proposed a new "guest worker" agreement that would provide for temporary legal residence for Mexican workers. Since the current immigration system does not provide enough workers to fill U.S. needs (Waslin, 2004), many newcomers are undocumented. However, it is estimated that 96% of undocumented men are in the labor force.

These workers primarily come from rural backgrounds, are skilled agriculturalists and accustomed to hard physical labor, and are rooted in a culture that values a strong work ethic and sense of responsibility to families. They are willing to take low-level, sometimes dangerous, low-wage jobs. Research on the meatpacking industry documents that workers are often injured to the point where they can no longer work, without access to medical care, insurance, or workers' compensation. Such workers are abandoned by the U.S. system that used their labor (Stull, Broadway, & Griffith, 1995). In some instances, employers simply refuse to pay workers.

In any migrant stream there are both "pull" and "push" factors. "Push" factors in Mexico and Central America include globalization forces that undermine rural economies, forcing farm workers off the land and into the international labor pool. Mexico's "closed society" offers limited upward mobility (Valdés, 1996), and economic struggles are compounded, some newcomers say, by hiring practices enmeshed in nepotism and graft. Central Americans in particular often come from countries such as Guatemala and Nicaragua that are still suffering the aftermath of years of war and civil disruption.

Community Issues and Responses

In regions where the Hispanic population is new, communities face many challenges with little experience and few resources. Growing newcomer immigrant communities need access to a variety of civic infrastructures, including medical care, housing, transportation, and schools. Spanish-speaking translators and people who are familiar with the needs of immigrant families become necessary in hospitals, courthouses, schools, and other civic institutions. In communities with few bilingual residents, these needs must often be initially met with scarce volunteers. With changes to the federal welfare system, states now have more decision-making power about providing social services, but they also have more of the financial burden (Passel, Capps, & Fix, 2004).

The new residents change the fabric of community life. While cities are affected by larger numbers of immigrants, in smaller communities the percentage change is greater and the entire civic life of a community is involved. Some receiving communities have at times felt overwhelmed, at a loss, or even resentful. Residents may believe that the Latino workers are taking jobs away from local workers. Local residents are often not fully aware of the reasons Spanish-speaking workers and families have appeared in their midst, and they may be unaware of the economic benefits these workers are bringing to the community. For example, some communities have invited a meatpacking industry to set up a plant, seeking the economic benefits of a new industry. They have then been surprised when Latino or other immigrant workers come in, or are brought in by the company itself, to help meet the plant's demand for workers (Stull et al., 1995).

Negative characterizations such as "dirty Mexicans" and stereotypes such as "they don't care about education" may be circulated. Established residents also raise the question, "Why don't they learn English?" It is clear, however, that immigrants know that they need English (Tse, 2001). If they do not succeed in learning English, it is not because they do not value it. Most often, adults working long hours in low-paying jobs while raising a family find little time or energy to study English.

Resentment causes some communities to resist providing social and civic resources to immigrants and discriminate against them in a variety of ways. Available housing may be substandard. Medical care may be difficult to find. Local institutions avoid hiring Spanish-speaking workers. Newcomers may suffer police harassment. Depending on local laws, there may be no way undocumented workers can get a driver's license, or the driver's license test may not be available in Spanish. Since in many communities driving a car is a necessity, police then arrest immigrants for driving without a license.

Just as local residents may not understand why Latino newcomers have settled in their community, the immigrants wonder why they are resented. From the newcomers' perspective, they are taking jobs others do not want, making very little and barely supporting themselves while being poorly treated on the job and in the community.

In addressing these challenges, churches and established social service agencies,

such as Catholic Charities and the YWCA, often provide leadership in helping newcomers. Immigrants turn to both Roman Catholic and Spanish-speaking Protestant congregations. There may be a few established Latinos and supporters in a community who can help create a base of support and build on it. Some school districts have taken the lead in bringing people together.

Newcomers actually represent a great resource for community renewal and development. Rural America has been on the decline in recent decades as factory farms and agribusiness have pushed families off the land. Contemporary meatpacking plants and other low-wage jobs do not offer the working conditions and salaries that local residents seek. As the children of longtime residents move away, many small towns are desperately seeking ways to stay alive. Mason City, Iowa, has actively recruited immigrants to settle there to offset a population exodus (Belsie, 2001). Latino families are, for the moment, offering a powerful new source of human capital.

Effect on Schools and Education

The New Latino Diaspora is significant for educational institutions because adults in their prime working years are immigrating to work, bringing families, and raising children here while leaving older family members at home. The Hispanic population is younger than the general U.S. population. In 2000 about one-third were under age 18 (the majority under age 15). This means that schools and other youth-serving institutions are and will continue to be especially affected by this new population. Hispanic families are also raising their children with limited financial resources. Households are larger than those of non-Hispanic whites, but about 75% of workers employed year-round make less than

$35,000. While Hispanic children are about one-fifth of the total U.S. population under 18, they represent one-third of the children living in poverty.

Schools have quickly reflected the presence of the newcomer families. Seemingly overnight, relatively homogeneous communities need Spanish-speaking staff and teachers. In Dalton, Georgia, Hispanic enrollment grew from less than 1% in 1987 to majority Hispanic in 2000–2001 (Hamann, 2003). A midwestern rural school district of 1,000 students in grades kindergarten through 12 went from a few families to one-third Hispanic enrollment in the same period.

The educational needs of the Latino Diaspora are twofold: both adults and children need access to educational services.

Education for Adults

Providing education to adults is important so they can support their families better, as well as support their children in doing well in school. Adults not only need English as a Second Language (ESL) but also may need literacy and adult basic education, and/or GED programs because schooling was not always available to them at home. Until the mid-1990s, only six years of schooling were mandated in Mexico. Although nine are now officially required, many children cannot stay in school because their families lack resources. Adults from Central America grew up during and after war's tremendous civil disruption. While one Latino parent project in Chicago serves participants with an average of a seventh grade education (personal communication, Flora Rodriguez Brown), other projects have found that many parents may have four years of schooling or less.

Many communities face difficulties in providing needed courses or use inappro-

priate materials and curricula developed for other kinds of adult students. The most often used approaches are literacy based, rather than focusing on oral communication. These teaching methods and materials do not address the needs of adult students who do not have much formal schooling, are not accustomed to using books to learn, and have low literacy in Spanish. Given family and work responsibilities, working adults also may find it difficult to attend classes at all, even if they are held at times when they are not working. Transportation to the teaching sites may be a problem.

K–12 Education

The public schools face a wide range of challenges in providing services to newcomer immigrant students. If the community has been part of the migrant worker "stream," there may be some resources and services in place that were developed as part of federal Migrant Education programs. Even so, these need to be adapted when families become year-round residents.

Perplexed school districts and teachers face the challenges of teaching children from cultural backgrounds different from the established community, with few resources available to them. Schools already under pressure from the struggling economies and reduced state support of the first years of the twenty-first century may be inadequately funded. Relatively quickly, schools find that they need Spanish-speaking staff. There may be none in the entire district. They need to communicate with parents, for very basic reasons, such as informing them where to go to register the child for school. They need translators for common kinds of parent communication letters. Districts often start with volunteer translators, but this can only be a temporary measure. The district must also hire

ESL teachers and, occasionally, staff bilingual or dual-language programs.

Providing access to the educational program is particularly problematic. Although bilingual education has been documented as the best way to teach immigrant students effectively, federal and state policies have dropped bilingual education in favor of "English immersion" approaches. Many districts are deciding to use "sheltered instruction," which places immigrant students in regular classrooms with ESL support, variously structured. Frequently, however, classroom teachers would like Spanish-speaking students to be in separate classrooms, rather than integrated into the "regular" classes. This is appropriate only if trained bilingual teachers are available to offer subject instruction in both Spanish and English. Many districts have only ESL teachers who are not qualified to teach subject matter. Usually there are not enough of them even to provide enough support to classroom teachers. Regular classroom teachers, unprepared to teach second language learners, are likely to provide less-demanding content to compensate for language-learning needs. Thus professional development for local faculty to learn how to teach second language learners is a critical need.

Tensions between established residents and newcomers affect schools as well. School policies and practices, as well as the students, may treat Latinos as "outsiders," even after the families have been in the district for some time. When Spanish-speaking families first start to settle in a school district, one ESL teacher may be traveling to several schools. Educators all over the Diaspora report that ESL classes may meet literally in closets. On the other hand, some districts meet the challenge by applying for the available funding and

developing appropriate programs, including dual-language approaches.

With such challenges in providing and gaining access to educational resources, it is not surprising that newcomer students encounter many of the same problems as Latinos in established communities. Nationally, 27% of Hispanics have not completed high school. Schools often hold low expectations for Latino students and do not provide full access to classes or information about further schooling or careers. It is more difficult for Latino students to participate in college preparatory work where such opportunities do exist. These conditions may contribute to low high school completion rates and college attendance.

Latino Immigrants' Perspectives on the Schools

To the students and their parents, the U.S. school system is very different from what they are used to. Students are coming from a different school day, a different grading system, and other "taken for granted" aspects of school. Parents do not understand such basics as how the schools are organized, when to expect report cards, how homework is given, and how students transition to the next higher school. Parents and students need initial orientation to all these issues.

Both parents and schools identify communication as a key issue. In Mexico, even parents with little formal education have access to communication with their children's schools and can participate in customary ways. They raise their children to be *bien educado*. While this term literally translates as "well-educated," it refers not to schooling but to someone who is respectful to others, carries out responsibilities to family, and is a decent person. Parents expect to send their children to school "ready to learn" in the sense that they will be well fed, clean, and clothed. "The teacher is your second mother," parents tell children, and the children are expected to be respectful and obedient as they are to their parents. In return, the teacher expects to take complete responsibility for students' academic development.

"Parent involvement" also differs from the concept held in U.S. schools. In Mexico, for example, mothers may come to the school to help with lunch; fathers contribute labor to school projects, such as painting classrooms, an activity is done by unionized employees in the U.S.; and whole families participate in school-sponsored events on national holidays. Parents supervise homework, but they do not necessarily help them work on assignments. When parents and schools cannot even communicate in the most basic fashion, these differences in cultural expectations may not be even recognized. Everyone involved may experience a great deal of frustration. Teachers mistakenly come to believe that "parents do not care about education."

Language issues are also crucial. Parents want their children to learn English. Most of the children do learn English, at least verbal communication, quickly and relatively fluently. (There is a range of the command of Standard English grammar and intonation patterns.) At the same time, they may "lose" their Spanish or not continue to develop Spanish into full adult usage. Parents say about their children, "They speak bad Spanish." Younger children may not develop as much Spanish and become literally unable to communicate directly with their own parents. When parents and children cannot communicate directly or cannot communicate fully and richly in the same native language, parenting becomes much more difficult (Kouritzin, 1999).

Some parents see school in the U.S. as a way to improve their children's life chances. They hope that the children can attend college and have a "career." However, their lack of knowledge of U.S. schools and preparation for careers may hamper these hopes. Helping parents understand the U.S. school system and occupations is another way to assist families in supporting their children's education. Interestingly, in the early 2000s several states passed laws allowing undocumented immigrant students to pay in-state college tuition.

Educational Responses So Far

There are no easy responses to these challenges. Some districts and states have responded more proactively than others. In Georgia, a school district developed a partnership with a Mexican university that included a teacher exchange program (Hamann, 2003). In the Upper Midwest, a community where a number of Southeast Asian refugee families had settled in the 1980s committed to relatively proactive outreach to Latino families and students. They felt they had made mistakes with the refugees that made it difficult for the young people to become integrated into the larger community. Some companies that have brought in immigrant workers also try to help the local community meet the new needs.

In many instances, however, educators and parents reinvent the wheel, addressing each challenge as it arises. Find a Spanish-speaking volunteer. Hire a Spanish-speaking aide. Develop an ESL program. While these are common problems that areas with established immigrant communities deal with on a regular basis, such resources are coupled with human resources—the people who know how to use them. Individual states and districts may not yet have resources, and educators are not familiar with how to access existing resources in other parts of the country.

Higher education also needs to pay attention to the needs of this growing community, both by preparing to serve the students as they enter college and by preparing teachers for the schools. Yet postsecondary institutions may be slow to respond to the new population. Teacher education programs, for example, may continue to prepare teachers for the area's longtime residents.

Implications for Communities and Schools

These new population dynamics call for attention to all these challenges. Receiving communities need to find ways to re-create themselves. The Latino Diaspora may be especially valuable in creating the new face of a rural America that has been on the decline in recent decades. Educators and educational institutions need to find ways to serve their changing communities. Universities and researchers can play key roles in the response to these new needs through providing support in terms of information and education for all these efforts. This remains an unfolding story of the twenty-first century.

References

Belsie, L. (2001). An Iowa Debate over Newcomers. *The Christian Science Monitor* 93(170), 1.

Hamann, E. T. (2003). *The Educational Welcome of Latinos in the New South*. Westport, CT: Praeger.

Hobbs, F., & Stoops, N. (2002). *Demographic Trends in the Twentieth Century*. Census 2000 Special Reports, Series CENSR-4. Washington, DC: U.S. Government Printing Office.

Kouritzin, S. G. (1999). *Face[t]s of First Language Loss*. Mahwah, NJ: Lawrence Erlbaum.

Passell, J. S., Capps, R., & Fix, M. E. (2004). *Undocumented Immigrants: Facts and Figures*. Washington, DC: The Urban Institute, January 12.

Stull, D. D., Broadway, M., & Griffith, D. (1995). *Anyway You Cut It: Meat Processing and Small-Town America*. Lawrence: University of Kansas Press.

Tse, L. (2001). *Why Don't They Learn English? Separating Fact from Fallacy in the Language Debate*. New York: Teachers College Press.

Valdes, G. (1996). *Con Respecto: Bridging the Distances between Culturally Diverse Families and Schools*. New York: Teachers College Press.

Waslin, M. (2004). Immigration. In *The State of Hispanic America 2004: Latino Perspectives on the American Agenda*. Washington, DC: National Council of La Raza.

Wortham, S., Murillo, E., Jr., & Hamann, E. T. (Eds.). (2002). *Education in the New Latino Diaspora: Policy and the Politics of Identity*. Westport, CT: Ablex.

Recommended Reading

Fix, M., Zimmermann, W., & Passel, J. S. (2001). *The Integration of Immigrant Families in the United States*. Washington, DC: The Urban Institute, July.

McLaughlin, H. J. (2002). *Schooling in Mexico: A Brief Guide for U.S. Educators*. Charleston, WV: ERIC Clearinghouse on Rural and Small Schools (EDO-RC-02-5).

Waslin, M. (2004). Immigration. In *The State of Hispanic America 2004: Latino Perspectives on the American Agenda*. Washington, DC: National Council of La Raza.

Margy McClain

NO CHILD LEFT BEHIND AND LATINO/A STUDENTS

No Child Left Behind (NCLB) is the George W. Bush administration's reauthorization of the 1965 Elementary and Secondary Education Act (ESEA). The original intent of the legislation, initiated during the Johnson administration's War on Poverty, was to provide equal access to educational opportunity through compensatory programs like Title I. Since that time, the legislation has undergone many revisions, across which the federal government has assumed increasing symbolic and material control of public schooling in the U.S. in spite of the fact that public education was constitutionally relegated to local and state entities.

Signed into law on January 8, 2001, at a Hamilton, Ohio, public elementary school, NCLB ushered in an era of sweeping federal demands in education, particularly as it required schools to demonstrate student achievement through extensive annual testing. Schools that did not meet demands of the law faced sanctions that ranged from paying for extra services like tutoring to complete reconstitution of schools. Of course, the law was highly controversial, and its critics crossed party lines. Orfield (2004) reported that 20 states have taken steps in opposition to the law. Utah's Republican-dominated house voted 64 to 8 in favor of a law forbidding the state to spend its own money on the NCLB requirements. In Virginia, the GOP-dominated legislature voted 98 to 1 in favor of a resolution that calls on Congress to exempt the state from the law. Vermont passed legislation similar to Utah's. Ohio and Minnesota have offered estimates of the millions of dollars needed to implement the unfunded mandates of the law (see Hoff, 2004).

With its specific demands for testing and English language requirements, NCLB will certainly affect public school education for Latino students who are members of a broad category of peoples who are Spanish speaking and living in the U.S. One notable example of protest against the detrimental effects of NCLB for Latino students oc-

curred in December 2003 when the Reading School District in Pennsylvania sued the Pennsylvania Department of Education to protect its schools from unfair sanctions directly related to the NCLB law. Seven of the district's schools were placed on a warning list because of low test scores, and the district faced takeover if the scores did not improve. In the lawsuit, three main points were argued: (1) there was insufficient technical and financial assistance for the district to comply with the act; (2) the district questioned how states determined subgroups for the disaggregated testing categories, including what constituted low-income or English proficient groups; and (3) the state did not offer the test in Spanish; therefore, students were judged on their math and reading abilities in English, not solely on their math and reading abilities (see Chute, 2003). Reading's student population is 64% Latino and 11% limited English proficient (LEP). Since this was the first lawsuit of its kind, educators throughout the country were monitoring it quite closely. Educators in Reading and other areas throughout the country are not interested in having lower standards for Latino students, or for any students. Instead, they are interested in helping children to learn in rigorous ways as they provide an equitable education that assures each student's Fourteenth Amendment rights of equal protection under the law. Yet, adequate resources, parental involvement, and quality educational experiences are necessary components to help students attain these educational goals.

It is necessary to state at the outset of this brief look at NCLB's impact on Latino students that the term Latino as used here does not necessarily reflect the differences among and across this group, including differences between Latinos who are born and raised in the U.S. and those who immigrate early or later in life and must acculturate into American society. The term *Latino* encapsulates many subgroups that may account for approximately 70 different variations depending on race, gender, language, and country of origin. What follows is primarily concerned with those students whose home language is Spanish and those who may face particular challenges in public education because of social class. Next are briefly discussed the challenges this legislation poses for students considered to be members of this broad and diverse group, as well as the consequences for the curriculum in schools that serve these Latino students. More specifically, the implications of this act are considered in relation to Latino students' language and culture, the implications of disaggregating test data for these students, and the effects on the programs and curriculum for Latino children. The entry concludes with suggestions for different policies that would better support Latino children in America's public schools.

Language and Culture

Quizas you don't	Maybe you don't
Understand lo que	understand what
Está pasando	is happening
Porque	why it is that our
es que nuestra	
Lengua	language
is slowing	is slowly
disappearing	disappearing
Es la programación	It's the programming
Que le han dado	that they have done
A nuestra nación	to our nation.

(excerpt from "Dos World—Two Mundos" by Henry J. Padron, as quoted in Darder, Torres, & Gutiérrez, 1997, p. 315)

NCLB has dramatic and potentially harmful consequences for the home language and culture of Latino students, especially as it functions to standardize language and curriculum in American public schools. Most notably, the law emphasizes the need to help students to learn English quickly and effectively so they can take exams in English after three years' instruction in English. While learning English is an important skill in American society, the law does not mention biliteracy, bicultural, or bilingual programs in substantive ways that value multilingualism or extend beyond the basic goal of helping English language learners (ELLs) meet high academic standards (Forrest, 2004), which is code for helping ELLs to score well on standardized tests. Nowhere in the legislation is there mention of preserving home cultures or the languages of students who come from homes where English is not the primary language.

Of course, this trend for English-only instruction is not unique to NCLB. In fact, it has precedence in state laws, most notoriously perhaps in California's controversial Proposition 227, which was passed into law in 1998. Proposition 227 eliminated the use of English learners' first language in public school classrooms. The claim for taking such action was that the students were not benefiting from these programs and that the only medium of instruction ought to be English. Parents across the state were misinformed, and they signed petitions that helped the passage of this proposition (González & Melis, 2000). However, eight years have passed since Proposition 227 eliminated bilingual programs in California, and English learners are not showing a significant improvement on standardized tests such as the SAT-9 (Gutierrez, 2002). Student test scores did not improve by eliminating bilingual and immersion programs, yet the legislation had dramatic effects on the education, culture, and language of Latino children (see González & Melis, 2000). NCLB continues this trend and its harmful consequences, limiting possibilities for bilingual programs to exist in schools that receive federal funding, stripping Latino students of their culture and language.

NCLB stands in stark contrast to other national curriculums that work to preserve the home languages and cultures of students, such as the Swedish National Curriculum for the compulsory school system, the preschool class, and the leisure-time center (Lpo-94), which is one of three national curriculums used in Sweden. This legislation contains specific language concerning the preservation of the Samic language and culture of an indigenous group in northern Sweden. While all students learn the Swedish language under the provisions of the national curriculum, they are encouraged to be multilingual. Swedish students are not tested and held accountable in ways that encourage them to lose their home language and culture (see http://www.skolverket.se/english/publ .shtml for texts of this legislation).

In addition to the detrimental effects of this legislation on children's home language and culture, test data are used in inappropriate ways to stigmatize and label children and schools as failing without full and accurate consideration of mitigating factors that would cause some students to do poorly on standardized tests. This is the next point considered here.

Testing and the Misuse of Data

One of the hallmarks of NCLB is that it forces schools to test all students. The problems with standardized testing and the cultural biases of the tests are well documented (see McNeil, 2000; Sacks, 1999). In addition, there are significant problems when curriculum and tests are not well aligned,

which has been the case in California in relation to the SAT-9 test (see NPR, 2002). Here students report being tested on content knowledge before they have had classes or instruction in particular areas.

NCLB requires all districts to disaggregate test data by racial and ethnic groups, by low-income groups, and by special needs students. While some lawmakers may argue that disaggregating data in this way will allow educators and others to see how particular groups are achieving (or not) in school so they can in turn be taught more effectively, this can be a very misleading practice requires no explanation of differences in scores (Abedi, 2004; Carlson, 2004; Paul, 2004).

Disaggregating test data according to ethnic and racial groups is problematic because it does not acknowledge the limitations of identifying a student as a member of a specific racial or ethnic group, particularly through broad and complex labels such as "Hispanic" or "Latino" that essentialize a variety of cultures, languages, values, socioeconomic groups, and more (Carlson, 2004). Further, disaggregation of test data is statistically problematic because the smaller numbers that are represented within a subgroup (such as Latinos or blacks) are difficult to compare to subgroups with larger numbers (such as whites) (see Abedi, 2004, for detailed discussion of these assessment and accountability concerns). Instead, disaggregating data tends to perpetuate misunderstandings about the perceived inferiority of particular groups when compared to white, middle-class students (Carlson, 2004).

At the same time, reports of increasing aggregate scores on tests often mask other issues, including high dropout rates among minority students. In Texas, for example, the Mexican American Legal Defense and

Education Fund attempted to demonstrate how the Texas Assessment of Academic Skills (TAAS) discriminated against African American and Hispanic children in Texas public schools. FairTest reported the following concerning this:

In one report, Professor Walt Haney of Boston College demonstrated that the gap in the pass rates between white students and minority students was large enough to be defined as a "racially discriminatory impact" under federal civil rights law. Haney also showed that the graduation rate for Latinos and African Americans dropped significantly, from about 60 percent to about 50 percent, after the state implemented the TAAS graduation requirement. After eight years, it still has not returned to the previous level. While the white graduation rate also declined initially, it rebounded to its previous level of 70 percent within a year. Each ten percent gap represents about 100,000 black and Hispanic students who do not graduate. Haney reported that a review of State Board of Education minutes revealed that the Board chose the passing score arbitrarily, ignoring accepted professional measurement procedures. The score that was set had the effect of maximizing the adverse impact of the TAAS on black and Hispanic students. (http://www.fairtest.org/examarts/fall99/The%20Case%20Against%20TAAS.html)

These concerns about the consequences of standardized testing do not stop at the Texas state border. Standardized testing has many flaws and shortcomings, and it is imperative that educators directly address the limitations of standardized testing and the legislation that endorses it in high-stakes decisions (see Kohn, 2000; Sacks, 1999), as well as the consequences it has for excluding children from public education in America (Paul, 2004).

Beyond concerns about the procedures and forms of testing, it is important to remember that child poverty rates for Latino children remain at an average of 28% (Paul, 2004). Test data, disaggregated or otherwise, do not give insight into the influences of poverty on children's learning or well-being, nor do such data support changes in education that will better care for children who come from homes with less than adequate money, food, or health care. While millions of dollars are spent on the testing requirements of NCLB, we can only wonder how this money could be spent differently to better to care for American children. At the same time, the education for those students who are economically poor and also English language learners continues to suffer: "English language learners receive a substantially inferior education when compared to English-speaking students who are as poor as they are . . . [and they] experience more extreme segregation in schools, classrooms, and programs than their peers" (Gutierrez, 2002, p. 18).

These concerns raise further questions concerning the Fourteenth Amendment rights of these children, many of whom are misidentified as learning disabled (Paul, 2004). These children are to be guaranteed equal protection under the law, a provision that should implicitly include equal access to quality public education.

Curriculum and Afterschool Programs for Latino Students

NCLB drives schools to focus primarily on reading, mathematics, and science instruction, the key areas that are tested in order for schools to continue to receive funding from the federal government. Even though the federal government offers on average only 7% of a school's overall budget, its influence is widely felt, particularly for those school districts that rely on the federal dollars that help them to meet the educational needs of their students. NCLB legislation potentially limits possibilities for a liberal arts education, and as a result many high minority school populations have decreased instructional time in foreign languages, the arts, and music (Foreign Language Annals, 2004). As Raymond Bartlett, Council for Basic Education, explained, "Truly high expectations cannot begin and end with math, science, and reading" (p. 167).

In addition to potentially limiting liberal arts aspects of a student's basic education, NCLB threatens opportunities for students to develop vocational and technical training (Coeyman, 2003). Instead of endorsing quality vocational and technical educational programs, the Bush administration forwards an expectation that was first articulated during the Clinton era, namely, that all students will go to college, and high school curriculum should be directed and aligned toward college preparation for all students (see President Clinton's February 4, 1997, State of the Union Address). Of course, this potentially affects every student, not just Latino students, but is yet another example of ways in which curriculum is narrowed and redirected in relation to this legislation.

This movement toward an emphasis on all students preparing for college has further implications for Latino students, who often find they are at a disadvantage when it comes to participating in rigorous curricula in order to meet the standards necessary for them to attend college and be successful at that level. As González (2002) noted, "Latinos are more likely than Whites to attend schools with inexperienced, ineffective teachers and less likely to have access to rigorous, properly aligned curricula" (p. 8). He goes on to observe that fully one in five Latino eighth grade students takes algebra, as opposed to more than one in four of their white peers. Latino students are usually enrolled in basic math courses that are designed to pass the math portion of the state's high school exam, but these courses rarely prepare them for little more. English as a Second Language (ESL) programs are not rigorous in some instances, particularly in terms of preparing students to think critically when reading in English. These classes are often a simplified version of the more rigorous English courses, and ESL students often read and answer questions that might be very simplistic in nature. This is also a disadvantage in terms of being able to think critically and become successful at the college level. But the most important issue concerning language learners is that once a student is placed in an ESL class, he or she is often tracked permanently into ESL programs that function to limit the opportunity for the student to access meaningful courses that will facilitate success at the academic level in postsecondary education (Gutierrez, 2002).

Education is important to Latino parents, and many are interested in participating in decisions about their child's education. However, only 38% of Latino parents feel they are being provided with adequate information concerning the academic standards of their child's school (González, 2002). Cultural synchronization, the harmony between "the cultural systems of the schools, diverse groups of learners, and the communities from which these learners come," is essential to the successful involvement of Latino parents in decisions about their children's education (Paul, 2004, p. 652).

Conclusion

The current constellation of educational reforms has created an educational straightjacket that simplifies a complex problem and results in solutions that are way too narrow to solve it (Gutierrez, 2002, p. 17).

The problem of how to best educate children who are part of the diverse and culturally rich group considered to be Latino in the U.S. is not well addressed through the NCLB legislation. Instead, we agree with González (2002) that the following actions would better support the education of children in Latino communities and schools across the U.S.:

• Equitable resource distribution
• Alignment of curricula and instruction with standards and assessments
• High-quality teachers
• Appropriate test use
• Utilization of multiple measures of student performance for making high-stakes decisions
• Fair treatment of special populations
• Supportive school organization and culture
• Active parent and community participation

These would be important steps toward guaranteeing that all Latino children are being served well through American public education. Clearly, NCLB falls significantly short of these goals.

References

Abedi, J. (2004). The No Child Left Behind Act and English Language Learners: Assessment and Accountability Issues. *Educational Researcher* 33(1), 4–14.

Carlson, K. (2004). Test scores by Race and Ethnicity. *Phi Delta Kappan* 85, 379.

Chute, E. (2003). School District Fights State; No Child Left Behind Sanctions Prompt Suit. *Pittsburgh Post-Gazette*, December 17, B1.

Coeyman, M. (2003). Practical Skills vs. 3R's: A Debate Revives. *Christian Science Monitor*, July 8. Available: http://www.csmonitor.com/2003/0708/p13s02-lepr.html (accessed February 26, 2005).

Darder, A., Torres, R. D., & Gutiérrez, H. (1997). *Latinos and Education*. New York: Routledge.

Foreign Language Annals. (2004). NCLB Leaves behind Liberal Arts, According to Study: Minority Students Most Affected by Curriculum Changes. *Foreign Language Annals* 37, 1.

Forrest, S. (2004). Implications of No Child Left Behind on Family Literacy in a Multicultural Community. *The Clearing House* 78(1), 41.

González, R., & Melis, I. (2000). *Language Ideologies: Critical Perspectives on the Official English Movement*. Urbana, IL: NCTE.

González, R. (2002). The No Child Left Behind Act: Implications for Local Educators and Advocates for Latino Students, Families, and Communities. Issues Brief. Washington, DC: National Council of La Raza.

Gutierrez, K. (2002). *Rethinking Educational Policy for English Learners*. Washington, DC: Aspen Institute.

Hoff, D. (2004). Debate Grows on True Costs of School Law. *Education Week* 23(21), 1, 22.

Kohn, A. (2000). *The Case Against Standardized Testing*. Portsmouth, NH: Heinemann.

McNeil, L. (2000). *Contradictions of School Reform: Educational Costs of Standardized Testing*. New York: Routledge.

National Public Radio (NPR). (2002). Testing Our Schools. *Frontline*. PBS.

Orfield, G. (2004). Law Is Leaving Children—and Education Reform—Behind. *Chicago Sun Tribune*, April 19, 51.

Paul, D. (2004). The Train Has Left: The No Child Left Behind Act Leaves Black and Latino Literacy Learners Waiting at the Station. *Journal of Adolescent and Adult Literacy* 47(8), 648–656.

Sacks, P. (1999). *Standardized Minds: The High Price of America's Testing Culture and What We Can Do to Change It*. New York: Perseus.

Recommended Reading

Garcia, G. (2003). *English Learners Reaching the Highest Level of English Literacy*. Newark, DE: International Reading Association.

González, R., & Melis, I. (2000). *Language Ideologies: Critical Perspectives on the Official English Movement*. Urbana, IL: NCTE.

Goodman, K., Shannon, P., Goodman, Y., & Rapoport, R. (2004). *Saving Our Schools: The Case for Public Education Saying No to "No Child Left Behind."* Berkeley, CA: RDR Books.

Sacks, P. (1999). *Standardized Minds: The High Price of America's Testing Culture and What We Can Do to Change It.* New York: Perseus.

Soto, L. (1996). *Language, Culture, and Power: Bilingual Families and the Struggle for Quality Education.* Albany, NY: SUNY Press.

*Rosita L. Rivera and
Jacqueline Edmondson*

NORMALISTAS/FOREIGN-TRAINED TEACHERS

Normalistas in this context are foreign-trained Mexican teachers pursuing teacher certification in the U.S. The field of teacher training continues to explore the importance and role of bilingual education in light of ever-changing demographics. The population of the U.S. now indicates that teacher training will need to change to meet the needs of children in the public school system. In analyzing the demographics, it is estimated that the Spanish-speaking group, both monolinguals and bilinguals, will soon be a majority group. In order to meet a pressing need, teacher-training programs must concentrate on increasing the number of teachers entering the field and helping them developing competencies that will prepare them to develop with the changing realities of the classroom of today and tomorrow.

Recent data indicate that most new teachers are members of the majority group and that the number of minorities entering the teaching profession continues to remain low. This trend is unlikely to change in the immediate future. Many school districts are experiencing English as a Second Language (ESL) and bilingual teacher shortages. The Urban Teacher Challenge (2000) recommended that preservice teacher-training programs should be improved to work with the majority minority schools and that the pool of teachers specializing in the education of limited English proficient (LEP) students be increased. In addressing the bilingual teacher shortage, it is imperative that the issue be examined from a multidimensional perspective. For example, efforts to increase minority prospective teachers may have a direct link in augmenting the number of bilingual educators. In addition, increasing the number of prospective bilingual teachers by tapping into the natural resource of immigrants who are trained teachers may be a viable plan.

The rationale for including teachers trained elsewhere is that there is a definite need to increase the number of competent bilingual educators. Certification of normalistas to address the bilingual educator shortage begins by recruiting those foreign-trained teachers who are legal residents, evaluating their coursework from Mexico, for example, developing a certification program for them, and putting them through a teacher education program. Normalistas have usually undergone training in a two- to four-year teacher preparation program. Petrovic and colleagues (1999) outline the different Mexican teacher-training programs in their typology:

1. Escuela normal básica (equivalent to a Bachelor's degree and certification for preschool or elementary education)

2. Escuela normal superior (equivalent to a Bachelor's degree and certification for secondary education)

3. Licenciatura en educación con especialización (equivalent to a Bachelor's degree and

certification with specialization; e.g., art, special education, physical education)

Documentation about normalista teacher preparation and how that preparation compares with U.S. teacher preparation is minimal. In some states foreign-trained teachers can obtain certification or licensure. Foreign-trained teachers seeking certification must be U.S. legal residents, demonstrate English proficiency, and have an equivalent to a bachelor's degree. They must submit their documents for evaluation to the state licensing board. Some states also require that they pass the state-mandated teacher competency test.

Smith (2001) indicates that nearly 20,000 teachers with licenciaturas from Mexico's Secretaría de Educación Pública (SEP) are residing in the U.S., though usually underemployed. They are underutilized human capital, usually earning minimum wages as restaurant workers, custodians, maids, or field workers. Little is known about the total number of U.S. resident who might have other types of teacher-training backgrounds.

School districts are looking to Spanish-speaking counties to supply bilingual education teachers. The rationale for inclusion of foreign-trained teachers in U.S. classrooms is that they have invaluable experience as educators and their ability to deliver content in Spanish is quite an asset (Petrovic et al., 1999). Principals and school directors feel that normalistas have good classroom teaching experience and possess advanced Spanish academic language proficiency. Normalistas, for the most part, are beginners or beginning intermediate speakers of English. They could be classified as having beginning basic interpersonal skills in English and having a full repertoire of cognitive academic language proficiency and literacy in Spanish.

Although few studies have been conducted with foreign-trained teachers, several criticisms are evident in the sparse extant literature. One criticism is that these teachers lack common linguistic and cultural experiences with U.S. language minority populations. A second criticism is that foreign-trained teachers often show negative attitudes toward the language minority's native language dialect (Valadez et al., 2000). Conversely, U.S.-born bilingual teachers are often taken to task for their lack of academic Spanish proficiency and for being required to demonstrate only minimal Spanish proficiency on state-mandated tests (Guerrero, 1997, 1998, 1999). Further, U.S. bilingual-teacher education preparation programs have been seen as lacking rigorous Spanish language requirements. Language use alone cannot be examined, however, when isolated from the sociocultural context.

Acknowledging the importance of shared ethnic identity between bilingual educators and their students, the existing criticism of foreign-trained teachers, and the dearth of empirical knowledge about U.S. resident normalistas, Clark and Flores (2000, 2001a, 2001b) and Clark, Flores, and McCoy (2002) conducted pilot studies. Focusing on examining the ethnic identity and teacher efficacy of normalistas, the researchers in these studies administered Spanish versions of the *Who Am I* (*WAI-S*) as a measure of self-concept and ethnic identity and the Teacher Self-Efficacy Quiz (TSQ-S) to normalista applicants. The researchers found that this group of normalistas had a strong national identity and prided themselves in being mexicanos. In a previous study with Mexican American, first-generation, ethnic minority, college-age students, Clark and Flores (2001b) noted that the students' self-reported ethnic identity reflected a continuum from Hispanic to Mexican.

Clark and colleagues (Clark & Flores, 2000; Clark et al., 2002) analyses of the normalistas' self-conceptualization, as reported on the *WAI-S*, depicted a positive and healthy well-being. Also noted was that most normalistas had both a high positive general teaching efficacy and personal teaching efficacy. Essentially, they felt they had the capacity to teach students regardless of outside factors and also felt their ability to teach affected the lives of their students. It is important to note, however, that there was a minority of applicants whose general teaching efficacy was determined by external factors, and their lack of confidence resulted in a low personal teaching efficacy. The researchers surmised that these types of individuals are likely to blame their inability to teach on external factors (i.e., the family, community, language variety, or socioeconomic status) and, as such, are not likely to be effective teachers.

Because Clark and Flores (2000) wanted to increase the power of their results in the determination of a relationship, if any, between the groups' self-conceptualizations and teacher efficacy, additional normalista applicants were interviewed for a subsequent study. In this study, Flores and Clark (2002) found that the "spiritual me" (James, 1920) category, which incorporated the self-conceptualizations of character and moral worth, did indeed have a significant effect on both general teaching efficacy and personal teaching efficacy. These findings are supported by the García and González study (2000), where Project Alianza normalistas viewed the teaching profession as a calling, a vocación, a moral commitment, and a *nací maestra*, and they also had a high sense of confidence in their ability to teach.

Normalistas' Attitudes

A previously mentioned concern is that normalistas might have preconceived notions regarding language minority students' language variety, bilingualism, and bilingual education. Initial interviews with normalista applicants revealed a minority of the applicants did indeed have pervasive negative attitudes toward the Spanish spoken in the U.S. (Clark & Flores, 2000). García and González (2000) also reported that normalistas did not think U.S. bilingual teachers had a strong command of the Spanish language. Clark and Flores (2000) noted that some of the normalista applicants had been against bilingual education because they felt that teachers did not have sufficient fluency in Spanish, were concerned that their children would not learn Spanish correctly, or would learn to speak English with an accent. Principals revealed that foreign-trained teachers working within the U.S. school system are confronted with differing educational philosophies, academic expectations, and parent-involvement expectations (Vallejo & García, 2001). Flores (2001) reminds us that normalistas were not prepared to be bilingual teachers and, as such, they are not likely to understand the rationale behind bilingual education.

In comparing the normalista and U.S. teacher preparation program, Petrovic and colleagues (1999) suggested that preparation was very similar. Likely, the only additional pedagogy needed would be that of bilingual education. English and test-taking skills should be emphasized. They state further that "we must employ teachers with the cross-cultural communication skills, which includes knowledge of the student's language and culture as well as knowledge of the myriad cultures in the U.S. whenever possible" (p. 57). Based on the previous study (Clark & Flores, 2000; Clark et al., 2002), Flores (2001) countered, suggesting that normalistas would also need to know the sociopolitical and historical experiences of the language minority student within the U.S. educational system.

For normalistas to become fully biliterate means they must attain the language and cultural literacy of the bicultural-bilingual community in addition to acquiring English literacy at the academic level. The normalistas need to understand what it means to be an ethnic minority in the U.S. and need to enhance their appreciation for dialectal and regional differences of Spanish in the Southwest. Having Spanish language proficiency does not necessarily mean that normalistas have the sociocultural knowledge to meet the needs of language minority children in the U.S. Calderón and Díaz (1993) noted that teachers working with Latino children must be prepared to understand and work with issues of cultural and linguistic differences in the U.S.

In the case of university teacher preparation programs, a pressing initial concern is the mechanisms for credentialing foreign-trained teachers as bilingual educators in order to augment the pool of competent teachers. However, since few studies focus on incorporating foreign-trained teachers into the existing pool of teachers, it is really not known whether they will be effective in U.S. urban settings. One of the biggest obstacles for most university teacher-training programs is the admission process for normalistas. A combination of elements such as state entry tests, foreign credentials, language assessment, and residency classifications create many of the admission barriers. Most universities have policies and well-established methods for dealing with foreign students, but not for dealing with U.S. residents with foreign credentials. Normalistas cannot be viewed either as foreign students or as international students simply because of their former educational experiences or residential status. In a study conducted by Flores and Clark (2002), a university director observes:

The major barrier was the lack of procedures that allow someone who has completed their higher education in another country to attend UTSA. This includes things such as transcripts, which we would not accept if they were not translated first. The translation of transcripts was not only a large expense for students but it also . . . took time, and that discouraged people from applying to the university.

Another director reflects:

Major barriers . . . probably had to do with reading and interpreting the normalistas' transcripts to ensure that they received proper credit for courses already taken. At the beginning of the Project, this was a major challenge. However, as we learned more about the Mexican school system and their teacher-preparation program, it became easier to handle.

When a normalista was told that a university would not accept her foreign credentials, a college advisor advised that she take a high school equivalency exam and attend a local community college to begin a degree program. Two years later her foreign credentials, equivalent to a bachelor's degree, were finally accepted. A director remembered similar incidents: "You have to wonder how many normalistas, licenciadas, the university has turned away over the years."

Further exploration of normalistas as prospective bilingual education teachers is needed. Successful recruitment, induction, and retention of non-traditional pools of foreign-born teachers into U.S. teacher preparation programs are sorely needed. Well-trained, highly qualified, and committed teachers for linguistically and culturally diverse classrooms increases access to equal educational opportunity for all students.

References

Calderón, M., & Díaz, E. (1993). Retooling Teacher Preparation Programs to Embrace Latino Realities in Schools. In R. E. Castro & Y. R. Ingle (Eds.), *Reshaping Teacher Education in the Southwest* (pp. 53–68). San Antonio, TX: The Tomás Rivera Center.

Clark, E. R., & Flores, B. B. (2000). Report on a Study of Normalistas' Ethnic Identity and Teaching Efficacy. *NABE News* 24(1), 20–22.

Clark, E. R., & Flores, B. B. (2001a). Is Spanish Proficiency Simply Enough? An Examination of Normalistas' Attitudes towards Spanish, Bilingualism, and Bilingual Teacher Pedagogy. *MEXTESOL Journal* 25(3), 13–27.

Clark, E. R., & Flores, B. B. (2001b). Who Am I? The Social Construction of Ethnic Identity and Self-Perceptions of Bilingual Preservice Teachers. *The Urban Review* 33(2), 69–86.

Clark, E. R., Flores, B. B., & McCoy, B. (2002). *Normalistas como maestras bilingües en los EUA: Un estudio sobre su concepto y eficacia.* Mexico: Universidad Pedagogical Nacional.

Flores, B. B. (2001). Thinking out of the Box: One University's Experience with Foreign-Trained Teachers. *Educational Policy Analysis Archives* 9(18). Available: http://www.olam.asu.edu/epaa/v9n18htm (accessed June 19, 2001).

Flores, B. B., & Clark, E. R. (2002). *El desarrollo de Proyecto Alianza: Lessons Learned and Policy Implications.* Tempe, AZ: Center for Bilingual Education.

García, A., & González, J. (2000). *The Views of Mexican Normalista and U.S. Bilingual Education Teachers: An Exploratory Study of Perceptions, Beliefs, and Attitudes.* Tempe, AZ: Center for Bilingual Education.

Guerrero, M. D. (1997). Spanish Academic Language Proficiency: The Case of Bilingual Education Teachers in the U.S. *Bilingual Research Journal* 21(1), 65–84.

Guerrero, M. D. (1998). Current Issues in the Spanish Language Proficiency of Bilingual Education Teachers. *Texas Papers in Foreign Language Education* 3(3), 135–149.

Guerrero, M. D. (1999). *Spanish Language Proficiency of Bilingual Education Teachers.* Tempe, AZ: Center for Bilingual Education.

James, W. (1920). *Collected Essays and Reviews.* New York: Longmans, Green and Company.

Petrovic, J. E., Orozco, G., González, E., & Díaz de Cossío, R. (1999). Mexican Normalista Teachers as a Resource for Bilingual Education in the United States: Connecting Two Models of Teacher Preparation. In J. M. González (Ed.), *CBER Exploration in Bi-national Education*, no. 1. Tempe, AZ: Center for Bilingual Education.

Smith, P. (2001). Tendencias en el desarrollo de licenciaturas en lenguas: Perspectivas desde la planificación lingüística. *MEXTESOL Journal* 25(1), 75–86.

The Urban Teacher Challenge: Teacher Demand and Supply in the Great City Schools. (2000). Available: http://www.rnt.org/quick/utc.pdf (accessed January 1, 2001).

Valadez, C., Etxeberría, F., Pescador, O., & Ambisca, A. (2000). International and Guest Teachers in American Schools: Teachers from Mexico and Spain in California Schools. Paper presented at the AERA Annual Meeting, New Orleans, LA, April 24–28.

Vallejo, C., & García, A. G. (2001). *Teacher Recruitment and Employment Practices in Selected States: Promising Prospects for Foreign-Trained Teachers.* Tempe, AZ: Center for Bilingual Education.

Recommended Reading

Cantu, L. (1999). Project Alianza: Tapping Community Resources for Bilingual Teachers. *IDRA Newsletter* 26, 1–2.

Flores, B. B., & Clark, E. R. (2004). Normalistas: A Critical Examination of Normalistas'

Self-Conceptualization and Teacher Efficacy. *Hispanic Journal of Behavioral Sciences* 26(2), 230–257.

Flores, B. B., Strecker, S., & Pérez, B. P. (2002). Critical Need for Bilingual Education Teachers: The Potentiality of Normalistas and Paraprofessionals. *Bilingual Research Journal* 26(3), 687–708.

Hewlett-Gómez, M. R., & Solis, A. (1995). Dual Language Instruction Design for Education of Recent Immigrant Secondary Students on the Texas-México Border. *Bilingual Research Journal* 19(3, 4), 429–452.

Molina Hernández, J. L. (1997). *Trabajando con profesores normalistas mexicanos en Long Beach, CA: Apuntes en torno a una experiencia docente*. Mexico: Intringulis.

Molina Hernández, J. L. (1999). Normalistas en universidades norteamericanas: Biculturales por partida doble. *La Crónica*, April 23. Columa: Reflexción Universitaria.

Peña, R. A. (1997). Cultural Differences and the Construction of Meaning: Implications for the Leadership and Organizational Context of Schools. *Education Policy Analysis Archives* 5(10). Available: http://olam.ed.asu.edu/epaa/v5n10.html (accessed August 21, 2000).

Valencia, R. R. (2000). Inequalities and the Schooling of Minority Students in Texas: Historical and Contemporary Conditions. *Hispanic Journal of Behavioral Sciences* 22(4), 445–459.

Valencia, R. R., & Aburto, S. (1991). Competency Testing and Latino Student Access to the Teaching Profession: An Overview of Issues. In G. D. Keller, J. R. Deneen, & R. J. Magallán (Eds.), *Assessment and Access: Hispanics in Higher Education* (pp. 167–193). Albany, NY: SUNY Press.

Valenzuela, A. (1999). *Subtractive Schooling: U.S.-Mexican Youth and the Politics of Caring*. Albany, NY: SUNY Press.

Varisco de García, N., & García, E. E. (1996). Teachers for Mexican Migrant and Immigrant Students: Meeting an Urgent Need. ERIC Document Reproduction Service No. ED 393639.

Ellen Riojas Clark and Belinda Flores

P

PARENTAL INVOLVEMENT

The involvement of Latino parents in their children's schooling and, more specifically, in support of their children's developing literacy is a topic of great concern in education today. Most often, when educators speak of such parental involvement, they privilege school literacy by advocating the participation of parents in literacy events in the home that replicate typical teacher-child literacy events in school classrooms. They expect to see a parent and child sitting together as the parent reviews homework or reads a picture book, asking open-ended questions. When literacy interactions in Latino homes occur but in different forms or occur but are unseen or "invisible," many educators assume that no valuable support is provided by parents. Guided by a deficit perspective, these educators conclude that Latino children and their families are deficient in language, culture, and the ability to contribute to their own learning. Research that investigates literacy in Latino homes by looking closely and respectfully at parent-child interactions and attending to their perspectives provides a different picture. The descriptions that follow are specific to the families studied but may also be representative of other Latino families as well as families from different marginalized groups.

Findings from three ethnographic research studies conducted with nine Puerto Rican kindergartners and their working-class families living in a large midwestern city on the U.S. mainland suggest that some young Latino children do engage actively in a variety of literacy events at home and may be people-rich in literacy resources. The developing literacy of the children studied was supported by a network of people including their parents, extended family members, siblings, peers in the neighborhood and at school, family friends, fictive kin such as "church brothers and sisters," and pastors and Sunday school teachers in addition to their classroom teachers. Both adults and children of differing abilities in Spanish and English and competencies as readers and writers participated in these networks.

In the homes, most of the parents studied used teacher-identified language to provide direct literacy instruction to their children and to engage them in meaningful literacy events such as reading letters from relatives. Some of the direct instruction was related to homework as the literature reports, but there were also instances initiated by parents or children that grew out of the families' daily activities. Fewer parents engaged their children in meaningful literacy experiences embedded in play. This role was undertaken by older siblings or cousins who frequently used the language and strategies learned in their schooling to teach school-related knowledge and skills during play. In some homes adults, including mothers, fathers, aunts, and uncles, read books to children; in others older siblings read the books or adults read the Bible to children or recited familiar poems. In the homes of families belonging to Protestant evangelical churches, collaborative Bible readings with adults and children were frequent and were sometimes transformed into reading lessons as adults provided finely tuned scaffolding for children's developing literacy abilities.

Parents explained that they valued education and communicated its importance to their children. Some felt their role in schooling consisted of getting their children to school on time, clean, and well fed. Some said that they did not remember educational terms and strategies learned years ago in school. Most parents, however, saw themselves as "adjunct teachers" who were capable of supporting the work of the classroom teacher by providing instruction, experiences, and literacy materials such as games, workbooks, and picture books.

In several homes, parents taught their children to read in Spanish with the *Cartilla fonética* (*Phonics Primer*) that they had used learning to read in Puerto Rico and that is still in use on the island. This approach is based on learning patterns of sounds in syllables and is dependant on the phonetic regularities of Spanish. Like other Latino families described in the literature, most parents explained that learning to read is a process of learning individual letters sounds and then blending them together. Nonetheless, many taught their children to read in Spanish and English balancing an approach that emphasized letter-sound correspondences and memorization of the alphabet with an approach that emphasized meaning

and drew on texts in the children's environments. For example, children might memorize individual vowel sounds one day and the next be helped to link the initial sounds of unfamiliar words with the names of family members.

Older siblings and cousins played an important role in these networks of support, often mediating the developing literacy of younger children with skill. Such adept teaching is described in the cross-cultural literature on siblings from varied cultures. In the families observed, siblings gave explicit directions about how to write or read written text, developed school-like worksheets matching words and pictures (including, for example, the word *mamá* with the name of the sisters' mother), provided text to repeat, and focused the developing reader's attention on pictures as clues to word meaning. Often they drew on Spanish as a resource, even when younger siblings were reading in English, by sharing the Spanish translations of the English words on the page or by using Spanish vowels sounds as cues to the irregular sounds of vowels in English. The younger siblings were typically active in these interactions; they initiated them, asked questions, and sometimes took on the teaching role.

Dramatic play was a favorite activity for children at home. Siblings might play "McDonald's," taking orders and selling food at an improvised drive-through or "school," practicing school routines and interacting with oral and written texts. In one home, the siblings and cousins played "church" together using Bibles and a microphone as well as literacy practices from church including the oral recitation of memorized psalms and prayers (holding the Bible up to read it), the singing of songs (mixing popular, secular songs into their services), and spontaneous preaching.

The assistance provided by older siblings and cousins seemed related in complex ways to their differing abilities to gauge the level of assistance needed, their age, gender, and school experiences, the focal children's competencies as developing readers, and their own literacy competencies in both Spanish and English. Family and cultural perspectives on literacy and sibling teaching also seemed relevant. In some homes, parents were observed modeling and providing oral cues to older children about the correct ways to help the younger ones (for example, by reminding them to ask younger siblings if they understood what they had read). In others, parents' beliefs about the interdependence of family members and the importance of *educación* (schooling plus correct moral and social upbringing) were the basis for creating an atmosphere in which everyone helped each other with school work and with other life tasks.

Literacy interactions with network members were often social events with multiple participants interacting with texts in the public spaces of their homes such as the kitchen and living room. In the community, public literacy events took place in church services, Sunday school, and in neighbors' living rooms. Although the parents and children occasionally interacted with print by themselves, most of the time they did so with others or in the company of others. This may reflect the collaborative nature of Latino families highlighted in the literature and a cultural understanding of literacy as often a social, rather than an individual, practice.

While the children read books with significant others, invented stories, songs, and poems, wrote messages and greeting cards, and read meaningful print in their environment, they also engaged in literacies at home and at church that involved memorization, oral recitation, and repetition. When reading the Bible they did not construct meaning but learned from more knowledgeable others about the meaning of the text. Notably, in other studies of developing literacy and religion in very different contexts, these literacy practices are described as providing young children with an induction into literacy. Children participated actively with people important in their lives around significant texts, often scaffolded by rituals with predictable patterns and melodies. They saw around them older and younger participants, all interacting competently though in different ways with the same texts, and they absorbed the adults' expectation that they, like the others, would learn to read as they continued to participate.

Many of the literacy events observed in the homes were syncretic as diverse languages and literacy practices were continually blended and reinvented. In this ongoing process, the children, along with the members of their networks of support, drew on Spanish and English, oral and written texts, from school and religious contexts as well as popular culture, encountered in their homes and in the community, on the U.S. mainland and in Puerto Rico. Their reinvention of literacy practices stands as a challenge to impoverished images of literacy learning in Latino children's homes. With the efforts of researchers and educators, these practices can be both visible and valued.

Recommended Reading

Compton-Lilly, C. (2003). *Reading Families: The Literate Lives of Urban Children*. New York: Teachers College Press.

Delgado-Gaitan, C. (2004). *Involving Latino Families in Schools: Raising Student Achievement through Home-School Partnerships*. Thousand Oaks, CA: Corwin.

Duranti, A., & Ochs, E. (1997). Syncretic Literacy in a Samoan American Family. In L. B. Resnick, R. Saljo, C. Pontecorvo, & B. Burge

(Eds.), *Discourse, Tools, and Reasoning: Essays on Situated Cognition* (pp. 169–202). Berlin: Springer-Verlag.

Dyson, A. H. (1999). Coach Bombay's Kids Learn to Write: Children's Appropriation of Media Material for School Literacy. *Research in the Teaching of English* 33, 367–402.

Farver, J.A.M. (1993). Cultural Differences in Scaffolding Pretend Play: A Comparison of American and Mexican-American Mother-Child and Sibling-Child Pairs. In K. MacDonald (Ed.), *Parent-Child Play: Descriptions and Implications* (pp. 349–366). Albany, NY: SUNY Press.

Gallimore, R., & Goldenberg, C. (1993). Activity Settings of Early Literacy: Home and School Factors in Children's Emergent Literacy. In E. A. Forman, N. Minick, & C. A. Stone (Eds.), *Contexts for Learning: Sociocultural Dynamics in Children's Development* (pp. 315–335). New York: Oxford University Press.

Gregory, E. (2001). Sisters and Brothers as Language and Literacy Teachers: Synergy between Siblings Playing and Working Together. *Journal of Early Childhood Literacy* 1(3), 301–322.

Gregory, E., Long, S., & Volk, D. (2004). *Many Pathways to Literacy: Young Children Learning with Siblings, Grandparents, Peers, and Communities*. London: Routledge-Falmer.

Hidalgo, N. M. (1994). Profile of a Puerto Rican Family's Support for School Achievement. *Equity and Choice* 10(2), 14–22.

Soto, L. D. (1990). *Language, Culture, and Power: Bilingual Families and the Struggle for Quality Education*. Albany, NY: SUNY Press.

Valdés, G. (1996). *Con respeto: Bridging the Distance between Culturally Diverse Families and Schools*. New York: Teachers College Press.

Van Kleek, A., Stahl, S. A., & Bauer, E. B. (2003). *On Reading Books to Children: Parents and Teachers*. Mahwah, NJ: Lawrence Erlbaum.

Volk, D., & de Acosta, M. (2001). "Many Differing Ladders, Many Ways to Climb . . .": Literacy Events in the Bilingual Classroom, Homes, and Community of Three Puerto Rican Kindergartners. *Journal of Early Childhood Literacy* 1(2), 193–224.

Volk, D., & de Acosta, M. (2003). Reinventing Texts and Contexts: Syncretic Literacy Events in Young Puerto Rican Children's Homes. *Research in the Teaching of English* 38(1), 8–48.

Zinsser, C. (1986). For the Bible Tells Me So: Teaching Children in a Fundamentalist Church. In B. B. Schieffelin & P. Gilmore (Eds.), *The Acquisition of Literacy: Ethnographic Perspectives* (pp. 55–71). Norwood, NJ: Ablex.

Dinah Volk

PARTICIPATORY ACTION RESEARCH

Participatory Action Research (PAR) can be considered as a promising approach to enhancing Latino education and facilitating community empowerment. PAR involves genuine participatory democracy in the interplay of education, research, and community development on the basis of equal rights, responsibilities, and benefits. PAR also involves transforming action, first of all for the benefit of the research participants. From this perspective, the Latino students, their parents, and their communities are, in principle, active participants in dialogues with school teachers and administrators and among themselves. In order for these dialogues to be genuinely democratic and hence authentic, participants should be active in studying their own educational and life conditions as well as the economic, political, and cultural factors that are contributing to their problems. The most important thing is that understanding should emanate from their own perspectives, not just the "official" interpretations of their problems. Latino communities should also be part of planning and implementing communal studies and the subsequent actions. These studies and actions are aimed at improving their life conditions, such as expanding educational opportunities; resisting and counteracting the power of domination, exploitation, and colonization; participating in shaping public policy; and holding their governmental representatives accountable.

Obviously, PAR contrasts with the conventional research *on* or *about* Latinos/as that ignores their agency, "funds of knowledge," and experiences in understanding their own realities. In addition, the conventional researcher's agenda is privileged over theirs. Hence, the results of this type of research often does more harm than good to Latinos because the researcher's understandings rarely coincide with participants' own perceptions of their problems and the solutions to them. This can be just an "intellectual colonization" of Latino realities. On the contrary, PAR emphasizes working *with* (Freire, 1992) participants (students and/or community members) toward understanding and enhancing their own situations and opportunities.

Philosophical Underpinnings of PAR

One of the defining principles of a genuine democracy is that it entails the "government of the people, by the people and for the people." This implies the people's informed, free, and full participation in the decisions that affect their lives. Participation is the key defining concept of democracy. Free and informed participation is not only a civil right but also a constitutive principle of being human. The Brazilian educator Paulo Freire (1992) defines humanness as *being-in-relation* with others through dialogue; that is, to participate with others in the understanding and remaking of their worlds on the basis of equal consciousnesses with equal rights and responsibilities.

There is a long history of failure of top-down measures for improving the education of minorities, especially Latinos, mainly because many of those programs are based on a "deficit thinking model" (Valencia, 1997). The end result of those measures has been de facto resegregation. Of common knowledge is the relentless resegregation of "minorities," especially Latinos, into "special education," lower-track classrooms and/or schools, with the accompanying "treatment" of low expectations, "at-risk" labels, unchallenging curricula, inadequate counseling, biased testing, and so on, and with the inevitable consequences of dropouts and "push-outs." Marginalization of poor and minority parents from having a genuine voice in the education of their children is commonplace, despite great efforts of parents and educator advocates for meaningful participation. There is plethora of studies, testimonials, documents, and rationales by many committed educators who are working with Latino communities in recording and cultivating what Moll (1992) refers to as "funds of knowledge" and Trueba (2002) names "a new cultural capital." The importance and necessity of this work is to involve the Latino community in understanding of their own realities and the possibilities of transforming them.

PAR is characterized as having the principles and tools to respond precisely to that necessity. By and large PAR is a response to widespread discontent with conventional empiricist research because of the lack of social change resulting from it. *Participation* refers to the actual engagement of research participants ("subjects" in conventional research) in the whole process of research, from formulating the research problem to using the results for betterment of the life conditions of the participants and their communities. This political character of participation asserts that participants "own" the information they provide, and so should be the first to benefit from it. Thus, participation is a way to demystify and democratize research. The *action* component refers to the use of such collective knowledge and understanding of the issue at hand, as research participants engage in *reflection* and *communal action,* to produce changes in their own communities concurrent with a vision of a more just society. These two attributes are the most distinctive defining principles of PAR. The principles of PAR are not precisely prescriptive characteristics, but are landmarks of its openness and contextual redefinition.

If conventional research *on* and *about* Latino issues may result in intellectual colonization of Latinos/as, PAR as understood here is a form of decolonization, from principles through methods, to the impact of its results. Participants are co-researchers of their own realities. They must participate in the decision of the *what, how,* and *what for* of the research project. Explanations concerning their problems and their solutions are co-constructed in dialogue among participants. Those same participants should benefit most from the study by using the results as a platform to engage in actions that will change their realities for the better. This approach to research is not new around the world; unfortunately, it has not prospered as many would hope. In the U.S., its practice is very marginal.

There are many pioneers of PAR around the world. To mention some: Freire contributed to the conceptualization and practice of PAR in Latin America and then in Africa (Freire, 1975, 1992). In Latin America there are some critical educators who have contributed to the development of the theoretical foundations of PAR, such as Fals-Borda (1978), Bosco-Pinto (1976), Ga-

jardo (1985), and de Schutter (1981). In the U.S., Miles Horton founded the Highlander Center (Appalachian Mountains) devoted to popular education through participatory research. Work in PAR is currently underway in Australia, at the University of Deakin (McTaggart, 1997). From the contributions of all these pioneers and their further developers one thing is clear: PAR is not just a methodology but a completely different view of what research in social contexts is about: its foundations, purposes, methods, and uses.

Another distinctive characteristic is that as we engage in PAR, there are more things done than written because usually those conducting the research need to "make the road by walking." There are often more important results than filling up the shelves with reports. What really matters is the understandings participants reach through dialogical research and the transformative actions they engage in to improve their life conditions.

PAR projects have been developed in many areas and contexts, such as active family involvement in literacy curriculum development, national literacy programs, urban settlements, public health, and students as researchers.

PAR: Model of Inquiry in Human and Social Sciences

Given the participatory character of PAR, the "outsider" researcher enters the community with no more than a framework of ideals concerning genuine participation in the study and transformation of the community's own reality. This conceptual framework is to be re-created in accordance with the specificities of the community and continuously revised in the light of the principles of PAR.

In the conventional approaches to research, the researcher plans ahead every aspect of the research process and then goes into the field for its implementation. In contrast, when we follow the PAR approach, planning cannot be carried out solely by the "outsider-researcher," since the participants are co-researchers with voice and decision power in defining and carrying out every step of the research agenda. One can, however, outline a general process that serves as a broad framework for entering and engaging community members in examining their reality and acting communally for transforming it:

1. *Enter into the community.* This step may take a long time. The whole idea is for the outsider researchers to become known by key members of the target community. The reason(s) for their presence should be explained, understood, and accepted as genuine by those community members. A good strategy is to participate in as many community events as possible. It is important to understand that the outsider will never become an insider, but he or she should aspire to become a trusted person in that specific community.

2. *Plan a community event.* Do this with the sole purpose of identifying the most deeply felt needs and concerns shared by most of the members of the community. This event should be scheduled a long time in advance. It needs to have a lot of publicity through the most effective channels in that community (word of mouth, church announcements, fliers, etc). The outsider researcher should facilitate the meeting. It is important that attendees meet in small groups to encourage the participation of all. Group reporters then present the summaries to the whole group so that the whole assembly may define priorities. Committees are organized and responsibilities are defined. The next meeting date to share progress in the different projects should be scheduled at this meeting. This first group of projects is usually aimed at studying and documenting in a systematic way the problems they have defined.

3. *Keep a field diary.* The outsider researchers and facilitators need to keep questionnaires, maps, and checklists developed by the different committees, with the assistance of the researchers and facilitators themselves, for the purpose of collecting information. The organization and analysis of the information are also collaborative tasks between researchers and facilitators and the co-researchers (members of the community) who have chosen to participate in the committees.

4. *Organize a second general meeting.* In this meeting studies carried out by the different committees are presented (displayed) and discussed by attendees. Communal actions are planned, to be implemented by the same or new committees.

5. *Continue the process.* The steps are repeated as new studies and actions are planned and implemented as community improvement endeavors. As noted above, PAR is an ongoing process of study, action, evaluation, reflection, and theorization.

6. *Make reports.* Reports may be elaborated addressing various audiences at different steps of the ongoing process. These reports may address the community itself, governmental social agencies, or other agencies with vested social interests in the community, as well as the academic community.

One of the most critical aspects in the practice of PAR is to facilitate the engagement of a significant proportion of the members of the target group or community in the design and implementation of the whole research process. In doing so, the outsider researcher(s) needs to devise conditions for a true dialogue among participants on several occasions and in various configurations (pairs, small groups, etc). He or she should be aware of the power relations that may come into play that silence or render invisible the concerns of those less privileged or articulate. A messianic attitude, most of all of the outsiders, needs to be avoided, since it may inhibit the real sense of democratic participation.

Why Is PAR Pertinent for the Education and Empowerment of Latino/a Communities?

As indicated, PAR is a three-dimensional pursuit inasmuch as it includes education, research, and community development; all three are aimed at collective and individual liberation through dialogue and communal action. This comprehensiveness and the over-arching goal of PAR contrast with the more conventional approaches to educational research, whose basic goal is to describe the existing phenomena (with numbers or with words), with little or no real benefit for the research subjects. PAR is led by the principle that the participants own the information, and therefore they should be the first to benefit from the study.

The participatory character of PAR moves researchers away from the "deficit thinking model" of "fixing" the "Latino/a problem." First, often the solutions proposed may be, irrelevant to the real problems this community faces, such as discrimination, segregation, and misrepresentation. Second, most research results on Latinos/as describe only the surface aspects and paint a grim picture of their conditions. By failing to address the roots of those problematic conditions and putting the blame on their lack of effort to succeed in this "land of opportunity," the research tends to disempower Latino/a students and their communities. PAR, on the contrary, facilitates the participation of Latinos/as in studying their own realities and in giving back to their communities by working for collective enhancement of their life conditions and opportunities.

In PAR genuine participation in the search for knowledge implies that all parties—researchers as well as participants—are together studying their situation and the possibilities for improving it. This is especially appropriate for Latino/a students and communities, because critical understanding of their own realities, and of the institutional, social, and economic structures that oppress them, is empowering. "Knowledge is power": to speak out, to challenge oppressive structures, and to mobilize and act collectively and individually is empowering. Becoming aware of shared experiences and struggles facilitates Latino/a cultural identity, which is a venue to collective action and social change.

Participatory search for knowledge is not only a research activity but also a pedagogical activity and may be the basis for building relevant and meaningful curricula. Paulo Freire (1992) in *Pedagogy of the Oppressed* talks about "Thematic Research," the prelude of PAR, which he characterizes as a rigorous and systematic dialogical process that allows participants to identify the themes that are significant for that specific community or group of students. There are several studies and experiences of educators and researchers (e.g., Reyes & Halcón, 2001) who have worked with Latinos/as on implementing participatory curriculum building and pedagogy based on participatory inquiry and have achieved extraordinary engagement, learning, and transformation of Latinos/as.

Becoming aware of the life conditions and the factors that impede Latino/a communities from participating in shaping their future is necessary but not sufficient to achieve liberation as social human beings. Communal actions facilitate a deeper understanding of reality through the transformation of that reality. When Latino/a students participate in action projects, they develop not only empathy with other people's suffering but also social responsibility as a constituting aspect of their life projects. In PAR the *action* component implies both the transformation of consciousnesses and the improvement of the actors' situation in particular and society at large. *Action* is also a defining characteristic of this research approach, as is its *participatory* character.

In conclusion, PAR is a promising alternative to conventional research approaches, especially concerning the education and empowerment of Latino/a students and their communities. PAR is promising because it embodies democratic participation, which allows Latinos/as to be active in the study and solution of their own problems. Active participation means that they are agents, not simply informants. PAR also facilitates the empowerment of Latino/a communities because it integrates education and pedagogy, research, and community-building empowerment.

References

Bosco-Pinto, J. (1976). *Educación liberadora: Dimensión, teoría y metodología.* Buenos Aires: Ediciones Búsqueda.

Fals-Borda, O. (1978). Por la praxis: El problema de cómo investigar la realidad para transformarla. In *Crítica y política en ciencias sociales: Memorias del Simposio Mundial de Cartagena* (pp. 209–242). Bogotá, Colombia: Editorial Punta de Lanza.

Freire, P. (1975). *Cartas a Guinea Bissau: Apuntes de una experiencia pedagógica en proceso.* Mexico City: Siglo XXI.

Freire, P. (1992). *Pedagogy of the Oppressed* (rev. ed.). New York: Continuum.

Freire, P. (1994). *Pedagogy of Hope.* New York: Continuum.

Gajardo, M. (1985). Evolución, situación actual y perspectivas de las estrategias de investigación participativa en América Latina. In M. Gajardo (Ed.), *Teoría y práctica de la educación popular* (pp. 395–450). Pátzcuaro, Michoacán, Mexico: PREDE-OEA / CREFAL / IDRC.

McTaggart, R. (Ed.). (1997). *Participatory Action Research: International Contexts and Consequences.* Albany, NY: SUNY Press.

Moll, L. C. (1992). Bilingual Classroom Studies and Community Analysis. *Educational Researcher* 21(2), 20–24.

Reyes, M. d. l. L., & Halcón, J. (Eds.). (2001). *The Best for Our Children: Critical Perspectives on Literacy for Latino Students.* New York: Teachers College Press.

Schutter, A. de. (1981). *Investigación participativa: Una opción metodológica para la educación de adultos.* Pátzcuaro, Michoacán, Mexico: CREFAL.

Trueba, H. T. (2002). Multiple Ethnic, Racial and Cultural Identities in Action: From Marginality to New Cultural Capital and Modern Society. *Journal of Latinos and Education* 1(1), 7–28.

Valencia, R. R. (1997). *Conceptualizing the Notion of Deficit Thinking.* London: Falmer.

Recommended Reading

Atweh, B., Christensen, C., & Dornan, L. (1998). Students as Action Researchers: Partnerships for Social Justice. In B. Atweh, S. Kemmis, & P. Weeks (Eds.), *Action Research in Practice: Partnerships for Social Justice in Education.* London: Routledge.

Davis, J., & Cooke, S. (1998). Parents as Partners for Educational Change: The Ashgrove Healthy School Environment Project. In B. Atweh, S. Kemmis, & P. Weeks (Eds.), *Action Research in Practice: Partnerships for Social Justice in Education.* London: Routledge.

Fals-Borda, O. (1978). Por la praxis: El problema de cómo investigar la realidad para transformarla. In *Crítica y política en ciencias sociales: Memorias del Simposio Mundial de Cartagena* (pp. 209–242). Bogotá, Colombia: Editorial Punta de Lanza.

Horton, M., & Freire, P. (1990). *We Make the Road by Walking: Conversations on Education and Social Change.* Philadelphia: Temple University Press.

Trueba, E. T. (1999). *Latinos unidos: From Cultural Diversity to the Politics of Solidarity.* Lanham, MD: Rowman & Littlefield.

Zou, Y., & Trueba, E. T. (Eds.). (1998). *Ethnic Identity and Power: Cultural Context of Political Action in School and Society*. Albany, NY: SUNY Press.

Myriam N. Torres, Luis-Vicente Reyes, María Mercado, and Luis Huerta-Charles

PEDRO ALBIZU CAMPOS HIGH SCHOOL (PACHS)

The following entry is based on ethnographic work that I conducted at this high school over a period of three years (1999–2002).

The Dr. Pedro Albizu Campos Alternative High School (PACHS), which currently enrolls 80 students and has an average class size of 12 students, was founded in 1972 as a response to the Eurocentric curricula and high dropout rates that Puerto Rican students had been experiencing in Chicago's public high schools. Historically, the dropout rates among Puerto Rican urban high school students in the U.S. has ranged anywhere between 45%–65% (Flores-González, 2002). An article published on April 8, 1973, in the *Chicago Tribune* titled, "Puerto Ricans Here Set Up Free School to Aid Dropouts," described the negative pedagogical conditions that many Puerto Rican high school students faced when the PACHS was founded. The high school was originally named "La Escuela Puertorriqueña" (the Puerto Rican School) and originated in the basement of a Chicago church. The article stated why the high school was founded.

The school, which opened in February [1972], is geared to aid Puerto Ricans who have dropped out of Tuley, Wells, and Lake View High Schools. It also serves as an alternative for Puerto Rican students who are considering leaving school because of academic or personal problems. . . . Puerto Rican students, parents, and community leaders have long complained that the Chicago public school system is counterproductive and generally apathetic to the real needs of Puerto Rican students.

Although the high school was originally established to address the educational needs of its mostly Puerto Rican student body (60 to 80 students), the school also currently enrolls students of Mexican, African American, and multiple Latino ethnicities from grades 9–12. Currently the PACHS serves as a citywide alternative high school and attracts students from different areas of the city. Because the high school does no formal advertising, most students come to the school by word of mouth, since a majority of the students who apply for admission are friends or relatives of current students or alumni. Because the high school wants to maintain a relatively small student body, a waiting list is maintained. At the time of this entry, this waiting list contained the names of more than 100 students.

Since 1974 the school has been located two miles northeast of the Puerto Rican community known as the Paseo Boricua. The high school itself is on the second floor of a two-story building that once housed a former Walgreen's photo-developing factory that was purchased by the Puerto Rican Cultural Center (PRCC). The PRCC is the umbrella organization under various community-based Puerto Rican agencies including the high school (refer to Ramos-Zayas, 1998). For example, VIDA/SIDA is an organization that provides awareness for HIV/AIDS prevention to the residents of the Puerto Rican community of Chicago. Another example of a PRCC-led community initiative is the Division Street Business Development Association (DSBDA). The DSBDA's main role is to encourage Puerto Ricans to relocate and operate their businesses on Division Street, which is the heart of Puerto Rican Chicago. Hence, the teachers at the PACHS are also part of a larger community organization that works for the cultural, economic, and educational interests of the Puerto Rican community of Chicago.

Funding and Accreditation

Although the high school is considered to be an independent private alternative high school, it is funded and accredited by several federal, state, and local agencies. For example, the students' lunches are federally subsidized through the free and reduced lunch program because the majority of the student body comes from families that fall beneath the federal poverty level. State funding, made available through the Title XX and the Illinois State Department of Child and Family Services, is used for the educational services of those students who may come from foster families. Local support is provided by the City of Chicago, which provides the school with funding for the mentoring of low income and at-risk students. The Mayor's Office of Workforce Development also disburses funding for student job placement and training.

The school also charges students yearly tuition. Ninth and tenth graders are charged $1,750. However, once students reach the eleventh and twelfth grades, they become eligible for a variety of scholarships made available through private donors. Consequently, a majority of the eleventh and twelfth grade students do not pay the annual tuition. Although the school has funding from various sources, the school has to be creative in order to limit their overhead costs. An example of this economic creativity is the fact that the school does not hire a janitor or lunchroom staff full time. Therefore, on a daily rotating schedule staff members participate in the school's maintenance, cleaning, and serving of breakfast and lunch to students.

Finally, the school is registered by the Illinois State Board of Education and ac-

credited by the National Association for the Legal Support of Alternative Schools (NALSAS). This accreditation enables the students to receive a regular high school diploma upon graduation. In addition, the school has a five-year program with the City of Chicago's Dual Enrollment Program so that select students, based on grade point average, have the opportunity to take college-level courses and earn college credit while still enrolled at the high school.

Administrative and Staff Structure

The school's administrative structure consists of a board of directors and a principal who believe that Puerto Ricans should lead their own school and community-based agencies. As the high school principal once indicated to me, whites are not encouraged to assume administrative positions because their leadership would only serve to implicitly perpetuate a colonizer-colonized relationship. The board of directors also reviews, revises, and legislates school policies. The high school's board of directors consists of 12 members and is composed of the various directors of Puerto Rican community agencies, business owners, a parent of a currently enrolled student, and a currently enrolled student. The high school principal is in charge of curricular issues, the implementation of board policies, and the general administration of the school. At the time of this study, the school's staff consisted of eight teachers, two office workers, two counselors, and a grant writer and accountant. A majority of the teaching staff is Puerto Rican, with the exception of two white teachers.

Educational Philosophy

The philosophy of the school reflects its educational mission, which is inherently focused on Puerto Rican pride and affirmation.

This philosophy is described in the PACHS teacher manual as follows:

This school is bilingual and bicultural because our community speaks both Spanish and English while fighting to maintain Puerto Rican culture. Living within the United States, the Puerto Rican people are pressured into assimilation. Neither our language or [sic] our culture is taught in schools. Our history is even more ignored. The emphasis of bilingual education in public schools has been to "mainstream"—to make Spanish-speaking students learn English. Puerto Rican students are told that their language and culture are impediments to their success. Teachers tell them that they may not speak Spanish in their classes. *At this school, we strive to regain our pride in our Puerto Ricaness. By studying their own history and culture, students are able to regain their self-esteem as Puerto Ricans and thus participate fully in their education.* (p. 2; emphasis mine)

The school's educational philosophy is also based on the work of Freire (1970) because of its emphasis on the concept of education as liberation. This concept encourages students to become agents of social change within the Puerto Rican community. This Freirian-based educational model involves a process by which students are encouraged by their teachers to question those social structures, beliefs, or "common-sense" assumptions that serve to perpetuate a status quo and maintain control over its students and community members. School documents explicitly address this educational philosophy.

To us, education is liberation. By this we mean that education is the development of a thinking human being with the capacity to change his or her environment. Students should take an active role in naming their world and transforming it for the betterment of all. Therefore, we believe education goes far beyond the categories of career, job, and acceptance of the status quo

without investigation. To do this, our method is student-centered and based on dialogue. The emphasis is critical thinking—to ask questions and to seek answers. The teacher acts a resource person/facilitator who kindles discussion and assists students in seeking the causes as well as solutions to problems. Much of this work is done with students seated in a circle where students face each other. Students are encouraged to participate and that what they say is not right or wrong, but rather the beginning of an analytical process in which they name their world. It is not the role of the teacher to extract answers that he or she wants to hear, but rather to encourage students to investigate and study what they say, so that they can shape their ideas and reach conclusions themselves. The teacher is not the provider of pre-packaged truth or preordained answers. (p. 3)

This active social analysis was especially evident in the school when I witnessed much dialogue between students and their facilitators in classes and community-based projects that encouraged students to research and analyze their immediate life circumstances, such as poverty, gang life, and police brutality. For instance, I noted how some students helped organize and carry out a protest march regarding police brutality against young Latinos/as. This particular march took place in the immediate Puerto Rican community. However, perhaps the most potent example of dialogical learning and teaching that I witnessed took place during the school's weekly *batey* sessions, which was part of the Unity for Social Analysis class that all students were required to take for credit.

The word *batey*, from the indigenous people of Puerto Rico, is the Taíno expression for "meeting area." The *batey* is an open space located in the middle of the second floor portion of the building in which the school is housed. Sofas and chairs line the outside perimeters of this space. It is here within the *batey* that the students and teachers would meet on Tuesday and Friday afternoons for one hour. This special space was designed to enable students and teachers to voice their sentiments on any topic imaginable. Usually these sessions are facilitated by teachers with student-driven agendas. This special space was also reserved for student poetry readings and artistic performances. I observed discussions revolving around a wide range of topics, such as the planning of field trips, problems that may have occurred between students and their teachers or fellow classmates during the school week, and discussions around topics such as patriarchy and feminism, gang life, as well as other topics of student interest. In instances where urgent issues could not be resolved in the one-hour allotted time period, a provision allowing for an extra weekly *batey* session was put into effect.

The Formal Curriculum

The PACHS curriculum is formally divided into three components: "Identity," "Cognitive Skills," and "Action." The "Identity" component of the curriculum stresses the importance of students analyzing their social realities as Puerto Ricans, Mexicans, African Americans, or students who may identify themselves as being of multiple Latino ethnicities. Student-based social analysis is done through the offering of Puerto Rican, Mexican, and African American history and literature courses. Most of the teachers utilized multiple texts that present topics through an alternative lens. For example, one U.S. history teacher used the work of Howard Zinn (*A People's History of the United States*) in his classes as a supplement to the main textbook. Other teachers used texts that specifically addressed African American and Mexican historical issues.

The "Cognitive Skills" component of the high school's curriculum reflects a more traditional public high school curriculum and includes Biology, Chemistry, Algebra, Basic Arithmetic, Geometry, Calculus, and Trigonometry, among other courses. The third and final component of the curriculum, "Action," is implemented through classes that encourage hands-on student experiences in areas such as photography, art, journalism, and video production. Other activities within this component involve student participation in community events such as community protest marches, community cleanups, and cultural events.

Finally, the PACHS is regarded by its students as a sanctuary (refer to a detailed account of the school-as-sanctuary concept in this volume) because of the value that students and teachers place on (1) caring relationships between students and teachers; (2) the importance of gang-free safe spaces; (3) the school's role as an extension of students' familial and community resources; and (4) the affirmation of students' Diasporic-based sociopolitical, cultural, and economic realities on behalf of Latinos/as and African American students.

Conclusion

As this entry goes to print, the PACHS is now located in a new building in the heart of the Puerto Rican neighborhood of Chicago—*Paseo Boricua*. The old building was sold to real estate developers who have built expensive loft apartments. The new PACHS has, besides its regular classrooms, state-of-the art computer labs and a science classroom with pods that enable students to perform experiments. Finally, in place of the murals of former and current Puerto Rican political prisoners, the new school building has a beige, stucco façade and is also home to the PRCC, the Puerto Rican Cultural Center, which houses a library and serves as a meeting space for cultural events.

References

Flores-González, N. (2002). *School Kids / Street Kids: Identity Development in Latino Students*. New York: Teachers College Press.

Freire, P. (1970). *Pedagogy of the Oppressed*. New York: Continuum.

Pedro Albizu Campos Alternative High School (PACHS) Teacher Manual. (n.d.) Chicago.

Ramos-Zayas, A. Y. (1998). Nationalist Ideologies, Neighborhood-Based Activism, and Educational Spaces in Puerto Rican Chicago. *Harvard Educational Review* 68(2), 164–192.

René Antrop-González

PLAY, LANGUAGE, AND LAUGHTER IN OUTDOOR SPACES

Children are eager to take their energy, laughter, and learning outside. Research has consistently shown the importance of play and the benefits of unstructured activities for young children. It is important to recognize, however, that the outdoor environments are keenly important spaces for learning, playing, and moving. Indoor and outdoor spaces need to respond to children's needs, development, and interests to effectively support young children's development.

The Importance of Play

Many people believe play is good for burning off energy and for physical growth. Research has shown, however, that play benefits all areas of development, and teachers are responding to this by examining outdoor spaces. Creative responsive play spaces need to support all areas of development and, more importantly, to foster a wide range of language and literacy skills. Therefore, traditional playgrounds are not sufficient in supporting the whole child. Play is key for child exploration, problem solving, language production, and socialization. We know that a significant amount of development and learning comes from unstructured activities.

Research has found that playgrounds are essential to not only physical strength but also cognitive and mental strength. Playgrounds help develop social, emotional, linguistic, and cognitive skills. Children need more than the traditional playgrounds, however. They need playgrounds that challenge their skills and provide opportunities to learn new ones. Given the diverse population of children in our country, children need more opportunities to engage in safe spaces where they can use their home language and learn and acquire new languages.

Numerous developmental benefits of play are critical considerations in unstructured outside play activities. These include cognitive development, language development, increased imagination and creativity, and increased problem solving and reasoning. Physical benefits clearly include small and large motor development.

Outdoor Play and Language

What happens with children's language during outdoor play? Children's language development in outdoor play is as critical as language development in indoor play. Although we expect language during outdoor play to sound a lot like language in indoor environments, there are some important differences. Some believe that language used during outdoor play tends to be more complex (Frost, Wortham, & Reifel, 2004). Others (Senda, 1992) have explored the importance of natural environments in fostering varied language structures and interactions. Many theorists have explored the importance of play for language development, production, and comprehension. Teachers who have worked with young children clearly understand the importance of socialization and play. Given the increasing awareness of obesity of young children, teachers are carefully turning their attention to ensuring that children have time and materials for outdoor play.

We do know that children playing outdoors may use more language for negotiating, since most of their outdoor play is self-directed and involves lots of decision making. Outdoor spaces provide a wealth of opportunities for problem solving, social interaction, and novel experiences. Children make decisions continuously on the playground: Where do I want to play? Who do I want to play with? For how long? What do I want to play, and for how long? How do I want to play? Who will I include in my play? What materials do I want to use, and where? How do I feel about playing in this particular place? Throughout play in outdoor environments, children are challenged with decisions to make, choices to take, problems to solve, and new experiences to engage in. Each poses an opportunity to use language. Therefore, it is important for children to have the language skills necessary to be able to express themselves, to convince others, and to negotiate their play. Often some play episode will be a continuation of play from the day before and will require a child to recall what happened previously, where the play episode ended, and how to continue with the same play episode.

Outdoor play offers a great opportunity for teachers to observe how children's language changes when youngsters play outdoors. Some children may use more language in outdoor play simply because of its informal or relaxed nature. Children who are English language learners (ELLs), for example, may feel more comfortable speaking to their peers in outdoor situations. Research has shown that children of diverse language backgrounds interact more frequently in outdoor spaces because they are informal spaces. This allows them to practice what new language they have learned and to build their vocabulary.

Interesting and Engaging Outdoor Spaces

For young children, inviting spaces need to respond to children's curiosity and afford the youngsters opportunities to express themselves in a variety of ways. Outdoor spaces certainly need to respond to the child's developmental needs. Outdoor learning environments need to include large areas that are diverse and provide adequate space for a variety of activities. Large areas need to provide opportunities to run, climb, roll, and gather. Rolling beams and zones for climbing are effective because they challenge children. The outdoor learning environment needs to provide clear boundaries and safe zones (Frost et al., 1997; Jambor, 1990). Frequently, in more traditional spaces the focus of the outdoor area is on equipment rather than on the child. Teachers, parents, and children understand all too well the need for interesting and engaging spaces where children can explore in a variety of zones and linguistically develop in natural spaces.

Play Zones

Outdoor play spaces or playgrounds are one of the few safe areas where children play and learn together on a regular basis. School buildings and classrooms have changed dramatically during the past 10 years, becoming concerned more about academics, than about the whole child. More schools are investing their capital in books and indoor environments, and ignoring the importance of outdoor spaces. Nationwide, playgrounds are becoming more and more impoverished and dangerous spaces for young children. Unfortunately, many regions invest in one playground for large elementary school children but neglect to recognize that the one playground may not meet the needs of very young children, pre–K to third grade. Children of different ages need different play opportunities to meet their social, intellectual, and physical needs.

These play zones should include but not be limited to a number of diverse areas:

1. A variety of natural spaces
2. Garden areas
3. Complex climbers for large motor skill
4. Trails, paths, connections
5. Small and large gathering zones
6. Art and drama areas
7. Specific science areas
8. Animal zones
9. Manipulative zones
10. Tricycle trails
11. Areas for push-pull toys
12. Water and sand zones

Outdoor Spaces and Outdoor Choices: Creative Materials

As children and teachers move outdoors, we need to revisit basic principles of material selections. The outdoor environment provides a wealth of natural choices, but we can extend and enhance these choices by carefully observing our children. Fundamentally, adding props and materials to each of the zones conceptually builds on the children's choices in play. Also, teachers should be mindful of the critical need for loose parts like old tires, lumber, crates, and other materials allowing the children to construct their own worlds of fantasy. In making decisions about materials, flexibility in using diverse materials is key in fostering and supporting the cognitive, social, and physical developments of young children.

Linguistic and Social Concerns

Studies (Marsh, 2004; Selim & Steinhagen, 2003) have shown that most children today spend more than three hours a day watching television or playing computer games. Clearly, this television time displaces the numerous hours that children could be engaged in other activities, among them reading or interacting with their peers outdoors. Other studies show that more than one-third of children never play outside. Nearly two-thirds of parents are worried about letting their children play outside. Other concerns include the lack of supervision, the poor quality of outdoor parks and playgrounds, and the various social dangers surrounding playgrounds.

The long-term effects of children spending less time playing outside are negative. A sedentary lifestyle is inevitably bad for children's social life and health. Outdoor activities, in contrast, encourage interaction between children and the development of social skills. The school playground constitutes an important site where children learn how to engage with one another and learn how to manage some of the risks associated with physical activity. Creative playgrounds are vitally important for many children who do not have access to a garden or live near a park, and playgrounds may be their only experience and opportunity to play with peers outside.

References

Frost, J. L., Wortham, S. C., & Reifel, S. (2004). *Play and Child Development*. Upper Saddle River, NJ: Prentice Hall.

Jambor, T. (1990). Promoting Perceptual Motor Development in Young Children. In S. C. Wortham & J. L. Frost (Eds.). *Playgrounds of Young Children: National Survey and Perspectives*. ERIC Manuscript, no. ED 326 492.

Marsh, J. (Ed.). (2004). *Popular Culture, New Media and Digital Literacy in Early Childhood*. London: RoutledgeFalmer.

Selim, I., & Steinhagen, R. (2003). *Where Do Our Children Play? The Importance and Design of Schoolyards*. Newark, NJ: Appleseed Public Interest Law Center.

Senda, M. (1992). *Design of Children's Play Environments*. New York: McGraw Hill.

Recommended Reading

Bruya, L. D., & Langendorfer, S. J. (1988). *Play Spaces for Children: A New Beginning*. Houston: North Texas State University Press.

Marsh, J. (Ed.). (2004). *Popular Culture, New Media and Digital Literacy in Early Childhood*. London: RoutledgeFalmer.

Moore, R. (1997). *Natural Learning*. Berkeley, CA: MIG Communications.

Vygotsky, L. S. (1994). Play and Its Role in the Mental Development of the Child. In *The Vygotsky Reader*. Oxford: Blackwell.

Georgianna Duarte and Cathy Gutierrez-Gomez

THE POLITICS OF ERASURE

The defining principle underlying national policy initiatives such as English-only propositions, anti-immigrant initiatives, and the No Child Left Behind Act of 2001 that implicitly and explicitly target the education of Latino students is what can be termed "the politics of erasure." Unilaterally designed to erase students' native language, national origin, and cultural formations, these initiatives arise out of an era marked by heightened nationalism and its attendant "fear factor" that views anyone outside of the xenophobic U.S. monoculture as a threat to the univocal cohesion and integration of U.S. citizenship. As a direct result of their magnitude and growing presence in the public domain, Latinos/as have become both objects of inclusion (through assimilationist efforts) and exclusion (by restricting their access and opportunity to a quality education) in educational politics. On the surface, the politics of erasure seeks to incorporate a burgeoning Latino population into the economic, social, and cultural spheres of U.S. society. But the repressed underside of such initiatives is reminiscent of efforts designed to safeguard the cultural and linguistic homogeneity of what Gilberto Gonzalez has termed the "Ideology and Practice of Empire" (2001). Within this framework, education is perceived as the main apparatus of assimilation and acculturation, (read exploitation) for a growing Latino/a population into the economic and social dimensions of an increasingly imperial and militaristic *Pax Americana*. Unearthing and naming the ostensibly hidden narratives and ideological underpinnings of education policy is a necessary counterpoint to the reigning initiatives that evoke, at times, the popular support of Latinos/as—and predominantly immigrant families[1]—in pursuit of achieving the material benefits associated with American nationality. It is essential, therefore, that policy initiatives be understood in terms of their historical specificity and in terms of their functional imperatives for nation-states "administering a commodity-centered economy and its class-determining division of social labor" (cited in San Juan, 2002). In education policy, the rhetoric of positive nationalism, that is, of equal opportunity for all, occludes both the racialized ideologies and class interests of the political elite who act—either willingly or unknowingly—in the service of maintaining internal cultural homogeneity and the empire chic status of the U.S.

As an instructive example, consider the recent arguments posited by Harvard professor Samuel Huntington, who the *New York Times* (Brooks, 2004) referred to as "one of the most eminent political scientists in the world." Huntington's (2004) commentary in *Who Are We?* is predictably aligned to the ideological imperatives of U.S. citizenship. Concerned with the "persistent flow of Hispanic immigrants" who, "unlike past immigrant groups . . . have not assimilated into mainstream U.S. culture, forming instead their own political and linguistic enclaves," he writes: "There is no Americano Dream. There is only the American Dream created by an Anglo-Protestant society. Mexican-Americans will share in that dream and in that society only if they dream in English" (2004, p.12). In linguistics we would refer to the aforementioned coupling as cognates, but in Huntington's context that speaks directly to the reactionary segments of the population that he depicts, they represent two separate and incommensurable worlds divided by language, culture, and values. In his enfeebled defense of the Anglosphere as the sacerdotal eyrie of U.S citizenship, Latinos/as, and primarily those of Mexican decent, are characterized as a monolithic cultural group that "lack initiative, self-reliance, and ambition" and have "little use for education; and acceptance of poverty as a virtue necessary for entrance into heaven" (cited in Huntington, 2004). Such views are neither new nor limited to depicting the Latino/a population. The rise of industrialization, the emergence of world wars, the collapse of statist communism and reformist social democracy, and the creation of the U.S. as the world's sole superpower have advanced an "us" versus "them" discourse that legitimizes political, military, and economic domination. Directly linked to economic exploitation is the cultural process of "othering," a process that is innately racialized, that places whiteness and the cultural values associated with it as the commanding method of "civil" society, while serving as a functioning principle of the imperial nation-state that seeks "asymmetrical distribution of social wealth and power" (San Juan, 2002, p. 93).

According to E. San Juan (2002), the object of nationalism signifies a community "just like us," which is inextricably linked to the nation-state's formation of classes and social groups. He writes:

What defines patria, or home for the victorious conquerors is their own self-validating attributes of gender, kinship or parentage, skin color, and the inexorable "natural" or naturalizing markers demarcating them from the subjugated and subordinated peoples. (p. 67)

San Juan elaborates on this position by unfolding the core roots of American national identity. He asserts that the development of American "patria" takes place along two primary dimensions: the systematic inclusion and exclusion of certain segments of the population; and the political management of social life forms according to the hierarchization of morals and codes of conduct (2002, p. 93). These identity formations are made manifest across multiple dimensions. The media, the electorate, pop culture, and education work symbiotically to sustain and proliferate hegemonic interpretations of what it means to be "American." Tensions do arise, however, when such formations are threatened by demographic shifts in the population—shifts of seismic proportions—that no longer secure a static or unyielding social configuration. It is during these times of flux and change across the geopolitical landscape that we witness an inversion in dominant discourses. The "colonizers" claim to be the "colonized," and consequently a systematic and sustained set of political initiatives makes its way into the legislative body as a necessary precaution or defense against the inclusion of "other" cultural arrangements.

In this contribution we argue that the once-regnant discourses of colonialism and imperialism have politically imploded as reactionary politicians are no longer speaking of conquering land, resources, and people adjacent to the southwest U.S. border but view themselves and the Anglo-American constituencies they represent as having been conquered by a burgeoning Latino/a population. As a result, numerous attempts have been made to erase any remnants of the motherland and to forcibly assimilate and acculturate Latinos/as to the "American way of life." Propelled by both state and national legislative initiatives, a politics of erasure is currently underway in our public schools. Addressing the historical and material antecedents of Latinos/as in the U.S., this entry highlights the necessity for a humanizing pedagogy of liberation that refutes either/or binaries (either you're American or you're not) and adopts a dialectical framework advanced by contemporary social movements and popular education initiatives in Latin America.

"Latino/a"—Historical and Material Dimensions

To understand the ways in which the education of Latino/a youth is being affected by what we term a politics of erasure it is necessary to fully define "Latino/a." We consider it important to highlight the arguments posited by Martha Gimenez (1997), who suggests that ethnic labels such as "Latino" or "Hispanic" work not only to solidify the negative stereotyping associated with that group (such as Huntington's views of Latino/a populations) but also to hide and de-emphasize both the differences and similarities across ethnic enclaves. By differences, we are suggesting that Latinos/as constitute a population of wide variation—across class and other social dimensions—and that they do not, by any measure, share or ascribe to an organic or pure cultural identity. By similarities, we are also suggesting that Latinos/as, when viewed as individuals situated along a historical and material continuum differentiated by class status, share traits, experiences, and values with other "non-Latino" groups. The process of Americanization, or what is often termed in academic circles acculturation and/or assimilation, is not a uniform process for Latinos/as in general. Gimenez is particularly insightful on this point: "Dialectically, however, culture is not a thing one learns or unlearns (thus becoming acculturated): It is the lived experience of people shaped by their location in the class and socioeconomic stratification systems" (1997, p. 231). Therefore, it is necessary to view Latinos/as as a social group in all their iterations and to consider the material backdrop of their cultural formations.

Latino/a, or Hispanic, is a cultural category that denotes both national origin (outside the U.S.) and generational status (for those born in the U.S.). Peoples of South American, Central American, Cuban, Dominican Republican, Puerto Rican, and Mexican origin (spanning across two continents and nineteen countries) classify as "Latino" as well as do native U.S. citizens from Latin American backgrounds. Often missed in census calculations that place the Latino population at over 35 million (Suárez-Orozco, 2001), however, are the various reasons behind their expatriation. For a limited number, their status in the U.S. will qualify as exilic, while others are delegated the indelible rank of "illegal aliens" or "immigrants." As Gimenez (2003) notes, exile, as a political construct, denotes the "forced removal from one's native country," whereas immigrants depart their countries of origin "voluntarily in search of economic opportunities and upward mobility." These two seemingly disparate definitions in fact transcend a false set of alternatives. Gimenez asserts, correctly in our view, that both "exiles" and "immigrants" share more than differ in the extent to which the social, material, and political factors demanding their expatriation can be linked to the processes of capitalist exploitation and accumulation. She claims thusly, "As capital speeds around the globe taking advantage of rapidly changing profit making opportunities the economic devastation it leaves behind compels millions of workers to uproot themselves and join local, regional and international migration flows" (2003, p. 1).

Since the Industrial Revolution, Latin America is representative of *weak* capitalism, situated along the periphery within an international capitalist system that forces the superexploitation of its laborers. As articulated by Enrique Dussel, "Within the international capitalist system, they [Latin-America] end up structurally transferring value to the central capital and its metropolitan centers, to England first, to the U.S. since 1945, and last to the giants of transnational capitalism such as Japan, Germany and the European Common Market" (1995, p. 129). Consequently, the region is now characterized as a host of economies dependent on the transnational firms and international structures of the World Trade Organization, World Bank, and International Monetary Fund. Rendered vulnerable by what Eduardo Galeano (2002) has referred to as the "mythology of the free market and consumer society," the false prophets of neoliberal policies have ushered in an era (from 1980 onward) characterized by the systematic economic collapse of Argentina, Bolivia, Brazil, Peru, and Venezuela. And in Mexico, the so-called poster boy of trade reform and economic liberalization, labor inequality has reached its highest level since 1984 (Bouillon, 2000). Although remarkable forces of working-class and indigenous mobilizations have accompanied these economic "crises,"[2] socially and economically, the region is in a relative state of instability and discord. With one-third of the population living in poverty and the wealthiest 20% receiving 60% of the region's wealth, Latin America boasts the greatest income inequality in the world next to Sub-Saharan Africa (IDB, 2003). Given these economic and social trajectories, it is not surprising to note that 40% of Latinos residing in the U.S. are foreign born (NCLR, 2004), an overwhelming majority (54%) of which have come from Mexico. Transnational labor recruiting networks, family reunification, and wage differentials across the southwestern U.S. border establish powerful contexts for Mexican immigration (Suárez-Orozco, 2001). Characterized as the "Neo-Bracero" program, the influx of undocumented workers into the U.S. functions to maintain the exploitation of a labor force who sell themselves at subhuman prices in exchange for the *possibility* of upward mobility or at least a better quality of life. In pursuit of personal and material dignity, it is their children who ultimately embody *esperanza*. Carrying the burden of the past and the hope for the future, children are offered—trustingly—to the institution that promises triumphalist visions of human sociality: education.

Education and the Politics of Erasure

Among U.S. institutions, public schools bear the greatest burden to bring youth and their families into the modernist regime. For educators such as Aronowitz (2004), schools serve as the primary mechanism to connect children and their families to the full spec-trum of social life. Social life, in these terms, includes broad notions of citizenship, but it also, and perhaps most importantly, suggests the cultivation of a laboring citizen body. He is worth quoting in extenso:

The common school is charged with the task of preparing children and youth for their dual responsibilities to the social order: citizenship and, perhaps its primary task, learning to labor. On the one hand, in the older curriculum on the road to citizenship in a democratic secular society, schools are supposed to transmit the jewels of the enlightenment, especially litera-ture and science. On the other hand, students are to be prepared for the work world by means of a loose but definitely stress on the redemptive value of work, the importance of family, and of course the imperative of love and loyalty on one's country. (Introduction 1.1)

We agree with Aronowitz's description of the public school and find it particularly relevant for Latinos/as and other immigrant groups struggling assiduously on the margins for full incorporation into the dominant landscape of U.S. society. The notion that schools ultimately shape and form future generations under the mantra of democracy building or "loving one's country" is a nec-essary tool for policymakers and other mem-bers of the bourgeois elite to justify pedagogical programs and initiatives de-signed to homogenize and unify a seemingly varied population. But what is often over-looked is the role schools play in serving as pallbearers of profit maximization and in sustaining a commodity-centered economy predicated on the social division of labor. It is here that the linkages between the expansion of capital and schooling become translucent— in terms of schools transforming into com-modities (through increased privatization) and in their role as commodity-producing (human labor-power) institutions.

The government itself clearly captures the interplay among schools, labor, capital, and citizenship. In a move not unprece-dented across presidential administrations, a report commissioned on behalf of the Bush Jr. administration, "From Risk to Opportu-nity, Hispanics in the U.S.," outlines these very relations. The President's Advisory Commission (2003) report states:

If the employment picture does not change, the economic consequences of an uneducated work-force will strain the economy of the United States. Hispanics are not maximizing their income potential or developing financial secu-rity. This leads to lost tax revenues, lower rates of consumer spending, reduced per capita sav-ings and increased social costs. (p. 3)

This narrative reduces Latinos/as' "failure" in the economy to a litany of discrete fac-tors in education. From factors such as limited parental involvement, poor aca-demic instruction, and a lack of English or accountability for results, an investment in school "improvement" is considered the only viable alternative toward eliminating the fiscal and social "crisis" associated with the Latinization of America. The President's Advisory Commission asserts, "School im-provement may be an expensive short-term investment, but the ultimate profit resulting from an educated Hispanic workforce is much greater" (2003, p. 3). When Latinos/as's participation in the labor market is contrasted against indicators that measure their integration in education and other as-pects of social life, the stage is set to "reform" or "rectify" the conditions asso-ciated with what is perceived as "failed assimilation." Across ethnic groups, Lati-nos/as have the highest high school dropout rate, nearly 28%, and for newly arrived immigrants the dropout rate stands at 40% (NCLR, 2004). Only one in ten Latinos ages 25 and over has received a bachelor's degree or higher, yet in the year 2002 nearly one in five of all those incarcerated in the U.S. were Latino (NCLR, 2004, p. 11). Of the close to 5 million English language learners (ELLs) residing in the U.S., an overwhelming majority are Spanish speakers; and in the year 2000–2001, Latinos/as represented 10% of the school-aged population, a proportion bound to increase exponentially. The "Latino experience" viewed against this backdrop provides the fuel and impetus for policymakers to create and implement educational initiatives to reverse the trend of so-called failure. Such is the rationale behind increased standardization (as a way to equalize educational inputs and outcomes) of curriculum, testing mechanisms, and instructional techniques. For Latinos/as and other segments of the population clinging to the rhetoric of positive nationalism, education policies in this vein are configured with irresistible appeal. But ultimately such efforts come at the expense of an often cruel and violent pedagogy of dehumanization that places the burden on the young and "unacculturated" to adopt "ways of being" that are—indeed—foreign and alien.

The very system that incorporates Latinos/as and other immigrant groups into the dominant whitestream society is the same system that seeks to alienate them from their local histories, their culture, and the location where their knowledge is inscribed: language (Maldonado-Torres, 2004). Language, which serves to classify, categorize, and label our human essence, is internalized. Language, as we are using the term, represents the core of our inner selves and the formation of our identities. In the words of Gloria Anzaldúa, "Ethnic identity is twin skin to linguistic identity—I am my language. Until I can take pride in my language, I cannot take pride in myself" (1987, p. 81). With language valorized as the essentialized component of nationality and identity, the Latino/a experience in public schools is most visibly affected by English-only movements. Starting in California with Proposition 227, an initiative that legally dismantled bilingual education instruction, and followed by similar propositions in Arizona (Proposition 226) and unsuccessful attempts in Colorado and Massachusetts, bilingual education is consistently thrust into the fetid sewers of wasteful pedagogy. While language policy has historically been sanctioned at the level of the state, the federal government's reauthorization of the Elementary and Secondary Education Act, through the No Child Left Behind Act of 2001, marked a reversal of language policy that stresses the acquisition of English skills only (Crawford, 2002). By eliminating any reference to the term "bilingual," by mandating achievement tests that measure, primarily, the acquisition of English over subject matter content (Abedi & Dietel, 2004), and by attaching a strict system of punishment and rewards to test results, the U.S. government has solidified a neocolonial model of education that legitimizes the sustained subordination of groups that fall short from gaining membership to the dominant discourses of U.S. citizenship. Gutierrez, Asato, Santos, & Gotanda (2001) have referred to this phenomena as "backlash pedagogy" rooted in "backlash politics, products of ideological and institutional structures that legitimize and thus maintain privilege, access and control of the sociopolitical terrain." Along a similar vein, Donaldo Macedo (2000) writes that English-only initiatives are present-day forms of colonialism, designed to subordinate groups through the loss of their human citizenship. In conjunction with initiatives that support anti-immigrant hysteria (Proposition 209 in

California, the elimination of the Immigrant Education Program in No Child Left Behind 2001), and measures to eradicate affirmative action programs, we are constantly reminded that becoming "American," from the standpoint of education policy, is an atrophic process that denies the full development of human subjectivity.

Toward a Humanizing Critical Pedagogy

As critical educators, we reject the notion that marginalized student groups must selectively choose between binary oppositions—of Americanism or un-Americanism. We also reject the notion that schools must ultimately service the needs of capital rather than the humanizing needs of children and their families. At the same time, we are aware of the complex set of social relations that have compelled millions of working-class and poor people from Latin America to leave their countries of origin in search of a viable alternative. The powerful notion of comprised national identities and the lived tensions and contradictions confronted in every aspect of social life in the U.S. by "immigrants" or "exiles" compels us to articulate a humanizing critical pedagogy that is rooted in the cultural, spiritual, and linguistic dimensions of everyday life. But a humanizing pedagogy is also grounded in material social relations and practices associated with contemporary capitalist formations. We have made an effort to note that the exploitation of human capacity to labor (labor-power) is not limited to regional or national geographical spaces alone. Rather, Latinos/as in the U.S. and abroad are implicated in a web of transnational relations linked to the accumulation of capital and extraction of surplus value. Moving from the center to the periphery, it is instructive for us to critically engage social movements and

popular education initiatives in Latin America as illustrative sites toward a humanizing critical pedagogy.

Raul Burgos (2002, p. 24) notes that popular struggles in Latin America have historically confronted the cultural ideological force of capitalism. He writes, "Neoliberalism exercises its dominion fundamentally on the cultural level, attacking the constitutive values of popular identity, national identity and the traditions of struggle contained in historical experience." Struggles and popular education initiatives across Latin America have responded to cultural dominion in numerous ways. From the Zapatistas in Chiapas, Mexico, to the *piqueteros* in the streets of Buenos Aires, Argentina, multiple groups have engaged in a process of reclaiming national and personal identity through collective *con-scientización*. The Zapatistas claim to have developed an alternative educational autonomous pedagogy that is defined and administered by the indigenous communities and which is independent of the ideological positions of those in power (Flores, 1999), whereas the *piqueteros* use alternative media in their commitment to "horizontal" and "non-hierarchical" forms of communication and organization in their struggle against capitalism and imperialism (Scatamburlo-D'Annibale, Suoranata, Jaramillo, & McLaren, in press). These movements differ in multiple ways and face a myriad of contradictions within and against the powers of the neoliberal state apparatus. The point we wish to illustrate, however, is the ethical radicalism that arises from collective human action such as that of the Zapatistas and the *piqueteros*. It is a radicalism that refutes ways of being that are imposed, rather than created by the people. It is a radicalism rooted in the sociohistorical reality of communities struggling against the totalizing power of global capitalism that, we argue, is the essence of a humanizing critical pedagogy.

A humanizing critical pedagogy respects students' language and cultural identity. It begins, in the words of Antonia Darder (2002), "with the view that all human beings participate actively in producing meaning and thus reinforces a dialectical and contextual view of knowledge" (p. 135). Cultural workers in this tradition ask students to recollect the past, to situate the present socially, politically, and economically, and to strive toward a future built upon a utopian universality that creates the conditions for groups to liberate themselves in their own contextually specific ways from all forms of oppression, domination, alienation, and degradation. A pedagogy built upon these perspectives and practices seeks to understand the underlying motives, interests, desires, and fears of draconian shifts in education policy, and it contests ascribed methods of producing knowledge. Rather than erasing students' cultural formations, a humanizing critical pedagogy unearths the debris of the dialectically fashioned self of capital from the oppressive strongholds of the state and the empire of capital and re-articulates what it means to be the subject rather than the object of history.

Notes

1. For an extensive survey of Latino beliefs on education see Pew Hispanic Center, "National Survey of Latinos: Education" (http://pewhispanic.org), 2004.

2. See P. McLaren & N. Jaramillo, "Critical Pedagogy as Organizational Praxis: Challenging the Demise of Civil Society in a Time of Permanent War" (http://gseis.ucla.edu), 2002.

References

Abedi, Jamal, & Dietel, Ron. (2004). Policy Brief: Challenges in the No Child Left Behind Act for English Language Learners. National Center for Research on Evaluation, Standards, and Student Testing (CRESST)/UCLA (Winter).

Anzaldúa, Gloria. (1987). *Borderlands/La Frontera: The New Mestiza*. San Francisco: Aunt Lute Books.

Aronowitz, Stanley. (2004). Against Schooling: Education and Social Class. *Journal for Academic Labor* (February). Available: http://www.louisville.edu/journal/workplace/issue 6p1/aronowitz04.html.

Bouillon, Cesar. (2000). *Inequality and Mexico's Labor Market After Trade Reform*. Washington, DC: Inter-American Development Bank.

Brooks, David. (2004). The Americano Dream. *New York Times*, February 24, section A, p. 25.

Burgos, Raul. (2002). The Gramscian Intervention in the Theoretical and Political Production of the Latin American Left. *Latin American Perspectives* 29(1), 9–37.

Crawford, James. (2002). The Bilingual Education Act 1968–2002 (Spring). Available: http://www.ourworld.compuserve.com/home pages/jwcrawford/T7obit.html.

Darder, Antonia. (2002). *Reinventing Paulo Freire*. Boulder, CO: Westview Press.

Dussel, Enrique. (1995). *Invention of the Americas*. Trans. Michel D. Barber. New York: Continuum.

Flores, Roberto. (1999). Breaking the Ideological Hold. In *Motion Magazine*. Available: http://www.inmotionmagazine.com/chbilin.html.

Galeano, Eduardo. (2002). The Upside-Down World. *The Progressive*. Available: http://www.progressive.org/dec02/gal1202.html.

Gimenez, Martha. (1997). Latino/"Hispanic"— Who Needs a Name? The Case against Standardized Labeling. In A. Darder, R. D. Torres, & H. Gutiérrez (Eds.), *Latinos and Education: A Critical Reader* (pp. 225–238). New York: Routledge.

Gimenez, Martha. (2003). The Politics of Exile: Class, Power, and the Exilic. *Cultural Logic* 6. Available: http://clogic.eserver.org/2003/2003.html.

Gonzalez, Gilberto. (2001). The Ideology and Practice of Empire: The U.S., Mexico, and the Education of Mexican Immigrants. *Cultural Logic* 4(1), 1.

Gutierrez, Kris, Asato, Jolynn, Santos, Maria, & Gotanda, Neil. (2002). Backlash Pedagogy: Language and Culture and the Politics of Reform. *Review of Education, Pedagogy and Cultural Studies* 24(4), 335–351.

Huntington, Samuel. (2004). *Who Are We? The Challenges to America's National Identity.* New York: Simon & Schuster.

Inter-American Development Bank (IDB). (2003). *Inequality, Exclusion and Poverty in Latin America and the Caribbean: Implications for Development.* Washington, DC: IDB.

Macedo, Donaldo. (2000). The Colonialism of the English Only Movement. *Educational Researcher* 29(3), 15–24.

Maldonado-Torres, Nelson. (2004). The Topology of Being and the Geopolitics of Knowledge: Modernity, Empire, Coloniality. *CITY Analysis of Urban Trends, Culture, Theory, Policy, Action* 8(1), 29–56.

National Council of La Raza (NCLR). (2004). *State of Hispanic America 2004.* Available: http://www.nclr.org.

President's Advisory Commission on Educational Excellence for Hispanic Americans. (2003). From Risk to Opportunity: Fulfilling the Educational Needs of Hispanic Americans in the 21st Century. Washington, DC: U.S. Government Printing Office, March 31.

San Juan, E. (2002). *Racism and Cultural Studies: Critiques of Multiculturalist Ideology and the Politics of Difference.* Durham, NC: Duke University Press.

Scatamburlo-D'Annibale, Valerie, Suoranta, Juha, Jaramillo, Nathalia, & McLaren, Peter. (in press). Farewell to the "Bewildered Herd": Paulo Freire's Revolutionary Dialogical Communication in the Age of Corporate Globalization, Forthcoming in Patrick D. Murphy & Clemencia Rodriguez (Eds.), *Communication and the Question of Culture in Latin America.*

Suárez-Orozco, Marcelo. (2001). Mexican Immigration . . . and the Latinization of the United States. *ReVista: Harvard Review of Latin America* (Fall). Available: http://drclas.fas.harvard.edu/publications/revista/mexico/suarezorozco.html.

Recommended Reading

For a historical and thorough analysis of assimilationist projects:

Gonzalez, Gilbert. (2004). *Culture of Empire.* Houston: University of Texas Press.

For an extensive analysis of language policy:

Gutierrez, Kris, Baquedano-Lopez, Patricia, & Alvarez, Hector (2000). The Crisis in Latino Education: The Norming of America. In C. Tejeda, Z. Leonardo, & C. Martinez (Eds.), *Charting New Terrains in Chicano(a) and Latino(a) Education* (pp. 213–232). Cresskill, NJ: Hampton Press.

Gutierrez, Kris et al. (2002). "Sounding American": The Consequences of New Reforms on English Language Learners. *Reading Research Quarterly* 37(3), 328–343.

For Critical Pedagogy

McLaren, Peter. (1997). *Revolutionary Multiculturalism: Pedagogies of Dissent for the New Millenium.* Boulder, CO: Westview Press.

McLaren, Peter. (2000). *Che Guevara, Paulo Freire, and the Pedagogy of the Revolution.* New York: Rowman & Littlefield.

Nathalia E. Jaramillo and
Peter McLaren

POVERTY

It was always a question of work, and work depended on the harvest, the car running, their health, the conditions of the road, how long the money held out, and the weather, which meant they could depend on nothing.

Helena María Viramontes,
Under the Feet of Jesus

Poverty is a social phenomenon that is inextricable from power and is an affliction affecting the powerless. Poverty, then, should be understood as a creation of the powerful for the exploitation of the powerless. It is no surprise that empowerment is central to a pedagogy for social justice. Empowerment should be understood, not in the patriarchal sense where someone with power or knowledge "empowers" the oppressed, but in the pedagogical sense whereby conditions are created to fathom the dynamics of power and poverty dialectically *with* the oppressed who empower themselves through their deeper awareness of the mechanisms that work to oppress them. Empowerment emerges through emancipation from internalized oppression that has resulted from dominant hegemonic structures and practices and a logic that blames the victim and convinces victims of their inferiority while equating privilege to superiority. Empowerment can be thought of as synonymous with choice. No one chooses to be poor, but a majority of the world's population finds itself living in poverty. The continuation of the status quo relies upon a "dance" between the oppressor and the oppressed. Once the oppressed work intellectually to demystify and name the sources of their oppression, they can begin to work counter-hegemonically to challenge the power structures of the status quo. Huffman (2004) captures the strategy of empowered groups in Africa: "The key element was non-cooperation with the colonial infrastructure," in other words, refusing to dance.

Language is a central issue in the politics of poverty, and rhetoric from the powerful makes promises designed to placate the oppressed but never intended to be kept. A language of deficit is employed to demonize and dehumanize victims and to identify character flaws (or to provide genetic explanations) to account for the economic woes of the powerless. A moment's reflection on how language is used illuminates terms used in schools such as "dropout," "atrisk,"

"culturally disadvantaged," and "discipline problem." This routinized way of speaking about marginalized students consistently accounts for their failure to learn as located with the victims, their families, or their cultural group. In the wider society "welfare queen," "homeless," "unemployed and unemployable," "trailer trash," "white trash," and "lazy" identify and demonize without interrogating who might have created and be benefiting from the human conditions these victims must endure.

One term to problematize here to demonstrate how the rhetoric of the status quo reveals its own hypocrisy and disjointed, almost schizophrenic "logic" is "compassionate conservative." Consider the oxymoronic relationship of these words. *To conserve* means "to keep things the way they are," as in preserving the status quo. Yet to improve the human conditions of the oppressed, to democratize wealth and power, change needs to occur. Compassion is about caring or agape. In combination one might interpret this term, coined by the powerful, as "We're sorry that you suffer so, but let's keep things the way they are anyway." In fact, not only have promises not been kept, but conditions have gotten worse as the concentration of wealth is becoming even more skewed in the favor of the powerful and the gap between rich and poor is ever widening.

In our present capitalist system, poverty is a category measured in financial terms. Poverty will be addressed in this material sense first. However, for the purposes of this operationalized definition, it would be appropriate to expand the conceptualization of poverty to delineate some of the positive aspects of the human beings who are normally demonized by those who create the desperate economic conditions so many are subjected to under the capitalist system.

Poverty is consistently addressed in government and social agencies from a deficit model, where the locus of the problem is within the victims. Research demonstrates, however, that poverty is a structural phenomenon, the result of an economic order that traps some people into poverty while it fails to provide the social safety nets to rescue others who fall into poverty through circumstances beyond their control. According to some recent studies (Berrick, 1995; Ehrenreich, 2001; Rank, 2004; Rothstein, 2004), poverty is not the result of character flaws (laziness, lack of ambition, dishonesty, or substance abuse, for example). Rank (2004) identifies three major reasons people fall into poverty: loss of job, radical change in family (divorce), and illness leading to insurmountable medical expenses. Whereas some are born into poverty and find it impossible to climb out, Rank asserts that nearly 75% of the population in the U.S. will experience poverty within their lifetimes. He argues that this demonstrates that structural weaknesses that leave people vulnerable, rather than character flaws, are the explanation.

The most vulnerable to poverty are women and children regardless of race (Berrick, 1995; Ehrenreich, 2001). Single mothers trying to raise a family without social safety nets in place fight an uphill struggle insurmountable to most. The consequences for their children are even more dire.

In a strictly capitalist sense, poverty is a condition identified by a line drawn in the financial sand and adjusted as economic conditions fluctuate. Recent trends demonstrate that more and more people are falling below the line (Berrick, 1995; Ehrenreich, 2001; Rank, 2004; Rothstein, 2004), with homelessness being close to the bottom of the category.

More important, since so many of those who are poor are consistently demonized and blamed for their own victimization, it is necessary to identify core characteristics of the majority of those who have been victimized and demonized in order to deconstruct the myths—generated out of ignorance—used to dehumanize these groups.

Myth: Parents Don't Care

That parents living in poverty fail to participate in the education of their children may be explained in many ways other than by accusing parents of indifference. The hours set aside for parents to come to the school, either for reasons of discipline or for school events such as plays, are often inflexible and biased toward the leisure class. That a parent cannot take off from work does not mean the parent does not care. Also, parents may harbor unpleasant memories from their own school experiences and feel uncomfortable returning to school. At the same time, educators can be intimidating through the professional jargon of IEPs (Individualized Education Plans) and not be effective communicating with parents. Further, homework and other schoolwork may not provide ways in which parents can become more involved in their children's education. To overcome such barriers, the ethnography of teaching can be used effectively, among other approaches, to engage parents in the education of their children so all can be successful.

In the case of Latinos, according to Rank (2004) 13.7% of the population of the U.S. is "Hispanic" but Latinos make up 24.7% of the poor. This disproportionate overrepresentation of Latinos living below the poverty line has structural explanations and far-reaching implications for education and employment opportunities. All the studies mentioned earlier recommend solutions such as affordable housing and livable wages.

No discussion of poverty would be complete without including a non-economic measure of a person's relative wealth. People who invest their life energies in the obscene accumulation of capital at the expense of others are morally bankrupt. On the other hand, poor families often provide solid moral foundations and loving environments for their children against all odds (Hayes, Bahruth, & Kessler, 1991; Valenzuela, 1999). Latino culture in particular teaches respect for teachers. The notion of *educación* demonstrates clearly the cultural foundations of ontological clarity in Latino households. "It refers to the family's role of inculcating in children a sense of moral, social, and personal responsibility and serves as the foundation for all other learning. Though inclusive of formal academic training, educación additionally refers to competence in the social world, wherein one respects the dignity and individuality of others" (Valenzuela, 1999, p. 23).

In conclusion, all of the studies recommend structural reforms necessary to address poverty (see Berrick, 1995; Ehrenreich, 2001; Rank, 2004; Rothstein, 2004). The ways poverty is discussed and approached must change radically if sincere reform is to occur. Studies such as these provide a voice to those most affected by the crisis of poverty in ways that dispel the myths associated with those victimized and demonized by the powerbrokers who regulate an economic system that produces poverty.

References

Berrick, J. D. (1995). *Faces of Poverty: Portraits of Women and Children on Welfare*. New York: Oxford University Press.

Ehrenreich, B. (2001). *Nickel and Dimed: On (Not) Getting By in America*. New York: Henry Holt.

Hayes, C. W., Bahruth, R., & Kessler, C. (1991). *Literacy con cariño* (new ed. 1998). Portsmouth, NH: Heinemann.

Huffman, V. (2004). Stories from the Cha Cha Cha. In P. L. Loeb (Ed.), *The Impossible Will Take a Little While*. New York: Basic Books.

Rank, M. (2004). *One Nation, Underprivileged: Why American Poverty Affects Us All*. New York: Oxford University Press.

Rothstein, R. (2004). *Class and Schools: Using Social, Economic, and Educational Reform to Close the Black-White Achievement Gap*. New York: Teachers College Press.

Valenzuela, A. (1999). *Subtractive Schooling: U.S.-Mexican Youth and the Politics of Caring*. Albany, NY: SUNY Press.

Recommended Reading

Chávez Chávez, R., & O' Donnell, J. (Eds.). (1998). *Speaking the Unpleasant*. Albany, NY: SUNY Press.

Chomsky, N. (1994). *The Prosperous Few and the Restless Many*. Berkeley, CA: Odonian Press.

Freire, P. (1970). *Pedagogy of the Oppressed*. New York: Continuum.

Gabbard, D. (2000). *Knowledge and Power in the Global Economy: Politics and the Rhetoric of School Reform*. Mahwah, NJ: Lawrence Erlbaum.

Galeano, E. (1989). *El libro de los abrazos*. Buenos Aires: Siglo XXI.

Giroux, H. (1996). *Fugitive Cultures: Race, Violence and Youth*. New York: Routledge.

Hayes, C. W., Bahruth, R., & Kessler, C. (1991). *Literacy con cariño* (new ed. 1998). Portsmouth, NH: Heinemann.

hooks, b. (1994). *Teaching to Transgress: Education as the Practice of Freedom*. London: Routledge.

Kohl, H. (1991). *I Won't Learn from You*. New York: New Press.

Kozol, J. (1990). *The Night is Dark and I Am Far from Home* (2nd ed.). New York: Touchstone.

Kozol, J. (1991). *Savage Inequalities*. New York: Crown Publishers.

Macedo, D. (1994). *Literacies of Power: What Americans Are Not Allowed To Know*. Boulder, CO: Westview Press.

Molnar, A. (1996). *Giving Kids the Business: The Commercialization of America's Schools*. Boulder, CO: Westview Press.

Morrison, T. (1992). *Race-ing Justice, Engendering Power*. New York: Pantheon Books.

O'Donnell, P. & Chávez Chávez, R. (2004). *Social Justice in These Times*. Greenwich, CT: Information Age Publishing.

Purpel, D. (2000). *Moral Outrage in Education*. New York: Peter Lang.

Robert Bahruth

PRESIDENT'S ADVISORY COMMISSION ON EDUCATIONAL EXCELLENCE FOR HISPANIC AMERICANS

On October 12, 2001, President George W. Bush created the President's Advisory Commission on Educational Excellence for Hispanic Americans. The commission was establish by the president's Executive Order 13230. The purpose of the commission was to target educational excellence for Hispanic Americans. Its mission was to "develop a multi-year plan to close the educational achievement gap facing Hispanic Americans and attain the goals established by the No Child Left Behind Act of 2001" (President's Advisory Commission, 2002, p. 23).

Members of the commission were appointed by the president, were non-partisan, and came from diverse backgrounds, including but not limited to educators, business entrepreneurs, and a religious leader. The 20 members were then divided into five working subcommittees, which focused on issues related to family, educator, public awareness and motivation, community and faith-based initiatives, and government resources and accountability (President's Advisory Commission, 2002, p. 2).

The first task assigned to the commission was an interim report to provide findings regarding the effectiveness of current practices related to (1) educational achievement, (2) parents in the education of their children, and (3) the role of federal agencies' education programs in helping parents successfully prepare their children to graduate from high school and attend postsecondary institutions. The interim report, *The Road to a College Diploma: The Complex Reality of Raising Educational Achievement for Hispanics in the United States,* in combination with an 18-month research review, town hall meetings, and dialogues with parents, teachers, and students, led to the creation of the final report.

From Risk to Opportunity: Fulfilling the Educational Needs of Hispanic Americans in the 21st Century was submitted to President Bush on March 31, 2003, thus concluding a plan to close the educational achievement gap for Hispanic American children.

The report set forth the following recommendations to achieve this goal:

- Establishing new and high expectations across America for Hispanic children by helping parents navigated the educational system

- Creating partnerships to provide additional options for children

- Implementing a nationwide public awareness and motivation campaign to address educational attainment and receiving a college education

- Full implementation and enforcement of No Child Left Behind

- Reinforcing a high-quality teaching profession by preparing teachers to address the diverse needs of the student population such as language proficiency and disabilities

- Providing incentives and compensation for teachers whose students show an improvement in academics

- Launching a national study to integrate formats employed by the colleges of education to prepare educators for reading instruction of diverse children

- Launching a coherent and comprehensive research agenda on the educational development of Hispanic Americans across the educational spectrum from Pre–K to Postsecondary

- Ensuring full access for Hispanic American students to enter college and demand greater accountability in higher education for Hispanic graduation rates by challenging the nation's postsecondary institutions to graduate 10% more of their students from colleges and universities each year

- Urging institutions to explore and increase development of retention programs that would benefit students

- Increasing accountability and coordination of programs within the federal government to better serve students and their families (President's Advisory Commission, 2003, pp. viii–ix)

Since the publication of this event, the White House Initiative on Educational Excellence for Hispanic Americans has worked in support of the implementation of these recommendations. Currently a new 1.5 billion High School Initiative to prepare students to graduate with the skills needed for college is currently on the Congress floor. If the High School Initiative passes as proposed, it would allow states and districts to use the resources for individual performance plans, dropout prevention efforts, and college awareness (Ed.Gov., 2005). In this matter the White House Initiative plays a crucial role not only to advocate for future funding to implement the recommendations by the schools but also to keep Hispanic students on the forefront of the educational platform.

On a similar note, the president's proposed budget 2006 includes $500 million for a Teacher Incentive fund to attract and reward the very best teachers for high-risk, high-poverty schools (Ed.Gov., 2005), thus

paving the road toward the implementation for improving teacher staff. The ongoing participation of the White House Initiative is vital because our Hispanic students are within these demographic areas. One needs to acknowledge the role that the White House Initiative has in enriching the education of Hispanic students, yet one must also follow up with recommendations set by the commission for the success of this multi-year plan.[1]

For example, several recommendations call for an in-depth research of the current situation of Hispanic students in the U.S. It is therefore indispensable that the White House Initiative on Educational Excellence for Hispanic Americans conduct qualitative studies of Hispanic students that focus on ethnic, generational, and demographic differences.

Some questions to frame these studies might include the following:

What is the social climate faced by Hispanic students and parents in our public schools that have led others to have low expectation of them?

What models of partnerships have been successful between Hispanic students, parents, business, and the community to provide students with a positive experience in their education?

Similarly, what partnerships have been detrimental to the students, parents, community, and businesses, thus negatively affecting the educational development of Hispanic students?

How have societal concerns such as poverty, gang violence, drug abuse, and incarceration affected Hispanic youth and their access to education K–16?

The road to close the educational achievement gap for Hispanic Americans does indeed require a multi-year plan. It consists of multiple fronts such as advocacy and research by the White House Initiative, public awareness of the educational situation of Hispanic students, and accountable partnerships among all sectors of society. If such work continues, then the implementation of the recommendations of *From Risk to Opportunity: Fulfilling the Educational Needs of Hispanic Americans in the 21st Century* will create positive changes toward closing the educational achievement gap facing Hispanic students in the U.S.

Note

1. Please note that the commission was terminated after submitting the final report to the president.

References

Ed.Gov. (2005). President's New High School Initiative, Other Proposed Programs Tackle Issues Important to Hispanics. Press release, February 23.

President's Advisory Commission on Educational Excellence for Hispanic Americans. (2002). *The Road to a College Diploma: The Complex Reality of Raising Educational Achievement for Hispanics in the United States*. Washington, DC: U.S. GPO.

President's Advisory Commission on Educational Excellence for Hispanic Americans. (2003). *From Risk to Opportunity: Fulfilling the Educational Needs of Hispanic Americans in the 21st Century*. Washington, DC: U.S. GPO.

Recommended Reading

Anyon, Jean. (1997). *Ghetto Schooling: A Political Economy of Urban Education Reform*. New York: Teachers College Press.

Miron, Louis F. (1996). *The Social Construction of Urban Schooling: Situating the Crisis*. Cresskill, NJ: Hampton Press.

Padilla, Felix M. (1992). *The Gang as an American Enterprise*. New Brunswick, NJ: Rutgers University Press.

Valenzuela, Angela. (1999). *Subtractive Schooling: U.S.-Mexican Youth and the Politics of Caring*. Albany, NY: SUNY Press.

Myrian Luis

PUERTO RICANS AT CARLISLE INDIAN SCHOOL

> Colonization carried forward by the armies of war is vastly more costly than that carried forward by the armies of peace, whose outpost and garrisons are the public schools.
>
> Samuel McCune Lindsay, 1902

During the last two years of the nineteenth century and the opening years of the twentieth, victorious in the Spanish American War, the U.S. government approved a series of grants and actions aimed at "Americanizing" the residents of their newest possession, Puerto Rico. In the process, at least 60 Puerto Rican youngsters were sent to be re-educated at the Carlisle Indian Industrial School, where the motto was, "Kill the Indian, save the man." Founded in 1878 by Captain Richard Henry Pratt, the purpose of the Carlisle School was to create a new mainstream identity for Indians, to change them into something "acceptable" for the society of the times.

It all began after the Indian Wars, when Captain Pratt was put in charge of a group of Indian prisoners who had been virtually exiled to Florida. There, Pratt engaged in reform practices still followed today in our prison system. He made certain that the Indians at Ft. Marion lived regimented lives, they had to work, learn to read and write in English, learn a trade, follow a strict military discipline, and even wear uniforms. After several years, and by an act of Congress, the Indian prisoners-of-war were pardoned. Some of them had no place to go and decided to stay with Pratt. Pratt developed a plan to "better" them as well as other Indians. Pratt took his group of ex-convicts to Hampton Institute in Virginia, an institution for the children of ex-slaves. After intense lobbying, Pratt convinced the U.S. government to give him the run-down facilities of Carlisle Barracks, located in Carlisle, Pennsylvania. Congress funded his project with money allocated from the "civilization fund." While preparing the school Pratt simultaneously engaged in a strong recruitment effort. Pratt held long meetings with the tribe leaders to convince them that their survival lay in the ability of a new generation to learn the American way. He stressed the need to learn to read and write English in order to maintain truthful communication with the white man. His strategy was as old as humanity, where the conqueror takes the children of the conquered, educates the new generation, and creates future leaders loyal to the new government.

Life at Carlisle Indian School

Everyday life at the Carlisle Industrial Indian School was totally regimented. A strict schedule was followed. In a bold move toward total acculturation the newly arrived youngsters were forbidden to speak their native languages, and their physical appearance was transformed the moment they stepped into the school. Indian regalia was discarded in favor of late-nineteenth-century attire handed out. The boys' long hair was cut short, and in some cases the girls' long hair was also cut. The children were taught to read and write English, were encouraged to join a Protestant Christian denomination, and were given vocational training in such areas as farming, baking, printing, and shoemaking.

The student's formal education was completed with an "outing" system. Students were sent out to live with local families for several months of the year. The stated purpose was to teach them to live and emulate the American life, but many of them were treated as servants and given no positive education—just shame came from the experience. It is important to mention, however, that some of the students were well treated and lived as members of the local family.

The Spanish-American War

By the end of the Indian Wars, the U.S. government had its eyes on the Caribbean. The sinking of the *Maine,* an event that is still a mystery to this date, unleashed what the U.S. leaders had wanted for a long time, an excuse to fight the Spaniards and expand into the Caribbean. Teddy Roosevelt called the Spanish-American War "a splendid little war." Cuba and Puerto Rico were conquered in record time, although the Philippines was a different story. Victorious Americans came to the Caribbean, mostly for strategic, military, and economic reasons, thinking that the islanders where grossly inferior to them.

Even educated blacks in the U.S. thought that the inhabitants of the Caribbean Islands were inferior. Booker T. Washington stated his interest in educating the Cubans and Puerto Ricans and, after the fact, mentioned the "elevating" benefits of industrial education in a letter published in 1900:

We now have the additional responsibility, either directly or indirectly, of educating and elevating about eight hundred thousand others of African descent in Cuba and Porto Rico, to say nothing of the white people of these islands, many of whom are in a condition about as deplorable as that of the Negroes.

The expansion of the U.S. grew after the Spanish-American War, to the dismay of many citizens who strongly criticized the government. It was at this historical juncture that the destinies of the African Americans, Native Americans, and Puerto Ricans collided.

Leaders behind the Carlisle Experiment

A small group of men were the architects of the idea to send Puerto Rican children to the Carlisle, Tuskegee, and Hampton Industrial Schools, an almost forgotten chapter of Puerto Rican history and colonialism. Richard Henry Pratt, John Eaton, and Nelson Miles knew each other well. They had served in the U.S. Army and rose through the ranks by using a mixture of intelligence, leadership, and effort. They had in common their service in the Civil War and the Indian Wars and were in charge of Indian Scout Units as well as Buffalo Soldier Units. Pratt convinced leaders of the U.S. government of the worthiness of his social experiment with the children of Indian chiefs.

The life of Miles, who was once described as a "brave peacock," was full of controversy, basically because he was loud and opinionated, and for his betrayal of his Indian scouts. After the Spanish-American War, Miles invited Eaton to be the first secretary of education of Puerto Rico. Eaton's stay in Puerto Rico was short, but his radical changes to the education system in Puerto Rico still remain today.

Meanwhile, Eaton rose rapidly through the government ranks and went from being director of the Freedman and Slaves Bureau to director of Indian Affairs; he was then called upon to organize a new Bureau of Education. Eaton was the moving intellectual force behind the plan to Americanize the Puerto Ricans using an offshoot of Pratt's Carlisle Plan that was already in place for the Indians. He was a close personal friend of Pratt; his frequent visits to Carlisle Indian School are well documented in the school's newspaper, *The Indian Helper*. As first secretary of education of Puerto Rico, Eaton implemented his brainchild, the

Carlisle Scholarship Program. He was unable to put it into full motion, however, because of serious health problems that forced him to leave the island very soon after his arrival. His successor, Dr. Martin Grove Brumbaugh, was the one who really carried the program.

Dr. Brumbaugh knew where he was sending the Puerto Rican youngsters because he was a native of Pennsylvania and later became governor of that state. Brumbaugh used the same proven program developed by Pratt and approached the elite families of Puerto Rico—the majority of the youngsters sent to Carlisle were the children of the upper-class families. Brumbaugh used a one-on-one personal approach, with arguments about the advantages of educating their children or losing them through ignorance of the new system.

The philosophy behind sending the children of elite Puerto Rican families to Carlisle School was the same one that Pratt stated in 1882: "The school serves a double purpose—first as an educating influence on those who are here and second as an educating and controlling influence"(Pratt, 1901). These men—Pratt, Eaton, Miles, and Brumbaugh—joined forces and put together a plan to "civilize" the Puerto Ricans.

Conflicting Stories

The stories of these youngsters are not told in history books, and until recently only a handful of people have known about the so-called Porto Rican Indians. A group of more than 60 Puerto Rican youngsters was sent to the city of Carlisle, Pennsylvania, to an Indian industrial boarding school. Who were these Puerto Rican youngsters? Who sent them to Carlisle? Who paid for their education? Why Carlisle? What kind of lives did they have after leaving Carlisle?

As answers were sought, a series of human stories began to unfold. Several answers were to be found within the records kept at the National Archives and Records Administration (NARA), folio 75. The Cumberland Historical Society located in Carlisle, Pennsylvania, also has many records with enlightening information about those students, including long letters answering school surveys about their lives after leaving the institution. Another part of the story came from three articles published in the U.S. and Puerto Rican press and from the school's newspaper, *The Indian Helper.*

Not long after their children arrived at Carlisle, many parents were surprised to receive letters from them telling about the bad conditions at the school. Several of the parents approached the well-known leader and politician Luis Muñoz Rivera, the Puerto Rican journalist and nationalist who had founded *La Democracia,* a newspaper later edited by his son Luis Muñoz Marín. Also a leader in the campaign for independence from Spain, in 1897 he had obtained a charter that granted some autonomy to Puerto Ricans, though it was never put into effect. Heading the first Puerto Rican cabinet under U.S. occupation, Muñoz Rivera opposed military governorship and pleaded for greater self-government, but faced with bitter opposition in Puerto Rico, he moved to New York City and there published the *Puerto Rican Herald,* which expounded the island's problems. Later, as resident commissioner of Puerto Rico in Washington, D.C. (1910–1916), he would obtain U.S. citizenship for Puerto Ricans. (*Columbia Encyclopedia,* 2001). Thus, Muñoz Rivera was the most likely individual who could help the parents. After reading the complaints, Muñoz Rivera went to inspect the school. His findings were published in the *Puerto Rican Herald* in 1901. He wrote about his visit in August of that year:

The letters of diverse students and their parents, from several places of the island, gave me a firm impression that the education was very bad and the food was detestable at the Indian School. Since I went there without any other purpose than rectifying or verifying those impressions, I asked each student individually about their personal experiences. All agreed with both extremes: "here we eat bad and we are not well." (Muñoz Rivera, 1901)

Apparently there had been a general perception among the Puerto Rican parents that they were sending their children to the school to receive a higher education. Muñoz Rivera addressed the controversy when he wrote:

Those who thought that their sons and daughters would become doctors, lawyers or architects were deceived. Some say that those careers were available to them in Puerto Rico. I resist admitting that Mr. Brumbaugh, whom I hold as an intelligent educator and serious person, had promised things that in reality could not be true. If those offers were to be confirmed, then a grave charge would result against the Department of Education. (Muñoz Rivera, 1901).

Muñoz Rivera offered to take the children back home, but the youngsters took a vote and decided to stay, arguing that they did not want to leave without first mastering the English language. One might infer that they wanted to return to Puerto Rico triumphant.

Two revealing sources are articles written by Angela Rivera-Tudó (1931) and Dr. Juan José Osuna (1949), two Puerto Ricans who were Carlisle alumni. Rivera-Tudó's article is titled "The Puerto Rican Indians." Here are some excerpts from what, at first sight, appears to be a simple invitation to a high school reunion:

Only those of us who went and experienced the misfortunes of this kind of experience in adolescence, since most of us had graduated from eighth grade as did others soon after their arrival in that land [the U.S.], I repeat, only we can attest to the suffering. (Rivera-Tudó, 1931)

Rivera-Tudó explains in detail her anguish and goes on to defend the worthiness of the students sent to Carlisle:

For me, the situation amounted to an unforgivable injustice, abusive treatment by our [U.S.] "masters," directed to denigrating Puerto Ricans further, by their choosing the only college they had for educating and civilizing the savage Redskin Indians for also educating and "civilizing" the wretched Puerto Ricans. And, to make matters worse, those of us who were there represented the best that Puerto Rico had. (Rivera-Tudó, 1931)

Leading scholar and Puerto Rican educator Dr. Juan José Osuna wrote about his misfortunes in Carlisle in the scholarly journal *Summer School Review* in 1932. His words paint a detailed picture of how he manipulated the outing system to stay out of Carlisle:

I worked there for the summer and went to school during the academic year of 1901–1902. Of the rest of my companions, some stayed like myself to work and study; some ran away and returned to Puerto Rico; and the parents of the well to do either sent for their children or transferred them to other schools. We were a very disappointed lot. I had decided to become a lawyer, but I did not see that in this school I would ever get nearer my goal. (Osuna, 1932)

It is sad and at the same time poignant to read his description of how he was treated:

As I was different from the Indians and also somewhat different from the Americans, I became a curiosity. On Sunday afternoons, people from all over that section of the country that came purposely to see Miss Mira's new boy visited the place. They had heard that he was not an Indian, that he had come from Puerto Rico; and they wanted to see what Puerto Ricans looked like. (Osuna, 1932)

Osuna closes his article by telling us about his last days as a Carlisle alumnus:

In the spring of 1905, I received a letter reminding me that I was still a Carlisle student, but that the authorities felt that I was advanced enough to graduate from the institution and sever my relationship with the Federal Government. . . . I went to Carlisle, attended commencement; . . . I received a diploma of the Carlisle Indian Industrial School. I graduated with the class of 1905; I am an alumnus of the Carlisle Indian Industrial School. I am an Indian in spite of myself. (Osuna, 1932)

Whereas these newspaper articles show one side of the Carlisle experience, documents found at NARA show another perspective. The first set of documents, created when the students first arrived at the school, was the *Descriptive and Historical Record of the Students*. These consisted of cards that included data such as name, parents' name, nation, blood (quantum), age at arrival, date of arrival, date of departure, reason for departure, and height and weight.

The first Puerto Ricans arrived at Carlisle Indian School in 1899. Most belonged to elite families and were youngsters between the ages of 12 and 19. Some families still had close ties to Spain. A group of at least 60 teenagers was sent to Carlisle Indian School between 1899 and 1906. Under the "tribe" category, the word "Porto Rican" was written. The Puerto Ricans who went to Carlisle were from mostly coastal towns, and if you follow the names of the municipalities and place them on a map of Puerto Rico, you can see the route of old Puerto Rico Road number 2, or the Military Road. The route of the train ran parallel to that road.

The average age of the youngsters sent was 15, and the youngest student, Olimpia Morales, was 12 years old. The children arrived in small groups ranging from 12 to 20 students. At least 5 of them ran away, and 11 students were requested to be returned to Puerto Rico by their parents. Three (maybe more) students joined the "Porto Rican Provisional Regiment" and were the first islanders who rose to the ranks of officers in the U.S. Army. The majority of the students returned to Puerto Rico, but a few of them, Paul Seguí and Vicente Figueroa among them, stayed in Pennsylvania for the rest of their adult lives.

Effects of the Carlisle Experience

In addition to letters and documents, a search of family records using genealogical research methodology uncovered many distinguished contributions of those Carlisle alumni. The surnames of the Puerto Rican students at Carlisle read like a *Who's Who* of the island's twentieth-century history. Surnames like Osuna, Seijo, Orriola, Rexach, Duchesne, Irrizary, Urrutia, and Nin, among others, are well known to this day in education, politics, arts, business, and music.

The investigation into what happened to those Puerto Ricans after their Indian School experience has resulted in an unexpected discovery. None of the descendants interviewed had known that their ancestors had attended the Carlisle Indian School—a well-kept secret unearthed after more than 100 years.

Elvira Vélez's story can be traced to the days just before the Spanish-American War. Her father, Francisco Vélez, was a rich landowner of a large sugar-cane plantation and the mayor of Lajas, a town located on the southwest coast of Puerto Rico. Besides Elvira, he also had two sons, whom he sent to medical school at Georgetown University. Elvira's only surviving child, retired engineer Gustavo Grana, knew that she attended

high school in Pennsylvania, but "she never mentioned the Indian School."

Concebida Duchesne came from a very musically talented family. Her father was a known musician during Spanish rule, and her brother Rafael Duchesne-Mondríguez was one of the great composers of "la danza puertorriqueña" (Puerto Rican waltz). Concebida's records at Carlisle mention that she was adopted by her patrons. One of the surveys the school sent her was answered by her patron, stating that she was studying to be a teacher and planning to return to Puerto Rico. She studied at Bloomsburg College, now Bloomsburg University. Her great grandnephew, a professor at the University of Puerto Rico, Dr. Juan Duchesne (2003), wrote:

Concebida ("titi Conci") returned to Puerto Rico in the 1920s with another sister named Francisca. Both were English teachers. They taught in the countryside of San Lorenzo, where they traveled on mule to school. Not long afterwards, both returned to the mainland, maybe before 1930. Paquita relocated to Boston and Concebida went to Poughkeepsie, NY . . . . she had been converted into an American and she could no longer speak in Spanish nor live in Puerto Rico. Concebida never again returned to Puerto Rico.

Dr. Juan Duchesne informed us that Concebida not only lost her ability to speak Spanish but also changed her religion and was a "fervent Protestant," causing shock among the Catholic members of her family.

Enrique Urrutia went to Carlisle even though his family had close ties to the Spanish crown. His great aunt was the wife of don Juan Dabán y Busterino, and her name was doña María Catalina de Urrútia y Montoya of Havana, Cuba. Don Juan Dabán was the governor of Puerto Rico in 1783. Peter Reilly, grandnephew of Urrutia, wrote: "The family has a rich military history and, in fact, was prominent in governing and protecting much of Spain's lands in the New World from the 17th century up to the Spanish-American War" (Reilly, 2003).

After leaving Carlisle, Enrique Urrutia joined the Porto Rico Provisional Regiment. He was one of the first group of Puerto Rican officers in the U.S. Army and retired as a colonel after serving in both world wars. His son and grandson followed in his footsteps as officers of the U.S. Army. Enrique is buried in Arlington National Cemetery. He never told his family that he attended the Carlisle Indian Industrial School.

Juan José Osuna went to Carlisle and, as noted, manipulated the system to stay out of the Indian School. A brilliant scholar, Osuna moved around for a while in the U.S. until he settled down and obtained a doctor's degree in education. He returned to Puerto Rico, worked at the University of Puerto Rico and was one of the co-founders of the university's publishing house, Editorial Universitaria. He was the dean of the University of Puerto Rico School of Education. His highly acclaimed book *A History of Education in Puerto Rico* is a well-researched, scholarly study of several hundred years of education on the island. He describes in his book the Carlisle Scholarship system, but he never mentions that he was a participant.

Carlisle Indian School changed the lives of that group of students. Some changed their religion; others acquired the ability to speak English, but some lost the use of their mother tongue—Spanish. The direct descendants of those Puerto Ricans knew their forebears had been sent to the continental U.S. to get an education, but were never told of their ties to the Indian School. Why? Shame to be associated with Native Americans? The need to forget a difficult time? Repression of bad memories? Trauma? We may never know the reasons behind this collective secret.

Conclusion

Why were those youngsters sent to Carlisle Indian School? Who sent them? They were sent to Carlisle as part of a very structured and open program to Americanize the Puerto Ricans following the Spanish-American War. "Council Bill 12, enacted in 1901, the Puerto Rican Legislature Bill 21 (1901), and later on House Bill 35, provided for scholarship money for twenty men and women to study at technical industrial schools in the U.S" (Silvestrini, 1992). Just as Pratt did with the Indians, Secretary of Education Brumbaugh convinced the Puerto Rican leaders to send their children not only to Carlisle Indian School but also to Tuskegee and Hampton, schools created to educate the ex-slaves, now traditional African American universities. Youngsters from Cuba were sent to Hampton and Tuskegee. The Indians, African Americans, and Puerto Ricans were forcibly mainstreamed, and education was used as a principle tool on the island of Puerto Rico as well as on the mainland: North American teachers arrived at the island for the sole purpose of teaching English. It was the intent not only to substitute the language but also change the value system and "Americanize" Puerto Ricans through the educational process.

José-Manuel Navarro (2002), in his book *Creating Tropical Yankees,* presents in detail the history of education in Puerto Rico and how the schools were openly used for the Americanizing the masses. The U.S. government had no qualms, like many other conquerors after their conquest, in creating a cadre of acculturated and assimilated youngsters. Those youngsters educated in the U.S. were very successful after returning to Puerto Rico, and their families still are. Their names are part of the intellectual, business, and political scene of the island.

The legacy of Carlisle is thus filled with contradictions. Some students spoke of the horrors and the prisonlike atmosphere, whereas others called it home and mentioned the school with fondness and warmth. Which accounts were sincere? Were some Carlisle graduates suffering from brainwashing or the Stockholm syndrome? Were they grateful for their professional successes?

A commemorative marker was inaugurated last September 1, 2003, in front of the Carlisle Barracks Cemetery. It reads:

This school was the model for a nationwide system of boarding schools intended to assimilate American Indians into mainstream culture. Over 10,000 indigenous children attended the school between 1879–1918. Despite idealistic beginnings, the school left a mixed and lasting legacy, creating opportunity for some students and conflicted identities for others. In this cemetery are 186 graves of students who died while at Carlisle.

None of the students buried in the Carlisle Barracks Cemetery are Puerto Ricans. They were the lucky ones! They were able to return home, probably with opportunity in one hand and conflicted identities in the other. The majority of the Puerto Rican kids, despite the pain, rose from the ashes stronger, and they took the education given at Carlisle and used it constructively to create a new and better life for themselves and their families. The Puerto Ricans at Carlisle Indian School left a legacy of resilience and strength.

References

Duchesne, Juan. (2003). Personal email to the author.

"Luis Muñoz Rivera." (2001–2004). *The Columbia Encyclopedia* (6th ed.). New York: Columbia University Press. Available: www.bartleby.com/65/.

Muñoz-Rivera, Luis. (1901). Untitled article, *Puerto Rican Herald.*

Navarro, José-Manuel. (2002). *Creating Tropical Yankees: Social Science Textbooks & US Ideological Control in Puerto Rico, 1898–1908.* New York: Routledge.

Osuna, José J. (1932). An Indian in Spite of Myself. *Summer School Review* 10(5).

Osuna, Juan J. (1949). *A History of Education in Puerto Rico.* Rio Piedras, PR: Editorial Universitaria.

Pratt, Richard H. (1901). *Pratt Papers.* New Haven, CT: Beinecke Library, Yale University.

Reilly, Peter. (2003). Personal email to the author.

Report of the Governor of Puerto Rico. (1909). NARA.

Rivera-Tudó, Angela. (1931). Translation by Vilma Irrizary. "The Puerto Rican Indians." *La Correspondencia de Puerto Rico,* January 3, p. 4.

Silvestrini, B. (1992). "Igualdad y proteccion: La legislacion sobre la mujer en Puerto Rico." In C. I. Rafucci, S. Alvarez Curbelo, & F. Pico (Eds.), *Senado de Puerto Rico, 1917–1992* (pp. 313–339). Rio Piedras, PR: Ediciones Huracan.

Washington, Booker T. (1900). *Signs of Progress among the Negroes.* Urbana: University of Illinois Press.

Recommended Reading

Library of Congress. Hispanic Americans in Congress: Luis Muñoz Rivera. Available: http://www.loc.gov/rr/hispanic/congress/munozrivera.html.

Muñoz-Rivera, Luis. (2000). Una visita al Indian School. *Revista de genealogía puertorriqueña* 1(2).

Navarro Rivera, Pablo. (2004). *The University of Puerto Rico: Colonialism and the Language of Teaching and Learning 1903–1952.* Available: http://www.lesley.edu/journals/jppp/4/navarro.html (accessed September 3, 2004).

Negrón de Montilla, Aida. (1971). *Americanization in Puerto Rico and the Public School System: 1900–1930.* Rio Piedras, PR: Editorial Edil.

Pennsylvania Historical and Museum Commission. Pennsylvania Governors Past to Present:

Governor Martin Grove Brumbaugh (1862–
1930). Available: http://www.phmc.state.
pa.us/bah/dam/governors/brumbaugh.asp?se
cid=31.

Silvestrini, Blanca G., & Luque de Sánchez,
María Dolores. (1988). *Historia de Puerto
Rico: Trayectoria de un pueblo*. San Juan, PR:
Editorial La Biblioteca.

Sonia Migdalia Rosa

PUERTO RICAN STUDENTS IN U.S. SCHOOLS

Puerto Rican students have been attending
U.S. schools since 1898, when residents of
the Caribbean island were handed over as
spoils of the Spanish-American War. The
Jones Act of 1917 afforded citizenship
against the will of the elected legislators on
the island (Rodriguez, 1989). It is crucial for
educators to understand the colonialism and
the massive migration of Puerto Ricans to the
U.S. during the twentieth century. Of the
32.8 million Latinos residing in the U.S., 9%
were Puerto Rican (U.S. Census Bureau,
March 2000). The Puerto Rican Diaspora
(close to 3.5 million) living on the U.S.
mainland represents half of all Puerto Ricans
(Institute for Puerto Rican Policy, 2006).

Puerto Rico remains a Commonwealth of
the U.S., which affects the education and
curricula of Puerto Rican learners both on
the island and in the metropolis. On the island U.S. Congress mandated English as the
language of instruction and the "American
way of life" leading to the importation of
U.S. ideals, teacher preparation, U.S. textbooks, imported structures of schooling,
English-only policies, and U.S. holidays.
(Negron de Montilla, 1971; Osuna, 1949).

In the metropolis Puerto Rican students
are rarely taken into account in the curricula
or textbooks. Sonia Nieto (1999a) reflects
on her daughters' education:

The curriculum in the schools they attended was
firmly monocultural and assimilationist. The
conventional understanding in most of those
settings was that schooling was to be a kind of
crucible where students were, if not melted, at
least treated to a common experience that would
homogenize them. This was almost uniformly
seen as a good thing by their teachers and by
society in general. (p. 2)

Issues of language, race, and social class
also affect the daily reality of Puerto Rican
children in the metropolis. Almost half of
Puerto Rican children live below the poverty level in spite of having working parents
(Children's Defense Fund, 2006). The continued pursuit of a monolingual, monocultural curriculum has meant linguistic and
cultural losses for our children. The struggle
of Puerto Rican parents for a quality education for their children has met with much
resistance (Soto, 1997a).

Return migration to and from the island
has also created challenges for learners who
describe themselves as "*los de aquí y los de
allá*," those who are from here and those who
are from there (Soto, 1997b). The Quality of
Education for Minorities project (1990) reported that 30% of New York City Puerto
Rican students reported changing from island to metropolis schools one to four times
between grades 7 and 9. There continues to
be a need to address how children can meet
this educational challenge.

Jonathan Kozol (1991) in his book *Savage
Inequalities* documents the disparities children face in New York City. This disparity is
evidenced in the academic achievement of
Puerto Rican children in the mainland schools
where the school's assumptions about children's intelligence is linked to the learner's
fluency in English and their knowledge of
middle-class norms (U.S. Commission on
Civil Rights, 1976). The myth that bilingualism is a barrier to academic success flies

in the face of research documenting the benefits of maintaining Spanish at home and at school (Soto, 1993; Zentella, 1997).

In order to best meet the needs of Puerto Rican learners schools can create what Nieto (1999a) refers to as "centering pedagogies." This approach ensures that children's identities are at the center of learning, with safe social spaces providing an opportunity for cultural and linguistic affirmations. The curriculum includes biculturalism as "natural," instruction in both the home language and English, meaningful parental involvement, bilingual/bicultural teachers, and materials reflecting the lives of the learners.

René Antrop (one of my former doctoral advisees) in his dissertation documents how Puerto Rican students find the nationalist curriculum of the Pedro Albizu Campos High School in Chicago as a "sanctuary" (see Gonzalez, 2003).

Reflecting on Bruner's notion of "ordinary practices of school," Nieto (1999b) suggests conditions for providing a meaningful community of learners: conditions should (1) be anti-racist and anti-bias; (2) reflect the understanding that all students have talents and strengths that can enhance their education; (3) based on the notion that those most intimately connected with students need to be meaningfully involved in their education; (4) reflect high expectations and rigorous standards for all learners; (5) be empowering and just (p. 20). Puerto Rican families interviewed elsewhere (Soto, 1997a) suggested that schools need to reflect a "caring curriculum" and children's home language and culture.

References

Children's Defense Fund. (2006). Available: http://www.childrensdefense.org.

Gonzalez, R. A. (2003). This School Is My Sanctuary. The Pedro Albizu Campos Alternative High School. JSRI Working paper, no. 57. Julian Samora Research Institute, Michigan State University, East Lansing, Michigan.

Institute for Puerto Rican Policy. (2006). Available: http://www.pridef.org/policy.htm.

Kozol, J. (1991). *Savage Inequalities*. New York: HarperCollins.

Negron de Montilla, A. (1971). *Americanization in Puerto Rico*. Rio Piedras, PR: Editorial Edil.

Nieto, S. (1999a). *Light in Their Eyes: Creating Multicultural Learning Communities*. New York: Teachers College Press.

Nieto, S. (1999b). *Affirming Diversity: The Sociopolitical Context of Multicultural Education*. New York: Addison Wesley.

Osuna, J. J. (1949). *A History of Education in Puerto Rico*. Rio Piedras: University of Puerto Rico.

The Quality of Education for Minorities (QEM Network). (1990). Available: http://qemnetwork.qem.org/pplc.htm.

Rodriguez, C. (1989). *Puerto Ricans: Born in the U.S.A.* Boston: Unwin Hyman.

Soto, L. D. (1993). Native Language For School Success. *Bilingual Research Journal* 17(1, 2).

Soto, L. D. (1997a). *Language, Culture, and Power: Bilingual Families Struggle for Quality Education*. New York: SUNY Press.

Soto, L. D. (1997b). Boricuas in America: The Struggle for Identity, Language, and Power. *Review of Education/Pedagogy/Cultural Studies* 19(4), 349–365.

U.S. Census Bureau. (March 2000). Available: http://www.census.gov.

U.S. Commission on Civil Rights. (1976). Report of the U.S. Commission on Civil Rights. Available: http://www.archives.gov/research/electronic-records/civil-rights.html.

Zentella, A. C. (1997). *Growing Up Bilingual*. Malden, MA: Blackwell.

Recommended Reading

Flores, J. (2000). *From Bomba to Hip-Hop: Puerto Rican Culture and Latino Identity*. New York: Columbia University Press.

Morales Carrión, Arturo. (1983). *Puerto Rico: A Political and Cultural History*. New York: W. W. Norton.

Negron de Montilla, A. (1990). *La americanización de Puerto Rico y el sistema de instrucción, 1900–1930*. Rio Piedras: Editorial de la Universidad de Puerto Rico.

Nieto, S. (2000). *Puerto Rican Students in U.S. Schools*. Mahwah, NJ: Lawrence Erlbaum.

Solís, J. (1994). *Public School Reform in Puerto Rico: Sustaining Colonial Models of Development*. Westport, CT: Greenwood Press, 1994.

Soto, L. D. (1997). *Language, Culture, and Power: Bilingual Families Struggle For Quality Education*. New York: SUNY Press.

Zentella, A. C. (1997). *Growing Up Bilingual*. Malden, MA: Blackwell.

Lourdes Diaz Soto

PUERTO RICO AND THE LANGUAGE ISSUE

English in Puerto Rico has been associated with the U.S. since the island became a U.S. territory in 1898, resulting in close political, military, and economic ties. In order for educators to understand the implications of the language issue for Puerto Ricans, it is necessary to look at the historical circumstances surrounding the problem. For more than 400 years before 1898, Puerto Rico had been a province of Spain, and therefore Spanish was the official language on the island. The majority of the population spoke only Spanish, so starting a relationship with a country that had a completely different language and religion was received with mixed feelings.

In 1902 both Spanish and English became official languages of Puerto Rico, but English was chosen as the medium of instructions in schools (Algren de Gutierrez, 1987). Not only was the island's economic and social situation "desperately low"

(Osuna, 1949) but also more than 75% of the population was illiterate. The intellectual elite was mainly formed by lawyers, doctors, and engineers who had studied in the U.S. and Europe (Osuna, 1949). Even though Puerto Rico was attractive to the North Americans in the sense that "Puerto Rico was clearly an economic and military asset" (Urciolli, 1998, p. 43), there were obvious differences between the two cultures: language, religion, and lifestyle. Because those who spoke English could effectively communicate their needs to those in positions of power, it can be said that English became a symbol of power and status on the island. The U.S. imposed English on Puerto Ricans, but the islanders refused to give up what they perceived as their cultural identity; thus for the majority of populace Spanish became the one symbol of Puerto Rican social and cultural identity—and it remains so today.

In 1949 English as a medium of instruction in schools was replaced by Spanish. English then became one of the required subjects taught at every grade level. When in 1991 Spanish was re-established as the only official language on the island, and then when both languages became official, it became very obvious that language in Puerto Rico was something more than just a medium of communication in schools. It had become a symbol of Puerto Rican identity. There have been many attempts to explain why Puerto Ricans are not able to speak English fluently after 12 years of formal instruction in schools. Many researchers have attributed the language problem to the conflict between language and Puerto Rican identity. This term, which Morris (1995) translated as "Puerto Ricanness," and later was categorized by Barreto (2001), refers to how Puerto Ricans see themselves and their surroundings. Puerto

Ricans are very proud of their culture, which is a mixture of their Spanish, African, and *Taíno* Indian heritage, but they cannot escape the reality that Puerto Ricans have been influenced by the U.S. because of the direct contact that the two countries have had for over a century. As a result of this, there is a sense of cultural ambiguity among Puerto Ricans. According to Zentella (1990) the explanation for the language identity controversy was that Puerto Ricans experienced the language change as cultural loss. She compared the way Puerto Ricans saw bilingualism on and off the island and concluded that Puerto Ricans on the island saw bilingualism as a symbol of assimilation rather than as a link to the outside world. This fear of losing their language and culture could be what influences Puerto Ricans the most when it comes to learning English.

Political parties have played an important role in the controversy, and according to Pousada (1996) this role focused on how each political party attempted to answer linguistic and cultural questions. There are three political parties on the island: the Popular Democratic Party (PPD), which supports the idea of maintaining Puerto Rico's present Commonwealth (ELA) status; the New Progressive Party (PNP), which supports the idea of statehood; and the Puerto Rican Independence Party (PIP), which supports the idea of independence for the island. Politicians from the different political parties have created competition between English and Spanish, and therefore "language has become an instrument to bring affiliates into their political party"(Crespo, 1991). Velez and Schweers (1993) suggested that the main reason for making Spanish the only official language in 1991 was to make statehood look like the "less feasible" political status for the Island, since at that time the political power was in the hands of the political parties opposed to statehood. Because language on the island is considered a marker of Puerto Rican identity, politicians have linked the language issue to the island's unresolved political status. Some politicians believe that when the island's status is decided, the language controversy will be solved as well.

This idea has influenced the ways in which Puerto Ricans see the reason for learning English on the island. Spanish is considered by many a main part of the Puerto Rican cultural identity, and many studies reveal that the majority Puerto Ricans believe that whether or not Puerto Rico ever becomes a state, Spanish should be kept as the official language of the island. English is seen as the language of the country that tried to impose on Puerto Ricans a new and different language and culture. Even though "English is the language most widely taught as a foreign language in over 100 countries, and English is now so widely established that it can no longer be thought of as owned by any single nation" (Crystal, 1997), for many Puerto Ricans English is still perceived as the language of the U.S.

Both Spanish and English should be promoted, not as identity markers, but as international languages necessary for communication. Politicians, language-planning developers, teachers, parents, and students should work together to modify the way Puerto Ricans look at the language issue. It is up to educators to take the initiative that will lead to effective language planning on the island.

References

Algren de Gutierrez, E. (1987). *The Movement Against the Teaching of English in Puerto Rico*. London, MD: University Press of America.

Barreto, A. (2001). *The Politics of Language in Puerto Rico*. Gainsville: University Press of Florida.

Crespo, M. (1991). Political Affiliation vs Language Maintenance, English Language Shift, and/or Bilingualism in Puerto Rico. Master's thesis, University of Puerto Rico, Mayagüez Campus.

Crystal, D. (1997). *English as a Global Language*. Cambridge: Cambridge University Press.

Morris, N. (1995). *Puerto Rico: Culture, Politics and Identity*. Westport, CT: Praeger.

Osuna, J. J. (1949). *A History of Education in Puerto Rico* (2nd. ed.). Rio Piedras: Editorial de la Universidad de Puerto Rico.

Pousada, A. (1996). Puerto Rico: On the Horns of a Language Dilemma. *TESOL Quarterly* 30(3), 499–509.

Urciolli, B. (1998). *Exposing Prejudice: Puerto Rican Experiences of Language, Race and Class*. Boulder, CO: Westview Press.

Velez, J., & Shweers, C. W. (1993). A U.S. Colony at a Linguistic Crossroads: The Decision to Make Spanish the Official Language in Puerto Rico. *Language Problems and Language Planning* 17(2), 117–139.

Zentella, A. (1990). Returned Migration, Language and Identity: Puerto Rican Bilinguals in dos mundos/Two Worlds. *Journal of Social Languages* 84, 81–100.

Nancy Vanessa Vicente

Many women in Puerto Rico were employed in needlework factories. Courtesy of the Library of Congress.

Carlos Campos studies in a kindergarten class, Texas, 1940s. The San Antonio Light Collection, UT Institute of Texan Cultures at San Antonio, No. L-2898-J. Courtesy of the Hearst Corporation.

A migrant farm worker holds her child in Texas. The San Antonio Light Collection, UT Institute of Texan Cultures at San Antonio, No. L-7090-71-12a. Courtesy of the Hearst Corporation.

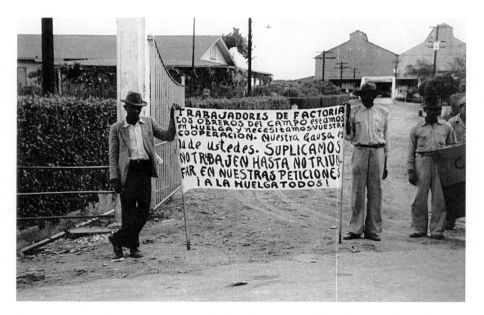

Factory workers in Puerto Rico hold a sign describing their strike. Courtesy of the Library of Congress.

Alicia Morales and Andres Cruz in a classroom at J. T. Brackenridge Elementary School in San Antonio, Texas, 1940s. The San Antonio Light Collection, UT Institute of Texan Cultures at San Antonio, No. L-3481-E. Courtesy of the Hearst Corporation.

An American Federation of Labor laundry worker, holding an umbrella, picketing outside the San Antonio Laundry, 1930s. The San Antonio Light Collection, UT Institute of Texan Cultures at San Antonio, No. L-1605-J. Courtesy of the Hearst Corporation.

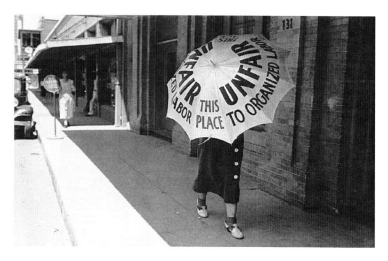

Sergeant J. E. Cassidy measures Lanier High School student Joe Gonzales for ROTC uniform, 1938. The San Antonio Light Collection, UT Institute of Texan Cultures at San Antonio, No. L-1980-Q. Courtesy of the Hearst Corporation.

Children standing outside of company housing, Puerto Rico. Courtesy of the Library of Congress.

Children in the slums of Las Monjas, Puerto Rico during the Depression. Courtesy of the Library of Congress.

The United Farm Workers Stamp reads "En Tejas Si Se Puede" ("In Texas it can be done"). The San Antonio Light Collection, UT Institute of Texan Cultures at San Antonio, No. L-7090-70-16a. Courtesy of the Hearst Corporation.

Children celebrate at a party in Corozal, Puerto Rico. Courtesy of the Library of Congress.

The Vieques Public School in Puerto Rico. Courtesy of the Library of Congress.

(*Left*) Matilde Elizondo and Salome Rodriquez during the Mexican Repatriation, 1931. The San Antonio Light Collection, UT Institute of Texan Cultures at San Antonio, No. L-1310-A. Courtesy of the Hearst Corporation. (*Right*) Frank Reyes sweeping trash into a dustpan, 1942. The San Antonio Light Collection, UT Institute of Texan Cultures at San Antonio, No. L-2898-K. Courtesy of the Hearst Corporation.

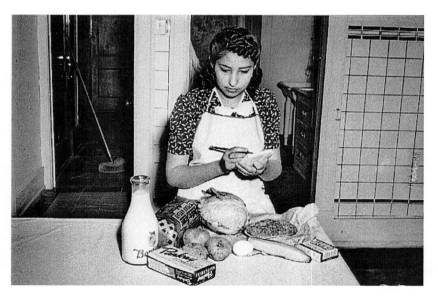

Aurora Moreno posed with grocery items, February 22, 1942. The San Antonio Light Collection, UT Institute of Texan Cultures at San Antonio, No. L-2898-G. Courtesy of the Hearst Corporation.

These boys are from the Sarco family. Courtesy of the Library of Congress.

Shoe shiners looking at a Christmas toy display, December 1939. The San Antonio Light Collection, UT Institute of Texan Cultures at San Antonio, No. L-2326-C. Courtesy of the Hearst Corporation.

A Puerto Rican laborer in front of a sugarcane field. Courtesy of the Library of Congress.

Schoolchildren from Vieques, Puerto Rico. Courtesy of the Library of Congress.

Pineapple farmers in Puerto Rico. Courtesy of the Library of Congress.

R

REPATRIATION OF MEXICANS DURING THE GREAT DEPRESSION

The Great Depression of the 1930s dislocated the lives of millions of unemployed Americans. The crisis also presented a great challenge to Mexican immigrants who had been so desirable as workers in the previous decade but were now discharged from their jobs by the thousands and then pressured to leave by community authorities. Between 1929 and 1936 at least 600,000 Mexican nationals and their children, many of whom were born in the U.S., returned to Mexico—this represented about one-third of the U.S. Mexican population. Mexicans living in large industrial cities ravaged by unemployment, such as Los Angeles, Chicago, and Detroit, were the most affected. Similar conditions existed in Texas and Arizona mining communities, where the collapsed market for raw materials forced a drastic curtailment of production.

The most zealous repatriation campaigns took place in Los Angeles. Charles P. Visel, Los Angeles County coordinator for unemployment relief, worked hand in hand with federal agents sent to Los Angeles by Secretary of Labor Doak and local Los Angeles police to arrest as many undocumented Mexicans as possible. Officials knew that even with beefed-up police presence, it would be impossible to corral all the undocumented Mexicans. A strategy was devised to intimidate aliens into leaving on their own by publicizing raids where hundreds of Mexicans were rounded up regardless of whether or not they carried documents. It turned out that only a small percentage of the Mexicans harassed in this manner were undocumented. As a solution to the unemployment problem, in 1931 President Hoover implemented the President's Emergency Committee for Employment (PECE), but it was no more than a public relations ploy to make people feel good about providing a marginal number of jobs through the private sector. But the PECE in Los Angeles, of which Charles Visel was a member, worked closely with county officials to coordinate the voluntary repatriation of Southern California Mexicans—that is, those who were not deportable under the 1929 act. In 1931, Visel traveled to Mexico hoping to arrange a program to settle in the thousands of Mexicans whom county officials and Visel hoped to repatriate.

The Mexican government did cooperate with various groups in the U.S., including Visel's program in Los Angeles County, which raised funds to send Mexicans to the border by promising to take responsibility for the repatriates once they crossed the border. Unfortunately, the engine of repatriation on the American side was more efficient than that south of the border and resulted in bottlenecks that left thousands of the discarded Mexicans marooned in border towns with little to eat and nowhere to sleep. Economic downturns had been a constant factor in their lives, but nothing compared to the suffering created by this crisis.

Recommended Reading

Balderrama, Francisco E., & Rodríguez, Raymond. (1995). *Decade of Betrayal: Mexican Repatriation in the 1930s.* Albuquerque: University of New Mexico Press.

Gutiérrez, David G. (1995). *Walls and Mirrors: Mexican Americans, Mexican Immigrants and the Politics of Ethnicity.* Berkeley: University of California Press.

Rosales, F. Arturo. (1996). *Chicano! A History of the Mexican American Civil Rights Movement.* Houston, TX: Arte Público Press.

F. Arturo Rosales

REPATRIATION OF MEXICANS FROM THE U.S.

The return of persons who are living abroad to their home countries is known as repatriation. Thus Mexican expatriates have constantly either repatriated voluntarily or forced to repatriate as long as their has been a border between Mexico and its northern neighbor, the U.S. Usually the desire to return to the home country or the desire of Americans to be rid of Mexicans occurred during economic downturns, but not always. About 80,000 Spanish-speaking settlers lived in the territories lost by Mexico as a consequence of the Texas Rebellion (1836), the Mexican War (1848), and the Gadsden Purchase (1853). The Mexican government offered Southwest Mexicans repatriation assistance south of the shrunken borders of the homeland. Those who felt insecure about provisions protecting Mexicans being honored decided to return. Others, who felt

embittered because they felt Mexico had betrayed them or who were willing to risk living under a new government, stayed. As a consequence, out of the tens of thousands of Mexicans living in the Southwest, about 3,000 took advantage of official Mexican attempts to repatriate them.

After 1880, because of the railroad, dramatic changes in the southwestern economy stimulated Mexican immigration tremendously. The two decades before 1900 saw 127,000 Mexicans entering the U.S. from Mexico, one and one-third times as many as the native Mexican population in 1848. By 1900 a railroad network integrated Texas, New Mexico, Arizona, and California with northern Mexico and parts of central and southern Mexico. The economic impact of the railroads soon drew Mexicans into the U.S. in a movement that dwarfed the influx of previous years. But the see-saw character of being wanted and then unwanted quickly became apparent.

During the 1907–1908 depression, for example, the Mexican government repatriated workers, appropriating 100,000 pesos for that purpose. In Los Angeles and San Francisco, consuls rallied expatriates to provide housing and food for thousands of unemployed compatriots. According to one report, San Francisco alone had close to 1,000 destitute Mexicans who could not find food or shelter. The Mexican government then paid for train fare through El Paso for families from various points in California. In 1914 farm prices dropped drastically and thousands of Mexicans wanted to return, but they were without funds. Texas, with three of four entry ports and railroad connections to the Mexican interior, had absorbed the lion's share of indigent and destitute immigrants. During April the Mexican Labor Ministry inquired among henequen producers in Yucatan if they could accommodate unemployed Mexican repatriates from Texas. In 1917 after the U.S. entered World War I, all young men over the age of 18 became eligible for military conscription. But local boards sometimes called up citizens of Mexico suspected of being Mexican Americans. The confusion provoked a mass exodus to Mexico. American employers who needed labor during wartime economic expansion became anxious about this voluntary repatriation. The Mexican government discouraged the return, as well, since emigration provided a safety valve for the unemployment problems in Mexico. Both governments joined in a widespread campaign to assure fearful Mexicans they would not be drafted.

Then early in 1921 definite signs of a postwar depression appeared, accompanied by a decrease in the desirability of Mexican immigrant labor. During the war years Mexicans had entered labor sectors where they supplied first-time competition with white workers. But 5 to 6 million workers in general were thrown out of work during 1921 in a malaise affecting Mexican immigrants more severely than white workers. Thousands were marooned in the U.S. in total destitution, unable to return home. This situation drained the energy and resources of the Mexican government, which had made a concerted effort to ease immigrant distress. The destitution, which affected Mexicans disproportionately during economic plunges, magnified their presence, fueling racism and encouraging nativist deportation sentiment. Mexicans were repatriated, however, because local governments did not want to take responsibility for the welfare of unemployed "undesirables" who, from their view point, did not have a right to charity, anyway. Deportations by the U.S. government increased during 1921

as thousands of Mexican workers were sought out throughout the country.

Nonetheless, the economy improved by 1923, easing repatriation pressures. But in 1926 an ailing Mexican economy combined with zealous over-recruitment to create an even greater incentive for emigration. Mexico declared the outflow as a threat to the nation's interests as well; newspapers, government officials, and union leaders alike lamented that the country was losing too many inhabitants. But by summer even U.S. employers looked askance at the saturated labor markets, prompting what the *Hispano Americano* of San Francisco called "massive deportations." That fall the need for Mexicans was reduced even further because the cotton yield in Texas and Arizona had fallen severely below normal expectations. As winter approached, destitute Mexicans from throughout the country clamored for repatriation.

The most dramatic repatriation of Mexicans took place during the Great Depression of the 1930s. This momentous event, which dislocated the lives of millions of unemployed Americans, presented the greatest challenge to Mexican immigrants, who had been so desirable as workers in the previous decade but were now discharged from their jobs by the thousands and then pressured to leave by community authorities. Between 1929 and 1936 at least 600,000 Mexican nationals and their children, many of whom were born in the U.S., returned to Mexico—this represented about one-third of the U.S. Mexican population. Mexicans living in large industrial cities ravaged by unemployment, such as Los Angeles, Chicago, and Detroit, were the most affected. Similar conditions existed in Texas and Arizona mining communities, where the collapsed market for raw materials forced a drastic curtailment of production.

The most zealous repatriation campaigns took place in Los Angeles. Charles P. Visel, Los Angeles County coordinator for unemployment relief, worked hand in hand with federal agents sent to Los Angeles by Secretary of Labor Doak and local Los Angeles police to arrest as many undocumented Mexicans as possible. Officials knew that even with beefed-up police presence, it would be impossible to corral all the undocumented Mexicans. A strategy was devised to intimidate aliens into leaving on their own by publicizing raids where hundreds of Mexicans were rounded up regardless of whether or not they carried documents. It turned out that only a small percentage of the Mexicans harassed in this manner were undocumented. As a solution to the unemployment problem, in 1931 President Hoover implemented the President's Emergency Committee for Employment (PECE), but it was no more than a public relations ploy to make people feel good about providing a marginal number of jobs through the private sector. But the Los Angeles PECE, of which Charles Visel was a member, worked closely with county officials to coordinate the voluntary repatriation of Southern California Mexicans—that is, those who were not deportable under the 1929 act. In 1931 Visel traveled to Mexico hoping to arrange a program to settle in the thousands of Mexicans whom county officials and Visel hoped to repatriate.

The Mexican government did cooperate with various groups in the U.S., including Visel's program in Los Angeles County, which raised funds to send Mexicans to the border by promising to take responsibility for the repatriates once they crossed the border. Unfortunately, the engine of repatriation on the American side was more efficient than that south of the border and resulted in bottlenecks that left thousands of the discarded Mexicans marooned in border towns with little to eat and nowhere to sleep. Economic downturns had been a constant factor in their lives, but nothing compared to the suffering created by this crisis.

With America's entry into World War II, the economy not only recovered but boomed and grew at an unprecedented rate. This, of course, meant that Mexicans again were needed to work in the U.S. This led to the Bracero program, where U.S. labor agents actually went into Mexico and recruited thousands of workers for the agricultural and railroad sectors. The Bracero program, however, inspired many others to immigrate on their own, often without documentation. Then after World War II the need for Mexican immigrant labor diminished; but the Korean War, which lasted two years, again raised the demand. A recession followed this latest international altercation, resulting in the predictable decline in Mexican worker desirability. In 1954 the U.S. federal government initiated Operation Wetback, in which Immigration and Naturalization Service (INS) officers rounded up thousands of undocumented workers and deported them to Mexico. In many cases they were sent back in airplanes to southern Mexico to prevent their return north. President Adolfo Ruiz Cortines protested the methods used, but he concurred with American authorities that the Bracero program should be the legitimate conduit by which Mexicans should enter to work in the U.S.

Repatriation continues to this day. Millions of undocumented workers are deported each year, mostly to Mexico. Exacerbating the problem is that in 1965 Congress passed a bill that reduced immigration from throughout the world. Mexico was disproportionally affected because it had never been on quota before. Overnight, it seems, the concept of the illegal alien became associated with Mexicans and deportation, and restriction is seen as the main solution among many Americans. But attempts have provided some relief. In 1986 the Immigration and Control Act allowed undocumented immigrants who had been in the U.S. before 1982 to acquire legal status. Some agricultural workers were given legal status as well. Even though millions qualified, however, the surge of undocumented entry continues, as does deportation of those caught without papers.

President George W. Bush unveiled an immigration plan in 2004 to allow foreign residents and undocumented workers who can prove they have a job or a job offer from a U.S. employer to qualify for a three-year temporary work visa. Workers who qualify for relief can renew their visas and stay an additional three years in the U.S. But this is a one-time renewal, and after the final three-year stint the workers are obliged to return to their home countries. Bush's idea, which must be legislated by Congress, has gone nowhere as of 2006, but most proposed blueprints to deal with the problem of immigration are similar. The initiative has been met with a mixed reception. Supporters claim that thousands of workers will be able to work without fear of deportation and that employers who are supposedly fined for hiring undocumented

persons would also rest easier. But according to union officials, any temporary amnesty would simply jeopardize the unions gains made since 1994 on behalf of low-wage workers who are largely undocumented. Civil rights activists feel that temporary admission robs immigrants, who are mainly Hispanics, from fulfilling their desire to achieve the American dream and condemns them and their families into a second-class strata in American life.

Recommended Reading

Balderrama, Francisco E., & Rodríguez, Raymond. (1995). *Decade of Betrayal: Mexican Repatriation in the 1930s.* Albuquerque: University of New Mexico Press.

García, Juan Ramón. (1980). *Operation Wetback: The Mass Deportation of Mexican Undocumented Workers in 1954.* Westport, CT: Greenwood Press.

Gutiérrez, David G. (1995). *Walls and Mirrors: Mexican Americans, Mexican Immigrants and the Politics of Ethnicity.* Berkeley: University of California Press.

Rosales, F. Arturo. (1996). *Chicano! A History of the Mexican American Civil Rights Movement.* Houston, TX: Arte Público Press.

Rosales, F. Arturo. (1999). *"Pobre raza!" Violence, Crime, Justice and Mobilization among Mexico Lindo Immigrants, 1900–1936.* Austin: University of Texas Press.

F. Arturo Rosales

S

SCHOOL AS SANCTUARY

> The "schools as sanctuary" concept is based on the experiences of students at the Dr. Pedro Albizu Campos Alternative High School (PACHS) in Chicago, Illinois.

The "school as sanctuary" concept describes the four components that are necessary within urban high schools if they are to create the conditions necessary for students to engage in the school-based learning process. These four components are (1) meaningful, interpersonal caring relationships between students and teachers, (2) psychologically and physically safe spaces, (3) the "school as family" notion; and (4) the affirmation of Diasporic-based sociopolitical, cultural, and economic realities on behalf of Latinos/as and African American urban students.

Meaningful, Interpersonal Caring Relationships between Students and Teachers

The kinds of student-teacher relationships that are valued by students at the PACHS manifest themselves in several ways. These ways include teachers holding their students to high academic expectations, sponsoring social outings that provide guidance and protection from negative urban street peer culture (i.e., gang recruitment and membership), and students

and teachers engaging themselves in a co-facilitative learning partnership where students feel that their teachers highly value the distinct home- and community-based epistemologies that students already bring with them to school.

School as Family

Another important component essential for school sanctuaries is to foment a family-like culture within the school that serves as an extension to the home and community support students bring to school. This type of school culture contributes to students' sense of belonging (Nieto, 1998) within school. Also, students who have extensive friendship networks in their schools are much more likely to develop and maintain a pro-school identity (Flores-González, 2002).

Psychologically and Physically Safe Spaces

Schools are also sanctuaries when they view their students' bilingual and bicultural life experiences not as deficits but as assets. In addition, it is of the utmost importance that schools support a culturally and linguistically additive curriculum (Valenzuela, 1999). A culturally and linguistically additive curriculum is one in which academic courses and teachers respect rather than denigrate the heritage languages and cultures their students bring to school. An additive curriculum also strives to critically call into question the notion that Eurocentric curricula are the only epistemological frameworks students should be exposed to.

Affirmation of Students' Racial/Ethnic and Political Realities and Beliefs

A school is a sanctuary when there exists a culture that uses students' racial/ethnic realities and political beliefs as grounds for solidarity within and outside the school. Moreover, it is crucial that academic courses seriously weave students' realities and make them grounds for critical reflection and dialogue. Hence, students are made to feel that their respective life experiences are not deficits but, rather, assets worthy of respect.

Implications for Latino/a Education

The "school as sanctuary" concept, with its four essential components, has various implications for Latino/a education within both large and small comprehensive high school reform contexts. When these components are in place, they help facilitate the school-based cultural conditions that make high schools become places where urban students of color are free of psychological and pedagogical neglect and hostilities based on race and ethnic origin.

References

Flores-González, N. (2002). *School Kids / Street Kids: Identity Development in Latino Students*. New York: Teachers College Press.

Nieto, S. (1998). Fact and Fiction: Stories of Puerto Ricans in U.S. Schools. *Harvard Educational Review*, 68(2), 133–163.

Valenzuela, A. (1999). *Subtractive Schooling: U.S.-Mexican Youth and the Politics of Caring*. Albany, NY: SUNY Press.

Recommended Reading

Antrop-González, R. (2003). This School Is My Sanctuary: The Dr. Pedro Albizu Campos Alternative High School. *Journal of the Center for Puerto Rican Studies* 15(2), 232–255.

René Antrop-González

SPANISH-ENGLISH CONTACT

The language situation and linguistic practices of heritage Spanish speakers in the U.S. are seldom regarded impassively; the ambiguity expressed in the title of Toribio (2004a), "Spanish/English Speech Practices: Bringing Chaos to Order," invokes the contradictory and conflictive fervor with which Spanish-English bilingual speech practices have been addressed by scholars, educators, and policymakers. On one representative position, the bilingualism and attendant linguistic manifestations that may result from the sustained contact of heritage and dominant language are lauded as essential to communication in bilingual communities, where speakers are commonly called on to access a continuum of grammatical, discursive, and sociolinguistic competencies in one or the other of two languages (cf., Valdés, 2000). However, as lamented by Zentella (1998, 2000), it is also, indeed much too frequently, attested that in the "linguistic logic" of U.S. society, heritage Spanish is a negative carryover that must be cancelled out, and the would-be benefit of possessing and deploying Spanish alongside English is equated with zero: "Those poor kids come to school speaking a hodgepodge. They are all mixed up and don't know any language well. As a result, they can't even think clearly" (quoted in Walsh, 1991, p. 106). The ensuing paragraphs elaborate a linguistically informed assessment of the contact Spanish, contact English, and Spanish-English bilingual speech of heritage Spanish speakers in the U.S.; the survey will make evident that rather than compensating for linguistic deficiency, "illicit language acts" signal the strategic and efficient use of linguistic and cognitive resources in the appropriation and management of two language systems.

Spanish-English Bilingual Speech

In most bilingual communities, members find themselves situated along a continuum that induces different "language modes" (Grosjean, 1998) within a "bilingual range" (Valdés, 2000). For instance, Zentella (1981, 1997), reports that in her long-term participant study of the linguistic practices of *el bloque,* a Puerto Rican community in *el barrio* of East Harlem, children could be observed to speak English with each other, but shifting to Spanish in deference to their elders. For these children, Spanish and English together constitute their linguistic competence in a singular sense, and their linguistic performance will draw primarily upon English or Spanish, as required by the "observables" of the speech situation (e.g., pragmatic norms, specific setting, and participants).[1] It is also commonplace in such communities that as bilingual speakers interact in bilingual mode, they will extend this ability to alternating languages in unchanged speech situations—that is, to code-switching (Zentella, 1981).

Gumperz, in his seminal work on discursive strategies, notes the important functions served by code-switching (1976, 1982).[2] The premise underlying his and many subsequent studies is that code-switching is a conscious choice on the part of the speaker. Since then, much research has been devoted to analyzing bilingual speech and imputing particular stylistic goals to specific code alternations. Parallel to studies focused on the

social and discursive factors that enter into its use are research efforts that have examined the grammatical properties of code-switched speech. Bilinguals are commonly heard to move between English and Spanish within the confines of a single clause, unveiling a mode that offers greater expressive possibilities without violating the grammatical rules of either Spanish or English. Consider in this respect the title to Poplack (1980): "Sometimes I'll Start a Sentence in English y termino en español." Such intra-sentential code-switched forms readily suggest a high degree of competence in the component languages. Nevertheless, as Poplack (1980) asserts, it is "precisely those switch types which have traditionally been considered most deviant" (p. 615). Indeed, the nomenclature—terms such as *Spanglish* and *Tex-Mex* for Spanish-English code-switching—carries pejorative connotations reflecting these misconceptions about the intellectual or linguistic abilities of those who code-switch. Perhaps most injuriously, the latter impressions are given voice by persons within the bilingual speech communities themselves; many heritage speakers internalize the stigma attached to their speech forms and ascribe only negative or covert prestige, if any, to their community speech norms (cf., Toribio, 2002; Wald, 1988; Zentella, 1998).

But it is by now well established among researchers in linguistics that intrasentential code-switching is not a random mixture of two flawed systems; rather, it is rule governed and systematic, demonstrating the operation of underlying grammatical restrictions.[3] Proficient bilinguals may be shown to exhibit a shared knowledge of what constitutes appropriate intrasentential code-switching. For example, Spanish-English bilingual speakers will agree that the code-switching title previously noted represents an acceptable bilingual form, whereas other language alternations do not (cf., Toribio, 2001b). Significantly, bilinguals proffer such judgments in the absence of overt instruction—speakers are not taught how to code-switch. Nevertheless, just as monolingual native speakers of Spanish and English have an intuitive sense of linguistic well-formedness in their language, Spanish-English bilinguals are able to rely on unconscious grammatical principles in producing and evaluating code-switched strings. Thus, contrary to common assumptions, code-switching patterns may be used as a measure of bilingual *ability,* rather than deficit. In fact, the degree of language proficiency that a speaker possesses in two languages has been shown to correlate with the type of code-switching engaged in.[4] In her research on bilinguals of diverse levels of competence, Poplack (1980) observes that those who reported to be dominant in one language tended to switch by means of taglike phrases (e.g., *sabes / you know* and *verdad? / right?*); in contrast, those who reported and demonstrated the greatest degree of bilingual ability favored intrasentential switches. This is corroborated by the ethnolinguistic research of Zentella (1981, 1997), which attests that proficient bilinguals display distinct behaviors in code-switching from their more Spanish-dominant or English-dominant community peers. Likewise, Montes-Alcalá's (2001) journal corpus demonstrates intersentential code-switching at the beginning of the sample, when the author's degree of bilingualism was more limited, and increased intrasentential code-switching in the later periods as the author reached a steady state of bilingualism, "building a bride between both languages"

(p. 198). Finally, similar patterns are attested among children acquiring two languages from birth (cf., De Houwer, 1995; Köppe & Meisel, 1995; Meisel, 1989, 1994) among children acquiring a second language in early childhood (cf., McClure, 1981), and among adult second language learners (cf., Bhatia & Ritchie, 1996; Rakowsky, 1989; Toribio, 2001a). Taken together, these investigations lead to the conclusion that, regardless of age, the bilingual's code-switching ability reflects the development of linguistic competence in the component languages (Babbe, 1995).

Consonant with the foregoing discussion, then, the appearance of English language elements in Spanish language contexts need not be interpreted as indicative of language impoverishment or erosion; it could simply be an instance of code-switching, in which case the grammatical autonomy and integrity of each language may be maintained. This is not to say, however, that the Spanish of proficient bilinguals is impervious to the incursions of the second language system. As affirmed by Silva-Corvalán (1986, 1994), among others, the permeability of a grammar to external influence depends on the existence of superficially parallel structures in the languages in contact (cf. Montrul, 2002, 2004). Although the differences between Spanish and English are significant, there is considerable syntactic parallelism between the two languages, which may lead to convergence. Two salient properties demonstrate the differences and emergent similarities at once. English allows only for preverbal positioning of subjects; Spanish accepts preverbal subjects but additionally sanctions postverbal placement (e.g., *Llegó Juan*). And English requires that subjects be overtly expressed; Spanish tolerates overt subjects but additionally licenses, and in some contexts requires, that subjects have no overt realization (e.g., *Hablo español*). Such equivalence is the basis for emergent convergence in Spanish-English bilingual settings—to be found in the reduction of grammatical options in the heritage language with greater allowance to those shared with the dominant linguistic system—and may be the basis for further structural convergence between the two linguistic systems (Muysken, 2000). This raises the important question of whether specific language forms are *further* favored when the languages are simultaneously deployed. The issue, then, is not whether the Spanish language is maintained while drifting toward or converging with the grammatical options shared with the English language system, but whether this drift is promoted by bilingual (versus monolingual) language modes (cf., Grosjean, 1998). In testing these claims of interlingual violability, Toribio (2004b) examines the variation that is attested in the Spanish speech data produced by code-switching bilinguals as they engage in Spanish and Spanish-English code-switched speech across two conditions. The positioning and (non) expression of subjects were selected for inquiry. The data reveal a use of pronouns that though not grammatically incorrect is discourse-pragmatically odd, being marked by a selection of available grammatical options that coincide with those of English. Thus, there is implicit in proficient bilingual speech behavior an appeal toward economy: the speaker reduces processing costs while enjoying the richness of bilingualism. Such a finding explains why Spanish-English bilingual speakers' Spanish language abilities may not be identical to those of native speakers who have acquired and used their Spanish in settings in which

only Spanish is employed for all interactions. Moreover, this outcome leads to a judgment against cries of corruption and degradation by the self-proclaimed conservators of the Spanish language. For it is uncertain, states Valdés (2000, p. 119) "whether linguistic conservatism is a predictor of language maintenance or whether the survival of a language in a minority-majority context requires the acceptance of 'interference' phenomena by its speakers" (cf., Silva-Corvalán, 1994; Woolard, 1992).

Pedagogical Implications

To be sure, much is to be gained by educators' understanding of the language diversity of heritage language students, especially as the former uphold the standardized linguistic varieties that are required for academic success (cf., Valdés, 2000). The ensuing paragraphs present pedagogical practices that further promote this positive disposition toward heritage language students, their particular speech forms, and their communities of practice.

Elementary school educators may examine the parallels in linguistic development and narrative performance in bilingual children through narrative descriptions of the events depicted in wordless picture books (e.g., Mercer Mayer's *Frog, Where Are You?*); Spanish heritage children may be asked to prepare their texts in Spanish, English, or varieties of each, as desired (cf., Berman & Slobin, 1994). Succeeding discussion should focus on their knowledge of specific language features, on their integration of cultural information, on their selection of specific language or code, and so on. A second exercise also drawing on picture books explores children's attitudes toward specific linguistic forms. For this activity, the teacher prepares three stories—one in Standard Spanish, one in Standard English, and one in a variety of the language(s) that most closely approximates the local vernacular. The stories are orally presented to students who subsequently respond to a series of questions probing language usage: Who authored each text? for which intended audience? What distinguishes the varieties of Spanish? Yet a third activity suitable for primary school children requires them to maintain a handout in which they document the languages deployed in different situations (e.g., at home, at school) and in carrying out key daily routines (e.g., doing homework, playing with sibling, or working with peers). As a follow-up, the children present a domain analysis of their language choice patterns—a "who speaks what to whom when and why"—and compare their findings with those of peers.

For middle school children, linguistic issues of voice may be highlighted in discussing prose narrative such as that excerpted from Norma Cantú's *Canícula,* in which Spanish lexical items function as echoes of a cultural tradition that remains inaccessible to the main language of the text, English.

Mami was the madrina one year; she sewed the most beautiful outfit for the baby Jesus—of white tulle, embroidered in white silk, complete with knitted cap and socks—we all helped with the preparativos, although we usually did anyway, even when it was some other neighbor who was the madrina. From the tamalada on Christmas Eve, for the acostar al niño, the singing of Mexican carols, and later because we kids insisted, English ones as well, the champurrado and the little bags of goodies (oranges, pecans, Mexican cookies), and the colaciones and other Christmas candy that fell from the star-shaped piñata that invariably Toño, the oldest of the neighborhood bullies, would break, Doña Carmen's posada was the best.

For teachers who serve high school Spanish heritage language students, examinations of bilingual materials may be carried out in concert with activities in subjects such as social studies and language arts. Suitable exemplars are readily available in the literary output of poets and writers. The linguistic inflections in Tato Laviera's bilingual poem "My Graduation Speech" render an enactment and commentary of the linguistic dilemma of Puerto Ricans in the U.S. (Flores, 1993).[5] Numerous and varied themes arise in the interpretation of this poem, some oriented toward content, and others focused on linguistic form: at one level, the poem is an indictment of the educational system; at another, the linguistic modulation of the poem represents the difficulty of marking out an "interlingual" space.[6]

My Graduation Speech
i think in spanish
i write in english
i want to go back to puerto rico,
but i wonder if my kink could live
in ponce, mayagüez and carolina
tengo las venas aculturadas
escribo en spanglish
abraham en español
abraham in english
tato in spanish
"taro" in english
tonto in both languages
how are you?
¿cómo estás?
i don't know if i'm coming
or si me fui ya
si me dicen barranquitas, yo reply,
"con qué se come eso?"
si me dicen caviar, i digo,
"a new pair of converse sneakers."
ahí supe que estoy jodío

ahí supe que estamos jodíos
english or spanish
spanish or english
spanenglish
now, dig this:
hablo lo inglés matao
hablo lo español matao
no sé leer ninguno bien
so it is, spanglish to matao
what i digo
¡ay, virgen, yo no sé hablar!

Other classroom activities could reference naturalistic language samples such as those afforded in personal narratives. Students could be asked to chronicle their own experiences, independently or in collaboration with siblings and other family members. The following brief entries, drawn from the personal history of an agricultural worker, are uniquely valuable in allowing for extensive cultural and linguistic analysis and discussion (Toribio, 2000). Perhaps the most immediately outstanding feature of the journal is in its form and what it reveals about the author and her social and linguistic disadvantages. In surviving largely as an oral language, the Spanish of this speaker may be attrited in isolation from the codified (written) norm and adapt in its contact with English.

Sali para D. en avion a las 2 de la tarde, pero ya mero no la hacía como antes de llegar al aeropuerto se nos fletio la llanta de la troca de J. Estuve en D. por cerca de 4 horas. estaba en "stand by." . . . además no tenemos agua caliente, ni baño para bañarnos y el servicío (escusado) se esta cayendo nomas con unas tablas delgadas sosteniendolo y la puerta del servicio esta toda quebrada; no la puedes cerrer porque si la sierras se quebra; *Nombre* si pisas un poca pesado . . . A. y D. no andan trabajando en la labor nomás se quedan en la troca porque todavia no se comienza la escuela para los migrantes creo que empieza hasta la semana que entra y nosotros no nos registramos porque ya nos vamos para Norte Kora y Minnestota. . . . Nomas va a la escuela A. y D., todos los demas vamos a trabajar en el betavel. Estuvimos levantados desde las cinco de la mañana y el (bus) autobus vino como a las 7:30 siete y media. [*sic*]

It should be patently evident that the introduction of materials and activities such as those outlined can provide the basis for teacher-facilitated peer discussions on a broad range of viable and vital issues—from civics to orthography—that are of personal relevance and educational merit to heritage language students. More than that, the mere act of acknowledging bilingual speech forms as worthy of examination will cultivate an affective environment that will translate into greater engagement on the part of the student.

Notes

1. Consult Zentella (1981, 2000) for a discussion of the principal communicative patterns—"who speaks what to whom"—that emerged in her study of the bilingual families of *el bloque*.

2. Gumperz provides a list of discourse functions marked by code-switching: quotation, addressee specification, interjections, reiteration, and message qualification. The listing is not exhaustive, as a review of the literature will demonstrate; subsequent research has corroborated Gumperz's classification and has revealed additional conversational strategies accomplished by code-switching. Especially noteworthy are the findings reported by Zentella (1997), who identified at least 22 communicative aims achieved by code alternation among Puerto Ricans in New York City.

3. Consult the syntactic-theoretical works of Woolford (1985), Belazi, Rubin, & Toribio (1994), MacSwan (1999, 2000), and Toribio (2001a).

4. It must not go unremarked, however, that although code-switching is subserved by bilin-

gual competence, it is not an essential feature of bilingual practice. Researchers such as Valdés (2000) and Lipski (1985) have observed that while competence in two languages is a necessary precondition, it is an insufficient prerequisite in determining successful code-switching performance: membership in a community in which code-switching is practiced may also be required. That is, code-switching practice requires social knowledge that is culturally specific and acquired through contextualized practice (cf. Toribio, 2002).

5. Consult Bruce-Novoa (1982) and L. Flores (1987) for insightful discussion on Chicano poetry.

6. Laviera presents a poet-persona who is silenced by the linguistic mismatch between English and Spanish, one who is inarticulate even in Spanglish, not only by assertion ("Spanglish to matao") but also by employing in his graduation speech such combinations as "yo reply," "or si me fui ya," and "what i digo"— switches, which, as noted, are unacceptable among bilingual speakers. Yet, writes Flores (1993), the closing line "must be understood ironically: the reader is by now aware that the speaker knows what he is saying and can say what he thinks in both languages and in a wide array of combinations of the two" (p. 176).

References

Babbe, M. (1995). Language Contact in Childhood Bilingualism. Master's thesis, University of California, Santa Barbara.

Belazi, H., Rubin, E., & Toribio, A. J. (1994). Code Switching and X-bar Theory: The Functional Head Constraint. *Linguistic Inquiry* 25(2), 221–237.

Berman, R., & Slobin, D. (1994). *Relating Events in Narrative: A Crosslinguistic Developmental Study*. Hillsdale, NJ: Lawrence Erlbaum.

Bhatia, T., & Ritchie, W. (1996). Bilingual Language Mixing, Universal Grammar, and Second Language Acquisition. In W. Ritchie & T. Bhatia (Eds.), *Handbook of Second Language Acquisition* (pp. 627–688). New York: Academic Press.

Bruce-Novoa, J. (1982). *Chicano Poetry: A Response to Chaos*. Austin: University of Texas Press.

Cantú, N. (2000). *Canícula*. Boston: Houghton Mifflin.

De Houwer, A. (1995). Bilingual Language Acquisition. In P. Fletcher & B. MacWhinney (Eds.), *The Handbook of Child Language* (pp. 219–250). Oxford: Blackwell.

Flores, J. (1993). *Divided Borders: Essays on Puerto Rican Identity*. Houston, TX: Arte Público Press.

Flores, L. (1987). Converging Languages in a World of Conflicts: Code-Switching in Chicano Poetry. *Visible-Language* 21, 130–152.

Grosjean, F. (1998). Studying Bilinguals: Methodological and Conceptual Issues. *Bilingualism: Language and Cognition* 1(2), 131–149.

Gumperz, J. (1976). The Sociolinguistic Significance of Conversational Code-Switching. *University of California Working Papers*, no. 46. Berkeley: University of California.

Gumperz, J. (1982). *Discourse Strategies*. Cambridge: Cambridge University Press.

Köppe, R., & Meisel, J. (1995). Code-Switching in Bilingual First Language Acquisition. In L. Milroy & P. Muysken (Eds.), *One Speaker, Two Languages* (pp. 276–301). Cambridge: Cambridge University Press.

Lipski, J. (1985). *Linguistic Aspects of Spanish-English Language Switching*. Tempe: Arizona State University, Center for Latin American Studies.

MacSwan, J. (1999). *A Minimalist Approach to Intra-sentential Code Switching*. Cambridge: Cambridge University Press.

MacSwan, J. (2000). The Architecture of the Bilingual Language Faculty: Evidence from Intrasentential Code-Switching. *Bilingualism: Language and Cognition* 3(1), 37–54.

McClure, E. (1981). Formal and Functional Aspects of the Code-Switched Discourse of Bilingual Children. In R. Durán (Ed.), *Latino Language and Communicative Behavior* (pp. 69–94). Norwood, NJ: Ablex.

Meisel, J. (1989). Early Differentiation of Languages in Bilingual Children. In K. Hyltenstam & L. Obler (Eds.), *Bilingualism across the Lifespan: Aspects of Acquisition, Maturity, and Loss* (pp. 13–40). Cambridge: Cambridge University Press.

Meisel, J. (1994). Code-Switching in Young Bilingual Children: The Acquisition of Grammatical Constraints. *Studies in Second Language Acquisition* 16(3), 413–439.

Mercer, M. (1969). *Frog, Where Are You?* New York: Dial Press.

Montes-Alcalá, C. (2001). Written Codeswitching: Powerful Bilingual Images. In R. Jacobson (Ed.), *Code-switching Worldwide II* (pp. 193–219). Berlin: Mouton de Gruyter.

Montrul, S. (2002). Incomplete Acquisition and Attrition of Spanish Tense/Aspect Distinctions in Adult Bilinguals. *Bilingualism: Language and Cognition* 5(1), 39–68.

Montrul, S. (2004). Subject and Object Expression in Spanish Heritage Speakers: A Case of Morphosyntactic Convergence. *Bilingualism: Language and Cognition* 7(2), 125–142.

Muysken, P. (2000). *Bilingual Speech*. Cambridge: Cambridge University Press.

Poplack, S. (1980). Sometimes I'll Start a Sentence in English y termino en español: Toward a Typology of Code-Switching. In J. Amastae & L. Elías-Olivares (Eds.), *Spanish in the United States: Sociolinguistic Aspects* (pp. 230–263). Cambridge: Cambridge University Press.

Rakowsky, A. (1989). A Study of Intra-Sentential Code-Switching in Spanish-English Bilinguals and Second Language Learners. Ph.D. dissertation, Brown University.

Silva-Corvalán, C. (1986). Bilingualism and Language Contact. *Language* 62(3), 587–608.

Silva-Corvalán, C. (1994). *Language Contact and Change: Spanish in Los Angeles*. Oxford: Oxford University Press.

Toribio, A. J. (2000). Migrant Language: Spanish Language Variation and Loss. Unpublished manuscript, The Pennsylvania State University.

Toribio, A. J. (2001a). On the Emergence of Code-Switching Competence. *Bilingualism: Language and Cognition* 4(3), 203–231.

Toribio, A. J. (2001b). Accessing Spanish-English Code-Switching Competence. *International Journal of Bilingualism* 5(4), 403–436.

Toribio, A. J. (2002). Spanish-English Code-Switching among U.S. Latinos. *International Journal of the Sociology of Language* 158, 89–119.

Toribio, A. J. (2004a). Spanish/English Speech Practices: Bringing Chaos to Order. *International Journal of Bilingual Education and Bilingualism* 7(2), 133–154.

Toribio, A. J. (2004b). Convergence as an Optimization Strategy in Bilingual Speech: Evidence from Code-Switching. *Bilingualism: Language and Cognition* 7(2), 165–173.

Valdés, G. (2000). Bilingualism and Language Use among Mexican Americans. In S. L. McKay & S.-L. C. Wong (Eds.), *New Immigrants in the United States* (pp. 99–136). Cambridge: Cambridge University Press.

Wald, B. (1988). Research on Dialects: Implications for Linguistic Theory. In J. Ornstein-Galicia, G. Green, & D. Bixler-Márquez (Eds.), *Research Issues and Problems in United States Spanish: Latin American and Southwestern Varieties* (pp. 57–73). Brownsville, TX: Pan American University at Brownsville.

Walsh, C. (1991). *Pedagogy and the Struggle for Voice: Issues of Language, Power, and Schooling for Puerto Ricans*. Westport, CT: Bergin & Garvey.

Woolard, K. A. (1992). Language Convergence and Language Death as Social Processes. In N. C. Dorian (Ed.), *Investigating Obsolescence: Studies in Language Contraction and Death* (pp. 365–367). Cambridge: Cambridge University Press.

Woolford, E. (1985). Bilingual Code-Switching and Syntactic Theory. *Linguistic Inquiry* 14(1), 520–536.

Zentella, A. C. (1981). Hablamos los dos. We Speak Both: Growing Up Bilingual in El Barrio. Ph.D. dissertation, University of Pennsylvania.

Zentella, A. C. (1997). *Growing Up Bilingual*. Malden, MA: Blackwell.

Zentella, A. C. (1998). Multiple Codes, Multiple Identities: Puerto Rican Children in New York City. In S. Hoyle & C. Temple Adger (Eds.), *Kids Talk: Strategic Language Use in Later Childhood* (pp. 95–112). Oxford: Oxford University Press.

Zentella, A. C. (2000). Puerto Ricans in the United States: Confronting the Linguistics Repercussions of Colonialism. In S. L. McKay & S.-L. C. Wong (Eds.), *New Immigrants in the United States* (pp. 99–164). Cambridge: Cambridge University Press.

Recommended Reading

Brutt-Griffler, J. (2002). *World English: A Study of Its Development*. Clevedon, UK: Multilingual Matters.

Lipski, J. (1985). *Linguistic Aspects of Spanish-English Language Switching*. Tempe: Arizona State University, Center for Latin American Studies.

Milroy, L., & Muysken, P. (1995). *One Speaker, Two Languages*. Cambridge: Cambridge University Press.

Poplack, S. (1980). Sometimes I'll Start a Sentence in Spanish y termino en español: Toward a Typology of Code-Switching. In J. Amastae & L. Elías-Olivares (Eds.), *Spanish in the United States: Sociolinguistic Aspects* (pp. 230–263). Cambridge: Cambridge University Press.

Poplack, S. (1981). Syntactic Structure and Social Function of Code-Switching. In R. Durán (Ed.), *Latino Language and Communicative Behavior* (pp. 169–184). Norwood, NJ: Ablex.

Timm, L. A. (1993). Bilingual Code-Switching: An Overview of Research. In B. Merino, H. Trueba, & F. Samaniego (Eds.), *Language and Culture in Learning* (pp. 94–112). Bristol, PA: Falmer.

Toribio, A. J., & Rubin, E. J. (1996). Code-Switching in Generative Grammar. In J. Jensen & A. Roca (Eds.), *Spanish in Contact* (pp. 203–226). Cambridge, MA: Cascadilla Press.

Zentella, A. C. (1997). *Growing Up Bilingual*. Malden, MA: Blackwell.

Almeida Jacqueline Toribio

SPECIAL EDUCATION RESTRICTIVENESS AND PLACEMENT PATTERNS

Latinos/as have become the largest non-white group in the U.S., numbering 39.9 million in July 2003 (U.S. Census Bureau, 2004). As a result of this growth, there is an increasing likelihood that Latino students will be designated with special needs (i.e., emotional disorder, mental retardation, specific learning disability, or speech impairment) (Artiles, Fierros, & Rueda, 2004). This coming reality is exacerbated by the large number of Latino English language learners (ELLs) mistakenly designated with special education labels. Historically, minority students with special needs have not enjoyed equal educational opportunities with their white counterparts (Fierros & Conroy, 2002; Finn, 1982).

This entry defines restrictiveness and describes placement patterns for U.S. Latino students with special needs. It examines recent research on special education contexts for Latino students with special needs, and it provides suggestions for teachers of these students.

Restrictiveness

Restrictiveness is a numerical value that describes the degree to which students with disabilities are educated outside of regular classrooms and isolated from their nondisabled peers (Fierros & Conroy, 2002). Restrictiveness rates are calculated using odds ratios. As shown in Figure 1, odds ratios reveal "the odds of an event occurring is the ratio of the probability of the event occurring to the probability of the

$$\psi = \frac{P_{00}P_{11}}{P_{01}P_{10}}$$

Figure 1
Odds Radio

event not occurring. The odds ratios reflect the extent to which membership in a given racial group affects the probability of being in the regular classroom (Fleiss, 1973; Siminoff, 2003; Wasserman, 2004). Odds ratios that are greater than 1.0 show that the odds of designation are larger than for the comparison group. An odds ratio of 1 indicates that there is no difference between the two groups, or $\psi = 1$. An odds ratio less than 1 indicates the comparison group (i.e., white students) has a greater chance of designation. Restrictiveness rates are generally higher for minority students with special needs than they are for whites students.

There has been much research demonstrating that students with special needs benefit when they are educated with regular education students (Harry, 1992; Losen & Orfield, 2002). Yet, students with special needs are often relegated to learning outside the regular classroom even though the Individuals with Disabilities Education Act (IDEA) mandates that they should be educated in the least restrictive environment (LRE) and also must receive a free and appropriate public education (FAPE). Students with special needs who do not enjoy learning in a regular classroom are said to be *restricted* from the regular classroom environment. This restriction violates inclusive practices that should be followed as part of the IDEA, yet numerous students find themselves stuck in a room outside the regular classroom. Although students with special needs from all different ethnic groups experience some level of restrictiveness from the regular education class-

room (i.e., being pulled out from the classroom), minority students with special needs have a greater chance of being restricted from the regular classroom than their white counterparts (Fierros & Conroy, 2002). The reality for these minority students with special needs is that they will be educationally shortchanged because of restrictive practices—a form of double jeopardy.

Double jeopardy occurs for minority students with special needs in classroom and school contexts in a number of different ways. Meyer and Patton (2001) point out that minority students are far more likely to

- Be taught by teachers who are not qualified to teach the core subjects
- Have teachers who completed an alternative certification program
- Have more substitute teachers
- Attend schools that are in substandard condition, lack state-of-the-art technology, and do not offer a rigorous and culturally responsive curriculum
- Have teachers who do not have access to sustained professional development opportunities
- Have teachers, administrators, and related service professionals who are not culturally competent
- Have inferior instructional materials (p. 7)

For minority students with special needs these classroom and school inequities present even greater challenges than students in more affluent districts who are more likely to be white (U.S. Department of Education, 2004).

Although researchers have tracked the evolution of disability incidence and ethnic minority placement rates, we know little about the representation of Latinos in contexts in which they represent a substantial proportion of the student population. Finn (1982), for example, reported that MR overrepresentation was a problem in districts with large Latino enrollment (i.e., + 70%); the largest mental retardation (MR) overrepresentation rates were observed in small districts with large Latino enrollment; Latino learning disabilities (LD) overrepresentation was also associated with this group's overrepresentation in MR. Moreover, the availability of programs to address the needs of ELLs (i.e., language minority students not yet fully proficient in English) seemingly mediates overrepresentation patterns, particularly in large school districts. Finn (1982) reported that the proportion of Latino students in bilingual programs was inversely associated with overrepresentation levels—that is, districts with the highest overrepresentation rates had smaller proportions of students in bilingual programs. He concluded, "It is possible that [Latino] students with poor English proficiency are misclassified as [mild MR] when bilingual programs are not available" (p. 372).

Placement Patterns for Latino Students with Special Needs

Placement patterns of Latino students with special needs are identified by comparing the percentage of Latino students in the given general population (i.e., school, district, or state) with the percentage of Latino students in the population of students with special needs and the comparable numbers by race and ethnicity in three placement categories (Fierros & Conroy, 2002; Finn, 1982).

- Overrepresentation: more students than expected in the population are designated with a special education label.
- Underrepresentation: fewer students than would be expected in the population are designated with a special education label.
- Proportional representation: the proportion of students in the population is equivalent to the

population designated with a special education label.

The U.S. Department of Education's Office of Special Education Programs (OSEP), the Office of Civil Rights (OCR), and the National Center for Education Statistics (NCES) conduct surveys of schools and districts across the U.S. to identify placement patterns of students by race and ethnicity. Survey completers choose from three placement categories: less than 20% time outside the regular classroom, between 21% and 60% time outside the classroom, and more than 60% outside the regular classroom.

Since these surveys began, there has been a consistent pattern of placements for disadvantage Latino and African American students with special needs (Artiles & Trent, 1994; Fierros & Conroy, 2002; Harry, 1992). These restrictive placements have meant that minority special education students' educational experiences are likely to be delivered in unequal and separate classroom environments (Crockett & Kauffman, 1999; Grossman, 1995). Couhtino and Repp (1999) reported that for the 1992–1993 school year, nearly 60% of students (ages 3 to 21) were taught outside the regular classroom. Lipsky and Gartner (1997) stated that "the negative consequences of the separate special education system are greater for students from racial minorities" (p. 33).

Studies on MR and specific learning disabilities (SLD) conducted since the early 1980s have found results that reflect the changing demographic patterns of U.S. Latinos. Generally, Latinos were underrepresented. The restrictiveness rates for the 1997–1998 school year were highest for students with MR and students with emotional disturbance (ED), where minorities and especially blacks are overrepresented

(U.S. Department of Education, 1999). Restrictiveness rates for students with MR were nearly 82%, with lower rates of restrictiveness for students with specific emotional disturbance (SED) (70%) and students with SLD (56%).

Latino students with special needs have been found to be underrepresented in special education placements in national- and state-level large-scale studies (Artiles & Trent, 1994; Fierros & Conroy, 2002). Yet, more recent district-level analyses of placement patterns for Latino students with special needs found that they are overrepresented in districts with relatively large numbers of Latino students. For example, in New York only 44% of Latino students with special needs were integrated into the regular classroom compared with 56% for white children and 51% for Asian children (Fierros & Conroy, 2002). Forty percent of African American students with special needs were integrated. These numbers are far worse than they appear because Latino and African American students are significantly overrepresented in the disabled population. What results is a double jeopardy for too many Latino and African American students with special needs.

Ruiz and Figueroa's (1995) work looking at the classroom-level realities of Latino students with special needs pointed out that the admirable and crucial work in the macro contexts (i.e., state- and district-level analyses) of special education for Latino students in the U.S. must continue. Their (1995) examination of the micro context of special education (i.e., classrooms) reported that

what sometimes gets lost in discussions of due process rights and systemic educational reform is precisely what leads many of us to continue our work with Latino students with disabilities: the quality of educational services provided to them and their families on a daily basis. Those

of us who spend time in classrooms with teachers and students occasionally see reason for hope, but most often we see reason to criticize: Spanish-speaking students in special education receive instruction that does not take into account their linguistic needs, that is linked to minimal academic growth, and that is the epitome of "dead end" classes. (p. 1)

Optimal Learning Environment (OLE) Classrooms

The special education classroom should be the instructional events and contexts created by the teacher. The OLE classrooms established in Rueda, Ruiz, and Figueroa (1996) have argued that OLE classrooms found in California use a set of very "specific non-reductionist" instructional strategies. A list of the OLE instructional principles follows:

1. Give students as much choice as possible in what they learn, read, write, and work on in the classroom, as opposed to always having the teacher select the topic, book, or project.

2. Be constructive. Build on the cultural knowledge and the interests of the student, as opposed to providing prepackaged materials, exercises, and drills.

3. Use a whole-part-whole approach to literature, writing, the arts, science, and mathematics, as opposed to requiring work on parts, fragments, or prerequisite skills.

4. Set up conditions for active student participation, as opposed to activities in which students are passive receptacles of "knowledge."

5. Attend to ideas first and then to mechanics, as opposed to giving issues of form, such as phonics, spelling, or grammar, a primary or exclusive focus.

6. As much as possible, have the students work for an authentic purpose, as opposed to teacher evaluation.

7. Immerse the students in a language- and print-rich environment, as opposed to an

impoverished one in terms of the quantity and quality of books and the amount of reading, writing, listening, and speaking.

8. Provide multiple opportunities for demonstrations of how to do the work, as opposed to giving verbal instructions.

9. Understand and accept the role of approximations in getting at the right answer, as opposed to reinforcing the "correct" answer on the first try.

10. Always give an immediate response to students' work products, as opposed to a future grade for the "right" response.

11. Create an atmosphere in which the classroom becomes a learning community, as opposed to a collection of individuals working on their individualized learning programs.

12. Have high expectations. Believe that the social and academic potential of underachieving pupils and of persons with disabilities is truly unlimited, as opposed to focusing on what they cannot do or on their previous grades, test scores, or labels.

In describing restrictiveness and revealing placement patterns for Latino students with special needs, this entry has sought to provide a descriptive portrait of Latino students with special needs through the examination of recent research on special education contexts for these students. It also provided effective teaching suggestions for teachers of Latino students with special needs.

References

Artiles, A., Fierros, E. G., & Rueda, R. (2004). Restrictiveness and Disproportionality in Top Ten Hispanic States. Paper presented at the Annual Meeting for the American Educational Research Association, April 15.

Artiles, A., & Trent, S. (1994). Overrepresentation of Minority Students in Special Education: A Continuing Debate. *Journal of Special Education* 27(4), 410–437.

Couhtino, M., & Repp, A. C. (1999). *Inclusion: The Integration of Students with Disabilities.* Belmont, CA: Wadsworth.

Crockett, J. B., & Kauffman, J. M. (1999). *The Least Restrictive Environment: Its Origins and Interpretations in Special Education.* Mahwah, NJ: Lawrence Erlbaum.

Fierros, E. G., & Conroy, J. (2002). Double Jeopardy: An Exploration of Restrictiveness and Race in Special Education. In D. Losen & G. Orfield (Eds.), *Racial Inequity in Special Education* (pp. 39–70). Cambridge, MA: The Civil Rights Project/Harvard Education Press.

Finn, J. D. (1982). Patterns in Special Education Placement as Revealed by the OCR Survey. In K. A. Heller, W. H. Holtzman, & S. Messick (Eds.), *Placing Children in Special Education: A Strategy for Equity* (pp. 322–381). Washington, DC: National Academy Press.

Fleiss, J. L. (1973). *Statistical Methods For Rates and Proportions.* New York: John Wiley & Sons.

Grossman, H. (1995). *Special Education In a Diverse Society.* Boston: Allyn & Bacon.

Harry, B. (1992). *The Disproportionate Representation of Minority Students in Special Education: Theories and Recommendations.* Project FORUM. Final report. Alexandria, VA: National Association of State Directors of Special Education. ERIC Document Reproduction Service, no. ED 374 637.

Lipsky, D. K., & Gartner, A. (1997). *Inclusion and School Reform: Transforming America's Classrooms.* Baltimore: Brookes.

Losen, D., & Orfield, G. (Eds.). (2002). *Racial Inequity in Special Education.* Cambridge, MA: The Civil Rights Project/Harvard Education Press.

Meyer, G., & Patton, J. M. (2001). *On Point. On the Nexus of Race, Disability, and Overrepresentation: What Do We Know? Where Do We Go?* Newton, MA: National Institute for Urban School Improvement.

Rueda, R., Ruiz, N. T., & Figueroa, N. T. (1996). Issues in the Implementation of Innovative Instructional Strategies. *Multiple*

Voices for Ethnically Diverse Exceptional Learners 1, 12–23.

Ruiz, N. T., & Figueroa, R. A. (1995). Learning-Handicapped Classrooms with Latino Students. *Education and Urban Society* 27, 463–483.

Siminoff, J. (2003). *Analyzing Categorical Data*. New York: Springer-Verlag.

U.S. Census Bureau. (2004). Small Area Income and Poverty Estimates Tables for School Districts by State and Income. *Housing and Household Economic Statistics Division, Small Area Estimates Branch*. Available: http://www.census.gov/hhes/www/saipe/sdtables/sd00links.html (accessed June 7, 2004).

U.S. Department of Education. (1999). *Twenty-first Annual Report to Congress on the Implementation of the Individuals with Disabilities Education Act*. Washington, DC: Office of Special Education Programs, U.S. Government Printing Office.

U.S. Department of Education. (2004). *Twenty-fourth Annual Report to Congress on the Implementation of the Individuals with Disabilities Education Act*. Washington, DC: Office of Special Education Programs, U.S. Government Printing Office.

Wasserman, L. (2004). *All of Statistics*. New York: Springer-Verlag.

Recommended Reading

Losen, D., & Orfield, G. (Eds.). (2002). *Racial Inequity in Special Education*. Cambridge, MA: The Civil Rights Project/Harvard Education Press.

Edward Garcia Fierros

STANDARDS

Standards outline what educators and policymakers believe K–12 students should know and be able to do in academic classes for successful achievement in school. Also called academic standards, or content and performance standards, standards are tied to both curricula and assessments. All students, including linguistically and culturally diverse learners in U.S. public schools—of which the majority are Latinos/as/Hispanics[1]—are expected to adhere to and attain competence in educational standards. Standards have grown out of discipline specific professional organizations such as the National Council of Teachers of Mathematics (NCTM), and they define minimum expectations of students in all content areas including math, language arts, science, social studies, and technology, as well as in the arts, foreign languages, and physical education. Because of the attention given to the academic standards in K–12 education, *standards* has become an important buzzword in today's educational environment.

The standards movement is comprised of two fundamental components: professional standards and state standards. Although both the professional and state strands work in concert to provide standardized education for elementary and secondary U.S. students, the two components have different goals and origins. Professional organizations approach standards as the professional consensus from content area specialists and educators as to what students must know and be able to do in the discipline at particular grade levels. State standards are mandates from policymakers that may or may not be aligned with professional standards. State content standards are a prescription to be followed by practitioners in the classrooms.

The standards movement came about in the late 1980s with the inception and development of the mathematical standards by NCTM (Gomez, 2000). Shortly thereafter, in the early 1990s, other professional organizations began to follow suit. Taking a cue from NCTM, the National Council of

Teachers of English (NCTE) and others, such as the International Reading Association (IRA), the National Council for the Social Studies (NCSS), and the American Council of Teachers of Foreign Languages (ACTFL), worked to develop standards in other content areas taught in schools.

First conceptualized in the early 1990s in George Bush Senior's term, and coming to fruition later, during Bill Clinton's tenure, the Goals 2000: Educate America Act mandated legislation that all students, including English as a second language (ESL) and bilingual learners, would be responsible for achieving high levels of content knowledge (Gomez, 2000). As a response to the "Call to Action" issued by Clinton in his State of the Union Address on February 4, 1997, the Department of Education developed a set of seven important priorities intended to reform education in the U.S. (U.S. Department of Education, 1997; Hopkins, 1997). One of these dealt specifically with educational standards and mandated that "all states and schools will have challenging and clear standards of achievement and accountability for all children, and effective strategies for reaching those standards" (Goals 2000, 1994). The Goals 2000: Reforming Education to Improve Student Achievement congressional report in April 1998 put the standards at center stage and both advocated and supported educational initiatives to promote high academic standards and ultimately high achievement of U.S. schoolchildren. Thus, the standards were afforded a higher and more valuable status in the federal, state, and local educational realms.

As a result of Goals 2000, individual states became responsible for outlining the necessary achievement guidelines for the learners in their domain. State standards, like many of the professional content area standards, began to take into account the demographic makeup of their student population. Some professional organization standards like those produced by NCTE, NCTM, and ACTFL, address issues specific to ethnically and linguistically diverse learners such as Latinos/as/Hispanics. These include nurturing the home language and culture (NCTE); respecting non-English-speaking cultures (ACTFL); and affording opportunities to learn to students who have traditionally been marginalized, such as women and English language learners (ELLs) (NCTM). The Teachers of English to Speakers of Other Languages (TESOL) standards are directed wholly toward ELLs in Pre-K–12 classrooms.

Education standards are central to George W. Bush's educational legislation, No Child Left Behind (NCLB). A principal component of NCLB mandates that states develop standards in the crucial content areas of math, science, language arts and reading, and English language proficiency. States are also required to develop standardized assessments to measure these content standards. State and school district funding serves as a carrot-and-stick for institutions to implement NCLB's guidelines. Schools and districts that do not make Adequate Yearly Progress (AYP) in meeting state educational standards (as measured by high-stakes tests) can—after a period of time—suffer punitive and often draconian consequences. Teachers at low-performing schools can be released from duty, and students in low-performing schools may move to same-district schools that are successful at meeting state standards (U.S. Department of Education, 2002). After a school fails to make AYP after three consecutive years, state funding can be diverted for use for supplemental educational services (SES), for students including individual student tutoring.

NCLB mandates that states must develop separate English language proficiency standards and create an English language proficiency assessment to measure those standards. As a result, ELLs, of which Latinos/as/Hispanics make up the vast majority, are required to attain proficiency not only in content areas but also in English. In states with high populations of Latinos/as/Hispanics, such as Texas, the state English language standards are specifically geared to Spanish speakers. Texas's general language arts standards are addressed in particular to speakers of both English and Spanish. In California, the U.S. state with the greatest number of ELLs, language standards include a component for English language development, which is separate from English standards. Unfortunately, restrictive anti-bilingual education laws and policies prevent many Latino/a/Hispanic ELLs from learning the content standards in the language they understand most—Spanish—while they are still learning English (Wright, 2005).

Distinct from English language proficiency standards, many states also have foreign language standards. While foreign language standards are not specifically tailored to ELLs, some address the needs of heritage language speakers. Courses such as Spanish for Spanish speakers are offered in states with large Latino/a/Hispanic populations. For example, Arizona's content standards includes standards for foreign and native languages, while its neighbor, New Mexico, provides educational standards for modern, classical, and native languages.

Despite their attempt to address the special needs of groups like Latinos/as/Hispanics, governmental policies that promote standards achievement such as NCLB have not been overly successful at meeting students' academic and language-learning needs (Wright, 2005). Latinos/as/Hispanics and other non-majority groups have traditionally performed poorly on the high-stakes tests used by the states and NCLB to measure student achievement of the content area standards (Taylor, 2000). Further, exceptions are not readily made for new immigrants and students from non-English-speaking households. NCLB allows ELLs only a one-year exemption on testing language arts and reading in English, and it mandates that content tests such as math must be given in the student's first year of enrollment. If English is the only language available in which students can take their math test, they will be tested in English. Under NCLB, English language proficiency tests are required for all first-year students.

Although many teachers favor standards and a standardization of the content areas, there are strong criticisms of the standards movement. Standards have been sharply criticized for advocating a "one size fits all" education (Ohanian, 1999), resembling a factory model of education. Standards have also come into question for representing and serving the dominant group in power (Keating, 1996), which is usually white, middle-class, and English speaking, because politicians play a critical role in the development of state content standards. As a result, standards typically reward those children who hail from homes whose norms, values, and background knowledge are most closely aligned with those in power; conversely, standards punish those from differing backgrounds, such as those in linguistically, culturally, and economically diverse homes.

The standards movement overlooks the fact that funding is often drastically unequal from school district to school district. Standards-based instruction holds all students to the same accountability standards, but it does not take into account the amount of resources schools have to pay and train teachers, purchase books and materials, keep up facilities, and provide services for disadvantaged students. Because many Latinos/as/Hispanics often attend underfunded schools, they are at a disadvantage in terms of reaching academic standards and, thus, ultimately being successful in school. The impact of the standards and standards-based instruction on Latinos/as/ Hispanics is not yet altogether clear. Although many state and professional standards in content areas address specific needs of certain populations, educational policies can ignore or exclude special considerations for some, including bilinguals and second language learners. Overall, however, the future of academic standards in K–12 education is bright. It is highly likely that federal education policy will continue to support and foster the development and implementation of academic standards. As the use of standardized assessments continues in U.S. schools, the incorporation of academic standards into K–12 curricula will also increase.

Note

1. I have included both terms *Hispanic* and *Latino/a* for inclusivity. Some object to one or the other label. And like R. Gutierrez, I employ the use of Latino/a to "decenter (the) paternalistic character (of Spanish)" (2002, p. 1083, n1) and also to highlight the importance and differences between genders with specific regard to learning (math) in institutional settings.

References

Goals 2000: Educate America Act. (1994). Public Law no. 103-227.

Gomez, Emily L. (2000). *A History of the ESL Standards for Pre-K–12 Students.* In Marguerite Ann Snow (Ed.), *Implementing the ESL Standards* (pp. 49–79). Alexandria, VA: TESOL.

Gutierrez, Rochelle. (2002). Beyond Essentialism: The Complexity of Language in Teaching Mathematics to Latina/o Students. *American Educational Research Journal* 39(4), 1047–1088.

Hopkins, Gary. (1997). A Primer: The Seven Priorities of the U.S. Department of Education. Education World. School Administrator's Article. Available: http://www .education-world.com/a_admin/admin025 .shtml (accessed March 2, 2005).

Keating, Daniel P. (1996). Habits of Mind for a Learning Society: Educating for Human Development. In David R. Olson & Nancy Torrance (Eds.), *Handbook of Education and Human Development: New Models of Learning, Teaching, and Schooling* (pp. 461–481). Oxford: Blackwell.

No Child Left Behind. (2001). Public Law no. 107-110.

Ohanian, Susan. (1999). *One Size Fits Few: The Folly of Educational Standards.* Portsmouth, NH: Heinemann.

Taylor, Judy. (2000). *Closing the Achievement Gap.* LINCletter Policy Publication, North Central Regional Educational Laboratory.

U.S. Department of Education. (1997). The Seven Priorities of the U.S. Department of Education. Available: http://www.ed.gov/ updates/7priorities/index.html (accessed February 17, 2005).

U.S. Department of Education. (1998). Goals 2000: Reforming Education to Improve Student Achievement. Archived Information: Goals 2000: Implementing Standards-Based Reform. Available: http://www.ed.gov/pubs/ G2KReforming/g2ch3.html (accessed February 17, 2005).

U.S. Department of Education. (2002). Dear Colleague Letter to State and Local Education Leaders Outlining Adequate Yearly Progress Provisions (Letter from Education Secretary Rod Paige). Available: http:// www.ed.gov/policy/elsec/guid/secletter/0207 24.html (accessed March 3, 2005).

U.S. Department of Education. (2004). Remarks of the U.S. Secretary Rod Paige at the Press Conference Announcing New Policies for ELLs (Press release). Washington, DC: Author.

Wright, Wayne. (2005). Language Policy Research Unit: Evolution of Federal Policy and Implications of No Child Left Behind for Language Minority Students. *Education Policy Studies Laboratory*. Tempe: Arizona State University.

Selected Content Area Standards Publications

Note: These standards publications can be accessed either in text form or through the Web sites of the professional organization.

Bilingual Education

sde.state.nm.us/div/learn.serv/Bilingual/dl/ . . . / 34.references.doc

www.emich.edu/coe/program_update/biling_sp/standards_matrix.html

www.emsc.nysed.gov/cial/biling/ESLbk.pdf

www.isbe.il.us/profpred/CASDvr/pdfs/28330_lbs2bilingual.pdf

www.njpep.org/standards

www.tea.state.tx.us/curriculum/biling/elps.html

English

National Council of Teachers of English (NCTE). (1996). *Standards for the English Language* Arts. Urbana, IL: NCTE. Available: http://www.ncte.org/about/over/standards/110846.htm.

English as a Second Language

Teachers of English to Teachers of Other Languages (TESOL). (1997). *ESL Standards for Pre-K–12 Students*. Alexandria, VA: TESOL. Available: http://www.tesol.org/s_tesol/sec css.asp?CID=113&DID=1583.

Fine Arts

Consortium of National Arts Education Associations. (1994). *National Standards for Arts Education: What Every Young American Should Know and Be Able to Do in the Arts*. Reston, VA: National Association for Music Education (MENC). Available: http://artsedge.kennedy-center.org/teach/standards/contents.cfm.

Foreign Language

American Council of Teachers of Foreign Languages (ACTFL). (1996). *Standards for Foreign Language Learning: Preparing for the 21st Century*. Lawrence, KS: ACTFL. Available: http://www.actfl.org/i4a/pages/index.cfm?pageid=3392.

American Council of Teachers of Foreign Languages (ACTFL). (1999). *Standards for Foreign Language Learning in the 21st Century*. Lawrence, KS: ACTFL.

Mathematics

National Council of Teachers of Mathematics (NCTM). (2000). *Principles and Standards for School Mathematics*. Reston, VA: NCTM. Available: http://standards.nctm.org/.

Physical Education

National Association for Sport and Physical Education (NASPE). (2004). *Moving into the Future: National Standards for Physical Education* (2nd ed.). Reston, VA: NASPE. Available: http://www.aahperd.org/naspe/template.cfm/template=publications-nationalstandards.html.

Science

National Academy of Sciences. (1996). *National Science Education Standards*. Washington, DC: National Academy Press. Available: http://books.nap.edu/html/nses/html/.

Social Studies

National Center for History in the Schools (NCHS). (1996). *The National Standards for History* (Basic ed.). Los Angeles: NCHS. Available: http://nchs.ucla.edu/standards/.

National Council for the Social Studies (NCSS). (1994). *Curriculum Standards for Social Studies: Expectations of Excellence*. Silver Spring, MD: NCSS. Available: http://www.socialstudies.org/standards/.

Holly Hansen-Thomas

SUBTRACTIVE SCHOOLING

In attempting to understand a pattern of achievement that distinguishes *regular-track*, Mexican immigrant youth from their U.S.-born, Mexican American counterparts, I devised the concept of subtractive schooling. *Subtractive Schooling: U.S.-Mexican Youth and the Politics of Caring* (1999) succinctly captures the central thesis that schools subtract resources from youth. My research findings are based on a three-year (1992–1995) case study of Juan Seguín High School (pseudonym), a virtually all-Latino, mostly Mexican, Houston, inner-city school. This resulted in a critique of the practice of cultural assimilation (or "Americanization") that characterizes most schooling for U.S.-Mexican youth.

Schools subtract resources from youth in two major ways. The first involves a process of "de-Mexicanization." By this I refer to the subtracting of students' culture and language through harmful and divisive school- and district-level practices, as well as local, state, and federal policies that not only fail to build on children's assets, but seek to erase them altogether. There is no neutral category for schooling because the status quo is subtractive and inscribed in public policy: The Texas Bilingual Education Code is a transitional policy framework. Similarly, the federal No Child Left Behind Act is similarly premised on children's rapid acquisition of the English language.

The second way concerns the role of caring and relationships between students and teachers. Specifically, teacher caring is conditional (Valenzuela, 1997). They expect students to *care about* school in a technical fashion before they *care for* them. In contrast, students' definition of caring is aligned to caring theory that posits that all learning should be premised on relation-ships (Noddings, 1984, 1992). Accordingly, students expect teachers to *care for* them in a respectful, holistic manner before they *care about* school. By disregarding students' definition of education—an orientation embodied in the Spanish language concept of *educación*—schooling subtracts resources from youth. Rather than helping them to be "well educated" in the Mexican sense (*ser bien educado*)—where schools are guided by a respectfulness toward their students' individuality—schools objectify them, treating children like objects.

Taken together, de-Mexicanization is corrosive, affecting not only the quality of schooling for students and teachers at Seguín High School but also the social capital that in a more ideal world (Coleman 1988, 1990) would connect Mexican immigrants and U.S.-born youth to each other. Given that students' academic skills and knowledge vary by generational status at Seguín, its relative presence among regular-track, immigrant youth and, conversely, its relative absence among their U.S.-born, Mexican American counterparts is of consequence to both groups' achievement.

Subtractive schooling policies and practices drive a wedge between these groups, fostering cultural de-identification to the degree that school-based resources and orientations are unable to develop constructively across groups. As in all such contexts, there is indeed a middling category of bilingual and bicultural youth; however, pressures to assimilate translate into pressures to choose between "more Mexicanized" or "more Americanized" friendship groups. The remedy to subtractive schooling is additive schooling, where language and culture are construed as assets, not deficits. In this space, a politically aware, authentically caring pedagogy occurs and there is no such thing as a standard child.

References

Coleman, James S. (1988). Social Capital in the Creation of Human Capital. *American Journal of Sociology* 94, 95–120.

Coleman, James S. (1990). *Foundations of Social Theory*. Cambridge, MA: Harvard University Press.

Noddings, Nel. (1984). *Caring: A Feminine Approach to Ethics and Moral Education*. Berkeley: University of California Press.

Noddings, Nel. (1992). *The Challenge to Care in Schools: An Alternative Approach to Education*. New York: Teachers College Press.

Valenzuela, Angela. (1997). Mexican American Youth and the Politics of Caring. In Elizabeth Long (Ed.), *From Sociology to Cultural Studies*: Vol. 2, *Sociology of Culture Annual Series*. London: Blackwell.

Valenzuela, Angela. (1999). *Subtractive Schooling: U.S.-Mexican Youth and the Politics of Caring*. Albany, NY: SUNY Press.

Recommended Reading

Valenzuela, Angela. (1999). *Subtractive Schooling: U.S.-Mexican Youth and the Politics of Caring*. Albany, NY: SUNY Press.

Angela Valenzuela

T

TEACHER EDUCATION USING ONLINE RESOURCES

Teacher candidates typically enter teacher preparation programs with some knowledge of the uses of technology in daily life but with relatively less understanding of its strategic and selective application to enhance the teaching-learning process. Teacher candidates also have little knowledge of the literary contributions of what was, until recently, the largest of the Latino communities in New York City. Our challenge as educators is to address these gaps within the timeframe of a 14-session semester at a time when we are required to meet a range of new and challenging teacher preparation requirements.

Similarly, teacher educators (and I include myself among these) need to develop technological literacy and to begin to find ways of integrating multimedia, online resources appropriately in all courses to broaden the learning opportunities of teacher candidates and to respond to the range of learning styles and individual differences found increasingly among them. Teacher educators also need to broaden their understandings of the contributions of groups that remain invisible in the knowledge base for teaching and that are misrepresented in the media. The recently televised, award-winning *American Writers* series on C-SPAN neglects the literary contributions of Puerto Rican intellectuals despite the role that Puerto Rican literati have played in influencing our nation's history, even though much media attention is given to the problems of youth identified with this community.

The online database Centro Library and Archives at Centro de Estudios Puertorriqueños, Hunter College, City University of New York (http://www.centropr.org), represents a vast and untapped resource for educators. Surprisingly, however, there are a number of other resources easily accessible online that provide a more balanced representation of the Puerto Rican community and its contributions to American society than typically presented in textbooks and the media. Thus, a number of excellent multimedia Web sites enable educators new to the uses of technology (again, I include myself among these) to experience directly its potential as a tool for learning and as a tool to enhance the teaching-learning process in ways that are developmentally appropriate. Clearly, while the use of multimedia technologies enhances the learning process, the use of these tools requires more than entry-level skills. For those who are new to the technology, interacting with good examples of multimedia Web sites appropriate for literacy instruction in the elementary schools represents a first step toward the creation of course-specific multimedia Web sites in teacher education. Through the exploration and use of these multimedia Web sites, all educators acquire skills and competencies to integrate them in creative new ways in their practice, even as we acquire greater skill and fluency in their application.

It is toward the development of these competencies and skills that the module described in this entry is designed. The module is geared toward preservice teachers and teacher educators with entry-level skills in the use of technology. It is a companion to the Nets.Work project developed by Centro de Estudios Puertorriqueños, and may also be presented independently. In either case, this module addresses a serious gap that needs to be bridged if we are to support teacher candidates in meeting new state certification requirements and national teacher preparation standards. Ultimately, however, our goal is to prepare teachers to build on the experiences and existing language and technological skills of elementary school students, and to enable all classroom participants to attain high standards of academic excellence no matter where they live or where they go to school.

Project Integration

Although activities will be incorporated into the course I teach, "Literacy across the Content Areas" (QSTA 410.80), they are also adaptable to other courses, including teaching social studies in the elementary school, educational technology, and children's literature. The incorporation of technology in courses that are highly interactive and that seek to address the underpreparation of teacher candidates also enables us to extend learning opportunities

beyond sessions that meet weekly for under two hours.

Assessment

In QSTA 410.80, assessment is approached as an ongoing process that is intended to inform the teaching-learning process, which requires that course participants keep a journal of their experiences of the course and the preparation of charts that chronicle learning experiences during each session. This written documentation has two purposes. First, the responses of teacher candidates during and across sessions will inform my activities as a mediator of learning and shape the modifications I make to my instructional roadmap, reflecting the belief that all instruction is context-specific and variable if we are to respond appropriately to the range of differences commonly found among learners. This understanding is even more important now that demographic changes have augmented the diversity of the New York City school population and just as new policies affecting graduation requirements and standards-based instruction have been imposed. Second, these responses also inform the actions of learners/teacher-candidates who need to become reflective, self-directed learners. Specifically, course participants are held responsible for monitoring and acting on their learning, which includes being aware of the support they need to understand and accomplish course requirements, and the actions they will take to address evolving needs. These experiences prepare teacher candidates to assume a similar stance in their own classrooms.

Entry skills of teacher candidates will be assessed using written responses to activities during session 1 (see the section "Seven-Part Instructional Sequence"). These responses will be recorded in individual journals of experiences and in charts prepared by me during each session. The final session of a seven-part instructional sequence will be devoted to reflections on changes teacher candidates have experienced throughout, using journal entries and charts resulting from each session.

Performance-based assessment will be employed to assess the skills of teacher candidates in applying what they have learned. Teacher candidates will participate in the preparation of a rubric to assess their emerging competencies in the use of multimedia online resources for teaching about Jésus Colón, as evidenced in self-formed team presentations scheduled for session 6. It is anticipated that this rubric will focus on teacher candidates' level of preparation (knowledge), competencies in the use of technology, and oral and written communication skills, as evidenced in their presentation style, the written handouts, and the media selected (e.g., PowerPoint).

Objectives for Teacher Candidates

- Use online multimedia resources to distinguish between primary and secondary sources and to understand that primary sources provide alternative perspectives on historical experiences and events, particularly on groups that have been marginalized in society.

- Use criteria in judging online multimedia resources to understand that Jesus Colon was one of the first Puerto Rican writers to portray, in English, the day-to-day experiences of Puerto Rican migrants in New York City during the decades prior to the 1950s.

- Make personal connections to and analyze the literary style and content of selections from the published (*A Puerto Rican in New York*, 1961) and unpublished writings (from the Jesus Colon Papers housed in the archives of Centro Library and Archives).

- Use technology tools (e.g., Web tools, digital cameras, scanners, and photographs) to create knowledge products (e.g., a multimedia PowerPoint presentation on Jesus Colon) for audiences inside and outside the classroom.

Seven-Part Instructional Sequence

Session 1: Initial Experience. This session is designed to assess teacher candidates' awareness of the importance of reader-text interactions and to elicit their entry-level knowledge of online resources as a tool for learning.

- Divide the class into three groups and assign a different selection from Jesus Colon's *A Puerto Rican in New York* ("Books that Never Get Returned"; "Sarah"; ("What D'ya Read?"). Do not identify the author or source.

- Reader Response (Making Text-to-Self Connections): Respond by saying how this selection speaks (or does not speak) to you at this moment. Conduct an uninterrupted read-aloud to capture the range of reactions.

- Evaluation: "Would you recommend this selection to a peer? Why/Why not?"

- Chart responses on newsprint and date chart for future reference.

- Categorize responses (e.g., genre, literary style, characters, common human experiences, and/or questions participants may have about the text and/or author). Summarize recommendations.

- Conclude by commenting on the text-to-self connections I made when I first read the selections and that motivated me to want to know more about the author and to share him in this class.

- Probe: (1) "Do you know who Jesus Colon is? Why do you suppose you have not heard of him?" (2) "Why is he important to include in this course? How can we use his writings to help motivate students to have better relationships with the texts they read?" (3) "What clues do you have about the historical period when he wrote from this selection?" (4) "Where could you go to find out more about him?" List responses on experience chart and date.

- Assignment: Review nine sources on Jesus Colon and select three that present different facts about this author whom you find interesting and informative. Provide printouts of online sources and summarize all three in no more than one page, 10-point font.

- Reflective Writing: Comment to the content and process of this session in a double-sided journal entry (one column for content learning and the other for how you acquired the insight). All charts and journal entries will be used as evidence for emerging competencies and skills in the use of technological resources in the fifth and seventh sessions.

Session 2: Using Primary and Secondary Sources of Print Information to Learn about Jesus Colon. The purpose of this session is to assist teacher candidates to locate accurate, relevant, and appropriate information on Jesus Colon by modeling the selective and strategic use of online resources. It is preferable to conduct this session from a classroom equipped with the technological tools needed to review interactive Web sites. It is possible, however, to conduct this session from a classroom that lacks this equipment, using instead a computer linked to the Internet through a projection device.

- Prepare a chart with the categories "Books," "The Internet," and "A friend or colleague" along the top, and "Primary and secondary sources" along the side to create 3 × 2 charts. Have participants summarize on large Post-it notes the information and sources they located on Jesus Colon and place appropriately. Wait to see if course participants request to have any terms defined before probing.

- Review the sources participants used before presenting my summary chart and, if possi-

ble, demonstrate use of multimedia technologies. Compare our two sets of sources and evaluate each for clues to accuracy (e.g., source), relevance (e.g., application to the teaching-learning process), appropriateness (developmental/age), comprehensiveness (dimensions emphasized), bias (unbalanced representation) of electronic information sources, and criteria derived from the Technology Foundation Standards for Students (http://cnets.iste.org/students/s_stands.html). Highlight and identify the multimedia tools employed (e.g., sound, movement, music, artifacts). Conclude by eliciting which Web sites participants would prefer to use as learners and recommend to their peers. List preferred sites, date, and save for future reference.

My list includes the following sources:

1. Centro Library and Archives (www.centropr .org)

2. The Yale–New Haven Teachers Institute. "The Hispanic View of the Urban Setting" by Myrella Lara (www.yale.edu/ynhti/ curriculum/units/1981/1/81.01.05.x.html)

3. Facing History and Ourselves Online Campus. "Little Things Are Big," by Jesus Colon; Little Things Are Big: Connection Questions (www.facinghistorycampus.org)

4. LOTUS Magazine. "Jesus Colon: 100 Years Later Afro, Proud, Legacy Lives," by Ishmael Nunez (http://www.lulu.com)

5. Writing and Rhetoric: 151. A Collaborative Writing Project Employing Hypertextual Links. Instructor: Anne Bennington, Ohio University (http://oak.cats.ohiou.edu/sm589 402/eng151)

6. Cyberlinks to *Borinquen's Barrios & Bateyes* (http://www.nyboricua.com)

- Assignment: Using double-sided journal entry, summarize key insights on the content and learning strategies used to facilitate learning in one or more of the following Web sites:

1. Annenberg/CPB (http://www.learner.org/channel/workshops/primary sources/edi.html)

2. *History Matters: The U.S. Survey Course on the Web*. "Making Sense of Letters and Diaries" by Steven Stowe (http://www.historymatters.gmu.edu/mse/letters); "Making Sense of Photographs" by Frank Goodyear (http://www.historymatters.gmu.edu/mse/sia/photo.htm)

3. Centro Web site primary documents (www.centropr.org)

4. C-SPAN, *American Writers II*. "The 20th Century: Zora Neale Hurston, Langston Hughes and the Harlem Renaissance Writers" (http://www.americanwriters.org/writers/hughes_hurston.asp).

Session 3: Understanding and Using Visual (Non-print) Texts: An Introduction to the Jesus Colon Archives. This session is intended to provide an orientation to the Jesus Colon Collection housed at Centro Library and Archives.

- In light of what we discussed last session, why have I have arranged for us to meet at Centro Library today?

Jot down any questions would you like the archivist to answer and see how many of these are answered during the course of this presentation? Check those off as they are answered and jot down any new questions as you view the PowerPoint presentation.

- The archivist will explain what an archive is and the range of primary documents stored in Hunter's collection. He or she will also present samples from the Jesus Colon Collection from Series I: Personal and Biographical Information; Series II: Correspondence; Series III: Writings; Series IX: Photographs; Series X: Clippings. The archivist will model how historians read photographs and other non-print sources as these are being presented.

- Assign participants to one of five groups to review a specific series in the collection. Each will complete a journal entry in which he or she summarizes what was reviewed in a specific series.

- Assignment: Summarize the information acquired from our visit to Centro Library and comment on the processes by which you acquired this knowledge. You may use a double-sided journal entry. Write an email to the archivist at Centro expressing appreciation from what you learned and request copies of documents from the Jesus Colon collection that you found interesting and informative as a future educator. Explain how you plan on using these documents. Make sure that you offer to pay for documents requested. Forward to me a copy of your email.

Session 4: The Writer as Historian and Social Critic. The purpose of this session is to re-examine selections from the works of Jesus Colon available at Centro Library and Archives (1) to understand the historical contexts in which Jesus Colon's writings emerged and (2) to examine how these writings serve both to make sense of and to change the world.

- Given what we have learned about Jesus Colon thus far, what kinds of things did he know very well that you expect him to write about? Chart the ideas. Hand out copies of the story "Little Things Are Big" for participants to read silently.

- Reader Response: What new insights do you acquire about the historical context in which Jesus Colon lived from this selection? How does this selection support or refute the statement, "Writers help us to understand the world and to change the world"?

- Connections to Other Writers: What other writers would you compare to Jesus Colon? (List suggestions and how they are perceived to be similar.) Draw a comparison between Jesus Colon and Langston Hughes, a contemporary who shared much in common with this writer—both, for example, were black, were bilingual, held blue-collar jobs, experimented with a range of genres, and wrote about the American experience from their position in the world. Why are these writers important to all Americans?

- Application to Teaching: What are the lessons for you as a future teacher?

- Assignment: Read information presented on these Web sites and jot down *three Big Ideas* that you acquired about writers as historian and social critics:

1. Yale–New Haven Teachers Institute. "Artistic Justice: The Artist as Historian and Social Critic," by Medria J. Blue (http://www.cis.yale.edu/ynhti/curriculum/guides/1996/1/96.01.02.x.html)
2. Facing History and Ourselves Online Campus. "Little Things Are Big," by Jesus Colon (http://www.facinghistorycampus.org)
3. C-SPAN, *American Writers II*: "The 20th Century: Zora Neale Hurston, Langston Hughes and the Harlem Renaissance Writers" (http://www.americanwriters.org/writers/hughes_hurston.asp)

Session 5: Planning a Multimedia Presentation on Jesus Colon. The purpose of this workshop session is to enable teacher candidates time to meet with their self-formed groups and to prepare their multimedia PowerPoint presentation on what that they have learned about Jesus Colon that is of relevance to their students and is in keeping with curriculum requirements and standards for social studies, language arts, and reading.

Teacher candidates are to fashion their presentations following the *American Writers* series. We will review this Web site (http://www.americanwriters.org) to identify how each featured writer is described and presented. For example:

1. The life and times of the writer, including connections to or relationships with other writers
2. His or her works in context using photos and videos
3. Examples of primary source documents such as drafts of work-in-progress or unpublished manuscripts
4. Interviews with leading authorities
5. Links to relevant Web sites

I will then consult with each team for 15 minutes, and the teams may arrange to meet with technology specialists on staff at Hunter.

Teacher candidates will collaborate in the creation of a rubric to assess their multimedia presentation using technological resources and tools modeled in class, on the Web, and during our visit to Centro Library and Archives.

Session 6: Multimedia Presentations. Each group will present a 15-minute multimedia PowerPoint presentation which utilize information and strategies from transacting with nine multimedia Web sites reviewed this semester. The primary audience will be students and the secondary audience will be other practitioners. The groups will receive written feedback from their peers and from the instructor, and they will also assess their own presentations using the rubric developed collaboratively in class. Thus teacher candidates will play an important role in assessing their own learning from multiple perspectives and using multiple sources of data.

Session 7: Reflections on Our Experiences. All charts and documents that we prepared during the semester and that relate to this activity will be displayed. Teacher candidates will come to class with written summative reflections (no longer than three pages, 10-point font) on their experiences in this unit, including suggestions as to how this experience may be modified for future participants in this course. Insights from summative reflections will be used to redesign this module the subsequent semester.

Web Resources

Annenberg/CPB, http://www.learner.org/channel/workshop/primarysources/edi.html.

Bennington, Anne. Writing and Rhetoric: 151. A Collaborative Writing Project Employing Hypertextual Links. Ohio University, http://oak.cats.ohiou.edu/sm589402/eng151.

Berea College, http://www.berea.edu/ENG/browner/ww.city/ww.city.

Blue, Medria J. Artistic Justice: The Artist as Historian and Social Critic. Yale–New Haven Teachers Institute, http://www.cis.yale.edu/ynhti/curriculum/guides/1996/1/96.01.02.x.html.

Borinquen's Barrios & Bateyes, http://www.nyboricua.com.

Centro Library and Archives, Centro de Estudios Puertorriqueños, Hunter College, City University of New York, http://www.centropr.org.

Colon, Jesus. Little Things Are Big. Facing History and Ourselves Online Campus, http://www.facinghistorycampus.org.

Goodyear, Frank. Making Sense of Photographs. *History Matters: The U.S. Survey Course on the Web*, http://www.historymatters.gmu.edu/mse/sia/photo.htm.

Lara, Myrella. The Hispanic View of the Urban Setting. Yale–New Haven Teachers Institute, http://yale.edu/ynhti/curriculum/units/1981/1/81.01.05.x.html.

Multimedia Mania 2003—Judges' Rubric. North Carolina State University, http://www.ncsu.edu/midlink/mm2002.rubric.htm.

Night, by Elie Wiesel: Taking Action Against Indifference, http://www.teachnet-lab.org/fklane/pmaslow/night/night2.htm.

Nunez, Ishmael. Jesus Colon: 100 Years Later Afro, Proud, Legacy Lives. *LOTUS Magazine*, http://www.lulu.com.

Stowe, Steven. Making Sense of Letters and Diaries. *History Matters: The U.S. Survey Course on the Web*, http://www.historymatters.gmu.edu/mse/letters.

Technology Foundation Standards for Students. ISTE NETS Project, http://cnets.iste.org/students/s_stands.html.

Zora Neale Hurston, Langston Hughes and the Harlem Renaissance Writers. C-SPAN, *American Writers II*: The 20th Century, http://www.americanwriters.org/writers/hughes_hurston.asp.

Recommended Reading

Acosta-Belen, E., & Sanchez-Korrol, V. (Eds.). (1993). *The Way It Was and Other Writings*. Houston, TX: Arte Público Press.

Colon, J. (1961). *A Puerto Rican in New York and other Sketches*. New York: International Publishers.

Delgado, L. (1988). Rufa Concepcion Fernandez: The Role of Gender in the Migration Process. In F. V. Matos Rodriguez & Linda Delgado (Eds.), *Puerto Rican Women's History: New Perspectives* (pp. 171–180). Armonk, NY: M. E. Sharpe.

The Jesus Colon archives at Centro Library and Archives, Hunter College, City University of New York.

Padilla Aponte, E. K. (Ed.). (2001). *Lo que el pueblo me dice*. Houston, TX: Arte Público Press.

Carmen Mercado

TEACHER LITERACY

In a research study of literacy teachers (Rummel & Quintero, 1997) we learned about these teachers' family histories and saw glimpses of what sociologists and anthropologists call "positive social context." In other words, the magic of what families across cultures do best—care for, attend to, and love each other, regardless of conditions—has a lifelong effect. The teachers in our study brought the effects of their own families to their relationships with their students and to their teaching. They showed us how positive it is when educators are informed by families' knowledge. Family knowledge and literacy are the interwoven fabric of cultural practices. The art of this family knowledge and related literacy practice promotes strength, encourages nurturance, and supports risk taking.

Many teachers, like many well-known writers and visionaries (Allen, 1992; Walker, 1990) talk about the importance of the passing on of stories by parents and grandparents. In our study (Rummel & Quintero, 1997) one teacher smiled as she reported that her West Indian grandmother passed on teaching through folk tales. She also spoke at length about her mother's influence on her reading, in terms of modeling, interest, and actually providing trips to bookstores and libraries. Another teacher talked about both grandfather and grandmother. He noted that passing on stories in his American Indian community during his youth was done orally. They would gather around a campfire, and the eldest would talk; often it was the grandmother.

Listening

- Reflect and write about how you describe or define your personal and family identity. Write about thoughts you have about your own ethnicity, neighborhood, spirituality, nationality, or language. What is important and not important to you about this aspect of yourself and why?
- Now write about your earliest memories of this part of yourself that you just wrote about. What was enjoyable or painful as you learned about these aspects of your identity?
- Read the poems "Roots/Raíces" and "Las canciones de mi abuela/My Grandma's Songs" by Francisco X. Alarcón (1997).

Dialogue

- With a partner, discuss your own family stories and these poems. What connections can you make between your stories and those of the poet?

Action

- Read the following memory of one teacher education student:

I have many literacy memories prior to age 9. The most memorable was my grandfather's storytelling. I can remember the times when my siblings and I would gather around him as he would tell stories and folktales. We made sure that we were always prepared and well behaved in order to have an opportunity to hear a "cuento" or story. Although the stories lasted about 10 minutes, I felt like I was in an imaginary world for that amount of time. My grandfather had a story for everything, and every night he would tell a different story. The stories were about animals, children, or stories of when he was a child. Some of the stories he told were based from our home country. The stories I enjoyed the most were the ones that were not so real (which I did not know then). The one thing that was captivating was that my grandfather was completely involved while storytelling through facial expressions, voice, and movements. He never read a storybook to us, but he was full of never-ending tales.

Sadly enough, I can remember more negative than positive literacy experiences at school. At the time, I was an ELL. I did not receive much support from my teachers until I managed to acquire some English skills. The first positive experience I can remember, was in the third grade. My teacher kept me in the classroom during recess time to give me an opportunity to complete my essay "the right way." When I handed it to her, she praised me on an essay well done. That was my first essay written in English.

References

Alarcón, Francisco X. (1997). *Laughing Tomatoes and Other Spring Poems: Jitomates risueños y otras poemas de primavera*. San Francisco: Children's Book Press.

Allen, Paula G. (1992). *Grandmothers of the Light*. Boston: Beacon Press.

Rummel, M. K., & Quintero, E. P. (1997). *Teachers' Reading / Teachers' Lives*. Albany, NY: SUNY Press.

Walker, A. (1990). *The Color Purple*. New York: Pocket Books.

Elizabeth Quintero

TEACHERS AND ETHNIC IDENTITY

A review of literature provides a conceptual framework establishing the importance of ethnic identity and teachers as related to Latino education. Perceivably, a shared ethnic identity is an advantage bilingual education teacher brings into the dynamics of a classroom (Jackson, 1986; Snow, 1990; Valencia & Aburto, 1991). Second, how teachers view themselves and their ability to teach are other factors affecting student success (Ashton & Webb, 1986; DiBella-McCarthy, McDaniel, & Miller, 1995; Goddard, Hoy, & Hoy, 2000). We assume that if teachers are empowered, then they can teach more effectively. This development of self leads teachers to a better understanding of others and enhances their communication and social relationships with their students. If this, then, is the role of an efficacious teacher in a linguistically and cultural diverse setting, it is necessary to ascertain the psychological profile of potential teachers. The realization that the U.S. school population ethnic makeup is neither monolingual nor monocultural is a challenge for teacher educators to reconsider how to prepare future teachers. One pressing need is to increase the number of competent teachers prepared to deal with the changing realities of the classroom of today and tomorrow; therefore, an aspect of such teacher education is an emphasis on ethnic identity.

Issues of ethnic and cultural identity are clearly at the forefront of interdisciplinary studies throughout the U.S. Scholars have examined the role of ethnic identity in relation to social class and power (Alba, 1999; Castillo-Speed, 1995; Walters, 1999). An increasing number of empirical studies focus on culture in regard to racial and ethnic boundaries (Lamont, 1999). Research demonstrates the complexity of the changing boundaries of ethnic and racial groups and the challenges of cultural identity in multicultural school settings (Anzaldúa, 1987; García, 1997; Hondagneu-Sotelo, 1994; Pettman, 1996). Since schools play such a crucial role in racial and ethnic relations, the training of teachers takes priority (Lucas, Henze, & Donato, 1997; Milk, 1990; Darling-Hammond, 1995). The key issues created by multicultural environments in contemporary classrooms provoke the construction of racial/ethnic identities, gender roles, and socioeconomic status; the relationship of teacher to children from diverse backgrounds; and teachers' own sense of ethnic identity (Romo, 1999). Thus, teachers must be aware of the ways language, culture, and ethnicity mediate the social construction of identity. Furthermore, how teachers perceive the interactions of these constructs may affect the expectations they have of students. The social construction of identity is at the core of how teachers will come to understand the role of culture in shaping racial and ethnic relations.

Ethnic identity is defined as a "construct or set of self-ideas about one's own ethnic group membership; . . . ethnic identity is

an important domain of self-concept"
(Bernal et al., 1993, p. 33). Ethnic identity
formation, ethnic identification, language,
self-esteem, and degrees of ethnic consciousness and ethnic unconsciousness are
elements that comprise this complex and
multidimensional construct (Devereux,
1980). Ethnic identity is important for minority individuals as a means of identification (See Portes, 1996).

Bautista de Domanico, Crawford, & De
Wolfe (1994) reveal a positive relation between bicultural identity and self-concept,
yet negative relation to psychological discomfort. Bautista de Domanico and others
(1994) contend that bicultural Mexican
Americans have reduced feelings of isolation. Other studies suggest that having a
strong sense of identity and a bicultural
perspective assist ethnic minorities in attaining a positive psychological adjustment
(Phinney, 1991; Phinney, Williamson, &
Chavira as cited in Phinney, 1991).

Specifically, for both high school and
college students, a positive relationship is
evident between self-esteem and bicultural
identity (Phinney, Chavira, & Williamson,
1992). Montgomery (1992) found that
Mexican American students with a bicultural perspective might still have genuine
concerns about losing their cultural heritage
and Mexican identity. However, there may
be qualitative differences in ethnic adolescents' definition of bicultural identity
(Phinney & Devich-Navarro, 1997).

The *Who Am I (WAI)* is a reflective
exercise that assists the individual in an
exploration of self. Specifically, studies
have used the *WAI* format with college
students of different ethnicities to understand the role of ethnic identity as a self-
conceptualization factor (Hurstfield, 1978;
Lay & Verkuyten, 1999). Hurstfield infers
that an individual's self-conceptualization

includes ethnic membership and status. She
suggests that in comparison to non-minority
students, ethnic minority students are more
likely to be conscious of racial or ethnic
identity. As compared to black and Chicano
students, whites view themselves as more
individualistic. Lay and Verkuyten's (1999)
findings indicate Chinese students identified themselves by their country of birth
rather than as Chinese Canadian. These
studies thus support the saliency of ethnicity as a self-conceptualization factor.

Ethnic identity and self-concept are issues that likely confront ethnic minority
college students pursuing teacher preparation. An analysis of preservice bilingual
education teachers' *WAI* responses reveal
that the participants used an ethnic identification label to identify themselves only
when prompted (Clark & Flores, 2001).
Since the majority of the participants did
not spontaneously list ethnic identity within
their *WAI* responses, Clark and Flores
(2001) did not consider it be one of the
most salient factors for this group of preservice bilingual teachers. Nevertheless,
they noted a significant association between
the prompted ethnic identity label and self-
conceptualization ($p < .001$). Further analysis suggests that the preservice teachers'
preferred ethnic labels that resembled a
continuum from Mexican to American.
These findings are similar to Montgomery's
(1992) and Bautista de Domanico and colleagues (1994). Clark and Flores (2001)
posit that for preservice bilingual education
teachers, ethnic self-identification may be
an individualistic conceptualization reflective of the heterogeneity found within the
group. Therefore, these researchers suggest
that ethnic labels may not be necessarily
interchangeable for some individuals.

Clark and Flores express concern with
the preservice bilingual teachers' lack of

spontaneous ethnic identification, especially when there appears to be a link between conscious identity and teacher beliefs (Flores, 2001). Moreover, other researchers have demonstrated that bilingual teachers' competence is dependent on exploring, validating, and employing these cultural experiences within their occupational role (Galindo, 1996; Galindo, Aragón, & Underhill, 1996). As a result, Clark and Flores argue for the development of a strong ethnic identity as being an essential component of the teacher identity.

Another series of studies examined the ethnic identity of Mexican foreign-trained teachers who aspired to be bilingual teachers in the U.S. (Clark & Flores, 2000; Flores & Clark, 2004). In these studies, the researchers administered a Spanish version of the *Who Am I* (*WAI-S*) as a measure of self-concept and ethnic identity. The researchers found that although this group lived in the U.S., they had a strong national identity and prided themselves in being *Mexicanos.* Considering the importance of conscious ethnic identity, the researchers recommend that the curriculum include the sociocultural, political, and history experiences of ethnic minorities. They surmised that this would assist in developing a shared ethnic identity between the foreign-born teachers and their U.S.-born ethnic minority students.

For Mexican Americans and Mexican immigrants pursuing teacher credentials, these findings appear to support the importance of ethnic identity in defining self. Moreover, for this group, like all others, the process toward positive self-concept development and psychological adjustment includes cultural understanding of self and one's own cultural group (Bernal et al., 1993; Phinney, 1991). Lastly, for teachers, their stance toward ethnic identity should not be dismissed, as their cultural experi-

ences will likely determine their interactions with their students (Galindo, 1996; Galindo et al., 1996; Galindo & Olguín, 1996).

In sum, teachers having a similar cultural framework as their students are more attuned to their students' needs (Peña, 1997). Teachers must have not only similar cultural experiences, however, but also a "conscious" ethnic identity (Flores, 2001) and use these cultural connections with their students (Flores, Strecker, & Pérez, 2002). Moreover, several studies have shown that when children are provided with teachers from their own language and cultural groups, their academic achievement improves (see Snow, 1990). Jiménez, Gersten, and Rivera's (1996) case study revealed how a bilingual education teacher modulated her teaching practices specifically to meet the needs of her language minority students, and they exhibited success. Quiocho and Rios (2000) poignantly argued that minority group teachers bring a unique critical perspective to schooling because of their experiences. Lastly, Galguera (1998) noted that ethnic minority students preferred teachers whose bilinguality, cultural, and gender characteristics matched their own characteristics.

Thus, for teachers, ethnic identity cannot simply be ignored, for their cultural experiences define how they will interact with others (Galindo, 1996; Galindo et al., 1996; Galindo & Olguín, 1996). Conceivably, teachers with a strong sense of ethnic identity likely have an enhanced self-concept, which, in turn, provides empowerment (i.e., a sense of internal power or self-efficacy). They will likely see the group as possessing high vitality (Gao, Schmidt, & Gudykunst, 1994). Moreover, the degree of school success for ethnic students is affected by how teachers, as official members of the school, view and respond to cultural differences (Peña, 1997).

References

Alba, R. (1999). Immigration and the American Realities of Assimilation and Multiculturalism. *Sociological Forum* 14(1), 3–25.

Anzaldúa, G. (1987). *Borderlands/La Frontera: The New Mestiza.* San Francisco: Aunt Lute Books.

Ashton, P. T., & Webb, R. B. (1986). *Making a Difference: Teachers' Sense of Efficacy and Student Achievement.* New York: Longman.

Bautista de Domanico, Y., Crawford, I., & De Wolfe, A. (1994). Ethnic Identity and Self-Concept in Mexican-American Adolescents: Is Bicultural Identity Related to Stress or Better Adjustment? *Child and Youth Care Forum* 23(3), 197–206.

Bernal, M. E., Knight, G. P., Ocampo, K. A., Garza, C. A., & Cota, M. K. (1993). Development of Mexican-American Identity. In M. E. Bernal & G. P. Knight (Eds.), *Ethnic Identity: Formation and Transmission among Hispanic and Other Minorities* (pp. 31–46). Albany, NY: SUNY Press.

Castillo-Speed, L. (Ed.). (1995). *Women's Voices from the Borderlands.* New York: Simon & Schuster.

Clark, E. R., & Flores, B. B. (2000). Report on a Study of Normalistas' Ethnic Identity and Teaching Efficacy. *NABE News* 24(1), 20–22.

Clark, E. R., & Flores, B. B. (2001). Who Am I? The Social Construction of Ethnic Identity and Self-Perceptions of Latino Preservice Teachers. *The Urban Review* 33(2), 69–86.

Darling-Hammond, L. (1995). Inequality and Access to Knowledge. In J. A. Banks & C. A. McGee Banks (Eds.), *Handbook of Research on Multicultural Education* (pp. 465–483). New York: Macmillian.

Devereux, G. (1980). *Basic Problems in Ethnopsychiatry.* Chicago: University of Chicago Press.

DiBella-McCarthy, H., McDaniel, E. A., & Miller, R. (1995). How Efficacious Are You? *Teaching Exceptional Children* 27(3), 68–73.

Flores, B. B. (2001). Bilingual Education Teachers' Beliefs and Their Relation to Self-Reported Practices. *Bilingual Research Journal* 25(3), 275–299.

Flores, B. B., & Clark, E. R. (2004). Normalistas: A Critical Examination of Normalistas' Self-Conceptualization and Teacher Efficacy. *Hispanic Journal of Behavioral Sciences* 26(2), 230–257.

Flores, B. B., Strecker, S., & Pérez, B. P. (2002). Critical Need for Bilingual Education Teachers: The Potentiality of *Normalistas* and Paraprofessionals. *Bilingual Research Journal* 26(3), 687–708.

Galguera, T. (1998). Students' Attitude Toward Teachers' Ethnicity, Bilinguality, and Gender. *Hispanic Journal of Behavioral Sciences* 20(4), 411–428.

Galindo, R. (1996). Reframing the Past in the Present: Chicana Teacher Role Identity as a Bridging Identity. *Education and Urban Society* 29(1), 85–102.

Galindo, R., Aragón, M., & Underhill, R. (1996). The Competence To Act: Chicana Teacher Role Identity in Life and Career Narratives. *The Urban Review* 28(4), 279–308.

Galindo, R., & Olguín, M. (1996). Reclaiming Bilingual Educators' Cultural Resources: An Autobiographical Approach. *Urban Education* 31(1), 29–56.

Gao, G., Schmidt, K. L., & Gudykunst, W. B. (1994). Strength of Ethnic Identity and Perceptions of Ethnolinguistic Vitality among Mexican Americans. *Hispanic Journal of Behavioral Sciences* 16(3), 332–341.

García, A. (1997). *Chicana Feminist Thought: The Basic Historical Writings.* New York: Routledge.

Goddard, R. D., Hoy, W. K., & Hoy, A. W. (2000). Collective Teacher Efficacy: Its Meaning, Measure, and Impact on Student Achievement. *American Educational Research Journal* 37(2), 479–507.

Hondagneu-Sotelo, P. (1994). *Gender Transitions: Mexican Experiences of Immigration.* Berkeley: University of California Press.

Hurstfield, J. (1978). Internal Colonialism: White, Black, and Chicano Self-Conceptions. *Ethnic and Racial Studies* 1, 6–79.

Jackson, P. W. (1986). *The Practice of Teaching*. New York: Teachers College Press.

Jiménez, R. T., Gersten, R., & Rivera, A. (1996). Conversations with a Chicana Teacher: Supporting Students' Transition from Native to English Language Instruction. *The Elementary School Journal* 96(3), 343–352.

Lamont, M. (Ed.). (1999). *The Cultural Territories of Race: Black and White Boundaries*. Chicago: University of Chicago Press.

Lay, C., & Verkuyten, M. (1999). Ethnic Identity and Its Relation to Personal Self-esteem: A Comparison of Canadian-Born and Foreign-Born Chinese Adolescents. *Journal of Social Psychology* 139(3), 288–299.

Lucas, T., Henze, R., & Donato, R. (1997). Promoting in Success of Latino Language Minority Students: An Exploratory Study of Six High Schools. In A. Darder, R. D. Torres, & H. Gutierrez (Eds.), *Latinos and Education: A Critical Reader* (pp. 373–397). New York: Routledge.

Milk, R. (1990). Preparing ESL and Bilingual Teachers for Changing Roles: Immersion for Teachers of LEP Children. *TESOL Quarterly* 24(3), 407–426.

Montgomery, G. T. (1992). Comfort with Acculturation Status among Students from South Texas. *Hispanic Journal of Behavioral Sciences* 14(2), 201–223.

Peña, R. A. (1997). Cultural Differences and the Construction of Meaning: Implications for the Leadership and Organizational Contexts of Schools. *Education Policy Analysis Archives* 5(10). Available: http://oalm.ed.asu/epaa/v5n10.html.

Pettman, J. (1996). Border Crossings/Shifting Identities: Minorities, Gender and the State International Perspective. In M. Shapiro and H. Alker (Eds.), *Challenging Boundaries* (pp. 261–283). Alker: University of Minnesota Press.

Phinney, J. S. (1991). Ethnic Identity and Self-Esteem: A Review and Integration. *Hispanic Journal of Behavioral Sciences* 13(2), 193–208.

Phinney, J. S., Chavira, V., & Williamson, L. (1992). Acculturation Attitudes and Self-Esteem among High School and College Students. *Youth & Society* 23(3), 299–312.

Phinney, J. S., & Devich-Navarro, M. (1997). Variations in Bicultural Identification among African American and Mexican American Adolescents. *Journal of Research on Adolescence* 7(1), 3–32.

Portes, P. R. (1996). Ethnicity and Culture in Educational Psychology. In D. Berlinger & R. C. Calfee (Eds.), *Handbook of Educational Psychology* (pp. 331–357). New York: Prentice Hall International.

Quiocho, A., & Rios, F. (2000). The Power of Their Presence: Minority Group Teachers and Schooling. *Review of Educational Research* 70(4), 485–528.

Romo, H. (1999). *Reaching Out: Best Practices for Educating Mexican-Origin Children and Youth*. Charleston, WV: ERIC, Clearinghouse on Rural Education and Small Schools.

Snow, C. E. (1990). Rationales for Native Language Instruction: Evidence from Research. In A. Padilla, H. H. Fairchild, & C. M. Valadez (Eds.), *Bilingual Education: Issues and Strategies* (pp. 60–74). Newbury Park, CA: Sage.

Valencia, R. R., & Aburto, S. (1991). Competency Testing and Latino Student Access to the Teaching Profession: An Overview of Issues. In G. D. Keller, J. R. Deneen, & R. J. Magallán (Eds.), *Assessment and Access: Hispanics in Higher Education* (pp. 167–193). Albany, NY: SUNY Press.

Walters, M. (1999). Ethnic and Racial Identities of Second-Generation Black Immigrants in New York City. In C. G. Ellison & W. A. Martin (Eds.), *Race and Ethnic Relations in the United States: Readings for the 21st Century* (pp. 476–485). Los Angeles: Roxbury Publishing Company.

Recommended Reading

Bernal M. E., Saenz, D. S., & Knight, G. P. (1991). Ethnic Identity and Adaptation of Mexican-American Youths in School

Settings. *Hispanic Journal of Behavioral Sciences* 13(2), 135–154.

Bullough, R. V., Knowles, J. G., & Crow, N. A. (1989). Teacher Self-Concept and Student Culture in the First Year of Teaching. *Teachers College Record* 91(2), 209–233.

Burke, E., & Gottesfield, H. (1986). Internal Power and Individuality. *Psychological Reports* 59(2, pt. 2), 792–794.

Clark, E. R., & Flores, B. B. (2001). Who Am I? The Social Construction of Ethnic Identity and Self-Perceptions of Latino Preservice Teachers. *The Urban Review* 33(2), 69–86.

Flores, B. B., & Clark, E. R. (2002). *El desarrollo de Proyecto Alianza: Lessons Learned and Policy Implications*. Tempe, AZ: Center for Bilingual Education.

James, W. (1920). The Self. In *Psychology: The Briefer Course* (pp. 41–49). New York: Henry Holt.

Lucas, J. R., & Stone, G. L. (1994). Acculturation and Competition among Mexican-Americans: A Reconceptualization. *Hispanic Journal of Behavioral Sciences* 16(2), 129–142.

Meyer, M. M., Linnville, M. E., & Reef, G. (1993). The Development of a Positive Self-Concept in Pre-service Teacher. *Action in Teacher Education* 25(1), 30–35.

Phinney, J. S., Cantu, L., & Kurtz, D. A. (1997). Ethnic and American Identity as Predictors of Self-Esteem Among African American, Latino, and White Adolescents. *Journal of Youth & Adolescence* 26(2), 165–187.

Phinney, J. S., Chavira, V., & Tate, J. D. (1993). The Effect of Ethnic Threat on Ethnic Self-Concept and Own-group Rating. *The Journal of Social Psychology* 133(4), 469–479.

Phinney, J. S., Ong, A., & Madden, T. (2000). Cultural Values and Intergenerational Discrepancies in Immigrant and Non-immigrant Families. *Child Development* 7(2), 528–539.

Rentsch, J., & Heffner, T. (1992). Measuring Self-Esteem: Validation of A New Scoring Technique for "Who Am I?" Responses. *Educational and Psychological Measurement* 52(3), 641–651.

Ellen Riojas Clark and Belinda Flores

TECHNOLOGY ADOPTION AND EDUCATION IN NEW MEXICO

According to Census 2000 population growth projections, in the next 15 to 20 years the Latino population in the U.S. will eventually become the first minority majority. The growth rate among Latinos is higher than that of any other ethnicity. Furthermore, New Mexico is a borderland state whose ethnic majority is actually Latino. A testament to this is reflected in the historical fact that New Mexico is the only state of the Union to have a constitution in which English and Spanish are together the state's official languages. New Mexico, as well as other borderland states, has the historical conjuncture of offering the rest of the nation its experiences in adopting technology in schools with a dominant Latino population. Differences in culture, worldviews, and understandings within the Latino population are key elements to making the use of technology in the classroom either a full-blown success or an embarrassing failure and misuse of public funds.

Today there is a definite push to adopt technologies as multiple facets of day-to-day life (Aronowitz, 2001; Dickens, 1998; Holton, 1998; Castells, 1998, 2000, 2004). Education has not been immune to the technological dissemination of late twentieth century and the emergent twenty-first century (Apple, 1998; Aronowitz, 2001; Noble, 1998; Streibel, 1998). What is the purpose of such dissemination? What is its driving force? Whose interest does it serve?

This entry focuses on a local borderland initiative—the New Mexico Laptop Learning Initiative (NMLLI)—and considers its ramifications for the extant global economic order. Supported by Governor Bill Richardson, the NMLLI initiative was implemented early in 2004. This entry analyzes the NMLLI to explore whether it is guided by critical pedagogy theory or is just a cosmetic patch on our extant educational problems. How to do this?

The first step is to analyze the text of the laptop initiative itself. This gives a concrete reference point to underlying philosophies behind this initiative. A next step is to consider an external evaluation report conducted by David Rutledge and James Duran (2004). This report, given to New Mexico's Governor Richardson, exposed some of the general findings, advantages, and limitations of the NMLLI. Finally, several questions must be considered to determine if the initiative was used to foment emancipatory pedagogy for those affected by the initiative (Freire, 1971, 1996, 1998a, 1998b). Was this initiative used in ways for self-empowerment as defined by the community? Was this a top-down initiative, or was the community the key instigator? What is the purpose of such initiative? Who benefits? Are unequal relations of oppression eliminated or perpetuated? These are issues addressed throughout this entry, but first let's find out what the NMLLI entails.

NMLLI: How Did This Come About?

The New Mexico Public Education Department engaged in a meta-analysis of research on how technologies can enhance, enrich, and optimize students' performance in school. Thus the NMLLI is articulated so that our students will do better in school. This nonetheless appears a bit contradictory, for if the general premise is students' school performance, then why does the first sentence of NMLLI's document begin with this statement:

Governor Richardson proposes a dramatic initiative on the premise that technology and innovation play key roles in New Mexico's economic future and in enhancing learning opportunities for students and teachers. One of the strategies proposed by the Governor is not only to prepare youth to be viable contributors to the state's economy but also to advance the ideals of substantive educational reform through a statewide program that provides every seventh grade student and their teachers with laptop computers. (New Mexico Public Education Department, 2003, p. 1)

This document in fact initiates its text with an epigraph that affirms the invaluable nature of technology in the educational setting. This may appear a bit confusing, but it is not. Scholars like Giroux, McLaren, hooks, Aronowitz, Freire, and Carnoy, among countless others, have written extensively on how education reproduces the extant social order. Some works have a Marxist twist, suggesting that extant education deals with class reproduction (Carnoy, 1988; Freire, 1996, 1998a, 1998b; McLaren, 2005). It comes as no surprise that educational policies, and hence this initiative, are guided by hegemonic ways to perpetuate the extant social, political, and economic order through education and educational policies (Carnoy, 1988). (This subject is the topic in subsequent pages.)

Whom Does the NMLLI Service?

NMLLI is a multilayered approach for introducing education technology in New Mexico schools that is symbolic and appropriate for contemporary innovation. Through this initiative, 717 seventh grade students and 80 of their teachers received laptops in six separate schools in an effort to improve student learning. It is cautionary to mention that NMLLI was implemented for six weeks of instruction for some schools but up to three months for others; therefore, the results demonstrate changes in student learning for a varying and limited phase. Nonetheless, the program has concrete reference points and models. For instance, this initiative mirrors the Maine Learning Technology Initiative. In fact, Maine's laptop initiative became the sole inspiration for this one. Both base their initiatives on the importance of education as a producer of citizens who will "guarantee a better and more solid economy for our future with the use of technology." For instance, in Maine the initiative was intended to "transform Maine into the premier state for utilizing technology in kindergarten to grade 12 education in order to prepare students for a future economy that will rely heavily on technology and innovation" (Task Force on Maine's Learning Technology Endowment, 2001, p. vi).

Technology as a sole guarantor of a solid and stable economy echoes the discourse of political economists, who refer to information and communication technologies as the lifeline of advanced global capitalism (Dickens, 1998; Castells, 1998, 2000, 2004). In fact, this condition existed when we shifted from a post-Fordist mode of production to a flexible mode, all within the sociohistorical context of the Information Age (Castells, 1998, 2000, 2004; Dickens, 1998; Holton, 1998; Kloby, 1997). So whom does the NMLL service? Paradoxically, it undeniably serves to give students the skills necessary to survive in the modern workforce while simultaneously big corporations use the educational system to produce ideal workers for the Information Age workplace, where digital skills and literacy are crucial (Tyner, 1998; van Dijk, 2000).

It is important to note that thus far, the Regional Educational Technology Assistance (RETA) project and Intel Teach to the Future have provided technical assistance and professional development for teachers and schools participating in the NMLLI. The project has been directed by the Governor's Office, the New Mexico Public Education Department (NMPED), and the New Mexico Council on Technology in Education. New Mexico and most of the U.S. live with the reality of corporate and government liaisons that materialize in grants, policies, and initiatives. In this case we have state and federal institutions of both economic development and public education working in cahoots with corporations such as Intel to implement initiatives of technology dissemination that traduces itself in a more digitally literate populace (Tyner, 1998). For instance, the National Telecommunications and Information Administration (NTIA), which is under the umbrella of the Department of Commerce, was responsible for the disturbing report concerning the digital divide and its detrimental effects on society and the economy. The NTIA produced three major reports called "Falling through the Gap." The first one was published in 1995, the second in 1998, and the last in 2000. Ironically, instead of decreasing, the digital divide has increased exponentially. Given such a reality, the NMLLI makes more sense than ever as a proactive driving force to minimize the digital divide.

Although to judge this initiative as either critical or not might be premature, certain elements of rhetoric, justification, structure, and philosophy are definitely just business as usual for corporations and educational institutions. Furthermore, the NMLLI has room for improvement; if driven by a critical pedagogy, such an initiative can break from the factory model of producing ideal workers. As such, NMLLI pedagogical methods need to go hand in hand with a critical theory lens, methodology, and curriculum. Before fully deconstructing and reconstructing the NMLLI, however, let's focus on what researchers have found out about it.

General Findings of the NMLLI Report

After extensive research Rutledge and Duran (2004) found what they considered a level of generalizability with respect to the Main Learning Technology Initiative as a peer example of the NMLLI Implementation and Evaluation Plan (Sánchez, 2003). Rutledge and Duran found similarities between the Maine initiative and the New Mexico laptop initiatives, as evidenced in the implementation plan of the Maine initiative, as enumerated here:

1. [T]eachers report using the laptop in lesson development and classroom instruction.

2. [They are] locating more up-to-date information, accessing information more easily and quickly, presenting lessons, [and] creating lessons [utilizing technology] . . .

3. [Their] lessons are more extensive, use more up-to-date resources, and provide more opportunities to explore knowledge in more depth.

4. [Teachers have] dramatically increased the use of technology within the classrooms.

5. [Students are] using their laptops to research information, complete assignments, create projects, and communicate with teachers and other students . . .

6. [Teachers] report an increase in the amount of work [students] are doing.

7. [Teachers] report that [students] are more focused and more interested in school.

8. [S]chools are finding ways to minimize costs, and possibly save money [as] laptops replace [other] materials. (Maine Education Policy Research Institute, 2003)

Duran and Rutledge (2004) concurred that the NMLLI has replicated these desired results. So how did such guidelines manifest themselves here in New Mexico? Consider the following sections on (1) teachers and teaching and (2) students and learning.

Teachers and Teaching

Most teachers interviewed in Rutledge and Duran's (2004) report indicated their lessons and classroom instruction were planned using laptop computers. Furthermore, in many instances the teachers with more computer knowledge have been utilized by NMLLI; because of this, teachers with more technology experience routinely gravitate toward the program.

According to the report, teachers in the NMLLI were pleased with the opportunity to use their technological skills to prepare activities and instruction using their laptops. Teachers also reported using the laptop computers for various activities where modern applications of technology have become frequent. For instance, consider the words of some teachers interviewed by Rutledge and Duran (2004): "In my class I have used them [laptops] for research, Internet, Encarta, and also, word processing," from one, and from another, "In my classroom . . . I've used them also for research, we have done a stock portfolio type of thing and they have also done reflection papers" (p. 12). Such teachers have modified their pedagogical styles in one way or another, declaring that their teaching has been enhanced because "the laptops encourage a more advance level of order for the learners in arranging student writings and readings" (Rutledge & Duran, 2004, p. 10).

According to Jean van Dijk (2000), the introduction of new technologies will produce a new dynamic of reservations, resistance, and skepticism from those whom it will affect. Rutledge and Duran (2004) report that many teachers were concerned with their abilities to use the new technologies but nonetheless demonstrated an interest in learning more technological teaching practices through professional development. Here is how one teacher articulated this notion in Rutledge and Duran's (2004) report:

We all need to improve and the training.... One of our teachers is really apprehensive about technology, but he was right in the middle of the frog dissection, and he was impressed with what was going on. And he was learning from the kids, and we learned from the kids. And even before the laptops initiative, we took that class, a class on computer repair maintenance because we knew there was a need for us to be techno-literate. (p. 15)

The NMLLI, teachers were not unified in a single voice, however. Some were pleased, others were more concerned, and yet others saw and experienced a major breakthrough in terms of their instructional techniques and their students' performance. For instance, some of the teachers felt they were exceedingly savvy about technology and its teaching applications. These advanced technology teachers felt they needed additional training as well (Rutledge and Duran, 2004). It thus appears that the NMLLI is just the beginning of a broader technology implementation initiative for New Mexico. Since the NMLLI is in its initial stages, it comes as no surprise that some of these concerns were communicated about professional development. In addition, it is important to point out that professional development is in its infancy as well for this pilot project of NMLLI. Some NMLLI recipients were planning their professional development activities at

the time the interviews and focus groups were scheduled. Future professional development projects will have an undeniable impact on the delivery and instruction of digital curricula throughout New Mexico. NMLLI is just the beginning of things to come, and inserting a critical pedagogy agenda creates a Pandora's box of emancipatory possibilities.

Students and Learning

According to Tyner (1998), digital literacy is indispensable in modern U.S. society. As those who control the modes of production demand digital literacy, the multiple tiers of the educational infrastructure does the same. In the process of such impending transformations many in the field of education incorporate a new form of literacy, which in this case is a digital language, no longer something considered outside of us or foreign, but rather an integral part of who we are (Faigley, 1999; Gates, 2000; Tyner, 1998). This premise drives the technological transformation found in our educational infrastructure (Apple, 1998; Noble, 1998; Streibel, 1998). In this context the hype on technology is understandable given the sociohistorical backdrop of information and communication technologies as the nuts and bolts of advanced global capital (Castells, 1998, 2000, 2004; Dickens, 1998; Holton, 1998). For digital literacy to become mainstream, it must become a commodified form of knowledge that not only is produced and embraced by academia and society in general but becomes a regime of truth and common sense (Foucault, 2000). From an educational standpoint the discourse of NMLLI and its execution achieves the pervasive goal of introducing digital literacy over many peripheries of society. According to Rutledge and Duran (2004), such a phenomenon can be seen in the New Mexican adoption of technology, as can be inferred from the following interview excerpt:

And also their parents are more involved and their siblings are more involved. This laptop is not being exclusively used by the students, but their siblings are using them at home, and I think that it is increasing the interaction between students and parents. A lot of them are sharing, and like a lot of them have to take their pre-lab home, and they have to go over it with their parents. (p. 15)

Furthermore, it has been argued that technology can free us from traditional forms of teaching and pedagogy. But is it doing so? How? According to Rutledge and Duran (2004), the NMLLI has transformed the educational setting. It gives a more creative, hands-on element that lectures do not facilitate or nurture. In their words, "The increased intensity that comes with the laptop initiative, contrary to traditional laboratory-styled classrooms, is that technology is augmented in non-traditional learning spaces in addition to the classroom" (Rutledge & Duran, 2004, p. 14). According to Rutledge and Duran (2004), traditional teaching ceases when the child leaves the classroom and a hands-on mode of learning continues until the next classroom session. Under such potential it appears to be the case that the only limit of self-learning is time.

In every NMLLI school student recipients are using their laptops in locations other than their classrooms. Furthermore, as Rutledge and Duran (2004) found, the students reported using laptops for activities other than classroom assignments—for example, listening to music, watching DVDs, or surfing the Internet. Although some individuals may consider this a misguided use of educational resources, these

activities are positive because they support other functions vital to audio, visual, and research and digital literacies (Tyner, 1998). As students play, they are immersed in the learning process; the job of the teacher is realized by teaching the process and not by middle-managing the details of the learning. This has serious room for expansion, and a critical theory and critical pedagogy version of this methodology can be articulated within initiatives such as NMLLI. In the context of extremely high dropout rates and lack of relevance of the education experience, the NMLLI has found that providing students with laptops "has actually been a motivator for the students also to improve themselves," and, in another instance, "it seems like they are taking more responsibility towards their own learning" (Rutledge & Duran, 2004).

Based on the exposition of Rutledge and Duran (2004), the NMLLI undeniable has constructivist elements to its pedagogy (Vygotsky, 1978). It is interesting to see to what degree. Is this program really focusing on the social construction of knowledge, or is it a hegemonic co-option of constructivist learning theory? It is misleading to assume that just because the initiative has a hands-on component, it incorporates by default a critical educational process.

Looking for the Critical in NMLLI

Are we looking for a needle in a haystack? Under the guiding philosophy of economic development, NMLLI appears to lack critical components. Its stated purpose of education is like that of scholars such as Freire, Carnoy (1988), and McLaren (2005), who refer to the perpetuation process of the values, norms, and beliefs of the social, political, and economic components of the current social order, known as capitalism sugarcoated as democracy.

Education here becomes one of the most ever-present institutions in the socialization of youth into a hegemonic social order.

Consistent with the gloomy educational scenario of federal policies such as the No Child Left Behind Act of 2001 (NCLB), the NMLLI appears to perpetuate a traditional understanding of the purpose of education. Furthermore, information and computer technology have been characterized as a punitive and intrusive technology within the workplace (Apple, 1998; Aronowitz & Menser, 1996; Noble, 1998; Streibel, 1998). It has been argued that technology systematically displaces workers into conditions of unemployment and harsher working conditions (Apple, 1998; Aronowitz & Menser, 1996; Virilio, 1997). Does this apply to the NMLLI?

It is difficult to answer this question. We face a conundrum, for we can answer both yes and no. Technology has not yet resulted in the downsizing of the educational workforce. Seeing how the NMLLI is cheered by teachers and administrators as an instance where teachers use technology for their pedagogy leads one to ask why there is such celebration. Although not actually stated in the laptop initiatives reports of Maine and New Mexico, once educators adopt technology, they will be expected to be more productive. Although teachers love the fact that through technology they can stay tuned in to the current events of their academic fields, they will in time be expected to do so without their working conditions being improved substantially, other than that they now possess laptops. Does this mean that teachers will be submerged into a neo-Tayloristic and Fordist mode of production education-style? In such a context it is only a matter of time before such a phenomenon is corroborated with further research.

In addition, NMLLI has been characterized as a catalytic element that motivates unmotivated students. This is actually a positive side of NMLLI. Nonetheless, what is the nature of the students' assignments? Are they a continuation of drill-and-kill tactics that compose 95% of extant educational software (Apple, 1998)? If this is the case, then we are looking for a needle in the haystack. What are critical components of the NMLLI? Although it is premature to come up with a definite answer, one can say the NMLLI does have critical pedagogy elements in the making.

As Rutledge and Duran (2004) reported, however, students in the program are interacting with class materials in a different way. If such processes are not tarnished by drill-and-kill tactics but, instead, are used as a problem-posing methodology that forces students to engage in research elements of a critical pedagogy that nurtures critical consciousness, then students will surely bloom. This tentative phenomenon affirms that NMLLI have a very strong potential for critical pedagogy.

Unfortunately critical pedagogues have to make a dollar out of 15 cents. Under the current social reality they have to envision creative ways to subvert the educational system within its extant supra and micro infrastructures. Critical pedagogues engaging with the NMLLI see in it the potential to become a serious driving force for critical pedagogy striving for critical consciousness (Freire, 1998a, 1998b). To do this we have to create the ideal conditions to equip our students with the social skills and knowledge they need to survive in the real world while being transformative agents of their own realities (Freire, 1996). How they choose to survive, with its respective implications, should be the focus of the general education process. For instance, tactics exposed by Paulo Freire (1971), Stanley Aronowitz (1996), bell hooks (2003), Peter McLaren (2005), Henry Giroux (1992), and Michael Apple (1998), among others, force us to envision and materialize curriculum and pedagogical techniques that nurture critical thinking and embrace problem-posing education. Under such a vision, instead of hindering our students' ability to survive in the real world, we enable them to become transformative agents of their material conditions of existence (Freire, 1996). Consequently, they should abhor hypocritical democracy, slave wages and labor, social injustices and inequity, and a myriad of other social issues we confront daily. Students with access to the Information Age have the potential to make this society much better than it is.

NMLLI and other technology-related initiatives can problematize how technology affects us. Does our society benefit from it? How does technology affect our natural environment? Is this something we want? Technology-related initiatives can help us embrace the critical dimensions they bring into the forefront of current educational practices, policies, and funding. If, on the other hand, technology initiatives just perpetuate education as a cultural imperialistic and hegemonic tool, then such initiatives should be imploded and boycotted.

Students and teachers who use their state-provided laptops to embrace a critical pedagogy framework are taking a step in the right direction. Nonetheless, the guiding light of policies like NMLLI is not critical pedagogy but creative dissemination of technologies into the world of the marginal have-nots in order to guarantee social and economic stability. The use of technology as a key tool for economic development is insufficiently challenged by either critical scholars or those affected by the technology adoption. That technology is negative for our economic system, the environment, education, or society is seldom at issue. Yet dialogue regarding this is critically needed. Indeed, teachers should be given the time and resources to engage in an effective dialogue (Freire, 1996). This Freirian-influenced dialogue should focus on why educators ought to implement technology in their classrooms. How will such implementation look? What is its driving force? Whom will it benefit?

Given that the NMLLI is in its germinal stage, it is too early to judge the laptop initiative. The NMLLI needs time to develop so further research and analysis can scrutinize whether such an initiative has components of critical pedagogy. There is always room for hope, and certainly countless emancipatory and revolutionary possibilities may emerge from technology. Electronic civil disobedience, political activism, hacktivism, independent media, media activism, and future forms of virtual political activism and revolutions within the sociohistorical context of the Information Age—these, critical pedagogue can embrace, nurture, and foment (CAE, 1996; Castells, 1998, 2000, 2004; Jordan, 2002; McCaughey & Ayers, 2003; Meikle, 2002). Under the scenario of emancipatory technologies, access to information and information dissemination is vital for any form of social transformation (Castells, 2004; Jordan, 2002; McCaughey & Ayer, 2003; Meikle, 2002). NMLLI is in its infancy and has serious room for a critical pedagogy curriculum and pedagogical tactics that can foment the creation of critical thinkers, problem solvers, and transformative agents of their own reality. Educators need to embrace and articulate emancipatory possibilities as they become proactive cultural workers (Freire, 1998a, 1998b). They need to do this without hesitation, for the alternative is to disintegrate into despair while systematically killing humanity's driving forces: emancipation and hope (Freire, 1998a, 1998b).

Things can be done differently. We can live in a different reality, a different society; everything could be different. To this end education can become the praxis of emancipation (Freire, 1971; hooks, 2004). Herein is the eternal hope that intellectuals become integral planners of educational policies, curricula, and praxis, thereby embracing a future when our society will nurture and embrace an educational system, with its respective policies and institutions, governed by a problem-posing critical pedagogy theory. By doing so, we are being realist in doing the impossible. What do you think?

References

Apple, M. (1998). Teaching and Technology: The Hidden Effects of Computers on Teachers and Students. In L. Beyer & M. Apple (Eds.), *The Curriculum: Problem, Politics and Possibilities*. Albany, NY: SUNY Press.

Aronowitz, S. (2001). *The Last Good Job in America: Work and Education in the Global Technoculture*. New York: Rowman & Littlefield.

Aronowitz, S., & Menser, M. (1996). On Cultural Studies, Science and Technology. In S. Aronowitz (Ed.), *Technoscience and Cyberculture*. New York: Routledge.

CAE. (1996). *Brain Virus: Electronic Civil Disobedience and Other Unpopular Ideas*. Brooklyn, NY: Autonomedia.

Carnoy, M. (1988). *La educación como imperialismo cultural*. Mexico: Siglo XXI.

Castells, M. (1998). *La era de la información: Economía, sociedad y cultura*: Vol. 3, *Fin del milenio*. Madrid: Alianza.

Castells, M. (2000). *The Information Age: Economy, Society and Culture*: Vol. 1, *The Rise of the Network Society*. Australia: Blackwell.

Castells, M. (2004). *The Information Age: Economy, Society and Culture*: Vol. 2, *The Power of Identity*. Australia: Blackwell.

Dickens, P. (1998). *The Global Shift: Transforming the World Economy*. New York: Guilford Press.

Faigley, L. (1999). Beyond Imagination: The Internet and Global Digital Literacy. In G. Hawisher & C. Selfe (Eds.), *Passions Pedagogies, and 21st Century Technologies*. Logan: Utah State University Press.

Foucault, M. (2000). *Ethics, Subjectivities and Truth* (vol. 1). New York: New Press.

Freire, P. (1971). *La educación como práctica de la libertad*. Mexico: Siglo XXI.

Freire, P. (1996). *Pedagogy of the Oppressed*. New York: Continuum.

Freire, P. (1998a). *Education for Critical Counciousness*. New York: Continuum.

Freire, P. (1998b). *Teachers as Cultural Workers: Letters to Those Who Dare to Teach*. Boulder, CO: Westview Press.

Gates, B. (1999). *Business @ the Speed of Thought: Suceeding in the Digital Economy*. New York: Warner Books.

Giroux, H. (1992). *Border Crossings: Cultural Workers and the Politics of Education*. London: Routledge.

Holton, R. J. (1998). *Globalization and the Nation State*. London: Macmillan.

hooks, b. (2003). *Teaching Community: A Pedagogy of Hope*. London: Routledge.

Jordan, T. (2002). *Activism! Direct Action, Hacktivism and the Future of Society*. London: Reaktion Books.

Maine Education Policy Research Institute. (2003). *The Maine Learning Technology Initiative: Teacher, Student and School Perspectives Midyear Evaluation Report*.

McCaughey, M., & Ayers, M. (2003). *CyberActivism: Online Activism in Theory and Practice*. London: Routledge.

McLaren, P. (2005). *Capitalists and Conquerors: Critical Pedagogy Against the Impire*. New York: Rowman & Littlefield.

Meikle, G. (2002). *Future Active: Media Activism and the Internet*. London: Routledge.

New Mexico Public Education Department. (2003). *New Mexico Learning Laptop Initiative*. Santa Fe: New Mexico State Board of Education.

Noble, D. (1998). The Regime of Technology in Education. In L. Beyer & M. Apple (Eds.), *The Curriculum: Problem, Politics and Possibilities*. Albany, NY: SUNY Press.

Rutledge, D., & Duran, J. (2004). *New Mexico Laptop Learning Initiative Research and Evaluation*. Report presented to Gov. Bill Richardson, Santa Fe, NM, March–August.

Sánchez, S. (2003). *The New Mexico Laptop Learning Initiative*. Report presented to Gov. Bill Richardson, Santa Fe, NM.

Streibel, M. (1998). A Critical Analysis of Three Approaches to the Use of Computers in Education. In L. Beyer & M. Apple (Eds.), *The Curriculum: Problem, Politics and Possibilities*. Albany, NY: SUNY Press.

Task Force on Maine's Learning Technology Endowment. (2001). Available: http://www.maine.gov/legis/opla/mlte.htm.

Tyner, K. (1998). *Literacy in a Digital World: Teaching and Learning in the Age of Information*. London: Lawrence Erlbaum.

Van Dijk, J. (2000). *The Network Society*. London: Sage Publications.

Virilio, P. (1997). *El Fin del Internet*. Barcelona: Editoriales Paidos.

Vygotsky, L. (1978). *Mind in Society*. Cambridge, MA: Harvard University Press.

Recommended Reading

Bowers, C. A. (2000). *Let Them Eat Data*. Athens Georgia: University of Georgia Press.

Carnoy, M. (1988). *La educación como imperialismo cultural*. Mexico: Siglo XXI.

Freire, P. (1998). *Teachers as Cultural Workers: Letters to Those Who Dare to Teach*. Boulder, CO: Westview Press.

Giroux, H. (2000). Posmodern Education and Disposable Youth. In P. Pericles-Trifonas (Ed.), *Revolutionary Pedagogies: Cultural Politics, Instituting Education, and the Discourse Theory*. London: RoutledgeFalmer.

hooks, b. (1994). *Teaching to Transgress: Education as the Practice of Freedom*. London: Routledge.

hooks, b. (2003). *Teaching Community: A Pedagogy of Hope*. London: Routledge.

Kloby, J. (1997). *Inequality, Power, and Development: The Task of Political Sociology*. Atlantic Highlands, NJ: Humanities Press.

McCaughey, M., & Ayers, M. (2003). *Cyber-Activism: Online Activism in Theory and Practice*. London: Routledge.

Joseph Carroll-Miranda

TESTING: LANGUAGE AND CULTURAL ISSUES

Although problems with the validity of psychoeducational measures for Latinos and other linguistic minorities in the U.S. have been documented for many decades beginning in the early 1930s (Sanchez, 1932), comprehensive, sustained efforts to study and tackle these issues in large-scale testing were not intitiated until the 1980s. Padilla (1992) and Keller (1991) attributed the increase in measurement research on Latinos to the emergence of a critical mass of Latino children in the schools and of Latino researchers trained in psychometrics. Subsequently, the accretion of a substantial body of measurement research on Latinos by both mainstream and Latino researchers led to the incorporation of many new standards that addressed language and cultural issues in the development and uses of tests (American Educational Research Association, American Psychological Association, & National Council on Measurement in Education, 1999).

Recently, the No Child Left Behind Act of 2001 (NCLB) gave special impetus to research on assessment in elementary and secondary schools for English language learners (ELLs) because it holds school districts and schools accountable for the progress of ELLs in academic content areas and in English language proficiency. This act explicitly acknowledges that we must be able to assess the educational development of ELLs accurately if we are to provide a quality education for these students. However, there is now ample evidence that instruments designed to measure knowledge of academic content for native speakers of English may not provide accurate information for ELLs and, in some cases, may seriously underestimate their true skills. Hence, states have begun to adapt these instruments in order to facilitate the participation of ELLs in state assessments. This entry first summarizes empirical evidence of threats to test validity in the assessment of Latino students and ELLs, and then evaluates efforts thus far to adapt content tests to the needs of ELLs.

Factors Associated with Lower Test Scores for Latino Students

There is consensus among researchers that there are three major classes of variables associated with the substantial gap between Latino and mainstream students in mean scores on English language psychoeducational tests: differences in language background, cultural experiences, and family socioeconomic levels (e.g., Abedi, 2003; Duran, 1989; Llabre, 1991; Loyola, McBride, & Loyola, 1991, Mestre & Royer, 1991; Pennock-Román, 1992; Rodriguez, 1992; Schmitt & Dorans, 1991). From a scientific research perspective, the existence of mean differences between Latinos and mainstream students associated with these factors is insufficient evidence by itself to demonstrate lower

validity or bias for tests. Instead, it is necessary to demonstrate that these factors cause a distortion in test scores that is unrelated to the characteristics or traits we intend to measure. This distortion is known as construct-irrelevant variance, that is, variation in test performance that is unrelated to the construct, the latent skill or trait, that the measure is intended to assess within a particular situation or context. When there is lower validity and bias due to construct-irrelevant variance, test scores cannot be interpreted in the same way for Latinos as they are for mainstream students.

The importance of context for the evaluation of construct irrelevancy is illustrated by the interpretations of findings concerning the influence of socioeconomic status (SES) on test scores. Zwick (2002) has pointed to the correlations between SES and school grades to substantiate that SES reflects the quality of schooling. In the context of predicting college success, she argues that the variation in test scores due to SES is not bias, but is instead an index of the quality of students' preparation necessary for college that is relevant to the intended construct. In contrast, when using test scores for the diagnostic evaluation of speech and hearing disabilities, one can justifiably claim that the influences of SES and of the quality of previous schooling on scores can be considered a distortion that interferes with the detection of a disability. In those diagnostic situations, test scores cannot be interpreted in the same way for children differing in SES.[1] The following review focuses on how test performance is affected by language background and other cultural differences that have been associated with variations in test scores that are construct irrelevant to traits measured in most educational contexts.

Effects of Language Background on Test Performance

Language Factors That Increase Test Difficulty for ELLs. One source of evidence about the effects of language background on test performance comes from comparisons of the difficulty of pairs of test items matched for content but differing in complexity of language. Abedi (2004) reviewed the linguistic features associated with greater item difficulty for ELLs in a number of studies on mathematics and science tests. These included unfamiliar and infrequent words, overly long words and sentences, and a number of sentence structures such as passive voice constructions and conditional clauses. He concluded that certain "linguistic features slow down the reader, make misinterpretation more likely, and add to the reader's cognitive load, interfering with concurrent tasks [in answering an item]" (p. 7).

Another source are studies that gathered self-report data from ELL test-takers about their interpretation of items and their difficulties with particular wording of items. In the summary by Mestre (1986), student self-reports revealed a number of syntax features of word problems in Algebra I that were found to cause a greater number of misinterpretations for ninth grade Latino bilinguals. For example, "the phrase 'six times as many students as professors' was interpreted by test-takers to mean that there was an equal number of professors and students ('as many as') . . . the 'six times' in front of the statement was interpreted to mean that each side [of the equation] S = P should be multiplied by 6" (p. 168). That is, students wrote "6S = 6P," when the correct answer was "S = 6P."

Kellagahan and MacNamara (1968) found that reading time for arithmetic word problems in the weaker language was much slower, even when students displayed an understanding of each separate component of an arithmetic problem. These findings were explained by MacNamara (1967) in terms of the additional burden placed on short-term memory by the longer decoding process required to understand the components of the problem. Duran's review (1989) found evidence that bilinguals process information more slowly in their weaker language for a variety of problem-solving tasks, not just arithmetic problems. Pennock-Román (1992) argued that most tests have less generous time limits than those allowed for homework and classroom tasks, and that tests tend to sample performance in an artificial, speeded context for ELLs. Hence, to the degree that stringent time limits and other test administration conditions differ from natural academic settings, there is construct-irrelevant variance in test scores if those scores are supposed to represent students' academic skills in real contexts.

Estimates of Proportion of Construct-Irrelevant Variance for ELLs. In two studies of students in Puerto Rico who were non-native speakers of English (Alderman 1982; Pennock-Román, 2002), it was possible to directly measure the degree to which testing in the weaker language introduces construct-irrelevant variance. For both studies, scores on tests for admission to higher education were available from instruments in both Spanish and English, as well as scores on an English language proficiency test. Using regression analyses, the variance in student scores on each English language admissions test (e.g., quantitative score on the Graduate Record Examinations) was decomposed into two components: (1) the proportion that was predicted by the test for the same skill when measured in the native language, Spanish; and (2) the proportion of additional variance that was predicted by the measure of English proficiency (over and beyond the prediction achieved with the Spanish language tests alone). Given that the skills intended to be measured were not knowledge of English per se but reasoning and content in various subject areas, the latter quantity was an index of the proportion of construct-irrelevant variance. It was found that *all* English language tests used had substantial proportions of construct-irrelevant variance due to limited proficiency in the language of the test (from 8% to 15% for quantitative tests to 34%–36% for verbal reasoning tests).

Language Factors That Affect Test Performance for Latinos Proficient in English. Schmitt and Dorans (1991) reviewed several studies on item performance on the Scholastic Aptitude Test (SAT) for Latino examinees whose preferred language was English, although many had Spanish language backgrounds. They found that the presence of cognates and homographs in analogies and antonym items affected the relative performance of these students who were matched to the non-Latino group on overall scores on the test. Cognates are words that appear to have the same Latin origin root in two languages but can have similar or different meanings in the two languages depending on the context of the item. Homographs are words that are spelled alike but which have different meanings (e.g., "bark"). Schmitt and Dorans found that items containing English words that are true cognates for Spanish words were differentially easier for Latinos than for non-Latinos, particularly if the word had a higher frequency of usage in Spanish. For example, an antonym containing the true cognate *facilitate* with the

keyed answer choice being the true cognate *complicate* was differentially easier for Latino examinees. Conversely, items containing false cognates were sometimes differentially harder for Latinos than for non-Latinos on experimentally developed tests. For example, an antonym item with the word *charlatan* meaning "quack" in English was shown to be differentially more difficult for Latino examinees because *charlatan* in Spanish can also mean "talkative" in addition to "quack."

The presence of homographs has also proved to increase item difficulty for most minority groups who may be less familiar with all the variety of meanings for certain words. These effects have been attributed to the lack of context in vocabulary items (O'Neill & McPeek, 1993). That is, reading comprehension items provide greater context for understanding the intended meanings of words and phrases as compared with antonyms and analogies. As a result, reading comprehension items are less likely to show differential item performance across groups.

Language Background and the Prediction of Academic Achievement. Few studies have explored how language background may affect the predictive validity of English language tests for U.S. Latinos (see the review by Pennock-Román, 1992). Most research predicting the academic performance of U.S. Latinos using tests such as the SAT have included Latinos of varying levels of English proficiency as one group without examining language background as one of the variables in the analysis (Breland, 1979; Duran, 1983; Fuertes & Sedlacek, 1994; Pearson, 1993; Whitworth & Barrientos, 1990). Generally, these studies have found a slightly lower degree of relationship between academic grade point average and test scores in English for Latinos as compared with non-Latinos.

The studies by Zwick and Schlemer (2004) and Pennock-Román (1990) are exceptions in that they did consider language background in their analyses. There were very few Latinos with low proficiency in English for the Pennock-Román study because recent immigrants were excluded, whereas the Zwick and Schlemer study participants were more variable in language background. Both studies found that Latinos' college grades tended to be slightly lower than expected from their test scores and high school grades as compared with non-Latino white examinees. Also, both studies found that the effects of language background were not consistent across different samples. Specifically, the effects of language background in the Pennock-Román study had non-trivial contributions to prediction for two out of six universities (those with higher proportions of students with limited proficiency). However, the directions of the effects were not consistent across the two universities. Zwick and Schlemer found some differences in the accuracy of prediction that were associated with language background, but the differences were not consistent across years (1997–1998) of data within the same university.

A clearer pattern emerges in the more numerous studies on the effects of English language proficiency for non-native speakers of English from a variety of foreign countries at U.S. institutions of higher learning (see the summaries by Hale, Stansfield, & Duran, 1984; Hendel & Doyle, 1978; Ramist, Lewis, & McCamley, 1994; Wilson, 1986). Two consequences of English proficiency on the predictive validity of English language tests have been seen consistently. One, there is a lower accuracy of prediction for non-native speakers having low proficiency in English as compared

with those having higher proficiency or having native-level fluency. Two, the actual grades of ELLs tend to be higher than expected from their verbal scores in English, particularly in quantitative fields.

In sum, studies on the effects of language background on test performance show that the validity of a test depends on the students' level of proficiency with the language of the test. There is evidence that the content knowledge of students limited in English proficiency is underestimated by tests in their weaker language (particularly verbal tests). For these students with low proficiency in English, the relationship between test scores and other measures of achievement external to the test is weaker. Such effects are more subtle and inconsistent, with bilingual students at higher levels of proficiency. Nevertheless, there is evidence of construct-irrelevant variance in test scores and item scores, even for bilinguals at higher levels of proficiency.

Cultural Differences and Familiarity with Tests

There are at least three different ways in which cultural differences are associated with group variations in test performance. One has to do with familiarity with tests. Duran (1989) and Solano-Flores and Trumbull (2003) cite research examples to document instances where American Indian and African American students, African tribespersons, or unschooled Westerners may be unable to understand what is required of them in assessment tasks. "To perform as expected on tasks, persons have to first understand the social and cultural context of assessment situations, the modes of thinking expected, and the ways in which language is used in an assessment context" (Duran, 1989, p. 574). Rodriguez (1992) has underscored why training in test-taking skills is so important for Latinos who are less acculturated to an American lifestyle. He states, "Steeped as immigrants in a traditional culture where test taking is not customary, Hispanics come to the testing situation with a cultural disadvantage . . . a traditionally minded Hispanic is [not test-wise and does not understand] the implications of tests for future life chances" (pp. 13–14).

Another way in which culture may affect test performance is related to the type of skills that are viewed as important by a particular group. Geisinger (1992) points out that "cognitive abilities . . . differ in both quantity and pattern across groups. . . . That different cultural groups adopt different value systems, engage in different activities based on their values, and that these varying activities differentially affect the development of specific skills and abilities appears to be a most plausible explanation for the different ability profiles across groups" (pp. 36–37). A third way in which culture may influence test performance has to do with the familiarity with, and interest in, particular content included in a test. For example, Mestre and Royer (1991) reviewed several studies that indicated that familiarity with cultural experiences included in reading passages affected reading comprehension. Moreover, Schmitt and Dorans (1991) found that items from reading passages with content of special interest to Latino groups were differentially easier for Latinos as compared with non-Latinos matched on total score.

Familiarity with Timed Tests. Of these factors, the issue of experience with tests—testwiseness—has attracted the most research on Latinos. In their review of several studies, Schmitt and Dorans (1991) found evidence that Latinos may guess perhaps too often when taking multiple-choice tests

and that they may have difficulty with budgeting their time and completing tests with stringent time limits. Llabre (1991) synthesized a number of studies of time-related issues in the test performance of Latinos. She concluded that the evidence for narrowing the gap in mean test scores between Latinos and non-Latinos by relaxing time limits was not always consistent. However, a re-examination of the studies she reported does show some clear trends if one classifies studies according to the Latinos' degree of acculturation. Specifically, the studies that included recent immigrants or students who were identified as being non-native speakers of English did find a narrowing of the performance gap under unspeeded conditions. On the other hand, the studies with more acculturated Latinos who were highly proficient in English showed no narrowing of the performance gap by relaxing time limits. Hence, it appears that both language background and degree of testwiseness associated with acculturation can influence how well Latinos perform on tests with stringent time limits.

To meet the need for greater test preparation, the Hispanic Higher Education Coalition and the College Board collaborated on a test familiarization kit called TestSkills (Gaire, 1991). Preliminary feedback from students who trained with TestSkills revealed that it was very well received and that the experience gave them more confidence and motivation to attempt the SAT (Pennock-Román, Powers, & Perez, 1991). Unfortunately, many Latinos are still not exposed to test preparation courses and to adequate college counseling about test taking, despite the availability of tools such as TestSkills. For example, Gándara and López (1998) found that college-bound Latino students with good academic records had low awareness about the importance of college admissions tests and lacked adequate preparation for the SAT.

Measuring Language Proficiency

One critical issue is the determination of the level of proficiency at which students with non-English language backgrounds can be validly tested with instruments designed for non-native speakers of English. Often the decision to include or exclude ELLs from participation in large-scale testing is made on the basis of the number of years during which a student receives instruction in English, on the basis of teachers' judgments, or on the basis of scores from standardized tests of English language proficiency.[2] Although a formal evaluation with valid tests of English language proficiency is more standardized and objective across settings, the tests have been criticized on a number of grounds.

Problems with Language Proficiency Measures. Bailey and Butler (2002) believe that currently available standardized tests fall short of measuring the right type of formal, academic language skills: "The content of currently available commercial language proficiency tests is not adequate to measure the level of language proficiency necessary for taking standardized achievement tests and for full participation in the mainstream classroom" (p. 14). In addition, Abedi (2004) points out that the domain of language skills intended to be measured has not been adequately specified for most tests, with different versions linked to different conceptual frameworks.

Duran (1989) indicates that there has been a failure to establish expected reliability of measures and few, if any, studies of the associations between test performance and authentic language behavior in criterion settings have been conducted. Instead, validity studies have focused on using scores on other instruments and course grades, criteria that are convenient but redundant or inappropriate. School grades are not adequate criteria because academic performance depends on academic skills, not just language proficiency.

Another crucial flaw of commonly used, commercially available English language proficiency tests outlined by Duran is that the classification according to level of English language proficiency has yielded inconsistent results from test to test. For example, Ulibarri, Spencer, and Rivas (1981) found that nearly one-quarter of the students in the study taking the same three published tests were classified at *different* proficiency levels according to the three tests. Without a common conceptual framework and lacking a common external criterion to mark milestones in achieved proficiency, it is understandable why different tests vary in their classification of the same students. Abedi (2004) warns that similar problems may occur with the new generation of English proficiency measures being developed by states in order to comply with the NCLB requirement.

If a student has insufficient experience with English for using English language tests, it may be appropriate to consider whether that student ought to be tested in his or her native language. However, Spanish language proficiency measures are plagued by psychometric flaws similar to those of English proficiency measures (e.g., see the critique of the Pre-Language Assessment Scales Español by MacSwan, Rolstad, & Glass, 2002). In addition to the poor psychometric research on these tests, there is the added problem of inappropriate attention to the dialectical variations in Spanish for Latino children who emigrate from many different countries. The kind of variations in vocabulary, frequency of word use, and pronunciation that exist among English speaking countries such as Australia, the United Kingdom, and the U.S. also occur among the more than 20 Spanish-speaking countries. However, tests of Spanish proficiency frequently are developed for only one country-origin group but are applied, without adaptation, to Latino groups from other countries not included in the original normative sample.

For children learning English and their native language simultaneously in the U.S., traditional measures of language proficiency developed for monolingual students may assess their language skills in an incomplete manner. Loyola and colleagues (1991) have argued that any monolingual test may lead to depressed scores and an erroneous classification of Latinos whose everyday language use includes considerable language mixing. Furthermore, many Latinos growing up in the U.S. have no exposure to high-quality, rigorous training in formal Spanish owing to limited availability of educational programs that maintain and develop literacy skills in native languages. Loyola and colleagues point to one of the consequences of the lack of instruction in formal Spanish— the frequent use of anglicisms (e.g., using the term *marketa* for "market" instead of *colmado*) that are not recognized as true Spanish words in dictionaries and standardized Spanish versions of instruments. Hence, for some bilingual students a dual-language test administration may be the most appropriate choice, rather than trying to determine which one of the languages is the dominant one.

Test Accommodations for Bilinguals and ELLs

Once it is acknowledged that a student's proficiency in English is below the thresh-

old necessary for valid testing using the standard versions of content area tests, one is faced with the dilemma of choosing the most appropriate alternative among the many options allowed by states for test accommodations. Accommodations are changes to a test or testing situation intended to facilitate students' access to the content of the test while preserving validity of the test scores (see the comprehensive list by Rivera, Collum, Shafer, & Sia, 2006). As detailed by Rivera and colleagues, linguistic accommodations include various strategies such as the use of glossaries or customized dictionaries, simplification of the syntax and vocabulary of items presented in English, translation of tests (directions and/or items), and provision of dual-language booklets.[3] The research base for the evaluation of these accommodations is under development, and no clear guidelines have yet emerged. Recent syntheses of research (Abedi, 2004; Rivera et al., 2006; Sireci, Li, & Scarpati, 2003) indicate that there are 13 non-overlapping experimental studies on school-aged children in the U.S. that have contrasted the scores of ELLs with and without test accommodations.[4] Owing to the recentness of this line of research, the majority are summarized in technical reports (Abedi, Courtney, & Leon, 2003a, 2003b; Abedi, Hofstetter, Baker, & Lord, 2001; Abedi, Lord, Kim, & Miyoshi, 2001; Albus, Bielinski, Thurlow, & Liu, 2001; Anderson et al., 2000; Castellon-Wellington, 2000; Garcia, 2000; Hafner, 2000; Kiplinger, Haug, & Abedi, 2000), although there are a few published in journals (Abedi & Lord, 2001; Hofstetter, 2003; Rivera & Stansfield, 2004).

Commonly, the mean test performance of ELLs with accommodations is compared with the mean for ELLs without accommodation in content areas such as mathematics and science, usually for eighth and fourth graders. The majority of studies also include contrasts with the performance of non-ELLs to see if the achievement gap is narrowed when accommodations are used. The gains in performance when using accommodations for ELLs as compared with no accommodation at all were usually small,[5] although there have been a few larger effects that appear promising.

In particular, Abedi and colleagues (2003b) found a moderately large improvement in fourth graders' mathematics scores when the items included a pop-up glossary delivered by computer. Hofstetter (2003) found that test items in Spanish resulted in large improvement in mathematics test scores for eighth grade students who received mathematics instruction in Spanish. (However, the Spanish version was detrimental to performance for ELLs receiving mathematics instruction in English.) Providing extended time to complete items increased the means for both ELLs and non-ELLs, so that the achievement gap was not necessarily reduced. It would be interesting to see if the scores from unspeeded test administrations were more valid in the sense of having a stronger relationship to performance in the classroom. However, none of the studies have examined correlations between accommodated test scores and other measures of achievement such as teachers' grades. The findings from the study by Kiplinger and colleagues (2000) suggest that linguistic simplification is more effective at moderate levels of English proficiency than it is at the extremes, but most researchers have not studied this type of interaction between accommodation and level of proficiency.

When evaluating accommodations, these preliminary results should be viewed with caution for a number of reasons. First, there are limitations in sample sizes per accommodation studied; that is, even in large studies with several hundred ELLs, when a variety of accommodations are considered, the sample size per condition was sometimes less than 20. Second, the improvement in test performance for non-ELLs when using accommodations may appear larger than it should be because former ELLs with less than native-level proficiency in English may have been grouped with non-ELLs in the control groups. In most studies, the categorization of students into ELL and non-ELL categories was often provided by the school, despite inconsistent procedures for classifications across school districts and schools. Researchers who controlled for English language reading proficiency reduced the heterogeneity in language proficiency within samples and found more statistically significant results for the effects of accommodations. Third, the educational context constrains how much improvement we can expect in test performance from test accommodations. For example, Duran and colleagues (2002) noted that ELLs' poor performance in mathematics despite accommodations reflected a lack of exposure in the ELLs' classrooms to content covered by the tests. When students do not know the content because it is not covered in the curriculum, no amount of test accommodation will be able to raise mean scores. Thus, some of the studies may have found small effects owing to similar restrictions in other states.

Conclusions

In the last 15 years, major progress has been made in research on international testing and the psychoeducational assessment of Latinos. There is much greater awareness of the complex problems involved in the accurate assessment of Latinos who are so heterogeneous in degree of proficiency in English, degree of acculturation, immigration history, country of origin, and quality of schooling. Measurement specialists now explicitly recognize how factors such as language background and cultural differences may introduce construct-irrelevant variation in tests, and they have developed standards for tests that take these issues into account. The statistical and research methodology for evaluating the equivalence of translated and original versions of tests has been greatly developed. Efforts such as the drive to include ELLs in the National Assessments of Educational Progress and the NCLB legislation have drawn particular attention to the test accommodations in the assessment of ELLs in the K–12 context. This awareness and greater arsenal of methodological tools is a large step forward, but the problems in the accurate assessment of Latinos and test misuse are far from being resolved.

Notes

1. A more detailed review of SES and test scores would exceed space limitations. Other important topics in the educational measurement of Latinos that were omitted include the validity of teacher competency tests (but see Farrell, 1990; Flores and Clark, 1997; and Valencia and Aburto, 1991a, 1991b) and of tests used for placement in special education (but see Demsky et al., 1998; Loyola et al., 1991; and Ulibarri, 1982). Also, a discussion of problems and solutions in establishing equivalence between translated and original tests is not included here (but see Artiola i Fortuny & Mullaney, 1997; Camara, 1992; Geisinger, 1994; Gierl, 2000; Gierl, Rogers, & Klinger, 1999; Hambleton, 1994; Lopez and Taussig, 1991; Olmedo, 1981; and Sireci, 1997).

2. If years of schooling are used as a proxy for English language proficiency, Collier's (1987) findings suggest one cannot apply the same cutoffs when identifying limited English proficiency for students who arrive at different ages. She found that young children adapted more quickly, but those who arrived "at ages 12–15 experienced the greatest difficulty and were projected to require as much as 6–8 years to reach grade level norms in academic achievement when schooled all in the second language" (p. 617).

An informal, teacher-based assessment of language proficiency may lead to the mistake of judging skills in face-to-face communication as being sufficient for test-taking. A number of researchers (Bailey & Butler. 2002; Chamot & O'Malley, 1994; Cummins, 1980, 2000) have emphasized the need to distinguish between the level of proficiency necessary for face-to-face communications and the literacy and sophistication necessary for valid measures of academic work and cognitive skills. As pointed out by Mestre and Royer (1991), "face-to-face communication is easier to achieve because it is 'context-embedded' in the sense that there are many cues to aid communication (e.g., gestures and intonation, opportunities for clarification) . . . [whereas] much academic work [including tests] takes place within a 'context-reduced situation' " (p. 43).

3. Nonverbal tests are not appropriate for content area tests and thus not discussed here owing to space limitations. For the use of nonverbal tests in evaluating overall intelligence or for placement in special education, see Demsky et al., 1998; Loyola et al., 1991; and Ulibarri, 1982.

4. These 15 studies randomly assigned ELLs to conditions and therefore contrasted comparable groups. Two additional studies have provided descriptive statistics on ELLs' performance where there was no random assignment of ELLs to conditions (Abedi, 2003; Duran, Brown, & McCall, 2002). In these studies, the students assigned to receive test accommodations had lower English proficiency and were not comparable to the groups receiving the standard booklets.

5. I have calculated Cohen's d (effect sizes), that is, the difference in means between groups placing the difference into units of standard

deviations for non-ELL students. The effect sizes were "small" according to Cohen's (1998) criteria for categorization of effect sizes (usually less than one-third of a standard deviation). Some were close to zero in both negative and positive directions.

References

Abedi, J. (2003). *Impact of Student Language Background on Content-Based Performance: Analyses of Extant Data* (CSE Technical Report No. 603). Los Angeles: National Center for Research on Evaluation, Standards, and Student Testing. Available: http://www.cse.ucla.edu/products/reports_set.htm (accessed December 1, 2004).

Abedi, J. (2004). The No Child Left Behind Act and English Language Learners: Assessment and Accountability Issues. *Educational Researcher* 33(1), 4–14.

Abedi, J., Courtney, M., & Leon, S. (2003a). *Effectiveness and Validity of Accommodations for English Language Learners in Large-Scale Assessments* (CSE Technical Report No. 608). Los Angeles: National Center for Research on Evaluation, Standards, and Student Testing. Available: http://www.cse.ucla.edu/products/reports_set.htm (accessed December 1, 2004).

Abedi, J., Courtney, M., & Leon, S. (2003b). *Research-Supported Accommodation for English Language Learners in NAEP* (CSE Technical Report No. 586). Los Angeles: University of California, National Center for Research on Evaluation, Standards, and Student Testing. Available: http://www.cse.ucla.edu/products/reports_set.htm (accesed December 1, 2004).

Abedi, J., Hofstetter, C., Baker, E., & Lord, C. (2001). *NAEP Math Performance and Test Accommodations: Interactions with Student Language Background* (CSE Technical Report No. 536). Los Angeles: National Center for Research on Evaluation, Standards, and Student Testing. Available: http://www.cse.ucla.edu/products/reports_set.htm (accessed December 1, 2004).

Abedi, J., & Lord, C. (2001). The Language Factor in Mathematics Tests. *Applied Measurement in Education* 14(3), 219–234.

Abedi, J., Lord, C., Kim, C., & Miyoshi, J. (2001). *The Effects of Accommodations on the Assessment of Limited English Proficient Students in the National Assessment of Educational Progress* (Publication No. NCES 2001–13). Washington, DC: National Center for Education Statistics. Available: http://nces.ed.gov/pubs2001/200113.pdf (accessed December 1, 2004).

Albus, D., Bielinski, J., Thurlow, M., & Liu, K. (2001). *The Effect of a Simplified English Language Dictionary on a Reading Test* (LEP Project Report No. 1). Minneapolis: University of Minnesota, National Center for Educational Outcomes. Available: http://education.umn.edu/NCEO/OnlinePubs/LEP1.html (accessed December 1, 2004).

Alderman, D. A. (1982). Language Proficiency as a Moderator Variable in Testing Academic Aptitude. *Journal of Educational Psychology* 74(4), 580–587.

American Educational Research Association, American Psychological Association, & National Council on Measurement in Education. (1999). *Standards for Educational and Psychological Tests.* Washington, DC: American Psychological Association.

Anderson, M., Liu, K., Swierzbin, B., Thurlow, M., & Bielinski, J. (2000). *Bilingual Accommodations for Limited English Proficient Students on Statewide Reading Tests: Phase 2* (Minnesota Report No. 31). Minneapolis: University of Minnesota, National Center for Educational Outcomes. Available: http://education.umn.edu/NCEO/OnlinePubs/MnReport31.html (accessed December 1, 2004).

Artiola i Fortuny, L., & Mullaney, H. A. (1997). Neuropsychology with Spanish Speakers: Language Use and Proficiency Issues for Test Development. *Journal of Clinical and Experimental Neuropsychology* 4, 615–622.

Bailey, F. A., & Butler, A. L. (2002). Equity in the Assessment of English Language

Learners K–12. *Idiom* 32(1), 1, 3. Available: http://www.nystesol.org (accessed November 18, 2004).

Breland, H. (1979). *Population Validity and College Entrance Examination Measures.* New York: College Entrance Examination Board.

Camara, W. J. (1992). Fairness and Fair Use in Employment Testing: A Matter of Perspective. In K. F. Geisinger (Ed.), *Psychological Testing of Hispanics* (pp. 215–231). Washington, DC: American Psychological Association.

Castellon-Wellington, M. (2000). *The Impact of Preference for Accommodations: The Performance of ELLs on Large-Scale Academic Achievement Tests* (Technical Report No. 524). Los Angeles: University of California, National Center for the Study of Evaluation, Standards, and Student Testing. Available: http://www.cse.ucla.edu/CRESST/Reports/TECH524.pdf (accessed December 1, 2004).

Chamot, A. U., & O'Malley, J. M. (1994). *The CALLA Handbook: Implementing the Cognitive Academic Language Learning Approach.* Reading, MA: Addison-Wesley.

Cohen, J. (1988). *Statistical Power Analysis for the Behavioral Sciences* (2nd ed.). Hillsdale, NJ: Lawrence Erlbaum.

Collier, V. P. (1987). Age and Rate Acquisition of Second Language for Academic Purposes. *TESOL Quarterly* 21, 617–641.

Cummins, J. (1980). The Construct of Proficiency in Bilingual Education. In J. E. Alatis (Ed.), *Current Issues in Bilingual Education* (pp. 81–103). Washington, DC: Georgetown University Press.

Cummins, J. (2000). *Language, Power and Pedagogy: Bilingual Children in the Crossfire.* Clevedon, UK: Multilingual Matters.

Demsky, Y. I., Mittenberg, W., Quintar, B., Katell, A. D., & Golden, C. J. (1998). Bias in the Use of Standard American Norms with Spanish Translations of the Wechsler Memory Scale—Revised. *Assessment* 5(2), 115–121.

Duran, R. P. (1983). *Hispanics' Education and Background: Predictors of College Achievement.* New York: College Entrance Examination Board.

Duran, R. P. (1989). Testing of Linguistic Minorities. In R. Linn (Ed.), *Educational Measurement* (3rd ed., pp. 573–587). New York: American Council of Education, Macmillan.

Duran, R. P., Brown, C., & McCall, M. (2002). Assessment of English Language Learners in the Oregon Statewide Assessment System: National and State Perspectives. In G. Tindal & T. Haladyna (Eds.), *Large-Scale Assessment Programs for All Students: Validity, Technical Adequacy, and Implementation* (pp. 371–394). Mahwah, NJ: Lawrence Erlbaum.

Farrell, E. J. (1990). On the Growing Shortage of Black and Hispanic Teachers. *English Journal* 79(1), 39–46.

Flores, B. B., & Clark, E. R. (1997). High-Stakes Testing: Barriers for Prospective Bilingual Education Teachers. *Bilingual Research Journal* 21(4), 335–357.

Fuertes, J. N., & Sedlacek, W. E. (1994). Predicting the Academic Success of Hispanic College Students Using SAT Scores. *College Student Journal* 28(3), 350–352.

Gaire, L. (1991). The Development of Test-Skills: A Test Familiarization Kit on the PSAT/NMSQT for Hispanic students. In G. D. Keller, J. R. Deneen, & R. J. Magallán (Eds.), *Assessment and Access: Hispanics in Higher Education* (pp. 235–242). Albany, NY: SUNY Press.

Gandara, P., & Lopez, E. (1998). Latino Students and College Entrance Exams: How Much Do They Really Matter? *Hispanic Journal of Behavioral Sciences* 20(1), 17–38.

Garcia, T., with del Rio Paraent, L., et al. (2000). *Study of a Dual Language Test Booklet in Eighth Grade Mathematics: Final Report.* Washington, DC: American Institutes for Research, November.

Geisinger, K. F. (1992). Fairness and Selected Psychometric Issues in the Psychological Testing of Hispanics. In K. F. Geisinger (Ed.), *Psychological Testing of Hispanics* (pp. 17–42). Washington, DC: American Psychological Association.

Geisinger, K. F. (1994). Cross-Cultural Normative Assessment: Translation and Adaptation Issues Influencing the Normative Interpretation of Assessment Instruments. *Psychological Assessment* 6, 303–312.

Gierl, M. J. (2000). Construct Equivalence on Translated Achievement Tests. *Canadian Journal of Education* 25, 280–296.

Gierl, M. J., Rogers, W. T., & Klinger, D. (1999). Using Statistical and Substantive Reviews to Identify and Interpret Translation DIF. *Alberta Journal of Educational Research* 45, 353–376.

Hafner, A. L. (2000). *Evaluating the Impact of Test Accommodations on Test Scores of LEP Students and Non-LEP Students*. Dover, DE: Delaware Department of Education. Available: http://www.doe.state.de.us (accessed December 1, 2004).

Hale, G. A., Stansfield, C. W., & Duran, R. P. (1984). *Summaries of Studies Involving the Test of English as a Foreign Language, 1963–1982*. Princeton, NJ: Educational Testing Service.

Hambleton, R. (1994). Guidelines for Adapting Educational and Psychological Tests: A Progress Report. *European Journal of Psychological Assessment* 10(3), 229–244.

Hendel, D. D., & Doyle, K. O., Jr. (1978). Predicting Success for Graduate Study in Business for English-Speaking and Non-English Speaking Students. *Educational and Psychological Measurement* 38(2), 411–414.

Hofstetter, C. H. (2003). Contextual and Mathematics Accommodation Test Effects for English Language Learners. *Applied Measurement in Education* 16(2), 159–188.

Kellagahan, J., & MacNamara, J. (1968). Reading in a Second Language in Ireland. In D. Jenkinson (Ed.), *Reading Instruction: An International Forum—Proceedings of the 1st World Congress on Reading* (pp. 231–240). Newark, DE: International Reading Association.

Keller, G. D. (1991). Introduction: Advances in Assessment and the Potential for Increasing the Number of Hispanics in Higher Education. In G. D. Keller, J. R. Deneen, & R. J. Magallán (Eds.), *Assessment and Access: Hispanics in Higher Education* (pp. 1–37). Albany, NY: SUNY Press.

Kiplinger, V. L., Haug, C. A., & Abedi, J. (2000). *A Math Assessment Should Test Math, Not Reading: One State's Approach to the Problem*. Paper presented at the 30th annual National Conference on Large-Scale Assessment, Snowbird, Utah, June.

Llabre, M. M. (1991). Time as a Factor in the Cognitive Test Performance of Latino College Students. In G. D. Keller, J. R. Deneen, & R. J. Magallán (Eds.), *Assessment and Access: Hispanics in Higher Education* (pp. 95–104). Albany, NY: SUNY Press.

Lopez, S. R., & Taussig, I. M. (1991). Cognitive-Intellectual Functioning of Spanish-Speaking Impaired and Non-impaired Elderly: Implications for Culturally Sensitive Assessment. *Psychological Assessment* 3, 448–453.

Loyola, J. L., McBride, D. F., & Loyola, L. J. (1991). Cognitive and Linguistic Abilities of Puerto Rican Bilingual Children: Implications for Assessment. *Journal of Educational Issues of Language Minority Students* 8, 31–52.

MacNamara, J. (1967). The Effects of Instruction in a Weaker Language. *Journal of Social Issues* 23, 121–135.

MacSwan, J., Rolstad, K., & Glass, G. V. (2002). Do Some School-Age Children Have No Language? Some Problems of Construct Validity in the Pre-LAS Español. *Bilingual Research Journal* 26(2), 395–420.

Mestre, J. P. (1986). The Latino Science and Engineering Student: Recent Research Findings. In K. F. Geisinger (Ed.), *Psychological Testing of Hispanics* (pp. 157–192). Washington, DC: American Psychological Association.

Mestre, J. P., & Royer, J. M. (1991). Cultural and Linguistic Influences on Latino Testing. In G. D. Keller, J. R. Deneen, & R. J. Magallán (Eds.), *Assessment and Access:*

Hispanics in Higher Education (pp. 39–66). Albany, NY: SUNY Press.

Olmedo, E. L. (1981). Testing Linguistic Minorities. *American Psychologist* 36, 1078–1085.

O'Neill, K. A., & McPeek, W. M. (1993). Items and Test Characteristics That Are Associated with Differential Item Functioning. In P. W. Holland & H. Wainer (Eds.), *Differential Item Functioning: Theory and Practice* (pp. 255–276). Hillsdale, NJ: Lawrence Erlbaum.

Padilla, A. M. (1992). Reflections on Testing: Emerging Trends and New Possibilities. In K. F. Geisinger (Ed.), *Psychological Testing of Hispanics* (pp. 271–284). Washington, DC: American Psychological Association.

Pearson, B. Z. (1993). Predictive Validity of the Scholastic Aptitude Test (SAT) for Hispanic Bilingual Students. *Hispanic Journal of Behavioral Sciences* 15(3), 342–356.

Pennock-Román, M. (1990). *Test Validity and Language Background: A Study of Hispanic American Students at Six Universities.* New York: The College Board.

Pennock-Román, M. (1992). Interpreting Test Performance in Selective Admissions for Hispanic Students. In K. F. Geisinger (Ed.), *Psychological Testing of Hispanics* (pp. 99–135). Washington, DC: American Psychological Association.

Pennock-Román, M. (2002). Relative Effects of English Proficiency on General Admissions Tests versus Subject Tests. *Research in Higher Education* 43(5), 601–623.

Pennock-Román, M., Powers, D. E., & Perez, M. (1991). A Preliminary Evaluation of TestSkills: A Kit to Prepare Hispanic Students for the PSAT/NMSQT. In G. D. Keller, J. R. Deneen, & R. J. Magallán (Eds.), *Assessment and Access: Hispanics in Higher Education* (pp. 243–264). Albany, NY: SUNY Press.

Ramist, L., Lewis, C., & McCamley, L. (1994). *Student Group Differences in Predicting College Grades: Sex, Language, and Ethnic Groups* (College Board Report No. 93-1 and

Educational Testing Service Research Report No. RR-94-27). Princeton, NJ: Educational Testing Service.

Rivera, C., Collum, E., Shafer, L., & Sia, J. K., Jr. (2006). An Analysis of State Assessment Policies Addressing the Accommodation of English Language Learners. In C. Rivera (Ed.), *A National Review of State Assessment Policy and Practice for English Language Learners.* Mahwah, NJ: Lawrence Erlbaum.

Rivera, C., & Stansfield, C. (2004). The Effects of Linguistic Simplification of Science Test Items on the Performance of Limited English Proficient and Monolingual English Speaking Students. *Educational Assessment* 9(3, 4), 79–105.

Rodriguez, O. (1992). Introduction to Technical and Societal Issues in the Psychological Testing of Hispanics. In K. F. Geisinger (Ed.), *Psychological Testing of Hispanics* (pp. 1–16). Washington, DC: American Psychological Association.

Sanchez, G. I. (1932). Group Differences and Spanish-Speaking Children—A Critical Review. *Journal of Applied Psychology* 16, 549–558.

Schmitt, A. P., & Dorans, N. J. (1991). Factors Related to Differential Item Functioning for Hispanic Examinees on the Scholastic Aptitude Test. In G. D. Keller, J. R. Deneen, & R. J. Magallán (Eds.), *Assessment and Access: Hispanics in Higher Education* (pp. 105–132). Albany, NY: SUNY Press.

Sireci, S. G. (1997). Problems and Issues in Linking Assessments across Languages. *Educational Measurement: Issues and Practices* 16(1), 12–19.

Sireci, S. G., Li, S., & Scarpati, S. (2003). The Effects of Test Accommodations on Test Performance [Review of the literature. *Center for Educational Assessment Research*] Report No. 485. Amherst, MA: School of Education, University of Massachusetts, Amherst.

Solano-Flores, G., & Trumbull, E. (2003). Examining Language in Context: The Need for New Research and Practice Paradigms in the

Testing of English-Language Learners. *Educational Researcher* 32(2), 3–13.

Ulibarri, D. M. (1982). A Neo-Piagetian Approach to Test Bias: Final Report (Report No. NIEG7980155). Larkspur, CA: De Avila, Duncan & Associates. ERIC Document Reproduction Service No. ED223711.

Ulibarri, D. M., Spencer, M. L., & Rivas, G. A. (1981). Language Proficiency and Academic Achievement: A Study of Language Proficiency Tests and Their Relationship to School Ratings as Predictors of Academic Achievement. *NABE Journal* 5(3), 47–80.

Valencia, R. R., & Aburto, S. (1991a). Competency Testing and Latino Student Access to the Teaching Profession: An Overview of Issues. In G. D. Keller, J. R. Deneen, & R. J. Magallán (Eds.), *Assessment and Access: Hispanics in Higher Education* (pp. 167–194). Albany, NY: SUNY Press.

Valencia, R. R., & Aburto, S. (1991b). Research Directions and Practical Strategies in Teacher Testing and Assessment: Implications for Improving Latino Access to Teaching. In G. D. Keller, J. R. Deneen, & R. J. Magallán (Eds.), *Assessment and Access: Hispanics in Higher Education* (pp. 195–232). Albany, NY: SUNY Press.

Whitworth, R. H., & Barrientos, G. A. (1990). Comparison of Hispanic and Anglo Graduate Record Examination Scores and Academic Performance. *Journal of Psychoeducational Assessment* 8, 128–130.

Wilson, K. M. (1986). *The Relationship of GRE General Test Scores to First-Year Grades for Foreign Graduate Students: Report of a Cooperative Study* (GRE Board Professional Report GREB No. 82-11P and Educational Testing Service Research Report RR-86-44). Princeton, NJ: Educational Testing Service.

Zwick, R. (2002). Is the SAT a "Wealth Test"? *Phi Delta Kappan* 84(4), 307–311.

Zwick, R., & Schlemer, L. (2004). SAT Validity for Linguistic Minorities at the University of California, Santa Barbara. *Educational Measurement: Issues and Practice* 23(1), 6–16.

María Pennock-Román

TRACKING

Tracking is a system of separating students in schools based on their supposed intelligence, academic abilities, attitude, or aptitudes. Students are assigned to different educational tracks, where they are placed in different classes or in different "ability groups" within the same classroom. Ability grouping is a tracking practice in education that places students in different groups according to what are deemed differences in their abilities. They thus receive different educational contents at different levels. During the twentieth century, tracking practices were presented as a solution to the challenges brought about by the growing diversity in schools. The rise of school enrollment and the increase of immigrant students in most Western countries have made our classrooms more plural, attended by children with diverse cultural backgrounds, languages, home practices, and so on. In response, schools often place different children in different groups according to performance and achievement and provide them with adapted curricula with different expectations and goals. School tracking is based, then, on adapting to diversity rather than on transforming schools and their contexts in order to overcome existing inequalities. Furthermore, one of the most significant consequences of tracking is labeling students, as well as creating higher or lower educational expectations of them and promoting better or worse school preparation.

Research demonstrates that minority students, such as blacks and Hispanics in the U.S. and Canada or Romà in Europe, tend to be overrepresented in the lower groups. Although based on the argument that tracked classes adapt to students' prior knowledge and assure meaningful learning processes, tracking practices infact condemn these students to lower academic goals, thereby perpetuating existing inequalities. In contrast, high achievers' groups are highly represented by students from the dominant culture.

According to Vygotsky (1978), the sociocultural context influences learning processes; Mead (1932) sheds light on the idea that our thoughts and actions are highly connected to our social interactions, particularly on the generalized other or the perception other people have about our performance. Separating students and providing them with different adapted curricula, learning expectations, and academic referents and stimulations leads to a range of learning experiences and outcomes. Most children in the lower groups perform at lower level and believe they do not have the capacity to perform at a higher level. Moreover, the access or lack of access to resources and tools like the Internet and books, belonging or not to a college-educated family, and the existence of positive references and people who in our capacities play decisive roles our learning processes.

Studies have distinguished between two opposite hidden tracks (Oakes, 1985, 1990; Oakes & Lipton, 1992): the track to educational success, the so-called college track, and the track to failure, or the so-called prison track. These studies demonstrated that likely students take steps in one direction or the other, for instance, toward college or toward marginal and criminal activities. Those who have been segregated into lower performance groups or lower performance classes are likely to look for success in non-academic activities, reject schooling, or develop a counter-school culture as part of their identity. Many may not feel identified with school rejection, but their low achievement leads them to drop

out from school and they will consequently have less opportunities in the labor market and society in general. In contrast, students who followed a high achievement track usually belong to the dominant culture and receive more preparation for high school and college. In the current information society, education is key to avoid social exclusion, and educational practices that segregate children and adolescents into ability groupings, performance groupings, or language and cultural groupings end up tracking them down to marginalization.

In many contexts, special education groupings were thought to help children with learning disabilities, that is, with mental and/or physical handicaps. Progressively, we have witnessed higher rates of ethnic and language minority students being tracked into these programs. Furthermore, there are also remedial and vocationally oriented tracks, focused on manual and practical activities, which far from providing any intellectual knowledge and skills are oriented to precarious jobs in the labor market. When placed in these programs, minority students have been not only "tracked to failure" but also treated as handicapped individuals who have "special" needs or are "less intelligent." This result has brought on much criticism from different sectors of society.

Opposite to these practices are programs that promote inclusive education. Rather than segregating students by performance level, they consider diversity to be an added value to the education process and bring the resources of (language teachers, tutors, special educators, volunteers, and others, into the classrooms to work this out. Thus, they promote high standards of learning for all children, regardless of their differences.

Tracking is a common practice worldwide and starts at an early age (Oakes, 1985). Although this practice often begins in middle school or high school, we can easily find schools that separate students as early as second or third grade. In the U.S. two-thirds of schools have some ability grouping at seventh grade, and one-fifth track in every subject.

The Debate About Tracking: Arguments For and Arguments Against

Does ability grouping help students' achievement or hinder it? Are we faced with an educational model that provides solutions for all students, or is it a path that perpetuates existing inequalities? Arguments in favor of promoting different academic routes state that it benefits all students: those who are attaining good results in school and those who have learning difficulties. The "good" students can receive a challenging curriculum and develop their potential, avoiding boredom or lack of motivation to study. These arguments often follow from the belief that children with lower performance slow down the standards of the better prepared.

A negative consequence is that over the years the gap between students in the low ability tracks and the higher tracks gradually increases. Some students receive a less-demanding curriculum that has often been defined as a "curriculum for happiness," or for social skills development, based on music, theater, and art at a an undemanding level, in contrast to a curriculum that requires of students effort and competency. In this framework, one part of the student body is likely to access the most-valued knowledge while the rest are offered happiness and sociability. As a result, when these students reach high school, they lack the necessary preparation and academic tools to follow the most advanced courses that prepare them for college and therefore drop out.

The consequence of labeling students is another factor to take into account. Labels such as "difficult," "hyperactive," "slow," "different," and "dull" verbally exchanged between teachers and/or family members create preconceived low expectations of a child. According to Mead (1932), these symbolic interactions come to be internalized by a child or adolescent as the "generalized other," characterized by an image of less capacity and failure.

Vocationally oriented groups or lower-track classes are overrepresented by high percentages of black, Hispanic, and Native American students, whereas the academic tracks have higher representation of white, upper-middle-class students. Tracking is in fact more common in schools where there are a large number of African American or Latino students. This practice fosters a polarized, segregated educational system based on ethnicity and race. This unequal distribution of students helps to perpetuate existing inequalities between advantaged and disadvantaged students, marked by race and class, and even to institutionalize the gap. Ethnic origin, English language proficiency, and cultural differences seem, therefore, to lead to an unequal education.

The debate about tracking has generated a serious questioning of the effectiveness of ability grouping and its results. However, while far from a consensus, there is much scientific and practical evidence that upholds the exclusionary consequences of tracking for disadvantage students. Many argue that it is also a loss for students in the higher tracks, who miss out on the richness of sharing learning activities with diverse peers through a diversity of interactions. Based on research findings and low educational results shown by some students and groups, an increasing number of schools are carrying out a process of "detracking"

(Oakes, 1990; Oakes & Lipton, 1992), which is also being considered in current educational proposals and reforms.

The Path to Exclusion, and
The Path to Inclusion

In the early 1970s the U.S. government forbade some forms of ability grouping; however, tracking remains authorized. In the 1990s many research projects demonstrated tracking's negative effects. Ability grouping and similar practices based on curriculum differentiation within the same class have been identified as the first step on the path to exclusion. Following this comes tracking the "different" students into separate classes, and then finally comes tracking outside the school. These steps are grounded in the assumption that some students have deficits instead of capacities; for example, cultural and linguistic differences are seen as a problem and not as an enriching element in mixed classes.

The consequences of tracking contribute to increasing inequities in opportunity, perpetuating the class and racial gap. Research on school dropout and multicultural and multilingual school contexts has demonstrated the negative impact of tracking on students from cultural minorities and low socioeconomic status. Educational experiences that fight inequities and promote the inclusion of marginalized groups, such as blacks and Hispanics, close the class and racial gaps that tracking have often opened, overcoming school failure and conflicts. Educators and schools are gradually implementing actions based on inclusion rather than segregation. As a result, they are currently detracking schools, moving toward practices that are inclusive and prioritize all students' academic success. Inclusive education practices and proposals depart from a critical standpoint that ques-

tions traditional homogeneous schooling. They defend that working in mixed classes or heterogeneous groups benefit all students, particularly when stressing cooperative learning and peer exchange and support. A student who explains to another how to do a particular task, for example, is not really repeating; rather, he or she is trying to organize knowledge and must rationalize it to be able to verbalize a comprehensible explanation. To explain a procedure or a concept to somebody who does not know it is an intellectually highly demanding task. This is possible when the student body is diverse. While sharing learning, students in heterogeneous classes are also developing aspects such as teamwork, solidarity, respect for difference, and communicative skills. This approach moves away from the competitiveness and stigmatization attached to tracking practices, and it offers dimensions of learning that are hardly present in homogeneous groups.

Experiences in the inclusive school culture—cooperative learning and dialogic learning, for example—are demonstrating that equal opportunities and inclusion can be guaranteed for all students (i.e., advantaged, disabled, from different cultural backgrounds, and of different socioeconomic status). The participation of other adults—that is, family and community members, other educators and volunteers—in the school and the classrooms is a common feature in many inclusive educational practices. One example such are *interactive groups* (Elboj, Puigdellívol, Soler, & Valls, 2002), a type of classroom organization involving heterogeneous groups (i.e., students of different cultures, languages, learning paces, etc.) work together in collaboration. Rather than segregating children at different levels or differentiating their curricula, a number of adults enter the classroom to help the teacher to promote peer interaction and cooperation among students to conduct and solve learning activities. Community members' to support of children's learning thus becomes an added value to schools through the inclusion of diverse discourses and languages and closer interactions linked with high motivation for schooling. Inclusive practices such as the interactive groups combine instrumental learning with the dynamics of solidarity, enhancing success and high academic standards for all and using the richness of diversity to achieve goals. This form of learning moves away from the exclusionary effects of tracking, and by drawing from a perspective of equality of differences and inclusion provides more educational opportunities for all children.

References

Elboj, C., Puigdellívol, I., Soler, M., & Valls, R. (2002). *Comunidades de aprendizaje: Transformar la educación.* Barcelona: Graó.

Mead, G. H. (1932). The Philosophy of the Present. Available: http://spartan.ac.brocku .ca/~lward/Mead/pubs2/philpres/ Mead_1932_toc.html.

Oakes, J. (1985). *Keeping Track: How Schools Structure Inequality.* New Haven, CT: Yale University Press.

Oakes, J. (1990). *Multiplying Inequalities: The Effects of Race, Class, and Tracking on Opportunities to Learn Math and Science.* Santa Monica, CA: RAND.

Oakes, J., & Lipton, M. (1992). Detracking Schools: Early Lessons from the Field. *Phi Delta Kappan* (February), 448–454.

Vygotsky, L. S. (1978). *Mind in Society. The Development of Higher Psychological Processes.* Cambridge, MA: Harvard University Press.

Recommended Reading

Aubert, A., Duque, E., Fisas, M., & Valls, R. (2004). *Dialogar y transformar: Pedagogía crítica del siglo XXI.* Barcelona: Graó.

Braddock, J. H. (1990). *Tracking: Implications For Student Race-Ethnic Groups* (Report no. 1). Baltimore: Johns Hopkins University, Center for Research on Effective Schooling for Disadvantaged Students (ED 325 600).

Oakes, J., & Lipton, M. (1992). Detracking Schools: Early Lessons from the Field. *Phi Delta Kappan* (February), 448–454.

Orfield, G., & Lee, Ch. (2004). *Brown* at 50: King's Dream or Plessy's Nightmare? (January). Available: http://www.civilrightsproject.harvard/reseg04/brown50.pdf (accessed April 20, 2005).

Willis, P. (1990). *Common Culture Symbolic Work at Play in the Everyday Cultures of the Young.* Boulder, CO: Westview Press.

Adriana Aubert

TRANSNATIONAL LATINO FAMILIES

In the U.S. today children of immigrants comprise the fastest-growing segment of the under-18 population—one out of every five children is the child of immigrants (Levitt & Waters, 2002). In addition, the fastest-growing group of children in U.S. public schools is Latino (Suárez-Orozco & Páez, 2002); over 60% of these Latino children are of immigrant stock, meaning that either they or one (or both) of their parents was born in another country (Rumbaut, 2002).

To be sure, present-day immigration is primarily comprised of the "new" or post-1965 wave of immigration—primarily composed of immigrants of color from Asian and Latin American countries. Most of these newcomers are Latino and becoming part of communities not traditionally viewed as immigrant-receiving (Wortham, Murillo, & Hamann, 2002) as well as settling in more traditional areas. Many of these immigrants, under globalization, can potentially live transnationally without having to sever ties to their countries of origin. Glick Schiller, Basch, & Blanc-Szanton (1992) advance the notion of transnationalism as a social process in which transmigrants develop and maintain "multiple relations"—familial, economic, social, organizational, religious, and so on—across two or more societies: the home country and the new nation of settlement.

Unlike many European immigrants who came to the U.S. at the turn of the century, immigrants in the twenty-first century are able to carry out transnational lives because of "shorter" distances between the U.S. and their natal communities. While the geographic space remains the same between immigrant-sending countries and the U.S., telecommunications, airplane transportation, money-wiring services, and improvements in basic infrastructure in home countries greatly reduce the time and space between immigrants here and family back home. This type of transnational migration is said to have accelerated in the last 20 years as a result of the communications revolution precipitated by the spread of capitalism and the fall of the Soviet Union (Giddens & Hutton, 2002).

These new ways of acculturating to the U.S., while maintaining close ties to countries of origin, are often left out of discussions and research on immigrant students and public schooling. What many educators do not realize is that globalization and transnationalism have changed the places and modes of incorporation for many recent immigrants, in particular Latinos. Thus, the implications for language and culture in this context are great and sorely understudied.

Brief Review of Immigration Scholarship and Transnationalism

Immigration scholars in the last century have utilized several theories to address the incorporation process of different immigrant groups in the U.S. This work has contributed to our views on how persons with different backgrounds (ethnicities, languages, cultures, and countries of origin) experience their settlement in the U.S. Efforts to document and describe the settlement process of newcomers have often coincided with the different waves of immigrants this country has experienced. In the earlier part of the twentieth century, for example, "classic assimilation" became prominent in describing different European immigrants during this wave of immigration.

Later on, immigration research began to pay closer attention to the "sending" and "receiving" context of immigrants' home countries and the new destination of settlement. Scholars advanced the notion that the factors that "pushed" immigrants to leave their home countries were as relevant as the factors that "pulled" them to settle in the U.S. The sending community factors included such variables as immigrants' levels of formal education, their past occupations, and the social and economic conditions of their countries of origin (war, civil strife, natural disaster, or unemployment crisis). But perhaps more importantly, researchers began to consider the social and economic climate of the receiving community experienced by immigrants. That is, they examined the immigrant social network (social capital and human resources) available to new arrivals as well as the government's reception of these immigrant groups (Brittain, 2002; Menjívar, 2000; Portes, 1995; Stepick, 2003). Four layers of reception were considered: individual human and social capital, the immigrant network or ethnic enclave, the local U.S. community, and the national or federal reception (Portes, 1995).

Much of the literature that looks at the sending and receiving context of immigrants in the U.S. has continued to gain momentum since the 1970s and 1980s. In the 1990s, however, Portes and Zhou (1993) put forth the concept of "segmented assimilation," which further delineates the paths of incorporation immigrant groups may follow in their new receiving context. These researchers contend that newcomers can enter one of three segments in society: (1) integration into the white middle class; (2) downward mobility and incorporation into the underclass; and (3) a middle space of economic advancement with preservation of certain ethnic traits. Segmented assimilation and classic assimilation (along with close examination of the sending and receiving context) help us understand in more detail the settlement process of immigrants in the U.S. These theories, however, do not shed any light on how newcomers maintain ties to their homelands if at all.

Today it is more common to understand how immigrants do in fact preserve strong links to their countries of origin. This new wave of studies has utilized "transnationalism" as a conceptual framework. Much of the literature on transnationalism has demonstrated that in an increasingly globalized world, many migrants have both the ability and the desire (as well as the need) to preserve connectivity to their countries of origin through an economic, political, religious, or familial manner while still becoming members of another nation-state. Indeed, to do justice to the multi-straddled lives that immigrants live today all across the world, it is critical that educators not only consider the traditional ways newcomers incorporate or assimilate but also closely look at the ways in which they maintain ties to their homelands. This is true not only of adult actors but also of children and youth and entire families as well.

The Case of Transnational Latino Families

In the case of Latino transmigrants, several groups have been immigrating, and in a sense, living "transnationally" for decades. This is particularly true for many Mexican and Dominican immigrants who have traditionally sustained close ties to their homeland through regular visits to *la patria* or *la república*. In the last 20 years or so—as a consequence of civil war and natural disaster—many Central Americans have immigrated to the U.S. and have begun to lead transnational lives as well. Cubans, in contrast, could be viewed as leading a unique "emotional transnationalism" (Espiritu & Tran, 2002) more akin to living in diaspora because of the difficulty of visiting Cuba resulting from U.S. sanctions or because of their rejection of their homeland because of personal political beliefs. Puerto Ricans, too—though often not considered "transnationals" because of Puerto Rico's status as a U.S. territory—lead lives of connection to their home community as migrants who circulate between the mainland and the island.

Within transnational Latino families there is as much heterogeneity as there is among Latinos themselves. In general, though, there are two configurations of families living a life of transnationalism: those whose members are physically spread across two countries and those who reside permanently in one country as a "family" but maintain close contact to the country of origin. In both cases, the type of transnationalism each family experiences is often predicated upon economic position and legal immigration status. In the case of some Dominicans, for example, there may be elite families whose fathers regularly conduct business in both the U.S. and the Dominican Republic and have the money and the legal status to shuttle across international borders regularly as an entire family. In another example, a working-class Guatemalan family may have one parent and two children in Florida while the other parent is in Guatemala raising another child, waiting to reunite with those in the U.S.

Still, other examples include working-class Mexican families whose immediate members live in California but have ties to extended family in Mexico so great that even undocumented status may not hinder their visiting their *pueblo* every three or four years; instead, these families save considerable money for their return entry into the U.S. In addition, families who have survived separation for two, three, or five years often reunite, with children undergoing many adjustments not only to their new country but to parent(s) whom they have not seen in a long time or stepparent(s) whom they have never met. In the latter case, these new guardians suddenly became authority figures in their lives because of a parent's remarriage upon immigration to the U.S.

While the social institution of family is an important lens through which to view transnational Latinos, the ways language and culture are strengthened and reshaped within this context are also critical in the study of immigrant students—whether they be first-, second-, or part of the 1.5-generation. Families experiencing their lives spread across two nation-states utilize transnationalism in their parenting, disciplining, and socialization strategies, as do their children in their shifting constructions of identity. These negotiations are spread over an entire childhood and even a lifetime. And as long as globalization proceeds at its current pace, many Latino immigrant families will continue to be reconfigured in the process.

References

Brittain, Carmina. (2002). *Transnational Messages: Experiences of Chinese and Mexican Immigrants in American Schools.* New York: LFB Scholarly Printing LLC.

Espiritu, Yen Le, & Tran, Thom. (2002). "Viet Nam, Nuoc Toi" ("Vietnam, My Country"): Vietnamese Americans and Transnationalism. In Peggy Levitt & Mary Waters (Eds.), *The Changing Face of Home: The Transnational Lives of the Second Generation* (pp. 367–398). New York: Russell Sage.

Giddens, A., & Hutton, W. (2002). *En el limite vivir en el capitalismo.* Barcelona: Tusquets.

Glick Schiller, Nina, Basch, Linda, & Blanc-Szanton, Cristina. (1992). Transnationalism: A New Analytic Framework for Understanding Migration. In Nina Glick Schiller, Linda Basch, & Cristina Blanc-Szanton (Eds.), *Towards a Transnational Perspective on Migration* (pp. 1–24). New York: New York Academy of Sciences.

Levitt, Peggy, & Mary C. Waters (Eds.). (2002). *The Changing Face of Home: The Transnational Lives of the Second Generation.* New York: Russell Sage Foundation.

Menjívar, Cecilia. (2000). *Fragmented Ties: Salvadoran Immigrant Networks in America.* Berkeley: University of California Press.

Portes, Alejandro. (1995). Segmented Assimilation among New Immigrant Youth: A Conceptual Framework. In R. Rumbaut & W. Cornelius (Eds.), *California's Immigrant Children: Theory, Research, and Implications* (pp. 71–77). San Diego: Center for U.S.-Mexican Studies, University of California.

Portes, Alejandro, & Zhou, Min. (1993). The New Second Generation: Segmented Assimilation and Its Variants. *Annals of the American Academy of Political and Social Science* 530 (November), 74–96.

Rumbaut, Rubén G. (2002). Severed or Sustained Attachments? Language, Identity, and

Imagined Communities in the Post-immigrant Generation. In Peggy Levitt & Mary C. Waters (Eds.), *The Changing Face of Home: The Transnational Lives of the Second Generation*. New York: Russell Sage Foundation.

Stepick, Alex. (2003). Immigrants, Race, and Power in Miami: Reconfiguring Relations. Paper presented at the University of California, Berkeley, Center for Latin American Studies, November 20.

Suárez-Orozco, Marcelo M., & Páez, Mariela M. (Eds.). (2002). *Latinos: Remaking America*. Berkeley: University of California Press.

Wortham, S., Murillo, E., Jr., & Hamann, E. T. (Eds.). (2002). *Education in the New Latino Diaspora: Policy and the Politics of Identity*. Westport, CT: Ablex.

Recommended Reading

Basch, Linda, Glick Schiller, Nina, & Szanton Blanc, Cristina. (1994). *Nations Unbound: Transnational Projects, Postcolonial Predicaments, and Deterritorialized Nation-States*. Amsterdam: Gordon & Breach Publishers.

Brittain, Carmina. (2003). Crossing Borders in the School Yard: The Formation of Transnational Social Spaces among Chinese and Mexican Immigrant Students. Center for Comparative Immigration Studies. Working Paper, no. 76. Available: http://repositories .cdlib.org/ccis/papers/wrkg76.

Dueñas C., Tomasa, Dueñas T., Tomasa, López, Montserrat, & Sánchez, Patricia. (forthcoming). *Recordando mis raíces y viviendo mis tradiciones/Remembering My Roots and Living My Traditions*. New York: Scholastic.

Fouron, Georges, & Glick Schiller, Nina. (2001). All in the Family: Gender, Transnational Migration, and the Nation-State. *Identities: Global Studies in Culture and Power* 7(4), 539–582.

Georges, Eugenia. (1992). Gender, Class, and Migration in the Dominican Republic: Women's Experiences in a Transnational Community. In Nina Glick Schiller, Linda Basch, & Cristina Blanc-Szanton (Eds.), *Towards a Transnational Perspective on Migration* (pp. 81–99). New York: New York Academy of Sciences.

Goldring, Luin. (1998). The Power of Status in Transnational Social Fields. In Michael P. Smith & Luis E. Guarnizo (Eds.), *Transnationalism from Below* (pp. 165–195). New Brunswick, NJ: Transaction Publishers.

Goldring, Luis. (2001). The Gender and Geography of Citizenship in Mexico-U.S. Transnational Social Spaces. *Identities: Global Studies in Culture and Power* 7(4), 501–537.

Guarnizo, Luis E., Portes, Alejandro, & Haller, William. (2002). Transnational Entrepreneurs: The Emergence and Determinants of an Alternative Form of Immigrant Economic Adaptation. *American Sociological Review* 67, 278–298.

Hondagneu-Sotelo, Pierrette, & Avila, Ernestine. (1997). "I'm Here, But I'm There": Transnational Latina Motherhood. *Gender & Society* 2(5), 548–571.

Levitt, Peggy. (2001). *The Transnational Villagers*. Berkeley: University of California Press.

Mahler, Sarah J. (2001). Transnational Relationships: The Struggle to Communicate across Borders. *Identities: Global Studies in Culture and Power* 7(4), 583–619.

Mahler, Sarah J., & Pessar, Patricia R. (2001). Gendered Geographies of Power: Analyzing Gender across Transnational Spaces. *Identities: Global Studies in Culture and Power* 7(4), 441–459.

Márquez, Raquel, & Romo, Harriet (Eds.). (forthcoming). *Transformations of La Familia on the U.S.-México Border Landscape*. Notre Dame, IN: University of Notre Dame Press.

Matthei, Linda M., & Smith, David A. (1998). "Belizean Boyz'n the 'Hood"? Garifuna Labor Migration and Transnational Identity. In Michael P. Smith & Luis E. Guarnizo (Eds.), *Transnationalism from Below* (pp. 270–290). New Brunswick, NJ: Transaction Publishers.

Orellana, Marjorie F., Thorne, Barrie, Chee, Anna, & Lam, Wam Shun Eva. Transnational Childhoods: The Participation of Children in Processes of Family Migration. *Social Problems* 48(4), 573–592.

Park, Kyeyoung. "I'm Floating in the Air": Creation of a Korean Transnational Space among Korean-Latino American Remigrants. In *Asian Transnationalities* (special issue) 7(3), 667–695.

Petrón, Mary A. (2003). "I'm bien pocha": Transnational Teachers of English in México. Ph.D. dissertation, University of Texas at Austin.

Rouse, Roger. (1992). Making Sense of Settlement: Class Transformation, Cultural Struggle, and Transnationalism among Mexican Migrants in the United States. In Nina Glick Schiller, Linda Basch, & Cristina Blanc-Szanton (Eds.), *Towards a Transnational Perspective on Migration* (pp. 25–52). New York: New York Academy of Sciences.

Sánchez, Patricia. (2001). Adopting Transnationalism Theory and Discourse: Making Space for a Transnational Chicana. *Discourse: Studies in the Cultural Politics of Education* 22(3), 375–381.

Sassen, Saskia. (1998). Toward a Feminist Analytics of the Global Economy. In S. Sassen (Ed.), *Globalization and Its Discontents: Essays on the New Mobility of People and Money* (pp. 81–109). New York: New Press.

Smith, Michael P., & Guarnizo, Luis E. (Eds.). (1998). *Transnationalism from Below*. New Brunswick, NJ: Transaction Publishers.

Smith, Robert C. (1998). Transnational Localities: Community, Technology and the Politics of Membership within the Context of Mexico and U.S. Migration. In Michael P. Smith & Luis E. Guarnizo (Eds.), *Transnationalism from Below* (pp. 196–240). New Brunswick, NJ: Transaction Publishers.

Srensen, Ninna Nyberg. (1998). Narrating Identity across Dominican Worlds. In Michael P. Smith & Luis E. Guarnizo (Eds.), *Transnationalism from Below* (pp. 241–269). New Brunswick, NJ: Transaction Publishers.

Suárez-Orozco, Marcelo M. (2001). Globalization, Immigration, and Education: The Research Agenda, *Harvard Educational Review* 71(3).

Suárez-Orozco, Marcelo M., & Qin-Hilliard, Desirée Baolian. (2004). *Globalization: Culture and Education in the New Millenium*. Berkeley: University of California Press.

Villenas, Sofía. (2002). Reinventing *Educación* in New Latino Communities: Pedagogies of Change and Continuity in North Carolina. In Stanton Wortham, Enrique Murillo Jr., & Edmund T. Hamman (Eds.), *Education in the New Latino Diaspora: Policy and the Politics of Identity* (pp. 17–35). Westport, CT: Ablex.

Patricia Sánchez

TWO-WAY BILINGUAL EDUCATION PROGRAMS

Our purpose in this entry is to build a case supporting two-way bilingual (TWB) education programs as (1) the best research-based and educationally applied model to meet the culturally and linguistically diverse needs of Latino/a students, who are immigrant English language learners (ELLs); (2) an equal educational opportunity for reducing the high dropout rates among Latino/a students and the academic achievement gap between majority and minority students.

The main section of this entry makes the case that TWB programs, when implemented effectively as high-quality research-based educational programs, can meet the No Child Left Behind (NCLB) Act of 2001 mandates by reducing the academic achievement gap of Latino students of low socioeconomic status (SES) who are immigrant ELLs. This section presents a synthesis of a critical literature review on TWB programs by discussing major data-based reports showing that TWB programs can effectively increase academic English language proficiency and academic achievement across content areas in Latino/a immigrant ELLs. TWB programs do work provided they are implemented by knowledgeable educators acting as committed advocates working under supportive administrative leadership at their local education agencies (LEAs) and state education agencies (SEAs), and within the supportive sociocultural context of a school and community partnership. It is important to understand that the use of first language (L1) for instruction can accelerate academic English language proficiency levels, resulting in higher developmental and learning outcomes and ultimately higher academic achievement levels. Thus, the main section synthesizes research studies supporting the use of L1 and second language (L2) as a method of instruction for stimulating ELLs to become additive bilinguals and for reducing their risk of underachievement because of their low SES and other family structure factors.

Bilingual Education: Equal Educational Opportunity for ELLs

The Bilingual Education Act of 1968 started the legitimization of the need to provide L1 instruction for ESL learners in order to provide equal educational opportunities for them. In the *Lau v. Nichols* case the Supreme Court ruled support of bilingual education for ELLs. The *Lau* suit validated the case of unequal educational opportunities suffered by Chinese American students in a public school district in San Francisco that offered English-only instruction.

Still today this social problem persists, with the hot political debate of offering non-English language instruction for new immigrant ESL students in public schools. Mainstream educational views still see schooling as the traditional social institution to "Americanize" or assimilate new immigrants. Minority leaders and contemporary educational data-based studies support maintenance of cultural and linguistic diversity in new immigrant and minority students as part of the rich multicultural, multilingual, multiracial "new mainstream America." Thus, the educational challenge of reducing the achievement gap among ELLs mandated by NCLB legislation is also tinted with a social and political debate of what are the best educational models to increase academic achievement in at-risk Latino students. Next is made a case for TWB educational programs as the best research-based educational alternative for providing an equal educational opportunity for Latino, immigrant, ELLs at risk of underachievement and dropping out of school.

A Case for Two-Way Bilingual Education Programs

The National Association for Bilingual Education (NABE) endorses as a best-quality education model those TWB programs that (1) use both L1 and L2 as a method of instruction; and (2) use valid and reliable authentic assessments linked to instructional goals, within a five-year timeline according to the readiness level of individual ELLs (Gonzalez, Yawkey, & Minaya-Rowe, in press). High-quality TWB programs comply with NCLB mandates because they promote academic English language proficiency and adequate academic achievement progress across content areas according to grade-level standards (Gonzalez et al., in press). The quality of TWB programs is squarely related to the quality of (1) training of teachers and their degree of cultural and linguistic competence to use L1 and L2 and the minority and mainstream cultures as methods of instruction and (2) school leadership and support to develop partnerships with the community and parents of ELLs.

Studies show that ELLs whose parents refuse bilingual or ESL educational services show large decreases in reading and math achievement by grade 5. Cross-sectional findings indicate that the largest number of ELL dropouts comes from this group, and those ELLs remaining finish school near the 12th percentile on standardized reading tests (National Center for Education Statistics, NCES; Thomas & Collier, 1997). School districts across the nation often struggle to convince parents that denying bilingual services to ELLs is detrimental to their long-term academic achievement and English academic language learning. Bilingual education continues to receive criticism in the local and national media, and as a result parents are misinformed and continue to deny these services to their children.

There are several reasons why denying bilingual education services to ELLs may have potentially negative effects on their academic achievement and English academic language learning. First, if bilingual education is denied, English monolingual instruction does not respond to the *educational needs* of Latino/a students, who are at risk of underachievement because of their low-SES backgrounds. Findings from a large number of research studies from the 1980s and 1990s (e.g., Bialystok, 1991; California State Department of Education, 1984; Collier, 1992; Collier & Thomas,

1989; Crawford, 1989; Cummins, 1981, 1989, 1991; Garcia, 1994; Genesee, 1987, 1994; Hakuta, 1988; Krashen, 1993; Lindholm, 1987, 2001; Ramirez, Yuen, & Ramey, 1991; Wong-Fillmore, 1991) provide strong evidence for the value of high-quality bilingual educational programs. The key issue is to offer high-quality TWB programs that respond to the educational needs of ELLs who come from economically disadvantaged backgrounds.

Second, bilingual education research findings from the last two decades support development of proficiency in L1 in order to accelerate English as a L2 acquisition in ELLs. Truly bilingual education programs seek to cultivate proficiency in two languages by using both languages as methods of instruction and tools for thinking, and research has shown that students' L1 can be maintained and developed at no cost to English. Actually, continued development of L1 helps to maintain adequate learning of content areas at grade level and enhances cognitive and social-affective development and progress in L2. When parents and educators of ELLs understand these basic research premises, they are typically in support of high-quality bilingual education programs that offer enriched educational opportunities for their language minority children.

More recent research patterns unveiled since 2000 (e.g., Calderon & Minaya-Rowe, 2003; Cloud, Genesee, & Hamayan, 2001; Collier & Thomas, 2004; Freeman, Freeman, & Mercuri, 2001; Thomas & Collier, 2000) reveal the steady longitudinal progress on academic achievement that ELLs exposed to TWB programs show, leading toward closing the academic achievement gap between minority and majority students. More specifically, research evidence (ibid.) shows that longitudinal exposure to a balanced L1 and L2 curriculum leads ELLs to higher levels of academic achievement in L2 and English academic language proficiency across grades and reduces dropout rates in comparison to matched groups being schooled in an English monolingual setting. For instance, literacy developed in L1 can be accessed and transferred to L2 because the general cognitive skills developed for reading processes can be abstracted and encoded in L1 and L2 as needed. According to Thomas and Collier (1997), when schools provide ELLs quality education in L1 and L2, they can develop higher levels of knowledge across content areas and literacy skills in L1 that help make the academic English they hear and read more comprehensible and further developed.

Third, external social factors may have a major influence on ELLs' English language acquisition at school. Examples are the *social and psychological distance* often created between L1 and L2 speakers, perceptions of each group in interethnic comparisons, cultural stereotyping, intergroup hostility, subordinate status of a minority group, or societal patterns of acculturation versus assimilation forces. Majority-minority and interethnic relations, as well as social class differences, are at the heart of these factors influencing ESL acquisition and academic achievement in school. Researchers such as Ogbu (1993), Oakes (1985), and Minucci and Olsen (1992) have found extensive evidence of institutionalized structures in U.S. schools that deny access to the foundation curriculum through tracking, ability grouping, and segregated school programs for ELLs. Moreover, segregated transitional bilingual classes and ESL classes can sometimes heighten the social inequities and maintain the status quo in majority-minority relations (Hernandez-

Chavez, 1984). Instead, by offering high-quality TWB programs, perceived as enrichment for both minority and mainstream students, U.S. public schools can serve as agents of *school reform* where teachers, students, and staff of many varied backgrounds join together and transform tensions between ethnic groups that currently exist in the broader society into nurturing and enriching classrooms that celebrate cultural and linguistic diversity.

The negative social perception about transitional bilingual and ESL programs in U.S. schools has led to ELLs' social isolation in "remedial" programs that deny them necessary instructional conditions for L2 acquisition to take place (Wong-Fillmore, 1991). To break the cycle of bilingual and ESL programs being perceived as remedial, they must be a permanent and integral part of the curriculum and must be taught through quality instruction that encourages the development of critical thinking and problem-solving skills in L1 and L2 as tools for learning across content areas (Gonzalez et al., in press). There is also research evidence supporting that high-quality TWB programs promote additive bilingualism that enhances cognitive development across several skills (e.g., Bialystok, 1991; Diaz, 1985; Diaz & Klingler, 1991; Diaz & Padilla, 1985; Hakuta, 1988). More specifically, additive bilingualism resulting from TWB programs increases creativity, concept formation, abstract thinking such as metalinguistic awareness (i.e., thinking about language or the meaning of symbols independently from linguistic forms, engaging in comparisons of symbols and meanings across languages and cultures, and developing humor) and metacognitive skills (i.e., thinking about thinking or the ability to monitor thinking and analyze and control mental processes), flexibility of thinking, increased readiness for reading and writing, and enhanced actual literacy skills. TWB programs promote integration of minority and majority students into a high-quality instructional environment that enhances academic achievement and bilingual academic competence for ELLs and *all* students.

Research from anthropology, sociology, sociolinguistics, psycholinguistics, and education has provided insights into the powerful and complex influence that sociocultural processes have on L1 and L2 acquisition. For example, undocumented and legal immigrant students fleeing war, political oppression, or severe economic conditions bring unique social, emotional, and academic needs, often having experienced interrupted schooling in their home countries. Students escaping war may exhibit symptoms of post-traumatic stress disorder, such as depression, withdrawal, hyperactivity, aggression, and intense anxiety in response to situations that recall traumatic events in their lives (Coelho, 1994). Studies of refugees' adaptation to life in the U.S. and success in school have emphasized the importance of a bicultural schooling context, integrating L1 and culture into the curriculum, as well as the importance of parents' maintenance of home language and cultural traditions (e.g., Tharp & Gallimore, 1988; Trueba, Jacobs, & Kirton, 1990).

Fourth, although data-based research studies have, since the early 1980s, reported a relationship between high-quality bilingual education and increased academic achievement across grade levels, there are still many unanswered questions in relation to current policy mandates and educationally applied decisions. Therefore, as pinpointed by Krashen (2005), there is need for additional research from methodologically well-conducted studies that respond to the specific mandates of current policy and dispels the myths of bilingual education for the American mainstream public as well as for minority parents of ELLs. Moreover, historically bilingual education research has *not* been done in the context of the integrated system of standards of current federal and state policy mandated in the NCLB Act of 2001. Thus, more research needs to be conducted in relation to specific instructional and assessment practices for ELLs within the current standard movement context provided by current legislation. As the NCLB mandates, educational decisions need to be based on research-based knowledge (and not just based on philosophical or political claims) about best educational practices for at-risk, low-SES immigrant ELLs, which can reduce the academic achievement gap between mainstream and minority students. As prior research has done, future research studies need to take into account external factors affecting learning and academic achievement; they also need to separate socioeconomic, cultural, and linguistic differences from underachievement. Research considering external at-risk factors for the underachievement of ELLs can help U.S. public schools reduce social inequality and provide genuine access to education as a social tool to become productive citizens within middle-class mainstream America. In this manner, research can support the civil rights movement and its derived policy of school reform (i.e., NCLB presently, and the Bilingual Education Act formerly) for supporting bilingual education as a best practice for academic excellence in ELLs (Gonzalez et al., in press).

Fifth, offering continuous professional development opportunities for all educators serving ELLs is a key component of educational success for this at-risk-of-underachievement population. Part of this training needs to be devoted to developing knowledge and strategies for strengthening partnerships between school, community, and parents. Educators also need to learn from research on best instructional and assessment practices for ELLs for enhancing academic English language proficiency and achievement. Educators also need to become sensitive to cultural and linguistic diversity, and they need to become willing to take risks and change educational practices. By becoming agents of change and school reform, educators accept their central role of committed, caring, and responsible or "morally accountable" professionals for the educational success of ELLs.

A sixth major trend in bilingual education research (e.g., Calderon & Minaya-Rowe, 2003; Cloud et al., 2001; Collier & Thomas, 2004; Tharp & Gallimore, 1988; Thomas & Collier, 2000; Trueba et al., 1990) points to the importance of developing strong partnerships among school and community and parents for supporting the academic achievement of ELLs within the U.S. public educational system. Bilingual and ESL teachers need to learn to function as cultural and linguistic mediators or bridges between the mainstream school culture and the minority home setting. The most important role of a teacher of an ESL student is to function as a role model for how to adapt culturally to the mainstream school setting while developing a bicultural and bilingual identity. It is challenging for ELLs to negotiate successfully the passage between cultures and languages as they go from their language minority home settings to the mainstream school cultures. Both teachers and parents need to collaborate to mediate the successful transition of ELLs between the home and school environments. An important mediational strategy is for ESL and mainstream teachers to develop opportunities for meaningful interactions with parents and community members and organizations. Teachers also need to value the culture and minority language of ELLs by representing its meaningful use in the curriculum and acknowledging and respecting diversity.

Overall these six major research trends in bilingual education studies represent the importance of interfacing research with policy and high-quality and research-based instructional practice for offering access and equality in the educational experience of ELLs. Presently there are still major gaps between these two cornerstones of the education of ELLs, that is, (1) research-based knowledge needs to inform practice through offering cutting-edge professional development to *all* educators serving ELLs, both mainstream and ESL and bilingual professionals; and (2) research needs to support and use policy as a tool for school reform representing the civil rights of language minority students.

Conclusions: Best Educational Practices for Latino/a Students

Based on the research patterns discussed in this entry, six major conclusions on best educational practices for TWB programs can be reached. First, Latino ELLs are at risk of underachievement mainly because of their low-SES backgrounds, and not directly because of their degree of English language acquisition or bilingualism. Poverty and related sociocultural factors puts them at risk of underachievement and dropping out of school (e.g., family structure factors such as low literacy levels and a low degree of acculturation at home; high number of siblings; quality of parent-child relationship; poor mental health of parents, etc.). Second, L1 development effectively increases and accelerates English academic language proficiency and academic achievement across content areas.

Third, given that external social factors affect English language acquisition, an integrated TWB high-quality education enhances academic achievement by reducing social and psychological distance and increasing cultural adaptation. A fourth pattern is the need for integration of policy and research, through using policy as a social tool for supporting research findings and, vice versa, developing research that helps implement policy in an educationally effective manner. A fifth emerging pattern is the need for providing professional development opportunities for *all* teachers to learn about research-based practices that increase the effectiveness of instruction and assessment for ELLs. Finally, the sixth trend points to the need for integrating community and school efforts through establishing collaborative partnerships between educators, parents, students, and community members and organizations.

In sum, research patterns synthesized in this article support the case for TWB education as an effective instructional model and practice. Research-based and high-quality TWB education can enhance academic achievement and English social and academic language development by enriching cognitive and social-affective development and skills in Latino immigrant ELLs. By using L1 and L2 as methods of instruction and tools for thinking, TWB education provides Latino immigrant ELLs with an enriched classroom that uses their cultural and linguistic diversity as a developmental and learning asset and provides additional resources and funding to compensate for the low-SES conditions that

place children from any ethnic group (even monolingual mainstream students) at risk for underachievement. Finally, as discussed in this entry, educational research is a social science that is contextualized within a social and political reality, so more research on TWB education needs to be done to respond to and affect current policy for providing genuine equal educational opportunities for ELLs. As ESL and bilingual educators, we have a "moral responsibility" to educate the American general public and our colleagues in best research-based practices for meeting the educational needs of low-SES immigrant ELLs at risk of underachievement within the sociocultural reality of U.S. public schools. We have to endure and persevere in this challenging task, always maintaining a link between research, policy and best educational practice, and we must always look to the future but maintain a link to our sociocultural history of Latino education in the U.S.

References

Bialystok, E. (1991). *Language Processing in Bilingual Children*. Cambridge: Cambridge University Press.

Calderon, M., & Minaya-Rowe, L. (2003). *Designing and Implementing Two-Way Bilingual Programs: A Step-by-Step Guide for Administrators, Teachers, and Parents*. Thousand Oaks, CA: Corwin Press.

California State Department of Education. (1984). *Studies on Immersion Education: A Collection for United States Educators*. Sacramento, CA: Author.

Cloud, N., Genesee, F., & Hamayan, E. (2001). *Dual Language Instruction: A Handbook for Enriched Education*. Boston: Heinle & Heinle.

Coelho, E. (1994). Social Integration of Immigrant and Refugee Children. In F. Genesee (Ed.), *Educating Second Language Children* (pp. 301–327). Cambridge: Cambridge University Press.

Collier, V. P. (1992). A Synthesis of Studies Examining Long-Term Language Minority Student Data on Academic Achievement. *Bilingual Research Journal* 16(1–2), 187–212.

Collier, V. P., & Thomas, W. P. (1989). How Quickly Can Immigrants Become Proficient in School English? *Journal of Educational Issues of Language Minority Students* 5, 26–38.

Collier, V. P., & Thomas, W. P. (2004). The Astounding Effectiveness of Dual Language Education for All. *NABE Journal of Research & Practice* 2(1), 1–19.

Crawford, J. (1989). *Bilingual Education. History, Politics, Theory, and Practice*. Trenton, NJ: Crane Publishing.

Cummins, J. (1981). The Role of Primary Language Development in Promoting Educational Success for Language Minority Students. In *Schooling and Language Minority Students: A Theoretical Framework* (pp. 3–49). Sacramento: California State Department of Education.

Cummins, J. (1989). *Empowering Minority Students*. Sacramento: California Association for Bilingual Education.

Cummins, J. (1991). Interdependence of First- and Second-Language Proficiency in Bilingual Children. In E. Bialystok (Ed.), *Language Processing in Bilingual Children* (pp. 70–89). Cambridge: Cambridge University Press.

Diaz, R. M. (1985). Bilingual Cognitive Development: Addressing Three Gaps in Current Research. *Child Development* 56, 1376–1388.

Diaz, R. M., & Klingler, K. (1991). Towards an Exploratory Model of the Interaction between Bilingualism and Cognitive Development. In E. Bialystok (Ed.), *Language Processing in Bilingual Children* (pp. 167–192). Cambridge: Cambridge University Press.

Diaz, R. M., & Padilla, K. A. (1985). The Self-regulatory Speech of Bilingual Preschoolers. Paper presented at the meeting of the Society for Research in Child Development, Toronto, Canada, April.

Freeman, Y. S., Freeman, D. E., & Mercuri, S. (2001). *Closing the Achievement Gap: How to Teach Limited-Formal-Schooling and Long-Term English Learners*. Portsmouth, NH: Heinemann.

Garcia, E. (1994). *Understanding and Meeting the Challenge of Student Cultural Diversity*. Boston: Houghton Mifflin.

Genesee, F. (1987). *Learning through Two Languages: Studies of Immersion and Bilingual Education*. Cambridge, MA: Newbury House.

Genesee, F. (1994). *Educating Second Language Children: The Whole Child, the Whole Curriculum, the Whole Community*. Cambridge: Cambridge University Press.

Gonzalez, V., Yawkey, T., & Minaya-Rowe, L. (in press). *English-as-a-Second-Language (ESL) Teaching and Learning: Classroom Applications for Pre-K through 12th Grade Students' Academic Achievement & Development*. Needham Heights, MA: Allyn & Bacon.

Hakuta, K. (1988). Why Bilinguals. In F. S. Kessel (Ed.), *The Development of Language and Language Researchers: Essays in Honor of Roger Brown* (pp. 229–318). Hillsdale, NJ: Lawrence Erlbaum.

Hernandez-Chavez, E. (1984). The Inadequacy of English Immersion Education as an Educational Approach for Language Minority Students in the United States. In *Studies on Immersion Education: A Collection for United States Educators* (pp. 144–183). Sacramento: California Department of Education.

Krashen, S. (1993). *The Power of Reading: Insights from the Research*. Englewood, CO: Libraries Unlimited.

Krashen, S. (2005). The Acquisition of Academic English by Children in Two-Way Programs: What Does the Research Say? In V. Gonzalez & J. V. Tinajero (Eds.), *NABE Review of Research & Practice* (vol. 3, pp. 3–19). Mahwah, NJ: Lawrence Erlbaum.

Lindholm, K. J. (1987). *Directory of Bilingual Immersion Programs: Two-Way Bilingual*

Education for Language Minority and Majority Students. Los Angeles: Center for Language Education and Research, University of California.

Lindholm, K. J. (2001). *Dual Language Education.* Clevedon, UK: Multilingual Matters. Available: www.ncela.gwu.edu.

National Center for Education Statistics (NCES). Official Web site, http://nces.ed.gov/nationsreportcard/sitemap.asp.

Minucci, C., & Olsen, L. (1992). *Programs for Secondary Limited English Proficient Students: A California Study.* Washington, DC: NCBE.

No Child Left Behind (NCLB) Act. (2001). *Official federal government* Web site, http://www.ed.gov/nclb/landing.html.

Oakes, J. (1985). *Keeping Track: How Schools Structure Inequality.* New Haven, CT: Yale University Press.

Ogbu, J. (1993). Variability in Minority School Performance: A Problem in Search of an Explanation. In E. Jacob & C. Jordan (Eds.), *Minority Education: Anthropological Perspectives* (pp. 83–111). Norwood, NJ: Ablex.

Ramirez, J. D., Yuen, S. D., & Ramey, D. R. (1991). Longitudinal Study of Structured English Immersion Strategy, Early-Exit and Late-Exit Transitional Bilingual Education Programs for Language-Minority Children. *Final Report to the U.S. Department of Education. Executive Summary and Vols. I and II.* San Mateo, CA: Aguirre International.

Tharp, R. G., & Gallimore, R. (1988). *Rousing Minds to Life: Teaching, Learning, and Schooling in Social Context.* Cambridge: Cambridge University Press.

Thomas, W. P., & Collier, V. P. (1997). *School Effectiveness for Language-Minority Students.* Washington, DC: National Clearinghouse for English Language Acquisition. Available: www.ncela.gwu.edu/ncbepubs/resource/effectiveness/index.html.

Thomas, W. P., & Collier, V. P. (2000). *A National Study of School Effectiveness for Language-Minority Students' Long-Term Academic Achievement.* Santa Cruz, CA, and Washington, DC: Center for Research on Education Diversity & Excellence (CREDE). Available: www.crede.ucsc.edu/research/llaa/l.l_final.htm.

Trueba, H. T., Jacobs, L., & Kirton, E. (1990). *Cultural Conflict and Adaptation: The Case of Hmong Children in American Society.* New York: Falmer.

Wong-Fillmore, L. (1991). Second Language Learning in Children: A Model of Language Learning in Social Context. In E. Bialystok (Ed.), *Language Processing in Bilingual Children* (pp. 49–69). Cambridge: Cambridge University Press.

Recommended Reading

Bruner, J. (1990). *Acts of Meaning.* Cambridge, MA: Harvard University Press.

Carnegie Task Force on Learning in the Primary Grades. (1996). *Years of Promise: A Comprehensive Learning Strategy for America's Children.* New York: Carnegie Corporation of New York.

Center for Research on Education, Diversity, and Excellence (CREDE). (2002). A Practical Guide to Understanding and Implementing Two-Way Immersion Programs. *Talking Leaves* 6(2), 1 & 9–10.

Cole, M. (1996). *Cultural Psychology: A Once and Future Discipline.* Cambridge, MA: Harvard University Press.

Doherty, W. D., Hilberg, R. S., Pinal, A., & Tharp, R. G. (2003). Five Standards and Student Achievement. In V. Gonzalez, & J. V. Tinajero (Eds.), *NABE Journal of Research and Practice* (vol. 1, pp. 1–24). Available: www.uc.edu/njrp.

Ensminger, M. E., & Slusarcick, A. L. (1992). Paths to High School Graduation or Dropout: A Longitudinal Study of a First-Grade Cohort. *Sociology of Education* 65(2), 95–113.

Felner, R. D., Kasak, D., Mulhall, P., & Flowers, N. (1997). The Project on High Performance Learning Communities: Applying the Land-Grant Model to School Reform. *Phi Delta Kappan*, March, 520–527.

Gonzalez, V. (2001). The Role of Socioeconomic and Sociocultural Factors in Language-Minority Children's Development: An Ecological Research View. *Bilingual Research Journal* 25 (1, 2), 1–30.

Gonzalez, V., Brusca-Vega, R., & Yawkey, T. D. (1997). *Assessment and Instruction of Culturally and Linguistically Diverse Students with or At-Risk of Learning Problems: From Research to Practice.* Needham Heights, MA: Allyn & Bacon.

Gonzalez, V., & Schallert, D. L. (1999). An Integrative Analysis of the Cognitive Development of Bilingual and Bicultural Children and Adults. In V. Gonzalez (Ed.), *Language and Cognitive Development in L2 Learning: Educational Implications for Children and Adults* (pp. 19–55). Needham Heights, MA: Allyn & Bacon.

Hatano, G., & Inagaki, K. (1986). Two Courses of Expertise. In H. Stevenson, H. Azuma, & K. Hakuta (Eds.), *Child Development and Education in Japan.* New York: Freedman.

Kaplan, J. L., & Luck, E. C. (1977). The Dropout Phenomenon as a Social Problem. *Educational Forum* 42(1), 41–56.

Lloyd, D. N. (1978). Prediction of School Failure from Third Grade Data. *Educational and Psychological Measurement* 38, 1193–1200.

National Research Council (1999a). *How People Learn.* Washington, DC: National Academy Press.

National Research Council. (1999b). *Improving Student Learning.* Washington, DC: National Academy Press.

Natriello, G. (1987). The Impact of Evaluation Processes on Students. *Educational Psychologist* 22, 155–175.

Piper, T. (1998). *Language and Learning: The Home and School Years.* Upper Saddler River, NJ: Prentice Hall.

Resnick, L. B., & Kloper, L. E. (1989). Toward the Thinking Curriculum: Current Cognitive Research. *Yearbook of the Association for Supervision and Curriculum Development.* Alexandria, VA: Association for Supervision and Curriculum Development.

Sheperd, L. A., & Smith, M. L. (1992). *Flunking Grades: Research and Policies on Retention.* New York: Felner.

Slavin, R. E. (1980). Effects of Individual Learning Expectations on Student Achievement. *Journal of Educational Psychology* 72(4), 520–524.

Stigler, J. R., Shweder, R., & Herdt, G. (1989). *Cultural Psychology: The Chicago Symposia on Culture and Development.* New York: Cambridge University Press.

Stroup, A. L., & Robins, L. N. (1972). Elementary School Predictors of High School Dropouts among Black Males. *Sociology of Education* 45(2), 212–212.

TESOL, (1997). *ESL Standards for Pre-K–12 Students.* Washington, DC: TESOL.

Tobin, J. J., Wu, D., & Davidson, D. (1989). *Preschool in Three Cultures: China, Japan, and the United States.* New Haven, CT: Yale University Press.

Virginia Gonzalez, Pauline Dow, and Josefina Villamil Tinajero

U

URBAN EDUCATION

The concept of urban education is critical to discuss, deconstruct, and explore when placing teaching and learning into the lived context of Latinos in the U.S. Schools do not exist in vacuums; instead, they exist within the larger social contexts of neighborhoods, cities, and even countries. In this time of changing Latino demographics in the U.S., urban education has been faced with intriguing challenges. From the early struggles and victories of the Latino communities across the country for education equity to current battles in schools for Latinos, urban schooling has played a primary role in the lives of Latinos today and in the history of the U.S. Some of the issues present for Latinos in urban schools include, but are not limited to, assimilative school practices, segregation and integration, native language instruction, and, most important, community activism and resistance by Latinos and others focused on addressing these issues.

Urban schools have been used to assimilate immigrant groups into the mainstream U.S. culture while native cultures and languages have been perceived as deficits. Assimilative school practices—and the resistance to these practices—are closely tied to the history of schooling in the U.S. The process of cultural and linguistic assimilation has been unfolding in U.S. schools since their inception. Latinos/as, among other non-white ethnic groups, have grappled against assimilative school practices that undermine their identities and ultimately their humanity.

School segregation is an issue urban schools have wrestled with for a long time. However, the discussion surrounding school segregation has not fully addressed the segregation of Latino children. Orfield (1988) found that in 1984, 31% of Latino/a children were learning in segregated schools across the U.S., and in the northeastern regions during this same period nearly half of all Latinos/as were in schools with 90%–100% minority populations. Moreover, in Orfield's (2001) later work, he provided the percentage of Latino/a children in 1998–1999 who were learning in segregated schools, and it has increased to 36.6%. Another component in his later research was a comparative look at schools with 50%–90% minority populations versus the 90%–100% minority population, schools he had also examined in the 1980s. What Orfield found was that in 1998–1999, at least three out of every four Latino/a students, or 75.6%, were enrolled in schools with 50%–100% minority populations, compared to 70.2% of African American students. More important is the trend of resegregation plaguing children of color across the U.S.

From 1968 through 1999 the percentage of Latinos/as learning in segregated schools has increased every school year. These segregation patterns did not stop the power of conservatives to turn back court-ordered desegregation policies in the 1970s. Furthermore, the current reality of school segregation, which reproduces the reality of separate and unequal education for youth of color, speaks to the lack of attention the courts pay to the lived realities of struggle in impoverished public schools in the U.S.

The Midwest had a wide increase in the percentage of Latino/a students in segregated schools from 1968 through 1999; thus, Latino/a children in Chicago received an inferior education that was being discussed on a national level. "National attention was focused on Chicago [in June 1988] when former Secretary of Education, William Bennett, called the Chicago public school system the worst in the nation" (Vasquez, 1994, p. 13).

The issue of desegregation policies was the basis of a series of recent decisions involving Atlanta, Oklahoma City, and Kansas City, as the U.S. Supreme Court has given its stamp of approval to this present configuration. Not only are public schools segregated, but in most American cities poor children have been consigned to schools that show little evidence of serving their educational needs. For example, in 1984, a study of Chicago high school dropouts showed a 75% dropout rate at two primarily Latino/a high schools. In addition, community organizations such as Latino/a Family Services estimate the dropout rate for Southwest Detroit to be close to 86% (Jose-Kampfner & Aparicio, 1998). "Large urban school districts which are 27% Latino tend to be chronically underfunded, spending an average of $5,200 per pupil in 1991, compared with $6,073 for

suburban schools" (ASPIRA Institute for Policy Research, 1993).

Language rights in schools have been evaded with the rapid replacement of bilingual programs for English immersion policies. Urban centers in the U.S. have historically and contemporarily received many immigrants from all around the world, but those who come from Spanish-speaking countries comprise the largest number. Yet, the preservation of Spanish has not been central to education policies that inform language practices within urban schools. Instead, education policies have pushed the implementation of English immersion practices that do not provide the resources or structures to maintain Spanish fluency. The most widely used bilingual education program in city schools with at least 20 students, who have the same native language, is the Transitional Bilingual Education (TBE) program. The average student in TBE will spend three years learning English, and the predictor for exiting is based on the English language skills that range from one to three years of transitional bilingual education. However, in New York City only 60% of limited English proficient (LEP) students in 1985 actually received appropriate services (Fine, 1991).

The struggle for school equity for Latinos/as has been coupled with a strong history of resistance rooted in community organizing and grassroots organizing. "From World War II to the 1990s [and today], Native Americans, Puerto Ricans, African Americans, and Mexican Americans have demanded that public schools recognize their distinct cultures and incorporate these cultures into curricula and textbooks" (Spring, 1994, p. 195). The resistance of Latinos/as has been overshadowed by talks of academic failure that is saturated with silence. Nevertheless, we must recall the history and current occurrences of resistance in order to create spaces where Latino/a identities can grow. We must remember that the Latino/a culture has not died, that the Spanish language still lives strong in urban Latino/a enclaves, and that this is the case because Latinos/as have resisted. As Gloria Anzaldúa (1999) puts it, "In leaving home I did not lose touch with my origins because *lo mexicano* is in my system. I am a turtle. Wherever I go I carry 'home' on my back" (p. 43).

References

Anzaldúa, G. (1999). *Borderlands / La frontera: The New Mestiza* (2nd ed.). San Francisco: Aunt Lute Books.

ASPIRA Institute for Policy Research. (1993). *Facing the Facts: The State of Hispanic Education.* Washington, DC: Author.

Fine, M. (1991). *Framing Dropouts: Notes on the Politics of Urban Public High School.* Albany, NY: SUNY Press.

Jose-Kampfner, C., & Aparicio, F. (1998). Rethinking Violence in the Educational Crisis of U.S. Latinos. *JSRI Research Report* no. 38. East Lansing: The Julian Samora Research Institute, Michigan State University.

Orfield, G. (1988). School Desegregation in the 1980's. *Equity and Choice* 4, 25–28.

Orfield, G. (2001). *Schools More Separate: Consequences of a Decade of Research.* Cambridge, MA: The Civil Rights Project, Harvard University.

Spring, J. (1994). *The American School.* New York: McGraw-Hill.

Vasquez, R. (1994). *Reforming Chicago Public Schools: The Intended and Unintended Consequences.* DeKalb: LEPS Press, Northern Illinois University.

Recommended Reading

Flores-Gonzalez, N. (2002). *School Kids/ Street Kids: Identity Development in Latino Students.* New York: Teachers College Press.

Laura, M., & Miron, L. (2005). *Urban Schools: The New Social Spaces of Resistance.* New York: Peter Lang.

Lipman, P. (2004). *High Stakes Education: Inequality, Globalization, and Urban School Reform.* New York: RoutledgeFalmer.

Noguera, P. A. (2003). *City Schools and the American Dream: Reclaiming the Promise of Public Education.* New York: Teachers College Press.

Valenzuela, A. (1999). *Subtractive Schooling: U.S.-Mexican Youth and the Politics of Caring.* Albany, NY: SUNY Press.

Erica R. Davila

W

WORKFORCE AND POSTSECONDARY TECHNICAL EDUCATION IN THE U.S.

Latinos are an increasingly vital part of the national economy and the fastest-growing segment of the U.S. population. Because of immigration and high birth rates, Latinos have displaced African Americans and become the largest minority population in the U.S. (U.S. Census Bureau, 2003). Now constituting 13% of the total population (U.S. Census Bureau, 2003), Latinos have high participation rates in America's labor force but tend to work in jobs that pay low wages, provide low economic mobility, and are less stable and more hazardous. Moreover, many of the low-wage jobs do not provide health benefits, a major reason for increased poverty levels among Latinos. This is true for both male and female workers and is the result of low educational attainment, language proficiency, lack of work experience, training and other employability skills ("Deadly Trend," 2002).

Definition of Latino

The term *Latino* is used "to denote all U.S. persons whose origins can be traced to the Spanish-speaking regions of Latin America, including the Caribbean, Mexico, Central America, and South America"
(Flores et al., 2002). It describes a very diverse group of people from all races and many nationalities. According to the U.S. Census Bureau (2000), the Latino population is made up of Mexicans (66.9%), Puerto Ricans (8.6%), Cuban (3.7%), Central and South American (14.3%), and other Hispanics (6.5%). In describing the differences within the Latino community, Vasquez (2001) emphasized that there are differences in each group's ethnic background and racial composition as well as social, economic, political, cultural, and linguistic differences. Chappa (1991) stated, "Hispanics are not a monolithic group. Many called what is now a part of the southwestern U.S. (states such as Arizona, California, Texas, etc.) their home well before the founding of Jamestown. Yet some also arrived within the last few years. The historical experience of each subgroup as it has developed in the United States is different" (p. 11). "However, because of their locations, education, and immigration histories, the various subgroups suffer in the labor market in different ways and to different degrees" (Arbona, 1995, p. 39). For example, as a result of their citizenship Puerto Ricans do not face many of the obstacles faced by other Latinos. Nonetheless, these differences, as well as level of acculturation and migration history, are important factors in understanding the career

development of Latinos. Such factors ultimately predicate occupational choice.

Latino Education

In general Latinos have low educational attainment and lag behind non-Hispanic groups in high school and college degree completion (National Survey of Latinos: Education, 2004). Large education gaps exist for Latinos, even beginning at preschool age. This perpetuates low educational attainment and reduced employment opportunity. As a result, Latinos are overrepresented in high-risk, low-skill/low-wage work. Various factors make Latinos the group with the least education and the highest high school dropout rate among all ethnic groups (U.S. Census Bureau, 2000; National Council of La Raza [NCLR], 2001). This high dropout rate limits their ability to pursue postsecondary education and obtain associate's, bachelor's, advanced degrees, and other kinds of training that lead to advanced employment.

Educational attainment, as reported by the U.S. Census Bureau (2000), indicates that the Hispanic population age 25 and over have attained less education than their non-Hispanic white counterparts. Twenty-seven percent have less than a ninth grade education compared to non-Hispanic whites (4.2%); 15.7% have not completed high school versus 7.3% for non-Hispanic whites; 27.9% have diplomas compared to 34.1%; and 29.1% have more than a high school education compared to 54.4% for non-Hispanic whites. These numbers are staggering, especially since the Latino population is growing faster than any other group and has the highest (35.5%) number of people younger than age 18 (NCLR, 2001). In the near future this group will be the largest segment of our workforce and will contribute more to a tax base upon which all Americans will increasingly come

to depend. Denying them the opportunity now hampers their future preparedness as they seek to make their mark as employers, employees, and entrepreneurs. As our society becomes older and as more baby-boomers begin to retire, we will become more dependent than ever on the economic contributions of Latinos to our society.

Latinos and Community Colleges

Latinos, more than other groups, tend to enroll in community colleges. In 2000, Latino students accounted for 14% of the students enrolled in two-year colleges and 7% of those in four-year institutions (National Center for Education Statistics, 2003). According to Brown, Santiago, and Lopez (2003), most Latino students are "first-generation college students, are low-income, have a less academic high school education than their peers, and enroll in community colleges" (p. 41). They continue by adding, "A large number of Latinos in higher education are also nontraditional students. They are older, work, attend college part-time, and often are also caring for family—all characteristics that influence the decisions Latino students make in participating in and completing higher education" (p. 42).

Although community colleges serve as the entry point for Latinos in their pursuit of postsecondary education, students who enroll in community colleges often attend part time, prolong their college education into their mid-twenties and beyond, and often have gaps in their attendance (Fry, 2002). These characteristics as well as those described above are all risk factors that contribute to non-completion of a postsecondary education. Attachment to family and community as well as economic need appear to be associated with high enrollments of Latinos in two-year institutions as well. Although the majority of the research on post-secondary educational outcome has reported that community colleges deter the completion of a four-year education for Latinos (Arbona, 1990; Rendon & Nora, 1994), Gray and Herr (1995) report, "The largest and fastest growing ranks of technical workers are not college-trained professionals; they are blue-collar technicians educated at the pre-baccalaureate postsecondary level, in high school vocational education programs, or in formal training programs in the workplace" (p. 30). They also indicated that many technical fields in which credentials are awarded at the postsecondary associate degree level and below were the largest projected job openings for 1990 and 2005. Two-year postsecondary institutions have the best potential for directing the Latino population into lucrative technical fields, namely, the blue-collar technical occupations (Gray & Herr, 1995). Some of these fields include agricultural business and production, agricultural sciences, business, communication technologies, computer and information sciences, construction, engineering, engineering technologies, health professions, home economics, mechanics and repair, personal services, precision production, protective services, science technologies, and transportation (Community College Research Center, 2004).

The Community College Research Center (CCRC, 2004), which looked at demographic characteristics of students in occupational programs using the National Postsecondary Student Aid Study (NPSAS) 1996 and 2000 survey data, indicated some of these trends: (1) There was a large increase in the proportion of computer and data-processing majors among occupational community college students; (2) There was an increase in community college students with previously earned degrees; and (3) There was a shift in the primary reason for enrolling among community college students. Interestingly, while many tout the benefits of the bachelor's degree, the research reported by CCRC (2004) states that the number of people who are enrolled as occupational students held another degree (>30%) and "the gain was the highest among those who held a bachelor's degree as their highest prior degree (increased from 2% to 9%)" (p. 5). In addition, "earning a degree or certificate is now the most commonly cited primary reason for enrolling among both occupational and academic students at two-year and less than two-year institutions, perhaps due to the expectations of employers in a competitive job market" (p. 5). It is significant that studies on Latinos and their participation in these types of programs are almost non-existent.

Career Development and Participation in Postsecondary Technical Education

Although Latinos are the fastest-growing minority group in the U.S., they are also the poorest and most undereducated when compared to other minority groups. Career development of Latinos, according to Arbona (1995), "has become a salient issue in the social sciences literature because it is believed that the quality of the future U.S. labor market will depend, to a great extent, on this group's education and job skills" (p. 38). If this is true, then research should focus on Latino education and access, and completion of higher education programs should be a priority.

A study by Maldonado and Farmer (2001) examined Latino participation in postsecondary technical education, a topic almost absent in the literature. The study utilized data from the National Center for

Education Statistics, National Education Longitudinal Study (1998) and a career development framework with which the theoretical underpinnings for this study were based. Career development is a life-long process and a determinant of educational attainment that leads to occupational attainment.

The NELS results indicated that, overall, Hispanic enrollment in postsecondary education in 1994 was approximately 72% of the total sample population in the twelfth grade in 1992. The total number decreased from 206,907 to 149,815, a drop of about 28%. Of those Hispanics in college, about 23% (34,595) identified themselves as pursuing technical and/or occupational programs. The largest Latino subgroup participating in technical and occupational programs was comprised of Mexicans (63%–21,840/34,595). Within each of the subgroups, the majority of students identified themselves as being enrolled in transfer programs: 68% Mexican, 63% Puerto Rican, 59% Cuban, and 66% other Hispanics (Maldonado & Farmer, 2001).

Of those enrolled in technical or occupational programs, the findings revealed, the largest enrollment of Latinos was in the following programs: Protective Services (3.1%), Mechanic (2.6%), Education (2.4%), and Dental/Medical Technician (2.3%). Programs such as Precision Production (.2%), Electronics (.6%), and Engineering Technology (1.1%) remained low (<2%). Programs such as Child Care and Guidance, Textiles, and Dietetics had no Hispanic enrollment (Maldonado & Farmer, 2001). This study showed that most Latinos graduating from high school tended to go on to receive some type of postsecondary education. However, most Latinos enrolled in academic programs that require a transfer to a university rather than the pursuit of technical or occupational programs. Although this is positive, the problem is that many students eventually drop out without either degree. The researchers believed that a history of tracking into vocational education programs in the past, the failure to recognize the changes in the economy and the demand for technical workers, and the belief that only a four-year education guarantees a good job in the future perpetuates large enrollments in academic and transfer programs at the community college.

Latino Participation in the Labor Force

Although many Latinos enter the workforce at an early age, working in low-skill jobs diminishes their opportunity to gain the kind of general work experience that brings about opportunities for better-paying low-risk positions. In 2000 almost one-fifth (19.4%) of Latino workers were employed in a service occupation, which includes food preparation, personal services, and cleaning or maintenance jobs as compared to one in nine non-Hispanic white workers (11.8%). Conversely, Latinos were less likely than non-Hispanic whites to work in high-paying managerial and professional specialty occupations. In 2000, 14% of Latinos were in managerial or professional occupations, compared with 33% of non-Hispanic whites. Among Latino subgroups, Mexicans (12%) were the least likely to work in managerial or professional occupations (NCLR, 2001, p. 18).

Language proficiency has a powerful impact on the type of work one has access to, as well as economic mobility. English language skills are necessary for almost all jobs in the U.S. data analyzed by Siles and

Pérez (2000) indicate that "a notable proportion of Latinos who speak Spanish do not have a level of English language ability that permits them to enter high-paying jobs in the current labor force" (p. 6). In addition, they state that "lack of English language skills can affect employment paths or job opportunities early in a worker's career" (p. 8) and "chances to move into high-wage jobs and industries projected to experience growth, are small if their English language skills are not at the level expected by the marketplace" (p. 8). With potential worker shortages being a concern for most U.S. businesses and as companies increasingly view their human capital as their greatest asset, such enterprises must concentrate more on employee development. Such development must include the nation's largest ethnic minority group, for in the future it will potentially form the largest segment of the workforce.

Summary

In summary, the educational attainment and the associated background factors are important considerations in Latinos' career development. Herr and Niles (1997), two distinguished scholars, stated that "decision making, development of self-identity, and life choices do not occur in a vacuum. They occur within political, economic, and social conditions that influence the achievement images and belief systems on which individuals base their actions" (pp. 157–176). Moreover, "factors such as poverty, poor education, and racism often combine to affect negatively the individual's self-concept, ambition, motivation, and self-efficacy, thereby diminishing the perceived utility of engaging in long-range future planning" (pp. 157–176). These factors and conditions demonstrate the complexities surrounding career development and educational attainment of Latino students.

However, it should be noted that career development among Latinos might vary depending upon how well an individual becomes acculturated to the dominant culture. Thomas and Alderfer (1989) described minorities as bicultural. Because they move between their culture and the dominant culture, most minorities experience difficulties functioning effectively. Latinos' ability to meet educational and occupational tasks is based on two predictors: migration history and socioeconomic background (Arbona, 1995; Maldonado & Farmer, 2001).

References

Arbona, C. (1990). Career Counseling Research and Hispanics: A Review of the Literature. *The Counseling Psychologist* 18(2), 300–323.

Arbona, C. (1995). Theory and Research on Racial and Ethnic Minorities: Hispanic Americans. In F.T.L. Leong (Ed.), *Career Development and Vocational Behavior of Racial and Ethnic Minorities* (pp. 37–66). Mahwah, NJ: Lawrence Erlbaum.

Brown, S. E., Santiago, D., & Lopez, E. (2003). Latinos in Higher Education: Today and Tomorrow [Electronic version]. *Change* 35(2), 40–46.

Chappa, J. (1991). Special Focus: Hispanic Demographics and Educational Trends. In D. J. Carter & R. Wilson (Eds.), *Minorities in Higher Education: Ninth Annual Status Report* (pp. 11–17). Washington, DC: American Council on Education.

Community College Research Center. (2004). *The Characteristics of Occupational Students in Postsecondary Education* (Issue Brief, no. 21). New York: Author.

"Deadly Trend" of Hispanic Worker Deaths on Top of Agenda at OSHA. (2002). *Labor Relations Week* 16(41), 1257.

Flores, G. et al. (2002). The Health of Latino Children: Urgent Priorities, Unanswered Questions, and a Research Agenda. *Journal of the American Medical Association* 288(1), 82–90.

Fry, R. (2002). *Latinos in Higher Education: Many Enroll, Too Few Graduate* [Electronic version]. Washington, DC: Pew Hispanic Center.

Gray, K., & Herr, E. (1995). *Other Ways to Win.* Thousand Oaks, CA: Corwin Press.

Herr, E. L., & Niles, S. (1997). Multicultural Career Guidance in the Schools. In Paul Pedersen & John C. Carey (Eds.), *Multicultural Counseling in Schools* (pp. 157–176). Boston: Allyn & Bacon.

Maldonado, C., & Farmer, E. (2001). Hispanic Students' Participation in Postsecondary Technical Programs in the United States. *International Journal of Vocational Education and Training* 9(1), 47–58.

National Center for Education Statistics (NCES). (2003). Available: http://nces.ed.gov/annuals/.

National Center for Education Statistics, National Education Longitudinal Study. (1998). Available: http://nces.ed.gov/annuals/.

National Council of La Raza (NCLR). (2001). *Beyond the Census: Hispanics and an American Agenda.* Washington, DC: Author. Available: www.nclr.org (accessed July 17, 2003).

National Survey of Latinos: Education. (2004). Available: http://www.pewtrusts.com/pdf/pew_hispanic_education_012304.pdf.

Pew Hispanic Center and the Kaiser Family Foundation. (2004). *National Survey of Latinos: Education.* Available: http://www.pewhispanic.org/site/docs/pdf/LatinoEducationSummaryandChartpackJan262004.pdf (accessed April 1, 2004).

Rendon, L. I., & Nora, A. (1994). A Synthesis and Application of Research on Hispanic Students in Community Colleges. In J. L. Ratcliff (Ed.), *Community Colleges* (pp. 287–293). Needham Heights, MA: Simon & Schuster.

Siles, M., & Peréz, S. M. (2000). What Latino Workers Bring to the Labor Market: How Human Capital Affects Employment Outcomes. In S. M. Peréz (Ed.), *Moving Up the Economic Ladder: Latino Workers and the Nation's Future Prosperity* (pp. 1–34). Washington, DC: National Council of La Raza.

Thomas, D. A., & Alderfer, C. P. (1989). The Influence of Race on Career Dynamics: Theory and Research on Minority Career Experiences. In M. B. Arthur, D. T. Hall, & B. S. Lawrence (Eds.), *Handbook of Career Theory* (pp. 133–158). New York: Cambridge University Press.

U.S. Census Bureau. (2000). *The Hispanic Population in the United States: Population Characteristics.* Available: www.census.gov (accessed July 17, 2003).

U.S. Census Bureau. (2003). *Annual Demographic Supplement to the March 2002 Current Population Survey.* Available: www.census.gov/Press-Release/www/2003/cb03-100.html (accessed February 3, 2005).

Vazquez, M. (2001). Latinos: ¡Viva la diferencia! *CRM*, 5, 22–24.

Recommended Reading

Farmer, E., Rojewski, J., & Farmer, B. (2004). *Diversity in America: Visions of the Future— Real Issues of Real People* (2nd ed.). Dubuque, IA: Kendall/Hunt.

Fry, R. (2003). Labor Market Outcomes of Hispanics by Generation (Report no. 188). New York: ERIC Clearinghouse on Urban Education. (ERIC Document Reproduction Service no. EDO-UD-03-7).

Llagas, C., & Snyder, T. D. (Eds.). (2003). Status and Trends in the Education of Hispanics (NCES 2003-008). Washington, DC: National Center for Education Statistics (NCES).

Maldonado, C., & Farmer, E. (2001). Hispanic Students' Participation in Postsecondary Technical Programs in the United States. *International Journal of Vocational Education and Training* 9(1), 47–58.

Pew Hispanic Center and the Kaiser Family Foundation. (2004). *National Survey of Lati-*

nos: Education. Available: http://www.pew
hispanic.org/site/docs/pdf/LatinoEducation
SummaryandChartpackJan262004.pdf (accessed April 1, 2004).

Schmidt, P. (2003). Academe's Hispanic Future. *Chronicle of Higher Education* 50(14),
A8–A13.

Cecilia Maldonado and Edgar I. Farmer

Y

THE YOUNG LORDS AND A PEDAGOGY OF FREEDOM

I want people to wonder at what forces created him, terrible, vindictive cold, calm man-child, courage in one hand, the machine gun in the other, scourge of the unrighteous—"an ox for the people to ride."

George Jackson

The legacies of the Young Lords Party (YLP) are felt in so many ways that they are hard to pinpoint, unless we focus on a process of continual struggle. Consciously avoiding the oversimplification of the multiple movements in 1960s and 1970s, we would do a great injustice not to recognize that some legacies attributed to the Young Lords (YL) can also be attributed to millions of activists. This entry focuses on a broad cast of actors and actresses present on the same revolutionary stage as the YL. To address this complex spectrum of activists and organizations, this entry briefly describes how the YL came into existence and what other organizations shaped the way they engaged in their revolutionary praxis during the late 1960s and early 1970s.

The purpose of this entry is to expose how the YLP legacies are seen today and how they are felt by new generations of Latino/a activists. Finally, this entry discusses how many of our Latino/a communities need our educational system to engage in pedagogies of freedom (Freire, 2001). The experience and histories of the YL can give us concrete examples to draw from. Based on some of the YL political projects we can envision, create, and materialize curricula, methodologies, and pedagogical praxis that nourish and encourage freedom.

"Revolution Is Gonna Come . . . Our Streets!"
by David Perez
Our cry is a very simple and logical one.
    Puerto Ricans
came to this country hoping to get a decent job and to
provide for their families; but it didn't take long to find out
that the American dream that was publicized so nicely
on our island turned out to be the Amerikkkan nightmare.

How We Got Here

To describe the late 1960s and 1970s in the inner city Latino/a communities means to talk about the Puerto Rican experience. Since the late nineteenth century there has been a constant migration of Puerto Ricans toward the U.S. (Flores, 1991; Sánchez-Korrol, 1994). Their experiences have changed culture and neighborhoods all over New York, New Jersey, New Haven, Boston, and Philadelphia. Dealing with stiff resistance, racism, and social injustice, Puerto Ricans needed to engage in community building as a mechanism for survival (Sánchez-Korrol, 1994). In time Puerto Rican neighborhoods had their own *bodegas* and *cuchifritos* stands. With the constant immigrational flux they brought Puerto Rico within them in ways that bled into their neighborhoods. The emerging Puerto Rican communities faced a great deal of resistance, struggle, and strife from mainstream society to (Flores, 1991; Sánchez-Korrol, 1994).

Puerto Rican migration reached a historical peak during the post–World War II years. It is estimated that between 1945 and 1955 an average of 53,000 Puerto Ricans migrated every year (Sánchez-Korrol, 1994). In fact, in 1940 the Puerto Rican population in the U.S. was approximately 69,967; by 1960 it reached an impressive 887,661, and in 1970 it was 1,391,463 (Sánchez-Korrol, 1994). In the 1960s most Latinos/as in urban cities were Puerto Ricans. With the exception of the Southwest, with its indigenous Mexican and immigrant Mexican populations, Puerto Ricans were the dominant Latino/a minority, especially on the East Coast.

In time Puerto Ricans and African Americans shared the same issues and struggles for they lived in the same or similar neighborhoods on the Lower East Side and in Harlem—which transformed itself into Spanish Harlem, or El Barrio—the South Bronx, and Brooklyn, all of which served as enclaves. Latino/a and African American populations were systematically marginalized, displaced in historically affluent neighborhoods that eventually transitioned into inner-city ghettoes and slums. Their shared experiences lead to common struggle and common cultural expressions (Flores, 2000).

A Culture That Spawned a Movement

Revolutions means change from the top to the bottom, and that includes the way we deal with each other as human beings.
Richie Perez

The numerous actors on the revolutionary stage of the 1960s and 1970s are so multidimensional it is impossible to consider them all here. Instead, this entry stresses those movements that contributed to the emergence of the Young Lord Organization (YLO) that eventually became the YLP. To suggest that activism for Puerto Ricans in the U.S. started with the YLP would be a great injustice, however. A great many works document the organizations and movements present since the nineteenth century; see, for example, Virginia Sánchez-Korrol (1994), Juan Flores (1991), and Jorge Duany (2002).

During the 1950s well over 200 organizations dealt with issues concerning the Puerto Rican community (Duany, 2002; Sánchez-Korrol, 1994), among them were the Puerto Rican Civic Club, the Puerto Rican Association for Communities Affairs, and the Puerto Rican Community Development Project. Puerto Ricans organized into a community, and notions of self-pride materialized in the first Puerto Rican Day parade in 1958 (Duany, 2002; Sánchez-Korrol, 1994).

In subsequent years the children of the big immigrations of the 1950s were knocking at the doors of higher-education institutions. Many YL members were involved with a myriad of organizations in the City University of New York (CUNY), the State University of New York (SUNY), the City College of New York (CCNY), and Columbia (Serrano, 1998). Early organizations like CUNY's SEEK (Search for Education Elevation and Knowledge), PREP

(Puerto Rican Educational Progress), SUNY's EOP (Education Opportunity Program) paved the way for future Puerto Rican–based student organizations (Serrano, 1998). Many clubs that had Latino/a members shape-shifted into the Puerto Rican Student Movement (PRSM), Puerto Rican Alliance (PRA), Aspira, and the Puerto Rican Student Union (PRSU) (Serrano, 1998). Many of these organizations worked hand in hand with multiple African American student organizations demanding African and Puerto Rican studies and curricula, and an open admissions policy within CUNY, NYCC, and SUNY.

The victories of these organizations during the late 1960s transformed higher education in many ways with the creation of African and Puerto Rican studies program that went hand in hand with other movements like the American Indian movement and the Brown Berets that each demanded Native American studies and Chicano/a studies. These movements together created the conditions for what we know as multicultural education, ethnic studies, Latino/a studies, and culturally relevant curricula.

> Let me say at the risk of seeming ridiculous that a true revolutionary is guided by great feelings of love.
>
> Ernesto "Che" Guevara

The Genesis

The common experiences of Puerto Ricans and African Americans created a spectrum of conditions that intertwined with each other. Major issues concerning social justice, exploitation, and oppression catapulted the creation of organizations that sparked the civil rights movements. The Student Non-Violent Coordinating Committee (SNCC) and the National Association for the Advancement of Colored People (NAACP) trained and inspired many Latinos/as into social justice and activism (Morales, 1996). For instance, Rodríguez-Morazzani (1998) states that the exposure of the African American community both in their own communities and through mass media lead African Americans to become involved in multiple student organizations. Many of these movements trained future YLP members (Serrano, 1998).

Urban Puerto Ricans were greatly inspired by the activism of African Americans (Rodríguez-Morazzani, 1998). Radical activism for Latinos/as and Puerto Ricans reached its apex in the 1960s. While being locked up in Sing Sing, Felipe Luciano held several talks with the Black Panthers Party leader Fred Hampton (Morales, 1996). The culmination of those talks dealt with creating revolutionary actions and forming solidarity movements defining the shared struggle of African Americans and Puerto Ricans. In 1968 a former street gang from Chicago became the YLO. Similar to the Black Panthers, the YL engaged in a program called Feed the People and took over a church to have a venue for their community-based programs (Morales, 1994, 1998). This action drew the attention of various Puerto Ricans in New York and eventually lead to the foundation of the East Coast chapter of the YLO in winter 1968 (Morales, 1996, 1998). With the YLO's foundation came a series of important events.

YLP Praxis

> We're trying to make a society where opportunity is the rule for everybody.
>
> Pablo "Yoruba" Guzman

From 1969 through 1972 the YL engaged in a series of actions that got them a great deal of attention from the mass media (Morales, 1996, 1998). They engaged with multiple issues such as community control, health, education, self-determination, and social justice. One of their first actions receiving national attention and thereby catapulting the YL into the living rooms of mainstream American, was the lack proper sanitation conditions faced by marginalized and ignored communities in the inner city. The sanitation department seldom picked up the garbage in many communities. So, the YL decided to take actions. They started sweeping garbage and cleaning their neighborhoods while concentrating the garbage in one area. After the third week the situation became unbearable, and they lit up the garbage to prove a point: "We will not be ignored and forced to live in these conditions."

Another media fiasco occurred when the YL took over a community church. They were engaging with their ever-growing Feed the People program of providing them with free breakfast and free clothes for winter. As the YL grew in popularity, more and more people joined them, soliciting their programs. They needed more space, so they thought it would be common sense that a church would lend its unused facilities to the people of the community it services. To their surprise, the reverend refused. Once again the YL decided to take matters into their own hands and tried to convince the congregation. While they were trying to address the congregation, the reverend called in the police, and 13 YL were arrested. Not giving up, a few weeks later the YL took over the church for three weeks. During this time the El Barrio community experienced what it means when someone shouts "Power to the People" (Morales, 1996, 1998). After three weeks the YL negotiated with the authorities and left. Over 106 YL and community members were arrested in this action; nonetheless, every-

body knew and felt they had won (Morales, 1998).

With the taking of the church in El Barrio, community support mushroomed. The YL were growing dramatically and became a source of pride to all Latinos/as and Puerto Ricans. Their support included many famous nuyorican poets and salsa musicians who where fomenting their own revolution in the worlds of music and art. Pedro Pietri, for example, engaged in his spoken-word style of poetry at YL activities. In fact, Pietri's "Puerto Rican Obituary" was published in the Young Lords' (1971) book *Pa' Lante: The Young Lords Party*. Also, YL member Pablo "Yoruba" Guzman was a member of the famous Last Poets group. Many of the cultural activities benefited from prominent talent like salsa legend Ray Barreto. The YL tapped into their own communities' cultural movements such as the booming salsa music scene. In this way the YL were so in tune with the artistic elements that Felipe Luciano states that salsa "is street music for street people, is the music of the people and the conscience of the people" (Berrios-Miranda, 2004).

Over time the health-related initiatives won the YL prestige. From their door-to-door preventive health services; their testing for led poisoning, tuberculosis, and anemia, and their detox initiatives to the physical takeover of Lincoln Hospital, the YL were concerned for the well-being of their communities. They took matters into their own hands for the benefit of their communities. Through their hard struggle concerning health issues with Latino/a and Puerto Rican communities, the YL forced New York City housing authorities to force landlords to remove cheap leaded paint, a serious health hazard to tenants. The YL had documented how one-third of children in El Barrio and the South Bronx had toxic level of lead in their blood and so forced more proactive health prevention measures and gave national spotlight to the deplorable health conditions Puerto Rican, Latino/a, and African American communities was forced to live with (Morales, 1996, 1998; YLP, 1971). The takeover of Lincoln Hospital lead to concrete victories. Lincoln Hospital created a detox program for heroin users, and few years later a new Lincoln Hospital in the South Bronx was constructed (Morales, 1996, 1998). These concrete victories sparked health reform movements that are alive and kicking to this day.

The YL promoted Puerto Ricans' drive for self-determination and the liberation of Puerto Rico. In September 1970, 102 years after El Grito de Lares, (1868 armed struggle against the Spaniards), the YL organized a conference in Columbia University titled Free Puerto Rico: Now. This conference hosted a myriad of organizations among them EL Comité, PRSU, and the Pro Independence Movement (MPI) (Morales, 1998). They engaged in multiple activities to shape Puerto Rico's future, initiating a decolonization process. Their efforts culminated a month later, on October 30, the historical date of armed insurrection against colonial powers in Puerto Rico in 1950. Well over 10,000 people marched in unison demanding the case of Puerto Rican decolonization to the United Nations, as well as the end of police brutality in their communities (Morales, 1996, 1998).

The YL continued with their struggle until the organization dissipated. In retrospect, many ex–Young Lords believe that their pro-independence initiative, which culminated in the YL's setting up in Puerto Rico, severed their community ties in the U.S. (Morales, 1996, 1998). The YL neglected the crucial community support that

got them to the where they were. After internal struggle and personal differences, many YL members left the organization. By 1972 the YL transmuted into the Puerto Rican Revolutionary Workers Organization as the group adopted more Marxist-Leninist approaches to their struggle. This organization lost steam by the mid-1970s.

There are a myriad of reasons for the YL disintegration. Many ex-members cite internal struggles, big egos, irreconcilable differences, and an acute case of paranoia. Multiple revolutionary movements became the government's public enemy number one. Under the FBI's COINTELPRO program, groups such as the Black Panther Party, Students for a Democratic Society, the American Indian movement, and the Puerto Rican pro-independence movement, and hence the YL, were targeted to be neutralized and destroyed (Churchill & Vander Wall, 1990). Under a strong 10-point process COINTELPRO used divide-and-conquer tactics combined with terror tactics of killing, kidnapping, and jailing key leaders of these organizations (Churchill, 1988). COINTELPRO also exploited internal differences to create factions that eventually left the organizations. According to various members of the YL, in retrospect they figure they were infiltrated from day one. In time they found out that many close friends were actually federal agents. In a climate of distrust, it is only a matter of time until an organization's cohesion disappears. Such was the case of the YL and countless organizations that planted the flag of social change and justice during the 1960s and 1970s.

"And They Don't Stop ... Cause They Can't Stop"

All over the world, the people know that
the streets

are ours, the moon is ours, the future is
  ours, man it's
all ours! All of it! And we here today will
  not rest until
it's won and placed firmly in the hands of
  the people.

Young Lords

Many of the revolutionary activists of the
1960s and 1970s are still engaging in
struggle. They are alive and kicking, organizing and working for better days. Those
who were once YL members are doing the
same. Most of their ex-leaders remain true to
their convictions. For example, Iris Morales
directs Union Square awards at the Fund for
the City of New York. This organization
gives funding to grassroots organization and
activists throughout the city. Morales has
also been involved in systemic educational
reform. Juan Gonzalez is a journalist and
former president of the National Congress
for Puerto Rican Rights (NCPRR). Richie
Perez is both former president and co-
founder of the NCPRR, is a co-founder of
the People's Justice 2000 coalition, and has
worked as a university professor in New
York. Activists all over this country suffered
a big blow when he passed away in 2004.
Minerva Solla is a union organizer for health
care workers. In an interesting twist of fate
Vicente "Panama" Alba is a union organizer and local representative of sanitation
workers in New York City. Felipe Luciano
is a consultant for corporations, government, and organizations that want to deal
with issues affecting Latinos/as in the U.S.
He is also the president of Luciano Pro-
ductions. Countless other ex–YL continue
to engage in day-to-day struggles to make
our world a better one.

As a result of the multiple struggles of the
1960s and 1970s, the YL included, a great
many organizations carry the legacies of
the struggles they incarnated. Andres Torres

(1998) states that "the radical experience
became a 'school' to thousands of future
leaders in all walks of life, people who went
on to become figures in areas: community
organizing, labor, education, culture and
politics" (p. 18). Many organizations and
institutions materialized out of the tumultuous revolutionary struggle of 1960s and
1970s activism. Just to mention a few, we
have the Museo del Barrio (New York), La
Casa de Chema (New York), Puerto Rican
Cultural Center and Casa Cultural Segundo
Ruiz Belvis (Chicago), Casa Don Pedro
(Newark, New Jersey), Taller Puertorriqueño (Philadelphia), Inquilinos Boricuas en
Accion (Boston), Center for Puerto Rican
Studies, Hostos Community College, Bor-
icua College, The Point, EL Puente, MUE-
VETE, Institute for Puerto Rican Policy,
Puerto Rican Legal Defense and Education
Fund, and a coterie of Puerto Rican, Latino,
Hispanic, and Caribbean studies departments
that continue to operate within academia.

The abundance of organizations reflects
the harsh reality that we live in a world
filled with a great deal of injustice, oppression, and exploitation. Many of the issues regarding education, health, and living
conditions that became the forefront of the
YL struggle thrive today. Some say that the
living conditions under advanced global
capitalism are actually worse (Kloby,
1997). The inequality gap of the haves and
have-not has grown exponentially (Kloby,
1997). Within this general context, the YL
could have come to a full circle. How?

Almost 30 years after the foundation of
the YL in 1968, we find ourselves again
with disenfranchised Latino/a youth. Just
like the YL, a street and prison gang known
as the Latin Kings shape-shifted in 1994 to
the Almighty Latin King and Queen Nation
(ALKQN). The documentary *Black and
Gold* (Rowley & Soohen, 1999) provides us

a glimpse of how the ALKQN emerged to eventually become a political organization. The ALKQN's history is much like that of YL's. Both organizations originated within street and gang life.

Furthermore, the documentary shows how organization members are deeply involved with their community. The ALKQN is a serious force of community organizing. In time, through them and other community organizers like former YL Richie Perez, the ALKQN created multiple coalitions against police brutality and demanded justice for the assassination of so many minority youth.

The AMLKQN have been a part of multiple struggles. Members of the AMLKQN are involved in education, school board and PTA meetings, the October 22nd movement, and the People's Justice 2000 coalition. They are engaged in the struggle for the liberation of Vieques and have had representatives in the Puerto Rican Day parade. Although not exactly like the YL, the AMLKQN have similar roots and experiences that create the surreal illusion that history is repeating itself. The spirit of the YL lives in Latino/a youth today, with the AMLKQN just one example of countless others. As long as we are not free from all forms of oppression and power is denied to the people, the struggle continues.

Liberation Schools: Young Lords and Education

America should never have taught us how to read, she should never have given eyes to see.

Felipe Luciano

The chains that have been taken off slaves' bodies are put back on their minds.

David Perez

Learning from the YL praxis, educators can embrace the notion of liberation schools. Drawing upon the pivotal works of Paulo Freire (1972, 1996, 1998, 2001) educators can nourish and implement a pedagogy of freedom. The works of critical pedagogues like Michael Apple, Stanley Aronowitz (2001, 2004), bell hooks (1994, 2004), Henry Giroux (1988), Peter McLaren (2001), and Donaldo Macedo (1994), just to name a few, can give educators a solid base to engage in an educational process that wishes to foster critical thinking, problem posing, and critical consciousness.

Based on the 13-point program the YL developed their own liberation schools. In them, they engaged in educational praxis that addressed main issues within their platform. These are (a) self-determination for Puerto Ricans and all Latinos/as; (b) liberation for all third world peoples; (c) opposition to racism; (d) equality for women; (e) community control of institutions (i.e., police, health services, churches, schools, housing, transportation, and social welfare); (f) true education of our Afro-Indio culture and Spanish language; (g) opposition to U.S. imperialist militarism; (h) opposition to the detrimental nature of capitalism; (i) self-defense by any means necessary. Educators can embrace a number of these main points that were the driving force for all YL praxis and incorporate them into their curricula.

Analyzing the YL 13-point platform, we can infer that the YL visionaries were critical pedagogues without the fancy rhetoric of academia. Within their platform they demanded the need for a society and hence an educational system that caters to the needs, experiences, and expectations of Latino/a communities. They demanded (a) curricular revisions that are at the heart of multicultural education and critical multiculturalism; (b) bilingual education; (c) communities controlling their own schools with their respective issues of proper funding, curriculum, pedagogical praxis, and strong community relations with the educators. In other words, the YL were advocating for anti-racist, anti-sexist education, for a curriculum that breaks from official versions of history by incorporating the voices of the other, demanding bilingual education, believing that communities should control the educational experiences of their children, that communities should demand ideal conditions for their children's education. They believed knowledge of self and knowledge of your own heritage is crucial for self-pride and self-determination and should always be present within schools and within society in general. These ideas are a reflection of the YL spirit.

Incorporating multiple points from the YL 13-point program are concrete examples of engaging in pedagogical praxis that aspires to create critical consciousness that may materialize itself in liberation and hence a pedagogy of freedom (Freire, 1972, 1996, 1998, 2001). Engaging in a pedagogy of freedom is a historical must (Aronowitz, 2001). Educators may have different visions of what freedom look like, but what constitute emancipation should be defined and articulated by those who are in the process of a pedagogy of freedom.

Drawing from Freire (1996), students must engage in constructing their own definition of what constitutes reality. They must come to a critical understanding through a problem-posing pedagogical praxis (Freire, 1996). Engaging in such pedagogy will create conditions enabling students and educators to reach a level of critical consciousness (Freire, 1998). Educators must break from traditional forms of pedagogical praxis to embrace a pedagogy that fuels from hope and aspires for the emancipation of humanity (Freire, 2001). Educators are thus burdened with deciding whether they are going to engage in pedagogical praxis that humanizes or dehumanizes (Freire, 1996). In restoring a process of humanizing our day-to-day reality, education can become an emancipatory act (Freire, 2001, hooks, 1994, 2004). But there is not a set blueprint for a pedagogy of freedom. We must build the road by walking. Educators must recognize that sometimes our biggest limitation is lack of imagination.

Needless to say, a pedagogy of freedom and pedagogy as an emancipatory act are historical necessities in times of unprecedented global injustices (Stiglitz, 2003; Aronowitz, 2004). We must embrace the YL slogan of "Pa' Lante Siempre Pa' Lante" until our educational system is of the utmost quality that produces grounded critical thinkers who are problem posers, problem solvers, and agents for social change (Freire, 1996). Until that day comes, just like the YL and countless others worldwide, let's work for better days: ¡Hasta la Victoria Siempre!

References

Aronowitz, S. (2001). *The Last Good Job in America*. New York: Basic Books.

Aronowitz, S. (2004). *Implicating Empire: Globalization and Resistance in the 21st Century*. New York: Basic Books & CUNY Press.

Berrios-Miranda, M. (2004). Salsa music as expressive liberation. *CENTRO (Journal)* 16(2), 159–173.

Churchill, W. (1998). *A Little Matter of Genocide*. Cambridge, MA: South End Press.

Churchill, W., & Vander Wall, J. (1990). *The COINTELPRO Papers*. Cambridge, MA: South End Press.

Duany, J. (2002). *Puerto Rican Nation on the Move: Identities on the Island and in the United States*. Chapel Hill: University of North Carolina Press.

Flores, J. (1991). *Divided Borders: Essays on Puerto Rican Identity.* Houston, TX: Arte Público Press.

Flores, J. (2000). *From Bomba to Hip-Hop: Puerto Rican Culture and Latino Identity.* New York: Columbia University Press.

Freire, P. (1972). *Pedagogia como la practica de la libertad.* Mexico: Editorial XXI.

Freire, P. (1996). *Pedagogy of the Oppressed.* New York: Continuum.

Freire, P. (1998). *Pedagogy for Critical Conciousness.* New York: Continuum.

Freire, P. (2001). *Pedagogy of Freedom.* New York: Rowman & Littlefield.

Giroux, H. (1998). *Schooling and the Struggle for Public Life: Democracy's Promise and Education's Challenge.* Minneapolis: University of Minnesota Press.

hooks, b. (1994). *Teaching to Transgress: Education as the Practice of Freedom.* London: Routledge.

hooks, b. (2004). *Teaching Community: A Pedagogy of Hope.* London: Routledge.

Kloby, J. (1997). *Inequality, Power and Development: The Task of Political Sociology.* Atlantic Highlands, NJ: Humanities Press.

Macedo, D. (1994). *Literacies of Power: What Americans Aren't Allowed to Know.* Boulder, CO: Westview Press.

McLaren, P. (2001). *Che Guevara, Paulo Freire and the Pedagogy of Revolution.* New York: Continuum.

Morales, I. (1996). *Pa'Lante Siempre Pa'Lante: The Young Lords* [Video Recording] New York: LENS Columbia University.

Morales, I. (1998). Pa'Lante Siempre Pa'Lante: The Young Lords. In A. Torres & J. Velazquez (Eds.), *The Puerto Rican Movement: Voices from the Diaspora.* Philadelphia: Temple University Press.

Rodríguez-Morazzani, R. (1998). Political Cultures of the Puerto Rican Left in the United States. In A. Torres & J. Velazquez (Eds.), *The Puerto Rican Movement: Voices from the Diaspora.* Philadelphia: Temple University Press.

Rowley, R., & Soohen, J. (1999). *Black and Gold.* [Video Recording]. New York: Big Noise Films.

Sánchez-Korrol, V. (1994). *From Colonia to Community: The History of Puerto Ricans in New York City.* Los Angeles: University of California Press.

Serrano, B. (1998). "Rifle, cañon y escopeta": A Chronicle of the Puerto Rican Student Union. In A. Torres & J. Velazquez (Eds.), *The Puerto Rican Movement: Voices from the Diaspora.* Philadelphia: Temple University Press.

Stiglitz, J. E. (2003). *Globalization and Its Discontents.* New York: W.W. Norton.

Torres, A. (1998). Introduction: Political Radicalism in the Diaspora: The Puerto Rican Experience. In A. Torres & J. Velazquez (Eds.), *The Puerto Rican Movement: Voices from the Diaspora.* Philadelphia: Temple University Press.

YLP. (1971). *Pa'Lante Young Lords Party.* New York: McGraw-Hill Books.

Recommended Reading

Torres, A., & Velazquez, J. (Eds.). (1998). *The Puerto Rican Movement: Voices from the Diaspora.* Philadelphia: Temple University Press.

Joseph Carroll-Miranda

Demographics

INTRODUCTION

Demographic information about people living in the U.S., and specifically those who identify themselves as Latino or Hispanic, is presented here in the form of census maps, tables, and a figure. The information has been taken from reports and publications issued by the U.S. Census Bureau, including Census 2000 and the annual American Community Survey, as well as from recent briefs concerned with matters of ethnicity and race. These sources contain total numbers of Latinos as well as growth rates and percentages of Latinos relative to the total population of the U.S.

Many of the tables provide information concerning key demographic variables such as educational attainment, socioeconomic status, and employment status, which are considered predictive of what sociologists refer to as "life chances." Many of these same variables are used to forecast social trends and form the basis for population projections.

Data from the U.S. Census Bureau is widely recognized as being among the highest quality of all sources of population data. One of the reasons for this recognition is the many attempts by Census Bureau staff and statisticians to keep abreast of changes in the demographic, lifestyle, and residential patterns of the U.S. population.

At the time of this writing, during Hispanic Heritage month 2005 (September 15–October 15), the U.S. Census has undertaken a major revision in the timing and collection of data.

Since 1790 a decennial census has been required by federal law, in what began as an attempt to apportion seats in the U.S. House of Representatives to approximately the same number of citizens and residents. While the decennial census is still used for that purpose, additional legal requirements have mandated that information, beyond the count and location of people, be collected as well. For example, the Voting Rights Act required that the census collect information about the race category to which respondents identified; the Civil Rights Act of 1964 required that information about ancestry be collected; and the Fair Housing Act required information about whether respondents identified themselves as Latino or Hispanic.

More recently, there was concern that the 10-year periods between the decennial censuses were too long to wait for the demographic, housing, and socioeconomic information that government and business leaders needed to meet the changing needs of their communities. In an attempt to modernize the census, utilizing technologies such as the Internet and modern scientific sampling techniques, the U.S. Census Bureau announced in January 2005 that it will streamline Census 2010 by using only the short form. In the past, approximately one in six addresses to which the census was mailed received the long form, consisting of approximately 60 questions, which took longer to fill out, resulting in a decreased response rate, but also collecting detailed information, such as language spoken at home, educational attainment, and commute times.

By using only the short form and incorporating more efficient data collection techniques (including handheld computers for field workers to eliminate data entry errors, as well as global positioning software to ensure workers are in the correct location), the U.S. Census Bureau expects to increase the accuracy and precision of the data it collects.

Beginning in 2005, the annual American Community Survey will include all the questions from the long form. This survey will be mailed monthly to a random, rolling sample of approximately 250,000 addresses throughout the U.S. and Puerto Rico, such that 2.5% of the population (about 1 in 40 addresses) will participate in the mandatory survey each year. The Census Bureau will release data for areas with populations of 65,000 or more annually, beginning in summer 2006. Smaller areas will have data released over a three to five-year period.

Such substantial changes in the primary data source for demographic information are relevant for two reasons: (1) demographic information from one period to another can be compared; and (2) the halfway point between the 2000 and 2010 decennial censuses has been reached, which presents the opportunity to update the numbers, patterns, and trends depicted in many of the tables in this section.

Interpretation of the demographic information must take into account that data collected by the U.S. Census Bureau had been changed with regard to the collection of information concerning racial and ethnic identification. Data on race in Census 2000 is not directly comparable to data collected from the 1990 and previous censuses. Census 2000 used federal standards established by the Office of Management and Budget (OMB) in October 1997 for presenting data on race and Hispanic origin, which require federal agencies to use a minimum of five race categories. The race categories used for collection of Census 2000 data included

1. White *alone*
2. Black or African American *alone*
3. American Indian and Alaska Native *alone*
4. Asian *alone*
5. Native Hawaiian and Other Pacific Islander *alone*
6. Some other race *alone*
7. Two or more races

In Census 2000 it is noteworthy that respondents were for the first time given the opportunity to select more than one race category, and that the category "Some other race" could constitute one of the races selected by respondents who also selected one or more of the other race categories. The consequences of this reconfiguration of race categories in Census 2000 included unexpected results, including that the overwhelming majority (97%) of those selecting "Some other race" were Latino, which suggests that many respondents considered Hispanic or Latino a racial as well as an ethnic identity.

This change in the collection of race data was accompanied by a switch in the order of questions with regard to Latino or Hispanic identification. Although the question on Latino origin was similar to the 1990 census question, it was asked directly before the question on race; whereas in the 1990 census the order was reversed, and it was separated by questions concerning age and marital status, further confounding the ability to compare the size of the Latino population in Census 2000 to the data from earlier censuses. Fortunately, sample data collected in years since the revised Census 2000 has retained its categories, so there is a comparative framework at the halfway point (to Census 2010).

Every census is designed to reflect changing lifestyles and issues of identity among the people in the U.S. Many Latinos in the U.S. consider their country or place of origin as their primary ethnic identity rather than the broader category (e.g., persons who think of themselves as Chicano or Puerto Rican rather than as Latino or Hispanic). Thus, demographic information in this section will include nationality or place of origin (ancestry) as well as ethnicity and race. By convention, the U.S. Census Bureau has been using "Hispanic or Latino," just as it uses "Black or African-American" as a more inclusive category.

GEOGRAPHY

Census Map 1, and other maps included in this chapter, utilize dual scaling, as is the case with two maps (i.e., of counties or municipios and of states).

Percent of Population, 2000

Hispanic or Latino Origin

All Races

All races: Hispanic or Latino population as a percent of total population by state

25.0 to 98.8
12.5 to 24.9
5.0 to 12.4
0.7 to 4.9

U.S. percent is 12.5

This map is one of a series of 14 "Percent of Population" maps with comparable categories for counties. Breaks defining map categories differ by small amounts among maps in the series to include the U.S. percent for the specific group mapped.

All races: Hispanic or Latino population as a percent of total population by county

95.0 to 99.7
70.0 to 94.9
50.0 to 69.9
25.0 to 49.9
12.5 to 24.9
5.0 to 12.4
1.0 to 4.9
0.1 to 0.9

U.S. percent is 12.5

0   100 Miles

Data Source: U.S. Census Bureau, Census 2000 Redistricting Data (PL 94-171) Summary File. Cartography: Population Division, U.S. Census Bureau. American FactFinder at factfinder.census.gov provides census data and mapping tools.

Census Map 1

Geographic Distribution of "Hispanics or Latinos," Census 2000, as Percentage of Total Population

Table 1
Places of 100,000 or More, Ranked by Percent "Hispanic or Latino"

				Hispanic or Latino	
Rank	Place Name[1]	State	Total Population	Number	Percent
1	East Los Angeles CDP[1]	CA	124,283	120,307	96.8
2	Laredo city	TX	176,576	166,216	94.1
3	Brownsville city	TX	139,722	127,535	91.3
4	Hialeah city	FL	226,419	204,543	90.3
5	McAllen city	TX	106,414	85,427	80.3
6	El Paso city	TX	563,662	431,875	76.6
7	Santa Ana city	CA	337,977	257,097	76.1
8	El Monte city	CA	115,965	83,945	72.4
9	Oxnard city	CA	170,358	112,807	66.2
10	Miami city	FL	362,470	238,351	65.8
11	Pomona city	CA	149,473	96,370	64.5
12	Salinas city	CA	151,060	96,880	64.1
13	Norwalk city	CA	103,298	64,965	62.9
14	Ontario city	CA	158,007	94,610	59.9
15	San Antonio city	TX	1,144,646	671,394	58.7
16	Downey city	CA	107,323	62,089	57.9
17	Fontana city	CA	128,929	74,424	57.7
18	Corpus Christi city	TX	277,454	150,737	54.3
19	Paterson city	NJ	149,222	74,774	50.1
20	Chula Vista city	CA	173,556	86,073	49.6
21	Elizabeth city	NJ	120,568	59,627	49.5
22	Pasadena city	TX	141,674	68,348	48.2
23	San Bernardino city	CA	185,401	88,022	47.5
24	Anaheim city	CA	328,014	153,374	46.8
25	Los Angeles city	CA	3,694,820	1,719,073	46.5
26	Inglewood city	CA	112,580	51,829	46.0
27	West Covina city	CA	105,080	48,051	45.7
28	Pueblo city	CO	102,121	45,066	44.1
29	Hartford city	CT	121,578	49,260	40.5
30	Albuquerque city	NM	448,607	179,075	39.9
31	Fresno city	CA	427,652	170,520	39.9
32	Escondido city	CA	133,559	51,693	38.7
33	Moreno Valley city	CA	142,381	54,689	38.4
34	Riverside city	CA	255,166	97,315	38.1
35	Palmdale city	CA	116,670	43,991	37.7
36	North Las Vegas city	NV	115,488	43,435	37.6
37	Houston city	TX	1,953,631	730,865	37.4
38	Long Beach city	CA	461,522	165,092	35.8
39	Tucson city	AZ	486,699	173,868	35.7
40	Corona city	CA	124,966	44,569	35.7
41	Dallas city	TX	1,188,580	422,587	35.6
42	Hayward city	CA	140,030	47,850	34.2
43	Phoenix city	AZ	1,321,045	449,972	34.1
44	Pasadena city	CA	133,936	44,734	33.4
45	Grand Prairie city	TX	127,427	42,038	33.0
46	Aurora city	IL	142,990	46,557	32.6
47	Stockton city	CA	243,771	79,217	32.5
48	Garden Grove city	CA	165,196	53,608	32.5
49	Bakersfield city	CA	247,057	80,170	32.5

(continued)

Table 1
(continued)

Rank	Place Name[1]	State	Total Population	Hispanic or Latino Number	Hispanic or Latino Percent
50	Orange city	CA	128,821	41,434	32.2
51	Bridgeport city	CT	139,529	44,478	31.9
52	Costa Mesa city	CA	108,724	34,523	31.8
53	Denver city	CO	554,636	175,704	31.7
54	Irving city	TX	191,615	59,838	31.2
55	Austin city	TX	656,562	200,579	30.5
56	Oceanside city	CA	161,029	48,691	30.2
57	Fullerton city	CA	126,003	38,014	30.2
58	San Jose city	CA	894,943	269,989	30.2
59	Providence city	RI	173,618	52,146	30.0
60	Fort Worth city	TX	534,694	159,368	29.8
61	Newark city	NJ	273,546	80,622	29.5
62	Jersey City city	NJ	240,055	67,952	28.3
63	Pembroke Pines city	FL	137,427	38,700	28.2
64	Rancho Cucamonga city	CA	127,743	35,491	27.8
65	Lubbock city	TX	199,564	54,786	27.5
66	Springfield city	MA	152,082	41,343	27.2
67	New York city[1]	NY	8,008,278	2,160,554	27.0
68	Chicago city	IL	2,896,016	753,644	26.0
69	Sunrise Manor CDP[1]	NV	156,120	40,619	26.0
70	Yonkers city	NY	196,086	50,852	25.9
71	Modesto city	CA	188,856	48,310	25.6
72	Garland city	TX	215,768	55,192	25.6
73	San Diego city	CA	1,223,400	310,752	25.4
74	Burbank city	CA	100,316	24,953	24.9
75	Glendale city	AZ	218,812	54,343	24.8
76	Allentown city	PA	106,632	26,058	24.4
77	San Buenaventura (Ventura) city	CA	100,916	24,573	24.3
78	Lancaster city	CA	118,718	28,644	24.1
79	Waco city	TX	113,726	26,885	23.6
80	Las Vegas city	NV	478,434	112,962	23.6
81	Paradise CDP[1]	NV	186,070	43,663	23.5
82	Hollywood city	FL	139,357	31,392	22.5
83	Daly City city	CA	103,621	23,072	22.3
84	Oakland city	CA	399,484	87,467	21.9
85	Amarillo city	TX	173,627	37,947	21.9
86	Concord city	CA	121,780	26,560	21.8
87	Waterbury city	CT	107,271	23,354	21.8
88	Sacramento city	CA	407,018	87,974	21.6
89	New Haven city	CT	123,626	26,443	21.4
90	Chandler city	AZ	176,581	37,059	21.0
91	Santa Clarita city	CA	151,088	30,968	20.5
92	Aurora city	CO	276,393	54,764	19.8
93	Mesa city	AZ	396,375	78,281	19.7
94	Glendale city	CA	194,973	38,452	19.7
95	Carrollton city	TX	109,576	21,400	19.5
96	Abilene city	TX	115,930	22,548	19.4
97	Tampa city	FL	303,447	58,522	19.3
98	Santa Rosa city	CA	147,595	28,318	19.2
99	Reno city	NV	180,480	34,616	19.2

Table 1
(continued)

| Rank | Place Name[1] | State | Total Population | Hispanic or Latino | |
				Number	Percent
100	Salt Lake City city	UT	181,743	34,254	18.8
101	Arlington CDP[1]	VA	189,453	35,268	18.6
102	West Valley City city	UT	108,896	20,126	18.5
103	Joliet city	IL	106,221	19,552	18.4
104	Arlington city	TX	332,969	60,817	18.3
105	Tempe city	AZ	158,625	28,473	17.9
106	Orlando city	FL	185,951	32,510	17.5
107	Simi Valley city	CA	111,351	18,729	16.8
108	Kansas City city	KS	146,866	24,639	16.8
109	Stamford city	CT	117,083	19,635	16.8
110	Santa Clara city	CA	102,361	16,364	16.0
111	Vallejo city	CA	116,760	18,591	15.9
112	Mesquite city	TX	124,523	19,500	15.7
113	Coral Springs city	FL	117,549	18,233	15.5
114	Sunnyvale city	CA	131,760	20,390	15.5
115	Peoria city	AZ	108,364	16,699	15.4
116	Westminster city	CO	100,940	15,369	15.2
117	Worcester city	MA	172,648	26,155	15.1
118	Alexandria city	VA	128,283	18,882	14.7
119	Huntington Beach city	CA	189,594	27,798	14.7
120	Salem city	OR	136,924	19,973	14.6
121	Lakewood city	CO	144,126	20,949	14.5
122	Boston city	MA	589,141	85,089	14.4
123	San Francisco city	CA	776,733	109,504	14.1
124	Lowell city	MA	105,167	14,734	14.0
125	Wichita Falls city	TX	104,197	14,570	14.0
126	Spring Valley CDP[1]	NV	117,390	16,165	13.8
127	Fremont city	CA	203,413	27,409	13.5
128	Thousand Oaks city	CA	117,005	15,328	13.1
129	Grand Rapids city	MI	197,800	25,818	13.1
130	Torrance city	CA	137,946	17,637	12.8
131	Rochester city	NY	219,773	28,032	12.8
132	Colorado Springs city	CO	360,890	43,330	12.0
133	Milwaukee city	WI	596,974	71,646	12.0
134	Gilbert town[1]	AZ	109,967	13,026	11.9
135	Henderson city	NV	175,381	18,785	10.7
136	Provo city	UT	105,166	11,013	10.5
137	Rockford city	IL	150,115	15,278	10.2
138	Oklahoma City city	OK	506,132	51,368	10.1
139	Plano city	TX	222,030	22,357	10.1
140	Lansing city	MI	119,128	11,886	10.0
141	Arvada city	CO	102,153	10,031	9.8
142	Berkeley city	CA	102,743	10,001	9.7
143	Wichita city	KS	344,284	33,112	9.6
144	Fort Lauderdale city	FL	152,397	14,406	9.5
145	Clearwater city	FL	108,787	9,754	9.0
146	Topeka city	KS	122,377	10,847	8.9
147	Fort Collins city	CO	118,652	10,402	8.8
148	Winston-Salem city	NC	185,776	16,043	8.6

(continued)

Table 1
(continued)

Rank	Place Name[1]	State	Total Population	Hispanic or Latino Number	Hispanic or Latino Percent
149	Durham city	NC	187,035	16,012	8.6
150	Philadelphia city	PA	1,517,550	128,928	8.5
151	South Bend city	IN	107,789	9,110	8.5
152	Cape Coral city	FL	102,286	8,521	8.3
153	Beaumont city	TX	113,866	9,028	7.9
154	St. Paul city	MN	287,151	22,715	7.9
155	Washington city	DC	572,059	44,953	7.9
156	Minneapolis city	MN	382,618	29,175	7.6
157	Buffalo city	NY	292,648	22,076	7.5
158	Omaha city	NE	390,007	29,397	7.5
159	Irvine city	CA	143,072	10,539	7.4
160	Charlotte city	NC	540,828	39,800	7.4
161	Cambridge city	MA	101,355	7,455	7.4
162	Cleveland city	OH	478,403	34,728	7.3
163	Metairie CDP[1]	LA	146,136	10,595	7.3
164	Tulsa city	OK	393,049	28,111	7.2
165	Green Bay city	WI	102,313	7,294	7.1
166	Raleigh city	NC	276,093	19,308	7.0
167	Scottsdale city	AZ	202,705	14,111	7.0
168	Kansas City city	MO	441,545	30,604	6.9
169	Tacoma city	WA	193,556	13,262	6.9
170	Portland city	OR	529,121	36,058	6.8
171	Des Moines city	IA	198,682	13,138	6.6
172	Athens-Clarke County[1]	GA	101,489	6,436	6.3
173	Vancouver city	WA	143,560	9,035	6.3
174	Clarksville city	TN	103,455	6,241	6.0
175	Fort Wayne city	IN	205,727	11,884	5.8
176	Anchorage municipality[1]	AK	260,283	14,799	5.7
177	Fayetteville city	NC	121,015	6,862	5.7
178	Toledo city	OH	313,619	17,141	5.5
179	Bellevue city	WA	109,569	5,827	5.3
180	Seattle city	WA	563,374	29,719	5.3
181	Syracuse city	NY	147,306	7,768	5.3
182	Eugene city	OR	137,893	6,843	5.0
183	Detroit city	MI	951,270	47,167	5.0
184	Gary city	IN	102,746	5,065	4.9
185	Manchester city	NH	107,006	4,944	4.6
186	Nashville-Davidson[1]	TN	569,891	26,091	4.6
187	Boise City city	ID	185,787	8,410	4.5
188	Atlanta city	GA	416,474	18,720	4.5
189	Columbus city	GA	186,291	8,372	4.5
190	Erie city	PA	103,717	4,572	4.4
191	Honolulu CDP[1]	HI	371,657	16,229	4.4
192	Greensboro city	NC	223,891	9,742	4.4
193	St. Petersburg city	FL	248,232	10,502	4.2
194	Newport News city	VA	180,150	7,595	4.2
195	Tallahassee city	FL	150,624	6,309	4.2
196	Virginia Beach city	VA	425,257	17,770	4.2
197	Jacksonville city	FL	735,617	30,594	4.2
198	Madison city	WI	208,054	8,512	4.1

Table 1
(continued)

Rank	Place Name[1]	State	Total Population	Hispanic or Latino Number	Hispanic or Latino Percent
199	Indianapolis city	IN	791,926	30,759	3.9
200	Norfolk city	VA	234,403	8,915	3.8
201	Overland Park city	KS	149,080	5,620	3.8
202	Independence city	MO	113,288	4,175	3.7
203	Lincoln city	NE	225,581	8,154	3.6
204	Ann Arbor city	MI	114,024	3,814	3.3
205	Lexington-Fayette[1]	KY	260,512	8,561	3.3
206	Naperville city	IL	128,358	4,160	3.2
207	New Orleans city	LA	484,674	14,826	3.1
208	Columbia city	SC	116,278	3,520	3.0
209	Flint city	MI	124,943	3,742	3.0
210	Spokane city	WA	195,629	5,857	3.0
211	Memphis city	TN	650,100	19,317	3.0
212	Hampton city	VA	146,437	4,153	2.8
213	Augusta-Richmond County[1]	GA	199,775	5,545	2.8
214	Little Rock city	AR	183,133	4,889	2.7
215	Richmond city	VA	197,790	5,074	2.6
216	Peoria city	IL	112,936	2,839	2.5
217	Sioux Falls city	SD	123,975	3,087	2.5
218	Columbus city	OH	711,470	17,471	2.5
219	Springfield city	MO	151,580	3,501	2.3
220	Savannah city	GA	131,510	2,938	2.2
221	Chattanooga city	TN	155,554	3,281	2.1
222	Chesapeake city	VA	199,184	4,076	2.0
223	Huntsville city	AL	158,216	3,225	2.0
224	St. Louis city	MO	348,189	7,022	2.0
225	Lafayette city	LA	110,257	2,071	1.9
226	Louisville city	KY	256,231	4,755	1.9
227	Portsmouth city	VA	100,565	1,748	1.7
228	Livonia city	MI	100,545	1,731	1.7
229	Baton Rouge city	LA	227,818	3,918	1.7
230	Cedar Rapids city	IA	120,758	2,065	1.7
231	Baltimore city	MD	651,154	11,061	1.7
232	Knoxville city	TN	173,890	2,751	1.6
233	Dayton city	OH	166,179	2,626	1.6
234	Shreveport city	LA	200,145	3,106	1.6
235	Binningham city	AL	242,820	3,764	1.6
236	Mobile city	AL	198,915	2,828	1.4
237	Warren city	MI	138,247	1,868	1.4
238	Sterling Heights city	MI	124,471	1,665	1.3
239	Pittsburgh city	PA	334,563	4,425	1.3
240	Cincinnati city	OH	331,285	4,230	1.3
241	Montgomery city	AL	201,568	2,484	1.2
242	Springfield city	IL	111,454	1,337	1.2
243	Akron city	OH	217,074	2,513	1.2
244	Evansville city	IN	121,582	1,392	1.1
245	Jackson city	MS	184,256	1,451	0.8

(continued)

Table 1
(continued)

				Hispanic or Latino	
Rank	Place Name[1]	State	Total Population	Number	Percent
	PUERTO RICO				
1	Ponce zona urbana[1]	PR	155,038	153,379	98.9
2	Bayamón zona urbana[1]	PR	203,499	200,742	98.6
3	Carolina zona urbana[1]	PR	168,164	165,334	98.3
4	San Juan zona urbana[1]	PR	421,958	413,328	98.0

1. In the U.S., there are 245 places with 100,000 or more population. These places include 234 incorporated places (232 cities, 1 municipality, and 1 town), 4 city-county consolidations with the county name included as part of the place name (Athens-Clarke County, GA; Augusta-Richmond County, GA; Lexington-Fayette, KY; and Nashville-Davidson, TN), and 7 census designated places (CDPs). CDPs are delineated for the decennial census and comprise densely settled concentrations of population which are identifiable by name, but which are not legally incorporated places. One of these CDPs is Arlington CDP, VA, which is coextensive with Arlington County. In Puerto Rico, there are 4 places with 100,000 or more population, all of which are CDPs identified as zonas urbans. There are no incorporated places in Hawaii or Puerto Rico.

If Miami–Dade County's nearly 1.2 million foreign-born residents comprised a city of their own, that city would be the 10th largest in the nation. In 2002, the American Community Survey revealed the nation has 33 million residents who are natives of other countries. Of the top 10 counties with the largest proportion of foreign-born, all but one (Hudson County, New Jersey) were located in New York or California.

Historically, it is common for recent immigrant groups to cluster geographically, before perhaps dispersing through internal migration. This pattern is apparent in census data, which indicate that 49% of the Latino-origin population lives in California and Texas, and that 43% of New Mexico's population is Hispanic, the highest of any state.

Number of People, 2000
Hispanic or Latino Origin
All Races

All races
Number of people
indicating Hispanic
or Latino origin
by state

■	10,000,000 to 10,970,000
	1,000,000 to 9,999,999
	10,000 to 969,999
	5,504 to 9,999

All races:
Number of people
indicating Hispanic
or Latino origin
by county

■	50,000 to 4,243,000
	10,000 to 49,999
	5,000 to 9,999
	1,000 to 4,999
	100 to 999
	1 to 99

0 ⊢———⊣ 100 Miles

Data Source: U.S. Census Bureau, Census 2000
Redistricting Data (PL 94-171) Summary File
Cartography: Population Division, U.S. Census Bureau
American Factfinder at *factfinder.census.gov*
provides census data and mapping tools.

0 ⊢———⊣ 100 Miles

0 ⊢———⊣ 100 Miles

Census Map 2
Geographic Distribution of "Hispanics or Latinos," Census 2000, as Total Number of Hispanics or Latinos

Table 2
Race and "Hispanic or Latino" Census 2000
Data Set: Census 2000 Summary File 1 (SF 1) 100–Percent Data
Geographic Area: U.S.—State; and Puerto Rico

						Percent of total population				
						Race				
				One race						
Geographic area	*Total population*	*White*	*Black or African American*	*American Indian and Alaska Native*	*Asian*	*Native Hawaiian and Other Pacific Islander*	*Some other race*	*Two or more races*	*Hispanic or Latino (of any race)*	*White alone, not Hispanic or Latino*
United States	281,421,906	75.1	12.3	0.9	3.6	0.1	5.5	2.4	12.5	69.1
Alabama	4,447,100	71.1	26.0	0.5	0.7	0.0	0.7	1.0	1.7	70.3
Alaska	626,932	69.3	3.5	15.6	4.0	0.5	1.6	5.4	4.1	67.6
Arizona	5,130,632	75.5	3.1	5.0	1.8	0.1	11.6	2.9	25.3	63.8
Arkansas	2,673,400	80.0	15.7	0.7	0.8	0.1	1.5	1.3	3.2	78.6
California	33,871,648	59.5	6.7	1.0	10.9	0.3	16.8	4.7	32.4	46.7
Colorado	4,301,261	82.8	3.8	1.0	2.2	0.1	7.2	2.8	17.1	74.5
Connecticut	3,405,565	81.6	9.1	0.3	2.4	0.0	4.3	2.2	9.4	77.5
Delaware	783,600	74.6	19.2	0.3	2.1	0.0	2.0	1.7	4.8	72.5
District of Columbia	572,059	30.8	60.0	0.3	2.7	0.1	3.8	2.4	7.9	27.8
Florida	15,982,378	78.0	14.6	0.3	1.7	0.1	3.0	2.4	16.8	65.4
Georgia	8,186,453	65.1	28.7	0.3	2.1	0.1	2.4	1.4	5.3	62.6
Hawaii	1,211,537	24.3	1.8	0.3	41.6	9.4	1.3	21.4	7.2	22.9
Idaho	1,293,953	91.0	0.4	1.4	0.9	0.1	4.2	2.0	7.9	88.0
Illinois	12,419,293	73.5	15.1	0.2	3.4	0.0	5.8	1.9	12.3	67.8
Indiana	6,080,485	87.5	8.4	0.3	1.0	0.0	1.6	1.2	3.5	85.8
Iowa	2,926,324	93.9	2.1	0.3	1.3	0.0	1.3	1.1	2.8	92.6
Kansas	2,688,418	86.1	5.7	0.9	1.7	0.0	3.4	2.1	7.0	83.1
Kentucky	4,041,769	90.1	7.3	0.2	0.7	0.0	0.6	1.1	1.5	89.3
Louisiana	4,468,976	63.9	32.5	0.6	1.2	0.0	0.7	1.1	2.4	62.5
Maine	1,274,923	96.9	0.5	0.6	0.7	0.0	0.2	1.0	0.7	96.5
Maryland	5,296,486	64.0	27.9	0.3	4.0	0.0	1.8	2.0	4.3	62.1
Massachusetts	6,349,097	84.5	5.4	0.2	3.8	0.0	3.7	2.3	6.8	81.9
Michigan	9,938,444	80.2	14.2	0.6	1.8	0.0	1.3	1.9	3.3	78.6
Minnesota	4,919,479	89.4	3.5	1.1	2.9	0.0	1.3	1.7	2.9	88.2
Mississippi	2,844,658	61.4	36.3	0.4	0.7	0.0	0.5	0.7	1.4	60.7

Missouri	5,595,211	84.9	11.2	0.4	1.1	0.1	0.8	1.5	2.1	83.8
Montana	902,195	90.6	0.3	6.2	0.5	0.1	0.6	1.7	2.0	89.5
Nebraska	1,711,263	89.6	4.0	0.9	1.3	0.0	2.8	1.4	5.5	87.3
Nevada	1,998,257	75.2	6.8	1.3	4.5	0.4	8.0	3.8	19.7	65.2
New Hampshire	1,235,786	96.0	0.7	0.2	1.3	0.0	0.6	1.1	1.7	95.1
New Jersey	8,414,350	72.6	13.6	0.2	5.7	0.0	5.4	2.5	13.3	66.0
New Mexico	1,819,046	66.8	1.9	9.5	1.1	0.1	17.0	3.6	42.1	44.7
New York	18,976,457	67.9	15.9	0.4	5.5	0.0	7.1	3.1	15.1	62.0
North Carolina	8,049,313	72.1	21.6	1.2	1.4	0.0	2.3	1.3	4.7	70.2
North Dakota	642,200	92.4	0.6	4.9	0.6	0.0	0.4	1.2	1.2	91.7
Ohio	11,353,140	85.0	11.5	0.2	1.2	0.0	0.8	1.4	1.9	84.0
Oklahoma	3,450,654	76.2	7.6	7.9	1.4	0.1	2.4	4.5	5.2	74.1
Oregon	3,421,399	86.6	1.6	1.3	3.0	0.2	4.2	3.1	8.0	83.5
Pennsylvania	12,281,054	85.4	10.0	0.1	1.8	0.0	1.5	1.2	3.2	84.1
Rhode Island	1,048,319	85.0	4.5	0.5	2.3	0.1	5.0	2.7	8.7	81.9
South Carolina	4,012,012	67.2	29.5	0.3	0.9	0.0	1.0	1.0	2.4	66.1
South Dakota	754,844	88.7	0.6	8.3	0.6	0.0	0.5	1.3	1.4	88.0
Tennessee	5,689,283	80.2	16.4	0.3	1.0	0.0	1.0	1.1	2.2	79.2
Texas	20,851,820	71.0	11.5	0.6	2.7	0.1	11.7	2.5	32.0	52.4
Utah	2,233,169	89.2	0.8	1.3	1.7	0.7	4.2	2.1	9.0	85.3
Vermont	608,827	96.8	0.5	0.4	0.9	0.0	0.2	1.2	0.9	96.2
Virginia	7,078,515	72.3	19.6	0.3	3.7	0.1	2.0	2.0	4.7	70.2
Washington	5,894,121	81.8	3.2	1.6	5.5	0.4	3.9	3.6	7.5	78.9
West Virginia	1,808,344	95.0	3.2	0.2	0.5	0.0	0.2	0.9	0.7	94.6
Wisconsin	5,363,675	88.9	5.7	0.9	1.7	0.0	1.6	1.2	3.6	87.3
Wyoming	493,782	92.1	0.8	2.3	0.6	0.1	2.5	1.8	6.4	88.9
Puerto Rico	3,808,610	80.5	8.0	0.4	0.2	0.0	6.8	4.2	98.8	0.9

At the midpoint between Census 2000 and Census 2010, 13 states contain at least one-half million Latino residents. These states are Arizona, California, Colorado, Florida, Georgia, Illinois, Nevada, New Jersey, New Mexico, New York, North Carolina, Texas, and Washington.

Next, a series of tables reveal the type of ancestry or nationality that was indicated by "Hispanics and Latinos" for the U.S. as well as on a region-by-region basis.

Table 3
"Hispanic or Latino" Origin by Type for the U.S. and Puerto Rico, Census 2000

Group	Number	Percent
HISPANIC OR LATINO ORIGIN		
Total population	281,421,906	100.0
Hispanic or Latino (of any race)	35,305,818	12.5
Not Hispanic or Latino	246,116,088	87.5
HISPANIC OR LATINO BY TYPE		
Hispanic or Latino (of any race).	35,305,818	100.0
Mexican	20,640,711	58.5
Puerto Rican	3,406,178	9.6
Cuban	1,241,685	3.5
Other Hispanic or Latino	10,017,244	28.4
Dominican (Dominican Republic)	764,945	2.2
Central American (excludes Mexican)	1,686,937	4.8
Costa Rican	68,588	0.2
Guatemalan	372,487	1.1
Honduran	217,569	0.6
Nicaraguan	177,684	0.5
Panamanian	91,723	0.3
Salvadoran	655,165	1.9
Other Central American	103,721	0.3
South American	1,353,562	3.8
Argentinean	100,864	0.3
Bolivian	42,068	0.1
Chilean	68,849	0.2
Colombian	470,684	1.3
Ecuadorian	260,559	0.7
Paraguayan	8,769	—
Peruvian	233,926	0.7
Uruguayan	18,804	0.1
Venezuelan	91,507	0.3
Other South American	57,532	0.2
Spaniard	100,135	0.3
All other Hispanic or Latino	6,111,665	17.3
Checkbox only, other Hispanic	1,733,274	4.9
Write-in "Spanish"	686,004	1.9
Write in "Hispanic"	2,454,529	7.0
Write-in "Latino"	450,769	1.3
Not elsewhere classified.	787,089	2.2

Note: Dash (—) represents zero or rounds to zero.
Source: U.S. Census Bureau, Census 2000, Summary File 1 and unpublished data.

Table 4
"Hispanic or Latino" Origin for East South Central Region, Census 2000

Group	Number	Percent
HISPANIC OR LATINO ORIGIN		
Total population	17,022,810	100.0
Hispanic or Latino (of any race)	299,176	1.8
Not Hispanic or Latino	16,723,634	98.2
HISPANIC OR LATINO BY TYPE		
Hispanic or Latino (of any race)	299,176	100.0
Mexican	174,895	58.5
Puerto Rican	25,975	8.7
Cuban	11,073	3.7
Other Hispanic or Latino	87,233	29.2
Dominican (Dominican Republic)	1,321	0.4
Central American (excludes Mexican)	17,253	5.8
Costa Rican	894	0.3
Guatemalan	6,698	2.2
Honduran	2,923	1.0
Nicaraguan	778	0.3
Panamanian	2,507	0.8
Salvadoran	2,843	1.0
Other Central American	610	0.2
South American	8,660	2.9
Argentinean	659	0.2
Bolivian	342	0.1
Chilean	684	0.2
Colombian	3,028	1.0
Ecuadorian	696	0.2
Paraguayan	140	—
Peruvian	1,239	0.4
Uruguayan	92	—
Venezuelan	1,375	0.5
Other South American	405	0.1
Spaniard	1,014	0.3
All other Hispanic or Latino	58,985	19.7
Checkbox only, other Hispanic	22,751	7.6
Write-in "Spanish"	6,841	2.3
Write in "Hispanic"	20,619	6.9
Write-in "Latino"	2,946	1.0
Not elsewhere classified	5,828	1.9

Note: Dash (—) represents zero or rounds to zero.
Source: U.S. Census Bureau, Census 2000, Summary File 1 and unpublished data.

Table 5
"Hispanic or Latino" Origin for South Atlantic Region, Census 2000

Group	Number	Percent
HISPANIC OR LATINO ORIGIN		
Total population	51,769,160	100.0
Hispanic or Latino (of any race)	4,243,946	8.2
Not Hispanic or Latino	47,525,214	91.8
HISPANIC OR LATINO BY TYPE		
Hispanic or Latino (of any race)	4,243,946	100.0
Mexican	1,074,939	25.3
Puerto Rican	645,530	15.2
Cuban	873,492	20.6
Other Hispanic or Latino	1,649,985	38.9
Dominican (Dominican Republic)	89,117	2.1
Central American (excludes Mexican)	419,046	9.9
Costa Rican	18,317	0.4
Guatemalan	68,229	1.6
Honduran	68,953	1.6
Nicaraguan	90,051	2.1
Panamanian	29,295	0.7
Salvadoran	128,660	3.0
Other Central American	15,541	0.4
South American	409,999	9.7
Argentinean	30,155	0.7
Bolivian	20,089	0.5
Chilean	20,285	0.5
Colombian	168,454	4.0
Ecuadorian	33,254	0.8
Paraguayan	2,128	0.1
Peruvian	67,510	1.6
Uruguayan	5,733	0.1
Venezuelan	48,627	1.1
Other South American	13,764	0.3
Spaniard	20,674	0.5
All other Hispanic or Latino	711,149	16.8
Checkbox only, other Hispanic	251,043	5.9
Write-in "Spanish"	77,743	1.8
Write in "Hispanic"	188,998	4.5
Write-in "Latino"	80,488	1.9
Not elsewhere classified	112,877	2.7

Source: U.S. Census Bureau, Census 2000, Summary File 1 and unpublished data.

Table 6
"Hispanic or Latino" Origin for West Region, Census 2000

Group	Number	Percent
HISPANIC OR LATINO ORIGIN		
Total population	63,197,932	100.0
Hispanic or Latino (of any race)	15,340,503	24.3
Not Hispanic or Latino	47,857,429	75.7
HISPANIC OR LATINO BY TYPE		
Hispanic or Latino (of any race)	15,340,503	100.0
Mexican	11,413,265	74.4
Puerto Rican	246,936	1.6
Cuban	105,994	0.7
Other Hispanic or Latino	3,574,308	23.3
Dominican (Dominican Republic)	9,944	0.1
Central American (excludes Mexican)	650,727	4.2
Costa Rican	17,274	0.1
Guatemalan	164,305	1.1
Honduran	37,607	0.2
Nicaraguan	56,276	0.4
Panamanian	17,225	0.1
Salvadoran	299,790	2.0
Other Central American	58,250	0.4
South American	212,371	1.4
Argentinean	29,941	0.2
Bolivian	8,404	0.1
Chilean	19,838	0.1
Colombian	45,393	0.3
Ecuadorian	22,071	0.1
Paraguayan	908	—
Peruvian	55,793	0.4
Uruguayan	2,439	—
Venezuelan	9,645	0.1
Other South American	17,939	0.1
Spaniard	35,978	0.2
All other Hispanic or Latino	2,665,288	17.4
Checkbox only, other Hispanic	705,081	4.6
Write-in "Spanish"	372,853	2.4
Write in "Hispanic"	1,045,706	6.8
Write-in "Latino"	211,375	1.4
Not elsewhere classified	330,273	2.2

Note: Dash (—) represents zero or rounds to zero.
Source: U.S. Census Bureau, Census 2000, Summary File 1 and unpublished data.

Table 7
"Hispanic or Latino" Origin for West North Central Region, Census 2000

Group	Number	Percent
HISPANIC OR LATINO ORIGIN		
Total population	19,237,739	100.0
Hispanic or Latino (of any race)	645,813	3.4
Not Hispanic or Latino	18,591,926	96.6
HISPANIC OR LATINO BY TYPE		
Hispanic or Latino (of any race)	645,813	100.0
Mexican	464,613	71.9
Puerto Rican	24,357	3.8
Cuban	9,251	1.4
Other Hispanic or Latino	147,592	22.9
Dominican (Dominican Republic)	1,559	0.2
Central American (excludes Mexican)	25,950	4.0
Costa Rican	989	0.2
Guatemalan	8,616	1.3
Honduran	3,570	0.6
Nicaraguan	1,180	0.2
Panamanian	2,297	0.4
Salvadoran	7,961	1.2
Other Central American	1,337	0.2
South American	16,871	2.6
Argentinean	1,257	0.2
Bolivian	638	0.1
Chilean	1,366	0.2
Colombian	4,839	0.7
Ecuadorian	3,338	0.5
Paraguayan	388	0.1
Peruvian	2,463	0.4
Uruguayan	165	—
Venezuelan	1,608	0.2
Other South American	809	0.1
Spaniard	1,606	0.2
All other Hispanic or Latino	101,606	15.7
Checkbox only, other Hispanic	30,597	4.7
Write-in "Spanish"	13,776	2.1
Write in "Hispanic"	39,251	6.1
Write-in "Latino"	6,479	1.0
Not elsewhere classified	11,503	1.8

Note: Dash (—) represents zero or rounds to zero.
Source: U.S. Census Bureau, Census 2000, Summary File 1 and unpublished data.

Table 8
"Hispanic or Latino" Origin for Mountain Division, Census 2000

Group	Number	Percent
HISPANIC OR LATINO ORIGIN		
Total population	18,172,295	100.0
Hispanic or Latino (of any race)	3,543,573	19.5
Not Hispanic or Latino	14,628,722	80.5
HISPANIC OR LATINO BY TYPE		
Hispanic or Latino (of any race)	3,543,573	100.0
Mexican	2,379,589	67.2
Puerto Rican	52,480	1.5
Cuban	24,852	0.7
Other Hispanic or Latino	1,086,652	30.7
Dominican (Dominican Republic)	2,937	0.1
Central American (excludes Mexican)	51,846	1.5
Costa Rican	2,537	0.1
Guatemalan	14,073	0.4
Honduran	4,986	0.1
Nicaraguan	3,500	0.1
Panamanian	3,811	0.1
Salvadoran	19,954	0.6
Other Central American	2,985	0.1
South American	35,535	1.0
Argentinean	5,087	0.1
Bolivian	1,234	—
Chilean	4,216	0.1
Colombian	8,198	0.2
Ecuadorian	2,800	0.1
Paraguayan	211	—
Peruvian	8,095	0.2
Uruguayan	604	—
Venezuelan	3,146	0.1
Other South American	1,944	0.1
Spaniard	9,559	0.3
All other Hispanic or Latino	986,775	27.8
Checkbox only, other Hispanic	210,511	5.9
Write-in "Spanish"	172,370	4.9
Write in "Hispanic"	493,405	13.9
Write-in "Latino"	26,445	0.7
Not elsewhere classified	84,044	2.4

Note: Dash (—) represents zero or rounds to zero.
Source: U.S. Census Bureau, Census 2000, Summary File 1 and unpublished data.

Table 9

"Hispanic or Latino" Origin for Mid-Atlantic Region, Census 2000

Group	Number	Percent
HISPANIC OR LATINO ORIGIN		
Total population	39,671,861	100.0
Hispanic or Latino (of any race)	4,378,862	11.0
Not Hispanic or Latino	35,292,999	89.0
HISPANIC OR LATINO BY TYPE		
Hispanic or Latino (of any race)	4,378,862	100.0
Mexican	418,996	9.6
Puerto Rican	1,645,638	37.6
Cuban	150,290	3.4
Other Hispanic or Latino	2,163,938	49.4
Dominican (Dominican Republic)	569,877	13.0
Central American (excludes Mexican)	272,217	6.2
Costa Rican	20,136	0.5
Guatemalan	48,388	1.1
Honduran	52,302	1.2
Nicaraguan	13,389	0.3
Panamanian	24,473	0.6
Salvadoran	99,815	2.3
Other Central American	13,714	0.3
South American	513,672	11.7
Argentinean	24,087	0.6
Bolivian	6,303	0.1
Chilean	16,218	0.4
Colombian	176,420	4.0
Ecuadorian	171,323	3.9
Paraguayan	3,678	0.1
Peruvian	77,605	1.8
Uruguayan	7,702	0.2
Venezuelan	14,198	0.3
Other South American	16,138	0.4
Spaniard	23,620	0.5
All other Hispanic or Latino	784,552	17.9
Checkbox only, other Hispanic	283,650	6.5
Write-in "Spanish"	83,074	1.9
Write in "Hispanic"	196,424	4.5
Write-in "Latino"	79,759	1.8
Not elsewhere classified	141,645	3.2

Source: U.S. Census Bureau, Census 2000, Summary File 1 and unpublished data.

Table 10
"Hispanic or Latino" Origin for Northeast Region, Census 2000

Group	Number	Percent
HISPANIC OR LATINO ORIGIN		
Total population	53,594,378	100.0
Hispanic or Latino (of any race)	5,254,087	9.8
Not Hispanic or Latino	48,340,291	90.2
HISPANIC OR LATINO BY TYPE		
Hispanic or Latino (of any race)	5,254,087	100.0
Mexican	479,169	9.1
Puerto Rican	2,074,574	39.5
Cuban	168,959	3.2
Other Hispanic or Latino	2,531,385	48.2
Dominican (Dominican Republic)	649,011	12.4
Central American (excludes Mexican)	336,523	6.4
Costa Rican	23,736	0.5
Guatemalan	74,377	1.4
Honduran	60,179	1.1
Nicaraguan	15,007	0.3
Panamanian	27,077	0.5
Salvadoran	119,491	2.3
Other Central American	16,656	0.3
South American	584,799	11.1
Argentinean	28,338	0.5
Bolivian	8,315	0.2
Chilean	19,549	0.4
Colombian	207,174	3.9
Ecuadorian	182,832	3.5
Paraguayan	4,166	0.1
Peruvian	88,396	1.7
Uruguayan	9,019	0.2
Venezuelan	18,047	0.3
Other South American	18,963	0.4
Spaniard	27,179	0.5
All other Hispanic or Latino	933,873	17.8
Checkbox only, other Hispanic	336,707	6.4
Write-in "Spanish"	104,008	2.0
Write in "Hispanic"	230,447	4.4
Write-in "Latino"	94,655	1.8
Not elsewhere classified	168,056	3.2

Source: U.S. Census Bureau, Census 2000, Summary File 1 and unpublished data.

Table 11
"Hispanic or Latino" Origin for New England Region, Census 2000

Group	Number	Percent
HISPANIC OR LATINO ORIGIN		
Total population	13,922,517	100.0
Hispanic or Latino (of any race)	875,225	6.3
Not Hispanic or Latino	13,047,292	93.7
HISPANIC OR LATINO BY TYPE		
Hispanic or Latino (of any race)	875,225	100.0
Mexican	60,173	6.9
Puerto Rican	428,936	49.0
Cuban	18,669	2.1
Other Hispanic or Latino	367,447	42.0
Dominican (Dominican Republic)	79,134	9.0
Central American (excludes Mexican)	64,306	7.3
Costa Rican	3,600	0.4
Guatemalan	25,989	3.0
Honduran	7,877	0.9
Nicaraguan	1,618	0.2
Panamanian	2,604	0.3
Salvadoran	19,676	2.2
Other Central American	2,942	0.3
South American	71,127	8.1
Argentinean	4,251	0.5
Bolivian	2,012	0.2
Chilean	3,331	0.4
Colombian	30,754	3.5
Ecuadorian	11,509	1.3
Paraguayan	488	0.1
Peruvian	10,791	1.2
Uruguayan	1,317	0.2
Venezuelan	3,849	0.4
Other South American	2,825	0.3
Spaniard	3,559	0.4
All other Hispanic or Latino	149,321	17.1
Checkbox only, other Hispanic	53,057	6.1
Write-in "Spanish"	20,934	2.4
Write in "Hispanic"	34,023	3.9
Write-in "Latino"	14,896	1.7
Not elsewhere classified	26,411	3.0

Source: U.S. Census Bureau, Census 2000, Summary File 1 and unpublished data.

Table 12

"Hispanic or Latino" Origin for West South Central Region, Census 2000

Group	Number	Percent
HISPANIC OR LATINO ORIGIN		
Total population	31,444,850	100.0
Hispanic or Latino (of any race)	7,043,574	22.4
Not Hispanic or Latino	24,401,276	77.6
HISPANIC OR LATINO BY TYPE		
Hispanic or Latino (of any race)	7,043,574	100.0
Mexican	5,298,247	75.2
Puerto Rican	87,800	1.2
Cuban	36,862	0.5
Other Hispanic or Latino	1,620,665	23.0
Dominican (Dominican Republic)	5,598	0.1
Central American (excludes Mexican)	174,151	2.5
Costa Rican	4,367	0.1
Guatemalan	23,515	0.3
Honduran	34,144	0.5
Nicaraguan	10,634	0.2
Panamanian	8,910	0.1
Salvadoran	84,337	1.2
Other Central American	8,244	0.1
South American	59,787	0.8
Argentinean	5,350	0.1
Bolivian	2,200	—
Chilean	3,406	—
Colombian	23,132	0.3
Ecuadorian	4,386	0.1
Paraguayan	350	—
Peruvian	9,438	0.1
Uruguayan	772	—
Venezuelan	7,763	0.1
Other South American	2,990	—
Spaniard	8,794	0.1
All other Hispanic or Latino	1,372,335	19.5
Checkbox only, other Hispanic	304,977	4.3
Write-in "Spanish"	78,876	1.1
Write in "Hispanic"	849,668	12.1
Write-in "Latino"	39,176	0.6
Not elsewhere classified	99,638	1.4

Note: Dash (—) represents zero or rounds to zero.
Source: U.S. Census Bureau, Census 2000, Summary File 1 and unpublished data.

Table 13

"Hispanic or Latino" Origin for North Central Region, Census 2000

Group	Number	Percent
HISPANIC OR LATINO ORIGIN		
Total population	45,155,037	100.0
Hispanic or Latino (of any race)	2,478,719	5.5
Not Hispanic or Latino	42,676,318	94.5
HISPANIC OR LATINO BY TYPE		
Hispanic or Latino (of any race)	2,478,719	100.0
Mexican	1,735,583	70.0
Puerto Rican	301,006	12.1
Cuban	36,054	1.5
Other Hispanic or Latino	406,076	16.4
Dominican (Dominican Republic)	8,395	0.3
Central American (excludes Mexican)	63,287	2.6
Costa Rican	3,011	0.1
Guatemalan	26,747	1.1
Honduran	10,193	0.4
Nicaraguan	3,758	0.2
Panamanian	4,412	0.2
Salvadoran	12,083	0.5
Other Central American	3,083	0.1
South American	61,075	2.5
Argentinean	5,164	0.2
Bolivian	2,080	0.1
Chilean	3,721	0.2
Colombian	18,664	0.8
Ecuadorian	13,982	0.6
Paraguayan	689	—
Peruvian	9,087	0.4
Uruguayan	584	—
Venezuelan	4,442	0.2
Other South American	2,662	0.1
Spaniard	4,890	0.2
All other Hispanic or Latino	268,429	10.8
Checkbox only, other Hispanic	82,118	3.3
Write-in "Spanish"	31,907	1.3
Write in "Hispanic"	79,840	3.2
Write-in "Latino"	15,650	0.6
Not elsewhere classified	58,914	2.4

Note: Dash (—) represents zero or rounds to zero.
Source: U.S. Census Bureau, Census 2000, Summary File 1 and unpublished data.

Table 14

"Hispanic or Latino" Origin for East South Central Region, Census 2000

Group	Number	Percent
HISPANIC OR LATINO ORIGIN		
Total population	17,022,810	100.0
Hispanic or Latino (of any race)	299,176	1.8
Not Hispanic or Latino	16,723,634	98.2
HISPANIC OR LATINO BY TYPE		
Hispanic or Latino (of any race)	299,176	100.0
Mexican	174,895	58.5
Puerto Rican	25,975	8.7
Cuban	11,073	3.7
Other Hispanic or Latino	87,233	29.2
Dominican (Dominican Republic)	1,321	0.4
Central American (excludes Mexican)	17,253	5.8
Costa Rican	894	0.3
Guatemalan	6,698	2.2
Honduran	2,923	1.0
Nicaraguan	778	0.3
Panamanian	2,507	0.8
Salvadoran	2,843	1.0
Other Central American	610	0.2
South American	8,660	2.9
Argentinean	659	0.2
Bolivian	342	0.1
Chilean	684	0.2
Colombian	3,028	1.0
Ecuadorian	696	0.2
Paraguayan	140	—
Peruvian	1,239	0.4
Uruguayan	92	—
Venezuelan	1,375	0.5
Other South American	405	0.1
Spaniard	1,014	0.3
All other Hispanic or Latino	58,985	19.7
Checkbox only, other Hispanic	22,751	7.6
Write-in "Spanish"	6,841	2.3
Write in "Hispanic"	20,619	6.9
Write-in "Latino"	2,946	1.0
Not elsewhere classified	5,828	1.9

Note: Dash (—) represents zero or rounds to zero.

Source: U.S. Census Bureau, Census 2000, Summary File 1 and unpublished data.

Percent of Population, 2000

Two or More Races

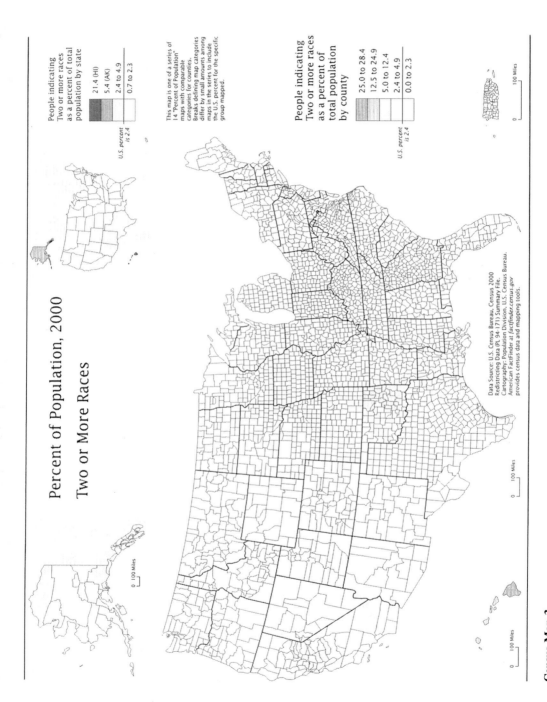

People indicating
Two or more races
as a percent of total
population by state

21.4 (HI)
5.4 (AK)
2.4 to 4.9
0.7 to 2.3

U.S. percent
is 2.4

This map is one of a series of
14 "Percent of Population"
maps with comparable
categories for counties.
Breaks defining map categories
differ by small amounts among
maps in the series to include
the U.S. percent for the specific
group mapped.

People indicating
Two or more races
as a percent of
total population
by county

25.0 to 28.4
12.5 to 24.9
5.0 to 12.4
2.4 to 4.9
0.0 to 2.3

U.S. percent
is 2.4

Data Source: U.S. Census Bureau, Census 2000
Redistricting Data (PL 94-171) Summary File.
Cartography: Population Division, U.S. Census Bureau.
American FactFinder at factfinder.census.gov
provides census data and mapping tools.

Census Map 3
Geographic Distribution of Biracial or Multiracial Identities, by Percent

Number of People, 2000
Two or More Races

Number of people indicating Two or more races by state

1,607,646 (CA)
100,000 to 999,999
10,000 to 99,999
7,335 to 9,999

Number of people indicating Two or more races by county

50,000 to 469,800
10,000 to 49,999
5,000 to 9,999
1,000 to 4,999
100 to 999
0 to 99

Data Source: U.S. Census Bureau, Census 2000 Redistricting Data (PL 94-171) Summary File. Cartography: Population Division, U.S. Census Bureau. American Factfinder at factfinder.census.gov provides census data and mapping tools.

Census Map 4
Geographic Distribution of Biracial or Multiracial Identities, by Number

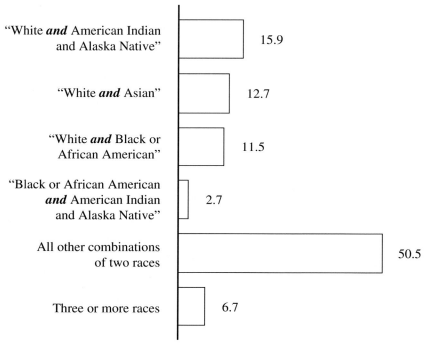

Figure 1
Distribution of Interracial Identities Selected in Census 2000
Note: Population reporting two or more races was 2.4% of the total population.
Source: U.S. Census Bureau, Census 2000 Redistricting (Public Law 94–171)
Summary File, Table PL1.

BIRACIAL OR MULTIRACIAL

Since 97% of respondents selecting "Some other race" identify themselves as "Hispanic or Latino" and over half (51%) of those selecting "Two or more races" included "Some other race" as one of the races selected, it can be inferred that the most common multiracial combination includes "Hispanic or Latino" and another race(s).

Figure 1 reveals that the most common (modal) combination of racial categories is "White" and "Native American/Alaska Native," but this masks the extent to which "Hispanic or Latino" identity has been construed simultaneously as a racial category (e.g., "Some other race" Latina married to a "White" Latino).

Table 15
Total U.S. Population by Age and Gender

United States	Total population			One race			Two or more races		
	Both sexes	Male	Female	Both sexes	Male	Female	Both sexes	Male	Female
FIVE-YEAR AGE GROUPS									
Total population	281,421,906	138,053,563	143,368,343	274,595,678	134,632,945	139,962,733	6,826,228	3,420,618	3,405,610
Under 5 years	19,175,798	9,810,733	9,365,065	18,227,583	9,328,579	8,899,004	948,215	482,154	466,061
5 to 9 years	20,549,505	10,523,277	10,026,228	19,719,732	10,101,978	9,617,754	829,773	421,299	408,474
10 to 14 years	20,528,072	10,520,197	10,007,875	19,824,608	10,164,015	9,660,593	703,464	356,182	347,282
15 to 19 years	20,219,890	10,391,004	9,828,886	19,597,998	10,075,286	9,522,712	621,892	315,718	306,174
20 to 24 years	18,964,001	9,687,814	9,276,187	18,411,917	9,405,807	9,006,110	552,084	282,007	270,077
25 to 29 years	19,381,336	9,798,760	9,582,576	18,868,887	9,537,752	9,331,135	512,449	261,008	251,441
30 to 34 years	20,510,388	10,321,769	10,188,619	20,026,210	10,074,647	9,951,563	484,178	247,122	237,056
35 to 39 years	22,706,664	11,318,696	11,387,968	22,235,945	11,079,394	11,156,551	470,719	239,302	231,417
40 to 44 years	22,441,863	11,129,102	11,312,761	22,021,176	10,917,323	11,103,853	420,687	211,779	208,908
45 to 49 years	20,092,404	9,889,506	10,202,898	19,754,156	9,720,917	10,033,239	338,248	168,589	169,659
50 to 54 years	17,585,548	8,607,724	8,977,824	17,316,932	8,476,692	8,840,240	268,616	131,032	137,584
55 to 59 years	13,469,237	6,508,729	6,960,508	13,280,566	6,417,290	6,863,276	188,671	91,439	97,232
60 to 64 years	10,805,447	5,136,627	5,668,820	10,662,421	5,068,659	5,593,762	143,026	67,968	75,058
65 to 69 years	9,533,545	4,400,362	5,133,183	9,421,591	4,349,182	5,072,409	111,954	51,180	60,774
70 to 74 years	8,857,441	3,902,912	4,954,529	8,766,843	3,863,245	4,903,598	90,598	39,667	50,931
75 to 79 years	7,415,813	3,044,456	4,371,357	7,348,823	3,016,865	4,331,958	66,990	27,591	39,399
80 to 84 years	4,945,367	1,834,897	3,110,470	4,904,714	1,819,570	3,085,144	40,653	15,327	25,326
85 years and over	4,239,587	1,226,998	3,012,589	4,205,576	1,215,744	2,989,832	34,011	11,254	22,757
SELECTED AGE GROUPS									
Under 18 years	72,293,812	37,059,196	35,234,616	69,436,926	35,608,943	33,827,983	2,856,886	1,450,253	1,406,633
Under 1 year	3,805,648	1,949,017	1,856,631	3,602,103	1,845,774	1,756,329	203,545	103,243	100,302
1 to 4 years	15,370,150	7,861,716	7,508,434	14,625,480	7,482,805	7,142,675	744,670	378,911	365,759
5 to 13 years	37,025,346	18,963,914	18,061,432	35,623,089	18,252,626	17,370,463	1,402,257	711,288	690,969
14 to 17 years	16,092,668	8,284,549	7,808,119	15,586,254	8,027,738	7,558,516	506,414	256,811	249,603
18 to 64 years	174,136,341	86,584,742	87,551,599	170,511,205	84,759,396	85,751,809	3,625,136	1,825,346	1,799,790
18 to 24 years	27,143,454	13,873,829	13,269,625	26,344,912	13,466,722	12,878,190	798,542	407,107	391,435
25 to 44 years	85,040,251	42,568,327	42,471,924	83,152,218	41,609,116	41,543,102	1,888,033	959,211	928,822
45 to 64 years	61,952,636	30,142,586	31,810,050	61,014,075	29,683,558	31,330,517	938,561	459,028	479,533
65 years and over	34,991,753	14,409,625	20,582,128	34,647,547	14,264,606	20,382,941	344,206	145,019	199,187

(continued)

Table 15
(continued)

United States	Total population			One race			Two or more races		
	Both sexes	Male	Female	Both sexes	Male	Female	Both sexes	Male	Female
16 years and over	217,149,127	105,134,229	112,014,898	212,931,366	103,037,343	109,894,023	4,217,761	2,096,886	2,120,875
18 years and over	209,128,094	100,994,367	108,133,727	205,158,752	99,024,002	106,134,750	3,969,342	1,970,365	1,998,977
21 years and over	196,899,193	94,737,132	102,162,061	193,295,686	92,952,379	100,343,307	3,603,507	1,784,753	1,818,754
50 years and over	76,851,985	34,662,705	42,189,280	75,907,466	34,227,247	41,680,219	944,519	435,458	509,061
55 years and over	59,266,437	26,054,981	33,211,456	58,590,534	25,750,555	32,839,979	675,903	304,426	371,477
60 years and over	45,797,200	19,546,252	26,250,948	45,309,968	19,333,265	25,976,703	487,232	212,987	274,245
62 years and over	41,256,029	17,373,013	23,883,016	40,830,934	17,189,857	23,641,077	425,095	183,156	241,939
67 years and over	31,101,522	12,594,818	18,506,704	30,805,496	12,472,139	18,333,357	296,026	122,679	173,347
72 years and over	21,794,764	8,366,229	13,428,535	21,601,789	8,289,809	13,311,980	192,975	76,420	116,555
75 years and over	16,600,767	6,106,351	10,494,416	16,459,113	6,052,179	10,406,934	141,654	54,172	87,482
Median age (years)	35.3	34.0	36.5	35.6	34.3	36.8	22.7	22.3	23.1
PERCENT DISTRIBUTION									
Total population	100.0	100.0	100.0	100.0	100.0	100.0	100.0	100.0	100.0
Under 18 years	25.7	26.8	24.6	25.3	26.4	24.2	41.9	42.4	41.3
Under 1 year	1.4	1.4	1.3	1.3	1.4	1.3	3.0	3.0	2.9
1 to 4 years	5.5	5.7	5.2	5.3	5.6	5.1	10.9	11.1	10.7
5 to 13 years	13.2	13.7	12.6	13.0	13.6	12.4	20.5	20.8	20.3
14 to 17 years	5.7	6.0	5.4	5.7	6.0	5.4	7.4	7.5	7.3
18 to 64 years	61.9	62.7	61.1	62.1	63.0	61.3	53.1	53.4	52.8
18 to 24 years	9.6	10.0	9.3	9.6	10.0	9.2	11.7	11.9	11.5
25 to 44 years	30.2	30.8	29.6	30.3	30.9	29.7	27.7	28.0	27.3
45 to 64 years	22.0	21.8	22.2	22.2	22.0	22.4	13.7	13.4	14.1
65 years and over	12.4	10.4	14.4	12.6	10.6	14.6	5.0	4.2	5.8

Source: U.S. Census Bureau, Census 2000 Summary File 1.

Table 16
Total Population in Households on Group Quarters

			In group quarters			
Subject	Total	In households	Total	Percent of total population in group quarters	Institutionalized population	Noninstitutionalized population
Both sexes	35,305,818	34,592,553	713,265	2.0	411,440	301,825
Under 18 years	12,342,259	12,278,397	63,862	0.5	26,108	37,754
18 to 29 years	8,129,214	7,800,047	329,167	4.0	151,083	178,084
30 to 49 years	10,029,379	9,802,051	227,328	2.3	167,540	59,788
50 years or more	4,804,966	4,712,058	92,908	1.9	66,709	26,199
Males	18,161,795	17,618,171	543,624	3.0	353,895	189,729
Under 18 years	6,334,844	6,292,992	41,852	0.7	20,860	20,992
18 to 29 years	4,424,498	4,172,641	251,857	5.7	142,329	109,528
30 to 49 years	5,207,769	5,010,625	197,144	3.8	153,472	43,672
50 years or more	2,194,684	2,141,913	52,771	2.4	37,234	15,537
Females	17,144,023	16,974,382	169,641	1.0	57,545	112,096
Under 18 years	6,007,415	5,985,405	22,010	0.4	5,248	16,762
18 to 29 years	3,704,716	3,627,406	77,310	2.1	8,754	68,556
30 to 49 years	4,821,610	4,791,426	30,184	0.6	14,068	16,116
50 years or more	2,610,282	2,570,145	40,137	1.5	29,475	10,662

Notes: For discussion of race and Hispanic origin concepts used in Census 2000, please see U.S. Census Bureau, Census 2000 Brief. "Overview of Race and Hispanic Origin: 2000," March 2001, CENBR/01-1. http://www.census.gov/prod/2001pub-cenbr01-1.pdf.

Data not adjusted based on the Accuracy and Coverage Evaluation. For Information on confidentiality protection, sampling error, nonsampling error, and definitions, see http://factfinder.census.gov/home/en/datanotes/expplu.html. For definitions of household and group quarters population, see below.

Household—A household includes all people who occupy a housing unit. People not living in households are classified as living in group quarters.

Group Quarters Population—The group quarters population includes all people not living in households. Two general categories of people in group quarters are recognized: (1) the institutionalized population which includes people under formally authorized, supervised care or custody in institutions at the time of enumeration (such as correctional institutions, nursing homes, and juvenile institutions) and (2) the noninstitutionalized population which includes all people who live in group quarters other than institutions (such as college dormitories, military quarters, and group homes).

Source: U.S. Census Bureau, Census 2000, unpublished tables.

Percent Under Age 18, 2000

Hispanic or Latino Origin

All Races

All Races:
Percent of people
indicating Hispanic
origin who are under
age 18 by state

	35.0 to 42.2
	25.7 to 34.9
	25.4 (DC)

U.S. percent
under 18 for
Hispanics is 35.0

U.S. percent under 18
for all people is 25.7

This map is one of a series of
14 "Percent Under Age 18"
maps with comparable
categories for counties. Only
the category break at the
U.S. percent for the specific
group mapped differs among
maps in the series.

All races:
Percent of people
indicating Hispanic or Latino
origin who are
under age 18
by county

	50.0 to 100.0
	40.0 to 49.9
	35.0 to 39.9
	25.7 to 34.9
	20.0 to 25.6
	0.0 to 19.9

High proportion of
Hispanics are young

U.S. percent under 18
for Hispanics is 35.0

U.S. percent under 18
for all people is 25.7

Low proportion of
Hispanics are young

| | Fewer than 100
people in county
indicating Hispanic
origin |

Data Source: U.S. Census Bureau, Census 2000
Redistricting Data (PL 94-171) Summary File.
Cartography: Population Division, U.S. Census Bureau.
American FactFinder at factfinder.census.gov
provides census data and mapping tools.

Census Map 5
Geographic Distribution of "Hispanic or Latino" Minors

530

Table 17
Categories of Race and Ancestry Used in American Community Surveys

Group	Number	Percent
RACE		
Total population	281,421,906	100.0
One race	274,595,678	97.6
White	211,460,626	75.1
Black or African American	34,658,190	12.3
American Indian and Alaska Native	2,475,956	0.9
American Indian	1,865,118	0.7
Alaska Native	97,876	0.0
Both American Indian and Alaska Native	1,002	0.0
American Indian or Alaska Native, not specified	511,960	0.2
Asian	10,242,998	3.6
Asian Indian	1,678,765	0.6
Chinese	2,432,585	0.9
Filipino	1,850,314	0.7
Japanese	796,700	0.3
Korean	1,076,872	0.4
Vietnamese	1,122,528	0.4
Other Asian category	1,061,646	0.4
Two or more Asian categories	223,588	0.1
Native Hawaiian and Other Pacific Islander	398,835	0.1
Native Hawaiian	140,652	0.0
Samoan	91,029	0.0
Guamanian or Chamorro	58,240	0.0
Other Pacific Islander category	99,996	0.0
Two or more Native Hawaiian or Other Pacific Islander categories	8,918	0.0
Some other race	15,359,073	5.5
Two or more races	6,826,228	2.4
Two races including Some other race	3,001,558	1.1
Two races excluding Some other race, and three or more races	3,824,670	1.4
Two races excluding Some other race	3,366,517	1.2
Three or more races	458,153	0.2
HISPANIC OR LATINO		
Total population	281,421,906	100.0
Hispanic or Latino (of any race)	35,305,818	12.5
Mexican	20,640,711	7.3
Puerto Rican	3,406,178	1.2
Cuban	1,241,685	0.4
Other Hispanic or Latino	10,017,244	3.6
Not Hispanic or Latino	246,116,088	87.5
RACE AND HISPANIC OR LATINO		
Total population	281,421,906	100.0
One race	274,595,678	97.6
Hispanic or Latino	33,081,736	11.8
Not Hispanic or Latino	241,513,942	85.8
Two or more races	6,826,228	2.4
Hispanic or Latino	2,224,082	0.8
Not Hispanic or Latino	4,602,146	1.6

The next table tracks patterns of recent immigration to the U.S., which is characterized by above average (for the overall population) growth rates for the nation's Hispanic and Asian populations. The "Hispanic or Latino" numbered 41.3 million on July 1, 2004, compared with 22.4 million in 1990 and 35 million in 2000. The projected Latino population as of July 1, 2050, is 102 million, which will constitute 24% of the nation's total population on that date.

Table 18
Nativity, Citizenship, Year of Entry, and Region of Birth, 2000
Data Set: Census 2000 Summary File 3 (SF 3)—Sample Data
Geographic Area: U.S.

Subject	Number	Percent
NATIVITY, CITIZENSHIP STATUS, AND YEAR OF ENTRY		
Total population	281,421,906	100.0
Native	250,314,017	88.9
Foreign born	31,107,889	11.1
Naturalized citizen	12,542,626	40.3
Not a citizen	18,565,263	59.7
Entered 1990 to March 2000	13,178,276	42.4
Naturalized citizen	1,759,386	13.4
Not a citizen	11,418,890	86.6
Entered 1980 to 1989	8,464,762	27.2
Naturalized citizen	3,777,456	44.6
Not a citizen	4,687,306	55.4
Entered before 1980	9,464,851	30.4
Naturalized citizen	7,005,784	74.0
Not a citizen	2,459,067	26.0
FOREIGN-BORN POPULATION BY REGION OF BIRTH AND YEAR OF ENTRY (excluding born at sea)		
Europe	4,915,557	100.0
1990 to March 2000	1,615,782	32.9
1980 to 1989	683,660	13.9
Before 1980	2,616,115	53.2
Asia	8,226,254	100.0
1990 to March 2000	3,533,010	42.9
1980 to 1989	2,604,031	31.7
Before 1980	2,089,213	25.4
Africa	881,300	100.0
1990 to March 2000	498,927	56.6
1980 to 1989	226,929	25.7
Before 1980	155,444	17.6
Oceania	168,046	100.0
1990 to March 2000	78,427	46.7
1980 to 1989	39,081	23.3
Before 1980	50,538	30.1
Latin America	16,086,974	100.0
1990 to March 2000	7,205,909	44.8
1980 to 1989	4,808,980	29.9
Before 1980	4,072,085	25.3
Northern America	829,442	100.0
1990 to March 2000	246,153	29.7
1980 to 1989	102,065	12.3
Before 1980	481,224	58.0

Place of Birth Code List (PDF 74KB).
Source: U.S. Census Bureau, Census 2000 Summary File 3, Matrices P21, P23, and PCT20.

Eleven percent of Latinos are under age 5, a higher proportion than any other racial or ethnic group in the U.S.

Percent Under Age 18, 2000

Two or More Races

Percent of people indicating Two or more races who are under age 18 by state

| 41.9 to 54.1 |
| 25.7 to 41.8 |
| 23.5 (DC) |

U.S. percent under 18 for Two or more races is 41.9

U.S. percent under 18 for all people is 25.7

This map is one of a series of 14 "Percent Under Age 18" maps with comparable categories for counties. Only the category break at the U.S. percent for the specific group mapped differs among maps in the series.

Percent of people indicating Two or more races who are under age 18 by county

| 50.0 to 100.0 |
| 41.9 to 49.9 |
| 25.7 to 41.8 |
| 20.0 to 25.6 |
| 0.0 to 19.9 |

High proportion of Two or more races are young

U.S. percent under 18 for Two or more races is 41.9

U.S. percent under 18 for all people is 25.7

Low proportion of Two or more races are young

Fewer than 100 people in county indicating Two or more races

0 ___ 100 Miles

Data Source: U.S. Census Bureau, Census 2000 Redistricting Data (PL 94-171) Summary File. Cartography: Population Division, U.S. Census Bureau. American FactFinder at *factfinder.census.gov* provides census data and mapping tools.

0 100 Miles

0 100 Miles

0 100 Miles

Census Map 6

Geographic Distribution of Biracial Minors

Table 19

Male Population by Age, Race, and "Hispanic or Latino" Origin for the U.S., 2000

Age	Total population	Race							Two or more races	Hispanic or Latino (of any race)	White alone, not Hispanic or Latino
		One race									
		Total	White	Black or African American	American Indian and Alaska Native	Asian	Native Hawaiian and Other Pacific Islander	Some other race			
FIVE-YEAR AGE GROUPS											
Total population	138,063,683	134,832,845	103,773,184	18,485,185	1,233,682	4,848,741	202,628	8,009,214	3,420,618	18,181,785	86,167,731
Under 5 years	9,810,733	9,328,579	6,597,764	1,424,275	108,669	337,149	17,254	843,478	482,154	1,900,431	5,747,742
5 to 9 years	10,523,277	10,101,978	7,159,656	1,627,475	120,954	348,856	18,702	826,335	421,299	1,851,885	6,321,695
10 to 14 years	10,520,197	10,164,015	7,361,650	1,554,518	125,260	352,071	18,376	722,140	356,182	1,617,185	6,623,228
15 to 19 years	10,391,004	10,075,286	7,288,058	1,492,765	119,350	380,560	19,394	785,159	315,718	1,688,556	6,530,937
20 to 24 years	9,687,814	9,405,807	6,675,522	1,280,628	102,116	407,855	20,243	919,033	282,007	1,875,139	5,865,075
25 to 29 years	9,798,760	9,537,752	6,846,202	1,211,753	95,441	484,136	18,385	681,835	261,008	1,826,145	6,038,628
30 to 34 years	10,321,769	10,074,647	7,490,728	1,239,755	94,245	461,712	16,883	771,324	247,122	1,668,064	6,723,177
35 to 39 years	11,318,696	11,079,394	8,544,270	1,328,309	99,900	439,179	16,638	651,098	239,302	1,474,462	7,835,996
40 to 44 years	11,129,102	10,917,323	8,631,912	1,267,177	92,141	398,450	14,650	512,953	211,779	1,178,548	8,058,013
45 to 49 years	9,889,506	9,720,917	7,855,623	1,056,143	77,577	345,873	11,717	373,984	168,589	885,695	7,410,884
50 to 54 years	8,607,724	8,476,692	7,023,516	831,065	62,799	288,810	9,479	261,023	131,032	664,235	6,669,501
55 to 59 years	6,508,729	6,417,290	5,415,680	588,262	43,962	203,331	6,642	159,413	91,439	456,165	5,151,858
60 to 64 years	5,136,627	5,068,659	4,292,670	468,895	32,324	160,314	4,908	109,548	67,968	347,409	4,079,327
65 to 69 years	4,400,362	4,349,182	3,753,923	374,454	22,837	119,499	3,747	74,712	51,180	268,184	3,578,792
70 to 74 years	3,502,512	3,453,245	3,407,201	291,976	16,163	92,659	2,452	52,774	39,667	205,691	3,267,502
75 to 79 years	3,044,456	3,016,865	2,696,297	206,915	10,701	67,074	1,537	34,341	27,591	135,463	2,603,467
80 to 84 years	1,834,897	1,819,570	1,643,745	116,030	5,489	36,339	907	17,061	15,327	67,919	1,597,046
85 years and over	1,226,998	1,215,744	1,088,377	54,780	4,065	24,824	695	13,003	11,254	49,617	1,054,863
SELECTED AGE GROUPS											
Under 18 years	37,059,188	35,808,843	26,481,922	6,632,176	427,912	1,268,016	86,678	2,833,341	1,450,253	6,334,844	22,827,848
Under 1 year	1,949,017	1,945,774	1,301,816	278,650	21,561	66,513	3,340	173,954	103,243	394,611	1,125,390
1 to 4 years	7,851,716	7,452,905	5,295,948	1,145,595	87,098	270,635	13,914	659,614	378,911	1,505,820	4,622,352
5 to 13 years	18,963,914	18,253,625	13,050,828	2,907,790	221,559	630,081	33,406	1,408,922	711,288	3,160,636	11,614,566
14 to 17 years	8,284,545	8,027,738	5,843,330	1,200,111	97,654	290,786	14,916	580,941	256,811	1,273,777	5,265,540

18 to 64 years	88,684,742	54,759,388	86,881,729	9,853,844	748,818	3,360,320	127,706	4,883,882	1,626,348	11,100,077	80,428,213
18 to 24 years	13,873,825	13,455,722	9,591,128	1,967,485	148,427	563,455	28,393	1,262,804	407,107	2,598,352	8,460,829
25 to 44 years	42,568,327	41,609,116	31,513,112	5,045,934	381,727	1,783,507	66,556	2,817,210	959,211	6,147,220	28,655,814
45 to 64 years	30,142,595	29,683,558	24,587,489	2,944,365	216,662	993,328	32,745	903,968	459,028	2,354,505	23,311,570
86 years and over	14,408,825	14,264,609	12,588,543	1,074,165	69,254	340,405	9,348	181,891	146,019	728,874	12,101,670
16 years and over	105,134,229	103,037,343	81,192,351	11,529,241	854,739	3,838,956	144,547	5,477,509	2,086,886	12,484,373	75,143,273
18 years and over	100,334,367	99,024,002	78,281,272	10,933,009	806,070	3,630,725	137,053	5,175,873	1,970,385	11,825,951	72,529,883
21 years and over	94,737,132	92,952,379	73,935,100	10,058,646	737,786	3,448,137	124,677	4,548,033	1,784,753	10,724,123	68,669,436
50 years and over	34,652,705	34,227,247	29,321,409	2,962,387	198,339	992,860	30,377	721,875	435,458	2,194,684	28,002,356
55 years and over	25,054,981	25,750,555	22,297,893	2,131,322	135,540	704,050	20,898	450,852	304,426	1,530,443	21,332,865
60 years and over	19,546,252	19,333,255	16,882,213	1,543,060	91,578	500,719	14,256	301,439	212,987	1,074,283	16,180,997
62 years and over	17,373,013	17,189,857	15,073,902	1,343,107	77,367	430,509	12,117	252,565	183,156	923,649	14,463,631
67 years and over	12,594,818	12,472,139	11,056,485	911,816	49,192	288,413	7,680	158,553	122,679	611,004	10,643,124
72 years and over	8,366,225	8,289,809	7,409,429	573,328	29,056	180,345	4,456	93,196	76,420	366,833	7,158,511
75 years and over	6,106,351	6,052,179	5,428,419	407,725	20,254	128,237	3,139	64,405	54,172	252,999	5,255,376
Medium age (years)	34.0	34.3	38.6	28.6	27.2	31.7	27.0	24.6	22.3	26.4	37.4

PERCENT DISTRIBUTION

Total population	100.0	100.0	100.0	100.0	100.0	100.0	100.0	100.0	100.0	100.0	100.0
Under 18 years	26.5	26.4	24.6	38.6	34.7	26.4	32.4	35.4	42.4	34.8	23.8
Under 1 year	1.4	1.4	1.3	1.7	1.7	1.3	1.6	2.2	3.0	2.2	1.2
1 to 4 years	5.7	5.6	5.1	7.0	7.1	5.5	6.9	8.4	11.1	8.3	4.9
5 to 13 years	13.7	13.6	12.6	17.7	18.0	12.7	16.5	17.6	20.8	17.4	12.2
14 to 17 years	6.0	6.0	5.6	7.3	7.9	5.9	7.4	7.3	7.5	7.0	5.5
18 to 64 years	62.7	63.0	63.3	68.9	80.6	87.7	63.0	82.2	63.4	61.1	63.6
18 to 24 years	10.0	10.0	9.2	11.3	12.0	11.5	14.0	15.8	11.9	14.3	8.9
25 to 44 years	30.8	30.9	30.4	30.7	30.9	36.0	32.5	35.2	23.0	33.3	30.1
45 to 64 years	21.5	22.0	23.7	17.9	17.6	20.2	16.2	11.3	13.4	13.0	24.5
86 years and over	10.4	10.6	12.1	8.5	4.8	8.9	4.6	2.4	4.2	4.0	12.7

Note: For information on confidentiality protection, nonsampling error, and definitions, see http://www.census.govprod/cen2000/doc/sf1./pdf.

Source: U.S. Census Bureau, Census 2000 Summary File 1.

535

Table 20

Educational Attainment for the Population 15 Years and Older, by Age and Hispanic Origin (Numbers in thousands; civilian non-institutionalized population)

Hispanic (of any race) and Both Sexes	Total	None	1st–4th grade	5th–6th grade	7th–8th grade	9th grade	10th grade	11th grade	High school graduate	Some college no degree	Associate degree, occupational	Associate degree, academic	Bachelor's degree	Master's degree	Professional degree	Doctorate degree
15 years and over	28,538	474	1,375	2,750	1,807	2,165	1,733	2,561	7,516	4,087	740	605	2,010	480	142	94
15 to 17 years	1,968	—	5	24	396	569	583	361	19	12	—	—	—	—	—	—
18 to 19 years	1,274	2	12	29	52	78	106	435	311	239	9	1	—	—	—	—
20 to 24 years	3,700	14	66	247	128	211	203	358	1,209	975	76	94	118	2	—	7
25 to 29 years	3,823	39	116	396	150	278	159	298	1,152	609	117	94	353	38	17	7
30 to 34 years	3,599	25	137	381	203	256	170	273	1,017	519	112	85	322	64	30	5
35 to 39 years	3,197	39	138	359	131	220	91	249	947	410	107	99	295	90	12	9
40 to 44 years	2,810	38	155	306	149	198	89	163	805	352	104	70	272	75	23	10
45 to 49 years	2,211	45	127	248	130	112	83	107	589	314	62	69	239	51	24	11
50 to 54 years	1,715	47	101	205	106	70	63	96	501	208	60	33	139	58	14	13
55 to 59 years	1,287	33	97	151	75	54	59	63	344	182	39	31	108	36	7	8
60 to 64 years	875	27	77	104	70	41	42	47	211	119	24	10	59	28	5	10
65 to 69 years	721	33	102	109	53	39	31	53	155	57	11	7	47	15	2	8
70 to 74 years	551	39	87	69	58	12	27	21	122	46	7	4	41	11	6	—
75 years and over	808	93	155	120	107	26	26	36	134	45	12	8	17	12	3	12
15 to 17 years	1,968	—	5	24	396	569	583	361	19	12	—	—	—	—	—	—
18 years and over	26,570	474	1,370	2,726	1,411	1,596	1,150	2,201	7,497	4,075	740	605	2,010	480	142	94
15 to 24 years	6,942	16	83	300	576	858	892	1,154	1,539	1,226	85	95	118	2	—	—
25 years and over	21,596	458	1,292	2,450	1,231	1,307	840	1,408	5,977	2,861	656	510	1,892	478	142	94
15 to 64 years	26,458	309	1,031	2,451	1,589	2,088	1,649	2,451	7,104	3,939	711	585	1,905	441	132	74
65 years and over	2,080	165	344	299	218	77	84	110	412	148	29	20	105	38	10	20

Educational Attainment

Note: Dash (—) represents zero or rounds to zero.
Source: U.S. Census Bureau, Census 2000, Current Population Survey.

Table 21
Educational Attainment of the Population 15 Years and Older, by Age and Hispanic Origin (Numbers in thousands; civilian non-institutionalized population)

Hispanic (of any race) and Male	Total	None	1st–4th grade	5th–6th grade	7th–8th grade	9th grade	10th grade	11th grade	High school graduate	Some college no degree	Associate degree, occupational	Associate degree, academic	Bachelor's degree	Master's degree	Professional degree	Doctorate degree
15 years and over	14,652	245	745	1,488	923	1,102	921	1,361	3,873	2,033	347	257	984	242	79	52
15 to 17 years	958	—	3	16	214	272	281	155	10	8	—	—	—	—	—	—
18 to 19 years	696	1	4	23	34	56	74	222	177	100	5	—	—	—	—	—
20 to 24 years	2,012	10	44	158	73	116	130	210	678	461	40	34	57	2	—	4
25 to 29 years	2,092	20	68	230	80	166	97	173	675	301	47	35	166	22	8	2
30 to 34 years	1,909	18	86	222	115	132	87	154	528	259	57	45	162	34	8	7
35 to 39 years	1,682	21	87	190	70	103	39	139	497	244	55	46	143	34	7	5
40 to 44 years	1,444	27	94	170	82	103	49	94	389	180	46	29	124	38	14	7
45 to 49 years	1,106	24	88	122	58	57	42	59	276	170	26	24	107	30	17	6
50 to 54 years	849	28	50	106	52	34	39	48	229	88	34	17	82	26	10	5
55 to 59 years	619	20	39	74	30	19	30	36	156	92	22	13	59	18	5	7
60 to 64 years	404	12	42	63	23	16	23	19	91	53	5	2	27	18	2	1
65 to 69 years	306	12	45	39	23	12	15	29	60	27	3	6	21	11	2	—
70 to 74 years	239	17	37	24	25	5	8	9	56	20	5	3	21	5	5	8
75 years and over	336	34	58	50	44	11	6	15	51	31	4	4	14	4	2	
15 to 17 years	958	—	3	16	214	272	281	155	10	8	—	—	—	—	—	—
18 years and over	13,694	245	741	1,472	709	830	640	1,207	3,864	2,025	347	257	984	242	79	52
15 to 24 years	3,666	11	51	197	320	444	485	586	864	569	45	34	57	2	—	—
25 years and over	10,986	234	694	1,291	603	658	436	775	3,009	1,464	303	224	926	240	79	52
15 to 64 years	13,772	182	605	1,375	831	1,073	891	1,308	3,706	1,955	336	245	928	221	71	43
65 years and over	881	63	140	112	92	28	29	53	167	78	11	12	56	21	9	9

Note: Dash (—) represents zero or rounds to zero.
Source: U.S. Census Bureau, Census 2000, Current Population Survey.

537

Table 22

Educational Attainment of the Population 15 Years and Over, by Age and Hispanic Origin, Census 2004 (Numbers in thousands; civilian non-institutionalized population)

Hispanic (of any race) and Female	Total	None	1st–4th grade	5th–6th grade	7th–8th grade	9th grade	10th grade	11th grade	High school graduate	Some college no degree	Associate degree, occupational	Associate degree, academic	Bachelor's degree	Master's degree	Professional degree	Doctorate degree
15 years and over	13,886	229	630	1,262	884	1,063	812	1,200	3,643	2,054	393	348	1,027	238	63	41
15 to 17 years	1,010	—	1	8	182	297	302	206	10	4	—	—	—	—	—	—
18 to 19 years	578	0	8	6	18	22	32	213	134	139	4	1	—	—	—	—
20 to 24 years	1,689	4	22	90	55	95	73	148	532	514	36	60	60	—	—	—
25 to 29 years	1,731	19	49	166	70	112	62	125	477	308	69	59	187	17	8	3
30 to 34 years	1,691	7	52	159	88	124	83	119	489	260	56	40	160	29	22	3
35 to 39 years	1,515	18	51	169	60	118	52	110	449	166	52	53	152	56	6	2
40 to 44 years	1,365	11	61	136	67	95	40	69	416	172	58	40	148	37	10	5
45 to 49 years	1,105	20	39	126	72	56	41	49	314	143	37	45	132	21	8	4
50 to 54 years	865	18	50	99	53	36	25	48	272	121	26	16	58	32	4	7
55 to 59 years	668	14	57	77	45	35	29	27	188	90	17	18	49	18	2	3
60 to 64 years	470	15	35	41	47	25	19	29	120	66	19	8	31	10	2	3
65 to 69 years	415	21	56	71	30	27	15	24	95	30	8	8	26	3	—	7
70 to 74 years	312	22	50	45	33	7	19	13	66	27	2	1	20	6	1	—
75 years and over	473	59	98	70	62	15	20	21	84	14	8	5	3	8	1	4
15 to 17 years	1,010	—	1	8	182	297	302	206	10	4	—	—	—	—	—	—
18 years and over	12,876	229	629	1,254	702	766	510	994	3,633	2,050	393	348	1,027	238	63	41
15 to 24 years	3,276	4	32	103	255	414	407	567	675	657	40	61	60	—	—	—
25 years and over	10,610	224	598	1,159	628	649	405	633	2,968	1,397	353	287	966	238	63	41
15 to 64 years	12,686	126	426	1,075	758	1,014	758	1,142	3,398	1,983	375	340	977	220	61	30
65 years and over	1,199	102	204	186	126	49	54	57	244	71	18	7	50	18	2	11

Note: Dash (—) represents zero or rounds to zero.
Source: U.S. Census Bureau, Census 2000, Current Population Survey.

A college degree nearly doubles annual earnings. The U.S. Census Bureau reported for that 2004, workers 18 and over with a bachelor's degree earned an average of $51,206, whereas those with a high school diploma earned $27,915. On July 2004 the U.S. Census Bureau estimated that 58% of Hispanics age 25 and older had at least a high school education and that 12% (2.7 million) of the "Latino or Hispanic" population age 25 or older had a bachelor's degree. Ten percent of college students in 2003 were Hispanic, compared with 4% two decades earlier. In 2004, 714,000 Latinos held advanced degrees (e.g., master's, professional such as doctor's and lawyer's, and doctoral).

The U.S. Census Bureau is conducting its 2005 National Census Test, which will investigate the possibility of a questionnaire in two languages, Spanish as well as English. Some households will be given the opportunity to fill out the questionnaire on the Internet.

Table 23

U.S.—Ability to Speak English by Language Spoken at Home for the Population 5 Years and Over

Language spoken at home	Total Number	Speak English "very well" Number	Percent	Speak English "well" Number	Percent	Speak English "not well" Number	Percent	Speak English "not at all" Number	Percent
Population 5 Years and older	262,375,150	(X)	(X)	(X)	(X)	(X)	(X)	(X)	(X)
Speak only English	215,423,555	(X)	(X)	(X)	(X)	(X)	(X)	(X)	(X)
Speak language other than English	46,951,595	25,631,190	54.6	10,333,555	22.0	7,620,720	16.2	3,366,130	7.2
Spanish or Spanish Creole	28,101,055	14,349,795	51.1	5,819,410	20.7	5,130,400	18.3	2,801,450	10.0
Other Indo-European languages	10,017,975	6,627,685	66.2	2,091,450	20.9	1,078,915	10.8	219,925	2.2
French (incl. Patois, Cajun)	1,643,840	1,228,800	74.8	269,460	16.4	138,000	8.4	7,580	0.5
French Creole	453,365	245,855	54.2	121,915	26.9	70,960	15.7	14,635	3.2
Italian	1,008,370	701,220	69.5	195,900	19.4	99,270	9.8	11,980	1.2
Portuguese or Portuguese Creole	564,630	320,445	56.8	125,465	22.2	90,410	16.0	28,310	5.0
German	1,383,440	1,079,695	78.0	219,465	15.9	79,560	5.8	4,720	0.3
Yiddish	178,940	123,160	68.8	35,455	19.8	17,295	9.7	3,030	1.7
Other West Germanic languages	251,135	182,050	72.5	58,290	23.2	9,420	3.8	1,375	0.6
Scandinavian languages	162,255	137,615	84.8	19,110	11.8	5,165	3.2	365	0.2
Greek	365,435	262,850	71.9	65,025	17.8	33,345	9.1	4,215	1.2
Russian	706,240	304,890	43.2	209,055	29.6	148,670	21.1	43,625	6.2
Polish	667,415	387,695	58.1	167,235	25.1	95,030	14.2	17,455	2.6
Serbo-Croatian	233,865	119,270	51.0	61,255	26.2	42,970	18.4	10,370	4.4
Other Slavic languages	301,080	176,715	58.7	72,945	24.2	41,860	13.9	9,560	3.2
Armenian	202,710	108,555	53.6	48,470	23.9	31,870	15.7	13,815	6.8
Persian	312,085	198,040	63.5	70,910	22.7	32,960	10.6	10,175	3.3
Gujarathi	235,985	155,010	65.7	50,635	21.5	22,520	9.5	7,820	3.3
Hindi	317,055	245,190	77.3	51,930	16.4	16,680	5.3	3,255	1.0
Urdu	262,900	180,020	68.5	56,735	21.6	20,815	7.9	5,330	2.0
Other Indic languages	439,285	274,140	62.4	108,510	24.7	43,395	9.9	13,240	3.0
Other Indo-European languages	327,945	196,470	59.9	83,685	25.5	38,720	11.8	9,070	2.8
Asian and Pacific Island languages	6,960,070	3,370,045	48.4	2,023,310	29.1	1,260,260	18.1	306,455	4.4
Chinese	2,022,140	855,690	42.3	595,330	29.4	408,595	20.2	162,525	8.0
Japanese	478,000	241,705	50.6	146,615	30.7	84,020	17.6	5,660	1.2
Korean	894,060	361,165	40.4	268,475	30.0	228,390	25.6	36,030	4.0
Mon-Khmer, Cambodian	181,890	77,620	42.7	51,650	28.4	41,460	22.8	11,160	6.1
Miao, Hmong	168,065	65,865	39.2	55,910	33.3	34,405	20.5	11,885	7.1
Thai	120,465	57,630	47.8	43,250	35.9	17,635	14.6	1,950	1.6

Laotian	149,305	67,565	45.3	43,175	28.9	32,100	21.5	6,465	4.3
Vietnamese	1,009,625	342,595	33.9	340,060	33.7	270,950	26.8	56,020	5.6
Other Asian languages	398,440	282,565	70.9	81,740	20.5	28,000	7.0	6,135	1.5
Tagalog	1,224,240	827,560	67.6	311,465	25.4	79,720	6.5	5,495	0.5
Other Pacific Island languages	313,840	190,085	60.6	85,640	27.3	34,985	11.2	3,130	1.0
Other languages	1,872,485	1,283,660	68.6	399,395	21.3	151,125	8.1	38,305	2.0
Navajo	178,015	115,025	64.6	42,975	24.1	14,390	8.1	5,625	3.2
Other Native North American languages	203,465	149,020	73.2	41,010	20.2	12,430	6.1	1,005	0.5
Hungarian	117,975	79,600	67.5	28,310	24.0	9,005	7.6	1,060	0.9
Arabic	614,580	403,395	65.6	140,055	22.8	58,595	9.5	12,535	2.0
Hebrew	195,375	158,450	81.1	28,575	14.6	7,770	4.0	580	0.3
African languages	418,500	294,455	70.4	87,135	20.8	30,875	7.4	6,035	1.4
Other and unspecified languages	144,575	83,715	57.9	31,335	21.7	18,060	12.5	11,465	7.9

Note: (X) Not applicable. Data based on a sample. For information on confidentiality protection, sampling error, nonsampling error, and definitions, see http://www.census.gov/prod/cen2000/doc/sf3.pdf.

Source: U.S. Census Bureau, Census 2000 PHC-T-37.

Table 24

"Hispanic or Latino" Voting-Age Population and Citizen Voting-Age Population by Sex, for the U.S.

Geographic area	Population, 18 years and over			Citizens, 18 years and over			Percent citizens, 18 years and over		
	Total	Male	Female	Total	Male	Female	Total	Male	Female
United States	22,974,271	11,753,553	11,220,718	14,300,581	6,950,535	7,350,046	62.2	59.1	65.5
Alabama	48,400	28,258	20,142	26,836	14,226	12,610	55.4	50.3	62.6
Alaska	15,592	8,318	7,274	13,064	6,906	6,158	83.8	83.0	84.7
Arizona	803,477	414,296	389,181	510,488	251,941	258,547	63.5	60.8	66.4
Arkansas	54,073	31,413	22,660	25,666	14,176	11,490	47.5	45.1	50.7
California	6,927,627	3,523,871	3,403,756	3,888,220	1,893,077	1,995,143	56.1	53.7	58.6
Colorado	478,593	251,846	226,747	344,804	171,310	173,494	72.0	68.0	76.5
Connecticut	204,683	100,142	104,541	160,336	75,257	85,079	78.3	75.2	81.4
Delaware	23,832	13,051	10,781	15,200	7,700	7,500	63.8	59.0	69.6
District of Columbia	33,832	17,724	16,108	13,687	6,287	7,400	40.5	35.5	45.9
Florida	1,985,145	975,873	1,009,272	1,250,363	585,540	664,823	63.0	60.0	65.9
Georgia	296,522	183,090	113,432	110,756	60,493	50,263	37.4	33.0	44.3
Hawaii	53,131	26,298	26,833	50,166	24,717	25,449	94.4	94.0	94.8
Idaho	59,117	32,210	26,907	35,749	18,334	17,415	60.5	56.9	64.7
Illinois	979,171	523,776	455,395	539,983	272,659	267,324	55.1	52.1	58.7
Indiana	136,266	75,817	60,449	88,321	45,154	43,167	64.8	59.6	71.4
Iowa	49,835	28,492	21,343	28,683	15,472	13,211	57.6	54.3	61.9
Kansas	113,675	61,656	52,019	68,603	35,028	33,575	60.4	56.8	64.5
Kentucky	38,571	24,267	14,304	22,249	12,863	9,386	57.7	53.0	65.6
Louisiana	77,512	38,892	38,620	58,428	28,086	30,342	75.4	72.2	78.6
Maine	5,783	2,952	2,831	5,093	2,586	2,507	88.1	87.6	88.6
Maryland	155,971	80,213	75,758	80,121	37,868	42,253	51.4	47.2	55.8
Massachusetts	272,359	130,015	142,344	188,318	85,973	102,345	69.1	66.1	71.9
Michigan	200,874	106,619	94,255	151,151	76,372	74,779	75.2	71.6	79.3
Minnesota	86,864	48,272	38,592	48,202	24,730	23,472	55.5	51.2	60.8
Mississippi	26,214	15,455	10,759	17,005	8,723	8,282	64.9	56.4	77.0
Missouri	74,235	39,341	34,894	51,770	25,839	25,931	69.7	65.7	74.3
Montana	10,789	5,136	5,653	9,958	4,746	5,212	92.3	92.4	92.2
Nebraska	57,117	31,939	25,178	31,756	16,583	15,173	55.6	51.9	60.3
Nevada	247,936	133,745	114,191	128,583	66,280	62,303	51.9	49.6	54.6
New Hampshire	12,654	6,565	6,089	9,558	4,744	4,814	75.5	72.3	79.1
New Jersey	780,683	389,768	390,915	495,223	236,122	259,101	63.4	60.6	66.3
New Mexico	507,187	246,677	260,510	441,359	212,498	228,861	87.0	86.1	87.9

542

New York	1,980,165	947,381	1,032,784	1,306,169	591,292	714,877	66.0	62.4	69.2
North Carolina	255,793	159,694	96,099	90,276	50,426	39,850	35.3	31.6	41.5
North Dakota	4,563	2,277	2,286	4,060	2,045	2,015	89.0	89.8	88.1
Ohio	135,609	70,499	65,110	113,792	56,498	57,294	83.9	80.1	88.0
Oklahoma	108,468	60,498	47,970	67,886	35,553	32,333	62.6	58.8	67.4
Oregon	167,230	95,079	72,151	79,297	40,866	38,431	47.4	43.0	53.3
Pennsylvania	244,602	123,664	120,938	206,077	100,995	105,082	84.2	81.7	86.9
Rhode Island	55,528	26,096	29,432	31,940	14,147	17,793	57.5	54.2	60.5
South Carolina	65,250	40,044	25,206	32,837	17,560	15,277	50.3	43.9	60.6
South Dakota	6,083	3,367	2,716	4,710	2,501	2,209	77.4	74.3	81.3
Tennessee	82,167	50,484	31,683	40,553	21,605	18,948	49.4	42.8	59.8
Texas	4,287,444	2,163,700	2,123,744	2,972,988	1,449,733	1,523,255	69.3	67.0	71.7
Utah	123,502	67,330	56,172	67,194	34,567	32,627	54.4	51.3	58.1
Vermont	3,612	1,753	1,859	3,322	1,603	1,719	92.0	91.4	92.5
Virginia	225,936	121,058	104,878	111,966	55,731	56,235	49.6	46.0	53.6
Washington	265,079	144,622	120,457	157,194	81,285	75,909	59.3	56.2	63.0
West Virginia	8,096	4,299	3,797	7,043	3,568	3,475	87.0	83.0	91.5
Wisconsin	117,061	65,224	51,837	75,997	39,590	36,407	64.9	60.7	70.2
Wyoming	20,363	10,497	9,866	17,581	8,680	8,901	86.3	82.7	90.2

Note: Data based on sample. For information on confidentiality protection, sampling error, nonsampling error, and definitions see www.census.gov/prod/cen2000/doc/sf4.pdf.

Source: U.S. Census Bureau, Census 2000, Summary File 4, Table PCT44.

FAMILY

The number of Hispanic families who reside in the U.S. is 9.3 million; of these, 63% include children under the age 18. Sixty-five percent of Latino children live with both parents. Eighteen percent of the nation's elementary and high school students are Hispanic, triple the proportion in 1970.

Kevin Ross

Glossary

Our intent here is not to propose fixed definitions, but instead to provide additional possibilities for discussion and critical analysis.

Acculturation. The process an individual goes through to become adapted to a different culture. For this to take place there need to be changes in both social and psychological behavior. Research has concentrated on the acculturation of immigrant workers to their host country (Byram, 2000, pp. 1, 2).

Additive Bilingualism. A situation where a second language is learned by an individual or a group without detracting from the maintenance and development of the first language; a situation where a second language adds to rather than replaces the first language. This is the opposite of *subtractive bilingualism* (Guzzetti, 2002, p. 698). Crawford (2000) tells us that research in second language acquisition has increasingly showcased the academic benefits of bilingual instruction. Indeed, when language minority students fail, it is more likely from too little instruction in their native language than too little English (p. 7). Crawford quotes a long-term national study that has documented higher student achievement in developmental bilingual classrooms. Admittedly, such findings are counterintuitive and poorly understood by a majority of the public. But this hardly explains the vehemence of the opposition, which typically has more to do with political than pedagogical considerations (2000, p. 7).

Americanization. Americanization refers to processes of "becoming American" and to organized efforts to encourage the transformation of immigrants into "Americans." The term is often used interchangeably with *assimilation* (http://find.galegroup.com/gvrl/infomark). Crawford (2000) explains that speaking English was featured in a campaign to "Americanize the immigrant" in the early 1900s, but such episodes were the exception (p. 2). Gradually, however, efforts to encourage assimilation became more coercive and overbearing. During World War I, Americanization received a substantial boost from the xenophobia unleashed against German Americans, who for the first time bore the brunt of repressive language policies. Suspicion toward foreign tongues broadened and deepened during the postwar "Red Scare" (p. 21). It was during this period that, for the first time, an ideological link was established between speaking "good English" and being a "good American" (p. 21). Crawford explains today's English-only campaign as a mainstream phenomenon. It would be more precise to call it a broad current fed by numerous social and ideological sources. These include class-based resentments toward prosperous immigrant groups as well as class-based fears about the poorest (p. 22).

Anti-racism. The psychological roots of racial prejudice and racial hostility are separate from the philosophical basis of multicultural education. Anti-racism and prejudice reduction are often included in a "strong" version of multicultural education. One can learn, for example, about other cultures and ethnic groups without confronting the racism that exists in one's own (and other) ethnic groups (Baker & Jones, 1998, p. 616; Cummins, 2000). Skutnabb-Kangas and Cummins (1988) indicated that multicultural education was not a big success. They stated that overt goals of multicultural education can be realized only when policymakers, educators, and communities acknowledge the subtle (and sometimes not so subtle) forms of institutionalized racism that permeate the structure of schools and mediate the interactions between educators and students (p. 127). In other words, unless it becomes "anti-racist education," multicultural education may serve only to provide a veneer of change that in reality perpetuates discriminatory educational structures (p. 128).

Assimilation. Assimilationist ideology is the belief that an effective, harmonious society can be achieved only if minority groups are absorbed into mainstream society. Harmony and equal opportunity depend on a shared language and culture (Guzzetti, 2002, p. 299). According to Kalantzis, Cope, and Slade (1989), some people negatively call the unifying process assimilation. Because they view culture as "ethnicity" rather than as a whole way of life, they claim that assimilation in places such as Australia is into a hybrid, ethnically defined Anglo-Celtic-ness. But it is, in a sense, a historical accident that Anglo-Celtic-ness is the dominant medium through which industrial society is organized in Australia. In Japan it is Japanese, but what remains of traditional, preindustrial Japanese culture is incorporated and commodified in a similar way to vestiges of preindustrial Anglo or Celtic culture, which remain in modern Australia.

At Promise. Swadener (1995) takes on a positive conterdiscourse proposed in the face of the self-blaming deficit model. Her research indicates that institutional practices create an exclusionary and discriminatory reaction for certain groups. At promise looks at the social issues critically, which creates discrepancies for different groups instead of blaming the victim for passive perpetuation.

At-Risk Students. "At-risk" has acquired many diverse meanings and has become a common expression used by educators, policymakers, and the media to describe children and adolescents who exhibit one or more of a broad range of social, familial, economic, linguistic, cultural, and educational conditions associated with school failure (Guzzetti, 2002, p. 33). According to Skutnabb-Kangas and Cummins (1988), the learning difficulties of minority students are often pedagogically induced in that children designated "at risk" frequently receive intensive instruction that confines them to a passive role and induces a form of "learned helplessness" (p. 143).

Bicultural. The dictionary definition of bicultural is "of, pertaining to, or combining two cultures and of or pertaining to biculturalism" (http://www.infoplease.com/dictionary/bicultural). Sometimes the terms *bilingual/education* and *bicultural education* are used interchangeably, referring to valuing and exercising more than one language and set of cultural values.

Bilingual Education. Bilingual education emerged in the 1970s and has become one of the dominant forms of educating language minority pupils in the U.S. and Canada. In 1974 in *Lau v. Nichols*, the U.S. Supreme Court ruled students who were not being taught the curriculum in a manner that they could understand—such as through their native language—were being denied their right to a public education as guaranteed by the equal protection provisions of the Civil Rights Act of 1964. Bilingual education thus began as a civil rights issue and only subsequently developed as an instructional approach to assist in teaching language minority students (Findlay, 1998, p. 21). Sánchez (1983) tells that after a century of suppressing the Spanish language in the schools of the Southwest, federal and state legislation finally recognized what UNESCO specialists in 1951 determined to be fundamental: that every effort be made to provide education in the mother tongue. Although instruction in the mother tongue is neither a new nor revolutionary idea in the Southwest, the mandate for bilingual education has provided a great deal of controversy and antagonism. Efforts are underway at the state and federal levels to eliminate subsidized bilingual education and substitute instead second language instruction. When one considers the low educational attainment of Hispanics under policies of English submersion, it seems illogical but unsurprising, given the discriminatory policies of this country, to find that the dominant group is more concerned with budgetary matters and with ensuring job tenure for English monolingual teachers than with facilitating the acquisition of academic skills by lingual minority groups. Bilingual education has become such a complex matter that it is often impossible to separate instructional objectives from political and economic considerations or even problems of implementation (p. 50).

Bilingualism. A situation where an individual or a community of speakers is competent or fluent in two or more languages. Bilingualism also refers to bilingual education—the practice and philosophy of teaching two or more languages (Findlay, 1998, p. 19). Swain (1982) quotes different theorists, such as Macnamara, Oestreicher, and Bloomfield, in defining bilingualism as those who possess at least one of the language skills (listening, speaking, reading, or writing) even to a minimal degree in their second language. At the other end of the scale, bilinguals have been defined as those who demonstrate complete mastery of two different languages without interference between two linguistic processes or who have native-like control of two or more languages.

Critical Pedagogy. Kincheloe (2004) asserts that the great denial in education is that politics can be kept out of the mainstream curricula. Critical pedagogy argues that such pronouncements are not grounded on an understanding of power. The political dimension of education should be pointed out in all teaching and learning (p. 10). Education simply cannot be neutral. Recognition of these educational poli-

tics suggests that teachers take a position and make it understandable to their students. They do not, however, have the right to impose these positions on their students. This is a central tenet of critical pedagogy (p. 11). The advocates of critical pedagogy are especially concerned with those groups and individuals who are suffering, whose lives are affected by the sting of discrimination and poverty (p. 11).

Cultural Invasion. Cultural invasion is always a systematic and deliberate form of action that operates upon the social structure to preserve that structure. It serves to silence, dominate, and oppress people by imposing a colonizing perspective (Freire, 2000).

Cultural Pluralism. The ownership of two or more sets of cultural beliefs, values, and attitudes. Multicultural education is often designed to encourage cultural pluralism in children (Guzzetti, 2002, p. 700). Advocates of multicultural education often compare U.S. society to a tossed salad or a patchwork quilt. Both metaphors suggest the use of an array of materials and objects of various sizes and shapes and colors. Each ingredient is dependent on the others, but each is still unique; together the ingredients form a collective total that is distinguished by its diversity. There are a number of formal definitions of cultural pluralism in the education literature. Although these definitions vary, all suggest that cultural pluralism includes the maintenance of diversity, a respect for differences, and the right to participate actively in all aspects of society without having to give up one's unique identity (Grant & Sleeter, 2003).

Deficit Model. The idea that some children have a deficiency in their language in vocabulary, grammar, or understanding, particularly in the classroom. The child has a perceived language "deficit" that has to be compensated for by remedial schooling or compensatory education. The problem is seen to be located in the child rather than in the school system or society or in the ideology of the perceiver. The opposite is an *enrichment model* (Guzzetti, 2002, p. 700).

Diaspora. The classic "old" diasporas were the Jews, the Greeks, and the Armenians, peoples who lost or were driven from their ancient homelands and then resided in different lands as dispersed minorities (diaspora is a Greek word meaning, appropriately, "scattered seeds") and yet continued to both dream and plan some day "return home." These classic diasporas have an ancient vintage—the Jewish diaspora has continued for more than 2,000 years, and Armenians too have lived in their diaspora for centuries. This list should also include the Gypsies, wanderers in their diaspora for many hundreds of years, and the black populations who, beginning in the fifteenth and sixteenth centuries, were brutally wrenched out of Africa and dispersed as slaves to different parts of the Americas. Today's "new" diasporas are considerably different. Depending upon the particular definition and usage, there are likely to be many more of them, and they are scattered about as a result of the global trends that shape the contemporary world. As we know, these new diasporas have emerged from the worldwide movement of millions of persons, which in turn has been caused by global inequalities, modern information and production technologies, and powerful multinational corporations that frequently shift production across the world, as well as the more familiar "old-fashioned" reasons of famine and war. At another level, diasporas can also be seen to thrive in a world made up of nation-states: inasmuch as they practice exclusivity, nation-states relegate "others" to long-term minority status at best, brutal elimination at worst (Levy & Weingrod, 2005).

Dual-Language Programs. According to Baker and Jones (1998), dual-language schools contain a balance of language majority and language minority children. Such schools use two languages approximately equally in the curriculum so that children become bilingual and biliterate (p. 616). Dual-language education programs have a variety of names in addition to dual language. These include bilingual immersion, two-way bilingual immersion, two-way immersion, two-way bilingual Spanish immersion (or whatever the target language is, combined with the word *immersion*), and developmental bilingual education. One reason some programs focus on the immersion aspect of the name is to affiliate it with enrichment or elitist programs. Another reason for focusing on the immersion aspect is to deemphasize the bilingual nature of the program because of the political connotations of bilingual education as a compensatory and lower-quality education program.

Emergent Literacy. This term designated new conceptions about the relationship between a growing child and literacy information from the environment and home literacy practices. The process of becoming literate starts before school intervention. Emergent literacy originally indicated concepts built by children through many encounters with print other than explicit teaching (http://find.galegroup.com/gvrl/infomark).

"English Only." An umbrella term for federal and state legislation or organizations that aim to make English the official language of the U.S. This includes two national organizations: U.S. English and English First (Guzzetti, 2002, p. 701). Crawford (2000) indicates that the major push for Anglo-conformity came in the first two decades of the twentieth century, as capitalists began to fear the revolutionary potential of immigrant workers.

"English Plus." A movement promoting the belief that all U.S. citizens should have the opportunity to become proficient in a language other than English (Guzzetti, 2002, p. 701). Crawford (2000) states that to better appreciate other cultures and to thrive in a global economy, it makes sense to encourage bilingualism: proficiency in English plus other languages. José Serrano, a Puerto Rican Democrat from the Bronx, proposed a legislative substitute for H.R. 123 along these lines. The bill recognized English as the "common language" of the U.S.—with no restrictive provisions—while instructing government to "conserve and develop the Nation's linguistic resources by encouraging all residents of this country to learn and maintain skills in a language other than English" (p. 46).

First Language. The term *first language* is used in different, overlapping ways, and can mean (1) the first language learned, (2) the stronger language, (3) the mother tongue, or (4) the language used most often (Guzzetti, 2002, p. 701).

Hispanics. Spanish speakers in the U.S. The term is officially used in the U.S. Census (Guzzetti, 2002, p. 701).

Language Acquisition. The process by which an individual acquires a comprehensive knowledge of a language (Findlay, 1998, p. 105).

Language Dominance. One language being the stronger or preferred language of an individual or the more prestigious language within a particular region (Guzzetti, 2002, p. 702). Language dominance occurs in situations in which one language is spoken more frequently by a larger number of people than is the case for other languages in a given region or country. The term *dominance* also implies that in such situations, minority languages can be viewed as less important by the dominant population (Findlay, 1998, p. 113).

Language Imperialism. The *Oxford English Dictionary* defines imperialism as "a policy of acquiring dependent territories or extending a country's influence over less powerful or less developed countries through trade, diplomacy, etc." One main agent of imperialism throughout the centuries has been language. When a dominant or colonizing power promotes or enforces its language on conquered territories, it facilitates the spread of its own culture and political, social, and sometimes religious ideologies (Guzzetti, 2002, p. 319).

Language Learning. The process by which a first or second language is internalized. Some authors restrict the use of the term to formal learning (e.g., in the classroom). Others include informal learning (e.g., in the home) (Guzzetti, 2002, p. 703).

Language Minority. A language community (or person) whose first language is different from the dominant language of the country; a group who speaks a language of low prestige; or low in power, or with low numbers in a society (Guzzetti, 2002, p. 703).

Latinos. Spanish speakers of Latin American extraction. This Spanish term is now used in English, especially by U.S. Spanish speakers themselves. Often preferred to "Hispanics" (Guzzetti, 2002, p. 703).

Migrant Education. The children of migrant agricultural workers are among the most educationally disadvantaged children in the U.S. The conditions associated with their migratory lifestyle, such as discontinuity in education, social and cultural isolation, strenuous work outside of school, extreme poverty, and poor health, impose multiple obstacles to educational success. Schools coping with temporary seasonal increases in enrollment can face significant challenges in addressing the migrant students' unique educational needs (http://find.galegroup.com/gvrl/infomark).

Multiculturalism. Multiculturalism embraces the ideal of equal, harmonious, mutually tolerant existence of different and diverse languages and of religious, cultural, and ethnic groups in a pluralistic society. A multicultural viewpoint is partly based on the idea that an individual can successfully hold two or more cultural identities (Guzzetti, 2002, p. 299). Sleeter and Grant (2003) define multiculturalism as follows: "People mean different things by the term multicultural education. For one thing, they do not always agree on what forms of diversity it addresses. Some people think only about racial or cultural diversity, whereas others conceptualize gender, social class, and additional forms of diversity" (Preface).

Multilingualism. The ability to speak several languages is sometimes called multilingualism. The term has also been used as a guiding concept in conjunction with bilingualism to refer to educational approaches and philosophies pertaining to the teaching of second languages or to the teaching of linguistically diverse populations (Findlay, 1998, pp. 124, 125).

Normalistas. Normalistas in this context are foreign-trained Mexican teachers pursuing teacher certification in the U.S. The field of teacher training continues to explore the importance and role of bilingual education in light of ever-changing demographics. The U.S. population now indicates that the field of teacher training will need to change to meet the needs of children in the public school system. In analyzing the demographics, it is estimated that the Spanish-speaking group, both monolinguals and bilinguals, will soon be a majority group. In order to meet a pressing need, teacher training programs need to concentrate on increasing the number of teachers entering the field and developing competencies for all teachers that will prepare them to develop with the changing realities of the classrooms of today and tomorrow (Clark & Flores, 2002, p. 1).

Nuyorican. Stavans (2003) defines Nuyorican as a "Puerto Rican person in the mainland" (p. 181). Mainlanders outside of New York do not identify with this term, nor does every Puerto Rican in New York. And many Nuyoricans have moved to Puerto Rico. Those who answer to the "Nuyorican" label with pride are primarily members of the second and third generations who remain bonded to each other and to Puerto Rico, New York, Spanish, and English by the linguistic inventions that took hold in the second half of the twentieth century and defined the "Nuyorican" (Zentella, 1997, pp. 1, 2).

Oppression. The result of arbitrary and cruel use of power on minority and disenfranchised populations. Forms of oppression include colonialism, imperialism, and totalitarianism.

Pedagogy of Freedom. In the introduction to Paulo Freire's *Pedadogy of Freedom* (1998), Stanley Aronowitz tells readers that this book is utopian text. He states that its utopianism consists of the wild and seemingly anachronistic idea that among other things education "is that specifically human act of intervening in the world." When Freire speaks of intervention, Aronowitz says, "I refer both to the aspiration for radical changes in society in such areas as economics, human relations, property, the right to employment, to land, to education, and to health, to the reactionary position whose aim is to immobilize history and maintain an unjust socio-economic and cultural order." In the foreword to Freire's *Pedagogy of the Oppressed* (2000), Donaldo Macedo tells the reader that Freire courageously challenges us to break with the rigidity of a technicist training approach to education in order to embrace those fundamental knowledges that will prevent us from deceiving our conscience. In the foreword to Freire's *Pedagogy of Freedom*, Macedo brilliantly reminds us about the social order that, according to Jean-Paul Sartre, "sanctions misery, chronic hunger, ignorance, or, in general sub-humanity." In essence, educators who refuse to transform the ugliness of human misery, social injustices, and inequalities invariably become educators for domestication who, as Sartre so poignantly suggested, "will change nothing and will serve no one, but will succeed only in finding moral comfort in malaise."

Subtractive Bilingualism. A situation in which a second language is learned at the expense of the first language and gradually replaces the first language (e.g., immigrants to a country or minority language pupils in submersion education) (Guzzetti, 2002, p. 706). Skutnabb-Kangas and Cummins (1988) indicate that educators who see their role as adding a second language and cultural affiliation to students' repertoire are likely to empower students more than those who see their role as replacing or subtracting students' primary language and culture in the process of assimilating them to the dominant culture. In addition to personal and future employment advantages of proficiency in two or more languages, there is considerable evidence that subtle educational advantages result from continued development of both languages among bilingual students.

Transnational. This term implies interconnections between the peoples of the world. New developments in telecommunication, immigration, and globalization have fostered closer boundaries with social, political, and economic ties.

References

Baker, C., & Jones, S. P. (Eds.). (1998). *Encyclopedia of Bilingualism and Bilingual Education*. Clevedon, UK: Multilingual Matters.

Byram, M. (2000). *Routledge Encyclopedia of Language Testing and Learning*. London: Routledge.

Clark, E. R., & Flores, N. (2002). *Normalistas/ Foreign-Trained Teachers*. San Antonio: University of Texas at San Antonio.

Crawford, J. (2000). *At War with Diversity: US Language Policy in an Age of Anxiety*. Clevedon, UK: Multilingual Matters.

Cummins, J. (2000). *Language, Power, and Pedagogy: Bilingual Children in the Crossfire*. Clevedon, UK: Multilingual Matters.

Findlay, M. S. (1998). *Language and Communication: A Cross-Cultural Encyclopedia*. Santa Barbara, CA: ABC-CLIO.

Freire, P. (1998). *Pedagogy of Freedom: Ethics, Democracy, and Civic Courage*. Lanham, MD: Rowman & Littlefield.

Freire, P. (2000). *Pedagogy of the Oppressed*. New York: Continuum.

Grant, C. A., & Sleeter, C. E. (2003). *Turning on Learning: Five Approaches for Multicultural Teaching Plans for Race, Class, Gender, and Disability*. New York: John Wiley & Sons.

Guzzetti, B. G. (Ed.). (2002). *Literacy in America: An Encyclopedia of History, Theory, and Practice*. Santa Barbara, CA: ABC-CLIO.

Kalantzis, M., Cope, B., & Slade, D. (1989). *Minority Languages and Dominant Culture: Issues of Education, Assessment, and Social Equity*. London: Falmer.

Kincheloe, J. L. (2004). *Critical Pedagogy Primer*. New York: Peter Lang.

Levy, A., & Weingrod, A. (2005). *Homelands and Diasporas: Holy Lands and Other Places*. Stanford, CA: Stanford University Press.

Sánchez, R. (1983). *Chicano Discourse: Sociohistoric Perspectives*. Rowley, MA: Newbury House.

Skutnabb-Kangas, T., & Cummins, J. (Eds.). (1988). *Minority Education: From Shame to Struggle*. Clevedon, UK: Multilingual Matters.

Sleeter, C. E., & Grant, C. A. (2003). *Making Choices for Multicultural Education: Five Approaches to Race, Class, and Gender* (4th ed.). New York: John Wiley & Sons.

Stavans, I. (2003). *Spanglish: The Making of a New American Language*. New York: Rayo.

Swadener, B. S. (1995). *Children and Families "At Promise": Deconstructing the Discourse of Risk*. Albany, NY: SUNY Press.

Swain, M. (1982). *Evaluating Bilingual Education: A Canadian Case Study*. Clevedon, UK: Multilingual Matters.

Zentella, A. C. (1997). *Growing Up Bilingual: Puerto Rican Children in New York*. Malden, MA: Blackwell.

Ozlem Zabitgil

Index

About the Editor and Contributors

THE EDITOR

LOURDES DIAZ SOTO is a graduate of Hunter College, City University of New York, and The Pennsylvania State University. She has taught and worked with families and children in Puerto Rico (Dorado Academy), Florida (Florida Atlantic University), New York City (Teachers College, Columbia University), and Pennsylvania (Lehigh University and The Pennsylvania State University). Scholarship and collegial opportunities have taken her to Puerto Rico, Costa Rica, Greece, Spain, Canada, Taiwan, and Uruguay. Her publications include *Language, Culture, and Power: Bilingual Families Struggle for Quality Education* (S.U.N.Y. Press) and two edited volumes published by Peter Lang entitled *Making a Difference in the Lives of Bilingual/Bicultural Learners* and *The Politics of Early Childhood Education*. A recent publication (2005) is a coedited volume with Beth Blue Swadener entitled *Power and Voice in Research with Children*, also published by Peter Lang. In addition, she has published numerous refereed articles and book chapters examining issues of social justice and equity. In August 2006 she joined the Education Faculty at the University of Texas at Austin.

THE CONTRIBUTORS

LUIS ALMEIDA is a doctoral candidate in Instructional Systems at The Pennsylvania State University. He received a Master of Science degree in Communication Education and Mass Media Technology from Clarion University of Pennsylvania. Mr. Almeida is also a recipient of numerous fellowships, awards, and titles, including the Puksar, Graham, and Miriam Gray fellowships, and in 2002 he received the lifetime title of Holmes Scholar from the Holmes Partnership organization in Washington, D.C. His research interests include user design, interface gaming design, systemic thinking in education, and Latino studies.

RENÉ ANTROP-GONZÁLEZ is an Assistant Professor in the Department of Curriculum and Instruction at the University of Wisconsin–Milwaukee. His teaching areas are in bilingual/second language education, and his principal research interests revolve around the impact of small school reform on the academic achievement of Latino/a high school students through the lenses of social capital and caring theory. His additional areas of research interest include the education of Puerto Rican/Latino urban high school students in the U.S., alternative education, and qualitative inquiry. Dr. Antrop-González's recent works include the forwarding of the "school as sanctuary concept" and its possible impact on Latino/a education in alternative multicultural high school settings and the factors that urban Puerto Rican high school students attribute to their high academic achievement. Finally, his most recent writings have been published in *Curriculum Inquiry*, the *International Journal of Qualitative Studies in Education*, the *Journal of the Center for Puerto Rican Studies*, the *Journal of Curriculum Theorizing*, the *Journal of Latinos and Education*, and *Taboo*.

CRISTIAN R. AQUINO-STERLING is a doctoral candidate in the Mary Lou Fulton College of Education at Arizona State University, completing a dissertation on the social justice discourse of resistance and critique around the No Child Left Behind Act. His academic and research interests pertain to critical and poststructural theories of discourse and education, and the schooling/education of Haitian and Haitian-Dominican children in his native Dominican Republic.

ANGELA E. ARZUBIAGA is an Assistant Professor in the Division of Psychology in Education at Arizona State University. She has been recognized for her work on family policy matters by the International Society for the Study of Behavioral Development. At the Vanderbilt Institute for Public Policy Studies she continued her research on immigrant families' adaptations. Currently she is a Spencer Grant investigator on the study "Children of Immigrants in U.S. Preschools: Parent and Teacher Perspectives."

ADRIANA AUBERT is Researcher of CREA (Center of Research in Theories and Practices that Overcome Inequalities) at the University of Barcelona and Tutor at the National University of Distance Education, Spain. Her main areas of research are the Romà population and the Learning Communities Project. She has participated in the national study *Brudila Callí: Romaní Women against Exclusion. Overcoming Absenteeism and School Failure of Romaní Girls and Adolescents* (Women's Institute, Spanish Ministry of Employment and Social Affairs). She is coauthor of the book *Dialogar y Transformar. Pedagogía crítica del siglo XXI*.

ROBERT BAHRUTH has taught at universities in Cuba, Israel, Ecuador, Colombia, Guatemala, Mexico, and Taiwan. While teaching in a bilingual fifth grade in Texas, he employed a humanistic approach with his students. *Literacy con Cariño* (Heinemann, 1991) is their success story. A new edition of *Literacy con Cariño*, released in 1998, includes a foreword by Paulo Freire and Donaldo Macedo. His Ph.D. is from the University of Texas at Austin, where he received the George I. Sanchez Endowed Presidential Scholarship for significant contributions to the field of minority education. He is a Professor at Boise State University and received the "Outstanding Faculty Award 1997–98" from the Associated Students of Boise State and the "Top Ten Scholars" Award in 2002.

ALFREDO H. BENAVIDES is Professor of Bilingual Education and Diversity Studies in the College of Education at Texas Tech University. Dr. Benavides has been in the field of bilingual education for over 30 years. The main thrust of his research and work has been in the area of teacher preparation. Prior to coming to Texas Tech he was at the University of Iowa and Arizona State University. Professor Benavides has published a variety of journal articles, book chapters, and two books. He has served on national and state committees through his involvement with the National Association for Bilingual Education and the American Educational Research Association. He is currently on the editorial board of the *Bilingual Review/Revista Bilingüe* and is co-editor of the *Bilingual Research Journal*, the premier journal in the field of bilingual education.

FAZILA BHIMJI is a lecturer in the Department of Humanities at the University of Central Lancashire, U.K. She received her Ph.D. in Applied Linguistics from the University of California, Los Angeles. Her research interests include looking at issues of race, ethnicity, and gender. More specifically, she explores the ways in which marginalized people live their everyday lives and combat racism and classism.

DANNY BRASSELL is an Associate Professor in the Teacher Education Department at California State University–Dominguez Hills. A prominent national speaker on literacy issues, he is the author of *Readers for Life: The Ultimate Reading Fitness Guide* (Heinemann, 2006) and is the founder of the Lazy Readers' Book Club (www.lazy readers.com).

MARGARITA E. CALDERÓN is a Senior Research Scientist and Professor at Johns Hopkins University's Center for Data-Driven Reform in Education. She has served on several national panels including the National Research Council's Committee on Teacher Preparation, the U.S. Department of Education Institute for Education Sciences' National Literacy Panel for Language Minority Children and Youth, the Carnegie Adolescent Literacy Panel, the Pacific Regional Educational Laboratory Panel on Early Literacy, and the California Pre-School Literacy Panel. She is principal investigator in a five-year study in middle and high schools, titled *Expediting Reading Comprehension for English Language Learners*, that focuses on professional development of science, social studies, and language arts teachers and the development of adolescent literacy within those content areas. She is co–principal investigator (with Robert Slavin) on the five-year Institute for Education Sciences' (IES) randomized evaluation of English immersion, transitional, and two-way bilingual programs and other Office of Educational Research and Improvement/IES projects. She is coeditor (with Robert Slavin) of *Effective Programs for Latino Students* and coauthor (with Liliana Minaya-Rowe) of *Designing and Implementing Two-Way Bilingual Programs* and *Expediting Comprehension for English Language Learners*. She has published over 100 articles, books, chapters, and teacher training manuals.

EVELYN CANABAL is Head of the World Languages Department at the Madeira School, McLean, Virginia. She developed the Spanish Heritage curriculum at the University of Maryland, College Park, where she taught for 17 years. In addtion to Heritage Language acquisition, her other research interests include U.S. Spanish legitimacy, content-based language instruction, and Latin American/Latino literatures and cultures.

CHRIS LISKA CARGER is an Associate Professor in the Department of Literacy Education at Northern Illinois University. She recently received the College of Education's Award for Outstanding Community Service and Partnership for her work with preservice teachers and bilingual children in the Reaching Out Through Art and Reading Program she directs. Her research has centered on responses to multicultural children's literature, bilingualism and reading, and the Latino academic achievement gap. In addition to her book *Of Borders and Dreams: A Mexican-American Experience of Urban Education*, she has written numerous articles for *Book Links*, *Educational Leadership*, and *Language Arts*.

ALISON A. CARR-CHELLMAN is Associate Professor of Instructional Systems in the Learning and Performance Systems department at the College of Education at The Pennsylvania State University. Her research interests include diffusion of innovations, systems change and systems theories, educational systems design, critiques of online learning, and user design. Her recent book, *Global Perspectives on E-learning: Rhetoric and Reality*, published by Sage, won an honorable mention in the Wedemeyer book competition in 2005.

JOSEPH CARROLL-MIRANDA has both a Ph.D. and M.A. in Curriculum and Instruction, with specialization in learning technology and critical pedagogy, from New Mexico State University. Originally from Puerto Rico, Joseph has engaged in research in areas dealing with youth culture. Some of his work deals with hip-hop and education, punk-hardcore culture and education, gang culture, activism and social justice, and techno-culture.

CHRISTINA CHÁVEZ is an Assistant Professor in the Liberal Studies department at California State Polytechnic University, Pomona. She teaches undergraduate teacher candidate courses in the history and politics of teaching, families and schools, and language, culture, and identity. Her research interests are in Latino families, later-generation Chicanos, minority teacher education, and language and literacy issues of

linguistic and racial minority students. Her forthcoming book, *In Their Own Words: A Five-Generation Mexican American Family in Los Angeles*, chronicles the home, work, and school lives of her own family.

ELLEN RIOJAS CLARK is a Professor in the Division of Bicultural Bilingual Studies at the University of Texas at San Antonio (UTSA). She has written extensively on the relationship between the constructs of self-concept, ethnic identity, self-efficacy, and good teaching. Another area of research is in the area of gifted language minority students. She has developed and presented many graduate summer institutes that focused on Latino literature and culture, multicultural education collaborative approaches, curriculum development, cooperative learning, and restructuring schools for language minority students at UTSA. Dr. Clark serves as Co–Principal Investigator for the Rockefeller Foundation Project: Knowledge, Culture, and Construction of Identity in a Transnational Community in San Antonio and is the Research Coordinator for the Academy for Teacher Excellence, a U.S. Department of Education project. She is the Educational Content Director for the Scholastic Entertainment PBS children's cartoon series *Maya and Miguel*.

ZULMARA CLINE is a Professor at California State University, San Marcos and Founding Director of the Center for the Study of Border Pedagogy. Dr. Cline completed her Ph.D. at the University of California, Santa Barbara, on the effects of socialization on school administrators. She is currently a scholar practitioner, writing extensively in the areas of border pedagogy, school policy, diversity, leadership, and multicultural education. She is an inspirational writer for Latinos/as, having authored a number of articles and poetry books dealing with issues of biculturalism and living in two worlds.

RUFINA CORTEZ is a doctoral student in Educational Policy Studies in the College of Education at the University of Illinois at Urbana–Champaign. Her research interests lie in the examination and interrogation of alternative educational methods mobilized by subordinate communities in response to the invisibility of their own histories within mainstream institutionalized educational settings. Her work has been featured in various books and periodicals.

ANTONIA DARDER is Professor of Educational Policy Studies and Latino and Latina Studies at the University of Illinois at Urbana–Champaign. Her scholarship and teaching focus on comparative studies of racism, class and society; questions of culture, identity, language, and popular culture; and the foundations of critical pedagogy, social justice theory, and the history of Puerto Rican feminism. Her books include *After Race, The Critical Pedagogy Reader, Culture and Difference, Culture and Power in the Classroom, The Latino Studies Reader, Latinos and Education*, and *Reinventing Paulo Freire*. As a cultural worker, poet, and artist, Professor Darder has been active in a variety of community grassroots efforts tied to education rights, worker's rights, bilingual education, women's issues, and immigration. In 2006 she established a radio collective that produces *Liberacion! The Local & Global Nexus of Politics, Art, and Struggle*, a public affairs radio program on WEFT 90.1, Champaign community radio.

ERICA R. DAVILA is an Assistant Professor in Education and the Coordinator of Urban Education at Arcadia University in Glenside, Pennsylvania.

REGINA DEIL-AMEN is an Assistant Professor of Educational Theory and Policy at The Pennsylvania State University. She is the author of several articles and a forthcoming book based on her research exploring how community colleges and private postsecondary vocational colleges structure students' educational experiences and prepare students for sub-baccalaureate careers. Her research interests include sociology of education, educational stratification and inequality, college aspirations and persistence, race/ethnicity, and social class.

ANTHONY DE JESÚS is an education researcher and interim director of the Center for Puerto Rican Studies at Hunter College, City University of New York. Born and raised in the Bronx, he has considerable experience working as a practitioner and researcher in urban schools, community-based organizations, and institutions of higher education. His research and teaching has focused primarily on addressing the social and cultural barriers that prevent Latino students from accessing postsecondary educational experiences and successfully transitioning to higher education.

CARLOS F. DIAZ is Professor of Multicultural Education at Florida Atlantic University. Formerly he taught at the secondary and community college levels. He has received five awards in his career for excellence in teaching. Dr. Diaz has been a member of the National Council for Accreditation of Teacher Education board of examiners since 1997. He is coauthor of *Global Perspectives for Educators* and editor and contributing author of *Multicultural Education for the 21st Century*, as well as various articles and chapters in other books. Over the past decade he has procured grants that have enabled approximately 300 South Florida educators to earn master's degrees with concentrations in multicultural education and English for Speakers of Other Languages on full scholarships.

GERARDO DIAZ is a doctoral candidate in Education Policy Studies at the University of Illinois at Urbana–Champaign. His scholarly interest involves tracing the historical interplay between education and the political economy. Specifically, his work examines the historical developments of Latino education in light of changing state/local economies, migration patterns, changing demographics, de facto/de jure segregation, and segmentation of labor markets.

PAULINE DOW is Associate Superintendent for the Canutillo Independent School District in El Paso County, Texas. Currently a doctoral student in Educational Leadership and Foundations at the University of Texas at El Paso, Ms. Dow's research focuses on the academic achievement of students participating in two-way bilingual programs in the El Paso region and the policy implications of cultivating a bilingual/biliterate community. She is Principal Investigator for Project AVANZA: A Two-Way Bilingual Education Program Initiative. This $1.4 million, five-year project is a systemwide effort to provide all students in grades K–12 in the Canutillo Independent School District with the opportunity to become academically proficient in both English and Spanish. Ms. Dow's professional service includes annual presentations at state and national conferences (for example, the Texas Association for Bilingual Education, the National Association for Bilingual Education, La Cosecha Two-Way Conference, and Texas Teachers of English to Speakers of Other Languages) and acting as conference chairperson for state and local conferences

(for example, Texas Association for Bilingual Education in 2000, Bilingual Education with an Emphasis in Math and Science annually since 1999, and Emerging Literature of the Southwest Culture in 1995, 1996, and 1997). In 1999 Ms. Dow was honored with the TEXTESOLER Award in recognition of her work in bilingual education.

GEORGIANNA DUARTE is Early Childhood Professor at the University of Texas at Brownsville & Texas Southmost College in Brownsville, Texas. She is a consultant, trainer, and reviewer for the Head Start Bureau as well as a member of the Sembrando Semillas, an Early Childhood Education committee for the National Council of La Raza. She is an active leader and member of the National Association for the Education of Young Children and the National Association of Bilingual Education, as well as a long-standing member of the International Play Association. She is currently involved in designing an ecological park in Ayacucho, Peru. She works extensively as a community partner and trainer in Migrant Head Start nationally and locally. She recently worked six months during her sabbatical in Ayacucho, Peru, training rural coordinators of an early childhood program. Through her collaborative projects in Peru, she will be teaching in Peru in July 2007.

MARTY DUCKENFIELD is affiliated with the National Dropout Prevention Center in the College of Health, Education, and Human Development at Clemson University (www.dropoutprevention.org). The National Dropout Prevention Center is the home of the Southern Regional Center for the National Service-Learning Exchange. Duckenfield's research interests are service-learning, resilience, and dropout prevention.

JACQUELINE EDMONDSON is Associate Professor of Education at The Pennsylvania State University, where she teaches undergraduate and graduate courses in reading and language arts, and she teaches graduate seminars on special topics that include situated literacies and education policy. Jackie's research is focused on education policy, rural schools and communities, and biography. Her books include *America Reads: A Critical Policy Study* (2000), *Prairie Town: Redefining Rural Life in an Age of Globalization* (2003), *Understanding and Applying Critical Policy Study: Reading Educators Advocating for Change* (2004), *Venus and Serena Williams: A Biography* (2005), *Reading Education Policy* (2005, coedited with Patrick Shannon), and *Condoleezza Rice: A Biography* (2006).

LAURA C. ENGEL is a Ph.D. candidate in Educational Policy Studies at the University of Illinois at Urbana–Champaign. With a background in bilingual education, her current research interests focus on globalization and the state, with specific emphasis on educational governance and policy production. Her dissertation addresses issues of educational policy production in Catalonia within the context of the emergence of a European Policy Space, and its relationship to national and subnational policy sites.

MIRYAM ESPINOSA-DULANTO is the Professor in charge of World Languages Education and Co-Director of the Program Specialist: English as a Second Language certificate at The Pennsylvania State University. Her writing and academic research explores the construction and transmission of knowledge in U.S schools. Professor Espinosa-Dulanto has taught in urban and rural settings, worked in teacher professional development, and had poetry readings in Asia, Europe, Latin America, and the U.S. Currently she is working on a poetry collection, "Finding Home in Memory: Stories of Immigration, Diaspora, and Dis/location."

JUDITH ESTRADA is an Educational Policy Studies graduate student at the College of Education at the University of Illinois at Urbana–Champaign. She received her B.A. in Latin American and Latina Latino Studies and Education from the University of California, Santa Cruz. Her current research cuts across critical theory, cultural studies, and critical pedagogy.

EDGAR I. FARMER is Professor of Education and Director of Postsecondary Technical & Community College Leadership in the Workforce Education & Development program at The Pennsylvania State University. He is also the Site Director for National Research and Dissemination Centers on Career & Technical Education. Dr. Farmer has worked extensively with school districts, government agencies, and other universities as a consultant in vocational education programs. His research interests are postsecondary technical education and vocational special needs, with emphasis on disadvantaged students as described in the Vocational Education Act.

EDWARD GARCIA FIERROS is an Assistant Professor in the Department of Education and Human Services at Villanova University. Professor Fierros coordinates the Masters program in Graduate Teacher Education and teaches graduate and undergraduate courses in Multicultural Education, Diversity and Inclusion, and Educational Research. His research interests focus on inclusive education for students of color, charter school education policy, and multiple intelligences theory. In addition to his scholarship in multicultural education and disability studies, Professor Fierros is coauthor of *Multiple Intelligences: Best Ideas from Research and Practice* (Pearson, 2004).

BELINDA FLORES is an Associate Professor and Department Chair at the University of Texas at San Antonio (UTSA). She completed her Ph.D. in Curriculum and Instruction at the University of Texas at Austin with specializations in Multilingual Studies and Educational Psychology. In 2000 she received the first place award for Outstanding Dissertation from the National Association for Bilingual Education, and she was awarded the 2004 UTSA President's Distinguished Award for Research Excellence. Her research is in the area of teacher preparation, specifically presage psychological factors (attitudes, ethnicity, epistemological beliefs, self-concept, and efficacy) and their impact on effective teacher behavior; high-stakes testing and its implications for teacher preparation; and family connections—identifying links for teachers to foster and build on children's prior knowledge. In 2003 she was funded for a Title V Grant from the U.S. Department of Education to create an Academy for Teacher Excellence at UTSA. In 2004 she also was funded for a Transition to Teaching Grant from the Department of Education.

LAURA GALICIA is a bilingual educator in East Los Angeles. Currently she is working on her Ph.D. in the Department of Education Policy Studies at the University of Illinois at Urbana–Champaign. Her research interests include critical pedagogy, literacy, and teacher education.

EUGENE E. GARCIA is Vice President for University-School Partnerships and Dean of the College of Education at Arizona State University. He served as a Senior Officer in the U.S. Department of Education from 1993 to 1995. He is Chair of the National Task Force on Early Education for Hispanics, funded by the Foundation for Child Development and the Mailman Family Foundation. His most recent books include *Hispanic Education in the United States: Raíces y Alas* (2001), *Student Cultural Diversity: Understanding and Meeting the Challenge* (2001), and *Teaching and Learning in Two Languages* (2005).

HERMÁN S. GARCÍA is Regents Professor of Curriculum and Instruction at New Mexico State University. He is a critical bilingual educator and has traveled extensively in Latin America.

ENCARNACION GARZA is an Assistant Professor in the Educational Leadership and Policy Studies Department at the University of Texas at San Antonio. His research has focused primarily on issues of social justice and the preparation of future school leaders who will serve minority children. He is the author of *Resiliency and Success: Migrant Children in the U.S.*

JOSUÉ M. GONZÁLEZ has worked in Latino education for over 40 years. He has played prominent roles in the National Association for Bilingual Education and in the Office of Bilgual Education and Minority Languages Affairs, the federal unit responsible for administering Title VII of the Elementary and Secondary Education Act. Currently he is Director of the Center for Education Equity and Language Diversity and Professor of Educational Leadership and Policy Studies in the Mary Lou Fulton College of Education at Arizona State University. He is a former editor of the *Bilingual Research Journal* and presently is

General Editor of the forthcoming *Encyclopedia of Bilingual Education in the United States*.

VIRGINIA GONZALEZ is Associate Professor of Education at the University of Cincinnati. She was formerly a faculty member at Texas A&M University and at the University of Arizona. She is an expert in second language learning and assessment and bilingual education. One of Dr. Gonzalez's major areas of expertise is the development of research models explaining cognitive and linguistic development in ESL Hispanic students and their implications for assessment, learning processes, and instructional programs. Dr. Gonzalez has published numerous books and journal articles, which have been applied for the assessment and instruction of diverse students and for the training of ESL/bilingual educators in higher education.

ELAISA SÁNCHEZ GOSNELL is Assistant Research Professor of Early Childhood Education at George Mason University. Her area of specialization is the assessment of culturally, linguistically, and ability diverse young children. She has extensive experience as a consultant and trainer at the local, state, and national levels on matters related to working with culturally and linguistically diverse children and their families.

CATHY GUTIERREZ-GOMEZ is an Associate Professor for the Early Childhood Multicultural Education program in the Department of Individual, Family, and Community Education at the University of New Mexico. She also teaches for the Department of Language, Literacy, and Sociocultural Studies and works in collaboration with the Teacher Education Department. She is an active member of some of the most prominent national early child-

hood organizations in the country, including the National Association for the Education of Young Children and the Association for Childhood Education International. Dr. Gutierrez-Gomez began her teaching career as a preschool teacher and gained extensive experience working in diverse capacities with Head Start at the local, state, and national levels. One of her first teaching experiences was in a Head Start program within a public school system. During graduate school at the University of North Texas she taught in the early childhood education program and was a clinical supervisor for the Professional Development Center.

HOLLY HANSEN-THOMAS is an Assistant Professor of TESOL and Literacy Education at Binghamton University. She has taught, studied, and conducted research in various countries, including Hungary, Germany, Spain, and the U.S., as a Fulbright Scholar. Supported by a dissertation grant from the American Educational Research Association and the Institute of Education Sciences, Holly was a National Association of Bilingual Education Outstanding Dissertation Award winner for 2005. She has published articles on second language writing, language ideology, and adolescent language learners in mainstream classes. Her current research interests examine issues encountered by second language learners in schools as well as the specialized forms of discourse used by minority language learners in content area classes.

LUIS HUERTA-CHARLES is an Assistant Professor who teaches Early Childhood/Bilingual Education in the Department of Curriculum and Instruction at New Mexico State University. He is coeditor (with Marc Pruyn) of *Teaching Peter McLaren: Paths of Dissent* (Peter Lang, 2005). His research interest focuses on the processes of early biliteracy, bilingual education, and teacher education related to socially just practices in the Borderlands. He also has been engaged in developing a research approach centered on viewing research as praxis within communities.

NATHALIA E. JARAMILLO is a doctoral candidate in the Graduate School of Education at the University of California, Los Angeles. She is author and coauthor of over a dozen articles on critical pedagogy and Marxist feminism and is coauthor (with Peter McLaren) of the forthcoming book, *Pedagogy and Praxis in the Age of Empire.*

HAROON KHAREM is Assistant Professor in the School of Education at Brooklyn College. He has written articles on African American history and education and is the author of *The Curriculum of Repression: A Pedagogy of Racial History in the United States* (2005).

ESTHER KOGAN is an Associate Professor of Education and Director of the Early Childhood Graduate Program at Adelphi University in Garden City, New York. She has been an advocate for children, teachers, and parents for the past 15 years with a focus on early childhood, gifted education, and bilingual education. Her research interests include the impact of family, culture, and school on child development, identity development in bilingual/bicultural children, teacher training, assessment of young children, and classrooms as respectful communities. Esther has presented at national and international conferences. She is the author of *Gifted Bilingual Students: A Paradox?* (Peter Lang, 2001) and coauthor, with Anne Mungai, of *Pathways to Inclusion: Voices from the Field* (University Press of America, 2005).

MANEL LACORTE is an Associate Professor of Spanish Applied Linguistics at the University of Maryland, College Park. He is also Director of the Spanish Language Program and a faculty member of the graduate program in Second Language Acquisition and Application, where he has taught courses in Spanish linguistics and sociolinguistics, second language methodology, curriculum development, and teacher education. He has presented and published papers in his areas of main interest (language classroom interaction and development, language use and identity, second language teacher education, and foreign-language teaching methodology), a teachers' guide on task-based teaching, and a collection of papers from an international conference held at the University of Maryland. He has recently coedited a volume on Spanish in the U.S. and in contact with other languages. He is now writing an academic book on interaction and context in foreign-language teaching and learning, and editing an introduction to Spanish applied linguistics.

HA LAM is a doctoral candidate in the Department of Curriculum and Instruction at Arizona State University. She received her M.A. in English for Speakers of Other Languages/Bilingual at the University of Maryland Baltimore County and her B.A. in Elementary Education at Goucher College. She has taught English as a Second Language at the high school and university level and English as a Foreign Language in Japan. She is currently teaching pre-service teachers. Her research interests include the maintenance and loss of heritage languages, the relationships between language, culture, and identity, and language policy.

JULIANA LASTA is a doctoral candidate in the Department of Curriculum and

Teaching at Teachers College, Columbia University. Born and raised in Argentina, she received her bachelor's degree in School Psychology with honors. While in Argentina she worked in a hospital for economically disadvantaged children, providing assessment to over 20 schools in the hospital district in math, language arts, and family therapy to promote social and learning abilities in children. She is currently an invited lecturer in the main universities in her country and continues her studies in her two main interests: education and family therapy.

KATHRYN J. LINDHOLM-LEARY is Professor of Child and Adolescent Development at San Jose State University, where she has taught for 19 years. She has worked with dual-language education programs for the past 20 years, and during that time she has evaluated over 25 programs and helped to establish programs in over 54 school districts in 11 states. She has presented her research results on dual-language education programs at many local, state, national, and international meetings, and her findings appear in newspapers, professional newsletters, professional journal articles, and book chapters. She has authored or co-authored two books on dual-language education and prepared a booklet for the U.S. Department of Education and the National Clearinghouse for Bilingual Education entitled *Biliteracy for a Global Society: An Idea Book on Dual Language Education.*

SARA LIPPI is a dual-language middle school teacher at the Cypress Hills Community School (Public School 89), a two-way Spanish-English immersion model in East New York, Brooklyn. As a New York City Teaching Fellow (2002–2004), she received her Masters in Education from Brooklyn College.

VIVIAN G. LÓPEZ is a doctoral candidate in the Literacy, Language, and Culture program in the Department of Curriculum and Instruction at New Mexico State University. Her research interests include critical literacy, bilingual and critical multicultural education, social justice and equity issues in education, parent voices within education, identity/language/culture, and education for indigenous peoples, Latinos, immigrants, and diverse populations. Ms. López has over 20 years of experience working with children, families, and educational practitioners. She has also taught classes, presented workshops, conducted public speaking engagements, served as a spokesperson, provided media interviews, and coordinated and managed educational and social service programs.

MYRIAN LUIS is in the doctoral program in the Department of Educational Policy Studies at the University of Illinois at Urbana–Champaign. Some of her awards include the Congressional Hispanic Caucus Institute Fellowship, the W. K. Kellogg Foundation & National Council for Community and Education Partnerships Fellowship, and recognition in the first edition of *The Chancellor's List.* Myrian's research interests include the history of education of Mexicans and Mexican Americans in the U.S., federal policy in relation to first-generation Mexicans in K–12, and educational remittances that occur within the transnational movement between Mexico and the U.S. She hopes one day to work for the Department of Education as an advocate for the Latino/a community.

CECILIA MALDONADO is an Assistant Professor in the Department of Educational Leadership at the University of Nevada, Las Vegas. She is the Coordinator for the Master's Degree program in Workforce

Training and Development. She is coauthor (with Dr. William Rothwell et al.) of *The Handbook of Training Technologies: An Introductory Guide to Facilitating Learning with Technology—Planning to Evaluation.* She has published a book chapter titled "Latinos at Work: Hispanics' Contribution to the Workplace and the Enhancement of the American Economy." This chapter is part of a book (now available in a second edition) titled *Diversity in America: Visions of the Future.* She is also an editor on an upcoming book titled *The Encyclopedia of Human Resource Management and Workplace Policy.* In addition, she has published scholarly articles, mostly surrounding Latino issues, in various professional journals.

ERIK MALEWSKI is an Assistant Professor of Curriculum Studies at Purdue University. He is interested in scholarship involving critical theory, multiculturalism, cultural studies, and post-structuralism as they inform the reconceptualization of curriculum and the social contexts of education. His most recent work has focused on technology and multiculturalism within teacher education; suicide, curriculum and public policy; and the internationalization of teacher education through study abroad. He is currently working on an edited book addressing intergenerational conversations on the state of the field of curriculum studies.

MARGY McCLAIN is an educational researcher and consultant based in Oklahoma City. She received her Ph.D. in Curriculum and Instruction from the University of Illinois at Chicago. Her research interests focus on issues of educational equity as pursued through policy initiatives, teacher education and professional development, parent engagement, and classroom practice.

PETER McLAREN is a Professor in the Division of Urban Schooling at the University of California, Los Angeles. Professor McLaren has published and edited over 40 books on critical education, and his writings have been translated into 17 languages. He is the inaugural recipient of the Paulo Freire Social Justice Award presented by Chapman University. Recently a group of education activists and scholars in Mexico created La Fundación McLaren de Pedagogía Crítica to promote critical pedagogy throughout Latin America.

CARMEN MEDINA is Assistant Professor of Literacy, Multicultural Children's Literature and Drama at the University of British Columbia. Her work examines children's responses to critical issues represented in Latino/a literature, particularly through drama in education practices. She has published this work in scholarly journals such as *Research in Drama in Education*, *Language Arts*, and *Theory into Practice*. In 2005 she was the recipient of the Virginia Hamilton Essay Award for an article that made a significant contribution to the professional literature concerning multicultural literary experiences for youth.

CARMEN MERCADO is Associate Professor in Curriculum and Teaching at Hunter College, City Unversity of New York. She teaches undergraduate, graduate, and doctoral courses and supervises students in their field placements. Since 1989 she has engaged in participatory action research with teachers, students, and families in multilingual, multidialectal modest-income communities in New York City to understand and build curricula around language and literacy funds of knowledge in students' homes and communities. She also has engaged in several cross-disciplinary collaborations, most recently with social scientists from El Centro de Estudios Puertorriquenos. El Centro's archives are a repository of primary sources (e.g., photographs, letters, newspaper articles, manuscripts, recordings) that document the experiences and intellectual (including literary) achievements of U.S.-based Puerto Ricans since the beginning of the twentieth century.

MARÍA MERCADO is an Associate Professor in the Department of Curriculum and Instruction at New Mexico State University, where she teaches undergraduate and graduate courses in bilingual education. She has over 20 years of teaching experience in bilingual education ranging from teaching kindergarteners to adults in higher education. Her teaching experiences in public schools have been concentrated in early childhood (K–3) bilingual education settings with Spanish/English speakers of the Southwest. Her research interests in bilingual education have focused on better understanding the social context of language education, specifically in dual-language immersion education, and biliteracy and bilingualism of young learners.

EVA MIDOBUCHE is an Associate Professor of Bilingual Education and Diversity Studies in the College of Education at Texas Tech University. Dr. Midobuche has had a long and distinguished career as a bilingual educator. Between 1980 and 2006 she held appointments and taught in elementary and Bilingual Education/ESL teacher preparation programs (both at the undergraduate and graduate levels) at Texas A&M University in Kingsville, the University of Texas at El Paso, the University of Oklahoma, Arizona State University, and now at Texas Tech University. Her experiences also include being a resource teacher and administrator in a large urban school district

as well as serving as the Associate Director of a federally funded Bilingual Education Multifunctional Resource Center at the University of Oklahoma. The center's activities included assisting the College of Education in administering and teaching courses that were provided by the Title VII Master's Grant and also serving 13 states by assisting them in addressing the educational needs of culturally and linguistically diverse populations, primarily through professional development activities. She has published extensively in journals such as *Educational Leadership*, *The Harvard Educational Review*, *The Bilingual Research Journal*, *and Teaching Children Mathematics*.

LILIANA MINAYA-ROWE is Associate Researcher at Johns Hopkins University's Center for Data-Driven Reform in Education. She is one of the 10 researchers on the National Research Synthesis Panel for the Center for Research in Education, Diversity & Excellence in charge of developing the research volume on Language Learning and Academic Achievement. She is co-principal investigator with Margarita Calderón on the Carnegie Foundation of New York *Project ExC-ELL: Expediting Comprehension for English-Language Learners* to design, implement, and refine a staff development program for middle and high school teachers of literature, science, mathematics, and social studies who have English-language learners in their classrooms. She is journal coeditor for the National Association of Bilingual Education's *Journal of Research and Practice*. Dr. Minaya-Rowe is also Professor Emeritus of the Neag School of Education at the University of Connecticut. Her research interests, publications, and teaching include teacher education, literacy, two-way bilingual and ESL program development and implementation, and first and second language acquisition and teaching methodology. Dr. Minaya-Rowe is editor of *Teacher Training and Effective Pedagogy in the Context of Student Diversity*, coauthor (with Margarita Calderón) of *Designing and Implementing Two-Way Bilingual Programs*, and coauthor (with Virginia González and Thomas Yawkey) of *English as a Second Language Teaching and Learning: Classroom Applications for Pre-K through 12th Grade Students*, and has published over 100 articles, chapters, books, and teacher training manuals and guidebooks.

ROSA MOLINA is the Assistant Superintendent of Instruction in the San Jose Unified School District. In her role, Rosa provides oversight of the district's preschool programs, 39 elementary schools, 6 middle schools, 7 high schools, and the Educational Options Programs. Rosa's career, which spans over 30 years, has been dedicated to working with culturally and linguistically diverse student populations in Santa Barbara, Oakland, and San Jose. She also served as the principal of one of California's first Two-Way Bilingual Education programs at River Glen School and brought the school to national and state prominence with the academic progress of the students in her charge. River Glen was granted a Title VII Academic Excellence grant to disseminate the Two-Way Bilingual Immersion (TWBI) program model across the country, and Rosa supported the development of over 27 programs in over 12 states. Rosa also serves as the President of California Association of Bilingual Education Two-Way Programs and has done so for more than 10 years. On the national and state level, Rosa has been responsible for training hundreds of teachers, staff members, parents, and administrators in the basic

elements of TWBI programs and continues to mark the progress and development of programs at the local, state, and national levels.

LUIS C. MOLL is a Professor in the Department of Language, Reading and Culture in the College of Education at the University of Arizona. Prior to that he worked at the Laboratory of Comparative Human Cognition and the Communications Department at the University of California, San Diego. His research addresses the connections among culture, psychology, and education, especially in relation to the education of Latino children in the U.S. Among other studies, he has analyzed the quality of classroom teaching, examined literacy instruction in English and Spanish, studied how literacy takes place in the broader social contexts of household and community life, and attempted to establish pedagogical relationships among these domains of study. Professor Moll has been the Associate Dean for Academic Affairs for the College of Education since January 2004.

MARTHA MONTERO-SIEBURTH is an Associate Professor in the Department of Leadership in Education at the Graduate College of Education of the University of Massachusetts–Boston, where she teaches in the Leadership in Urban Schools Doctoral Program and the Educational Administration Masters Program. Her expertise is in the area of anthropology and sociology of education, curriculum and instructional development, and bilingual, multicultural, and international education. She has published extensively in English and Spanish and coedited *The Struggle for a New Paradigm: Qualitative Research in Latin America* (with Gary L. Anderson) and *Latino Adolescents: Making the Invisible, Visible* (with Francisco A. Villarruel, both from Garland

Press). Her research has been in U.S. urban schools and communities in the greater Boston metropolitan area and in rural and urban schools in Costa Rica, Honduras, Mexico, and Guatemala with diverse international agencies and national educational ministries. Dr. Montero-Sieburth received the Research in Elementary, Secondary or Postsecondary Education Award 2005 from the Hispanic Research Issues Special Interest Group of the American Educational Research Association.

MARCELA A. K. MOVIT is a Ph.D. candidate in the Education Theory and Policy department at The Pennsylvania State University. Her dissertation will consider questions of equal educational opportunity for linguistically diverse students, particularly addressing the question of differences in access to linguistic resources in schools for students from various backgrounds.

ENRIQUE G. MURILLO JR. is a tenured faculty member for the Educational Research Methods and Foundations in Education position at California State University, San Bernardino. He is a first-generation Chicano, born and raised on the greater east side of Los Angeles, and a native bilingual speaker in Spanish/English. He has successfully served during the last two decades in the capacity of schoolteacher, counselor, social-service worker, community organizer, director/consultant in various community-based projects, lecturer, manager and editor for several academic journals, researcher, and university instructor.

JUAN NECOCHEA is a Professor at California State University, San Marcos, Cocoordinator of the Center for the Study of Border Pedagogy, and Principal Investigator of the College Assistance Migrant Program. Dr. Necochea has conducted research in the areas of border pedagogy, school reform, policy implementation, leadership, bilingual education, and diversity, with a scholar practitioner perspective. He is currently coordinating the Teacher Diversity Program, helping to promote diversity among the teaching profession.

DEBORAH PALMER is an Assistant Professor of Bilingual Education in the Department of Curriculum and Instruction at the University of Texas at Austin. Her research interests include bilingual education programs, policy, and practice; ethnography and discourse analysis in diverse multilingual settings; dual-language education; and bilingual teacher preparation. She was a bilingual teacher at Adelante Two-Way Immersion School in Redwood City, California before Proposition 227, and subsequently worked on the Proposition 227 Research Project at the Center for Latino Policy Research at the University of California, Berkeley, while pursuing her doctorate.

JAVIER DÍEZ PALOMAR is Fulbright Visiting Scholar in the Department of Mathematics at the University of Arizona. He has published works on themes interconnecting adult education, mathematics education and literacy, and the support of information and communication technologies in mathematics learning. He participated in research projects such as *ALNET: Dialogic Numeracy on the NET* (Socrates Program, European Commission), and *EMMA: European Network for Motivational Mathematics for Adults* (Socrates Program, European Commission).

MARÍA PENNOCK-ROMÁN is a psychometric and statistical consultant (MPR Psychometric and Research Consulting). She has taught psychometric and statistical courses at The Pennsylvania State University (1996–2002) and at the University of Pennsylvania Graduate School of Education (1977–1985). She also has 12 years of research experience in the Applied Measurement Research division of the Educational Testing Service (1985–1996), where she authored the most comprehensive study to date on the validity of the SAT test for Hispanic students. Her recent journal articles have appeared in the *Journal of Exposure Science and Environmental Epidemiology*, the *American Journal of Speech and Language Pathology*, and *Research in Higher Education*.

ELVA CERDA PÉREZ is an Associate Professor of Bilingual and ESL Education at the University of Texas/TSC at Brownsville. She has been a supervisor of student teachers; a coordinator, chair, and co-chair of the annual binational conference held once a year; a presenter at local, regional, state, national, and international conferences; and a consultant for school districts at the local, state and national levels. She also has served on educational committees at the local, state, national levels. Her research areas of interest are in first and second language acquisition, culture, parental involvement, reading/language arts, and higher-order thinking skills. She was awarded the title of "Honorary Faculty Member for Life" by the faculty of the Universidad Autonoma de Matamoros, and she was nominated and awarded a plaque to "Who's Who Among American Universities" in 2005. In 2006 she was nominated "Best Professor of the Year" by the Academic Affairs Office of the University of Texas and Texas Southmost College. Her most recent publication appears in *Revista trimestral de la Universidad Pedagógica en Tamaulipas* (2005).

JOHN PETROVIC is a former ESL teacher and currently Assistant Professor in the Social and Cultural Foundations of Education at the University of Alabama. His work related to bilingual education has appeared in *The Philosophy of Education Yearbook*, *Bilingual Research Journal*, and *Language Policy*.

MIQUEL ÁNGEL PULIDO is Teaching Assistant and Researcher in Communication Studies at the University of Lleida, Spain. He has been involved in the development of research projects in the areas of digital literacy, information and communication technologies, and cultural groups. He participated in the research project *NODAT: Perceptions and Possibilities of Public Internet Access Points*, funded by the Secretary of Telecommunications and Information Society of the Catalan government.

ELIZABETH QUINTERO is Associate Professor of Early Childhood Education, chair of the doctoral committee in the Department of Teaching and Learning, and Director of the Early Childhood Masters program in the Steinhardt School of Education at New York University. Dr. Quintero's research, teaching, and service involve critical literacy in multilingual, multicultural communities. She is the author of *Problem Posing with Multicultural Children's Literature: Developing Critical Early Childhood Curricula* (Peter Lang, 2004) and *Refugee and Immigrant Family Voices: Experience, and Education* (Sense Publishers, forthcoming), and coauthor of *Literacy to Cross the Generations: Immigrant Learners and Their Families*

(Center for Applied Linguistics, 1993), *Teachers' Reading/Teachers' Lives* (SUNY Press, 1997), *American Voices: Webs of Diversity* (Merrill Education/Prentice Hall, 1998), and *Becoming a Teacher in the New Society: Bringing Communities and Classrooms Together* (Peter Lang, 2003).

A. Y. "FRED" RAMIREZ is an Associate Professor of Education at California State University, Fullerton, where he teaches educational methods, multicultural education, and a course on families and schools. His research interests include parental involvement, rethinking multicultural education, and social justice. In his spare time he is active on a school site council, coaches his kids in their sports, mentors first offender youth from his community, is a part of a nonprofit organization that focuses on schools and communities, and teaches scuba diving as a certified scuba instructor.

LUIS-VICENTE REYES is an Assistant Professor at New Mexico State University, a Carnegie I Research Hispanic Institution, where he teaches in the areas of early childhood, bilingual education, and educational learning technologies. Dr. Reyes's research interests are in early biliteracy, family literacy, leadership, and technology.

ROSITA L. RIVERA recently finished her studies leading to a Ph.D. in Curriculum and Instruction with a minor in English as a Second Language (ESL) and Applied Linguistics. She has taught ESL and Spanish in schools in California, Puerto Rico, and Pennsylvania. She is also an army veteran. She is currently working at the University of Puerto Rico in Mayaguez. Her research interests include ESL teachers with a military background, narrative analysis, discourse analysis, and language policies.

BEATRIZ RIVERA-BARNES is an Assistant Professor of Spanish at The Pennsylvania State University. Her scholarly essays and articles have appeared in journals such as *Letras Hispanas*, *The Multicultural Review*, *Istmo*, and *Dialog*. She is also the author of two novels and a collection of short stories published by Arte Público Press. Her third novel, entitled *Do Not Pass GO*, is forthcoming.

GLORIA RODRIGUEZ is an Assistant Professor in the School of Education at the University of California, Davis. Dr. Rodriguez specializes in school finance and educational leadership from a critical, social justice perspective, as well as the equity status of Latino/a students in the U.S. Dr. Rodriguez was recognized in 1998 as a recipient of the American Education Finance Association's Jean Flanigan Outstanding Dissertation Award for her study, *Getting to Educational Equity through School Finance: The Status of Latinos in California* (1997). Recent publications include "Vertical Equity in School Finance and the Potential for Increasing School Responsiveness to Student and Staff Needs," *The Peabody Journal of Education* (2004) and a coauthored chapter with Russell Rumberger, "Chicano Dropouts: An Update of Research and Policy Issues," in *Chicano School Failure and Success: Review of Research and Policies*, 2nd ed. (Routledge/Falmer, 2002).

KELLIE ROLSTAD is Associate Professor of Language and Literacy and Early Childhood Education at Arizona State University, and she has served as Visiting Scholar in the Graduate School of Education at both Harvard University and the University of California, Los Angeles. Her research interests include early childhood bilingualism, language diversity, language of instruction programs and theory, academic use of language, and two-way immersion. Her work has appeared in the *Bilingual Research Journal, Teachers College Record, Hispanic Journal of Behavioral Sciences,* and *Educational Policy*, among others.

SONIA MIGDALIA ROSA holds a B.A. in secondary education with a specialty in Spanish and a Master's degree in Spanish Literature with a specialty in Puerto Rican Literature from the University of Puerto Rico at Mayagüez. Her forthcoming book is titled *Los Mitos Taínos: Espejo de los mitos de América* (The Taíno Myths: Mirror of the American Myths). Sonia resides in northern Virginia, where she works as an educator, writer, and independent researcher.

F. ARTURO ROSALES is Professor of History at Arizona State University. He has researched and published on the Mexican experience in the U.S. and on Mexican immigration to the Chicago area and to Houston, Texas. In 1996 he published *Chicano! A History of the Mexican American Civil Rights Movement.* It is a companion text to a Public Broadcasting Service television series, and it was named an Outstanding Book on Human Rights in North America by the Gustavus Myers Foundation. He also is author of *"Pobre Raza!" Violence, Justice, and Mobilization among México Lindo Immigrants, 1900–1936* (University of Texas Press, 1999), *Testimonio: A Documentary History of the Mexican American Struggle for Civil Rights* (Arte Público Press, 2000), and *Dictionary of Latino Civil Rights History* (Arte Público Press, 2006).

GRACIELA ROSENBERG is a Professor of Bilingual/ESL Education at the University of Texas at Brownsville and Texas Southmost College. She has a doctorate in curriculum and instruction bilingual and ESL education. She has assisted in developing new undergraduate bilingual and ESL courses.

KEVIN ROSS is a doctoral candidate in Educational Psychology at The Pennsylvania State University.

ALMA RUBAL-LOPEZ earned her first master's degree in the area of Guidance and Counseling from the Consortium for Bilingual Counselor Education, sponsored by the City University of New York. She later earned her second master's degree from Yeshiva University in the field of Psychology and subsequently earned a combined doctorate degree in Developmental Psychology and Linguistics in 1991.

PATRICIA SÁNCHEZ is an Assistant Professor in Culture, Literacy, and Language in the Division of Bicultural-Bilingual Studies at the University of Texas at San Antonio. In her research, Dr. Sánchez uses a sociocultural lens to examine issues related to globalization, transnationalism, and immigrant students and families. Her recently published work includes a co-authored book on social policy, *Beyond "Bilingual" Education: New Immigrants and Public School Policies in California* (Urban Institute Press, 2004). She also co-authored a bilingual children's book with Latina youth, published by Scholastic, titled *Recuerdo mis raíces y vivo mis tradiciones* (Remembering My Roots and Living My Traditions).

SHIRLEY R. STEINBERG is an Associate Professor at the McGill University Faculty of Education. She is the author and editor of numerous books and articles and coedits several book series. The founding editor of *Taboo: The Journal of Culture and Educa-*

tion, Steinberg has recently finished editing *Teen Life in Europe*, and with Priya Parmar and Birgit Richard *The Encyclopedia of Contemporary Youth Culture*. She is the editor of *Multi/Intercultural Conversations: A Reader*. She is coeditor (with Joe Kincheloe) of *Kinderculture: The Corporate Construction of Childhood* and *The Miseducation of the West: How Schools and the Media Distort Our Understanding of the Islamic World*; coauthor (with Joe Kincheloe) of *Changing Multiculturalism: New Times, New Curriculum*; and coauthor (with Joe Kincheloe and Patrick Slattery) of *Contextualizing Teaching*. Her areas of expertise and research are in critical media literacy, social drama, and youth studies.

TOM T. STRITIKUS is Assistant Professor in the College of Education at the University of Washington. He is author of *Immigrant Children and the Politics of English-Only* (LFB Scholarly Publishing, 2002). His teaching and research focuses on policy and practice issues for culturally and linguistically diverse students. He has published articles in the *Bilingual Research Journal*, *Teachers College Record*, *Educational Policy*, and the *Journal of Language, Identity, and Education*.

SABINE E. TEAVER is a doctoral candidate in the Division of Educational Studies at Emory University in Atlanta, Georgia. She was a high school teacher of foreign languages (French, German, and Spanish) and English as a Second Language for 10 years in Northeast Georgia before becoming a doctoral student. Her research focus in multicultural education is the academic orientation and achievement of undocumented Mexican high school students in the New Latino Diaspora, new immigrant gateway states that have not traditionally hosted Latino immigrants.

JOSEFINA VILLAMIL TINAJERO is a Professor of Bilingual Education and Dean of the College of Education at the University of Texas at El Paso. Her major area of expertise is the development of innovative models and educational applications for instruction of English language learners. She specializes in staff development and school-university partnership programs, and has consulted with school districts and publishing companies to design ESL, bilingual, literacy, and biliteracy programs. She has served on state and national advisory committees for standards development, including the English as a New Language Advisory Panel of the National Board for Professional Teaching Standards and the Texas Reading Academies. She is past president of the National Association for Bilingual Education and currently serves on the Board of Directors of the American Association of Colleges for Teacher Education. Most recently, Dr. Tinajero was named one of the 80 Most Influential Hispanics in the U.S. by *U.S. Hispanic Business Magazine*, the 2004 Outstanding U.S. Bilingual Educator by the Education Ministry of Spain, and the 2002 Texas Professor of the Year by the Carnegie Foundation for the Advancement of Teaching and the Council for the Advancement and Support of Education.

ALMEIDA JACQUELINE TORIBIO is Professor of Linguistics in the Department of Spanish, Italian, and Portuguese at The Pennsylvania State University. Her major fields of inquiry are linguistic theory, Spanish syntax, and contact linguistics, with specializations in language variation and change, bilingualism, and attrition. Her publications appear in *Bilingualism: Language & Cognition*, *International Journal of Bilingualism*, *International Journal of the*

Sociology of Language, Lingua, Linguistic Inquiry, Linguistics, and *Probus*. Her current research program is focused on the linguistic factors that constrain the mechanisms and outcomes of language contact, with particular attention devoted to convergence in the domains of phonology and morpho-syntax.

MYRIAM N. TORRES is an Assistant Professor in the Department of Curriculum and Instruction at New Mexico State University. She teaches multiple critical literacies, language arts methods, praxis and reflexivity, curriculum and pedagogy, and educational research including action research/teacher research. Her research interests and publications are Latino education, family literacy, pedagogy of language, critical media literacy, critical discourse analysis, and research as praxis.

ROBERTO P. TREVIÑO is the founder of the Bienestar Health Program, a school-based multicomponent intervention to reduce type II diabetes in fourth grade Hispanic children living in San Antonio. The program has received national acclaim and has been instituted into school curriculums in the Harlandale, Edgewood, and San Antonio Independent School Districts, among others. Dr. Treviño will be inducted into the Texas Diabetes Institute's "Wall of Honor" for his efforts. He is at the forefront of diabetes education and prevention and works tirelessly to help educate the community about the debilitating effects of diabetes.

ANGELA VALENZUELA is a Professor in both the Cultural Studies in Education Program within the Department of Curriculum & Instruction and the Educational Policy and Planning Program within the Department of Educational Administration at the University of Texas at Austin. A Stanford University graduate, her previous teaching positions were in Sociology at Rice University in Houston, Texas (1990–1998) and as a Visiting Scholar at the Center for Mexican American Studies at the University of Houston (1998–1999). Valenzuela's research and teaching interests are in the sociology of education, minority youth in schools, educational policy, and urban education reform. She is the author of *Subtractive Schooling: U.S. Mexican Youth and the Politics of Caring* (SUNY Press, 1999) and editor of *Leaving Children Behind: How "Texas-Style" Accountability Fails Latino Youth* (SUNY Press, 2004).

ALEJANDRA VELASCO is affiliated with the Graduate School of Education and Information Studies at the University of California, Los Angeles.

NANCY VANESSA VICENTE is a Ph.D. candidate at The Pennsylvania State University. She started her teaching career in Puerto Rico, where she has taught English at all levels. Prior to coming to Penn State, she worked as an instructor at the University of Puerto Rico at Mayagüez. She currently supervises World Languages pre-service teachers around Centre County, Pennsylvania. Some of her research interests include the politics of teaching English around the world, decolonizing methodologies, race/class/gender issues, and critical pedagogy. Her dissertation explores the role of the English language teacher in Puerto Rico.

DINAH VOLK is a Professor and Coordinator of the Early Childhood Program in the College of Education at Cleveland State University, Cleveland, Ohio. She has been a teacher of young children in the U.S. and Latin America. Her research on the language and literacy practices of young bilingual children has been published in

Language and Education, Research in the Teaching of English, Journal of Early Childhood Literacy, Early Childhood Research Quarterly, and *Anthropology and Education Quarterly.* She is coeditor (with Eve Gregory and Susi Long) of *Many Pathways to Literacy: Young Children Learning with Siblings, Grandparents, Peers, and Communities* (RoutledgeFalmer, 2004).

GAY WILGUS is Assistant Professor of Early Childhood Education at City College, City University of New York, where she teaches infant/toddler development and curriculum and sociology of education. She has spent many years as head teacher for two-year-olds and as a music and movement consultant for preschool-aged children. Past research has centered on the academic writing issues of early childhood education teacher candidates and on programs for young immigrant children in the French public schools. She is currently involved in an international collaboration on this topic.

OZLEM ZABITGIL earned a Master's degree in Applied Linguistics/Teaching English as a Second Language at The Pennsylvania State University with a Fulbright scholarship, and she is currently a Ph.D. candidate in Adult Education with a minor in Language and Literacy, also at Penn State. She has taught various ESL and writing classes. She was recently awarded the David H. Nicholson Graduate Fellowship in Adult Education at Penn State. Her research interests are educational reform and social justice as it relates to language learning, adult literacy, and identity research. She has presented at various research conferences on literacy and educational reform. Her current dissertation focuses on Turkish Village Institutes, a unique form of educational and social reform in 1930s Turkey.

CLARA V. ZAMORA is an eighth grader at O'Henry Middle School in Austin, Texas, taking Advanced Placement courses. She enjoys writing, playing girl's basketball, singing in the school choir, and playing electric guitar. In July 2006 she played a lead acting role in *Petra's Cuento 2006*, an Austin Mexican American theatrical comedy.

LUZ VALENZUELA ZAMORA is a fifth grader at Barton Hills Elementary School in Austin, Texas. She enjoys writing, soccer, dancing, acting, and singing, and has performed in *La Pastorela*, an Austin Christmas play. In July 2006 she played a lead acting role in *Petra's Cuento 2006*, an Austin Mexican American theatrical comedy.

ANA CELIA ZENTELLA is a Professor in the Department of Ethnic Studies at the University of California, San Diego. She is one of the foremost researchers in what she has named "anthro-political linguistics." She is a central figure in the study of U.S. Latino varieties of Spanish and English, Spanglish, and language socialization in Latino families, and a respected critic of the linguistic profiling facilitated by English-only laws and anti–bilingual education legislation.